Europe

phrasebooks

Europe phrasebook
4th edition – September 2009

Published by
Lonely Planet Publications Pty Ltd ABN 36 005 607 983
90 Maribyrnong St, Footscray, Victoria 3011, Australia

Lonely Planet Offices
Australia Locked Bag 1, Footscray, Victoria 3011
USA 150 Linden St, Oakland CA 94607
UK 2nd Floor, 186 City Rd, London ECV1 2NT

Cover Illustration
Europhile…Euromance by Mik Ruff

ISBN 978 1 74179 973 6
text © Lo
cover illus

Printed th
Printed in

Ann Arbor
District Library
aadl.org

acknowledgments

This book is based on existing editions of Lonely Planet's phrasebooks. It was developed with the help of the following people:

- Ronelle Alexander for the Bulgarian chapter
- Gordana Ivetac for the Croatian chapter
- Richard Nebeský for the Czech chapter
- Michael Janes for the French chapter
- Gunter Muehl for the German chapter
- Thanasis Spilias for the Greek chapter
- Christina Mayer for the Hungarian chapter
- Karina Coates, Pietro Iagnocco and Susie Walker for the Italian chapter
- Piotr Czajkowski for the Polish chapter
- Robert Landon and Anabela de Azevedo Teixeira Sobrinho for the Portuguese chapter
- Anamaria Beligan and Dana Lovinesku for the Romanian chapter
- James Jenkin and Grant Taylor for the Russian chapter
- Marta López for the Spanish chapter
- Emma Koch for the Swedish chapter
- Arzu Kürklü for the Turkish chapter

Lonely Planet Language Products

Associate Publisher: Ben Handicott
Project Manager: Jane Atkin, Kate Mórgan
Editor: Branislava Vladisavljevic

Managing Editor: Annelies Mertens
Layout Designer: Carlos Solarte
Cover Illustration: Mik Ruff

europe – at a glance

One of the most rewarding things about travelling through Europe is the rich variety of cuisine, customs, architecture and history. Adding to this variety is the number of very different languages you'll encounter on your travels. Most languages spoken in Europe, including English, belong to what's known as the Indo-European language family, believed to have originally developed from one language spoken thousands of years ago. A number of European languages are represented in Roman script, which can make them a little more accessible for English-speaking travellers. Other alphabets in use include Cyrillic (used for Russian, for example) and Greek. They can be a little confusing, given their vaguely (and often misleadingly) recognisable shapes, but learning their scripts is easily achievable.

The Romance languages (French, Italian, Spanish and Portuguese) all developed from Vulgar Latin, which spread through Western Europe during the rule of the Roman Empire. The freedom with which English has borrowed Latin-based vocabulary means you'll quickly recognise many words from these languages. The Germanic languages – Dutch and German – are more closely related to English. The Scandinavian languages form the northern branch of the Germanic languages tree, having developed from Old Norse, the language of the Vikings. Their big advantage is that, being so closely related, once you've got the hang of one language, the others should seem quite familiar. Greek, the language of the Iliad and the Odyssey, forms a single branch of the Indo-European language family and uses Greek script.

The Slavic languages are a branch of the Indo-European language family and share a large amount of basic vocabulary. They originated north of the Carpathian mountains and are now divided into Eastern (Russian), Western (Czech and Polish) and Southern (Bulgarian and Croatian) subgroups. The languages traditionally associated with the Orthodox Church (Russian, Bulgarian and Macedonian) use Cyrillic alphabet, while those influenced by the Catholic Church (Czech, Slovak, Polish, Croatian and Slovene) use Roman alphabet. Romanian, the only representative of the Romance languages in Eastern Europe, is more closely related to French, Italian or Spanish.

Finally, Turkish and Hungarian are part of the Ural-Altaic language family, which includes languages spoken from the Balkan Peninsula to northeast Asia.

Bulgarian

bulgarian alphabet

А а a	Б б buh	В в vuh	Г г guh	Д д duh
Е е e	Ж ж zhuh	З з zuh	И и ee	Й й ee *krat*·ko
К к kuh	Л л luh	М м muh	Н н nuh	О о o
П п puh	Р р ruh	С с suh	Т т tuh	У у oo
Ф ф fuh	Х х huh	Ц ц tsuh	Ч ч chuh	Ш ш shuh
Щ щ shtuh	Ъ ъ uh	ь er *ma*·luhk	Ю ю yoo	Я я ya

bulgarian

introduction

Surprisingly, the name of the oldest South Slavic literary language, Bulgarian (български *buhl*-gar-skee), isn't of Slavic origin. It's one of a handful of words remaining in Bulgarian from the language of the Bulgars, a Turkic people who invaded the eastern Balkans in the late 7th century. Together with their language, they were assimilated by the local Slavs, who had crossed the Danube and settled in the peninsula at the start of the 6th century.

As a member of the South Slavic group of languages, Bulgarian has Macedonian and Serbian as its closest relatives. However, it also shows similarities with the non-Slavic languages in the so-called Balkan linguistic union (Romanian, Albanian and Greek), as a result of multilingualism and interaction among the Balkan nations. These foreign influences explain many of its grammatical features – for example, the lack of noun cases, which sets Bulgarian (and Macedonian) apart from the other Slavic languages. In addition, numerous Turkish words entered the Bulgarian vocabulary during five centuries of Ottoman rule. During the 19th century, many of the loanwords from Turkish were eliminated from the language. Their place was partially filled by Russian words, as Russian has influenced Bulgarian through both Bulgaria's ties with the Orthodox Church and long-standing cultural ties with Russia.

Old Bulgarian (also known as Old Church Slavonic) was the first Slavic language recorded in written form, in religious literature from the 9th century. The central figures in the development of the Slavic literary language were Saints Cyril and Methodius, Byzantine Orthodox missionaries who invented the Glagolitic alphabet around 863 AD and used it to translate Greek liturgical texts into Old Church Slavonic. Their disciples devised the Cyrillic alphabet (based on Greek and Glagolitic) in which Bulgarian has been written ever since. In its modern version, standardised after the last spelling reform in 1945, it's very similar to the Russian Cyrillic alphabet. Today, Bulgarians celebrate St Cyril and Methodius Day as a national holiday on 24 May (also known as the Day of Bulgarian Culture or the Cyrillic Alphabet Day).

Modern Bulgarian has about 9 million speakers and is the official language of Bulgaria, with Bulgarian-speaking minorities in Ukraine, Moldova, Romania, Serbia, Hungary, Greece and Turkey. The literary standard is based on the northeastern dialects. The transitional dialects spoken around the borders between Bulgaria, Serbia and Macedonia are very similar and the political issues arising from this linguistic similarity have been sensitive throughout history.

pronunciation

vowel sounds

The vowels in Bulgarian all have equivalents in English, so you shouldn't have any problems. To make yourself sound like a native, just remember that in Bulgarian, vowels in unstressed syllables are generally pronounced shorter and weaker than they are in stressed syllables.

symbol	english equivalent	bulgarian example	transliteration
a	father	дата	*da*·ta
ai	aisle	май	mai
e	bet	лек	lek
ee	see	бира	*bee*·ra
o	pot	вода	vo·*da*
oo	zoo	тук	took
uh	ago	къде	kuh·*de*

word stress

There's no general rule regarding word stress in Bulgarian – it can fall on any syllable and sometimes changes in different grammatical forms of the same word. Just follow our coloured pronunciation guides, in which the stressed syllable is always in italics.

consonant sounds

The consonant sounds in Bulgarian are pretty straightforward, as they all have equivalents in English. The only sound you might trip over is ts, which can occur at the start of words. Try saying 'cats', then 'ats', then 'ts' to get the idea.

symbol	english equivalent	bulgarian example	transliteration
b	bed	брат	brat
ch	cheat	чист	cheest
d	dog	душ	doosh
f	fat	фенерче	fe·ner·che
g	go	гума	goo·ma
h	hat	хотел	ho·tel
k	kit	карта	kar·ta
l	lot	билет	bee·let
m	man	масло	mas·lo
n	not	нула	noo·la
p	pet	грип	greep
r	run	утро	oot·ro
s	sun	син	seen
sh	shot	шест	shest
t	top	сто	sto
ts	hats	крадец	kra·dets
v	very	вчера	vche·ra
y	yes	брой	broy
z	zero	зад	zad
zh	pleasure	плаж	plazh

tools

language difficulties

Do you speak English?
Говорите ли английски? — go·vo·ree·te lee ang·lees·kee

Do you understand?
Разбирате ли? — raz·bee·ra·te lee

I (don't) understand.
(Не) разбирам. — (ne) raz·bee·ram

What does (механа) mean?
Какво значи (механа)? — kak·vo zna·chee (me·ha·na)

How do you ...? — Как се ...? — kak se ...
  pronounce this — произнася това — pro·eez·nas·ya to·va
  write (спирка) — пише (спирка) — pee·she (speer·ka)

Could you please ...? — Моля ...? — mol·ya ...
  repeat that — повторете това — pov·to·re·te to·va
  speak more slowly — говорете бавно — go·vo·re·te bav·no
  write it down — напишете това — na·pee·she·te to·va

essentials

Yes.	Да.	da
No.	Не.	ne
Please.	Моля.	*mol·*ya
Thank you	Благодаря	bla·go·dar·*ya*
(very much).	(много).	(*mno·*go)
You're welcome.	Няма защо.	*nya·*ma zash·*to*
Excuse me.	Извинете.	iz·vee·*ne·*te
Sorry.	Съжалявам.	suh·zhal·*ya·*vam

numbers

0	нула	*noo*-la	15	петнайсет	pet-*nai*-set
1	един/една m/f	ed-*een*/ed-*na*	16	шестнайсет	shes-*nai*-set
	едно n	ed-*no*	17	седемнайсет	se-dem-*nai*-set
2	два/две m/f&n	dva/dve	18	осемнайсет	o-sem-*nai*-set
3	три	tree	19	деветнайсет	de-vet-*nai*-set
4	четири	*che*-tee-ree	20	двайсет	*dvai*-set
5	пет	pet	21	двайсет и едно	*dvai*-set ee ed-*no*
6	шест	shest	22	двайсет и две	*dvai*-set ee dve
7	седем	*se*-dem	30	трийсет	*tree*-set
8	осем	*o*-sem	40	четирийсет	che-*tee*-ree-set
9	девет	*de*-vet	50	петдесет	pet-de-*set*
10	десет	*de*-set	60	шестдесет	shest-de-*set*
11	единайсет	e-dee-*nai*-set	70	седемдесет	se-dem-de-*set*
12	дванайсет	dva-*nai*-set	80	осемдесет	o-sem-de-*set*
13	тринайсет	tree-*nai*-set	90	деветдесет	de-vet-de-*set*
14	четири-найсет	*che*-tee-ree-*nai*-set	100	сто	sto
			1000	хиляда	hee-*lya*-da

time & dates

What time is it?	Колко е часът?	*kol*-ko e cha-*suht*
It's one o'clock.	Часът е един.	cha-*suht* e e-*deen*
It's (two) o'clock.	Часът е (два).	cha-*suht* e (dva)
Quarter past (one).	(Един) и петнайсет.	(e-*deen*) ee pet-*nai*-set
Half past (one).	(Един) и половина.	(e-*deen*) ee po-lo-*vee*-na
Quarter to (eight).	(Осем) без петнайсет.	(*o*-sem) bez pet-*nai*-set
At what time ...?	В колко часа ...?	v *kol*-ko cha-*suh* ...
At ...	В ...	v ...
am	сутрин	*soo*-treen
pm	следобед	sle-*do*-bed
Monday	понеделник	po-ne-*del*-neek
Tuesday	вторник	*vtor*-neek
Wednesday	сряда	*srya*-da
Thursday	четвъртък	chet-*vuhr*-tuhk
Friday	петък	*pe*-tuhk
Saturday	събота	*suh*-bo-ta
Sunday	неделя	ne-*del*-ya

tools – BULGARIAN

11

January	януари	ya·noo·*a*·ree
February	февруари	fev·roo·*a*·ree
March	март	mart
April	април	ap·*reel*
May	май	mai
June	юни	*yoo*·nee
July	юли	*yoo*·lee
August	август	*av*·goost
September	септември	sep·*tem*·vree
October	октомври	ok·*tom*·vree
November	ноември	no·*em*·vree
December	декември	de·*kem*·vree

What date is it today?
  Коя дата е днес? — ko·*ya da*·ta e dnes

It's (15 December).
  Днес е (петнайсти декември). — dnes e (pet·*nai*·stee de·*kem*·vree)

| since (May) | от (май) | ot (mai) |
| until (June) | до (юни) | do (*yoo*·nee) |

last/	миналата/	*mee*·na·la·ta/
next ...	следващата ...	*sled*·vash·ta·ta ...
night	вечер	*ve*·cher
week	седмица	*sed*·mee·tsa
year	година	go·*dee*·na

| last month | миналия месец | *mee*·na·lee·ya *me*·sets |
| next month | следващия месец | *sled*·vash·tee·ya *me*·sets |

yesterday/	вчера/утре ...	*vche*·ra/*oot*·re ...
tomorrow ...		
morning	сутринта	soot·reen·*ta*
afternoon	следобед	sle·*do*·bed
evening	вечерта	ve·cher·*ta*

weather

What's the weather like?	Какво е времето?	kak·vo e vre·me·to
It's ...	... е.	... e
cloudy	Облачно	*ob*·lach·no
cold	Студено	stoo·*de*·no
hot	Горещо	go·*resh*·to
raining	Дъждовно	duhzh·*dov*·no
snowing	Снеговито	sne·go·*vee*·to
sunny	Слънчево	*sluhn*·che·vo
warm	Топло	*top*·lo
windy	Ветровито	vet·tro·*vee*·to

spring	пролет f	*pro*·let
summer	лято n	*lya*·to
autumn	есен f	*e*·sen
winter	зима f	*zee*·ma

border crossing

I'm here ...	Тука съм ...	*too*·ka suhm ...
on business	по работа	po *ra*·bo·ta
on holiday	във ваканция	vuhv va·*kan*·tsee·ya

I'm here for ...	Тука съм за ...	*too*·ka suhm za ...
(10) days	(десет) дена	(*de*·set) *de*·na
(two) months	(два) месеца	(dva) me·*se*·tsa
(three) weeks	(три) седмици	(tree) *sed*·mee·tsee

I'm going to (Gabrovo).
Отивам в (Габрово).   o·*tee*·vam v (*gab*·ro·vo)

I'm staying at the (Serdika).
Отседнал/Отседнала   ot·*sed*·nal/ot·*sed*·na·la
съм в (Сердика). m/f   suhm v (*ser*·dee·ka)

I have nothing to declare.
Нямам нищо да декларирам.   *nya*·mam *neesh*·to da dek·la·*ree*·ram

I have something to declare.
Имам нещо да декларирам.   *ee*·mam *nesh*·to da dek·la·*ree*·ram

That's (not) mine.
Това (не) е мое.   to·*va* (ne) e *mo*·ye

transport

tickets & luggage

Where can I buy a ticket?
Къде мога да си купя билет?   kuh·*de mo*·ga da see *koop*·ya bee·*let*

Do I need to book a seat?
Трябва ли да запазя място?   *tryab*·va lee da za·*paz*·ya *myas*·to

One ... ticket **(to Varna), please.**	Един билет ... (за Варна), моля.	e·*deen* bee·*let* ... (za *var*·na) *mol*·ya
one-way	в едната посока	v ed·*na*·ta po·*so*·ka
return	за отиване и връщане	za o·*tee*·va·ne ee *vruhsh*·ta·ne

I'd like to ... my **ticket, please.**	Искам да ... своя билет, моля.	ees·kam da ... *svo*·ya bee·*let mol*·ya
cancel	върна	*vuhr*·na
change	сменя	smen·*ya*
collect	взема	*vze*·ma
confirm	потвърдя	pot·vuhr·*dya*

I'd like a ... seat, **please.**	Искам място ..., моля.	ees·kam *myas*·to ... *mol*·ya
nonsmoking	за непушачи	za ne·poo·*sha*·chee
smoking	за пушачи	za poo·*sha*·chee

How much is it?
Колко струва?   *kol*·ko *stroo*·va

Is there air conditioning?
Има ли климатична
инсталация?   *ee*·ma lee klee·ma·*teech*·na
een·sta·*la*·tsee·ya

Is there a toilet?
Има ли тоалетна?   *ee*·ma lee to·a·*let*·na

How long does the trip take?
Колко трае пътуването?   *kol*·ko *tra*·ye puh·*too*·va·ne·to

Is it a direct route?
Има ли прекачване?   *ee*·ma lee pre·*kach*·va·ne

I'd like a luggage locker.
Искам да оставя багажа
си на гардероб.   ees·kam da os·*tav*·ya ba·*ga*·zha
see na gar·de·*rob*

My luggage has been ...	Багажът ми е ...	ba·ga·zhuht mee e ...
damaged	повреден	po·vre·den
lost	загубен	za·goo·ben
stolen	откраден	ot·kra·den

getting around

Where does flight (355) arrive?
Къде пристига полет (355)?   kuh·de prees·tee·ga po·let (tree pet pet)

Where does flight (355) depart?
Откъде тръгва полет (355)?   ot·kuh·de truhg·va po·let (tree pet pet)

Where's (the) ...?	Къде се намира ...?	kuh·de se na·mee·ra ...
arrivals hall	терминал	ter·mee·nal
	'пристигане'	pree·stee·ga·ne
departures hall	терминал	ter·mee·nal
	'заминаване'	za·mee·na·va·ne
duty-free shop	безмитен магазин	bez·mee·ten ma·ga·zeen
gate (12)	изход (дванайсет)	ees·hod (dva·nai·set)

Is this the ...	Това ли е ...	to·va lee e ...
to (Burgas)?	за (Бургас)?	za (boor·gas)
boat	корабът	ko·ra·buht
bus	автобусът	av·to·boo·suht
plane	самолетът	sa·mo·le·tuht
train	влакът	vla·kuht

What time's	В колко часа	v kol·ko cha·suh
the ... bus?	е ... автобус?	e ... av·to·boos
first	първият	puhr·vee·yat
last	последният	po·sled·nee·yat
next	следващият	sled·vash·tee·yat

At what time does it arrive/leave?
В колко часа пристига/тръгва?   v kol·ko cha·suh prees·tee·ga/truhg·va

How long will it be delayed?
Колко закъснение има?   kol·ko za·kuhs·ne·nee·ye ee·ma

What station/stop is this?
Коя е тази гара/спирка?   ko·ya e ta·zee ga·ra/speer·ka

Does it stop at (Plovdiv)?
Спира ли в (Пловдив)?   spee·ra lee v (plov·deev)

Please tell me when we get to (Smoljan).

Кажете ми моля когато
пристигнем в (Смолян).

ka·*zhe*·te mee *mol*·ya ko·*ga*·to
prees·*teeg*·nem v (*smol*·yan)

How long do we stop here?

След колко време тръгваме оттук?

sled *kol*·ko *vre*·me *truhg*·va·me ot·*took*

Is this seat available?

Това място свободно ли е?

to·*va myas*·to svo·*bod*·no lee e

That's my seat.

Това е моето място.

to·*va* e *mo*·ye·to *myas*·to

I'd like a taxi …	Искам да поръчам такси …	ees·kam da po·*ruh*·cham tak·*see* …
at (9am)	в (девет часа сутринта)	v (*de*·vet cha·*sa* soo·treen·*ta*)
now	сега	se·*ga*
tomorrow	за утре	za *oot*·re

Is this taxi available?

Таксито свободно ли е?

tak·*see*·to svo·*bod*·no lee e

How much is it to …?

Колко струва до …?

kol·ko *stroo*·va do …

Please put the meter on.

Моля да включите таксиметъра.

mol·ya da vklyoo·chee·te tak·see·*me*·tuh·ra

Please take me to (this address).

Моля да ме докарате
до (този адрес).

mol·ya da me do·*ka*·ra·te
do (*to*·zi ad·*res*)

Please …	Моля …	*mol*·ya …
slow down	намалете	na·ma·*le*·te
stop here	спрете тук	*spre*·te took
wait here	чакайте тук	*cha*·kai·te took

car, motorbike & bicycle hire

I'd like to hire a …	Искам да взема под наем …	ees·kam da *vze*·ma pod *na*·em …
bicycle	един велосипед	e·*deen* ve·lo·see·*ped*
car	една кола	e·*dna* ko·la
motorbike	един мотопед	e·*deen* mo·to·*ped*

with ...	с ...	s ...
a driver	шофьор	sho-*fyor*
air conditioning	климатична	klee-ma-*teech*-na
	инсталация	een-sta-*la*-tsee-ya
antifreeze	антифриз	an-tee-*freez*
snow chains	вериги за сняг	ve-*ree*-gee za snyag

How much for	Колко струва на ...	*kol*-ko *stroo*-va na ...
... hire?	да се наеме?	da se na-*e*-me
hourly	час	chas
daily	ден	den
weekly	седмица	*sed*-mee-tsa

air	въздух m	*vuhz*-dooh
oil	масло n	*mas*-lo
petrol	бензин m	ben-*zeen*
tyres	гуми f pl	*goo*-mee

I need a mechanic.
Трябва ми монтьор.   *tryab*-va mee mon-*tyor*

I've run out of petrol.
Нямам бензин.   *nya*-mam ben-*zeen*

I have a flat tyre.
Пукнала ми се е гумата.   *pook*-na-la mee se e *goo*-ma-ta

directions

Where's the ...?	Къде се намира ...?	kuh-*de* se na-*mee*-ra ...
bank	банката	*ban*-ka-ta
city centre	центърът на града	*tsen*-tuh-ruht na gra-*duh*
hotel	хотелът	ho-*te*-luht
market	пазарът	pa-*za*-ruht
police station	полицейският	po-lee-*tsey*-skee-uht
	участък	oo-*chas*-tuhk
post office	пощата	*po*-shta-ta
public toilet	една градска	ed-*na grad*-ska
	тоалетна	to-a-*let*-na
tourist office	бюрото за	*byoo*-ro-to za
	туристическа	too-ree-stee-*ches*-ka
	информация	een-for-*ma*-tsee-ya

Is this the road to (Rila)?
Това ли е пътят за (Рила)? — to-*va* lee e *puh*-tyat za (*ree*-la)

Can you show me (on the map)?
Можете ли да ми покажете — *mo*-zhe-te lee da mee po-*ka*-zhe-te
(на картата)? — (na *kar*-ta-ta)

What's the address?
Какъв е адресът? — ka-*kuhv* e ad-*re*-suht

How far is it?
На какво разстояние е? — na kak-*vo* ras-to-*ya*-nee-e e

How do I get there?
Как се ходи до там? — kak se *ho*-dee do tam

Turn …	Завийте …	za-*veey*-te …
at the corner	на следващия	na *sled*-vash-tee-ya
	ъгъл	*uh*-guhl
at the traffic lights	при светофара	pree sve-to-*fa*-ra
left/right	наляво/надясно	na-*lya*-vo/na-*dyas*-no

It's …	Това е …	to-*va* e …
behind …	зад …	zad …
far away	далече	da-*le*-che
here	тука	*too*-ka
in front of …	пред …	pred …
left	наляво	na-*lya*-vo
near (to …)	близо (до …)	*blee*-zo (do …)
next to …	до …	do …
on the corner	на ъгъла	na *uh*-guh-luh
opposite …	срещу …	*sresh*-too …
right	надясно	na-*dyas*-no
straight ahead	право	*pra*-vo
there	там	tam

by bus	с автобус	s av-to-*boos*
by taxi	с такси	s tak-*see*
by train	с влак	s vlak
on foot	пеша	pe-*sha*

north	север	*se*-ver
south	юг	yoog
east	изток	*ees*-tok
west	запад	*za*-pad

signs

Вход/Изход	vhod/*ees*·hod	**Entrance/Exit**
Отворено/Затворено	ot·*vo*·re·no/zat·*vo*·re·no	**Open/Closed**
Свободни стаи	svo·*bod*·nee *sta*·yee	**Rooms Available**
Няма стаи	*nya*·ma *sta*·yee	**No Vacancies**
Информация	een·for·*ma*·tsee·ya	**Information**
Полиция	po·*lee*·tsee·ya	**Police Station**
Забранено	za·bra·*ne*·no	**Prohibited**
Тоалетни	to·a·*let*·nee	**Toilets**
Мъже	muh·*zhe*	**Men**
Жени	zhe·*nee*	**Women**
Горещо/Студено	go·*resh*·to/stoo·*de*·no	**Hot/Cold**

accommodation

finding accommodation

Where's a ...?	Къде има ...?	kuh·*de ee*·ma ...
camping ground	къмпинг	*kuhm*·peeng
guesthouse	пансион	pan·see·*on*
hotel	хотел	ho·*tel*
youth hostel	общежитие	ob·shte·*zhee*·tee·ye

Can you	Можете ли	*mo*·zhe·te lee
recommend	да препоръчате	da pre·po·*ruh*·cha·te
somewhere ...?	нещо ...?	*nesh*·to ...
cheap	евтино	*ev*·tee·no
good	хубаво	*hoo*·ba·vo
nearby	наблизо	na·*blee*·zo

I have a reservation.
Имам резервация.   ee·mam re·zer·*va*·tsee·ya

My name's ...
Казвам се ...   *kaz*·vam se ...

I'd like to book a room, please.
Искам да взема една стая, моля.   *ees*·kam da *vze*·ma ed·*na sta*·ya *mol*·ya

Do you have a ... room?	Имате ли стая с ...?	ee·ma·te lee sta·ya s ...
single	едно легло	ed·no leg·lo
double	едно голямо легло	ed·no go·lya·mo leg·lo
twin	две легла	dve leg·la

How much is it per ...?	Колко е на ...?	kol·ko e na ...
night	вечер	ve·cher
person	човек	cho·vek

Can I pay ...?	Мога ли да платя ...?	mo·ga lee da pla·tya ...
by credit card	с кредитна карта	s kre·deet·na kar·ta
with a travellers cheque	с пътнически чекове	s puht·nee·ches·kee che·ko·ve

I'd like to stay for (two) nights.
Искам стаята за (две) нощи. ees·kam sta·ya·ta za (dve) nosh·ti

From (2 July) to (6 July).
От (втори юли) до (шести юли). ot (vto·ree yoo·lee) do (shes·tee yoo·lee)

Can I see it?
Мога ли да я видя? mo·ga lee da ya vee·dya

Am I allowed to camp here?
Мога ли да си сложа
палатката тук? mo·ga lee da see slo·zha
 pa·lat·ka·ta took

Is there a camp site nearby?
Има ли къмпинг наблизо? ee·ma lee kuhm·peeng na·blee·zo

requests & queries

When/Where is breakfast served?
Кога/Къде сервират закуската? ko·ga/kuh·de ser·vee·rat za·koos·ka·ta

Please wake me at (seven).
Моля събудете ме в (седем). mol·ya suh·boo·de·te me v (se·dem)

Could I have my key, please?
Дайте ми ключа, моля. dai·te mee klyoo·cha mol·ya

Can I get another (blanket)?
Дайте ми моля още едно
(одеяло). dai·te mee mol·ya osh·te ed·no
 (o·de·ya·lo)

Is there an elevator/a safe?
Има ли асансьор/сейф? ee·ma lee a·san·syor/seyf

The room is too ...	Стаята е прекалено ...	sta·ya·ta e pre·ka·le·no ...
expensive	скъпа	skuh·pa
noisy	шумна	shoom·na
small	малка	mal·ka

The ... doesn't work.	Не работи ...	ne ra·bo·tee ...
air conditioning	климатичната	klee·ma·teech·na·ta
	инсталация	een·sta·la·tsee·ya
fan	вентилаторът	ven·tee·la·to·ruht
toilet	тоалетната	to·a·let·na·ta

This ... isn't clean.	Тази ... не е чиста.	ta·zee ... ne e chees·ta
pillow	възглавница	vuhz·glav·nee·tsa
towel	кърпа	kuhr·pa

This sheet isn't clean.	Този чаршаф не е чист.	to·zee char·shaf ne e cheest

checking out

What time is checkout?
Кога трябва да напусна стаята?   ko·ga tryab·va da na·poos·na sta·ya·ta

Can I leave my luggage here?
Мога ли да оставя своя   mo·ga lee da os·tav·ya svo·ya
багаж тук?   ba·gazh took

Could I have my ...?	Дайте ми ..., моля.	dai·te mee ... mol·ya
deposit	моя депозит	mo·ya de·po·zeet
passport	моя паспорт	mo·ya pas·port
valuables	моите ценности	mo·yee·te tsen·nos·tee

communications & banking

the internet

Where's the local Internet café?
Къде се намира най-близкият   kuh·de se na·mee·ra nai·blees·kee·yat
интернет?   een·ter·net

How much is it per hour?
Колко се плаща на час?   kol·ko se pla·shta na chas

I'd like to ...	Искам да ...	*ees*·kam da ...
check my email	проверя и-мейла си	pro·ver·*ya ee*·*mey*·la see
get Internet access	използвам интернета	iz·*polz*·vam een·ter·*ne*·ta
use a printer	използвам принтер	iz·*polz*·vam *preen*·ter
use a scanner	използвам скенер	iz·*polz*·vam *ske*·ner

mobile/cell phone

I'd like a ...	Искам ...	*ees*·kam ...
mobile/cell phone for hire	да взема под наем един мобилен телефон	da *vze*·ma pod *na*·em e·*deen* mo·*bee*·len te·le·*fon*
SIM card for your network	предплатена карта за мобилни телефони за вашата мрежа	pred·*pla*·te·na *kar*·ta za mo·*beel*·nee te·le·*fo*·nee za *va*·sha·ta *mre*·zha
What are the rates?	Какви са цените?	kak·*vee* sa tse·*nee*·te

telephone

What's your phone number?

Какъв е вашият телефонен номер?

ka·*kuhv* e *va*·shee·yat te·le·*fo*·nen *no*·mer

The number is ...

Номерът е ...

no·me·ruht e ...

Where's the nearest public phone?

Къде се намира най-близката телефонна будка?

kuh·*de* se na·*mee*·ra nai·*blees*·ka·ta te·le·*fon*·na *bood*·ka

I'd like to buy a phonecard.

Искам да си купя една телефонна карта.

ees·kam da see *koop*·ya ed·*na* te·le·*fon*·na *kar*·ta

I want to ...	Искам да ...	*ees*·kam da ...
call (Singapore)	се обадя в (Сингапур)	se o·*bad*·ya v (seen·ga·*poor*)
make a local call	се обадя някъде в града	se o·*bad*·ya *nya*·kuh·de v gra·*duh*
reverse the charges	се обадя на тяхната сметка	se o·*bad*·ya na *tyah*·na·ta *smet*·ka

How much does ... cost?	Колко струва ...?	kol·ko stroo·va ...
a (three)-minute call	разговор от (три) минути	raz·go·vor ot (tree) mee·noo·tee
each extra minute	всяка допълнителна минута	vsya·ka do·puhl·nee·tel·na mee·noo·ta

(Five) leva per minute.
(Пет) лева една минута.   (pet) le·va ed·na mee·noo·ta

post office

I want to send a ...	Искам да изпратя ...	ees·kam da eez·prat·ya ...
letter	едно писмо	ed·no pees·mo
parcel	един колет	e·deen ko·let
postcard	една пощенска картичка	ed·na posh·ten·ska kar·teech·ka

I want to buy a/an ...	Искам да купя ...	ees·kam da koop·ya ...
envelope	един плик	e·deen pleek
stamp	една марка	ed·na mar·ka

Please send it (to Australia) by ...	Моля да се изпрати (в Австралия) ...	mol·ya da se eez·pra·tee (v av·stra·lee·ya) ...
airmail	с въздушна поща	s vuhz·doosh·na posh·ta
express mail	с бърза поща	s buhr·za posh·ta
registered mail	препоръчано	pre·po·ruh·cha·no
surface mail	с обикновена поща	s o·beek·no·ve·na posh·ta

Is there any mail for me?
Има ли писма за мене?   ee·ma lee pees·ma za me·ne

bank

Where's a/an ...?	Къде има ...?	kuh·de ee·ma ...
ATM	банкомат	ban·ko·mat
foreign exchange office	обмяна на валута	ob·mya·na na va·loo·ta

I'd like to ...	Искам да ...	ees·kam da ...
Where can I ...?	Къде мога да ...?	kuh·de mo·ga da ...
arrange a transfer	уредя да ми се изпратят пари чрез банков превод	oo·red·ya da mee se eez·prat·yat pa·ree chrez ban·kov pre·vod
cash a cheque	осребря чек	os·reb·ryuh chek
change a travellers cheque	осребря пътнически чек	os·reb·ryuh puht·nee·ches·kee chek
change money	обмена пари	ob·men·ya pa·ree
get a cash advance	изтегля пари от кредитната си карта	eez·teg·lya pa·ree ot kre·deet·na·ta see kar·ta
withdraw money	тегля пари в брой	teg·lya pa·ree v broy

What's the ...?	Каква е ...?	kak·va e ...
charge for that	таксата	ko·mee·see·on·na
commission	комисионна	tak·sa·ta

It's ...	... е.	... e
(10) leva	(Десет) лева	(de·set) le·va
free	Безплатно	bez·plat·no

What's the exchange rate?
Какъв е валутен курс?   ka·kuhv e va·loo·ten koors

What time does the bank open?
В колко часа се отваря банката?   v kol·ko cha·suh se ot·var·ya ban·ka·ta

Has my money arrived yet?
Парите ми пристигнаха ли вече?   pa·ree·te mee prees·teeg·na·ha lee ve·che

sightseeing

getting in

What time does it open/close?
В колко часа се отваря/затваря?   v kol·ko cha·suh se ot·var·ya/zat·var·ya

What's the admission charge?
Каква е входната такса?   kak·va e vhod·na·ta tak·sa

Is there a discount for students/children?
Има ли намаление за студенти/деца?   ee·ma lee na·ma·le·nee·ye za stoo·den·tee/det·sa

I'd like a ...	Искам ...	*ees*·kam ...
catalogue	един каталог	e·*deen* ka·ta·*log*
guide	един гид	e·*deen* geed
map	една карта на района	ed·*na kar*·ta na ra·*yo*·na

I'd like to see ...	Искам да видя ...	*ees*·kam da *veed*·ya ...
What's that?	Какво е онова?	kak·*vo* e o·no·*va*
Can I take a photo?	Мога ли да направя снимка?	*mo*·ga lee da na·*prav*·ya *sneem*·ka

tours

When's the next ...?	Кога тръгва следващата ...?	ko·*ga truhg*·va *sled*·vash·ta·ta ...
day trip	еднодневна	ed·no·*dnev*·na
	екскурзия	eks·*koor*·zee·ya
tour	обиколка	o·*bee*·kol·ka

Is ... included?	Включена ли е ...?	vklyoo·che·na lee e ...
accommodation	нощувката	nosh·*toov*·ka·ta
the admission charge	входната такса	*vhod*·na·ta *tak*·sa
food	храната	hra·*na*·ta

Is transport included?
Включен ли е транспортът? — *vklyoo*·chen lee e trans·*por*·tuht

How long is the tour?
Колко трае екскурзията? — *kol*·ko *tra*·e eks·*koor*·zee·ya·ta

What time should we be back?
В колко часа ще се върнем? — v *kol*·ko cha·*suh* shte se *vuhr*·nem

sightseeing		
church	църква f	*tsuhrk*·va
main square	централен площад m	tsen·*tra*·len plosh·*tad*
monastery	манастир m	ma·nas·*teer*
monument	паметник m	*pa*·met·nik
museum	музей m	moo·*zey*
old city	стария град m	*sta*·ree·yuht grad
palace	дворец m	dvo·*rets*
ruins	развалини f pl	raz·va·lee·*nee*
stadium	стадион m	sta·dee·*on*
statue	статуа f	*sta*·too·a

shopping

enquiries

Where's a ... ?	Къде има ...?	kuh·de ee·ma ...
bank	банка	ban·ka
bookshop	книжарница	knee·zhar·nee·tsa
camera shop	магазин за	ma·ga·zeen za
	фотоапарати	fo·to·a·pa·ra·tee
department store	универсален	oo·nee·ver·sa·len
	магазин	ma·ga·zeen
grocery store	гастроном	gas·tro·nom
market	пазар	pa·zar
newsagency	киоск	kee·osk
supermarket	супермаркет	soo·per·mar·ket

Where can I buy ...?
Къде мога да си купя
(един катинар)?
kuh·de mo·ga da see koop·ya
(e·deen ka·nee·tar)

I'm looking for ...
Търся ...
tuhr·sya ...

Can I look at it?
Мога ли да го разгледам?
mo·ga lee da go raz·gle·dam

Do you have any others?
Имате ли още?
ee·ma·te lee osh·te

Does it have a guarantee?
Има ли гаранция?
ee·ma lee ga·ran·tsee·ya

Can I have it sent abroad?
Можете ли да го изпратите
в чужбина?
mo·zhe·te lee da go eez·pra·tee·te
v choozh·bee·na

Can I have my ... repaired?
Можете ли да поправите
моя ...?
mo·zhe·te lee da po·pra·vee·te
mo·ya ...

It's faulty.
Не е на ред.
ne e na red

I'd like ..., please.	Искам ..., моля.	*ees*·kam ... *mol*·ya
a bag	един плик	e·*deen* pleek
a refund	да ми се вратят	da mee se *vrat*·yuht
	парите	pa·*ree*·te
to return this	да върна това нещо	da *vuhr*·na to·*va nesh*·to

paying

How much is it?

Колко струва?   *kol*·ko *stroo*·va

Can you write down the price?

Моля, напишете цената.   *mol*·ya na·pee·*she*·te tse·*na*·ta

That's too expensive.

Скъпо е.   *skuh*·po e

What's your lowest price?

Каква е най-низката ви цена?   kak·*va* e nai·*neez*·ka·ta vee tse·*na*

I'll give you (five) euros.

Ще ви дам (пет) евро.   shte vee dam (pet) *ev*·ro

I'll give you (15) leva.

Ще ви дам (петнайсет) лева.   shte vee dam (pet·*nai*·set) *le*·va

There's a mistake in the bill.

Има грешка в сметката.   *ee*·ma *gresh*·ka v *smet*·ka·ta

Do you accept ...?	Приемате ли ...?	pree·*e*·ma·te lee ...
credit cards	кредитни карти	kre·*deet*·nee *kar*·tee
debit cards	дебитни карти	de·*beet*·nee *kar*·tee
travellers cheques	пътнически	puht·*nee*·ches·kee
	чекове	*che*·ko·ve

I'd like ..., please.	Дайте ми моля ...	*dai*·te mee *mol*·ya ...
a receipt	квитанция	kvee·*tan*·tsee·ya
my change	ресто	*res*·to

clothes & shoes

Can I try it on?	Мога ли да го пробвам?	*mo*·ga lee da go *prob*·vam
My size is (42).	Номерът ми е	*no*·me·ruht mee e
	(четирийсет и два).	(che·*tee*·ree·set ee dva)
It doesn't fit.	Не ми става.	ne mee *sta*·va

small	малко	*mal*·ko
medium	средно	*sred*·no
large	голямо	gol·*ya*·mo

books & music

I'd like a ...	Искам ...	*ees*·kam ...
newspaper	един вестник	e·*deen vest*·neek
(in English)	(на английски)	(na an·*glee*·skee)
pen	една писалка	ed·*na* pee·*sal*·ka

Is there an English-language bookshop?

Има ли книжарница с ee·ma lee knee·*zhar*·nee·tsa s
книги на английски? *knee*·gee na ang·*lees*·kee

I'm looking for something by (Ivan Vazov).

Търся нещо от (Иван Вазов). *tuhr*·sya *nesh*·to ot (ee·*van* va·zov)

Can I listen to this?

Мога ли да слушам това? *mo*·ga lee da *sloo*·sham to·*va*

photography

Can you ...?	Можете ли да ...?	mo·*zhe*·te lee da ...
burn a CD from	запишете на	za·*pee*·she·te na
my memory card	компактен диск от	kom·*pak*·ten deesk ot
	моя флешдрайв	*mo*·ya *flesh*·draiv
develop this film	проявите този филм	pro·*ya*·vee·te *to*·zee film
load my film	заредите моя филм	za·*re*·dee·te *mo*·ya film

I need a ... film	Трябви ми ... филм	*tryab*·va mee ... film
for this camera.	за този фотоапарат.	za *to*·zee fo·to·a·pa·*rat*
APS	АПС	a puh suh
B&W	черно-бял	cher·no·*byal*
colour	цветен	*tsve*·ten

I need a ... film	Трябви ми филм ...	*tryab*·va mee film ...
for this camera.	за този фотоапарат.	za *to*·zee fo·to·a·pa·*rat*
slide	за диапозитиви	za dee·a·po·zee·*tee*·vee
(200) speed	за скорост (двеста)	za *sko*·rost (*dve*·sta)

When will it be ready? Кога ще бъде готов? ko·*ga* shte *buh*·de go·*tov*

meeting people

greetings, goodbyes & introductions

Hello/Hi.	Здравейте/Здравей.	zdra·vey·te/zdra·vey
Good night.	Лека нощ.	le·ka nosht
Goodbye/Bye.	Довиждане/Чао.	do·veezh·da·ne/cha·o

| Mr/Mrs | господин/госпожа | gos·po·deen/gos·po·zha |
| Miss | госпожица | gos·po·zhee·tsa |

How are you?	Как си/сте? inf/pol	kak si/ste
Fine, thanks.	Добре, благодаря.	do·bre bla·go·da·rya
And you?	А ти/вие? inf/pol	a te/vee·e
What's your name?	Как се казваш/	kak se kaz·vash/
	казвате? inf/pol	kaz·va·te
My name is …	Казвам се …	kaz·vam se …
I'm pleased to	Приятно ми е да се	pree·yat·no mee e da se
meet you.	запозная с вас.	za·poz·na·ya s vas

This is my …	Това е …	to·va e …
boyfriend	моят приятел	mo·yat pree·ya·tel
brother	моят брат	mo·yat brat
daughter	моята дъщеря	mo·ya·ta duh·shter·ya
father	моят баща	mo·yat bash·ta
friend	мой приятел m	moy pree·ya·tel
	моя приятелка f	mo·ya pree·ya·tel·ka
girlfriend	моята приятелка	mo·ya·ta pree·ya·tel·ka
husband	моят съпруг	mo·yat suh·proog
mother	моята майка	mo·ya·ta mai·ka
partner (intimate)	моят приятел m	mo·yat pree·ya·tel
	моята приятелка f	mo·ya·ta pree·ya·tel·ka
sister	моята сестра	mo·ya·ta ses·tra
son	моят син	mo·yat seen
wife	моята съпруга	mo·ya·ta suh·proo·ga

Here's my …	Ето моя …	e·to mo·ya …
What's your …?	Какъв е вашият …?	ka·kuhv e va·shee·yat …
(email) address	(и-мейл) адрес	(ee·meyl) a·dres
fax number	факс	faks
phone number	телефонен номер	te·le·fo·nen no·mer

occupations

What's your occupation?	Какво работите?	kak·vo ra·bo·tee·te
I'm a/an ...	Аз съм ...	az suhm ...
artist	художник m	hoo·dozh·neek
	художничка f	hoo·dozh·neech·ka
businessperson	бизнесмен m	beez·nes·men
	бизнесменка f	beez·nes·men·ka
farmer	фермер m	fer·mer
	фермерка f	fer·mer·ka
office worker	чиновник m	chee·nov·neek
	чиновничка f	chee·nov·neech·ka
scientist	учен m&f	oo·chen

background

Where are you from?	Откъде сте?	ot·kuh·de ste
I'm from ...	Аз съм от ...	az suhm ot ...
Australia	Австралия	av·stra·lee·ya
Canada	Канада	ka·na·da
England	Англия	ang·lee·ya
New Zealand	Нова Зеландия	no·va ze·lan·dee·ya
the USA	Съединените	suh·e·dee·ne·nee·te
	Щати	sha·tee
Are you married?	Женен/Омъжена ли сте? m/f	zhe·nen/o·muh·zhe·na lee ste
I'm married.	Женен/Омъжена съм. m/f	zhe·nen/o·muh·zhe·na suhm
I'm single.	Не съм женен/омъжена. m/f	ne suhm zhe·nen/o·muh·zhe·na

age

How old ...?	На колко години ...?	na kol·ko go·dee·nee ...
are you	си/сте inf/pol	si/ste
is your daughter	е дъщеря ти/ви inf/pol	e duhsh·ter·ya tee/vee
is your son	е синът ти/ви inf/pol	e see·nuht tee/vee

| I'm ... years old. | На ... години съм. | na ... go-*dee*-nee suhm |
| He/She is ... years old. | Той/Тя е на ... години. | toy/tya e na ... go-*dee*-nee |

feelings

I'm ...	Аз съм ...	az suhm ...
I'm not ...	Не съм ...	ne suhm ...
happy	щастлив	shtast-*leev*
hungry	гладен	*gla*-den
sad	тъжен	*tuh*-zhen
thirsty	жаден	*zha*-den
tired	уморен	oo-mo-*ren*

I'm ...	На мене ми е ...	na *me*-ne mee e ...
I'm not ...	Не ми е ...	ne mee e ...
cold	студено	stoo-*de*-no
hot	топло	*top*-lo
OK	добре	do-*bre*

Are you ...?	... ли ви е?	... lee vee e
cold	Студено	stoo-*de*-no
hot	Топло	*top*-lo
OK	Добре	do-*bre*

entertainment

going out

Where can I find ...?	Къде има ...?	kuh-*de* ee-*ma* ...
clubs	нощни заведения	*nosht*-nee za-ve-*de*-nee-ya
gay venues	гей клубове	gey *kloo*-bo-ve
pubs	кръчми	*kruch*-mee

I feel like going to a/the ...	Ходи ми се на ...	*ho*-dee mee se na ...
concert	концерт	kon-*tsert*
movies	кино	*kee*-no
party	един купон	e-*deen* koo-*pon*
restaurant	ресторант	res-to-*rant*
theatre	театър	te-*a*-tuhr

interests

Do you like ...?	Харесвате ли ...?	ha-*res*-va-te lee ...
I (don't) like ...	(Не) Харесвам ...	(ne) ha-*res*-vam ...
art	изкуството	iz-*koost*-vo-to
movies	киното	*kee*-no-to
reading	четенето	*che*-te-ne-to
sport	спорта	*spor*-tuht
travelling	пътуването	puh-*too*-va-ne-to
Do you like to ...?	Обичате ли да ...?	o-*bee*-cha-te lee da ...
dance	танцувате	tan-*tsoo*-va-te
go to concerts	ходите на концерти	*ho*-dee-te na kon-*tser*-tee
listen to music	слушате музика	*sloo*-sha-te *moo*-zee-ka

food & drink

finding a place to eat

Can you recommend a ...?	Можете ли да препоръчате ...?	*mo*-zhe-te lee da pre-po-*ruh*-cha-te ...
bar	един бар	e-*deen* bar
café	едно кафене	ed-*no* ka-fe-*ne*
restaurant	един ресторант	e-*deen* res-to-*rant*
I'd like ..., please.	Искам ..., моля.	*ees*-kam ... *mol*-ya
a table for (four)	една маса за (четирма)	ed-*na* ma-sa za (che-*teer*-ma)
the (non)smoking section	в залата за (не)пушачи	v *za*-la-ta za (ne-)poo-*sha*-chee

ordering food

breakfast	закуска f	za-*koos*-ka
lunch	обед m	*o*-bed
dinner	вечеря f	ve-*cher*-ya
snack	закуска f	za-*koos*-ka
What would you recommend?	Какво ще препоръчате?	kak-*vo* shte pre-po-*ruh*-cha-te

I'd like (the) ..., please.	Дайте ми ..., моля.	*dai*·te mee ... *mol*·ya
bill	сметката	*smet*·ka·ta
drink list	листата с напитките	*lees*·ta·ta s na·*peet*·kee·te
menu	менюто	men·*yoo*·to
that dish	онова блюдо	o·no·*va blyoo*·do

drinks

(cup of) coffee/tea ...	(чаша) кафе/чай ...	(*chas*·ha) ka·*fe*/chai ...
with milk	с мляко	s *mlya*·ko
without sugar	без захар	bez *za*·har
(orange) juice	(портокалов) сок m	(por·to·*ka*·lov) sok
soft drink	безалкохолна напитка f	bez·al·ko·*hol*·na na·*peet*·ka
... water	... вода	... vo·*da*
boiled	преварена	pre·va·*re*·na
mineral	минерална	mee·ne·*ral*·na

in the bar

I'll have ...	Ще взема ...	shte *vze*·ma ...
I'll buy you a drink.	Ще ти/ви	shte tee/vee
	почерпя. inf/pol	po·*cher*·pya
What would you like?	Какво ще вземеш/	kak·*vo* shte *vze*·mesh/
	вземете? inf/pol	*vze*·me·te
Cheers!	Наздраве!	na·*zdra*·ve
brandy	ракия f	ra·*kee*·ya
cocktail	коктейл m	kok·*teyl*
cognac	коняк m	kon·*yak*
a shot of (whisky)	едно малко (уиски)	ed·*no mal*·ko (oo·*ees*·kee)
a ... of beer	... бира	... *bee*·ra
bottle	едно шише	ed·*no* shee·*she*
glass	една чаша	ed·*na* cha·sha
a bottle of ... wine	едно шише ... вино	ed·*no* shee·*she* ... *vee*·no
a glass of ... wine	една чаша ... вино	ed·*na* cha·sha ... *vee*·no
red	червено	cher·*ve*·no
sparkling	шумящо	shoo·*myash*·to
white	бяло	*bya*·lo

self-catering

What's the local speciality?

Има ли някакъв	ee·ma lee nya·ka·kuhv
местен специалитет?	mes·ten spe·tsee·a·lee·tet

How much is (a kilo of cheese)?

Колко струва (един	kol·ko stroo·va (e·deen
килограм кашкавал)?	kee·lo·gram kash·ka·val)

I'd like ...	Дайте ми ...	dai·te mee ...
(100) grams	(сто) грама	(sto) gra·ma
(two) kilos	(два) килограма	(dva) kee·lo·gra·ma
(three) pieces	(три) парчета	(tree) par·che·ta
(six) slices	(шест) парчета	(shest) par·che·ta

Less.	По-малко.	po·mal·ko
Enough.	Достатъчно.	dos·ta·tuch·no
More.	Повече.	po·ve·che

special diets & allergies

Is there a vegetarian restaurant near here?

Има ли наблизо	ee·ma lee nab·lee·zo
вегетериански ресторант?	ve·ge·te·ree·an·skee res·to·rant

Do you have vegetarian food?

Имате ли вегетерианска храна?	ee·ma·te lee ve·ge·te·ree·an·ska hra·na

Could you	Можете ли да	mo·zhe·te lee da
prepare a meal	приготвите	pree·got·vee·te
without ...?	яденето без ...?	ya·de·ne·to bez ...
butter	краве масло	kra·ve mas·lo
eggs	яйца	yai·tsa
meat stock	месен бульон	me·sen bool·yon

I'm allergic to ...	Алергичен/Алергична	a·ler·gee·chen/a·ler·geech·na
	съм към ... m/f	suhm kuhm ...
dairy produce	млечни продукти	mlech·nee pro·dook·tee
gluten	глутен	gloo·ten
MSG	МСГ	muh suh guh
nuts	ядки	yad·kee
seafood	морски продукти	mor·skee pro·dook·tee

emergencies

basics

Help!	Помощ!	*po*·mosht
Stop!	Стоп!	stop
Go away!	Махайте се!	*ma*·hai·te se
Thief!	Крадец!	kra·*dets*
Fire!	Пожар!	po·*zhar*
Watch out!	Внимавайте!	vnee·*ma*·vai·te

Call ...!	Повикайте ...!	po·*vee*·kai·te ...
a doctor	лекар	*le*·kar
an ambulance	бърза помощ	*buhr*·za *po*·mosht
the police	полицията	po·*lee*·tsee·ya·ta

It's an emergency!
Има спешен случай!   ee·ma *spe*·shen *sloo*·chai

Could you help me, please?
Бихте ли ми помогнали?   *beeh*·te lee mee po·*mog*·na·lee

I have to use the telephone.
Трябва да телефонирам.   *tryab*·va da te·le·fo·*nee*·ram

I'm lost.
Загубих се.   za·*goo*·beeh se

Where are the toilets?
Къде има тоалетни?   kuh·*de* ee·ma to·a·*let*·nee

police

Where's the police station?
Къде е полицейският участък?   kuh·*de* e po·lee·*tsey*·skee·yat oo·*chas*·tuhk

I want to report an offence.
Искам да съобщя за едно   *ees*·kam da suh·obsh·*tya* ed·*no*
нарушение.   na·roo·*she*·nee·ye

I have insurance.
Имам застраховка.   ee·mam za·stra·*hov*·ka

I've been ...	... ме.	... me
assaulted	Нападнаха	na·*pad*·na·ha
raped	Изнасилиха	eez·na·*see*·lee·ha
robbed	Ограбиха	o·*gra*·bee·ha

I've lost my ...	Изгубих си ...	eez-*goo*-beeh see ...
My ... was/were stolen.	Откраднаха ми ...	ot-*krad*-na-ha mee ...
backpack	раница	*ra*-nee-tsa
bags	чантите	*chan*-tee-te
credit card	кредитната карта	kre-*deet*-na-ta *kar*-ta
handbag	чантата	*chan*-ta-ta
jewellery	бижутата	bee-*zhoo*-ta-ta
money	парите	pa-*ree*-te
passport	паспорта	pas-*por*-ta
travellers cheques	пътническите чекове	puht-*nee*-ches-kee-te *che*-ko-ve
wallet	портфейла	port-*fey*-la
I want to contact my ...	Искам да се свържа с нашето ...	*ees*-kam da se *svuhr*-zha s *na*-she-to ...
consulate	консулство	*kon*-sools-tvo
embassy	посолство	po-*sols*-tvo

health

medical needs

Where's the nearest ...?	Къде е най-близкият/ най-близката ...? m/f	kuh-*de* e nai-*bleez*-kee-yat/ nai-*bleez*-ka-ta ...
dentist	зъболекар m	zuh-bo-*le*-kar
doctor	лекар m	*le*-kar
hospital	болница f	*bol*-nee-tsa
(night) pharmacist	(нощна) аптека f	(*nosht*-na) a-po-*te*-ka

I need a doctor (who speaks English).
Трябва ми лекар
(говорещ английски).

tryab-va mee *le*-kar
(go-*vo*-resht ang-*lees*-kee)

Could I see a female doctor?
Може ли да ме прегледа лекарка?

mo-zhe lee da me pre-*gle*-da *le*-kar-ka

I've run out of my medication.
Свърши ми се е лекарството.

svuhr-shee mee se e le-*karst*-vo-to

conditions, symptoms & allergies

I'm sick.	Болен/Болна съм. m/f	bo·len/bol·na suhm
It hurts here.	Тук ме боли.	took me bo·lee
I have a headache/	Боли ме глава/	bo·lee me gla·va/
toothache.	зъб.	zuhb

I have (a) ...	Имам ...	ee·mam ...
asthma	астма	ast·ma
bronchitis	бронхит	bron·heet
constipation	запек	za·pek
cough	кашлица	kash·lee·tsa
diarrhoea	диария	dee·a·ree·ya
fever	температура	tem·pe·ra·too·ra
heart condition	болно сърце	bol·no suhr·tse
pain	болки	bol·kee
sore throat	възпалено гърло	vuhz·pa·le·no guhr·lo

I'm allergic to ...	Алергичен/Алергична	a·ler·gee·chen/a·ler·geech·na
	съм на ... m/f	suhm na ...
antibiotics	антибиотици	an·tee·bee·o·tee·tsee
anti-	противо-	pro·tee·vo·
inflammatories	възпалителни	vuhz·pa·lee·tel·nee
	лекарства	le·karst·va
aspirin	аспирин	as·pee·reen
bees	пчели	pche·lee
codeine	кодеин	ko·de·een
penicillin	пеницилин	pe·nee·tsee·leen

antiseptic	антисептичен m	an·tee·sep·tee·chen
bandage	бинт m	beent
condoms	презервативи m pl	pre·zer·va·tee·vee
contraceptives	противозачатъчни	pro·tee·vo·za·cha·tuhch·nee
	средства n pl	sred·stva
diarrhoea medicine	лекарство против	le·karst·vo pro·teev
	разтройство n	raz·troyst·vo
insect repellent	средство срещу	sredst·vo pro·teev
	насекоми n	na·se·ko·mee
laxatives	пургатив m	poor·ga·teev
painkillers	обезболяващо n	o·bez·bo·lya·va·shto
rehydration salts	соли за оводняване f pl	so·lee za o·vod·nya·va·ne
sleeping tablets	приспивателно n	pree·spee·va·tel·no

english–bulgarian dictionary

Bulgarian nouns in this dictionary have their gender indicated by ⓜ (masculine), ⓕ (feminine) or ⓝ (neuter). If it's a plural noun, you'll also see pl. Adjectives are given in the masculine form only. Words are also marked as a (adjective), v (verb), sg (singular), pl (plural), inf (informal) or pol (polite) where necessary.

A

accident катастрофа ⓕ ka-tas-*tro*-fa
accommodation нощувка ⓕ nosh-*toov*-ka
adaptor адаптер ⓜ a-*dap*-ter
address адрес ⓜ ad-*res*
after след sled
air-conditioned с климатична инсталация
  s klee-ma-*teech*-na een-sta-*la*-tsee-ya
airplane самолет ⓜ sa-mo-*let*
airport летище ⓝ le-*teesh*-te
alcohol алкохол ⓜ al-ko-*hol*
all всичко *vseech*-ko
allergy алергия ⓕ a-*ler*-gee-ya
ambulance линейка ⓕ lee-*ney*-ka
and и ee
ankle глезен ⓜ *gle*-zen
arm ръка ⓕ ruh-*ka*
ashtray пепелница ⓕ pe-pel-*nee*-tsa
ATM банкомат ⓜ ban-ko-*mat*

B

baby бебе ⓝ *be*-be
back (body) гръб ⓜ gruhb
backpack раница ⓕ *ra*-nee-tsa
bad лош losh
bag чанта ⓕ *chan*-ta
baggage claim подаване на багаж ⓝ
  po-*da*-va-ne na ba-*gazh*
bank банка ⓕ *ban*-ka
bar бар ⓜ bar
bathroom баня ⓕ *ban*-ya
battery батерия ⓕ ba-*te*-ree-ya
beautiful красив kra-*seev*
bed легло ⓝ leg-*lo*
beer бира ⓕ *bee*-ra
before пред pred
behind зад zad
bicycle колело ⓝ ko-le-*lo*
big голям gol-*yam*
bill банкнота ⓕ bank-*no*-ta

black черен *che*-ren
blanket одеяло ⓝ o-de-*ya*-lo
blood group кръвна група ⓕ *kruhv*-na *groo*-pa
blue син seen
boat кораб ⓜ *ko*-rab
book (make a reservation) v запазвам za-*paz*-vam
bottle шише ⓝ shee-*she*
bottle opener отварачка ⓕ ot-va-*rach*-ka
boy момче ⓝ mom-*che*
brakes (car) спирачки ⓕ pl spee-*rach*-kee
breakfast закуска ⓕ za-*koos*-ka
broken (faulty) развален raz-va-*len*
Bulgaria България ⓕ buhl-*ga*-ree-ya
Bulgarian (language) български *buhl*-gar-skee
Bulgarian a български *buhl*-gar-skee
bus автобус ⓜ av-to-*boos*
business търговия ⓕ tuhr-*go*-vee-ya
buy купувам koo-*poo*-vam

C

café кафене ⓝ ka-fe-*ne*
camera фотоапарат ⓜ fo-to-a-pa-*rat*
camp site къмпинг ⓜ *kuhm*-peeng
cancel отказвам ot-*kaz*-vam
can opener отварачка ⓕ ot-va-*rach*-ka
car кола ⓕ ko-*la*
cash пари ⓕ pa-*ree*
cash (a cheque) v осребрявам os-reb-*rya*-vam
cell phone мобилен телефон ⓜ mo-*bee*-len te-le-*fon*
centre център ⓜ *tsen*-tuhr
change (money) v сменям *smen*-yam
cheap евтин *ev*-teen
check (bill) сметка ⓕ *smet*-ka
check-in регистрация ⓕ re-gees-*tra*-tsee-ya
chest гърди ⓕ *guhr*-dee
child дете ⓝ de-*te*
cigarette цигара ⓕ tsee-*ga*-ra
city град ⓜ grad
clean a чист cheest
closed затворен zat-*vo*-ren
coffee кафе ⓝ ka-*fe*
coins монети ⓕ pl mo-*ne*-tee

cold a студен stoo-*den*
collect call обаждане за тяхна сметка ⓝ
o-*bazh*-da-ne na *tyah*-na *smet*-ka
come идвам *eed*-vam
computer компютър ⓜ kom-*pyoo*-tuhr
condom презерватив ⓜ pre-zer-va-*teev*
contact lenses контактни лещи ⓕ pl
kon-*takt*-nee *lesh*-tee
cook v готвя *got*-vya
cost цена ⓕ tse-*na*
credit card кредитна карта ⓕ *kre*-deet-na *kar*-ta
cup чаша ⓕ cha-sha
currency exchange обмяна на валута ⓕ
ob-*mya*-na na va-*loo*-ta
customs (immigration) митница ⓕ *meet*-neet-sa

D

dangerous опасен o-*pa*-sen
date (time) дата ⓕ *da*-ta
day ден ⓜ den
delay закъснение ⓝ za-kuhs-*nee*-nee-ye
dentist зъболекар ⓜ zuh-bo-le-kar
depart тръгвам truhg-vam
diaper пелена ⓕ pe-le-*na*
dictionary речник ⓜ rech-neek
dinner вечеря ⓕ ve-*cher*-ya
direct пряк pryak
dirty мръсен mruh-sen
disabled (person) инвалид ⓜ een-va-*leed*
discount намаление ⓝ na-ma-*le*-nee-ye
doctor лекар ⓜ *le*-kar
double bed двойно легло ⓝ *dvoy*-no leg-*lo*
double room стая с две легла ⓕ *sta*-ya s dve leg-*la*
drink пия ⓕ *pee*-ya
drive v карам ka-ram
drivers licence шофьорска книжка ⓕ
sho-*fyor*-ska *kneesh*-ka
drug (illicit) наркотик ⓜ nar-ko-*teek*
dummy (pacifier) биберон ⓜ bee-be-*ron*

E

ear ухо ⓝ oo-*ho*
east изток ⓜ *eez*-tok
eat ям yam
economy class втора класа ⓕ *vto*-ra *kla*-sa
electricity електричество ⓝ e-lek-*tree*-chest-vo
elevator асансьор ⓜ a-san-*syor*
email и-мейл ⓜ *ee*-meyl
embassy посолство ⓝ po-*sols*-tvo

emergency спешен случай ⓜ *spe*-shen *sloo*-chai
English (language) английски ⓜ ang-*lees*-kee
entrance вход ⓜ vhod
evening вечер ⓕ *ve*-cher
exchange rate валутен курс ⓜ va-*loo*-ten koors
exit изход ⓜ *eez*-hod
expensive скъп skuhp
express mail бърза поща ⓕ *buhr*-za *posh*-ta
eye око ⓝ o-*ko*

F

far далече da-*le*-che
fast бърз buhrz
father баща ⓜ bash-*ta*
film (camera) филм ⓜ feelm
finger пръст ⓜ pruhst
first-aid kit първа помощ ⓕ *puhr*-va po-*mosht*
first class първа класа ⓕ *puhr*-va *kla*-sa
fish риба ⓕ *ree*-ba
food храна ⓕ hra-*na*
foot крак ⓜ krak
fork вилица ⓕ *vee*-lee-tsa
free (of charge) безплатно bez-*plat*-no
friend приятел/приятелка ⓜ/ⓕ
pree-*ya*-tel/pree-*ya*-tel-ka
fruit плод ⓜ plod
full пълен *puh*-len
funny смешен *sme*-shen

G

gift подарък ⓜ po-*da*-ruhk
girl момиче ⓝ mo-*mee*-che
glass (drinking) чаша ⓕ *cha*-sha
glasses очила ⓝ pl o-chee-*la*
go отивам o-*tee*-vam
good добър do-*buhr*
green зелен *ze*-len
guide гид ⓜ geed

H

half половина ⓕ po-lo-*vee*-na
hand ръка ⓕ ruh-*ka*
handbag дамска чанта ⓕ *dam*-ska chan-*ta*
happy щастлив shtast-*leev*
have имам ee-*mam*
he той toy
head глава ⓕ gla-*va*

heart сърце ⓝ *suhr-tse*
heat горещина ⓕ *go-resh-tee-na*
heavy тежък *te-zhuhk*
help v помагам *po-ma-gam*
here тук *too-ka*
high висок *vee-sok*
highway шосе ⓝ *sho-se*
hike v ходя пеш *hod-ya pesh*
holiday ваканция ⓕ *va-kan-tsee-ya*
homosexual а хомосексуален *ho-mo-sek-soo-a-len*
hospital болница ⓕ *bol-nee-tsa*
hot горещ *go-resht*
hotel хотел ⓜ *ho-tel*
hungry гладен *gla-den*
husband мъж ⓜ *muhzh*

I

I аз *az*
identification (card) легитимация ⓕ *le-gee-tee-ma-tsee-ya*
ill болен *bo-len*
important важен *va-zhen*
included включен *vklyoo-chen*
injury щета ⓕ *shte-ta*
insurance застраховка ⓕ *za-stra-hov-ka*
Internet интернет ⓜ *een-ter-net*
interpreter преводач ⓜ *pre-vo-dach*

J

jewellery бижутерия ⓕ *bee-zhoo-te-ree-ya*
job работа ⓕ *ra-bo-ta*

K

key ключ ⓜ *klyooch*
kilogram килограм ⓜ *kee-lo-gram*
kitchen кухня ⓕ *kooh-nya*
knife нож ⓜ *nozh*

L

laundry (place) пералня ⓕ *pe-ral-nya*
lawyer адвокат ⓜ *ad-vo-kat*
left (direction) ляво *lya-vo*
left-luggage office гардероб ⓜ *gar-de-rob*
leg крак ⓜ *krak*
lesbian а лезбийски *lez-bee-skee*

less по-малко *po-mal-ko*
letter (mail) писмо ⓝ *pees-mo*
lift (elevator) асансьор ⓜ *a-san-syor*
light светлина ⓕ *svet-lee-na*
like v харесвам *ha-res-vam*
lock брава ⓕ *bra-va*
long дълъг *duh-luhg*
lost загубен *za-goo-ben*
lost-property office бюро за загубени вещи ⓝ
  byoo-ro za za-goo-be-nee vesh-tee
love v обичам *o-bee-cham*
luggage багаж ⓜ *ba-gazh*
lunch обяд ⓜ *o-byad*

M

mail поща ⓕ *posh-ta*
man мъж ⓜ *muhzh*
map карта ⓕ *kar-ta*
market пазар ⓜ *pa-zar*
matches кибрит ⓜ *kee-breet*
meat месо ⓝ *me-so*
medicine лекарство ⓝ *le-karst-vo*
menu меню ⓝ *men-yoo*
message съобщение ⓝ *suh-ob-shte-nee-ye*
milk мляко ⓝ *mlya-ko*
minute минута ⓕ *mee-noo-ta*
mobile phone мобилен телефон ⓜ
  mo-bee-len te-le-fon
money пари ⓕ *pa-ree*
month месец ⓜ *me-sets*
morning сутрин ⓕ *soot-reen*
mother майка ⓕ *mai-ka*
motorcycle мотоциклет ⓜ *mo-to-tseek-let*
motorway магистрала ⓕ *ma-gee-stra-la*
mouth уста ⓕ *oos-ta*
music музика ⓕ *moo-zee-ka*

N

name име ⓝ *ee-me*
napkin салфетка ⓕ *sal-fet-ka*
nappy пелена ⓕ *pe-le-na*
near близък *blee-zuhk*
neck врат ⓜ *vrat*
new нов *nov*
news новина ⓕ *no-vee-na*
newspaper вестник ⓜ *vest-neek*
night нощ ⓕ *nosht*
no не *ne*

noisy шумен *shoo-*men
nonsmoking за непушачи za ne-poo-*sha*-chee
north север ⓜ *se-*ver
nose нос ⓜ nos
now сега se-*ga*
number число ⓝ chees-*lo*

O

oil (engine) масло ⓝ *mas-*lo
old стар star
one-way ticket еднопосочен билет ⓜ
ed-no-po-*so-*chen *bee-*let
open а отворен ot-*vo-*ren
outside навън na-*vuhn*

P

package колет ⓜ ko-*let*
paper хартия ⓕ har-*tee*-ya
park (car) v паркирам par-*kee-*ram
passport паспорт ⓜ pas-*port*
pay плащам *plash-*tam
pen писалка ⓕ pee-*sal-*ka
petrol бензин ⓜ ben-*zeen*
pharmacy аптека ⓕ ap-*te-*ka
phonecard телефонна карта ⓕ te-le-*fon-*na *kar-*ta
photo снимка ⓕ *sneem-*ka
plate чиния ⓕ chee-*nee-*ya
police полиция ⓕ po-*leet-*see-ya
postcard пощенска карта ⓕ *posh-*ten-ska *kar-*ta
post office поща ⓕ *posh-*ta
pregnant бременна *bre-*men-na
price цена ⓕ tse-*na*

Q

quiet тих teeh

R

rain дъжд ⓜ duhzhd
razor самобръсначка ⓕ sa-mo-bruhs-*nach-*ka
receipt квитанция ⓕ kvee-*tan-*tsee-ya
red червен cher-*ven*
refund връщане на парите ⓝ
*vruhsh-*ta-ne na pa-*ree-*te
registered mail препоръчано писмо ⓝ
pre-po-*ruh-*cha-no pees-*mo*
rent v вземам под наем *vze-*mam pod *na-*em

repair v поправям po-*prav-*yam
reservation резервация ⓕ re-zer-*va-*tsee-ya
restaurant ресторант ⓜ res-to-*rant*
return v връщам *vrush-*tam
return ticket билет за отиване и връщане ⓜ
*bee-*let za o-tee-va-ne ee *vrush-*ta-ne
right (direction) дясно *dyas-*no
road път ⓜ puht
room стая ⓕ *sta-*ya

S

safe а безопасен be-zo-*pa-*sen
sanitary napkin дамска превръзка ⓕ
*dam-*ska pre-*vruhz-*ka
seat място ⓝ *myas-*to
send пращам *prash-*tam
service station бензиностанция ⓕ
ben-zee-no-*stan-*tsee-ya
sex секс ⓜ seks
shampoo шампоан ⓜ sham-po-*an*
share a room живея в една стая с
zhee-*ve-*ya v ed-*na sta-*ya s
shaving cream крем за бръснене ⓜ
krem za bruhs-*ne-*ne
she тя tya
sheet (bed) чаршаф ⓜ char-*shaf*
shirt риза ⓕ *ree-*za
shoes обувки ⓕ pl o-*boov-*kee
shop магазин ⓜ ma-ga-*zeen*
short къс kuhs
shower душ ⓜ doosh
single room стая с едно легло ⓕ *sta-*ya s ed-*no* leg-*lo*
skin кожа ⓕ *ko-*zha
skirt пола ⓕ po-*la*
sleep v спя spyuh
slowly бавно *bav-*no
small малък *mal-*uhk
smoke (cigarettes) v пуша *poo-*sha
soap сапун ⓜ sa-*poon*
some някои *nya-*ko-yee
soon скоро *sko-*ro
south юг ⓜ yoog
souvenir shop магазин за сувенири ⓜ
ma-ga-*zeen* za soo-ve-*nee-*ree
speak говоря go-*vor-*ya
spoon лъжица ⓕ luh-*zhee-*tsa
stamp марка ⓕ *mar-*ka
stand-by ticket билет на търси се ⓜ
*bee-*let na *tuhr-*see se
station (train) гара ⓕ *ga-*ra
stomach стомах ⓜ sto-*mah*

stop v спря spryuh
stop (bus) спирка ① speer-ka
street улица ① oo-leet-sa
student студент/студентка ⓜ/① stoo-dent/stoo-dent-ka
sun слънце ⓝ sluhn-tse
sunscreen крем против загаряне ⓜ krem pro-teev za-ga-rya-ne
swim v плувам ploo-vam

T

tampons тампони ⓜ pl tam-po-nee
taxi такси ① tak-see
teaspoon лъжичка ① luh-zheech-ka
teeth зъби ⓜ pl zuh-bee
telephone телефон ⓜ te-le-fon
television телевизия ① te-le-vee-zee-ya
temperature (weather) температура ① tem-pe-ra-too-ra
tent палатка ① pa-lat-ka
that (one) онова o-no-va
they те te
thirsty жаден zha-den
this (one) това to-va
throat гърло ⓝ guhr-lo
ticket билет ⓜ bee-let
time време ⓝ vre-me
tired уморен oo-mo-ren
tissues хартиени носни кърпички ① pl har-teey-nee nos-nee kuhr-peech-kee
today днес dnes
toilet тоалетна ① to-a-let-na
tomorrow утре oot-re
tonight довечера do-ve-che-ra
toothbrush четка за зъби ① chet-ka za zuh-bee
toothpaste паста за зъби ① pas-ta za zuh-bee
torch (flashlight) фенерче ⓝ fe-ner-che
tour екскурзия eks-koor-zee-ya
tourist office бюро за туристическа информация ⓝ byoo-ro za too-rees-tee-ches-ka een-for-ma-tsee-ya
towel кърпа ① kuhr-pa
train влак ⓜ vlak
translate превеждам pre-vezh-dam
travel agency туристическа агенция ① too-rees-tee-ches-ka a-gen-tsee-ya
travellers cheque пътнически чек ⓜ puht-nee-ches-kee chek
trousers панталони ⓜ pl pan-ta-lo-nee
twin beds двойни легла ⓝ pl dvoy-nee leg-la
tyre гума ① goo-ma

U

underwear бельо ⓝ bel-yo
urgent спешен spe-shen

V

vacant свободен svo-bo-den
vacation ваканция ① va-kan-tsee-ya
vegetable зеленчук ⓜ ze-len-chook
vegetarian a вегетериански ve-ge-te-ree-an-skee
visa виза ① vee-za

W

waiter сервитьор ⓜ ser-vee-tyor
walk v ходя ho-dya
wallet портфейл ⓜ port-feyl
warm a топъл to-puhl
wash (something) мия mee-ya
watch часовник ⓜ cha-sov-neek
water вода ① vo-da
we ние nee-ye
weekend събота и неделя ① suh-bo-ta ee ne-del-ya
west запад ⓜ za-pad
wheelchair инвалидна количка ① een-va-leed-na ko-leech-ka
when кога ko-ga
where къде kuh-de
white бял byal
who кой koy
why защо zash-to
wife жена ① zhe-na
window прозорец ⓜ pro-zo-rets
wine вино ⓝ vee-no
with с/със s/suhs
without без bez
woman жена ① zhe-na
write пиша pee-sha

Y

yellow жълт zhult
yes да da
yesterday вчера vche-ra
you sg inf ти tee
you sg pol & pl вие vee-ye

Croatian

croatian & serbian alphabets

croatian	serbian	croatian	serbian	croatian	serbian	croatian	serbian
A a a	A a	*E e* e	E e	*Lj lj* l'	Љ љ	*Š š* sh	Ш ш
B b be	Б б	*F f* ef	Ф ф	*M m* em	М м	*T t* te	Т т
C c tse	Ц ц	*G g* ge	Г г	*N n* en	Н н	*U u* u	У у
Č č tch	Ч ч	*H h* ha	Х х	*Nj nj* n'	Њ њ	*V v* ve	В в
Ć ć ch	Ћ ћ	*I i* i	И и	*O o* o	О о	*Z z* zed	З з
D d de	Д д	*J j* y	Ј ј	*P p* pe	П п	*Ž ž* zh	Ж ж
Dž dž dzh	Џ џ	*K k* ka	К к	*R r* er	Р р		
Đ đ j	ђ ђ	*L l* el	Л л	*S s* es	С с		

■ croatian/serbian

introduction

Did you know that the words *Dalmatian* and *cravat* come from Croatian (*hrvatski* hr·vat·ski), which is also referred to as Serbo-Croatian? Croatian isn't really a separate language from Serbian or Bosnian. Linguists commonly refer to the varieties spoken in Croatia, Bosnia-Hercegovina, Montenegro and Serbia with the umbrella term 'Serbo-Croatian' while acknowledging dialectical differences between them. Croats, Serbs and Bosnians themselves generally maintain that they speak different languages, however – a reflection of their desire to retain separate ethnic identities.

As the language of about 5 million people in one of the world's newest countries, Croatian has an intriguing, cosmopolitan and at times fraught history. Its linguistic ancestor was brought to the region in the 6th and 7th centuries by the South Slavs, who may have crossed the Danube from the area now known as Poland. This ancestral language split off into two branches: East South Slavic, which later evolved into Bulgarian and Macedonian, and West South Slavic, of which Slovene, Serbian and Croatian are all descendants.

Croatia may be a peaceful country today but the Balkan region to which it belongs has a long history of invasion and conflict. These upheavals have enriched and politicised the language. The invasion by Charlemagne's armies and the conversion of Croats to the Roman Church in AD 803 left its mark on Croatian in the form of words borrowed from Latin and the adoption of the Latin alphabet rather than the Cyrillic alphabet (with which Serbian is written). Subsequent invasions by the Hapsburg, Ottoman and Venetian empires added vibrancy to the language through an influx of German, Turkish and Venetian dialect words. Many words from the standard Italian of Croatia's neighbour Italy have also been absorbed.

The good news is that if you venture into Serbia or Montenegro, you'll be able to enrich your travel experience there by using this chapter. In case of the most common differences between Croatian and Serbian, both translations are given and indicated with ©/Ⓢ. The Cyrillic alphabet (used alternatively with the Latin alphabet in Serbia and Montenegro) is also included on the page opposite. Croatian is a handy lingua franca in any of the other states that made up part of the former Yugoslavia, as it's an official language in Bosnia-Hercegovina (along with Serbian and Bosnian) and people in Macedonia and Slovenia, who speak closely related languages, generally understand Croatian. In other words (often heard throughout this region) – *nema problema* ne·ma pro·ble·ma (no problem)!

pronunciation

vowel sounds

In written Croatian, vowels that appear next to each other don't run together as in English. When you see two or more vowels written next to each other in a Croatian word, pronounce them separately.

symbol	english equivalent	croatian example	transliteration
a	**father**	*zdravo*	*zdra*-vo
ai	**aisle**	*ajvar*	*ai*-var
e	**bet**	*pet*	pet
i	**hit**	*sidro*	*si*-dro
o	**pot**	*brod*	brod
oy	**toy**	*tvoj*	tvoy
u	**put**	*skupo*	*sku*-po

word stress

As a general rule, in two-syllable words in Croatian stress usually falls on the first syllable. In words of three or more syllables, stress may fall on any syllable except the last. In our pronunciation guides, the stressed syllable is italicised.

Croatian also has what's known as 'pitch accent'. A stressed vowel may have either a rising or a falling pitch and be long or short. The combination of stress, pitch and vowel length in a given syllable occasionally affects the meaning of a word, but you don't need to worry about reproducing this feature of Croatian and we haven't indicated it in this book. In the few cases where it's important, it should be clear from the context what's meant. You may notice though that the speech of native speakers has an appealing musical lilt to it.

consonant sounds

Croatian consonant sounds all have close equivalents in English. The rolled r sound can be pronounced in combination with other consonants as a separate syllable – eg *Hrvat* hr-vat (Croat). If the syllables without vowels look a bit intimidating, try inserting a slight 'uh' sound before the r to help them run off your tongue more easily.

symbol	english equivalent	croatian example	transliteration
b	**bed**	*glazba*	*glaz*·ba
ch	**ch**eat	*četiri, ćuk*	*che*·ti·ri, chuk
d	**d**og	*doručak*	*do*·ru·chak
f	**f**at	*fotograf*	*fo*·to·graf
g	**g**o	*jagoda*	*ya*·go·da
h	**h**at	*hodnik*	*hod*·nik
j	**j**oke	*džep, đak*	jep, jak
k	**k**it	*krov*	krov
l	**l**ot	*lutka*	*lut*·ka
ly	mil**li**on	*nedjelja*	*ned*·ye·lya
m	**m**an	*mozak*	*mo*·zak
n	**n**ot	*nafta*	*naf*·ta
ny	ca**ny**on	*kuhinja*	*ku*·hi·nya
p	**p**et	*petak*	*pe*·tak
r	**r**un (rolled)	*radnik*	*rad*·nik
s	**s**un	*sastanak*	*sas*·ta·nak
sh	**sh**ot	*košta*	*kosh*·ta
t	**t**op	*sat*	sat
ts	ha**ts**	*prosinac*	*pro*·si·nats
v	**v**ery	*viza*	*vi*·za
y	**y**es	*svjetlost*	*svyet*·lost
z	**z**ero	*zec*	zets
zh	plea**s**ure	*koža*	*ko*·zha
'	a slight y sound	*kašalj, siječanj*	*ka*·shal', *si*·ye·chan'

tools

language difficulties

Do you speak English?
Govorite/Govoriš li engleski? **pol/inf**   go·vo·ri·te/go·vo·rish li en·gle·ski

Do you understand?
Da li razumijete/razumiješ? **pol/inf**   da li ra·zu·mi·ye·te/ra·zu·mi·yesh

I (don't) understand.
Ja (ne) razumijem.   ya (ne) ra·zu·mi·yem

What does (*dobro*) mean?
Što znači (dobro)?   shto zna·chi (do·bro)

How do you ...?	*Kako se ...?*	ka·ko se ...
pronounce this	*ovo izgovara*	o·vo iz·go·va·ra
write (*dobro*)	*piše (dobro)*	pi·she (do·bro)

Could you please ...?	*Možete li ...?* **pol**	mo·zhe·te li ...
	Možeš li ...? **inf**	mo·zhesh li ...
repeat that	*to ponoviti*	to po·no·vi·ti
speak more slowly	*govoriti sporije*	go·vo·ri·ti spo·ri·ye
write it down	*to napisati*	to na·pi·sa·ti

essentials

Yes.	*Da.*	da
No.	*Ne.*	ne
Please.	*Molim.*	mo·lim
Thank you	*Hvala vam/ti*	hva·la vam/ti
(very much). **pol/inf**	*(puno).*	(pu·no)
You're welcome.	*Nema na čemu.*	ne·ma na che·mu
Excuse me.	*Oprostite.*	o·pro·sti·te
Sorry.	*Žao mi je.*	zha·o mi ye

numbers

0	*nula*	*nu*·la	14	*četrnaest*	che·*tr*·na·est
1	*jedan* m	*ye*·dan	15	*petnaest*	*pet*·na·est
	jedna f	*yed*·na	16	*šesnaest*	*shes*·na·est
	jedno n	*yed*·no	17	*sedamnaest*	se·*dam*·na·est
2	*dva* m&n	dva	18	*osamnaest*	o·*sam*·na·est
	dvije f	*dvi*·ye	19	*devetnaest*	de·*vet*·na·est
3	*tri*	tri	20	*dvadeset*	*dva*·de·set
4	*četiri*	che·ti·ri	21	*dvadeset jedan*	*dva*·de·set *ye*·dan
5	*pet*	pet	30	*trideset*	*tri*·de·set
6	*šest*	shest	40	*četrdeset*	che·*tr*·de·set
7	*sedam*	se·dam	50	*pedeset*	pe·*de*·set
8	*osam*	o·sam	60	*šezdeset*	shez·*de*·set
9	*devet*	de·vet	70	*sedamdeset*	se·dam·*de*·set
10	*deset*	de·set	80	*osamdeset*	o·sam·*de*·set
11	*jedanaest*	ye·*da*·na·est	90	*devedeset*	de·ve·*de*·set
12	*dvanaest*	*dva*·na·est	100	*sto*	sto
13	*trinaest*	*tri*·na·est	1000	*tisuću/hiljadu* ©/⑤	*ti*·su·chu/*hi*·lya·du

time & dates

What time is it?	*Koliko je sati?*	ko·*li*·ko ye *sa*·ti
It's one o'clock.	*Jedan je sat.*	*ye*·dan ye *sa*·t
It's (10) o'clock.	*(Deset) je sati.*	(*de*·set) ye *sa*·ti
Quarter past (10).	*(Deset) i petnaest.*	(*de*·set) i *pet*·na·est
Half-past (10).	*(Deset) i po.*	(*de*·set) i *po*
Quarter to (10).	*Petnaest do (deset).*	*pet*·na·est do (*de*·set)
At what time?	*U koliko sati?*	u ko·*li*·ko *sa*·ti
At ...	*U ...*	u ...
am	*prijepodne*	*pri*·ye·*pod*·ne
pm	*popodne*	po·*pod*·ne
Monday	*ponedjeljak*	po·*ne*·dye·lyak
Tuesday	*utorak*	*u*·to·rak
Wednesday	*srijeda*	sri·*ye*·da
Thursday	*četvrtak*	chet·*vr*·tak
Friday	*petak*	*pe*·tak
Saturday	*subota*	*su*·bo·ta
Sunday	*nedjelja*	*ne*·dye·lya

January	siječanj	si·ye·chan'
February	veljača	ve·lya·cha
March	ožujak	o·zhu·yak
April	travanj	tra·van'
May	svibanj	svi·ban'
June	lipanj	li·pan'
July	srpanj	sr·pan'
August	kolovoz	ko·lo·voz
September	rujan	ru·yan
October	listopad	li·sto·pad
November	studeni	stu·de·ni
December	prosinac	pro·si·nats

What date is it today?	Koji je danas datum?	ko·yi ye da·nas da·tum
It's (18 October).	(Osamnaesti listopad).	(o·sam·na·e·sti li·sto·pad)
since (May)	od (svibnja)	od (svib·nya)
until (June)	do (lipnja)	do (lip·nya)
last night	sinoć	si·noch
last week	prošlog tjedna ©️	prosh·log tyed·na
	prošle nedelje ⑤	prosh·le ne·de·lye
last month	prošlog mjeseca	prosh·log mye·se·tsa
last year	prošle godine	prosh·le go·di·ne
next week	idućeg tjedna ©️	i·du·cheg tyed·na
	iduće nedelje ⑤	i·du·che ne·de·lye
next month	idućeg mjeseca	i·du·cheg mye·se·tsa
next year	iduće godine	i·du·che go·di·ne
yesterday/	jučer/	yu·cher/
tomorrow ...	sutra ...	su·tra ...
morning	ujutro	u·yu·tro
afternoon	popodne	po·pod·ne
evening	uvečer	u·ve·cher

weather

What's the weather like?	Kakvo je vrijeme?	kak·vo ye vri·ye·me
It's ...	... je.	... ye
cloudy	Oblačno	o·blach·no
cold	Hladno	hlad·no
hot	Vruće	vru·che
raining	Kišovito	ki·sho·vi·to
snowing	Snjegovito	snye·go·vi·to
sunny	Sunčano	sun·cha·no
warm	Toplo	to·plo
windy	Vjetrovito	vye·tro·vi·to
spring	proljeće n	pro·lye·che
summer	ljeto n	lye·to
autumn	jesen f	ye·sen
winter	zima f	zi·ma

border crossing

I'm here ...	Ja sam ovdje ...	ya sam ov·dye ...
in transit	u prolazu	u pro·la·zu
on business	poslovno	po·slov·no
on holiday	na odmoru	na od·mo·ru
I'm here for ...	Ostajem ovdje ...	o·sta·yem ov·dye ...
(10) days	(deset) dana	(de·set) da·na
(two) months	(dva) mjeseca	(dva) mye·se·tsa
(three) weeks	(tri) tjedna ©	(tri) tyed·na
	(tri) nedelje ⑤	(tri) ne·de·lye

I'm going to (Zagreb).
 Ja idem u (Zagreb). ya i·dem u (za·greb)

I'm staying at the (Intercontinental).
 Odsjesti ću u (Interkontinentalu). od·sye·sti chu u (in·ter·kon·ti·nen·ta·lu)

I have nothing to declare.
 Nemam ništa za prijaviti. ne·mam nish·ta za pri·ya·vi·ti

I have something to declare.
 Imam nešto za prijaviti. i·mam nesh·to za pri·ya·vi·ti

That's (not) mine.
 To (ni)je moje. to (ni)·ye mo·ye

tools – CROATIAN

51

transport

tickets & luggage

Where can I buy a ticket?
Gdje mogu kupiti kartu?
gdye mo·gu ku·pi·ti kar·tu

Do I need to book a seat?
Trebam li rezervirati mjesto?
tre·bam li re·zer·vi·ra·ti myes·to

One ... ticket	*Jednu ... kartu*	yed·nu ... kar·tu
(to Split), please.	*(do Splita), molim.*	(do spli·ta) mo·lim
one-way	*jednosmjernu*	yed·no·smyer·nu
return	*povratnu*	po·vrat·nu

I'd like to ... my	*Želio/Željela bih ...*	zhe·li·o/zhe·lye·la bih ...
ticket, please.	*svoju kartu, molim.* m/f	svoy·u kar·tu mo·lim
cancel	*poništiti*	po·ni·shti·ti
change	*promijeniti*	pro·mi·ye·ni·ti
collect	*uzeti*	u·ze·ti
confirm	*potvrditi*	pot·vr·di·ti

I'd like a ...	*Želio/Željela bih ...*	zhe·li·o/zhe·lye·la bih ...
seat, please.	*sjedište, molim.* m/f	sye·dish·te mo·lim
nonsmoking	*nepušačko*	ne·pu·shach·ko
smoking	*pušačko*	pu·shach·ko

How much is it?
Koliko stoji?
ko·li·ko stoy·i

Is there air conditioning?
Imate li klima-uređaj?
i·ma·te li kli·ma·u·re·jai

Is there a toilet?
Imate li zahod/toalet? ©/⑤
i·ma·te li za·hod/to·a·let

How long does the trip take?
Koliko traje putovanje?
ko·li·ko trai·e pu·to·va·nye

Is it a direct route?
Je li to direktan pravac?
ye li to di·rek·tan pra·vats

Where can I find a luggage locker?
Gdje se nalazi pretinac/sanduče ©/⑤
za odlaganje prtljage?
gdye se na·la·zi pre·ti·nats/san·du·che
za od·la·ga·nye prt·lya·ge

My luggage has been …	Moja prtljaga je …	moy·a prt·lya·ga ye …
damaged	oštećena	osh·te·che·na
lost	izgubljena	iz·gub·lye·na
stolen	ukradena	u·kra·de·na

getting around

Where does flight (10) arrive?
Gdje stiže let (deset)? · gdye *sti·*zhe let (*de·*set)

Where does flight (10) depart?
Odakle kreće let (deset)? · o·dak·le *kre·*che let (*de·*set)

Where's (the) …?	Gdje se nalazi …?	gdye se na·la·zi …
arrivals hall	dvorana za dolaske	dvo·ra·na za do·las·ke
departures hall	dvorana za odlaske	dvo·ra·na za od·las·ke
duty-free shop	duty-free	dyu·ti·fri
	prodavaonica	pro·da·va·o·ni·tsa
gate (12)	izlaz (dvanaest)	iz·laz (dva·na·est)

Which … goes to (Dubrovnik)?	Koji … ide za (Dubrovnik)?	koy·i … i·de za (du·brov·nik)?
boat	brod	brod
bus	autobus	a·u·to·bus
plane	zrakoplov/avion ©/⑤	zra·ko·plov/a·vi·on
train	vlak/voz ©/⑤	vlak/voz

What time's the … bus?	Kada ide … autobus?	ka·da i·de … a·u·to·bus
first	prvi	pr·vi
last	zadnji	zad·nyi
next	slijedeći	sli·ye·de·chi

At what time does it arrive/leave?
U koliko sati stiže/kreće? · u ko·*li·*ko *sa·*ti *sti·*zhe/*kre·*che

How long will it be delayed?
Koliko kasni? · ko·*li·*ko *kas·*ni

What station/stop is this?
Koja stanica je ovo? · koy·a *sta·*ni·tsa ye *o·*vo

What's the next station/stop?
Koja je slijedeća stanica? · koy·a ye sli·*ye·*de·cha *sta·*ni·tsa

Does it stop at (Zadar)?
Da li staje u (Zadru)? · da li *sta·*ye u (*zad·*ru)

Please tell me when we get to (Pula).
Molim vas recite mi — mo·lim vas re·tsi·te mi
kada stignemo u (Pulu). — ka·da stig·ne·mo u (pu·lu)

How long do we stop here?
Koliko dugo ostajemo ovdje? — ko·li·ko du·go o·stai·e·mo ov·dye

Is this seat available?
Da li je ovo sjedište slobodno? — da li ye o·vo sye·dish·te slo·bod·no

That's my seat.
Ovo je moje sjedište. — o·vo ye moy·e sye·dish·te

I'd like a taxi ...	*Trebam taksi ...*	tre·bam tak·si ...
at (9am)	*u (devet prijepodne)*	u (de·vet pri·ye·pod·ne)
now	*sada*	sa·da
tomorrow	*sutra*	su·tra

Is this taxi available?
Da li je ovaj taksi slobodan? — da li ye o·vai tak·si slo·bo·dan

How much is it to ...?
Koliko stoji prijevoz do ...? — ko·li·ko stoy·i pri·ye·voz do ...

Please put the meter on.
Molim uključite taksimetar. — mo·lim uk·lyu·chi·te tak·si·me·tar

Please take me to (this address).
Molim da me odvezete — mo·lim da me od·ve·ze·te
na (ovu adresu). — na (o·vu a·dre·su)

Please ...	*Molim vas ...*	mo·lim vas ...
slow down	*usporite*	u·spo·ri·te
stop here	*stanite ovdje*	sta·ni·te ov·dye
wait here	*pričekajte ovdje*	pri·che·kai·te ov·dye

car, motorbike & bicycle hire

I'd like to	*Želio/Željela*	zhe·li·o/zhe·lye·la
hire a ...	*bih iznajmiti ... m/f*	bih iz·nai·mi·ti ...
bicycle	*bicikl*	bi·tsi·kl
car	*automobil*	a·u·to·mo·bil
motorbike	*motocikl*	mo·to·tsi·kl
with ...	*sa ...*	sa ...
a driver	*vozačem*	vo·za·chem
air conditioning	*klima-uređajem*	kli·ma·u·re·jai·em

How much for ... hire?	*Koliko stoji najam po ...?*	ko·*li*·ko *stoy*·i *nai*·am po ...
hourly	*satu*	*sa*·tu
daily	*danu*	*da*·nu
weekly	*tjednu/nedelji* ©/⑤	*tyed*·nu/*ne*·de·lyi

air	*zrak/vazduh* m ©/⑤	zrak/*vaz*·duh
oil	*ulje* n	*u*·lye
petrol	*benzin* m	*ben*·zin
tyres	*gume* f pl	*gu*·me

I need a mechanic.
   Trebam automehaničara.   *tre*·bam *a*·u·to·me·*ha*·ni·cha·ra

I've run out of petrol.
   Nestalo mi je benzina.   *ne*·sta·lo mi ye ben·*zi*·na

I have a flat tyre.
   Imam probušenu gumu.   *i*·mam *pro*·bu·she·nu *gu*·mu

directions

Where's the ...?	*Gdje je ...?*	*gdye* ye ...
bank	*banka*	*ban*·ka
city centre	*gradski centar*	*grad*·ski *tsen*·tar
hotel	*hotel*	*ho*·tel
market	*tržnica/pijaca* ©/⑤	*trzh*·ni·tsa/*pi*·ya·tsa
police station	*policijska stanica*	po·*li*·tsiy·ska *sta*·ni·tsa
post office	*poštanski ured*	*po*·shtan·ski *u*·red
public toilet	*javni zahod/toalet* ©/⑤	*yav*·ni za·hod/to·a·*let*
tourist office	*turistička agencija*	tu·*ris*·tich·ka a·*gen*·tsi·ya

Is this the road to (Pazin)?
   Je li ovo cesta/put za (Pazin)? ©/⑤   ye li *o*·vo *tse*·sta/put za (*pa*·zin)

Can you show me (on the map)?
   Možete li mi to   *mo*·zhe·te li mi to
   pokazati (na karti)?   po·*ka*·za·ti (na *kar*·ti)

What's the address?
   Koja je adresa?   *koy*·a ye a·*dre*·sa

How far is it?
   Koliko je udaljeno?   ko·*li*·ko ye *u*·da·lye·no

How do I get there?
   Kako mogu tamo stići?   *ka*·ko *mo*·gu *ta*·mo *sti*·chi

Turn ...	Skrenite ...	skre·ni·te ...
at the corner	na uglu	na u·glu
at the traffic lights	na semaforu	na se·ma·fo·ru
left/right	lijevo/desno	li·ye·vo/de·sno

It's ...	Nalazi se ...	na·la·zi se ...
behind ...	iza ...	i·za ...
far away	daleko	da·le·ko
here	ovdje	ov·dye
in front of ...	ispred ...	i·spred ...
left	lijevo	li·ye·vo
near ...	blizu ...	bli·zu ...
next to ...	pored ...	po·red ...
on the corner	na uglu	na u·glu
opposite ...	nasuprot ...	na·su·prot ...
right	desno	de·sno
straight ahead	ravno naprijed	rav·no na·pri·yed
there	tamo	ta·mo

by bus	autobusom	a·u·to·bu·som
by taxi	taksijem	tak·si·yem
by train	vlakom/vozom ©/ⓢ	vla·kom/vo·zom
on foot	pješke	pyesh·ke

north	sjever m	sye·ver
south	jug m	yug
east	istok m	is·tok
west	zapad m	za·pad

signs

Ulaz/Izlaz	u·laz/iz·laz	Entrance/Exit
Otvoreno/Zatvoreno	ot vo·re·no/zat vo·re·no	Open/Closed
Slobodna Mjesta	slo·bod·na mye·sta	Rooms Available
Bez Slobodnih Mjesta	bez slo·bod·nih mye·sta	No Vacancies
Informacije	in·for·ma·tsi·ye	Information
Policijska Stanica	po·li·tsiy·ska sta·ni·tsa	Police Station
Zabranjeno	za·bra·nye·no	Prohibited
WC	ve·tse	Toilets
Muški	mush·ki	Men
Ženski	zhen·ski	Women
Toplo/Hladno	to·plo/hlad·no	Hot/Cold

accommodation

finding accommodation

Where's a ...?	Gdje se nalazi ...?	gdye se na·la·zi ...
camping ground	kamp	kamp
guesthouse	privatni smještaj	pri·vat·ni smyesh·tai
	za najam	za nai·am
hotel	hotel	ho·tel
youth hostel	prenoćište za	pre·no·chish·te za
	mladež	mla·dezh
Can you recommend	Možete li	mo·zhe·te li
somewhere ...?	preporučiti negdje ...?	pre·po·ru·chi·ti neg·dye ...
cheap	jeftino	yef·ti·no
good	dobro	do·bro
nearby	blizu	bli·zu

I'd like to book a room, please.
Želio/Željela bih rezervirati   zhe·li·o/zhe·lye·la bih re·zer·vi·ra·ti
sobu, molim. m/f   so·bu mo·lim

I have a reservation.
Imam rezervaciju.   i·mam re·zer·va·tsi·yu

My name's ...
Moje ime je ...   moy·e i·me ye ...

Do you have a ...	Imate li ...?	i·ma·te li ...
room?		
single	jednokrevetnu sobu	yed·no·kre·vet·nu so·bu
double	sobu sa duplim	so·bu sa dup·lim
	krevetom	kre·ve·tom
twin	dvokrevetnu sobu	dvo·kre·vet·nu so·bu
How much is it per ...?	Koliko stoji po ...?	ko·li·ko sto·yi po ...
night	noći	no·chi
person	osobi	o·so·bi
Can I pay by ...?	Mogu li platiti sa ...?	mo·gu li pla·ti·ti sa ...
credit card	kreditnom	kre·dit·nom
	karticom	kar·ti·tsom
travellers cheque	putničkim čekom	put·nich·kim che·kom

For (three) nights.
Na (tri) noći. — na (tri) *no*-chi

From (2 July) to (6 July).
Od (drugog srpnja) do — od (*dru*-gog *srp*-nya) do
(šestog srpnja). — (*she*-stog *srp*-nya)

Can I see it?
Mogu li je vidjeti? — *mo*-gu li ye *vi*-dye-ti

Am I allowed to camp here?
Mogu li ovdje kampirati? — *mo*-gu li *ov*-dye kam-*pi*-ra-ti

Where can I find the nearest camp site?
Gdje se nalazi najbliže — gdye se *na*-la-zi *nai*-bli-zhe
mjesto za kampiranje? — *mye*-sto za kam-*pi*-ra-nye

requests & queries

When/Where is breakfast served?
Kada/Gdje služite doručak? — *ka*-da/gdye *slu*-zhi-te *do*-ru-chak

Please wake me at (seven).
Probudite me u (sedam), molim. — pro-*bu*-di-te me u (*se*-dam) *mo*-lim

Could I have my key, please?
Mogu li dobiti moj — *mo*-gu li *do*-bi-ti moy
ključ, molim? — klyuch *mo*-lim

Could I have another (blanket)?
Mogu li dobiti jednu dodatnu — *mo*-gu li *do*-bi-ti *yed*-nu *do*-dat-nu
(deku)? — (*de*-ku)

Is there a/an ...?	*Imate li ...?*	*i*-ma-te li ...
elevator	*dizalo/lift* ©/®	*di*-za-lo/lift
safe	*sef*	sef
The room is too ...	*Suviše je ...*	*su*-vi-she ye ...
expensive	*skupo*	*sku*-po
noisy	*bučno*	*buch*-no
small	*malo*	*ma*-lo
The ... doesn't work.	*... je neispravan.*	... ye *ne*-i-spra-van
air conditioning	*Klima-uređaj*	*kli*-ma-u-*re*-jai
fan	*Ventilator*	ven-ti-*la*-tor
toilet	*Zahod/Toalet* ©/®	*za*-hod/to-a-*let*

This ... isn't clean.	Ova ... nije čista.	o·va ... ni·ye chis·ta
blanket	deka	de·ka
sheet	plahta ©	plah·ta

This ... isn't clean.	Ovaj ... nije čist.	o·va ... ni·ye chist
sheet	čaršav ⓢ	char·shav
towel	ručnik/peškir ©/ⓢ	ruch·nik/pesh·kir

checking out

What time is checkout?
U koliko sati treba napustiti sobu?   u ko·*li*·ko *sa*·ti *tre*·ba na·*pu*·sti·ti *so*·bu

Can I leave my luggage here?
Mogu li ovdje ostaviti svoje torbe?   mo·gu li ov·dye o·sta·vi·ti svoy·e tor·be

Could I have my ..., please?	Mogu li dobiti ..., molim?	mo·gu li do·bi·ti ... mo·lim
deposit	svoj depozit	svoy de·po·zit
passport	svoju putovnicu/pasoš ©/ⓢ	svoy·u pu·tov·ni·tsu/pa·sosh
valuables	svoje dragocjenosti	svo·ye dra·go·tsye·no·sti

communications & banking

the internet

Where's the local Internet café?
Gdje je mjesni internet kafić?   gdye ye mye·sni in·ter·net ka·fich

How much is it per hour?
Koja je cijena po satu?   koy·a ye tsi·ye·na po sa·tu

I'd like to ...	Želio/Željela bih ... m/f	zhe·li·o/zhe·lye·la bih ...
check my email	provjeriti svoj email	pro·vye·ri·ti svoy i·meyl
get Internet access	pristup internetu	pri·stup in·ter·ne·tu
use a printer	koristiti pisač/štampač ©/ⓢ	ko·ri·sti·ti pi·sach/shtam·pach
use a scanner	koristiti skener	ko·ri·sti·ti ske·ner

mobile/cell phone

I'd like a ...	*Trebao/Trebala bih ... m/f*	tre·ba·o/tre·ba·la bih ...
mobile/cell phone for hire	*iznajmiti mobilni telefon*	iz·*nai*·mi·ti mo·*bil*·ni te·*le*·fon
SIM card for your network	*SIM karticu za vašu mrežu*	sim *kar*·ti·tsu za *va*·shu *mre*·zhu

What are the rates?
Koje su cijene telefoniranja?　　*ko*·ye su tsi·*ye*·ne te·le·fo·*ni*·ra·nya

telephone

What's your phone number?		
Koji je vaš/tvoj broj telefona? pol/inf		*koy*·i ye vash/tvoy broy te·le·*fo*·na
The number is ...		
Broj je ...		broy ye ...
Where's the nearest public phone?		
Gdje je najbliži javni telefon?		gdye ye *nai*·bli·zhi *yav*·ni te·*le*·fon
I'd like to buy a phonecard.		
Želim kupiti telefonsku karticu.		*zhe*·lim *ku*·pi·ti te·*le*·fon·sku *kar*·ti·tsu

I want to ...	*Želim ...*	*zhe*·lim ...
call (Singapore)	*nazvati (Singapur)*	*naz*·va·ti (*sin*·ga·pur)
make a (local) call	*obaviti (lokalni) poziv*	o·ba·vi·ti (*lo*·kal·ni) *po*·ziv
reverse the charges	*obaviti poziv na račun pozvanog*	o·ba·vi·ti *po*·ziv na *ra*·chun *poz*·va·nog

How much does ... cost?	*Koliko košta ...?*	ko·*li*·ko *kosh*·ta ...
a (three)-minute call	*poziv od (tri) minute*	*po*·ziv od (tri) mi·*nu*·te
each extra minute	*svaka naknadna minuta*	*sva*·ka *nak*·nad·na mi·*nu*·ta
(3 kuna) per (30) seconds.	*(3 kune) po (30) sekundi.*	(tri *ku*·ne) po (*tri*·de·set) se·*kun*·di

60

post office

I want to send a ...	Želim poslati ...	zhe·lim po·sla·ti ...
fax	telefaks	te·le·faks
letter	pismo	pi·smo
parcel	paket	pa·ket
postcard	dopisnicu	do·pi·sni·tsu

I want to buy a/an ...	Želim kupiti ...	zhe·lim ku·pi·ti ...
envelope	omotnicu/koverat ©/⑤	o·mot·ni·tsu/ko·ve·rat
stamp	poštansku marku	posh·tan·sku mar·ku

Please send it by ... to (Australia).	Molim da pošaljete to ... u (Australiju).	mo·lim da po·sha·lye·te to ... u (a·u·stra·li·yu).
airmail	zračnom/vazdušnom poštom ©/⑤	zrach·nom/vaz·dush·nom posh·tom
express mail	ekspres poštom	eks·pres posh·tom
registered mail	preporučenom poštom	pre·po·ru·che·nom posh·tom
surface mail	običnom poštom	o·bich·nom posh·tom

Is there any mail for me?
Ima li bilo kakve pošte za mene?   i·ma li bi·lo kak·ve posh·te za me·ne

bank

Where's a/an ...?	Gdje se nalazi ...?	gdye se na·la·zi ...
ATM	bankovni automat	ban·kov·ni a·u·to·mat
foreign exchange office	mjenjačnica za strane valute	mye·nyach·ni·tsa za stra·ne va·lu·te

Where can I ...?	Gdje mogu ...?	gdye mo·gu ...
I'd like to ... m/f	Želio/Željela bih ... m/f	zhe·li·o/zhe·lye·la bih ...
arrange a transfer	obaviti prijenos novca	o·ba·vi·ti pri·ye·nos nov·tsa
cash a cheque	unovčiti ček	u·nov·chi·ti chek
change a travellers cheque	zamijeniti putnički ček	za·mi·ye·ni·ti put·nich·ki chek
change money	zamijeniti novac	za·mi·ye·ni·ti no·vats
get a cash advance	uzeti predujam/avans u gotovini ©/⑤	u·ze·ti pre·du·yam/a·vans u go·to·vi·ni
withdraw money	podignuti novac	po·dig·nu·ti no·vats

What's the ...?	Koji/Kolika je ...? m/f	koy·i/ko·li·ka ye ...
charge for that	pristojba/tarifa	pri·stoy·ba/ta·ri·fa
	za to f ©/⑤	za to
exchange rate	tečaj/kurs	te·chai/kurs
	razmjene m ©/⑤	raz·mye·ne

It's ...	To je ...	to ye ...
(50) kuna	(pedeset) kuna	(pe·de·set) ku·na
free	besplatno	bes·plat·no

What time does the bank open?
U koliko sati se otvara banka?   u ko·li·ko sa·ti se ot·va·ra ban·ka

Has my money arrived yet?
Da li je moj novac stigao?   da li ye moy no·vats sti·ga·o

sightseeing

getting in

What time does it open/close?
U koliko sati se otvara/zatvara?   u ko·li·ko sa·ti se ot·va·ra/zat·va·ra

What's the admission charge?
Koliko stoji ulaznica?   ko·li·ko stoy·i u·laz·ni·tsa

Is there a discount for students/children?
Imate li popust za   i·ma·te li po·pust za
studente/djecu?   stu·den·te/dye·tsu

I'd like a ...	Želio/Željela bih ... m/f	zhe·li·o/zhe·lye·la bih ...
catalogue	katalog	ka·ta·log
guide	turistički vodič	tu·ri·stich·ki vo·dich
local map	kartu mjesta	kar·tu mye·sta

I'd like to see ...
Želio/Željela bih vidjeti ... m/f   zhe·li·o/zhe·lye·la bih vi·dye·ti ...

What's that?
Što je to?   shto ye to

Can I take a photo?
Mogu li slikati?   mo·gu li sli·ka·ti

tours

When's the next ...?	*Kada je idući/ iduća ...?* m/f	*ka·da ye i·du·chi/ i·du·cha ...*
day trip	*dnevni izlet* m	*dnev·ni iz·let*
tour	*turistička ekskurzija* f	*tu·ri·stich·ka ek·skur·zi·ya*
Is ... included?	*Da li je ... uključen/ uključena?* m/f	*da ye ... uk·lyu·chen/ uk·lyu·che·na*
accommodation	*smještaj* m	*smye·shtai*
the admission charge	*ulaznica* f	*u·laz·ni·tsa*
food	*hrana* f	*hra·na*
transport	*prijevoz* m	*pri·ye·voz*

How long is the tour?
Koliko traje ekskurzija? ko·*li*·ko *trai*·e ek·*skur*·zi·ya

What time should we be back?
U koje bi se vrijeme trebali vratiti? u *koy*·e bi se vri·*ye*·me *tre*·ba·li *vra*·ti·ti

sightseeing

castle	*dvorac* m	*dwa*·rats
cathedral	*katedrala* f	ka·te·*dra*·la
church	*crkva* f	*tsr*·kva
main square	*glavni trg* m	*glav*·ni trg
monastery	*samostan/manastir* m ©/⑤	*sa*·mo·stan/*ma*·nas·tir
monument	*spomenik* m	*spo*·me·nik
museum	*muzej* m	*mu*·zey
old city	*stari grad* m	*sta*·ri grad
palace	*palača* f	*pa*·la·cha
ruins	*ruševine* f pl	*ru*·she·vi·ne
stadium	*stadion* m	*sta*·di·on
statue	*kip* m	kip

shopping

enquiries

Where's a ...?	*Gdje je ...?*	gdye ye ...
bank	*banka*	*ban*-ka
bookshop	*knjižara*	*knyi*-zha-ra
camera shop	*prodavaonica*	pro-da-va-o-ni-tsa
	fotoaparata	fo-to-a-pa-*ra*-ta
department store	*robna kuća*	*rob*-na *ku*-cha
grocery store	*prodavaonica*	pro-da-va-o-ni-tsa
	namirnica	na-*mir*-ni-tsa
market	*tržnica/pijaca* ©/⑤	*tr*-zhni-tsa/*pi*-ya-tsa
newsagency	*prodavaonica*	pro-da-va-o-ni-tsa
	novina	no-*vi*-na
supermarket	*supermarket*	su-per-*mar*-ket

Where can I buy (a padlock)?
Gdje mogu kupiti (lokot)?   gdye *mo*-gu *ku*-pi-ti (*lo*-kot)

I'm looking for ...
Tražim ...   *tra*-zhim

Can I look at it?
Mogu li to pogledati?   *mo*-gu li to po-*gle*-da-ti

Do you have any others?
Imate li bilo kakve druge?   i-ma-te li *bi*-lo *kak*-ve *dru*-ge

Does it have a guarantee?
Ima li ovo garanciju?   i-ma li o-vo ga-*ran*-tsi-yu

Can I have it sent abroad?
Možete li mi to   *mo*-zhe-te li mi to
poslati u inozemstvo?   po-*sla*-ti u i-no-*zemst*-vo

Can I have my (backpack) repaired?
Mogu li popraviti svoj (ranac)?   *mo*-gu li po-*pra*-vi-ti svoy (*ra*-nats)

It's faulty.
Neispravno je.   ne-*is*-prav-no ye

I'd like ..., please.	*Želio/Željela bih ...* m/f	*zhe*-li-o/*zhe*-lye-la bih ...
a bag	*vrećicu*	*vre*-chi-tsu
a refund	*povrat novca*	*pov*-rat *nov*-tsa
to return this	*ovo vratiti*	*o*-vo *vra*-ti-ti

paying

How much is it?
Koliko stoji/košta? ©/⑤   ko·*li*·ko *sto*·yi/*kosh*·ta

Can you write down the price?
Možete li napisati cijenu?   *mo*·zhe·te li na·*pi*·sa·ti tsi·*ye*·nu

That's too expensive.
To je preskupo.   to ye *pre*·sku·po

Do you have something cheaper?
Imate li nešto jeftinije?   *i*·ma·te li *nesh*·to yef·*ti*·ni·ye

I'll give you (five kuna).
Dati ću vam (pet kuna).   *da*·ti chu vam (pet *ku*·na)

There's a mistake in the bill.
Ima jedna greška na računu.   *i*·ma *yed*·na *gresh*·ka na ra·*chu*·nu

Do you accept …?   *Da li prihvaćate …?*   da li *pri*·hva·cha·te …
  credit cards   *kreditne kartice*   *kre*·dit·ne *kar*·ti·tse
  debit cards   *debitne kartice*   *de*·bit·ne *kar*·ti·tse
  travellers cheques   *putničke čekove*   *put*·nich·ke *che*·ko·ve

I'd like …, please.   *Želio/Željela bih …* m/f   zhe·li·o/zhe·lye·la bih …
  a receipt   *račun*   *ra*·chun
  my change   *moj ostatak novca*   moy o·*sta*·tak *nov*·tsa

clothes & shoes

Can I try it on?   *Mogu li to probati?*   *mo*·gu li to *pro*·ba·ti
My size is (40).   *Moja veličina je (četrdeset).*   *moy*·a ve·li·*chi*·na ye (che·tr·*de*·set)
It doesn't fit.   *Ne odgovara mi to.*   ne od·*go*·va·ra mi to

small   *sitna*   *sit*·na
medium   *srednja*   *sred*·nya
large   *krupna*   *krup*·na

books & music

I'd like (a) ...	Želio/Željela bih ... m/f	zhe·li·o/zhe·lye·la bih ...
newspaper	novine	no·vi·ne
(in English)	(na engleskom)	(na en·gles·kom)
pen	kemijsku	ke·miy·sku

Is there an English-language bookshop?

Postoji li knjižara za — po·stoy i li knyi·zha·ra za
engleski jezik? — en·gle·ski ye·zik

I'm looking for something by (Oliver Dragojević).

Tražim nešto od — tra·zhim nesh·to od
(Olivera Dragojevića). — (o·li·ve·ra dra·goy·e·vi·cha)

Can I listen to this?

Mogu li ovo poslušati? — mo·gu li o·vo po·slu·sha·ti

photography

Can you ...?	Možete li ...?	mo·zhe·te li ...
develop this film	razviti ovaj film	raz·vi·ti o·vai film
load my film	staviti moj film	sta·vi·ti moy film
	u foto-aparat	u fo·to·a·pa·rat
transfer photos	prebaciti	pre·ba·tsi·ti
from my	fotografije sa	fo·to·gra·fi·ye sa
camera to CD	mog aparata na CD	mog a·pa·ra·ta na tse·de

I need a/an ... film	Trebam ... film	tre·bam ... film
for this camera.	za ovaj foto-aparat.	za o·vai fo·to·a·pa·rat
APS	APS	a·pe·es
B&W	crno-bijeli	tsr·no·bi·ye·li
colour	kolor	ko·lor

I need a ... film	Trebam film ...	tre·bam film ...
for this camera.	za ovaj foto-aparat.	za o·vai fo·to·a·pa·rat
slide	za dijapozitive	za di·ya·po·zi·ti·ve
(200) speed	brzine (dvijesto)	br·zi·ne (dvi·ye·sto)

When will it	Kada će to biti	ka·da che to bi·ti
be ready?	gotovo?	go·to·vo

meeting people

greetings, goodbyes & introductions

Hello.	Bog/Zdravo. ©/⑤	bog/zdra·vo
Hi.	Ćao.	cha·o
Good night.	Laku noć.	la·ku noch
Goodbye.	Zbogom.	zbo·gom
Bye.	Ćao.	cha·o
See you later.	Doviđenja.	do·vi·je·nya
Mr	Gospodin	go·spo·din
Mrs	Gospođa	go·spo·ja
Miss	Gospođica	go·spo·ji·tsa
How are you?	Kako ste/si? pol/inf	ka·ko ste/si
Fine. And you?	Dobro. A vi/ti? pol/inf	do·bro a vi/ti
What's your name?	Kako se zovete/zoveš? pol/inf	ka·ko se zo·ve·te/zo·vesh
My name is ...	Zovem se ...	zo·vem se ...
I'm pleased to meet you.	Drago mi je da smo se upoznali.	dra·go mi ye da smo se u·poz·na·li

This is my ...	Ovo je moj/moja ... m/f	o·vo ye moy/moy·a ...
boyfriend	dečko	dech·ko
brother	brat	brat
daughter	ćerka	cher·ka
father	otac	o·tats
friend	prijatelj/prijateljica m/f	pri·ya·tel'/pri·ya·te·lyi·tsa
girlfriend	cura/devojka ©/⑤	tsu·ra/de·voy·ka
husband	muž	muzh
mother	majka	mai·ka
partner (intimate)	suprug/supruga m/f	su·prug/su·pru·ga
sister	sestra	ses·tra
son	sin	sin
wife	žena	zhe·na

Here's my ...	Ovo je moj/moja ... m/f	o·vo ye moy/moy·a ...
What's your ...?	Koji je tvoj ...? m	koy·i ye tvoy ...
	Koja je tvoja ...? f	koy·a ye tvoy·a ...
(email) address	(email) adresa f	(i·meyl) a·dre·sa
fax number	broj faksa m	broy fak·sa
phone number	broj telefona m	broy te·le·fo·na

occupations

What's your occupation?	*Čime se bavite?*	*chi*·me se *ba*·vi·te
I'm a/an ...	*Ja sam ...*	ya sam ...
artist	*umjetnik* m	*um*·yet·nik
	umjetnica f	*um*·yet·ni·tsa
businessperson	*poslovna osoba*	*po*·slo·vna *o·so·*ba
farmer	*poljodjelac* ©	po·lyo·*dye·*lats
	zemljoradnik ⑤	zem·lyo·*rad·*nik
office worker	*službenik* m	*sluzh*·be·nik
	službenica f	*sluzh*·be·ni·tsa
scientist	*znanstvenik* ©	*znans*·tve·nik
	naučnik ⑤	*na*·uch·nik
tradesperson	*zanatlija*	za·*nat*·li·ya

background

Where are you from?	*Odakle ste?*	o·*da*·kle ste
I'm from ...	*Ja sam iz ...*	ya sam iz ...
Australia	*Australije*	a·u·*stra*·li·ye
Canada	*Kanade*	ka·na·de
England	*Engleske*	*en*·gles·ke
New Zealand	*Novog Zelanda*	*no*·vog *ze*·lan·da
the USA	*Amerike*	a·*me*·ri·ke
Are you married?	*Jeste li vi vjenčani?*	*ye*·ste li vi *vyen*·cha·ni
I'm married.	*Ja sam u braku.*	ya sam u *bra*·ku
I'm single.	*Ja sam neoženjen.* m	ya sam ne·*o*·zhe·nyen
	Ja sam neudata. f	ya sam *ne*·u·da·ta

age

How old ...?	*Koliko ... godina?*	ko·*li*·ko ... *go*·di·na
are you	*imate/imaš* pol/inf	*i*·ma·te/*i*·mash
is your daughter	*vaša kći ima*	*va*·sha k·*chi i*·ma
is your son	*vaš sin ima*	vash sin *i*·ma
I'm ... years old.	*Imam ... godina.*	*i*·mam ... *go*·di·na
He/She is ... years old.	*On/Ona ima ... godina.*	on/*o*·na *i*·ma ... *go*·di·na

feelings

I'm (not) …	Ja (ni)sam …	ya (ni·)sam …
Are you …?	Jeste li …?	ye·ste li …
happy	sretni	sret·ni
hungry	gladni	glad·ni
OK	dobro	dob·ro
sad	tužni	tuzh·ni
thirsty	žedni	zhed·ni
tired	umorni	u·mor·ni

Are you hot/cold?
Je li vam toplo/hladno?   ye li vam to·plo/hlad·no

I'm (not) hot/cold.
Meni (ni)je toplo/hladno.   me·ni (ni·)ye to·plo/hlad·no

entertainment

going out

Where can	Gdje mogu	gdye mo·gu
I find …?	pronaći …?	pro·na·chi …
clubs	noćne klubove	noch·ne klu·bo·ve
gay venues	gay lokale	gey lo·ka·le
pubs	gostionice	go·sti·o·ni·tse
I feel like going	Želim otići …	zhe·lim o·ti·chi …
to a/the …		
concert	na koncert	na kon·tsert
movies	u kino/bioskop ©/⑤	u ki·no/bi·os·kop
party	na zabavu	na za·ba·vu
restaurant	u restoran	u re·sto·ran
theatre	u kazalište	u ka·za·lish·te

Do you like ...?	Volite li ...?	vo·li·te li ...
I (don't) like ...	Ja (ne) volim ...	ya (ne) vo·lim ...
art	umjetnost	um·yet·nost
cooking	kuhanje	ku·ha·nye
movies	filmove	fil·mo·ve
reading	čitanje	chi·ta·nye
shopping	kupovanje	ku·po·va·nye
sport	sport	sport
travelling	putovanja	pu·to·va·nya
Do you like to ...?	Da li volite da ...?	da li vo·li·te da ...
dance	plešete	ple·she·te
listen to music	slušate glazbu/	slu·sha·te glaz·bu/
	muziku ©/ⓢ	mu·zi·ku

food & drink

finding a place to eat

Can you	Možete li preporučiti	mo·zhe·te li pre·po·ru·chi·ti
recommend a ...?	neki ...?	ne·ki ...
bar	bar	bar
café	kafić	ka·fich
restaurant	restoran	re·sto·ran
I'd like ...	Želim ...	zhe·lim ...
a table for (five)	stol za (petoro)	stol za (pe·to·ro)
the (non)smoking	(ne)pušačko	(ne·)pu·shach·ko
section	mjesto	mye·sto

ordering food

breakfast	doručak m	do·ru·chak
lunch	ručak m	ru·chak
dinner	večera f	ve·che·ra
snack	užina f	u·zhi·na
today's special	specijalitet dana m	spe·tsi·ya·li·tet da·na

What would you recommend?	Što biste nam preporučili?	shto bi·ste nam pre·po·ru·chi·li
I'd like (the) ..., please.	Mogu li dobiti ..., molim?	mo·gu li do·bi·ti ... mo·lim
bill	račun	ra·chun
drink list	cjenik pića	tsye·nik pi·cha
menu	jelovnik	ye·lov·nik
that dish	ono jelo	o·no ye·lo

drinks

coffee/tea ...	kava/čaj ...	ka·va/chai ...
with milk	sa mlijekom	sa mli·ye·kom
without sugar	bez šećera	bez she·che·ra
(orange) juice	sok (od naranče) m	sok (od na·ran·che)
mineral water	mineralna voda f	mi·ne·ral·na vo·da
soft drink	bezalkoholno piće m	be·zal·ko·hol·no pi·che
(hot) water	(topla) voda f	(to·pla) vo·da

in the bar

I'll have ...	Želim naručiti ...	zhe·lim na·ru·chi·ti ...
I'll buy you a drink.	Častim vas/te pićem. pol/inf	cha·stim vas/te pi·chem
What would you like?	Što želite/želiš? pol/inf	shto zhe·li·te/zhe·lish
Cheers!	Živjeli!	zhi·vye·li
brandy	rakija f	ra·ki·ya
champagne	šampanjac m	sham·pa·nyats
cocktail	koktel m	kok·tel
plum brandy	šljivovica f	shlyi·vo·vi·tsa
a bottle/glass of beer	boca/čaša piva	bo·tsa/cha·sha pi·va
a shot of (whiskey)	jedna čašica (viskija)	yed·na cha·shi·tsa (vi·ski·ya)
a bottle/glass of ... wine	boca/čaša ... vina	bo·tsa/cha·sha ... vi·na
red	crnog	tsr·nog
sparkling	pjenušavog	pye·nu·sha·vog
white	bijelog	bi·ye·log

self-catering

What's the local speciality?
Što je ovdje područni/lokalni ©/⑤   shto ye *ov*-dye po-*druch*-ni/*lo*-kal-ni
specijalitet? ©/⑤   spe-tsi-ya-*li*-tet

What's that?
Što je to?   shto ye to

How much is (a kilo of cheese)?
Koliko stoji/košta (kila sira)? ©/⑤   ko-*li*-ko *sto*-yi/*kosh*-ta (*ki*-la *si*-ra)

I'd like ...	*Želim ...*	*zhe*-lim ...
(200) grams	*(dvijesto) grama*	(dvi-*ye*-sto) *gra*-ma
(two) kilos	*(dvije) kile*	(dvi-ye) *ki*-le
(three) pieces	*(tri) komada*	(tri) ko-*ma*-da
(six) slices	*(šest) kriška*	(shest) *kri*-sha-ka

Less.	*Manje.*	*ma*-nye
Enough.	*Dosta.*	*do*-sta
More.	*Više.*	*vi*-she

special diets & allergies

Is there a vegetarian restaurant near here?
Da li znate za vegetarijanski da li *zna*-te za ve-ge-ta-ri-*yan*-ski
restoran ovdje blizu? re-*sto*-ran *ov*-dye *bli*-zu

Do you have vegetarian food?
Da li imate vegetarijanski obrok? da li *i*-ma-te ve-ge-ta-ri-*yan*-ski *o*-brok

Could you prepare a	*Možete li prirediti*	mo-*zhe*-te li pri-*re*-di-ti
meal without ...?	*obrok koji ne sadrži ...?*	*o*-brok koy-i ne *sa*-dr-zhi ...
butter	*maslac*	*ma*-slats
eggs	*jaja*	*yai*-a
meat stock	*mesni bujon*	*mes*-ni *bu*-yon

I'm allergic	*Ja sam alergičan/*	ya sam a-*ler*-gi-chan/
to ...	*alergična na ... m/f*	a-*ler*-gich-na na ...
dairy produce	*mliječne proizvode*	mli-*yech*-ne pro-*iz*-vo-de
gluten	*gluten*	*glu*-ten
MSG	*glutaminat*	glu-ta-mi-*nat*
nuts	*razne orahe*	*raz*-ne *o*-ra-he
seafood	*morske plodove*	*mor*-ske *plo*-do-ve

emergencies

basics

Help!	*Upomoć!*	u·po·moch
Stop!	*Stanite!*	sta·ni·te
Go away!	*Maknite se!*	mak·ni·te se
Thief!	*Lopov!*	lo·pov
Fire!	*Požar!*	po·zhar
Watch out!	*Pazite!*	pa·zi·te
Call ...!	*Zovite ...!*	zo·vi·te ...
a doctor	*liječnika/lekara* ©/Ⓢ	li·yech·ni·ka/le·ka·ra
an ambulance	*hitnu pomoć*	hit·nu po·moch
the police	*policiju*	po·li·tsi·yu

It's an emergency!
Imamo hitan slučaj. — i·ma·mo hi·tan slu·chai

Could you help me, please?
Molim vas, možete li mi pomoći? — mo·lim vas mo·zhe·te li mi po·mo·chi

Can I use your phone?
Mogu li koristiti vaš telefon? — mo·gu li ko·ri·sti·ti vash te·le·fon

I'm lost.
Izgubio/Izgubila sam se. m/f — iz·gu·bi·o/iz·gu·bi·la sam se

Where are the toilets?
Gdje se nalaze zahodi/toaleti? ©/Ⓢ — gdye se na·la·ze za·ho·di/to·a·le·ti

police

Where's the police station?
Gdje se nalazi policijska stanica? — gdye se na·la·zi po·li·tsiy·ska sta·ni·tsa

I want to report an offence.
Želim prijaviti prekršaj. — zhe·lim pri·ya·vi·ti pre·kr·shai

I have insurance.
Imam osiguranje. — i·mam o·si·gu·ra·nye

I've been ...	*Ja sam bio/bila ...* m/f	ya sam bi·o/bi·la ...
assaulted	*napadnut/napadnuta* m/f	na·pad·nut/na·pad·nu·ta
raped	*silovan/silovana* m/f	si·lo·van/si·lo·va·na
robbed	*opljačkan* m	op·lyach·kan
	opljačkana f	op·lyach·ka·na

My ... was/were stolen.	*Ukrali su mi ...*	*u·kra·li su mi ...*
I've lost my ...	*Izgubio/Izgubila*	*iz·gu·bi·o/iz·gu·bi·la*
	sam ... m/f	*sam ...*
backpack	*svoj ranac*	*svoy ra·nats*
bags	*svoje torbe*	*svoy·e tor·be*
credit card	*svoju kreditnu*	*svoy·oo kre·dit·nu*
	karticu	*kar·ti·tsu*
jewellery	*svoj nakit*	*svoy na·kit*
money	*svoj novac*	*svoy no·vats*
passport	*svoju putovnicu* ©	*svoy·oo pu·tov·ni·tsu*
	svoj pasoš ⑤	*svoy pa·sosh*
travellers cheques	*svoje putničke*	*svoy·e put·nich·ke*
	čekove	*che·ko·ve*
I want to contact	*Želim stupiti u*	*zhe·lim stu·pi·ti u*
my ...	*kontakt sa ...*	*kon·takt sa ...*
consulate	*svojom ambasadom*	*svoy·om am·ba·sa·dom*
embassy	*svojim konzulatom*	*svoy·im kon·zu·la·tom*

health

medical needs

Where's the	*Gdje je najbliži/*	*gdye ye nai·bli·zhi/*
nearest ...?	*najbliža ...?* m/f	*nai·bli·zha ...*
dentist	*zubar* m	*zu·bar*
doctor	*liječnik/lekar* m ©/⑤	*li·yech·nik/le·kar*
hospital	*bolnica* f	*bol·ni·tsa*
(night) pharmacist	*(noćna) ljekarna/*	*(noch·na) lye·kar·na*
	apoteka f ©/⑤	*a·po·te·ka*

I need a doctor (who speaks English).
Trebam liječnika/lekara   *tre·bam li·yech·ni·ka/le·ka·ra*
(koji govori engleski). ©/⑤   *(koy·i go·vo·ri en·gle·ski)*

Could I see a female doctor?
Mogu li dobiti ženskog   *mo·gu li do·bi·ti zhen·skog*
liječnika/lekara? ©/⑤   *li·yech·ni·ka/le·ka·ra*

I've run out of my medication.
Nestalo mi je lijekova.   *ne·sta·lo mi ye li·ye·ko·va*

symptoms, conditions & allergies

I'm sick.	Ja sam bolestan/ bolesna. m/f	ya sam *bo*·le·stan/ *bo*·le·sna
It hurts here.	Boli me ovdje.	*bo*·li me *ov*·dye
I have ...	Imam ...	*i*·mam ...
asthma	astma f	*ast*·ma
bronchitis	bronhitis m	bron·*hi*·tis
constipation	zatvorenje n	zat·vo·*re*·nye
cough	kašalj m	*ka*·shal'
diarrhoea	proljev m	*pro*·lyev
fever	groznica f	*gro*·zni·tsa
headache	glavobolja f	gla·*vo*·bo·lya
heart condition	poremećaj srca m	po·re·me·chai *sr*·tsa
nausea	mučnina f	much·*ni*·na
pain	bol m	bol
sore throat	grlobolja f	gr·*lo*·bo·lya
toothache	zubobolja f	zu·*bo*·bo·lya
I'm allergic to ...	Ja sam alergičan/ alergična na ... m/f	ya sam a·*ler*·gi·chan/ a·*ler*·gich·na na ...
antibiotics	antibiotike	an·ti·bi·o·*ti*·ke
anti-inflammatories	lijekove protiv upale	li·*ye*·ko·ve *pro*·tiv *u*·pa·le
aspirin	aspirin	a·*spi*·rin
bees	pčele	*pche*·le
codeine	kodein	ko·*de*·in
penicillin	penicilin	pe·ni·*tsi*·lin
antiseptic	antiseptik m	an·ti·*sep*·tik
bandage	zavoj m	*za*·voy
contraceptives	sredstva za spriječavanje trudnoće n pl	*sreds*·tva za spri·ye·*cha*·va·nye trud·*no*·che
diarrhoea medicine	lijekovi protiv proljeva m pl	li·*ye*·ko·vi *pro*·tiv *pro*·lye·va
insect repellent	sredstvo za odbijanje insekata n	*sreds*·tvo za od·*bi*·ya·nye in·se·ka·ta
laxatives	laksativi m pl	lak·sa·ti·vi
painkillers	tablete protiv bolova f pl	ta·*ble*·te *pro*·tiv *bo*·lo·va
rehydration salts	soli za rehidrataciju f	*so*·li za re·hi·dra·*ta*·tsi·yu
sleeping tablets	tablete za spavanje f pl	ta·*ble*·te za *spa*·va·nye

english–croatian dictionary

Croatian nouns in this dictionary have their gender indicated by ⓜ (masculine), ⓕ (feminine) or ⓝ (neuter). If it's a plural noun, you'll also see pl. Adjectives are given in the masculine form only. Words are also marked as a (adjective), v (verb), sg (singular), pl (plural), inf (informal), pol (polite), ⓒ (Croatian) or ⓢ (Serbian) where necessary.

A

accident *nezgoda* ⓕ *nez-go-da*
accommodation *smještaj* ⓜ *smye-shtai*
adaptor *konverter* ⓜ *kon-ver-ter*
address *adresa* ⓕ *a-dre-sa*
after *poslije* *po-sli-ye*
air-conditioned *klimatiziran* *kli-ma-ti-zi-ran*
airplane *zrakoplov/avion* ⓜ *zra-ko-plov/a-vi-on* ⓒ/ⓢ
airport *zračna luka* ⓕ */aerodrom* ⓜ *zrach-na lu-ka/a-e-ro-drom* ⓒ/ⓢ
alcohol *alkohol* ⓜ *al-ko-hol*
all *sve* sve
allergy *alergija* ⓕ *a-ler-gi-ya*
ambulance *hitna pomoć* ⓕ *hit-na po-moch*
and *i* i
ankle *gležanj/članak* ⓜ *gle-zhan'/chla-nak* ⓒ/ⓢ
arm *ruka* ⓕ *ru-ka*
ashtray *pepeljara* ⓕ *pe-pe-lya-ra*
ATM *bankovni automat* ⓜ *ban-kov-ni a-u-to-mat*

B

baby *beba* ⓕ *be-ba*
back (body) *leđa* ⓝ pl *le-ja*
backpack *ranac* ⓜ *ra-nats*
bad *loš* losh
bag *torba* ⓕ *tor-ba*
baggage claim *šalter za podizanje prtljage* ⓜ *shal-ter za po-di-za-nye prt-lya-ge*
bank *banka* ⓕ *ban-ka*
bar *bar* ⓜ bar
bathroom *kupaonica* ⓕ *ku-pa-o-ni-tsa*
battery (car) *akumulator* ⓜ *a-ku-mu-la-tor*
battery (general) *baterija* ⓕ *ba-te-ri-ya*
beautiful *lijep* li-yep
bed *krevet* ⓜ *kre-vet*
beer *pivo* ⓝ *pi-vo*
before *prije* *pri-ye*
behind *iza* *i-za*
bicycle *bicikl* ⓜ *bi-tsi-kl*
big *velik* ve-lik
bill *račun* ⓜ *ra-chun*

black *crn* tsrn
blanket *deka* ⓕ *de-ka*
blood group *krvna grupa* ⓕ *krv-na gru-pa*
blue *plav* plav
boat (ship) *brod* ⓜ brod
boat (smaller/private) *čamac* ⓜ *cha-mats*
book (make a reservation) v *rezervirati* *re-zer-vi-ra-ti*
Bosnia-Hercegovina *Bosna i Hercegovina* ⓕ *bos-na i her-tse-go-vi-na*
Bosnian (language) *bosanski jezik* ⓜ *bo-san-ski ye-zik*
bottle *boca* ⓕ *bo-tsa*
bottle opener *otvarač za boce* ⓜ *ot-va-rach za bo-tse*
boy *dječak* ⓜ *dye-chak*
brakes (car) *kočnice* ⓕ pl *koch-ni-tse*
breakfast *doručak* ⓜ *do-ru-chak*
broken (faulty) *pokvaren* *po-kva-ren*
bus *autobus* ⓜ *a-u-to-bus*
business *biznis* ⓜ *biz-nis*
buy *kupiti* *ku-pi-ti*

C

café *kafić/kavana* ⓜ/ⓕ *ka-fich/ka-va-na*
camera *foto-aparat* ⓜ *fo-to-a-pa-rat*
camp site *mjesto za kampiranje* ⓜ *mye-sto za kam-pi-ra-nye*
cancel *poništiti* *po-ni-shti-ti*
can opener *otvarač za limenke/konzerve* *ot-va-rach za li-men-ke/kon-zer-ve* ⓒ/ⓢ
car *automobil* ⓜ *a-u-to-mo-bil*
cash *gotovina* ⓕ *go-to-vi-na*
cash (a cheque) v *unovčiti* *u-nov-chi-ti*
cell phone *mobilni telefon* ⓜ *mo-bil-ni te-le-fon*
centre *centar* ⓜ *tsen-tar*
change (money) v *zamijeniti* *za-mi-ye-ni-ti*
cheap *jeftin* *yef-tin*
check (bill) *račun* ⓜ *ra-chun*
check-in *prijemni šalter* ⓜ *pri-yem-ni shal-ter*
chest *prsa/grudi* ⓕ pl *pr-sa/gru-di* ⓒ/ⓢ
child *dijete* ⓝ *di-ye-te*
cigarette *cigareta* ⓕ *tsi-ga-re-ta*
city *grad* ⓜ grad
clean a *čist* chist
closed *zatvoren* *zat-vo-ren*
coffee *kava* ⓕ *ka-va*

76

coins *novčići* ⓜ pl *nov-chi-chi*
cold a *hladan* *hla-dan*
collect call *poziv na račun nazvane osobe* ⓜ
  po-ziv na ra-chun naz-va-ne o-so-be
come *doći* *do-chi*
computer *računalo* ⓝ/*kompjuter* ⓜ
  ra-chu-na-lo/komp-yu-ter ©/⑤
condom *prezervativ* ⓜ *pre-zer-va-tiv*
contact lenses *kontakt leće* ① pl/*kontaktna sočiva*
  ⓝ pl *kon-takt le-che/kon-takt-na so-chi-va* ©/⑤
cook v *kuhati* *ku-ha-ti*
cost *cijena* ① *tsi-ye-na*
credit card *kreditna kartica* ① *kre-dit-na kar-ti-tsa*
Croatia *Hrvatska* ① *hr-vat-ska*
Croatian (language) *hrvatski* ⓜ *hr-vat-ski*
Croatian a *hrvatski* *hr-vat-ski*
cup *šalica/šoljica* ① *sha-li-tsa/sho-l'i-tsa* ©/⑤
currency exchange *tečaj/kurs stranih valuta* ⓜ
  te-chai/kurs stra-nih va-lu-ta ©/⑤
customs (immigration) *carinarnica* ① *tsa-ri-nar-ni-tsa*

D

dangerous *opasan* *o-pa-san*
date (time) *datum* ⓜ *da-tum*
day *dan* ⓜ *dan*
delay *zakašnjenje* ① *za-kash-nye-nye*
dentist *zubar* ⓜ *zu-bar*
depart *otići* *o-ti-chi*
diaper *pelene* ① pl *pe-le-ne*
dictionary *rječnik* ⓜ *ryech-nik*
dinner *večera* ① *ve-che-ra*
direct *direktan* *di-rek-tan*
dirty *prljav* *pr-lyav*
disabled *onesposobljen* *one-spo-sob-lyen*
discount *popust* ⓜ *po-pust*
doctor *liječnik/lekar* ⓜ *li-yech-nik/le-kar* ©/⑤
double bed *dupli krevet* ⓜ *du-pli kre-vet*
double room *dvokrevetna soba* ① *dvo-kre-vet-na so-ba*
drink *piće* ① *pi-che*
drive v *voziti* *vo-zi-ti*
drivers licence *vozačka dozvola* ① *vo-zach-ka doz-vo-la*
drug (illicit) *droga* ① *dro-ga*
dummy (pacifier) *duda/cucla* ① *du-da/tsu-tsla* ©/⑤

E

ear *uho* ⓝ *u-ho*
east *istok* ⓜ *i-stok*
eat *jesti* *ye-sti*
economy class *drugi razred* ⓜ *dru-gi raz-red*
electricity *struja* ① *stru-ya*
elevator *dizalo* ⓝ/*lift* ⓜ *di-za-lo/lift* ©/⑤

email *e-mail* ⓜ *i-me-il*
embassy *ambasada* ① *am-ba-sa-da*
emergency *hitan slučaj* ⓜ *hi-tan slu-chai*
English (language) *engleski* ⓜ *en-gle-ski*
entrance *ulaz* ⓜ *u-laz*
evening *večer* ① *ve-cher*
exchange rate *tečaj/kurs razmjene* ⓜ
  te-chai/kurs raz-mye-ne©/⑤
exit *izlaz* ⓜ *iz-laz*
expensive *skup* *skup*
express mail *ekspres pošta* ① *eks-pres posh-ta*
eye *oko* ⓝ *o-ko*

F

far *daleko* *da-le-ko*
fast *brz* *brz*
father *otac* ⓜ *o-tats*
film (camera) *film* ⓜ *film*
finger *prst* ⓜ *prst*
first-aid kit *pribor za prvu pomoć* ⓜ
  pri-bor za pr-vu po-moch
first class *prvi razred* ⓜ *pr-vi raz-red*
fish *riba* ① *ri-ba*
food *hrana* ① *hra-na*
foot *stopalo* ⓝ *sto-pa-lo*
fork *viljuška* ① *vi-lyush-ka*
free (of charge) *besplatan* *be-spla-tan*
friend *prijatelj/prijateljica* ⓜ/①
  pri-ya-tel'/pri-ya-te-lyi-tsa
fruit *voće* ⓝ *vo-che*
full *pun* *pun*
funny *smiješan* *smye-shan*

G

gift *dar/poklon* ⓜ *dar/pok-lon* ©/⑤
girl *djevojčica* ① *dye-voy-chi-tsa*
glass (drinking) *čaša* ① *cha-sha*
glasses *naočale* ① pl *na-o-cha-le*
go *ići* *i-chi*
good *dobar* *do-bar*
green *zelen* *ze-len*
guide *vodič* ⓜ *vo-dich*

H

half *polovina* ① *po-lo-vi-na*
hand *ruka* ① *ru-ka*
handbag *ručna torbica* ① *ruch-na tor-bi-tsa*
happy *sretan* *sre-tan*
have *imati* *i-ma-ti*
he *on* *on*

head *glava* ① *gla*-va
heart *srce* ① *sr*-tse
heat *vrućina* ① *vru*-chi-na
heavy *težak* te-zhak
help v *pomoći* po-*mo*-chi
here *ovdje* ov-dye
high *visok* vi-sok
highway *autoput* ① *a*-u-to-put
hike v *pješačiti* pye-sha-chi-ti
holidays *praznici* ① pl *praz*-ni-tsi
homosexual *homoseksualac/homoseksualka* ⑩/① ho-mo-sek-su-a-lats/ho-mo-sek-su-al-ka
hospital *bolnica* ① *bol*-ni-tsa
hot *vruć* vruch
hotel *hotel* ⑩ ho-*tel*
hungry *gladan/gladna* ⑩/① *gla*-dan/*gla*-dna
husband *muž* ⑩ muzh

I

I *ja* ya
identification (card) *osobna iskaznica/lična karta* ① o-*sob*-na i-*skaz*-ni-tsa/*lich*-na *kar*-ta ©/⑤
ill *bolestan* bo-le-stan
important *važan* va-zhan
included *uključen* uk-lyu-chen
injury *povreda* ① po-*vre*-da
insurance *osiguranje* ① o-si-gu-*ra*-nye
Internet *internet* ⑩ in-ter-net
interpreter *tumač* ⑩ *tu*-mach

J

jewellery *nakit* ⑩ *na*-kit
job *posao* ⑩ *po*-sa-o

K

key *ključ* ⑩ klyuch
kilogram *kilogram* ⑩ *ki*-lo-gram
kitchen *kuhinja* ① *ku*-hi-nya
knife *nož* ⑩ nozh

L

laundry (place) *praonica* ① pra-o-ni-tsa
lawyer *pravnik* ⑩ *prav*-nik
left (direction) *lijevi* li-ye-vi
left-luggage office *ured za odlaganje prtljage* ⑩ u-*red* za od-*la*-ga-nye prt-*lya*-ge
leg *noga* ① *no*-ga
lesbian *lezbijka* ① *lez*-biy-ka
less *manje* *ma*-nye

letter (mail) *pismo* ⑩ *pi*-smo
lift (elevator) *dizalo* ⑩/*lift* ⑩ di-za-lo/lift ©/⑤
light *svjetlost* ① *svyet*-lost
like v *dopadati se* do-pa-da-ti se
lock *brava* ① *bra*-va
long *dugačak* du-gub-chak
lost *izgubljen* iz-gub-lyen
lost-property office *ured za izgubljene stvari* ⑩ u-*red* za iz-*gub*-lye-ne stva-ri
love v *voljeti* vo-lye-ti
luggage *prtljaga* ① prt-*lya*-ga
lunch *ručak* ⑩ *ru*-chak

M

mail *pošta* ① *posh*-ta
man *čovjek* ⑩ *cho*-vyek
map (of country) *karta* ① *kar*-ta
map (of town) *plan grada* ⑩ plan *gra*-da
market *tržnica/pijaca* ① *trzh*-ni-tsa ©/⑤
matches *šibice* ① pl *shi*-bi-tse
meat *meso* ⑩ *me*-so
medicine *lijekovi* ⑩ pl li-ye-ko-vi
menu *jelovnik* ⑩ *ye*-lov-nik
message *poruka* ① po-*ru*-ka
milk *mlijeko* ⑩ mli-ye-ko
minute *minuta* ① mi-*nu*-ta
mobile phone *mobilni telefon* ⑩ mo-bil-ni te-*le*-fon
money *novac* ⑩ *no*-vats
Montenegro *Crna Gora* ① tsr-na *go*-ra
month *mjesec* ⑩ *mye*-sets
morning *jutro* ⑩ *yu*-tro
mother *majka* ① *mai*-ka
motorcycle *motocikl* ⑩ mo-to-*tsi*-kl
motorway *autoput* ⑩ *a*-u-to-put
mouth *usta* ① pl *u*-sta
music *glazba* ① *glaz*-ba

N

name *ime* ⑩ *i*-me
napkin *salveta* ① sal-*ve*-ta
nappy *pelene* ① pl *pe*-le-ne
near *blizu* *bli*-zu
neck *vrat* ⑩ vrat
new *nov* nov
news *vijesti* ① pl *vi*-ye-sti
newspaper *novine* ① pl *no*-vi-ne
night *noć* ① noch
no *ne* ne
noisy *bučan* *bu*-chan
nonsmoking *nepušački* ⑩ *ne*-pu-shach-ki
north *sjever* ⑩ *sye*-ver

nose *nos* ⓜ nos
now *sada* sa-da
number *broj* ⓜ broy

O

oil (engine) *ulje* ⓝ u-lye
old *star* star
one-way ticket *jednosmjerna karta* ⓕ
   yed-no-smyer-na kar-ta
open ⓐ *otvoren* ot-vo-ren
outside *vani/napolju* va-ni/na-po-l'u ©/Ⓢ

P

package *paket* ⓜ pa-ket
paper *papir* ⓜ pa-pir
park (car) v *parkirati* par-ki-ra-ti
passport *putovnica* ⓕ/*pasoš* ⓜ
   pu-tov-ni-tsa/pa-sosh ©/Ⓢ
pay *platiti* pla-ti-ti
pen *kemijska* ⓕ ke-miy-ska
petrol *benzin* ⓜ ben-zin
pharmacy *ljekarna/apoteka* ⓕ
   lye-kar-na/a-po-te-ka ©/Ⓢ
phonecard *telefonska kartica* ⓕ
   te-le-fon-ska kar-ti-tsa
photo *fotografija* ⓕ fo-to-gra-fi-ya
plate *tanjur* ⓜ ta-nyur
police *policija* ⓕ po-li-tsi-ya
postcard *dopisnica* ⓕ do-pi-sni-tsa
post office *poštanski ured* ⓜ posh-tan-ski u-red
pregnant *trudna* trud-na
price *cijena* ⓕ tsi-ye-na

Q

quiet *tih* tih

R

rain *kiša* ⓕ ki-sha
razor *brijač* ⓜ bri-yach
receipt *račun* ⓜ ra-chun
red *crven* tsr-ven
refund *povrat novca* ⓜ pov-rat nov-tsa
registered mail *preporučena pošta* ⓕ
   pre-po-ru-che-na posh-ta
rent v *iznajmiti* iz-nai-mi-ti
repair v *popraviti* po-pra-vi-ti
reservation *rezervacija* ⓕ re-zer-va-tsi-ya
restaurant *restoran* ⓜ re-sto-ran
return v *vratiti se* vra-ti-ti se

return ticket *povratna karta* ⓕ po-vra-tna kar-ta
right (direction) *desno* de-sno
road *cesta* ⓕ/*put* ⓜ tse-sta/put ©/Ⓢ
room *soba* ⓕ so-ba

S

safe ⓐ *siguran* si-gu-ran
sanitary napkin *higijenski uložak* ⓜ
   hi-gi-yen-ski u-lo-zhak
seat *sjedište* ⓝ sye-dish-te
send *poslati* po-sla-ti
Serbia *Srbija* ⓕ sr-bi-ya
Serbian (language) *srpski jezik* ⓜ srp-ski ye-zik
service station *benzinska stanica* ⓕ
   ben-zin-ska sta-ni-tsa
sex *seks* ⓜ seks
shampoo *šampon* ⓜ sham-pon
share (a dorm) *dijeliti* di-ye-li-ti
shaving cream *pjena za brijanje* ⓕ
   pye-na za bri-ya-nye
she *ona* o-na
sheet (bed) *plahta* ⓕ/*čaršav* ⓜ
   pla-hta/char-shav ©/Ⓢ
shirt *košulja* ⓕ ko-shu-lya
shoes *cipele* ⓕ pl tsi-pe-le
shop *prodavaonica* ⓕ pro-da-va-o-ni-tsa
short *kratak* kra-tak
shower *tuš* ⓜ tush
single room *jednokrevetna soba* ⓕ
   yed-no-kre-vet-na so-ba
skin *koža* ⓕ ko-zha
skirt *suknja* ⓕ suk-nya
sleep v *spavati* spa-va-ti
slowly *sporo* spo-ro
small *mali* ma-li
smoke (cigarettes) v *pušiti* pu-shi-ti
soap *sapun* ⓜ sa-pun
some *malo* ma-lo
soon *uskoro* u-sko-ro
south *jug* ⓜ yug
souvenir shop *prodavaonica suvenira* ⓕ
   pro-da-va-o-ni-tsa su-ve-ni-ra
speak *govoriti* go-vo-ri-ti
spoon *žlica/kašika* ⓕ zhli-tsa/ka-shi-ka ©/Ⓢ
stamp *poštanska marka* ⓕ posh-tan-ska mar-ka
stand-by ticket *uvjetna/uslovna karta* ⓕ
   uv-yet-na/us-lov-na kar-ta ©/Ⓢ
station (train) *stanica* ⓕ sta-ni-tsa
stomach *želudac* ⓜ zhe-lu-dats
stop v *zaustaviti* za-u-sta-vi-ti
stop (bus) *stanica* ⓕ sta-ni-tsa
street *ulica* ⓕ u-li-tsa

student *student* ⓜ & ⓕ *stu*-dent
sun *sunce* ⓝ *sun*-tse
sunscreen *losion za zaštitu od sunca* ⓜ
lo-si-on za *zash*-ti-tu od *sun*-tsa
swim v *plivati* *pli*-va-ti

T

tampon *tampon* ⓜ *tam*-pon
taxi *taksi* ⓜ *tak*-si
teaspoon *žličica/kašičica* ⓕ
zhli-chi-tsa/*ka*-shi-chi-tsa ©/Ⓢ
teeth *zubi* ⓝ pl *zu*-bi
telephone *telefon* ⓜ te-*le*-fon
television *televizija* ⓕ te-le-*vi*-zi-ya
temperature (weather) *temperatura* ⓕ tem-pe-ra-*tu*-ra
tent *šator* ⓜ *sha*-tor
that (one) *ono* o-no
they *oni/one/ona* ⓜ/ⓕ/ⓝ o-ni/o-ne/o-na
thirsty *žedan* *zhe*-dan
this (one) *ovo* o-vo
throat *grlo* ⓝ *gr*-lo
ticket *karta* ⓕ *kar*-ta
time *vrijeme* ⓝ *vri*-ye-me
tired *umoran* u-mo-ran
tissues *papirnati rupčići* ⓜ pl *pa*-pir-na-ti *rup*-chi-chi ©
papirne maramice ⓕ pl *pa*-pir-ne *ma*-ra-mi-tse Ⓢ
today *danas* da-nas
toilet *zahod/toalet* ⓜ *za*-hod/to-a-*let* ©/Ⓢ
tomorrow *sutra* *su*-tra
tonight *večeras* ve-che-ras
toothbrush *četkica za zube* ⓕ *chet*-ki-tsa za *zu*-be
toothpaste *pasta za zube* ⓕ *pa*-sta za *zu*-be
torch (flashlight) *ručna svjetiljka* ⓕ *ruch*-na *svye*-til'-ka
tour *ekskurzija* ⓕ ek-*skur*-zi-ya
tourist office *turistička agencija* ⓕ
tu-*ri*-stich-ka a-*gen*-tsi-ya
towel *ručnik/peškir* ⓜ *ruch*-nik/*pesh*-kir ©/Ⓢ
train *vlak/voz* ⓜ vlak/voz ©/Ⓢ
translate *prevesti* pre-ve-sti
travel agency *putna agencija* ⓕ *put*-na a-*gen*-tsi-ya
travellers cheque *putnički ček* ⓜ *put*-nich-ki chek
trousers *hlače/pantalone* ⓕ pl
hla-che/pan-ta-lo-ne ©/Ⓢ
twin beds *dva kreveta* ⓜ pl dva *kre*-ve-ta
tyre *guma* ⓕ *gu*-ma

U

underwear *donje rublje* ⓝ *do*-nye *rub*-lye
urgent *hitan* *hi*-tan

V

vacant *prazan* *pra*-zan
vacation *praznici* ⓜ pl *praz*-ni-tsi
vegetable *povrće* ⓝ *po*-vr-che
vegetarian a *vegetarijanski* ve-ge-ta-*ri*-yan-ski
visa *viza* ⓕ *vi*-za

W

waiter *konobar* ⓜ *ko*-no-bar
walk v *hodati* ho-da-ti
wallet *novčanik* ⓜ *nov*-cha-nik
warm a *topao* to-pa-o
wash (something) *oprati* o-pra-ti
watch *sat* ⓜ sat
water *voda* ⓕ *vo*-da
we *mi* mi
weekend *vikend* ⓜ *vi*-kend
west *zapad* za-pad
wheelchair *invalidska kolica* ⓕ pl in-*va*-lid-ska ko-*li*-tsa
when *kada* ka-da
where *gdje* gdye
white *bijel* bi-yel
who *tko* tko
why *zašto* zash-to
wife *žena* ⓕ *zhe*-na
window *prozor* ⓜ *pro*-zor
wine *vino* ⓝ *vi*-no
with *sa* sa
without *bez* bez
woman *žena* ⓕ *zhe*-na
write *napisati* na-*pi*-sa-ti

Y

yellow *žut* zhut
yes *da* da
yesterday *jučer* *yu*-cher
you sg inf *ti* ti
you sg pol & pl *vi* vi

Czech

czech alphabet

A a uh	Á á a	B b bair	C c tsair	Č č chair
D d dair	Ď ď dyair	E e e	É é *dloh*-hair air	Ě ě e s *hach*-kem
F f ef	G g gair	H h ha	Ch ch cha	I i ee
Í í *dloh*-hair ee	J j yair	K k ka	L l el	M m em
N n en	Ň ň en'	O o o	P p pair	Q q kair
R r er	Ř ř erzh	S s es	Š š esh	T t tair
Ť ť tyair	U u u	Ú ú *dloh*-hair u	Ů ů u s *krohzh*-kem	V v vair
W w *dvo*-yi-tair vair	X x iks	Y y *ip*-si-lon	Ý ý *dloh*-hee *ip*-si-lon	Z z zet
Ž ž zhet				

czech

introduction

Czech (*čeština* chesh-tyi-nuh), the language which gave us words such as *dollar*, *pistol* and *robot*, has a turbulent history. The Czech Republic may now be one of the most stable and well-off Eastern European countries, but over the centuries the land and the language have been regularly swallowed and regurgitated by their neighbours. In 1993 the Velvet Divorce ended the patched-together affair that was Czechoslovakia, and allowed Czech to go its own way after being tied to Slovak for over 70 years.

Both Czech and Slovak belong to the western branch of the Slavic language family, pushed westward with the Slavic people by the onslaught of the Huns, Avars, Bulgars and Magyars in the 5th and 6th centuries. Czech is also related to Polish, though not as closely as to Slovak – adults in Slovakia and the Czech Republic can generally understand one another, although younger people who have not been exposed to much of the other language may have more difficulty.

The earliest written literature dates from the 13th century upswing in Czech political power, which continued for several centuries. In the 17th century, however, the Thirty Years War nearly caused literature in Czech to become extinct. Fortunately, the national revival of the late 18th century brought it to the forefront again, at least until the 20th century, when first Nazi and then Communist rule pressed it into a subordinate position once more.

Many English speakers flinch when they see written Czech, especially words like *prst* prst (finger) and *krk* krk (neck) with no apparent vowels, and the seemingly unpronounceable clusters of consonants in phrases like *čtrnáct dní* chtr-natst dnyee (fortnight). Don't despair! With a little practice and the coloured pronunciation guides in this chapter you'll be enjoying the buttery mouthfeel of Czech words in no time. Czech also has one big advantage in the pronunciation stakes – each Czech letter is always pronounced exactly the same way, so once you've got the hang of the Czech alphabet you'll be able to read any word put before you with aplomb. Thank religious writer and martyr Jan Hus for this – he reformed the spelling system in the 15th and 16th centuries and introduced the *háček* ha-chek (ˇ) and the various other accents you'll see above Czech letters.

So, whether you're visiting the countryside or marvelling at Golden Prague, launch into this Czech chapter and your trip will be transformed into a truly memorable one.

pronunciation

vowel sounds

The Czech vowel system is relatively easy to master and most sounds have equivalents in English.

symbol	english equivalent	czech example	transliteration
a	**father**	*já*	ya
ai	**aisle**	*krajka*	*krai*-kuh
air	**hair**	*veliké*	ve-lee-*kair*
aw	**law**	*balcón*	*bal*-kawn
e	**bet**	*pes*	pes
ee	**see**	*prosím*	*pro*-seem
ey	**hey**	*dej*	dey
i	**bit**	*kolik*	*ko*-lik
o	**pot**	*noha*	*no*-huh
oh	**oh**	*koupit*	*koh*-pit
oo	**zoo**	*ústa*	*oo*-stuh
oy	**toy**	*výstroj*	*vee*-stroy
ow	**how**	*autobus*	*ow*-to-bus
u	**put**	*muž*	muzh
uh	**run**	*nad*	nuhd

word stress

Word stress in Czech is easy – it's always on the first syllable of the word. Stress is marked with italics in the pronunciation guides in this chapter as a reminder.

consonant sounds

The consonants in Czech are mostly the same as in English, with the exception of the kh sound, the r sound (which is rolled as it is in Spanish) and the rzh sound.

symbol	english equivalent	czech example	transliteration
b	**b**ed	*bláto*	*bla·to*
ch	**ch**eat	*odpočinek*	*ot·po·chi·nek*
d	**d**og	*nedávný*	*ne·dav·nee*
f	**f**at	*vyfotit*	*vi·fo·tit*
g	**g**o	*vegetarián*	*ve·ge·tuh·ri·an*
h	**h**at	*zahrady*	*zuh·hruh·di*
k	**k**it	*navěky*	*na·vye·ki*
kh	lo**ch**	*kuchyně*	*ku·khi·nye*
l	**l**ot	*loni*	*lo·nyi*
m	**m**an	*menší*	*men·shee*
n	**n**ot	*nízký*	*nyeez·kee*
p	**p**et	*dopis*	*do·pis*
r	**r**un (rolled)	*rok*	*rok*
rzh	rolled r followed by zh	*řeka*	*rzhe·kuh*
s	**s**un	*slovo*	*slo·vo*
sh	**sh**ot	*pošta*	*posh·tuh*
t	**t**op	*fronta*	*fron·tuh*
ts	ha**ts**	*co*	*tso*
v	**v**ery	*otvor*	*ot·vor*
y	**y**es	*již*	*yizh*
z	**z**ero	*zmiz*	*zmiz*
zh	plea**s**ure	*už*	*uzh*
'	a slight y sound	*promiňte*	*pro·min'·te*

tools

language difficulties

Do you speak English?
Mluvíte anglicky?   mlu·vee·te uhn·glits·ki

Do you understand?
Rozumíte?   ro·zu·mee·te

I understand.
Rozumím.   ro·zu·meem

I don't understand.
Nerozumím.   ne·ro·zu·meem

What does (knedlík) mean?
Co znamená (knedlík)?   tso znuh·me·na (kned·leek)

How do you ...?	*Jak se ...?*	yuhk se ...
pronounce this	*toto vyslovuje*	*toh*·to *vis*·lo·vu·ye
write (krtek)	*píše (krtek)*	*pee*·she (*kr*·tek)

Could you please ...?	*Prosím, můžete ...?*	pro·seem moo·zhe·te ...
repeat that	*to opakovat*	to o·puh·ko·vuht
speak more slowly	*mluvit pomaleji*	mlu·vit po·muh·le·yi
write it down	*to napsat*	to nuhp·suht

essentials		
Yes.	*Ano.*	uh·no
No.	*Ne.*	ne
Please.	*Prosím.*	pro·seem
Thank you	*(Mnohokrát)*	(mno·ho·krat)
(very much).	*Děkuji.*	dye·ku·yi
You're welcome.	*Prosím.*	pro·seem
Excuse me.	*Promiňte.*	pro·min'·te
Sorry.	*Promiňte.*	pro·min'·te

numbers

0	*nula*	*nu·*luh	16	*šestnáct*	*shest·*natst
1	*jeden* m	*ye·*den	17	*sedmnáct*	*se·*dm·natst
	jedna f	*yed·*na	18	*osmnáct*	*o·*sm·natst
	jedno n	*yed·*no	19	*devatenáct*	*de·*vuh·te·natst
2	*dva/dvě* m/f&n	dvuh/dvye	20	*dvacet*	*dvuh·*tset
3	*tři*	trzhi	21	*dvacet jedna*	*dvuh·*tset *yed·*nuh
4	*čtyři*	*chti·*rzhi		*jednadvacet*	*yed·*nuh·*dvuh·*tset
5	*pět*	pyet	22	*dvacet dva*	*dvuh·*tset dvuh
6	*šest*	shest		*dvaadvacet*	*dvuh·*uh·*dvuh·*tset
7	*sedm*	*se·*dm	30	*třicet*	*trzhi·*tset
8	*osm*	*o·*sm	40	*čtyřicet*	*chti·*rzhi·tset
9	*devět*	*de·*vyet	50	*padesát*	*puh·*de·sat
10	*deset*	*de·*set	60	*šedesát*	*she·*de·sat
11	*jedenáct*	*ye·*de·natst	70	*sedmdesát*	*se·*dm·de·sat
12	*dvanáct*	*dvuh·*natst	80	*osmdesát*	*o·*sm·de·sat
13	*třináct*	*trzhi·*natst	90	*devadesát*	*de·*vuh·de·sat
14	*čtrnáct*	*chtr·*natst	100	*sto*	sto
15	*patnáct*	*puht·*natst	1000	*tisíc*	*tyi·*seets

time & dates

What time is it?	*Kolik je hodin?*	*ko·*lik ye *ho·*dyin
It's one o'clock.	*Je jedna hodina.*	ye *yed·*nuh *ho·*dyi·nuh
It's (10) o'clock.	*Je (deset) hodin.*	ye (*de·*set) *ho·*dyin
Quarter past (10).	*Čvrt na (jedenáct).*	chtvrt nuh (*ye·*de·natst)
	(lit: quarter of eleven)	
Half past (10).	*Půl (jedenácté).*	pool (*ye·*de·nats·tair)
	(lit: half eleven)	
Quarter to (eleven).	*Tříčtvrtě na (jedenáct).*	*trzhi·*chtvr·tye nuh (*ye·*de·natst)
At what time?	*V kolik hodin?*	f *ko·*lik *ho·*dyin
At …	*V …*	f …
am (midnight–8am)	*ráno*	*ra·*no
am (8am–noon)	*dopoledne*	*do·*po·led·ne
pm (noon–7pm)	*odpoledne*	*ot·*po·led·ne
pm (7pm–midnight)	*večer*	*ve·*cher

Monday	pondělí	pon-dye-lee
Tuesday	úterý	oo-te-ree
Wednesday	středa	strzhe-duh
Thursday	čtvrtek	chtvr-tek
Friday	pátek	pa-tek
Saturday	sobota	so-bo-tuh
Sunday	neděle	ne-dye-le

January	leden	le-den
February	únor	oo-nor
March	březen	brzhe-zen
April	duben	du-ben
May	květen	kvye-ten
June	červen	cher-ven
July	červenec	cher-ve-nets
August	srpen	sr-pen
September	září	za-rzhee
October	říjen	rzhee-yen
November	listopad	li-sto-puht
December	prosinec	pro-si-nets

What date is it today?
   Kolikátého je dnes?   ko-li-ka-tair-ho ye dnes

It's (18 October).
   Je (osmnáctého října).   ye (o-sm-nats-tair-ho rzheey-nuh)

last night	včera v noci	fche-ruh v no-tsi
last week/month	minulý týden/měsíc	mi-nu-lee tee-den/mye-seets
last year	vloni	vlo-nyi

next ...	příští ...	przheesh-tyee ...
week	týden	tee-den
month	měsíc	mye-seets
year	rok	rok

tomorrow/yesterday ...	zítra/včera ...	zee-truh/fche-ruh ...
morning (early/late)	ráno/dopoledne	ra-no/do-po-led-ne
afternoon	odpoledne	ot-po-led-ne
evening	večer	ve-cher

weather

What's the weather like?	*Jaké je počasí?*	yuh·kair ye po·chuh·see
It's ...		
cloudy	*Je zataženo.*	ye zuh·tuh·zhe·no
cold	*Je chladno.*	ye khluhd·no
hot	*Je horko.*	ye hor·ko
raining	*Prší.*	pr·shee
snowing	*Sněží.*	snye·zhee
sunny	*Je slunečno.*	ye slu·nech·no
warm	*Je teplo.*	ye tep·lo
windy	*Je větrno.*	ye vye·tr·no
spring	*jaro* n	yuh·ro
summer	*léto* n	lair·to
autumn	*podzim* m	pod·zim
winter	*zima* f	zi·muh

border crossing

I'm here ...	*Jsem zde ...*	ysem zde ...
in transit	*v tranzitu*	f truhn·zi·tu
on business	*na služební cestě*	nuh slu·zheb·nyee tses·tye
on holiday	*na dovolené*	nuh do·vo·le·nair
I'm here for ...	*Jsem zde na ...*	ysem zde nuh ...
(10) days	*(deset) dní*	(de·set) dnyee
(three) weeks	*(tři) týdny*	(trzhi) teed·ni
(two) months	*(dva) měsíce*	(dvuh) mye·see·tse

I'm going to (Valtice).
Jedu do (Valtic).   ye·du do (vuhl·tyits)

I'm staying at the (Hotel Špalíček).
Jsem ubytovaný/á v   ysem u·bi·to·vuh·nee/a v
(Hotelu Špalíček). m/f   (ho·te·lu shpuh·lee·chek)

I have nothing to declare.
Nemám nic k proclení.   ne·mam nyits k prots·le·nyee

I have something to declare.
Mám něco k proclení.   mam nye·tso k prots·le·nyee

That's not mine.
To není moje.   to ne·nyee mo·ye

transport

tickets & luggage

Where can I buy a ticket?
Kde koupím jízdenku? · gde koh·peem yeez·den·ku

Do I need to book a seat?
Potřebuji místenku? · pot·rzhe·bu·yi mees·ten·ku

One ... ticket to (Telče), please.	... do (Telče), prosím.	... do (tel·che) pro·seem
one-way	Jednosměrnou jízdenku	yed·no·smyer·noh yeez·den·ku
return	Zpáteční jízdenku	zpa·tech·nyee yeez·den·ku

I'd like to ... my ticket, please.	Chtěl/Chtěla bych ... moji jízdenku, prosím. m/f	khtyel/khtye·luh bikh ... mo·yee yeez·den·ku pro·seem
cancel	zrušit	zru·shit
change	změnit	zmye·nyit
collect	vyzvednout	vi·zved·noht
confirm	potvrdit	pot·vr·dyit

I'd like a ... seat, please.	Chtěl/Chtěla bych ... m/f	khtyel/khtye·luh bikh ...
nonsmoking	nekuřácké místo	ne·ku·rzhats·kair mees·to
smoking	kuřácké místo	ku·rzhats·kair mees·to

How much is it?
Kolik to stojí? · ko·lik to sto·yee

Is there a toilet?
Je tam toaleta? · ye tuhm to·uh·le·tuh

Is there air conditioning?
Je tam klimatizace? · ye tuhm kli·muh·ti·zuh·tse

How long does the trip take?
Jak dlouho trvá cesta? · yuhk dloh·ho tr·va tses·tuh

Is it a direct route?
Je to přímá cesta? · ye to przhee·ma tses·tuh

Where can I find a luggage locker?
Kde mohu najít zavazadlová schránka? · gde mo·hu nuh·yeet zuh·vuh·zuhd·lo·va skhran·kuh

My luggage	Moje zavazadlo	mo·ye zuh·vuh·zuhd·lo
has been ...	bylo ...	bi·lo ...
damaged	poškozeno	posh·ko·ze·no
lost	ztraceno	ztruh·tse·no
stolen	ukradeno	u·kruh·de·no

getting around

Where does flight (OK25) arrive?
Kam přiletí let (OK25)?   kuhm przhi·le·tyee let (aw·ka dvuh·tset pyet)

Where does flight (OK25) depart?
Kde odlítá let (OK25)?   gde od·lee·ta let (aw·ka dvuh·tset pyet)

Where's (the) ...?	Kde je ...?	gde ye ...
arrivals hall	příletová hala	przhee·le·to·va huh·luh
departures hall	odletová hala	od·le·to·va huh·luh
duty-free shop	prodejna	pro·dey·nuh
	bezcelního zboží	bez·tsel·nyee·ho zbo·zhee
gate (12)	východ k letadlu	vee·khod k le·tuhd·lu
	(dvanáct)	(dvuh·natst)

Is this the ...	Jede tento/tato ...	ye·de ten·to/tuh·to ...
to (Mělník)?	do (Mělníka)? m/f	do (myel·nyee·kuh)
bus	autobus m	ow·to·bus
train	vlak m	vluhk
tram	tramvaj f	truhm·vai
trolleybus	trolejbus m	tro·ley·bus

When's the	V kolik jede	f ko·lik ye·de
... bus?	... autobus?	... ow·to·bus
first	první	prv·nyee
last	poslední	po·sled·nyee
next	příští	przhee·shtyee

At what time does the bus/train leave?
V kolik hodin odjíždí   f ko·lik ho·dyin od·yeezh·dyee
autobus/vlak?   ow·to·bus/vluhk

How long will it be delayed?
Jak dlouho bude mít zpoždění?   yuhk dloh·ho bu·de meet zpozh·dye·nyee

What's the next station/stop?
Která je příští stanice/zastávka?   kte·ra ye przheesh·tyee stuh·nyi·tse/zuhs·taf·kuh

Does it stop at (Cheb)?
Zastaví to v (Chebu)?   zuhs·tuh·vee to f (*khe*·bu)

Please tell me when we get to (Přerov).
Prosím vás řekněte mi   pro·seem vas rzhek·nye·te mi
kdy budeme v (Přerově).   kdi *bu*·de·me f (*przhe*·ro·vye)

How long do we stop here?
Jak dlouho zde budeme stát?   yuhk *dloh*·ho zde *bu*·de·me stat

Is this seat available?
Je toto místo volné?   ye *to*·to *mees*·to *vol*·nair

That's my seat.
To je mé místo.   to ye mair *mees*·to

I'd like a taxi ...	*Potřebuji taxíka ...*	po·trzhe·bu·yi *tuhk*·see·kuh ...
at (9am)	*v (devět hodin*	f (*de*·vyet *ho*·dyin
	dopoledne)	*do*·po·led·ne)
now	*teď*	ted'
tomorrow	*zítra*	*zee*·truh

Is this taxi available?
Je tento taxík volný?   ye *ten*·to *tuhk*·seek *vol*·nee

How much is it to ...?
Kolik stojí jízdenka do ...?   *ko*·lik *sto*·yee *yeez*·den·kuh do ...

Please put the meter on.
Prosím zapněte taxametr.   pro·seem *zuhp*·nye·te *tuhk*·suh·me·tr

Please take me to (this address).
Prosím odvezte mě na (tuto adresu).   pro·seem *od*·ves·te mye na (*tu*·to *uh*·dre·su)

Please ...	*Prosím ...*	pro·seem ...
slow down	*zpomalte*	*spo*·muhl·te
stop here	*zastavte zde*	zuhs·*tuhf*·te zde
wait here	*počkejte zde*	poch·*key*·te zde

car, motorbike & bicycle hire

I'd like to hire a ...	*Chtěl/Chtěla bych si půjčit ...* m/f	khtyel/*khtye*·luh bikh si *pooy*·chit ...
bicycle	*kolo*	*ko*·lo
car	*auto*	*ow*·to
motorbike	*motorku*	*mo*·tor·ku

with ...	s ...	s ...
a driver	*řidičem*	*rzhi*-dyi-chem
air conditioning	*klimatizací*	*kli*-muh-ti-zuh-tsee
antifreeze	*nemrznoucí směsí*	ne-mrz-noh-tsee smye-see
snow chains	*sněhovými řetězy*	snye-ho-vee-mi *rzhe*-tye-zi

How much for	*Kolik stojí*	ko-lik *sto*-yee
... hire?	*půjčení na ...?*	pooy-che-nyee nuh ...
hourly	*hodinu*	*ho*-dyi-nu
daily	*den*	den
weekly	*týden*	*tee*-den

air	*vzduch* m	*vz*-dukh
oil	*olej* m	*o*-ley
petrol	*benzin* m	*ben*-zin
tyre	*pneumatika* f	*pne*-u-muh-ti-kuh

I need a mechanic.	*Potřebuji mechanika.*	pot-rzhe-bu-yi me-khuh-ni-kuh
I've run out of petrol.	*Došel mi benzin.*	do-shel mi *ben*-zin
I have a flat tyre.	*Mám defekt.*	mam de-fekt

directions

Where's the ...?	*Kde je ...?*	gde ye ...
bank	*banka*	*buhn*-kuh
city centre	*centrum*	*tsen*-trum
hotel	*hotel*	*ho*-tel
market	*trh*	trh
police station	*policejní stanice*	po-li-tsey-nyee *stuh*-nyi-tse
post office	*pošta*	*posh*-tuh
public toilet	*veřejný záchod*	ve-rzhey-nee *za*-khod
tourist office	*turistická informační kancelář*	tu-ris-tits-ka in-for-muhch-nyee kuhn-tse-larzh

Is this the road to (Cheb)?
Vede tato silnice do (Chebu)?   ve-de tuh-to sil-ni-tse do (khe-bu)

Can you show me (on the map)?
Můžete mi to ukázat (na mapě)?   moo-zhe-te mi to u-ka-zuht (nuh muh-pye)

What's the address?
Jaká je adresa?　　　　　　　　　yuh-ka ye uh-dre-suh

How far is it?
Jak je to daleko?　　　　　　　　yuhk ye to duh-le-ko

How do I get there?
Jak se tam dostanu?　　　　　　yuhk se tuhm dos-tuh-nu

Turn ...	*Odbočte ...*	od-boch-te ...
at the corner	*za roh*	zuh rawh
at the traffic lights	*u semaforu*	u se-muh-fo-ru
left/right	*do leva/prava*	do le-vuh/pruh-vuh

It's ...	*Je to ...*	ye to ...
behind ...	*za ...*	zuh ...
far away	*daleko*	duh-le-ko
here	*zde*	zde
in front of ...	*před ...*	przhed ...
left	*na levo*	nuh le-vo
near	*blízko*	bleez-ko
next to ...	*vedle ...*	ved-le ...
on the corner	*na rohu*	nuh ro-hu
opposite ...	*naproti ...*	nuh-pro-tyi ...
right	*na pravo*	nuh pruh-vo
straight ahead	*přímo*	przhee-mo
there	*tam*	tuhm

by bus	*autobusem*	ow-to-bu-sem
by taxi	*taxikem*	tuhk-si-kem
by train	*vlakem*	vluh-kem
on foot	*pěšky*	pyesh-ki
north	*sever*	se-ver
south	*jih*	yih
east	*východ*	vee-khod
west	*západ*	za-puhd

Vchod/Východ	vkhod/*vee*-khod	**Entrance/Exit**
Otevřeno/Zavřeno	o-te-vrzhe-no/*zuh*-vrzhe-no	**Open/Closed**
Volné pokoje	vol-nair po-ko-ye	**Rooms Available**
Obsazeno	op-suh-ze-no	**No Vacancies**
Informace	in-for-muh-tse	**Information**
Policejní stanice	po-li-tsey-nyee *stuh*-nyi-tse	**Police Station**
Zakázáno	zuh-ka-za-no	**Prohibited**
Záchody	za-kho-di	**Toilets**
Páni	pa-nyi	**Men**
Ženy	zhe-ni	**Women**
Horké/Studené	hor-kair/*stu*-de-nair	**Hot/Cold**

accommodation

finding accommodation

Where's a …?	*Kde je …?*	gde ye …
camping ground	*tábořiště*	ta-bo-rzhish-tye
guesthouse	*penzion*	pen-zi-on
hotel	*hotel*	ho-tel
youth hostel	*mládežnická*	mla-dezh-nyits-ka
	ubytovna	u-bi-tov-nuh
Can you recommend	*Můžete mi doporučit*	moo-zhe-te mi do-po-ru-chit
somewhere …?	*něco …?*	nye-tso …
cheap	*levného*	lev-nair-ho
good	*dobrého*	dob-rair-ho
nearby	*nejbližšího*	ney-blizh-shee-ho

I'd like to book a room, please.
Chtěl/Chtěla bych   khtyel/*khtye*-luh bikh
rezervovat pokoj, prosím. m/f   re-zer-vo-vuht po-koy pro-seem

I have a reservation.
Mám rezervaci.   mam re-zer-vuh-tsi

My name is …
Mé jméno je …   mair ymair-no ye …

Do you have a double room?
Máte pokoj s manželskou postelí?   ma-te po-koy s muhn-zhels-koh pos-te-lee

Do you have a ... room?	*Máte ... pokoj?*	ma·te ... po·koy
single	*jednolůžkový*	yed·no·loozh·ko·vee
twin	*dvoulůžkový*	dvoh·loozh·ko·vee

How much is it per ...?	*Kolik to stojí ...?*	ko·lik to sto·yee ...
night	*na noc*	nuh nots
person	*za osobu*	zuh o·so·bu

Can I pay ...?	*Mohu zaplatit ...?*	mo·hu zuh·pluh·tyit ...
by credit card	*kreditní kartou*	kre·dit·nyee kuhr·toh
with a travellers cheque	*cestovním šekem*	tses·tov·nyeem she·kem

For (three) nights/weeks.
Na (tři) noci/týdny.   nuh (trzhi) no·tsi/*teed*·ni

From (2 July) to (6 July).
Od (druhého července)   od (*dru*·hair·ho *cher*·ven·tse)
do (šestého července).   do (*shes*·tair·ho *cher*·ven·tse)

Can I see it?
Mohu se na něj podívat?   mo·hu se na nyey po·dyee·vuht

Am I allowed to camp here?
Mohu zde stanovat?   mo·hu zde stuh·no·vuht

Where can I find a camping ground?
Kde mohu najít stanový tábor?   gde mo·hu nuh·yeet stuh·no·vee ta·bor

requests & queries

When's breakfast served?
V kolik se podává snídaně?   f ko·lik se po·da·va snyee·duh·nye

Where's breakfast served?
Kde se podává snídaně?   gde se po·da·va snyee·duh·nye

Please wake me at (seven).
Prosím probuďte mě v (sedm).   pro·seem pro·bud'·te mye f (se·dm)

Could I have my key, please?
Můžete mi dát můj klíč, prosím?   moo·zhe·te mi dat mooy kleech pro·seem

Can I get another (blanket)?
Mohu dostat další (deku)?   mo·hu dos·tuht duhl·shee (de·ku)

Do you have a/an ...?	Máte ...?	ma·te ...
elevator	výtah	vee·tah
safe	trezor	tre·zor

The room is too ...	Je moc ...	ye mots ...
expensive	drahý	druh·hee
noisy	hlučný	hluch·nee
small	malý	muh·lee

The ... doesn't work.	... nefunguje.	... ne·fun·gu·ye
air conditioning	Klimatizace	kli·muh·ti·zuh·tse
fan	Větrák	vye·trak
toilet	Toaleta	to·uh·le·tuh

This ... isn't clean.	Tento ... neni čistý.	ten·to ... ne·nyi chis·tee
pillow	polštář	pol·shtarzh
towel	ručník	ruch·nyeek

checking out

What time is checkout?
V kolik hodin máme vyklidit pokoj? f ko·lik ho·dyin ma·me vi·kli·dyit po·koy

Can I leave my luggage here?
Mohu si zde nechat zavazadla? mo·hu si zde ne·khuht zuh·vuh·zuhd·luh

Could I have my ..., please?	Můžete mi vratit ..., prosím?	moo·zhe·te mi vra·tyit ... pro·seem
deposit	zálohu	za·lo·hu
passport	pas	puhs
valuables	cennosti	tse·nos·tyi

communications & banking

the internet

Where's the local Internet café?
Kde je místní internetová kavárna? gde ye meest·nyee in·ter·ne·to·va kuh·var·nuh

How much is it per hour?
Kolik to stojí na hodinu? ko·lik to sto·yee nuh ho·dyi·nu

I'd like to ...	Chtěl/Chtěla bych ... m/f	khtyel/khtye·luh bikh ...
check my email	zkontrolovat můj email	skon·tro·lo·vuht mooy ee·meyl
get Internet access	přístup na internet	przhees·tup nuh in·ter·net
use a printer	použít tiskárnu	po·u·zheet tyis·kar·nu
use a scanner	použít skener	po·u·zheet ske·ner

mobile/cell phone

I'd like a ...	Chtěl/Chtěla bych ... m/f	ktyel/khtye·luh bikh ...
mobile/cell phone for hire	si půjčit mobil	si pooy·chit mo·bil
SIM card for your network	SIM kartu pro vaší síť	sim kuhr·tu pro vuh·shee seet'

| What are the rates? | Jaké jsou tarify? | yuh·kair ysoh tuh·ri·fi |

telephone

What's your phone number?
Jaké je vaše telefonní číslo? yuh·kair ye vuh·she te·le·fo·nyee chees·lo

The number is ...
Číslo je ... chees·lo ye ...

Where's the nearest public phone?
Kde je nejbližší veřejný telefon? gde ye ney·blizh·shee ve·rzhey·nee te·le·fon

I'd like to buy a phonecard.
Chtěl/Chtěla bych koupit ktyel/khtye·luh bikh koh·pit
telefonní kartu. m/f te·le·fo·nyee kuhr·tu

I want to ...	Chtěl/Chtěla bych ... m/f	ktyel/khtye·luh bikh ...
call (Singapore)	telefonovat do (Singapůru)	te·le·fo·no·vuht do sin·guh·poo·ru
make a local call	si zavolat místně	si zuh·vo·luht meest·nye
reverse the charges	telefonovat na účet volaného	te·le·fo·no·vuht na oo·chet vo·luh·nair·ho

How much does ... cost?	Kolik stojí ...?	ko-lik sto-yee ...
a (three)-minute	(tří) minutový	(trzhee) mi-nu-to-vee
call	hovor	ho-vor
each extra minute	každá další	kuhzh-da duhl-shee
	minuta	mi-nu-tuh

(Seven crowns) per minute.
(Sedm korun) za jednu minutu.   (se-dm ko-run) zuh yed-nu mi-nu-tu

post office

I want to send a ...	Chci poslat ...	khtsi po-sluht ...
fax	fax	fuhks
letter	dopis	do-pis
parcel	balík	buh-leek
postcard	pohled	po-hled

I want to buy a/an ...	Chci koupit ...	khtsi koh-pit ...
envelope	obálku	o-bal-ku
stamp	známku	znam-ku

Please send it by	Prosím vás pošlete	pro-seem vas po-shle-te
... to (Australia).	to ... do (Austrálie).	to ... do (ow-stra-li-ye)
airmail	letecky poštou	le-tets-ki posh-toh
express mail	expresní poštou	eks-pres-nyee posh-toh
registered mail	doporučenou poštou	do-po-ru-che-noh posh-toh
surface mail	obyčejnou poštou	o-bi-chey-noh posh-toh

Is there any mail for me?
Mám zde nějakou poštu?   mam zde nye-yuh-koh posh-tu

bank

I'd like to ...	Chtěl/Chtěla bych ... m/f	kthyel/khtye-luh bikh ...
Where can I ...?	Kde mohu ...?	gde mo-hu ...
arrange a transfer	převést peníze	przhe-vairst pe-nyee-ze
cash a cheque	proměnit šek	pro-mye-nyit shek
change a travellers	proměnit	pro-mye-nyit
cheque	cestovní šek	tses-tov-nyee shek
change money	vyměnit peníze	vi-mye-nyit pe-nyee-ze
get a cash advance	zálohu v hotovosti	za-lo-hu v ho-to-vos-tyi
withdraw money	vybrat peníze	vi-bruht pe-nyee-ze

Where's a/an ...?	*Kde je ...?*	*gde ye ...*
ATM	*bankomat*	*buhn·ko·muht*
foreign exchange office	*směnárna*	*smye·nar·nuh*

What's the ...?	*Jaký je ...?*	*yuh·kee ye ...*
charge for that	*poplatek za to*	*po·pluh·tek zuh to*
exchange rate	*devizový kurz*	*de·vi·zo·vee kurz*

It's ...	*Je to ...*	*ye to ...*
(12) crowns	*(dvanáct) korun*	*(dvuh·natst) ko·run*
(five) euros	*(pět) eur*	*(pyet) e·ur*
free	*bez poplatku*	*bez po·pluht·ku*

What time does the bank open?
Jaké jsou úřední hodiny? — *yuh·kair ysoh oo·rzhed·nyee ho·dyi·ni*

Has my money arrived yet?
Přišly už moje peníze? — *przhi·shli uzh mo·ye pe·nyee·ze*

sightseeing

getting in

What time does it open/close?
V kolik hodin otevírají/ zavírají? — *f ko·lik ho·dyin o·te·vee·ruh·yee/ zuh·vee·ruh·yee*

What's the admission charge?
Kolik stojí vstupné? — *ko·lik sto·yee vstup·nair*

Is there a discount for students/children?
Máte slevu pro studenty/děti? — *ma·te sle·vu pro stu·den·ti/dye·tyi*

I'd like a ...	*Chtěl/Chtěla bych ...* m/f	*khtyel/khtye·luh bikh ...*
catalogue	*katalog*	*kuh·tuh·log*
guide	*průvodce*	*proo·vod·tse*
local map	*mapu okolí*	*ma·pu o·ko·lee*

I'd like to see ...
Chtěl/Chtěla bych vidět ... m/f
khtyel/*khtye*·luh bikh *vi*·dyet ...

What's that?
Co je to?
tso ye to

Can I take a photo of this?
Mohu toto fotografovat?
mo·hu to·to fo·to·gruh·fo·vuht

Can I take a photo of you?
Mohu si vás vyfotit?
mo·hu si vas *vi*·fo·tyit

tours

When's the next ...? | *Kdy je příští ...?* | gdi ye *przheesh*·tyee ...
day trip | *celodenní výlet* | *tse*·lo·de·nye *vee*·let
tour | *okružní jízda* | o·kruzh·nye *yeez*·duh

Is ... included? | *Je zahrnuto/a ...?* n/f | ye zuh·hr·nu·to/a ...
accommodation | *ubytování* n | u·bi·to·va·nye
the admission charge | *vstupné* n | fstup·nair
food | *strava* f | struh·vuh
transport | *doprava* f | do·pruh·vuh

How long is the tour?
Jak dlouho bude trvat
tento zájezd?
yuhk *dloh*·ho *bu*·de tr·vuht
ten·to za·yezd

What time should we be back?
V kolik hodin se máme vrátit?
f ko·lik ho·dyin se *ma*·me *vra*·tyit

sightseeing		
castle	*hrad* m	hruhd
cathedral	*katedrála* f	kuh·te·dra·luh
church	*kostel* m	kos·tel
main square	*hlavní náměstí* n	*hluhv*·nye *na*·myes·tyee
monastery	*klášter* m	klash·ter
monument	*památník* m	puh·mat·nyeek
museum	*muzeum* f	mu·ze·um
old city	*staré město* n	*stuh*·rair myes·to
palace	*palác* m	puh·lats
ruins	*zříceniny* f pl	zrzhee·tse·nyi·ni
stadium	*stadion* m	*stuh*·di·yon
statue	*socha* f	so·khuh

shopping

enquiries

Where's a ...?	Kde je ...?	gde ye ...
bank	banka	buhn-kuh
bookshop	knihkupectví	knyikh-ku-pets-tvee
camera shop	foto potřeby	fo-to pot-rzhe-bi
department store	obchodní dům	op-khod-nyee doom
grocery store	smíšené zboží	smee-she-nair zbo-zhee
market	tržnice	tr-zhnyi-tse
newsagency	tabák	tuh-bak
supermarket	samoobsluha	suh-mo-op-slu-huh

Where can I buy (a padlock)?
Kde si mohu koupit (zámek)?   gde si mo-hu koh-pit (za-mek)

I'm looking for ....
Hledám ...   hle-dam ...

Can I look at it?
Mohu se na to podívat?   mo-hu se nuh to po-dyee-vuht

Do you have any others?
Máte ještě jiné?   ma-te yesh-tye yi-nair

Does it have a guarantee?
Je na to záruka?   ye nuh to za-ru-kuh

Can I have it sent abroad?
Můžete mi to poslat   moo-zhe-te mi to pos-luht
do zahraničí?   do zuh-hruh-nyi-chee

Can I have my ... repaired?
Můžete zde opravit ...?   moo-zhe-te zde o-pruh-vit ...

It's faulty.
Je to vadné.   ye to vuhd-nair

I'd like ..., please.	Chtěl/Chtěla bych	khtyel/khtye-la bikh
	..., prosím. m/f	... pro-seem
a bag	tašku	tuhsh-ku
a refund	vrátit peníze	vra-tyit pe-nyee-ze
to return this	toto vrátit	to-to vra-tyit

paying

How much is it?
Kolik to stojí? — ko·lik to *sto*·yee

Can you write down the price?
Můžete mi napsat cenu? — *moo*·zhe·te mi *nuhp*·suht *tse*·nu

That's too expensive.
To je moc drahé. — to ye mots *druh*·hair

What's your lowest price?
Jaká je vaše konečná cena? — *yuh*·ka ye *vuh*·she *ko*·nech·na *tse*·nuh

I'll give you (200 crowns).
Dám vám (dvěstě korun). — dam vam (*dvye*·stye *ko*·run)

There's a mistake in the bill.
Na účtu je chyba. — nuh *ooch*·tu ye *khi*·buh

Do you accept ...?	*Mohu platit ...?*	*mo*·hu *pluh*·tyit ...
credit cards	*kreditními kartami*	*kre*·dit·nyee·mi *kuhr*·tuh·mi
debit cards	*platebními*	*pluh*·teb·nyee·mi
	kartami	*kuhr*·tuh·mi
travellers cheques	*cestovními šeky*	*tses*·tov·nyee·mi *she*·ki
I'd like ..., please.	*Můžete mi dát*	*moo*·zhe·te mi dat
	..., prosím?	... *pro*·seem
a receipt	*účet*	*oo*·chet
my change	*mé drobné*	mair *drob*·nair

clothes & shoes

Can I try it on?	*Mohu si to zkusit?*	*mo*·hu si to *sku*·sit
My size is (40).	*Mám číslo (čtyřicet).*	mam *chee*·slo (*chti*·rzhi·tset)
It doesn't fit.	*Nepadne mi to.*	ne·*puhd*·ne mi to
small	*malý*	*muh*·le
medium	*střední*	*strzhed*·nye
large	*velký*	*vel*·keeh

books & music

I'd like a ...	Chtěl/Chtěla bych ... m/f	khtyel/khtye·luh bikh ...
newspaper	noviny	no·vi·ni
(in English)	(v angličtině)	(f uhn·glich·tyi·nye)
pen	propisovací pero	pro·pi·so·vuh·tsee pe·ro

Is there an English-language bookshop?
Je tam knihkupectví   ye tuhm *knyih*·ku·pets·tvee
s anglickýma knihama?   s *uhn*·glits·kee·muh *knyi*·huh·muh

I'm looking for something by (Kabát).
Hledám něco od (Kabátu).   *hle*·dam *nye*·tso od (*kuh*·ba·tu)

Can I listen to this?
Mohu si to poslechnout?   *mo*·hu si to *po*·slekh·noht

photography

Can you ...?	Můžete ...?	moo·zhe·te ...
develop this film	vyvolat tento film	vi·vo·luht ten·to film
load my film	vložit můj film	vlo·zhit mooy film
transfer photos	uložit fotografie	u·lo·zhit fo·to·gruh·fi·ye
from my camera	z mého	z mair·ho
to CD	fotoaparátu	fo·to·uh·puh·ra·tu
	na CD	nuh tsair·dairch·ko

I need a/an ... film	Potřebuji ... film	pot·rzhe·bu·yi ... film
for this camera.	pro tento fotoaparát.	pro ten·to fo·to·uh·puh·rat
APS	APS	a·pair·es
B&W	černobílý	cher·no·bee·lee
colour	barevný	buh·rev·nee
slide	diapozitivní	di·uh·po·zi·tiv·nyee
(200) speed	film s citlivostí	film s tsit·li·vos·tyee
	(dvěstě)	(dvye·stye)

When will it be ready? *Kdy to bude hotové?*   gdi to bu·de ho·to·vair

meeting people

greetings, goodbyes & introductions

Hello/Hi.	*Ahoj/Čau.*	uh-hoy/chow
Good night.	*Dobrou noc.*	do-broh nots
Goodbye.	*Na shledanou.*	nuh-skhle-duh-noh
Bye.	*Ahoj/Čau.*	uh-hoy/chow
See you later.	*Na viděnou.*	nuh vi-dye-noh
Mr/Mrs	*pan/paní*	puhn/puh-nyee
Miss	*slečna*	slech-nuh
How are you?	*Jak se máte/máš?* pol/inf	yuhk se ma-te/mash
Fine. And you?	*Dobře. A vy/ty?* pol/inf	dob-rzhe a vi/ti
What's your name?	*Jak se jmenujete/ jmenuješ?* pol/inf	yuhk se yme-nu-ye-te/ yme-nu-yesh
My name is ...	*Jmenuji se ...*	yme-nu-yi se ...
I'm pleased to meet you.	*Těší mě.*	tye-shee mye
This is my ...	*To je můj/moje ...* m/f	to ye mooy/mo-ye ...
boyfriend	*přítel*	przhee-tel
brother	*bratr*	bruh-tr
daughter	*dcera*	dtse-ruh
father	*otec* m	o-tets
friend	*přítel* m	przhee-tel
	přítelkyně f	przhee-tel-ki-nye
girlfriend	*přítelkyně*	przhee-tel-ki-nye
husband	*manžel*	muhn-zhel
mother	*matka*	muht-kuh
partner (intimate)	*partner/partnerka* m/f	puhrt-ner/puhrt-ner-kuh
sister	*sestra*	ses-truh
son	*syn*	sin
wife	*manželka*	muhn-zhel-kuh
Here's my ...	*Zde je moje ...*	zde ye mo-ye ...
What's your ...?	*Jaké/Jaká je vaše ...?* n/f	yuh-kair/yuh-ka ye vuh-she ...
(email) address	*(email) adresa* f	(ee-meyl) uh-dre-suh
fax number	*faxové číslo* n	fuhk-so-vair chees-lo
phone number	*telefonní číslo* n	te-le-fo-nyee chees-lo

occupations

What's your occupation?
Jaké je vaše povolání? yuh·kair ye *vuh*·she po·vo·la·nyee

I'm a/an ...	*Jsem ...*	ysem ...
artist	*umělec/umělkyně* m/f	u·mye·lets/u·myel·ki·nye
businessperson	*obchodník* m&f	ob·khod·nyeek
farmer	*zemědělec* m	ze·mye·dye·lets
	zemědělkyně f	ze·mye·dyel·ki·nye
manual worker	*dělník* m&f	dyel·nyeek
office worker	*úředník* m	oo·rzhed·nyeek
	úřednice f	oo·rzhed·nyi·tse
scientist	*vědec/vědkyně* m/f	vye·dets/vyed·ki·nye

background

Where are you from?	*Odkud jste?*	ot·kud yste
I'm from ...	*Jsem z ...*	ysem s ...
Australia	*Austrálie*	ow·stra·li·ye
Canada	*Kanady*	kuh·nuh·di
England	*Anglie*	uhn·gli·ye
New Zealand	*Nového Zélandu*	no·vair·ho zair·luhn·du
the USA	*Ameriky*	uh·meh·ri·ki

Are you married?	*Jste ženatý/vdaná?* m/f	yste zhe·nuh·tee/fduh·na
I'm married.	*Jsem ženatý/vdaná.* m/f	ysem zhe·nuh·tee/fduh·na
I'm single.	*Jsem svobodný/á.* m/f	ysem svo·bod·nee/a

age

How old ...?	*Kolik ...?*	ko·lik ...
are you	*je vám let* pol	ye vam let
	ti je let inf	ti ye let
is your daughter	*let je vaší dceři*	let ye *vuh*·shee dtse·rzhi
is your son	*let je vašemu synovi*	let ye *vuh*·she·mu si·no·vi

I'm ... years old.	*Je mi ... let.*	ye mi ... let
He's ... years old.	*Je mu ... let.*	ye mu ... let
She's ... years old.	*Jí je ... let.*	yee ye ... let

feelings

Are you ...?	Jste ...?	yste ...
I'm/I'm not ...	Jsem/Nejsem ...	ysem/ney·sem ...
happy	šťastný/šťastná m/f	shtyuhst·nee/shtyuhst·na
hungry	hladový/hladová m/f	hluh·do·vee/hluh·do·va
sad	smutný/smutná m/f	smut·nee/smut·na
thirsty	žíznivý/žíznivá m/f	zheez·nyi·vee/zheez·nyi·va

Are you ...?	Je vám ...?	ye vam ...
I'm/I'm not ...	Je/Není mi ...	ye/ne·nyi mi ...
cold	zima	zi·muh
hot	horko	hor·ko

entertainment

going out

Where can I find ...?	Kde mohu najít ...?	gde mo·hu nuh·yeet ...
clubs	kluby	klu·bi
gay venues	homosexuální	ho·mo·sek·su·al·nyee
	zábavné podniky	za·buhv·nair pod·ni·ki
pubs	hospody	hos·po·di

I feel like going	Rád bych šel ... m	rad bikh shel ...
to a/the ...	Ráda bych šla ... f	ra·duh bikh shluh ...
concert	na koncert	nuh kon·tsert
movies	do kina	do ki·nuh
party	na mejdan/	nuh mey·duhn/
	večírek	ve·chee·rek
theatre	na hru	nuh hru
restaurant	do restaurace	do res·tow·ruh·tse

interests

Do you like to ...?		
go to concerts	Chodíte na koncerty?	kho·dyee·te nuh kon·tser·ti
dance	Tancujete?	tuhn·tsu·ye·te
listen to music	Posloucháte hudbu?	po·sloh·kha·te hud·bu

Do you like ...?	Máte rád/ráda ...? m/f	ma-te rad/ra-duh ...
I like ...	Mám rád/ráda ... m/f	mam rad/ra-duh ...
I don't like ...	Nemám rád/ráda ... m/f	ne-mam rad/ra-duh ...
art	umění	u-mye-nyee
cooking	vaření	vuh-rzhe-nyee
movies	filmy	fil-mi
reading	čtení	chte-nyee
sport	sport	sport
travelling	cestování	tses-to-va-nyee

food & drink

finding a place to eat

Can you	Můžete	moo-zhe-te
recommend a ...?	doporučit ...?	do-po-ru-chit ...
café	kavárnu	kuh-var-nu
pub	hospodu	hos-po-du
restaurant	restauraci	res-tow-ruh-tsi
I'd like ..., please.	Chtěl/Chtěla bych	khtyel/khtye-luh bikh
	..., prosím. m/f	... pro-seem
a table for (five)	stůl pro (pět)	stool pro (pyet)
the nonsmoking	nekuřáckou	ne-ku-rzhats-koh
section	místnost	meest-nost
the smoking section	kuřáckou místnost	ku-rzhats-koh meest-nost

ordering food

breakfast	snídaně f	snee-duh-nye
lunch	oběd m	o-byed
dinner	večeře f	ve-che-rzhe
snack	občerstvení n	ob-cherst-ve-nyee
What would you	Co byste doporučil/	tso bis-te do-po-ru-chil/
recommend?	doporučila? m/f	do-po-ru-chi-luh

I'd like (the) ..., please.	Chtěl/Chtěla bych ..., prosím. m/f	khtyel/khtye-luh bikh ... pro-seem
bill	účet	oo-chet
drink list	nápojový lístek	na-po-yo-vee lees-tek
menu	jídelníček	yee-del-nyee-chek
that dish	ten pokrm	ten po-krm

drinks

(cup of) coffee ...	(šálek) kávy ...	(sha-lek) ka-vi ...
(cup of) tea ...	(šálek) čaje ...	(sha-lek) chuh-ye ...
with milk	s mlékem	s mlair-kem
without sugar	bez cukru	bez tsu-kru
(orange) juice	(pomerančový) džus m	(po-me-ruhn-cho-vee) dzhus
soft drink	nealkoholický nápoj m	ne-uhl-ko-ho-lits-kee na-poy
(hot) water	(horká) voda f	(hor-ka) vo-duh
... mineral water	... minerální voda f	... mi-ne-ral-nyee vo-duh
sparkling	perlivá	per-li-va
still	neperlivá	ne-per-li-va

in the bar

I'll have a ...	Dám si ...	dam si ...
I'll buy you a drink.	Zvu vás/tě na sklenku. pol/inf	zvu vas/tye nuh sklen-ku
What would you like?	Co byste si přál/přála? m/f	tso bis-te si przhal/przha-la
Cheers!	Na zdraví!	nuh zdruh-vee
brandy	brandy f	bruhn-di
champagne	šampaňské n	shuhm-puhn'-skair
cocktail	koktejl m	kok-teyl
a shot of (whisky)	panák (whisky)	puh-nak (vis-ki)
a bottle/jug of beer	láhev/džbán piva	la-hef/dzhban pi-vuh
a bottle/glass of ... wine	láhev/skleničku ... vína	la-hef/skle-nyich-ku ... vee-nuh
red	červeného	cher-ve-nair-ho
sparkling	šumivého	shu-mi-vair-ho
white	bílého	bee-lair-ho

self-catering

What's the local speciality?
Co je místní specialita?   tso ye *meest*-nyee spe-tsi-uh-li-tuh

What's that?
Co to je?   tso to ye

How much is (500 grams of cheese)?
Kolik stojí (padesát   ko-lik sto-yee (*puh*-de-sat
deka sýra)?   de-kuh see-ruh)

I'd like ...	Chtěl/Chtěla bych ... m/f	khtyel/*khtye*-luh bikh ...
200 grams	dvacet deka	*dvuh*-tset de-kuh
(two) kilos	(dvě) kila	(dvye) ki-luh
(three) pieces	(tři) kusy	(trzhi) ku-si
(six) slices	(šest) krajíců	(shest) *kruh*-yee-tsoo

Less.	Méně.	*mair*-nye
Enough.	Stačí.	*stuh*-chee
More.	Trochu více.	*tro*-khu *vee*-tse

special diets & allergies

Is there a vegetarian restaurant near here?
Je zde blízko vegetariánská   ye zde *blees*-ko ve-ge-tuh-ri-ans-ka
restaurace?   *res*-tow-ruh-tse

Do you have vegetarian food?
Máte vegetariánská jídla?   *ma*-te ve-ge-tuh-ri-ans-ka *yeed*-luh

Could you prepare a meal without ...?
Mohl/Mohla by jste   *mo*-hl/*mo*-hluh bi yste
připravit jídlo bez ...? m/f   *przhi*-pruh-vit *yeed*-lo bez ...

butter	máslo n	*mas*-lo
eggs	vejce n pl	*vey*-tse
meat stock	bujón m	*bu*-yawn

I'm allergic to ...	Mám alergii na ...	mam uh-*ler*-gi-yi nuh ...
dairy produce	mléčné výrobky	*mlair*-chnair *vee*-rob-ki
gluten	lepek	*le*-pek
MSG	glutaman sodný	*glu*-tuh-muhn sod-nee
nuts	ořechy	*o*-rzhe-khi
seafood	plody moře	*plo*-di mo-rzhe

emergencies

basics

Help!	*Pomoc!*	*po*-mots
Stop!	*Zastav!*	*zuhs*-tuhf
Go away!	*Běžte pryč!*	*byezh*-te prich
Thief!	*Zloděj!*	*zlo*-dyey
Fire!	*Hoří!*	*ho*-rzhee
Watch out!	*Pozor!*	*po*-zor
Call ...!	*Zavolejte ...!*	*zuh*-vo-ley-te ...
a doctor	*lékaře*	*lair*-kuh-rzhe
an ambulance	*sanitku*	*suh*-nit-ku
the police	*policii*	*po*-li-tsi-yi

It's an emergency.
To je naléhavý případ. — to ye nuh-*lair*-huh-vee *przhee*-puhd

Could you help me, please?
Můžete prosím pomoci? — moo-zhe-te *pro*-seem *po*-mo-tsi

Can I use the phone?
Mohu si zatelefonovat? — mo-hu si *zuh*-te-le-fo-no-vuht

I'm lost.
Zabloudil/Zabloudila jsem. m/f — *zuh*-bloh-dyil/*zuh*-bloh-dyi-luh ysem

Where are the toilets?
Kde jsou toalety? — gde ysoh *to*-uh-le-ti

police

Where's the police station?
Kde je policejní stanice? — gde ye *po*-li-tsey-nyee *stuh*-nyi-tse

I want to report an offence.
Chci nahlásit trestný čin. — khtsi *nuh*-hla-sit *trest*-nee chin

I have insurance.
Jsem pojištěný/pojištěná. m/f — ysem *po*-yish-tye-nee/*po*-yish-tye-na

I've been ...	... *mě.*	... mye
assaulted	*Přepadli*	*przhe*-puhd-li
raped	*Znásilnili*	*zna*-sil-nyi-li
robbed	*Okradli*	*o*-kruhd-li

I've lost my ...	Ztratil/Ztratila jsem ... m/f	ztruh-tyil/ztruh-tyi-luh ysem ...
My ... was/were stolen.	Ukradli mě ...	u-kruhd-li mye ...
backpack	batoh	buh-tawh
credit card	kreditní kartu	kre-dit-nyee kuhr-tu
bag	zavazadlo	zuh-vuh-zuhd-lo
handbag	kabelku	kuh-bel-ku
jewellery	šperky	shper-ki
money	peníze	pe-nyee-ze
passport	pas	puhs
travellers cheques	cestovní šeky	tses-tov-nyee she-ki
wallet	peněženku	pe-nye-zhen-ku
I want to contact my ...	Potřebuji se obrátit na ...	pot-rzhe-bu-yi se o-bra-tyit nuh ...
consulate	můj konzulát	mooy kon-zu-lat
embassy	mé velvyslanectví	mair vel-vi-sluh-nets-tvee

health

medical needs

Where's the nearest ...?	Kde je nejbližší ...?	gde ye ney-blizh-shee ...
dentist	zubař	zu-buhrzh
doctor	lékař	lair-kuhrzh
hospital	nemocnice	ne-mots-nyi-tse
(night) pharmacist	(non-stop) lékárník	(non-stop) lair-kar-nyeek

I need a doctor (who speaks English).

Potřebuji (anglickomluvícího) doktora.   pot-rzhe-bu-yi (uhn-glits-kom-lu-vee-tsee-ho) dok-to-ruh

Could I see a female doctor?

Mohla bych být vyšetřená lékařkou?   mo-hluh bikh beet vi-shet-rzhe-na lair-kuhrzh-koh

I've run out of my medication.

Došly mi léky.   dosh-li mi lair-ki

112

symptoms, conditions & allergies

I'm sick.	Jsem nemocný/ nemocná. m/f	ysem ne·mots·nee/ ne·mots·na
It hurts here.	Tady to bolí.	tuh·di to bo·lee
I have (a) ...	Mám ...	mam ...

asthma	astma n	uhst·muh
bronchitis	zánět průdušek m	za·nyet proo·du·shek
constipation	zácpa f	zats·puh
cough n	kašel m	kuh·shel
diarrhoea	průjem m	proo·yem
fever	horečka f	ho·rech·kuh
headache	bolesti hlavy f	bo·les·tyi hluh·vi
heart condition	srdeční porucha f	sr·dech·nyee po·ru·khuh
nausea	nevolnost f	ne·vol·nost
pain n	bolest f	bo·lest
sore throat	bolest v krku f	bo·lest f kr·ku
toothache	bolení zubu n	bo·le·nyee zu·bu

I'm allergic to ...	Jsem alergický/ alergická na ... m/f	ysem uh·ler·gits·kee/ uh·ler·gits·ka nuh ...
antibiotics	antibiotika	uhn·ti·bi·o·ti·kuh
anti-inflammatories	protizánětlivé léky	pro·tyi·za·nyet·li·vair lair·ki
aspirin	aspirin	uhs·pi·rin
bees	včely	fche·li
codeine	kodein	ko·deyn
penicillin	penicilin	pe·ni·tsi·lin

antiseptic	antiseptický prostředek m	uhn·ti·sep·tits·kee prost·rzhe·dek
bandage	obvaz m	ob·vuhz
condoms	prezervativy m pl	pre·zer·vuh·ti·vi
contraceptives	antikoncepce f	uhn·ti·kon·tsep·tse
diarrhoea medicine	lék na průjem m	lairk nuh proo·yem
insect repellent	prostředek na hubení hmyzu m	pros·trzhe·dek nuh hu·be·nyee hmi·zu
laxatives	projímadla m pl	pro·yee·muhd·la
painkillers	prášky proti bolesti m pl	prash·ki pro·tyi bo·les·tyi
rehydration salts	iontový nápoj m	yon·to·vee na·poy
sleeping tablets	prášky na spaní m pl	prash·ki nuh spuh·nyee

english–czech dictionary

Czech nouns in this dictionary have their gender indicated by ⓜ (masculine), ⓕ (feminine) or ⓝ (neuter). If it's a plural noun, you'll also see pl. Adjectives are given in the masculine form only. Words are also marked as a (adjective), v (verb), sg (singular), pl (plural), inf (informal) or pol (polite) where necessary.

A

accident *nehoda* ⓕ ne-ho-duh
accommodation *ubytování* ⓝ
u-bi-to-va-nyee
adaptor *adaptor* ⓜ uh-duhp-tor
address *adresa* ⓕ uh-dre-suh
after *po* po
air-conditioned *klimatizovaný* kli-muh-ti-zo-vuh-nee
airplane *letadlo* ⓝ le-tuhd-lo
airport *letiště* ⓝ le-tyish-tye
alcohol *alkohol* ⓜ uhl-ko-hol
all a *všichni* vshikh-nyi
allergy *alergie* ⓕ uh-ler-gi-ye
ambulance *ambulance* ⓕ uhm-bu-luhn-tse
and a uh
ankle *kotník* ⓜ kot-nyeek
arm *paže* ⓕ puh-zhe
ashtray *popelník* ⓜ po-pel-nyeek
ATM *bankomat* ⓜ buhn-ko-muht

B

baby *nemluvně* ⓝ nem-luv-nye
back (body) *záda* ⓝ za-duh
backpack *batoh* ⓜ buh-tawh
bad *špatný* shpuht-nee
bag *taška* ⓕ tuhsh-kuh
baggage claim *výdej zavazadel* ⓜ
vee-dey zuh-vuh-zuh-del
bank *banka* ⓕ buhn-kuh
bar *bar* ⓜ buhr
bathroom *koupelna* ⓕ koh-pel-nuh
battery *baterie* ⓕ buh-te-ri-ye
beautiful *krásný* kras-nee
bed *postel* ⓕ pos-tel
beer *pivo* ⓝ pi-vo
before *před* przhed
behind *za* zuh
bicycle *kolo* ⓝ ko-lo
big *velký* vel-kee
bill *účet* ⓜ oo-chet
black *černý* cher-nee

blanket *deka* ⓕ de-kuh
blood group *krevní skupina* ⓕ
krev-nyee sku-pi-nuh
blue *modrý* mod-ree
book (make a reservation) v *objednat* ob-yed-nuht
bottle *láhev* ⓕ la-hef
bottle opener *otvírák na láhve* ⓜ
ot-vee-rak nuh lah-ve
boy *chlapec* ⓜ khluh-pets
brakes (car) *brzdy* ⓕ pl brz-di
breakfast *snídaně* ⓕ snee-duh-nye
broken (faulty) *zlomený* zlo-me-nee
bus *autobus* ⓜ ow-to-bus
business *obchod* ⓜ op-khod
buy *koupit* koh-pit

C

café *kavárna* ⓕ kuh-var-nuh
camera *fotoaparát* ⓜ fo-to-uh-puh-rat
camp site *autokempink* ⓜ ow-to-kem-pink
cancel *zrušit* zru-shit
can opener *otvírák na konzervy* ⓜ
ot-vee-rak nuh kon-zer-vi
car *auto* ⓝ ow-to
cash *hotovost* ⓕ ho-to-vost
cash (a cheque) v *inkasovat šek* in-kuh-so-vuht shek
cell phone *mobil* ⓜ mo-bil
centre *střed* ⓜ strzhed
change (money) v *vyměnit* vi-mye-nyit
cheap *levný* lev-nee
check (bill) *účet* ⓜ oo-chet
check-in *recepce* ⓕ re-tsep-tse
chest *hruď* ⓕ hrud'
child *dítě* ⓝ dyee-tye
cigarette *cigareta* ⓕ tsi-guh-re-tuh
city *město* ⓝ myes-to
clean a *čistý* chis-tee
closed *zavřený* zuh-vrzhe-nee
coffee *káva* ⓕ ka-vuh
coins *mince* ⓕ min-tse
cold a *chladný* khluhd-nee
collect call *hovor na účet volaného* ⓜ
ho-vor nuh oo-chet vo-luh-nair-ho

DICTIONARY

A

come *přijít przhi-yeet*
computer *počítač* ⓜ *po-chee-tuhch*
condom *prezervativ* ⓜ *pre-zer-vuh-tif*
contact lenses *kontaktní čočky* ⓕ pl
  kon-tuhkt-nyee choch-ki
cook v *vařit vuh-rzhit*
cost *cena* ⓕ *tse-nuh*
credit card *kreditní karta* ⓕ
  kre-dit-nyee kuhr-tuh
cup *šálek* ⓜ *sha-lek*
currency exchange *směnárna* ⓕ *smye-nar-nuh*
customs (immigration) *celnice* ⓕ *tsel-ni-tse*
Czech a *český ches-kee*
Czech (language) *čeština* ⓕ *chesh-tyi-nuh*
Czech Republic *Česká republika* ⓕ
  ches-ka re-pu-bli-kuh

D

dangerous *nebezpečný ne-bez-pech-nee*
date (time) *schůzka* ⓕ *skhoaz-kuh*
day *den* ⓜ *den*
delay *zpoždění* ⓝ *zpozh-dye-nyee*
dentist *zubař/zubařka* ⓜ/ⓕ *zu-buhrzh/zu-buhrzh-kuh*
depart *odjet od-yet*
diaper *plénka* ⓕ *plairn-kuh*
dictionary *slovník* ⓜ *slov-nyeek*
dinner *večeře* ⓝ *ve-che-rzhe*
direct *přímý przhee-mee*
dirty *špinavý shpi-nuh-vee*
disabled *invalidní in-vuh-lid-nyee*
discount *sleva* ⓕ *sle-vuh*
doctor *doktor/doktorka* ⓜ/ⓕ *dok-tor/dok-tor-kuh*
double bed *manželská postel* ⓕ *muhn-zhels-ka pos-tel*
double room *dvoulůžkový pokoj* ⓜ
  dvah-loozh-ko-vee po-koy
drink *nápoj* ⓜ *na-poy*
drive v *řídit rzhee-dyit*
drivers licence *řidičský průkaz* ⓜ
  rzhi-dyich-skee proo-kuhz
drugs (illicit) *drogy* ⓕ pl *dro-gi*
dummy (pacifier) *dudlík* ⓜ *dud-leek*

E

ear *ucho* ⓝ *u-kho*
east *východ* ⓜ *vee-khod*
eat *jíst yeest*
economy class *turistická třída* ⓕ *tu-ris-tits-ka trzhee-duh*
electricity *elektřina* ⓕ *e-lek-trzhi-nuh*
elevator *výtah* ⓜ *vee-tuh*
email *email* ⓜ *ee-meyl*

embassy *velvyslanectví* ⓝ *vel-vi-sluh-nets-tvee*
emergency *pohotovost* ⓕ *po-ho-to-vost*
English (language) *angličtina* ⓕ *uhn-glich-tyi-nuh*
entrance *vstup* ⓜ *vstup*
evening *večer* ⓜ *ve-cher*
exchange rate *směnný kurs* ⓜ *smye-nee kurz*
exit *východ* ⓜ *vee-khod*
expensive *drahý druh-hee*
express mail *expresní zásilka* ⓕ *eks-pres-nyee za-sil-kuh*
eye *oko* ⓝ *o-ko*

F

far *daleko duh-le-ko*
fast *rychlý rikh-lee*
father *otec* ⓜ *o-tets*
film (camera) *film* ⓜ *film*
finger *prst* ⓜ *prst*
first-aid kit *lékárnička* ⓕ *lair-kar-nyich-kuh*
first class *první třída* ⓕ *prv-nyee trzhee-duh*
fish *ryba* ⓕ *ri-buh*
food *jídlo* ⓝ *yeed-lo*
foot *chodidlo* ⓝ *kho-dyid-lo*
fork *vidlička* ⓕ *vid-lich-kuh*
free (of charge) *bezplatný bez-pluht-nee*
friend *přítel/přítelkyně* ⓜ/ⓕ
  przhee-tel/przhee-tel-ki-nye
fruit *ovoce* ⓝ *o-vo-tse*
full *plný pl-nee*
funny *legrační le-gruhch-nyee*

G

gift *dar* ⓜ *duhr*
girl *dívka* ⓕ *dyeef-kuh*
glass (drinking) *sklenička* ⓕ *skle-nyich-kuh*
glasses *brýle* ⓕ pl *bree-le*
go *jít yeet*
good *dobrý do-bree*
green *zelený ze-le-nee*
guide *průvodce* ⓜ *proo-vod-tse*

H

half *polovina* ⓕ *po-lo-vi-nuh*
hand *ruka* ⓕ *ru-kuh*
handbag *kabelka* ⓕ *kuh-bel-kuh*
happy *šťastný shtyast-nee*
have *mít meet*
he *on on*
head *hlava* ⓕ *hluh-vuh*
heart *srdce* ⓝ *srd-tse*

heat *horko* ⓝ *hor-ko*
heavy *těžký* *tyezh-kee*
help v *pomoci* *po-mo-tsi*
here *tady* *tuh-dy*
high *vysoký* *vi-so-kee*
highway *dálnice* ⓕ *dal-nyi-tse*
hike v *trampovat* *truhm-po-vuht*
holiday *svátek* ⓜ *sva-tek*
homosexual *homosexuál* ⓜ *ho-mo-sek-su-al*
hospital *nemocnice* ⓕ *ne-mots-nyi-tse*
hot *horký* *hor-kee*
hotel *hotel* ⓜ *ho-tel*
hungry *hladový* *hluh-do-vee*
husband *manžel* ⓜ *muhn-zhel*

I

I *já* *ya*
identification (card) *osobní doklad* ⓝ
o-sob-nyee dok-luhd
ill *nemocný* *ne-mots-nee*
important *důležitý* *doo-le-zhi-tee*
included *včetně* *fchet-nye*
injury *zranění* ⓝ *zruh-nye-nyee*
insurance *pojištění* ⓝ *po-yish-tye-nyee*
Internet *internet* ⓜ *in-ter-net*
interpreter *tlumočník/tlumočnice* ⓜ/ⓕ
tlu-moch-nyeek/tlu-moch-nyi-tse

J

jewellery *šperky* ⓜ pl *shper-ki*
job *zaměstnání* ⓝ *zuh-myest-na-nyee*

K

key *klíč* ⓜ *kleech*
kilogram *kilogram* ⓜ *ki-lo-gruhm*
kitchen *kuchyň* ⓕ *ku-khin'*
knife *nůž* ⓜ *noozh*

L

laundry (place) *prádelna* ⓕ *pra-del-nuh*
lawyer *advokát/advokátka* ⓜ/ⓕ
uhd-vo-kat/uhd-vo-kat-kuh
left (direction) *levý* *le-vee*
left-luggage office *úschovna zavazadel* ⓕ
oos-khov-nuh zuh-vuh-zuh-del
leg *noha* ⓕ *no-huh*

lesbian *lesbička* ⓕ *les-bich-kuh*
less *menší* *men-shee*
letter (mail) *dopis* ⓜ *do-pis*
lift (elevator) *výtah* ⓜ *vee-tah*
light *světlo* ⓝ *svyet-lo*
like v *mít rád* *meet rad*
lock *zámek* ⓜ *za-mek*
long *dlouhý* *dloh-hee*
lost *ztracený* *ztruh-tse-nee*
lost-property office *ztráty a nálezy* ⓕ
ztra-ti uh na-le-zi
love v *milovat* *mi-lo-vuht*
luggage *zavazadlo* ⓝ *zuh-vuh-zuhd-lo*
lunch *oběd* ⓜ *o-byed*

M

mail *pošta* ⓕ *posh-tuh*
man *muž* ⓜ *muzh*
map (of country) *mapa* ⓕ *muh-puh*
map (of town) *plán* ⓜ *plan*
market *trh* ⓜ *trh*
matches *zápalky* ⓕ pl *za-puhl-ki*
meat *maso* ⓝ *muh-so*
medicine *lék* ⓜ *lairk*
menu *jídelní lístek* ⓜ *yee-del-nyee lees-tek*
message *zpráva* ⓕ *zpra-vuh*
milk *mléko* ⓝ *mlair-ko*
minute *minuta* ⓕ *mi-nu-tuh*
mobile phone *mobil* ⓜ *mo-bil*
money *peníze* ⓜ pl *pe-nyee-ze*
month *měsíc* ⓜ *mye-seets*
morning *ráno* ⓝ *ra-no*
mother *matka* ⓕ *muht-kuh*
motorcycle *motorka* ⓕ *mo-tor-kuh*
motorway *dálnice* ⓕ *dal-nyi-tse*
mouth *ústa* ⓕ *oos-tuh*
music *hudba* ⓕ *hud-buh*

N

name *jméno* ⓝ *ymair-no*
napkin *ubrousek* ⓜ *u-broh-sek*
nappy *plenka* ⓕ *plen-kuh*
near *blízko* *bleez-ko*
neck *krk* ⓜ *krk*
new *nový* *no-vee*
news *zprávy* ⓕ pl *zpra-vi*
newspaper *noviny* ⓕ pl *no-vi-ni*
night *noc* ⓕ *nots*
no *ne* *ne*

noisy *hlučný* hluch-nee
nonsmoking *nekuřácký* ne-ku-rzhats-kee
north *sever* ⑩ se-ver
nose *nos* ⑩ nos
now *teď* teď
number *číslo* ⑪ chees-lo

O

oil (engine) *olej* ⑩ o-ley
old *starý* stuh-ree
one-way ticket *jednoduchá jízdenka* ①
   yed-no-du-kha yeez-den-kuh
open a *otevřená* o-tev-rzhe-nee
outside *venku* ven-ku

P

package *balík* ⑩ buh-leek
paper *papír* ⑩ puh-peer
park (car) v *parkovat* puhr-ko-vuht
passport *pas* ⑩ puhs
pay *platit* pluh-tyit
pen *propiska* ① pro-pis-kuh
petrol *benzín* ⑩ ben-zeen
pharmacy *lékárna* ① lair-kar-nuh
phonecard *telefonní karta* ①
   te-le-fo-nyee kuhr-tuh
photo *fotka* ① fot-kuh
plate *talíř* ⑩ tuh-leerzh
police *policie* ① po-li-tsi-ye
postcard *pohled* ⑩ po-hled
post office *pošta* ① posh-tuh
pregnant *těhotná* tye-hot-na
price *cena* ① tse-nuh

Q

quiet *tichý* tyi-khee

R

rain *déšť* ⑩ dairsht'
razor *břitva* ① brzhit-vuh
receipt *stvrzenka* ① stvr-zen-kuh
red *červený* cher-ve-nee
refund *vrácení peněz* ⑪ vruh-tse-nyee pe-nyez
registered mail *doporučená zásilka* ①
   do-po-ru-che-na za-sil-kuh
rent v *pronajmout* pro-nai-moht

repair v *opravit* o-pruh-vit
reservation *rezervace* ① re-zer-vuh-tse
restaurant *restaurace* ① res-tow-ruh-tse
return v *vrátit se* vra-tyit se
return ticket *zpáteční jízdenka* ①
   zpa-tech-nyee yeez-den-kuh
right (direction) *pravý* pruh-vee
road *silnice* ① sil-nyi-tse
room *pokoj* ⑩ po-koy

S

safe a *bezpečný* bez-pech-nee
sanitary napkins *dámské vložky* ① pl
   dams-kair vlozh-ki
seat *místo* ⑪ mees-to
send *poslat* pos-luht
service station *benzínová pumpa* ①
   ben-zee-no-va pum-puh
sex *pohlaví* ⑪ po-hluh-vee
shampoo *šampon* ⑩ shuhm-pon
share (a dorm) *spoluobývat* spo-lu-o-bee-vuht
shaving cream *pěna na holení* ①
   pye-nuh nuh ho-le-nyee
she *ona* o-nuh
sheet (bed) *prostěradlo* ⑪ pros-tye-ruhd-lo
shirt *košile* ① ko-shi-le
shoes *boty* ① pl bo-ti
shop *obchod* ⑩ op-khod
short *krátký* krat-kee
shower *sprcha* ① spr-khuh
single room *jednolůžkový pokoj* ⑪
   yed-no-loozh-ko-vee po-koy
skin *kůže* ① koo-zhe
skirt *sukně* ① suk-nye
sleep v *spát* spat
slowly *pomalu* po-muh-lu
small *malý* muh-lee
smoke (cigarettes) v *kouřit* koh-rzhit
soap *mýdlo* ⑪ meed-lo
some *několik* nye-ko-lik
soon *brzy* br-zi
south *jih* ⑩ yih
souvenir shop *obchod se suvenýry* ⑩
   op-khod se su-ve-nee-ri
speak *říci* rzhee-tsi
spoon *lžíce* ① lzhee-tse
stamp *známka* ① znam-kuh
station (train) *nádraží* ⑪ na-druh-zhee
stomach *žaludek* ⑩ zhuh-lu-dek

stop v *zastavit* zuhs·tuh·vit
stop (bus) *zastávka* ⓕ zuhs·taf·kuh
street *ulice* ⓕ u·li·tse
student *student/studentka* ⓜ/ⓕ
　　stu·dent/stu·dent·kuh
sun *slunce* ⓕ slun·tse
sunscreen *opalovací krém* ⓜ o·puh·lo·vuh·tsee krairm
swim v *plavat* pluh·vuht

T

tampons *tampon* ⓜ tuhm·pon
taxi *taxík* ⓜ tuhk·seek
teaspoon *lžička* ⓕ lzhich·kuh
teeth *zuby* ⓜ pl zu·bi
telephone *telefon* ⓜ te·le·fon
television *televize* ⓕ te·le·vi·ze
temperature (weather) *teplota* ⓕ te·plo·tuh
tent *stan* ⓜ stuhn
that (one) *tamten* tuhm·ten
they *oni* o·nyi
thirsty *žíznivý* zheez·nyi·vee
this (one) *tenhle* ten·hle
throat *hrdlo* ⓜ hrd·lo
ticket *vstupenka* ⓕ fstu·pen·kuh
time *čas* ⓜ chuhs
tired *unavený* u·nuh·ve·nee
tissues *kosmetické kapesníčky* ⓜ pl
　　kos·me·tits·kair kuh·pes·neech·ki
today *dnes* dnes
toilet *toaleta* ⓕ to·uh·le·tuh
tomorrow *zítra* zeet·ruh
tonight *dnes večer* dnes ve·cher
toothbrush *zubní kartáček* ⓜ zub·nyee kuhr·ta·chek
toothpaste *zubní pasta* ⓕ zub·nyee puhs·tuh
torch (flashlight) *baterka* ⓕ buh·ter·kuh
tour *okružní jízda* ⓕ o·kruzh·nyee yeez·duh
tourist office *turistická informační kancelář* ⓕ
　　tu·ris·tits·ka in·for·muhch·nyee kuhn·tse·larzh
towel *ručník* ⓜ ruch·nyeek
train *vlak* ⓜ vluhk
translate *přeložit* przhe·lo·zhit
travel agency *cestovní kancelář* ⓕ
　　tses·tov·nyee kuhn·tse·larzh
travellers cheque *cestovní šek* ⓜ tses·tov·nyee shek
trousers *kalhoty* ⓕ pl kuhl·ho·ti
twin beds *dvoupostel* ⓕ dvoh·pos·tel
tyre *pneumatika* ⓕ pne·u·muh·ti·kuh

U

underwear *spodní prádlo* ⓝ spod·nyee prad·lo
urgent *naléhavý* nuh·lair·huh·vee

V

vacant *volný* vol·nee
vacation (from school) *prázdniny* ⓕ prazd·nyi·ni
vacation (from work) *dovolená* ⓕ do·vo·le·na
vegetable *zelenina* ⓕ ze·le·nyi·nuh
vegetarian a *vegetariánský* ve·ge·tuh·ri·yans·kee

W

waiter/waitress *číšník/číšnice* ⓜ/ⓕ
　　cheesh·nyeek/cheesh·nyi·tse
wallet *peněženka* ⓕ pe·nye·zhen·ka
walk v *jít* yeet
warm a *teplý* tep·lee
wash (something) *umýt* u·meet
watch *hodinky* ⓕ pl ho·dyin·ki
water *voda* ⓕ vo·duh
we *my* mi
weekend *víkend* ⓜ vee·kend
west *západ* ⓜ za·puhd
wheelchair *invalidní vozík* ⓜ in·vuh·lid·nyee vo·zeek
when *kdy* gdi
where *kde* gde
white *bílý* bee·lee
who *kdo* gdo
why *proč* proch
wife *manželka* ⓕ muhn·zhel·kuh
window *okno* ⓝ ok·no
wine *víno* ⓝ vee·no
with s s
without *bez* bez
woman *žena* ⓕ zhe·nuh
write *psát* p·sat

Y

yellow *žlutý* zhlu·tee
yes *ano* uh·no
yesterday *včera* fche·ruh
you sg inf *ty* ti
you sg pol&pl *vy* vi

French

french alphabet

A a a	*B b* be	*C c* se	*D d* de	*E e* eu
F f ef	*G g* zhe	*H h* ash	*I i* i	*J j* zhi
K k ka	*L l* el	*M m* em	*N n* en	*O o* o
P p pe	*Q q* kew	*R r* er	*S s* es	*T t* te
U u ew	*V v* ve	*W w* dubl ve	*X x* iks	*Y y* i grek
Z z zed				

french

FRANÇAIS

introduction

What do you think of when the word 'French' comes up? A *bon vivant*, drinking an *apéritif tête-à-tête* with a friend at a *café*, while studying the *à la carte* menu and making some witty *double entendres*? Are you getting *déjà vu* yet? Chances are you already know a few fragments of French (*français* fron·sey) – bonjour, oui, au revoir, bon voyage and so on. Even if you missed out on French lessons, though, that first sentence (forgive the stereotyping) is evidence that you probably know quite a few French words without realising it. And thanks to the Norman invasion of England in the 11th century, many common English words have a French origin – some estimate, in fact, that three-fifths of everyday English vocabulary arrived via French.

So, after centuries of contact with English, French offers English speakers a relatively smooth path to communicating in another language. The structure of a French sentence won't come as a surprise and the sounds of the language are generally common to English as well. The few sounds that do differ will be familiar to most through television and film examples of French speakers – the silent 'h' and the throaty 'r', for example. French is a distant cousin of English, but is most closely related to its Romance siblings, Italian and Spanish. These languages developed from the Latin spoken by the Romans during their conquests of the 1st century BC.

Almost 30 countries cite French as an official language (not always the only language, of course), in many cases due to France's colonisation of various countries in Africa, the Pacific and the Caribbean. It's the mother tongue of around 80 million people in places like Belgium, Switzerland, Luxembourg, Monaco, Canada and Senegal as well as France, and another 50 million speak it as a second language. French was the language of international diplomacy until the early 20th century, and is still an official language of a number of international organisations, including the Red Cross, the United Nations and the International Olympic Committee.

As well as the advantage of learning a language that's spoken all around the world, there are more subtle benefits to French. Being told of a wonderful vineyard off the tourist track, for example, or discovering that there's little truth in the cliché that the French are rude. And *regardez* the significant body of literature (the Nobel Prize for Literature has gone to French authors a dozen times), film and music … You'll find the reasons to speak French just keep growing.

pronunciation

vowel sounds

Generally, French vowel sounds are short and don't glide into other vowels. Note that the ey in *café* is close to the English sound, but it's shorter and sharper.

symbol	english equivalent	french example	transliteration
a	run	*tasse*	tas
ai	aisle	*travail*	tra·vai
air	fair	*faire*	fair
e	bet	*fesses*	fes
ee	see	*lit*	lee
eu	nurse	*deux*	deu
ew	ee pronounced with rounded lips	*tu*	tew
ey	as in 'bet', but longer	*musée*	moo·zey
o	pot	*pomme*	pom
oo	moon	*chou*	shoo

There are also four nasal vowels in French. They're pronounced as if you're trying to force the sound out of your nose rather than your mouth. In French, nasal vowels cause the following nasal consonant sound to be omitted, but a 'hint' of what the implied consonant is can sometimes be heard. We've used nasal consonant sounds (m, n, ng) with the nasal vowel to help you produce the sound with more confidence. Since the four nasal sounds can be quite close, we've simplified it this way:

symbol	english equivalent	french example	transliteration
om/on/ong	like the 'o' in 'pot', plus nasal conso-nant sound	*mouton*	moo·ton
um/un/ung	similar to the 'a' in 'bat', plus nasal consonant sound	*magasin*	ma·ga·zun

consonant sounds

symbol	english equivalent	french example	transliteration
b	**bed**	*billet*	bee·yey
d	**dog**	*date*	dat
f	**fat**	*femme*	fam
g	**go**	*grand*	gron
k	**kit**	*carte*	kart
l	**lot**	*livre*	leev·re
m	**man**	*merci*	mair·see
n	**not**	*non*	non
ny	ca**ny**on	*signe*	see·nye
ng	ri**ng**	*cinquante*	sung·kont
p	**pet**	*parc*	park
r	**run** (throaty)	*rue*	rew
s	**sun**	*si*	see
sh	**sh**ot	*changer*	shon·zhey
t	**top**	*tout*	too
v	**very**	*verre*	vair
w	**win**	*oui*	wee
y	**yes**	*payer*	pe·yey
z	**zero**	*vous avez*	voo·za·vey
zh	plea**s**ure	*je*	zhe

word stress

Syllables in French words are, for the most part, equally stressed. English speakers tend to stress the first syllable, so try adding a light stress on the final syllable to compensate. The rhythm of a French sentence is based on breaking the phrase into meaningful sections, then stressing the final syllable pronounced in each section. The stress at these points is characterised by a slight rise in intonation.

tools

language difficulties

Do you speak English?
Parlez-vous anglais? — par·ley·voo ong·gley

Do you understand?
Comprenez-vous? — kom·pre·ney·voo

I understand.
Je comprends. — zhe kom·pron

I don't understand.
Je ne comprends pas. — zhe ne kom·pron pa

What does (*beaucoup*) mean?
Que veut dire (beaucoup)? — ke veu deer (bo·koo)

How do you ...?	*Comment ...?*	ko·mon ...
pronounce this	*le prononcez-vous*	le pro·non·sey voo
write (*bonjour*)	*est-ce qu'on écrit (bonjour)*	es kon ey·kree (bon·zhoor)

Could you please ...?	*Pourriez-vous ..., s'il vous plaît?*	poo·ree·yey voo ... seel voo pley
repeat that	*répéter*	rey·pey·tey
speak more slowly	*parler plus lentement*	par·ley plew lon·te·mon
write it down	*l'écrire*	ley·kreer

essentials

Yes.	*Oui.*	wee
No.	*Non.*	non
Please.	*S'il vous plaît.*	seel voo pley
Thank you (very much).	*Merci (beaucoup).*	mair·see (bo·koo)
You're welcome.	*Je vous en prie.*	zhe voo zon·pree
Excuse me.	*Excusez-moi.*	ek·skew·zey·mwa
Sorry.	*Pardon.*	par·don

FRANÇAIS – tools

numbers

0	*zéro*	zey·ro	16	*seize*	sez
1	*un*	un	17	*dix-sept*	dee·set
2	*deux*	deu	18	*dix-huit*	dee·zweet
3	*trois*	trwa	19	*dix-neuf*	deez·neuf
4	*quatre*	ka·tre	20	*vingt*	vung
5	*cinq*	sungk	21	*vingt et un*	vung tey un
6	*six*	sees	22	*vingt-deux*	vung·deu
7	*sept*	set	30	*trente*	tront
8	*huit*	weet	40	*quarante*	ka·ront
9	*neuf*	neuf	50	*cinquante*	sung·kont
10	*dix*	dees	60	*soixante*	swa·sont
11	*onze*	onz	70	*soixante-dix*	swa·son·dees
12	*douze*	dooz	80	*quatre-vingts*	ka·tre·vung
13	*treize*	trez	90	*quatre-vingt-dix*	ka·tre·vung·dees
14	*quatorze*	ka·torz	100	*cent*	son
15	*quinze*	kunz	1000	*mille*	meel

time & dates

What time is it?	*Quelle heure est-il?*	kel eur ey·teel
It's one o'clock.	*Il est une heure.*	ee·ley ewn eu
It's (10) o'clock.	*Il est (dix) heures.*	ee·ley (deez) eu
Quarter past (one).	*Il est (une) heure et quart.*	ee·ley (ewn) eu ey kar
Half past (one).	*Il est (une) heure et demie.*	ee·ley (ewn) eu ey de·mee
Quarter to (one).	*Il est (une) heure*	ee·ley (ewn) eu
	moins le quart.	mwun le kar
At what time …?	*À quelle heure …?*	a kel eu …
At …	*À …*	a …
in the morning	*du matin*	dew ma·tun
in the afternoon	*de l'après-midi*	de la·prey·mee·dee
in the evening	*du soir*	dew swar
Monday	*lundi*	lun·dee
Tuesday	*mardi*	mar·dee
Wednesday	*mercredi*	mair·kre·dee
Thursday	*jeudi*	zheu·dee
Friday	*vendredi*	von·dre·dee
Saturday	*samedi*	sam·dee
Sunday	*dimanche*	dee·monsh

January	*janvier*	zhon-vyey
February	*février*	feyv-ryey
March	*mars*	mars
April	*avril*	a-vreel
May	*mai*	mey
June	*juin*	zhwun
July	*juillet*	zhwee-yey
August	*août*	oot
September	*septembre*	sep-tom-bre
October	*octobre*	ok-to-bre
November	*novembre*	no-vom-bre
December	*décembre*	dey-som-bre

What date is it today?
   C'est quel jour aujourd'hui?   sey kel zhoor o-zhoor-dwee

It's (18 October).
   C'est le (dix-huit octobre).   sey le (dee-zwee tok-to-bre)

| since (May) | *depuis (mai)* | de-pwee (mey) |
| until (June) | *jusqu'à (juin)* | zhoos-ka (zhwun) |

| today | *aujourd'hui* | o-zhoor-dwee |
| tonight | *ce soir* | se swar |

last ...		
night	*hier soir*	ee-yair swar
week	*la semaine dernière*	la se-men dair-nyair
month	*le mois dernier*	le mwa dair-nyey
year	*l'année dernière*	la-ney dair-nyair

next ...		
week	*la semaine prochaine*	la se-men pro-shen
month	*le mois prochain*	le mwa pro-shen
year	*l'année prochaine*	la-ney pro-shen

yesterday/tomorrow ...	*hier/demain ...*	ee-yair/de-mun ...
morning	*matin*	ma-tun
afternoon	*après-midi*	a-pre-mee-dee
evening	*soir*	swar

weather

What's the weather like?	Quel temps fait-il?	kel tom fey·teel

It's ...

cloudy	Le temps est couvert.	le tom ey koo·vair
cold	Il fait froid.	eel fey frwa
hot	Il fait chaud.	eel fey sho
raining	Il pleut.	eel pleu
snowing	Il neige.	eel nezh
sunny	Il fait beau.	eel fey bo
warm	Il fait chaud.	eel fey sho
windy	Il fait du vent.	eel fey dew von

spring	printemps m	prun·tom
summer	été m	ey·tey
autumn	automne m	o·ton
winter	hiver m	ee·vair

border crossing

I'm here ...	Je suis ici ...	zhe swee zee·see ...
in transit	de passage	de pa·sazh
on business	pour le travail	poor le tra·vai
on holiday	pour les vacances	poor ley va·kons

I'm here for ...	Je suis ici pour ...	zhe swee zee·see poor ...
(10) days	(dix) jours	(dees) zhoor
(three) weeks	(trois) semaines	(trwa) se·men
(two) months	(deux) mois	(deu) mwa

I'm going to (Paris).
Je vais à (Paris). zhe vey a (pa·ree)

I'm staying at the (Hotel Grand).
Je loge à (l'hotel Grand). zhe lozh a (lo·tel gron)

I have nothing to declare.
Je n'ai rien à déclarer. zhe ney ryun a dey·kla·rey

I have something to declare.
J'ai quelque chose à déclarer. zhey kel·ke·shoz a dey·kla·rey

That's not mine.
Ce n'est pas à moi. se ney pa a mwa

transport

tickets & luggage

Where can I buy a ticket?
Où peut-on acheter un billet?   oo pe·ton ash·tey um bee·yey

Do I need to book a seat?
Est-ce qu'il faut réserver une place?   es·keel fo rey·zer·vey ewn plas

One ... ticket	*Un billet ... (pour*	um bee·yey ... (poor
(to Bordeaux), please.	*Bordeaux), s'il vous plaît.*	bor·do) seel voo pley
one-way	*simple*	sum·ple
return	*aller et retour*	a·ley ey re·toor

I'd like to ... my	*Je voudrais ... mon*	zhe voo·drey ... mom
ticket, please.	*billet, s'il vous plaît.*	bee·yey seel voo pley
cancel	*annuler*	a·new·ley
change	*changer*	shon·zhey
collect	*retirer*	re·tee·rey
confirm	*confirmer*	kon·feer·mey

I'd like a ... seat,	*Je voudrais une place*	zhe voo·drey ewn plas
please.	*..., s'il vous plaît.*	... seel voo pley
(non)smoking	*non-fumeur*	non few·me
smoking	*fumeur*	few·me

How much is it?
C'est combien?   sey kom·byun

Is there air conditioning?
Est-qu'il y a la climatisation?   es·keel ya la klee·ma·tee·za·syon

Is there a toilet?
Est-qu'il y a des toilettes?   es·keel ya dey twa·let

How long does the trip take?
Le trajet dure combien de temps?   le tra·zhey dewr kom·byun de tom

Is it a direct route?
Est-ce que c'est direct?   es·ke sey dee·rekt

I'd like a luggage locker.
Je voudrais une   zhe voo·drey ewn
consigne automatique.   kon·see·nye o·to·ma·teek

My luggage	Mes bagages	mey ba-gazh
has been ...	ont été ...	on tey-tey ...
damaged	endommagés	on-do-ma-zhey
lost	perdus	per-dew
stolen	volés	vo-ley

getting around

Where does flight (008) arrive?
Où atteri le vol (008)?　　oo a-te-ree le vol (zey-ro zey-ro weet)

Where does flight (008) depart?
D'où décolle le vol (008)?　　doo dey-kol le vol (zey-ro zey-ro weet)

Where's (the) ...?	Où se trouve ...?	oo se troo-ve ...
arrivals hall	le hall d'arrivée	le hol da-ree-vey
departures hall	le hall des departs	le hol dey dey-par
duty-free shop	le magasin duty-free	le ma-ga-zun dyoo-tee free
gate (12)	porte (douze)	port (dooz)

Is this the ... to (Nice)?	Est ce ... pour (Nice)?	es se ... poor (nees)
boat	le bateau	le ba-to
bus	le bus	le bews
plane	l'avion	la-vyon
train	le train	le trun

What time's	Le ... bus passe	le ... bews pas
the ... bus?	à quelle heure?	a kel e
first	premier	pre-myey
last	dernier	dair-nyey
next	prochain	pro-shun

At what time does it arrive/leave?
A quelle heure est ce qu'il arrive/part?　　a kel eur es se keel a-ree-ve/par

How long will it be delayed?
De combien de temps est-il retardé?　　de kom-byun de tom es-teel re-tar-dey

What station is this?
C'est quelle gare?　　sey kel gar

What's the next station?
Quelle est la prochaine gare?　　kel ey la pro-shen gar

Does it stop at (Amboise)?
Est-ce qu'il s'arrête à (Amboise)?　　es-kil sa-ret a (om-bwaz)

Please tell me when we get to (Nantes).
Pouvez-vous me dire quand
nous arrivons à (Nantes)?
poo·vey·voo me deer kon
noo za·ree·von a (nont)

How long do we stop here?
Combien de temps on s'arrête ici?
kom·byun de tom on sa·ret ee·see

Is this seat available?
Est-ce que cette place est libre?
es·ke set plas ey lee·bre

That's my seat.
C'est ma place.
sey ma plas

I'd like a taxi …	*Je voudrais un taxi …*	zhe voo·drey un tak·see …
at (9am)	*à (neuf heures*	a (neu veur
	du matin)	dew ma·tun)
now	*maintenant*	mun·te·non
tomorrow	*demain*	de·mun

Is this taxi available?
Vous êtes libre?
voo·zet lee·bre

How much is it to …?
C'est combien pour aller à …?
sey kom·byun poor a·ley a …

Please put the meter on.
Mettez le compteur, s'il vous plaît.
me·tey le kon·teseel voo pley

Please take me to (this address).
Conduisez-moi à (cette adresse),
s'il vous plaît.
kon·dwee·zey mwa a (set a·dres)
seel voo pley

Please	*…, s'il vous plaît.*	… seel voo pley
slow down	*Roulez plus lentement*	roo·ley plew lont·mon
stop here	*Arrêtez-vous ici*	a·rey·tey voo ee·see
wait here	*Attendez ici*	a·ton·dey ee·see

car, motorbike & bicycle hire

I'd like to hire a …	*Je voudrais louer …*	zhe voo·drey loo·wey …
bicycle	*un vélo*	un vey·lo
car	*une voiture*	ewn vwa·tewr
motorbike	*une moto*	ewn mo·to

with …	*avec …*	a·vek …
a driver	*un chauffeur*	un sho·feur
air conditioning	*climatisation*	klee·ma·tee·za·syon

How much for ... hire?	Quel est le tarif par ...?	kel ey le ta·reef par ...
hourly	heure	eur
daily	jour	zhoor
weekly	semaine	se·men

air	air m	air
oil	huile f	weel
petrol	essence f	es·sons
tyres	pneus f pl	pneu

I need a mechanic.
J'ai besoin d'un mécanicien.   zhey be·zwun dun mey·ka·nee·syun

I've run out of petrol.
Je suis en panne d'essence.   zhe swee zon pan de·sons

I have a flat tyre.
Mon pneu est à plat.   mom pneu ey ta pla

directions

Where's the ...?	Où est-ce qu'il y a ...?	oo es·keel ya ...
bank	la banque	la bongk
city centre	le centre-ville	ler son·tre·veel
hotel	l'hôtel	lo·tel
market	le marché	le mar·shey
police station	le commissariat	le kom·mee·sar·ya
	de police	de po·lees
post office	le bureau de poste	le bew·ro de post
public toilet	des toilettes	dey twa·let
tourist office	l'office de tourisme	lo·fees de too·rees·me

Is this the road to (Toulouse)?
C'est la route pour (Toulouse)?   sey la root poor (too·looz)

Can you show me (on the map)?
Pouvez-vous m'indiquer (sur la carte)?   poo·vey·voo mun·dee·key (sewr la kart)

What's the address?
Quelle est l'adresse?   kel ey la·dres

How far is it?
C'est loin?   sey lwun

How do I get there?
Comment faire pour y aller?   ko·mon fair poor ee a·ley

Turn ...	Tournez ...	toor-ney ...
at the corner	au coin	o kwun
at the traffic lights	aux feux	o feu
left/right	à gauche/droite	a gosh/drwat

It's ...	C'est ...	sey ...
behind ...	derrière ...	dair-yair ...
far away	loin d'ici	lwun dee-see
here	ici	ee-see
in front of ...	devant ...	de-von ...
left	à gauche	a gosh
near (to ...)	près (de ...)	prey (de ...)
next to ...	à côté de ...	a ko-tey de ...
opposite ...	en face de ...	on fas de ...
right	à droite	a drwat
straight ahead	tout droit	too drwa
there	là	la

north	nord m	nor
south	sud m	sewd
east	est m	est
west	ouest m	west

by bus	en bus	om bews
by taxi	en taxi	on tak-see
by train	en train	on trun
on foot	à pied	a pyey

signs

Entrée/Sortie	on-trey/sor-tee	Entrance/Exit
Ouvert/Fermé	oo-vair/fair-mey	Open/Closed
Chambre Libre	shom-bre lee-bre	Rooms Available
Complet	kom-pley	No Vacancies
Renseignements	ron-sen-ye-mon	Information
Commissariat De Police	ko-mee-sar-ya de po-lees	Police Station
Interdit	in-teyr-dee	Prohibited
Toilettes	twa-let	Toilets
Hommes	om	Men
Femmes	fam	Women
Chaude/Froide	shod/frwad	Hot/Cold

accommodation

finding accommodation

Where's a ...?	*Où est-ce qu'on peut trouver ...?*	oo es·kon peu troo·vey ...
camping ground	*un terrain de camping*	un tey·run de kom·peeng
guesthouse	*une pension*	ewn pon·see·on
hotel	*un hôtel*	un o·tel
youth hostel	*une auberge de jeunesse*	ewn o·bairzh de zhe·nes
Can you recommend somewhere ...?	*Est-ce que vous pouvez recommander un logement ...?*	es·ke voo poo·vey re·ko·mon·dey un lozh·mon ...
cheap	*pas cher*	pa shair
good	*de bonne qualité*	de bon ka·lee·tey
nearby	*près d'ici*	prey dee·see

I'd like to book a room, please.
Je voudrais réserver   zhe voo·drey rey·zair·vey
une chambre, s'il vous plaît.   ewn shom·bre seel voo pley

I have a reservation.
J'ai une réservation.   zhey ewn rey·zair·va·syon

My name is ...
Mon nom est ...   mon nom ey ...

Do you have a ... room?	*Avez-vous une chambre ...?*	a·vey·voo ewn shom·bre ...
single	*à un lit*	a un lee
double	*avec un grand lit*	a·vek ung gron lee
twin	*avec des lits jumeaux*	a·vek dey lee zhew·mo
Can I pay by ...?	*Est-ce qu'on peut payer avec ...?*	es·kom peu pey·yey a·vek ...
credit card	*une carte de crédit*	ewn kart de krey·dee
travellers cheque	*des chèques de voyage*	dey shek de vwa·yazh
How much is it per ...?	*Quel est le prix par ...?*	kel ey le pree par ...
night	*nuit*	nwee
person	*personne*	pair·son

I'd like to stay for (two) nights.
Je voudrais rester pour (deux) nuits.   zhe voo·drey res·tey poor (der) nwee

From (July 2) to (July 6).
Du (deux juillet) au (six juillet).   dew (de zhwee·yey) o (see zhwee·yey)

Can I see it?
Est-ce que je peux la voir?   es·ke zhe peu la vwar

Am I allowed to camp here?
Est-ce que je peux camper ici?   es·ke zhe peu kom·pey ee·see

Where's the nearest camp site?
Où est le terrain de camping   oo ey ler tey·run de kom·peeng
le plus proche?   le plew prosh

requests & queries

When/Where is breakfast served?
Quand/Où le petit   kon/oo le pe·tee
déjeuner est-il servi?   dey·zhe·ney ey·teel sair·vee

Please wake me at (seven).
Réveillez-moi à (sept)   rey·vey·yey·mwa a (set)
heures, s'il vous plaît.   eur seel voo pley

Could I have my key, please?
Est-ce que je pourrais avoir   es·ke zhe poo·rey a·vwar
la clé, s'il vous plaît?   la kley seel voo pley

Can I get another (blanket)?
Est-ce que je peux avoir   es·ke zhe pe a·vwar
une autre (couverture)?   ewn o·tre (koo·vair·tewr)

Is there a/an ...?	*Avez-vous un ...?*	a·vey·voo un ...
elevator	*ascenseur*	a·son·seur
safe	*coffre-fort*	ko·fre·for

The room is too ...	*C'est trop ...*	sey tro ...
expensive	*cher*	shair
noisy	*bruyant*	brew·yon
small	*petit*	pe·tee

134

The ... doesn't work.	... ne fonctionne pas.	... ne fong·syon pa
air conditioning	La climatisation	klee·ma·tee·za·syon
fan	Le ventilateur	le von·tee·la·teur
toilet	Les toilettes	le twa·let

This ... isn't clean.	... n'est pas propre.	... ney pa pro·pre
pillow	Cet oreiller	set o·rey·yey
sheet	Ce drap	se drap
towel	Cette serviette	set sair·vee·et

checking out

What time is checkout?
Quand faut-il régler?
kon fo·teel rey·gley

Can I leave my luggage here?
Puis-je laisser mes bagages?
pweezh ley·sey mey ba·gazh

Could I have my	Est-ce que je pourrais	es·ke zhe poo·rey
..., please?	avoir ..., s'il vous plaît?	a·vwar ... seel voo pley
deposit	ma caution	ma ko·syon
passport	mon passeport	mon pas·por
valuables	mes biens précieux	mey byun prey·syeu

communications & banking

the internet

Where's the local Internet café?
Où est le cybercafé du coin?
oo ey le see·bair·ka·fey dew kwun

How much is it per hour?
C'est combien l'heure?
sey kom·byun leur

I'd like to ...	Je voudrais ...	zhe voo·drey ...
check my email	consulter mon	kon·sewl·tey mong
	courrier électronique	koor·yey ey·lek·tro·neek
get Internet	me connecter	me ko·nek·tey a
access	à l'internet	lun·tair·net
use a printer	utiliser une	ew·tee·lee·zey ewn
	imprimante	um·pree·mont
use a scanner	utiliser un scanner	ew·tee·lee·zey un ska·nair

mobile/cell phone

I'd like a ...	Je voudrais ...	zhe voo·drey ...
mobile/cell phone for hire	louer un portable	loo·ey um por·ta·ble
SIM card for your network	une carte SIM pour le réseau	ewn kart seem poor le rey·zo

What are the rates?	Quels sont les tarifs?	kel son ley ta·reef

telephone

What's your phone number?
Quel est votre numéro de téléphone? kel ey vo·tre new·mey·ro de tey·ley·fon

The number is ...
Le numéro est ... le new·mey·ro ey ...

Where's the nearest public phone?
Où est le téléphone public le plus proche? oo ey le tey·ley·fon pewb·leek le plew prosh

I'd like to buy a phone card.
Je voudrais acheter une carte téléphonique. zhe voo·drey ash·tey ewn kart tey·ley·fo·neek

I want to ...	Je veux ...	zhe ve ...
call (Singapore)	téléphoner avec préavis (à Singapour)	tey·ley·fo·ney a·vek prey·a·vee (a sung·ga·poor)
make a local call	faire un appel local	fair un a·pel lo·kal
reverse the charges	téléphoner en PCV	tey·ley·fo·ney om pey·sey·vey

How much does ... cost?	Quel est le prix ...?	kel ey le pree ...
a (three)-minute call	d'une communication de (trois) minutes	dewn ko·mew·nee·ka·syon de (trwa) mee·newt
each extra minute	de chaque minute supplémentaire	de shak mee·newt sew·pley·mon·tair

It's (one euro) per (minute).
(Un euro) pour (une minute). (un eu·ro) poor (ewn mee·newt)

post office

I want to send a ...	Je voudrais envoyer ...	zhe voo-drey on-vwa-yey ...
fax	un fax	un faks
letter	une lettre	ewn le-tre
parcel	un colis	ung ko-lee
postcard	une carte postale	ewn kart pos-tal

I want to buy a/an ...	Je voudrais acheter ...	zhe voo-drey ash-tey ...
envelope	une enveloppe	ewn on-vlop
stamp	un timbre	un tum-bre

Please send it (to Australia) by ...	Envoyez-le (en Australie) ..., s'il vous plaît.	on-vwa-yey-le (on os-tra-lee) ... seel voo pley
airmail	par avion	par a-vyon
express mail	en exprès	on neks-pres
registered mail	en recommandé	on re-ko-mon-dey
surface mail	par voie de terre	par vwa de tair

Is there any mail for me?
Y a-t-il du courrier pour moi?   ya-teel dew koor-yey poor mwa

bank

Where's a/an ...?	Où est ...?	oo ey ...
ATM	le guichet automatique	le gee-shey o-to-ma-teek
foreign exchange office	le bureau de change	le bew-ro de shonzh

I'd like to ...	Je voudrais ...	zhe voo-drey ...
arrange a transfer	faire un virement	fair un veer-mon
cash a cheque	encaisser un chèque	ong-key-sey un shek
change a travellers cheque	changer des chèques de voyage	shon-zhey dey shek de vwa-yazh
change money	changer de l'argent	shon-zhey de lar-zhon
get a cash advance	une avance de crédit	ewn a-vons de krey-dee
withdraw money	retirer de l'argent	re-tee-rey de lar-zhon

What's the ...?	Quel est ...?	kel ey ...
charge for that	le tarif	le ta-reef
exchange rate	le taux de change	le to de shonzh

It's ...	C'est ...	sey ...
(12) euros	(douze) euros	(dooz) eu-ro
free	gratuit	gra-twee

What time does the bank open?
À quelle heure ouvre la banque? a kel eur oo-vre la bongk

Has my money arrived yet?
Mon argent est-il arrivé? mon ar-zhon ey-teel a-ree-vey

sightseeing

getting in

What time does it ...?	Quelle est l'heure ...?	kel ey leur ...
close	de fermeture	de fer-me-tewr
open	d'ouverture	doo-vair-tewr

What's the admission charge?
Quel est le prix d'admission? kel ey le pree dad-mee-syon

Is there a discount for children/students?
Il y a une réduction pour les eel ya ewn rey-dewk-syon poor ley
enfants/étudiants? zon-fon/zey-tew-dyon

I'd like a ...	Je voudrais ...	zhe voo-drey ...
catalogue	un catalogue	ung ka-ta-log
guide	un guide	ung geed
local map	une carte de la région	ewn kart de la rey-zhyon

I'd like to see ...	J'aimerais voir ...	zhem-rey vwar ...
What's that?	Qu'est-ce que c'est?	kes-ke sey
Can I take photos?	Je peux prendre	zhe peu pron-dre
	des photos?	dey fo-to

tours

When's the next ...?	C'est quand la prochaine ...?	sey kon la pro-shen ...
day trip	excursion	eks-kewr-syon
	d'une journée	dewn zhoor-ney
tour	excursion	eks-kewr-syon

Is ... included?	Est-ce que ... est inclus/incluse? m/f	es·ke ... ey tung·klew/tung·klewz
accommodation	le logement m	le lozh·mon
the admission charge	l'admission f	lad·mee·syon
food	la nourriture f	la noo·ree·tewr
transport	le transport m	le trons·por

How long is the tour?
L'excursion dure combien de temps?   leks·kewr·syon dewr kom·byun de tom

What time should we be back?
On doit rentrer pour quelle heure?   on dwa ron·trey poor kel eur

sightseeing

castle	château m	sha·to
cathedral	cathédrale f	ka·tey·dral
church	église f	ey·gleez
main square	place centrale f	plas son·tral
monastery	monastère m	mo·na·stair
monument	monument m	mo·new·mon
museum	musée m	mew·zey
old city	vieille ville f	vyey veel
palace	palais m	pa·ley
ruins	ruines f pl	rween
stadium	stade m	stad
statues	statues f pl	sta·tew

shopping

enquiries

Where's a ...?	Où est ...?	oo es ...
bank	la banque	la bongk
bookshop	la librairie	la lee·brey·ree
camera shop	le magasin photo	le ma·ga·zun fo·to
department store	le grand magasin	le gron ma·ga·zun
grocery store	l'épicerie	ley·pee·sree
market	le marché	le mar·shey
newsagency	le marchand de journaux	le mar·shon de zhoor·no
supermarket	le supermarché	le sew·pair·mar·shey

Where can I buy (a padlock)?
Où puis-je acheter (un cadenas)?   oo pweezh ash·tey (un kad·na)

I'm looking for ...
Je cherche ...   zhe shairsh ...

Can I look at it?
Est-ce que je peux le voir?   es·ke zhe peu le vwar

Do you have any others?
Vous en avez d'autres?   voo zon a·vey do·tre

Does it have a guarantee?
Est-ce qu'il y a une garantie?   es keel ya ewn ga·ron·tee

Can I have it sent overseas?
Pouvez-vous me l'envoyer   poo·vey·voo me lon·vwa·yey
à l'étranger?   a ley·tron·zhey

Can I have my ... repaired?
Puis-je faire réparer ...?   pwee·zhe fair rey·pa·rey ...

It's faulty.
C'est défectueux.   sey dey·fek·tweu

I'd like ..., please.   *Je voudrais ...,*   zhe voo·drey ...
         s'il vous plaît.   seel voo pley
   a bag   *un sac*   un sak
   a refund   *un remboursement*   un rom·boors·mon
   to return this   *rapporter ceci*   ra·por·tey se·see

paying

How much is it?
C'est combien?   sey kom·byun

Can you write down the price?
Pouvez-vous écrire le prix?   poo·vey·voo ey·kreer le pree

That's too expensive.
C'est trop cher.   sey tro shair

Can you lower the price?
Vous pouvez baisser le prix?   voo poo·vey bey·sey le pree

I'll give you (five) euros.
Je vous donnerai (cinq) euros.   zhe voo don·rey (sungk) eu·ro

There's a mistake in the bill.
Il y a une erreur dans la note.   eel ya ewn ey·reur don la not

Do you accept ...?	Est-ce que je peux payer avec ...?	es·ke zhe pe pey·yey a·vek ...
credit cards	une carte de crédit	ewn kart de krey·dee
debit cards	une carte de débit	ewn kart de dey·bee
travellers cheques	des chèques de voyages	dey shek de vwa·yazh
I'd like ..., please.	Je voudrais ..., s'il vous plaît.	zhe voo·drey ... seel voo pley
a receipt	un reçu	un re·sew
my change	ma monnaie	ma mo·ney

clothes & shoes

Can I try it on?	Puis-je l'essayer?	pwee·zhe ley·sey·yey
My size is (42).	Je fais du (quarante-deux).	zhe fey dew (ka·ront·deu)
It doesn't fit.	Ce n'est pas la bonne taille.	se ney pa la bon tai
small	petit	pe·tee
medium	moyen	mwa·yen
large	grand	gron

books & music

I'd like a ...	Je voudrais ...	zhe voo·drey ...
newspaper	un journal	un zhoor·nal
(in English)	(en anglais)	(on ong·gley)
pen	un stylo	un stee·lo

Is there an English-language bookshop?
Y a-t-il une librairie anglaise?   ya·teel ewn lee·brey·ree ong·gleyz

I'm looking for something by (Camus).
Je cherche quelque chose de (Camus).   zhe shairsh kel·ke shoz de (ka·mew)

Can I listen to this?
Je peux l'écouter ici?   zhe peu ley·koo·tey ee·see

photography

Can you ...?	*Pouvez-vous ...?*	poo·vey·voo ...
burn a CD from my memory card	*copier un CD de ma carte memoire*	ko·pyey un se·de de ma kart mey·mwar
develop this film	*développer cette pellicule*	dey·vlo·pey set pey·lee·kewl
load my film	*charger ma pellicule*	shar·zhey ma pey·lee·kewl
I need a/an ...	*J'ai besoin d'une ...*	zhey be·zwun dewn ...
film for this camera.	*pellicule ... pour cet appareil.*	pey·lee·kewl ... poor sey·ta·pa·rey
APS	*APS*	a·pey·es
B&W	*en noir et blanc*	on nwar ey·blong
colour	*couleur*	koo·leur
slide	*diapositive*	dya·po·zee·teev
(200) speed	*rapidité (deux cent)*	ra·pee·dee·tey (deu son)

When will it be ready?
Quand est-ce que cela sera prêt?   kon tes·ke se·la se·ra prey

meeting people

greetings, goodbyes & introductions

Hello.	*Bonjour.*	bon·zhoor
Hi.	*Salut.*	sa·lew
Good night.	*Bonsoir.*	bon·swar
Goodbye.	*Au revoir.*	o re·vwar
See you later.	*À bientôt.*	a byun·to
Mr	*Monsieur*	me·syeu
Mrs	*Madame*	ma·dam
Miss	*Mademoiselle*	mad·mwa·zel
How are you?	*Comment allez-vous?*	ko·mon ta·ley·voo
Fine, thanks. And you?	*Bien, merci. Et vous?*	byun mair·see ey voo
What's your name?	*Comment vous appelez-vous?*	ko·mon voo za·pley·voo
My name is ...	*Je m'appelle ...*	zhe ma·pel ...
I'm pleased to meet you.	*Enchanté/Enchantée.* m/f	on·shon·tey

This is my ...	Voici mon/ma ... m/f	vwa-see mon/ma ...
boyfriend	petit ami	pe-tee ta-mee
brother	frère	frair
daughter	fille	fee-ye
father	père	pair
friend	ami/amie m/f	a-mee
girlfriend	petite amie	pe-teet a-mee
husband	mari	ma-ree
mother	mère	mair
partner (intimate)	partenaire	par-te-nair
sister	sœur	seur
son	fils	fees
wife	femme	fam

Here's my ...	Voici mon ...	vwa-see mon ...
What's your ...?	Quel est votre ...? pol	kel ey vo-tre ...
	Quel est ton ...? inf	kel ey ton ...
address	adresse	a-dress
email address	e-mail	ey-mel
fax number	numéro de fax	new-mey-ro de faks
phone number	numéro de	new-mey-ro de
	téléphone	tey-ley-fon

occupations

What's your occupation?

Vous faites quoi comme métier? pol	voo fet kwa kom mey-tyey
Tu fais quoi comme métier? inf	tew fey kwa kom mey-tyey

I'm a/an ...	Je suis un/une ... m/f	zhe swee zun/zewn ...
artist	artiste m&f	ar-teest
businessperson	homme/femme	om/fem
	d'affaires m/f	da-fair
farmer	agriculteur m	a-gree-kewl-teur
	agricultrice f	a-gree-kewl-trees
manual worker	ouvrier/ouvrière m/f	oo-vree-yey/oo-vree-yair
office worker	employé/employée	om-plwa-yey
	de bureau m/f	de bew-ro
scientist	scientifique m&f	syon-tee-feek
student	étudiant/étudiante m/f	ey-tew-dyon/ey-tew-dyont
tradesperson	ouvrier qualifié m&f	oo-vree-yey ka-lee-fyey

background

Where are you from?	*Vous venez d'où?* pol	voo ve·ney doo
	Tu viens d'où? inf	tew vyun doo
I'm from ...	*Je viens ...*	zhe vyun ...
Australia	*d'Australie*	dos·tra·lee
Canada	*du Canada*	dew ka·na·da
England	*d'Angleterre*	dong·gle·tair
New Zealand	*de la Nouvelle-Zélande*	de la noo·vel·zey·lond
the USA	*des USA*	dey zew·es·a
Are you married?		
	Est-ce que vous êtes marié(e)? m/f	es·ke voo zet mar·yey
	Est-ce que tu es marié(e)? m/f inf	es·ke tew ey mar·yey
I'm married.		
	Je suis marié/mariée. m/f	zhe swee mar·yey
I'm single.		
	Je suis célibataire. m&f	zhe swee sey·lee·ba·tair

age

How old ...?	*Quel âge ...?*	kel azh ...
are you	*avez-vous* pol	a·vey·voo
	as-tu inf	a·tew
is your daughter	*a votre fille* pol	a vo·tre fee·ye
is your son	*a votre fils* pol	a vo·tre fees
I'm ... years old.	*J'ai ... ans.*	zhey ... on
He/She is ... years old.	*Il/Elle a ... ans.*	eel/el a ... on

feelings

I'm (not) ...	*Je (ne) suis (pas)...*	zhe (ne) swee (pa) ...
Are you ...?	*Êtes-vous ...?* pol	et voo ...
	Es-tu ...? inf	ey·tew ...
happy	*heureux/heureuse* m/f	er·reu/er·reuz
sad	*triste* m&f	treest

I'm ...	J'ai ...	zhey ...
I'm not ...	Je n'ai pas ...	zhe ney pa ...
Are you ...?	Avez-vous ...? pol	a·vey voo ...
	As-tu ...? inf	a·tew ...
cold	froid/froide m/f	frwa/frwad
hot	chaud/chaude m/f	sho/shod
hungry	faim m&f	fum
thirsty	soif m&f	swaf

entertainment

going out

Where can I find ...?	Où sont les ...?	oo son ley ...
clubs	clubs	kleub
gay venues	boîtes gaies	bwat gey
pubs	pubs	peub
I feel like going	Je voudrais	zhe voo·drey
to a/the ...	aller ...	a·ley ...
concert	à un concert	a ung kon·sair
movies	au cinéma	o see·ney·ma
party	à la fête	a la feyt
restaurant	au restaurant	o res·to·ron
theatre	au théâtre	o tey·a·tre

interests

Do you like ...?	Aimes-tu ...? inf	em·tew ...
I like ...	J'aime ...	zhem ...
I don't like ...	Je n'aime pas ...	zhe nem pa ...
art	l'art	lar
cooking	cuisiner	kwee·zee·ney
movies	le cinéma	le see·ney·ma
nightclubs	les boîtes	ley bwat
reading	lire	leer
shopping	faire des courses	fair dey koors
sport	le sport	le spor
travelling	voyager	vwa·ya·zhey

Do you like to ...?	Aimes-tu ...? inf	em·tew ...
dance	danser	don·sey
go to concerts	aller aux concerts	a·ley o kon·sair
listen to music	écouter de	ey·koo·tey de la
	la musique	mew·zeek

food & drink

finding a place to eat

Can you	Est-ce que vous pouvez	es·ke voo poo·vey
recommend a ...?	me conseiller ...?	me kon·sey·yey ...
bar	un bar	um bar
café	un café	ung ka·fey
restaurant	un restaurant	un res·to·ron

I'd like ..., please.	Je voudrais ...,	zhe voo·drey ...
	s'il vous plaît.	seel voo pley
a table for (five)	une table pour	ewn ta·ble poor
	(cinq) personnes	(sungk) pair·son
the (non)smoking	un endroit pour	un on·drwa poor
section	(non-)fumeurs	non·few·me

ordering food

breakfast	petit déjeuner m	pe·tee dey·zhe·ney
lunch	déjeuner m	dey·zhe·ney
dinner	dîner m	dee·ney
snack	casse-croûte m	kas·kroot

What would you recommend?
Qu'est-ce que vous conseillez?   kes·ke voo kon·sey·yey

I'd like (the) ...,	Je voudrais ...,	zhe voo·drey ...
please.	s'il vous plaît.	seel voo pley
bill	l'addition	la·dee·syon
drink list	la carte des boissons	la kart dey bwa·son
menu	la carte	la kart
that dish	ce plat	ser pla
wine list	la carte des vins	la kart dey vun

FRANÇAIS – food & drink

drinks

(cup of) coffee ...	*(un) café ...*	(ung) ka·fey ...
(cup of) tea ...	*(un) thé ...*	(un) tey ...
with milk	*au lait*	o ley
without sugar	*sans sucre*	son sew·kre
(orange) juice	*jus (d'orange)* m	zhew (do·ronzh)
soft drink	*boisson non-alcoolisée* f	bwa·son non·al·ko·lee·zey
... water	*eau ...*	o ...
hot	*chaude*	shod
sparkling mineral	*minérale gazeuse*	mee·ney·ral ga·zeuz
still mineral	*minérale non-gazeuse*	mee·ney·ral nong·ga·zeuz

in the bar

I'll have ...	*Je prends ...*	zhe pron ...
I'll buy you a drink.	*Je vous offre un verre.*	zhe voo zo·fre un vair
What would you like?	*Qu'est-ce que vous voulez?*	kes·ke voo voo·ley
Cheers!	*Santé!*	son·tey
brandy	*cognac* m	ko·nyak
champagne	*champagne* m	shom·pan·ye
cocktail	*cocktail* m	kok·tel
a shot of (whisky)	*un petit verre de (whisky)*	um pe·tee vair de (wees·kee)
a bottle of ... wine	*une bouteille de vin ...*	ewn boo·tey de vun ...
a glass of ... wine	*un verre de vin ...*	un vair de vun ...
red	*rouge*	roozh
sparkling	*mousseux*	moo·seu
white	*blanc*	blong
a ... of beer	*... de bière*	... de byair
glass	*un verre*	un vair
bottle	*une bouteille*	ewn boo·tey

food & drink – FRENCH

147

self-catering

What's the local speciality?
Quelle est la spécialité locale? — kel ey la spey·sya·lee·tey lo·kal

What's that?
Qu'est-ce que c'est, ça? — kes·ke sey sa

How much is (a kilo of cheese)?
C'est combien (le kilo de fromage)? — sey kom·byun (le kee·lo de fro·mazh)

I'd like ...	*Je voudrais ...*	zhe voo·drey ...
(200) grams	*(deux cents) grammes*	(deu son) gram
(two) kilos	*(deux) kilos*	(deu) kee·lo
(three) pieces	*(trois) morceaux*	(trwa) mor·so
(six) slices	*(six) tranches*	(sees) tronsh

Less.	*Moins.*	mwun
Enough.	*Assez.*	a·sey
More.	*Plus.*	plew

special diets & allergies

Is there a vegetarian restaurant near here?
Y a-t-il un restaurant végétarien par ici? — ya·teel un res·to·ron vey·zhey·ta·ryun par ee·see

Do you have vegetarian food?
Vous faites les repas végétarien? — voo fet ley re·pa vey·zhey·ta·ryun

Could you prepare a meal without ...?	*Pouvez-vous préparer un repas sans ...?*	poo·vey·voo prey·pa·rey un re·pa son ...
butter	*beurre*	beur
eggs	*œufs*	zeu
meat stock	*bouillon gras*	boo·yon gra

I'm allergic to ...	*Je suis allergique ...*	zhe swee za·lair·zheek ...
dairy produce	*aux produits laitiers*	o pro·dwee ley·tyey
gluten	*au gluten*	o glew·ten
MSG	*au glutamate de sodium*	o glew·ta·mat de so·dyom
nuts	*au noix*	no nwa
seafood	*aux fruits de mer*	o frwee de mair

emergencies

basics

Help!	*Au secours!*	o skoor
Stop!	*Arrêtez!*	a·rey·tey
Go away!	*Allez-vous-en!*	a·ley·voo·zon
Thief!	*Au voleur!*	o vo·leur
Fire!	*Au feu!*	o feu
Watch out!	*Faites attention!*	fet a·ton·syon

Call ...!	*Appelez ...!*	a·pley ...
a doctor	*un médecin*	un meyd·sun
an ambulance	*une ambulance*	ewn om·bew·lons
the police	*la police*	la po·lees

It's an emergency!
C'est urgent!
sey tewr·zhon

Could you help me, please?
*Est-ce que vous pourriez
m'aider, s'il vous plaît?*
es·ke voo poo·ryey
mey·dey seel voo pley

Could I use the telephone?
*Est-ce que je pourrais utiliser
le téléphone?*
es·ke zhe poo·rey ew·tee·lee·zey
le tey·ley·fon

I'm lost.
Je suis perdu/perdue. m/f
zhe swee pair·dew

Where are the toilets?
Où sont les toilettes?
oo son ley twa·let

police

Where's the police station?
Où est le commissariat de police?
oo ey le ko·mee·sar·ya de po·lees

I want to report an offence.
Je veux signaler un délit.
zhe veu see·nya·ley un dey·lee

I have insurance.
J'ai une assurance.
zhey ewn a·sew·rons

I've been assaulted.
J'ai été attaqué/attaquée. m/f
zhey ey·tey a·ta·key

I've been raped.
J'ai été violé/violée. m/f — zhey ey·tey vyo·ley

I've been robbed.
On m'a volé. — on ma vo·ley

I've lost my ...	*J'ai perdu ...*	zhey pair·dew ...
My ... was/were stolen.	*On m'a volé ...*	on ma vo·ley ...
backpack	*mon sac à dos*	mon sak a do
bags	*mes valises*	mey va·leez
credit card	*ma carte de crédit*	ma kart de krey·dee
handbag	*mon sac à main*	mon sak a mun
jewellery	*mes bijoux*	mey bee·zhoo
money	*mon argent*	mon ar·zhon
passport	*mon passeport*	mom pas·por
travellers cheques	*mes chèques de voyage*	mey shek de vwa·yazh
wallet	*mon portefeuille*	mom por·te·feu·ye

I want to contact my ...	*Je veux contacter mon ...*	zher veu kon·tak·tey mon ...
consulate	*consulat*	kon·sew·la
embassy	*ambassade*	om·ba·sad

health

medical needs

Where's the nearest ...?	*Où y a t-il ... par ici?*	oo ee a teel ... par ee·see
dentist	*un dentiste*	un don·teest
doctor	*un médecin*	un meyd·sun
hospital	*un hôpital*	u·no·pee·tal
(night) pharmacist	*une pharmacie (de nuit)*	ewn far·ma·see (de nwee)

I need a doctor (who speaks English).
J'ai besoin d'un médecin (qui parle anglais). — zhey be·zwun dun meyd·sun (kee parl ong·gley)

Could I see a female doctor?
Est-ce que je peux voir une femme médecin? — es·ke zhe peu vwar ewn fam meyd·sun

I've run out of my medication.
Je n'ai plus de médicaments. — zhe ney plew de mey·dee·ka·mon

symptoms, conditions & allergies

I'm sick.	Je suis malade.	zhe swee ma·lad
It hurts here.	J'ai une douleur ici.	zhey ewn doo·leur ee·see
I have (a) …	J'ai …	zhey …
asthma	de l'asthme	de las·me
bronchitis	la bronchite	la bron·sheet
constipation	la constipation	la kon·stee·pa·syon
cough	la toux	la too
diarrhoea	la diarrhée	la dya·rey
fever	la fièvre	la fyev·re
headache	mal à la tête	mal a la tet
heart condition	maladie de cœur	ma·la·dee de keur
nausea	la nausée	la no·zey
pain	une douleur	ewn doo·leur
sore throat	mal à la gorge	mal a la gorzh
toothache	mal aux dents	mal o don
I'm allergic to …	Je suis allergique …	zhe swee za·lair·zheek …
antibiotics	aux antibiotiques	o zon·tee·byo·teek
anti-inflammatories	aux antiinflammatoires	o zun·tee·un·fla·ma·twar
aspirin	à l'aspirine	a las·pee·reen
bees	aux abeilles	o za·bey·ye
codeine	à la codéine	a la ko·dey·een
penicillin	à la pénicilline	a la pey·nee·see·leen
antiseptic	antiseptique m	on·tee·sep·teek
bandage	pansement m	pons·mon
condoms	préservatifs m pl	prey·zair·va·teef
contraceptives	contraceptifs m pl	kon·tre·sep·teef
diarrhoea medicine	médecine pour la diarrhée f	med·seen poor la dya·ey
insect repellent	repulsif anti-insectes m	rey·pewl·seef on·tee·un·sekt
laxatives	laxatifs m pl	lak·sa·teef
painkillers	analgésiques m pl	a·nal·zhey·zeek
rehydration salts	sels de réhydratation m pl	seyl de rey·ee·dra·ta·syon
sleeping tablets	somnifères m pl	som·nee·fair

english–french dictionary

French nouns and adjectives in this dictionary have their gender indicated by ⑩ (masculine) or ① (feminine). If it's a plural noun, you'll also see pl. Words are also marked as n (noun), a (adjective), v (verb), sg (singular), pl (plural), inf (informal) and pol (polite) where necessary.

A

accident *accident* ⑩ ak-see-don
accommodation *logement* ⑩ lozh-mon
adaptor *adaptateur* ⑩ a-dap-ta-teur
address *adresse* ① a-dres
after *après* a-prey
air-conditioned *climatisé* kee-ma-tee-zey
airplane *avion* ⑩ a-vyon
airport *aéroport* ⑩ a-ey-ro-por
alcohol *alcool* ⑩ al-kol
all a *tout/toute* ⑩/① too/toot
allergy *allergie* ① a-lair-zhee
ambulance *ambulance* ① om-bew-lons
and *et* ey
ankle *cheville* ① she-vee-ye
arm *bras* ⑩ bra
ashtray *cendrier* ⑩ son-dree-yey
ATM *guichet automatique de banque* ⑩
gee-shey o-to-ma-teek de bonk

B

baby *bébé* ⑩ bey-bey
back (body) *dos* ⑩ do
backpack *sac à dos* ⑩ sak a do
bad *mauvais/mauvaise* ⑩/① mo-vey/mo-veyz
bag *sac* ⑩ sak
baggage claim *retrait des bagages* ⑩
re-trey dey ba-gazh
bank *banque* ① bonk
bar *bar* ⑩ bar
bathroom *salle de bain* ① sal de bun
battery (car) *batterie* ① bat-ree
battery (general) *pile* ① peel
beautiful *beau/belle* ⑩/① bo/bel
bed *lit* ⑩ lee
beer *bière* ① byair
before *avant* a-von
behind *derrière* dair-yair
Belgium *Belgique* ① bel-zheek
bicycle *vélo* ⑩ vey-lo

big *grand/grande* ⑩/① gron/grond
bill *addition* ① a-dee-syon
black *noir/noire* ⑩/① nwar
blanket *couverture* ① koo-vair-tewr
blood group *groupe sanguin* ⑩ groop song-gun
blue *bleu/bleue* ⑩/① bler
book (make a reservation) v *réserver* rey-zair-vey
bottle *bouteille* ① boo-tey
bottle opener *ouvre-bouteille* ① oo-vre-boo-tey
boy *garçon* ⑩ gar-son
brakes (car) *freins* ⑩ frun
breakfast *petit déjeuner* ⑩ pe-tee dey-zheu-ney
broken (faulty) *défectueux/défectueuse* ⑩/①
dey-fek-tweu/dey-fek-tweuz
bus (auto) *bus* ⑩ (o-to)bews
business *affaires* ① a-fair
buy *acheter* ash-tey

C

café *café* ⑩ ka-fey
camera *appareil photo* ⑩ a-pa-rey fo-to
camp site *terrain de camping* ⑩ tey-run de kom-peeng
cancel *annuler* a-new-ley
can opener *ouvre-boîte* ⑩ oo-vre-bwat
car *voiture* ① vwa-tewr
cash *argent* ⑩ ar-zhon
cash (a cheque) v *encaisser* ong-key-sey
cell phone *téléphone portable* ⑩ tey-ley-fon por-ta-ble
centre *centre* ⑩ son-tre
change (money) v *échanger* ey-shon-zhey
cheap *bon marché* ⑩ bon mar-shey
check (bill) *addition* ① la-dee-syon
check-in n *enregistrement* ⑩ on-re-zhee-stre-mon
chest *poitrine* ① pwa-treen
child *enfant* ⑩&① on-fon
cigarette *cigarette* ① see-ga-ret
city *ville* ① veel
clean a *propre* ⑩&① pro-pre
closed *fermé/fermée* ⑩/① fair-mey
coffee *café* ⑩ ka-fey
coins *pièces* ① pyes
cold a *froid/froide* ⑩/① frwa/frwad

collect call *appel en PCV* ⓜ a·pel on pey·sey·vey
come *venir* ve·neer
computer *ordinateur* ⓜ or·dee·na·teur
condom *préservatif* ⓜ prey·zair·va·teef
contact lenses *verres de contact* ⓜ vair de kon·takt
cook v *cuire* kweer
cost *coût* ⓜ koo
credit card *carte de crédit* ⓕ kart de krey·dee
cup *tasse* ⓕ tas
currency exchange *taux de change* ⓜ to de shonzh
customs (immigration) *douane* ⓕ dwan

D

dangerous *dangereux/dangereuse* ⓜ/ⓕ
    don·zhreu/don·zhreuz
date (time) *date* ⓕ dat
day *date de naissance* ⓕ dat de ney·sons
delay *retard* ⓜ re·tard
dentist *dentiste* ⓕ don·teest
depart *partir* par·teer
diaper *couche* ⓕ koosh
dictionary *dictionnaire* ⓜ deek·syo·nair
dinner *dîner* ⓜ dee·ney
direct *direct/directe* ⓜ/ⓕ dee·rekt
dirty *sale* ⓜ&ⓕ sal
disabled *handicapé/handicapée* ⓜ/ⓕ on·dee·ka·pey
discount *remise* ⓕ re·meez
doctor *médecin* ⓜ meyd·sun
double bed *grand lit* ⓜ gron lee
double room *chambre pour deux personnes* ⓕ
    shom·bre poor de pair·son
drink *boisson* ⓕ bwa·son
drive v *conduire* kon·dweer
drivers licence *permis de conduire* ⓜ
    pair·mee de kon·dweer
drugs (illicit) *drogue* ⓕ drog
dummy (pacifier) *tétine* ⓕ tey·teen

E

ear *oreille* ⓕ o·rey
east *est* ⓜ est
eat *manger* mon·zhey
economy class *classe touriste* ⓕ klas too·reest
electricity *électricité* ⓕ ey·lek·tree·see·tey
elevator *ascenseur* ⓜ a·son·seur
email *e-mail* ⓜ ey·mel
embassy *ambassade* ⓕ om·ba·sad
emergency *cas urgent* ⓜ ka ewr·zhon

English (language) *anglais/anglaise* ⓜ/ⓕ
    ong·gley/ong·gleyz
entrance *entrée* ⓕ on·trey
evening *soir* ⓜ swar
exchange rate *taux de change* ⓜ to de shonzh
exit *sortie* ⓕ sor·tee
expensive *cher/chère* ⓜ/ⓕ shair
express mail *exprès* eks·pres
eye *œil* ⓜ eu·yee

F

far *lointain/lointaine* ⓜ/ⓕ lwun·tun/lwun·ten
fast *rapide* ⓜ&ⓕ ra·peed
father *père* ⓜ pair
film (camera) *pellicule* ⓕ pey·lee·kewl
finger *doigt* ⓜ dwa
first-aid kit *trousse à pharmacie* ⓕ troos a far·ma·see
first class *première classe* ⓕ pre·myair klas
fish *poisson* ⓜ pwa·son
food *nourriture* ⓕ noo·ree·tewr
foot *pied* ⓜ pyey
fork *fourchette* ⓕ foor·shet
France *France* frons
free (of charge) *gratuit/gratuite* ⓜ/ⓕ
    gra·twee/gra·tweet
French (language) *Français* fron·sey
friend *ami/amie* ⓜ/ⓕ a·mee
fruit *fruit* ⓜ frwee
full *plein/pleine* ⓜ/ⓕ plun/plen
funny *drôle* ⓜ&ⓕ drol

G

gift *cadeau* ⓜ ka·do
girl *fille* ⓕ fee·ye
glass (drinking) *verre* ⓜ vair
glasses *lunettes* ⓕ pl lew·net
go *aller* a·ley
good *bon/bonne* ⓜ/ⓕ bon
green *vert/verte* ⓜ/ⓕ vairt
guide n *guide* ⓜ geed

H

half *moitié* ⓕ mwa·tyey
hand *main* ⓕ mun
handbag *sac à main* ⓜ sak a mun
happy *heureux/heureuse* ⓜ/ⓕ eu·reu/eu·reuz
have *avoir* a·vwar

he *il* eel
head *tête* ① tet
heart *cœur* ⓜ keur
heat *chaleur* ① sha-leur
heavy *lourd/lourde* ⓜ/① loor/loord
help v *aider* ey-dey
here *ici* ee-see
high *haut/haute* ⓜ/① o/ot
highway *autoroute* ① o-to-root
hike v *faire la randonnée* fair la ron-do-ney
holiday *vacances* ① pl va-kons
homosexual n *homosexuel/homosexuelle* ⓜ/①
o-mo-sek-swel
hospital *hôpital* ⓜ o-pee-tal
hot *chaud/chaude* ⓜ/① sho/shod
hotel *hôtel* ⓜ o-tel
(be) hungry *avoir faim* a-vwar fum
husband *mari* ⓜ ma-ree

I

I *je* zhe
identification (card) *carte d'identité* ①
kart dee-don-tee-tey
ill *malade* ⓜ&① ma-lad
important *important/importante* ⓜ/①
um-por-ton/um-por-tont
included *compris/comprise* ⓜ/①
kom-pree/kom-preez
injury *blessure* ① bley-sewr
insurance *assurance* ① a-sew-rons
Internet *Internet* ⓜ un-tair-net
interpreter *interprète* ⓜ&① un-tair-pret

J

jewellery *bijoux* ⓜ pl bee-zhoo
job *travail* ⓜ tra-vai

K

key *clé* ① kley
kilogram *kilogramme* ⓜ kee-lo-gram
kitchen *cuisine* ① kwee-zeen
knife *couteau* ⓜ koo-to

L

laundry (place) *blanchisserie* ① blon-shees-ree
lawyer *avocat/avocate* ⓜ/① a-vo-ka/a-vo-kat

left (direction) *à gauche* a gosh
left-luggage office *consigne* ① kon-see-nye
leg *jambe* ① zhomb
lesbian n *lesbienne* ① les-byen
less *moins* mwun
letter (mail) *lettre* ① ley-trer
lift (elevator) *ascenseur* ⓜ a-son-seur
light *lumière* ① lew-myair
like v *aimer* ey-mey
lock *serrure* ① sey-rewr
long *long/longue* ⓜ/① long(k)
lost *perdu/perdue* ⓜ/① pair-dew
lost-property office *bureau des objets trouvés* ⓜ
bew-ro dey zob-zhey troo-vey
love v *aimer* ey-mey
luggage *bagages* ⓜ pl ba-gazh
lunch *déjeuner* ⓜ dey-zheu-ney

M

mail *courrier* ⓜ koo-ryey
man *homme* ⓜ om
map *carte* ① kart
market *marché* ⓜ mar-shey
matches *allumettes* ① pl a-lew-met
meat *viande* ① vyond
medicine *médecine* ① med-seen
menu *carte* kart
message *message* ⓜ mey-sazh
milk *lait* ⓜ ley
minute *minute* ① mee-newt
mobile phone *téléphone portable* ⓜ
tey-ley-fon por-ta-ble
money *argent* ⓜ ar-zhon
month *mois* ⓜ mwa
morning *matin* ⓜ ma-tun
mother *mère* ① mair
motorcycle *moto* ⓜ mo-to
motorway *autoroute* ① o-to-root
mouth *bouche* ① boosh
music *musique* ① mew-zeek

N

name *nom* ⓜ nom
napkin *serviette* ① sair-vyet
nappy *couche* ① koosh
near *près de* prey de
neck *cou* ⓜ koo
new *nouveau/nouvelle* ⓜ/① noo-vo/noo-vel

news *les nouvelles* ley noo-vel
newspaper *journal* ⓜ zhoor-nal
night *nuit* ⓕ nwee
no *non* non
noisy *bruyant/bruyante* ⓜ/ⓕ brew-yon/brew-yont
nonsmoking *non-fumeur* non-few-meur
north *nord* ⓜ nor
nose *nez* ⓜ ney
now *maintenant* mun-te-non
number *numéro* ⓜ new-mey-ro

O

oil (engine) *huile* ⓕ weel
old *vieux/vieille* ⓜ/ⓕ vyeu/vyey
one-way ticket *billet simple* ⓜ bee-yey sum-ple
open a *ouvert/ouverte* ⓜ/ⓕ oo-vair/oo-vairt
outside *dehors* de-or

P

package *paquet* ⓜ pa-key
paper *papier* ⓜ pa-pyey
park (car) v *garer (une voiture)* ga-rey (ewn vwa-tewr)
passport *passeport* ⓜ pas-por
pay *payer* pey-yey
pen *stylo* ⓜ stee-lo
petrol *essence* ⓕ ey-sons
pharmacy *pharmacie* ⓕ far-ma-see
phonecard *télécarte* ⓕ tey-ley-kart
photo *photo* ⓕ fo-to
plate *assiette* ⓕ a-syet
police *police* ⓕ po-lees
postcard *carte postale* ⓕ kart pos-tal
post office *bureau de poste* ⓜ bew-ro de post
pregnant *enceinte* on-sunt
price *prix* ⓜ pree

Q

quiet *tranquille* ⓜ&ⓕ trong-keel

R

rain n *pluie* ⓕ plwee
razor *rasoir* ⓜ ra-zwar
receipt *reçu* ⓜ re-sew
red *rouge* roozh
refund *remboursement* ⓜ rom-boor-se-mon
registered mail *en recommandé* on re-ko-mon-dey

rent v *louer* loo-ey
repair v *réparer* rey-pa-rey
reservation *réservation* ⓕ rey-zair-va-syon
restaurant *restaurant* ⓜ res-to-ron
return v *revenir* rev-neer
return ticket *aller retour* ⓜ a-ley re-toor
right (direction) a *droite* a drwat
road *route* ⓕ root
room *chambre* ⓕ shom-bre

S

safe a *sans danger* ⓜ&ⓕ son don-zhey
sanitary napkin *serviette hygiénique* ⓕ
    sair-vyet ee-zhyey-neek
seat *place* ⓕ plas
send *envoyer* on-vwa-yey
service station *station-service* ⓕ sta-syon-sair-vees
sex *sexe* ⓜ seks
shampoo *shampooing* ⓜ shom-pwung
share (a dorm) *partager* par-ta-zhey
shaving cream *mousse à raser* ⓕ moos a ra-zey
she *elle* el
sheet (bed) *drap* ⓜ dra
shirt *chemise* ⓕ she-meez
shoes *chaussures* ⓕ pl sho-sewr
shop *magasin* ⓜ ma-ga-zun
short *court/courte* ⓜ/ⓕ koor/koort
shower *douche* ⓕ doosh
single room *chambre pour une personne* ⓕ
    shom-bre poor ewn pair-son
skin *peau* ⓕ po
skirt *jupe* ⓕ zhewp
sleep v *dormir* dor-meer
slowly *lentement* lon-te-mon
small *petit/petite* ⓜ/ⓕ pe-tee/pe-teet
smoke (cigarettes) v *fumer* few-mey
soap *savon* ⓜ sa-von
some *quelques* kel-ke
soon *bientôt* byun-to
south *sud* ⓜ sewd
souvenir shop *magasin de souvenirs* ⓜ
    ma-ga-zun de soov-neer
speak *parler* par-ley
spoon *cuillère* ⓕ kwee-yair
stamp *timbre* ⓜ tum-bre
stand-by ticket *billet stand-by* ⓜ bee-yey stond-bai
station (train) *gare* ⓕ gar
stomach *estomac* ⓜ es-to-ma
stop v *arrêter* a-rey-tey

DICTIONARY

T

stop (bus) *arrêt* ⓜ a-rey
street *rue* ① rew
student *étudiant/étudiante* ⓜ/①
  ey-tew-dyon/ey-tew-dyont
sun *soleil* ⓜ so-ley
sunscreen *écran solaire* ⓜ ey-kron so-lair
swim v *nager* na-zhey
Switzerland *Suisse* swees

T

tampons *tampons* ⓜ pl tom-pon
taxi *taxi* ⓜ tak-see
teaspoon *petite cuillère* ① pe-teet kwee-yair
teeth *dents* ① don
telephone n *téléphone* ⓜ tey-ley-fon
television *télé(vision)* ① tey-ley(vee-zyon)
temperature (weather) *température* ①
  tom-pey-ra-tewr
tent *tente* ① tont
that (one) *cela* se-la
they *ils/elles* ⓜ/① eel/el
(be) thirsty *avoir soif* a-vwar swaf
this (one) *ceci* se-see
throat *gorge* ① gorzh
ticket *billet* ⓜ bee-yey
time *temps* ⓜ tom
tired *fatigué/fatiguée* ⓜ/① fa-tee-gey
tissues *mouchoirs en papier* ⓜ pl
  moo-shwar om pa-pyey
today *aujourd'hui* o-zhoor-dwee
toilet *toilettes* ① pl twa-let
tomorrow *demain* de-mun
tonight *ce soir* se swar
toothbrush *brosse à dents* ① bros a don
toothpaste *dentifrice* ⓜ don-tee-frees
torch (flashlight) *lampe de poche* ① lomp de posh
tour *voyage* ⓜ vwa-yazh
tourist office *office de tourisme* ⓜ
  o-fees-de too-rees-me
towel *serviette* ① sair-vyet
train *train* ⓜ trun
translate *traduire* tra-dweer
travel agency *agence de voyage* ①
  a-zhons de vwa-yazh
travellers cheque *chèque de voyage* ⓜ
  shek de vwa-yazh
trousers *pantalon* ⓜ pon-ta-lon

twin beds *lits jumeaux* ⓜ pl dey lee zhew-mo
tyre *pneu* ⓜ pneu

U

underwear *sous-vêtements* ⓜ soo-vet-mon
urgent *urgent/urgente* ⓜ/① ewr-zhon/ewr-zhont

V

vacant *libre* ⓜ&① lee-bre
vacation *vacances* ① pl va-kons
vegetable n *légume* ⓜ ley-gewm
vegetarian a *végétarien/végétarienne* ⓜ/①
  vey-zhey-ta-ryun/vey-zhey-ta-ryen
visa *visa* ① vee-za

W

waiter *serveur/serveuse* ⓜ/① sair-veur/sair-veurz
walk v *marcher* mar-shey
wallet *portefeuille* ① por-te-feu-ye
warm a *chaud/chaude* ⓜ/① sho/shod
wash (something) *laver* la-vey
watch *montre* ① mon-tre
water *eau* ① o
we *nous* noo
weekend *week-end* ⓜ week-end
west *ouest* ⓜ west
wheelchair *fauteuil roulant* ⓜ fo-teu-ye roo-lon
when *quand* kon
where *où* oo
white *blanc/blanche* ⓜ/① blong/blonsh
who *qui* kee
why *pourquoi* poor-kwa
wife *femme* ① fam
window *fenêtre* ① fe-ney-tre
wine *vin* ⓜ vun
with *avec* a-vek
without *sans* son
woman *femme* ① fam
write *écrire* ey-kreer

Y

yellow *jaune* zhon
yes *oui* wee
yesterday *hier* ee-yair
you sg inf *tu* tew
you sg pol *vous* voo
you pl *vous* voo

German

german alphabet

A a a	*B b* be	*C c* tse	*D d* de	*E e* e
F f ef	*G g* ge	*H h* ha	*I i* i	*J j* yot
K k ka	*L l* el	*M m* em	*N n* en	*O o* o
P p pe	*Q q* ku	*R r* er	*S s* es	*T t* te
U u u	*V v* fau	*W w* ve	*X x* iks	*Y y* *ewp·si·lon*
Z z tset				

■ **german**

introduction

Romantic, flowing, literary ... not usually how German (*Deutsch* doytsh) is described, but maybe it's time to reconsider. After all, this is the language that's played a major role in the history of Europe and remains one of the most widely spoken languages on the continent. It's taught throughout the world and chances are you're already familiar with a number of German words that have entered English – *kindergarten*, *kitsch* and *hamburger*, for example, are all of German origin.

German is spoken by around 100 million people, and is the official language of Germany, Austria and Liechtenstein, as well as one of the official languages of Belgium, Switzerland and Luxembourg. German didn't spread across the rest of the world with the same force as English, Spanish or French. Germany only became a unified nation in 1871 and never established itself as a colonial power. After the reunification of East and West Germany, however, German has become more important in global politics and economics. Its role in science has long been recognised and German literature lays claim to some of the most famous written works ever printed. Just think of the enormous influence of Goethe, Nietzsche, Freud and Einstein.

German is usually divided into two forms – Low German (*Plattdeutsch* plat-doytsh) and High German (*Hochdeutsch* hokh-doytsh). Low German is an umbrella term used for the dialects spoken in Northern Germany. High German is considered the standard form and is understood throughout German-speaking communities, from the Swiss Alps to the cosy cafés of Vienna; it's also the form used in this phrasebook.

Both German and English belong to the West Germanic language family, along with a number of other languages including Dutch and Yiddish. The primary reason why German and English have grown apart is that the Normans, on invading England in 1066, brought with them a large number of non-Germanic words. As well as the recognisable words, the grammar of German will also make sense to an English speaker. Even with a slight grasp of German grammar, you'll still manage to get your point across. On the other hand, German tends to join words together (while English uses a number of separate words) to express a single notion. You shouldn't be intimidated by this though – after a while you'll be able to tell parts of words and recognising 'the Football World Cup qualifying match' hidden within *Fussballweltmeisterschaftsqualifikationsspiel* won't be a problem at all!

pronunciation

vowel sounds

German vowels can be short or long, which influences the meaning of words. They're pronounced crisply and distinctly, so *Tee* (tea) is tey, not *tey-*ee.

symbol	english equivalent	german example	transliteration
a	**run**	*hat*	hat
aa	**father**	*habe*	*haa*·be
ai	**aisle**	*mein*	main
air	**fair**	*Bär*	bair
aw	**saw**	*Boot*	bawt
e	**bet**	*Männer*	*me*·ner
ee	**see**	*fliegen*	*flee*·gen
eu	**nurse**	*schön*	sheun
ew	ee pronounced with rounded lips	*zurück*	tsu·*rewk*
ey	as in 'bet', but longer	*leben*	*ley*·ben
i	**hit**	*mit*	mit
o	**pot**	*Koffer*	*ko*·fer
oo	**zoo**	*Schuhe*	*shoo*·e
ow	**now**	*Haus*	hows
oy	**toy**	*Leute, Häuser*	*loy*·te, *hoy*·zer
u	**put**	*unter*	*un*·ter

word stress

Almost all German words are pronounced with stress on the first syllable. While this is a handy rule of thumb, you can always rely on the coloured pronunciation guides, which show the stressed syllables in italics.

consonant sounds

All German consonant sounds exist in English except for the kh and r sounds. The kh sound is generally pronounced at the back of the throat, like the 'ch' in 'Bach' or the Scottish 'loch'. The r sound is pronounced at the back of the throat, almost like saying g, but with some friction, a bit like gargling.

symbol	english equivalent	german example	transliteration
b	bed	*Bett*	bet
ch	cheat	*Tschüss*	chews
d	dog	*dein*	dain
f	fat	*vier*	feer
g	go	*gehen*	*gey*·en
h	hat	*helfen*	*hel*·fen
k	kit	*kein*	kain
kh	loch	*ich*	ikh
l	lot	*laut*	lowt
m	man	*Mann*	man
n	not	*nein*	nain
ng	ring	*singen*	*zing*·en
p	pet	*Preis*	prais
r	run (throaty)	*Reise*	*rai*·ze
s	sun	*heiß*	hais
sh	shot	*schön*	sheun
t	top	*Tag*	taak
ts	hits	*Zeit*	tsait
v	very	*wohnen*	*vaw*·nen
y	yes	*ja*	yaa
z	zero	*sitzen*	*zi*·tsen
zh	pleasure	*Garage*	ga·*raa*·zhe

tools

language difficulties

Do you speak English?
Sprechen Sie Englisch?   shpre·khen zee *eng*·lish

Do you understand?
Verstehen Sie?   fer·*shtey*·en zee

I (don't) understand.
Ich verstehe (nicht).   ikh fer·*shtey*·e (nikht)

What does (*Kugel*) mean?
Was bedeutet (Kugel)?   vas be·*doy*·tet (*koo*·gel)

How do you ...?	*Wie ...?*	vee ...
pronounce this	*spricht man dieses*	shprikht man *dee*·zes
	Wort aus	vort ows
write (*Schweiz*)	*schreibt man (Schweiz)*	shraipt man (shvaits)

Could you please ...?	*Könnten Sie ...?*	*keun*·ten zee ...
repeat that	*das bitte wiederholen*	das *bi*·te vee·der·*haw*·len
speak more	*bitte langsamer*	*bi*·te *lang*·za·mer
slowly	*sprechen*	shpre·khen
write it down	*das bitte aufschreiben*	das *bi*·te *owf*·shrai·ben

essentials

Yes.	*Ja.*	yaa
No.	*Nein.*	nain
Please.	*Bitte.*	*bi*·te
Thank you.	*Danke.*	*dang*·ke
Thank you very much.	*Vielen Dank.*	*fee*·len dangk
You're welcome.	*Bitte.*	*bi*·te
Excuse me.	*Entschuldigung.*	ent·*shul*·di·gung
Sorry.	*Entschuldigung.*	ent·*shul*·di·gung

numbers

0	*null*	nul	16	*sechzehn*	*zeks·tseyn*
1	*eins*	ains	17	*siebzehn*	*zeep·tseyn*
2	*zwei*	tsvai	18	*achtzehn*	*akht·tseyn*
3	*drei*	drai	19	*neunzehn*	*noyn·tseyn*
4	*vier*	feer	20	*zwanzig*	*tsvan·tsikh*
5	*fünf*	fewnf	21	*einundzwanzig*	*ain·unt·tsvan·tsikh*
6	*sechs*	zeks	22	*zweiundzwanzig*	*tsvai·unt·tsvan·tsikh*
7	*sieben*	zee·ben	30	*dreißig*	*drai·tsikh*
8	*acht*	akht	40	*vierzig*	*feer·tsikh*
9	*neun*	noyn	50	*fünfzig*	*fewnf·tsikh*
10	*zehn*	tseyn	60	*sechzig*	*zekh·tsikh*
11	*elf*	elf	70	*siebzig*	*zeep·tsikh*
12	*zwölf*	zveulf	80	*achtzig*	*akht·tsikh*
13	*dreizehn*	*drai·tseyn*	90	*neunzig*	*noyn·tsikh*
14	*vierzehn*	*feer·tseyn*	100	*hundert*	*hun·dert*
15	*fünfzehn*	*fewnf·tseyn*	1000	*tausend*	*tow·sent*

time & dates

What time is it?	*Wie spät ist es?*	vee shpeyt ist es
It's one o'clock.	*Es ist ein Uhr.*	es ist ain oor
It's (10) o'clock.	*Es ist (zehn) Uhr.*	es ist (tseyn) oor
Quarter past (one).	*Viertel nach (eins).*	fir·tel naakh (ains)
Half past (one).	*Halb (zwei).* (lit: half two)	halp (tsvai)
Quarter to (one).	*Viertel vor (eins).*	fir·tel fawr (ains)
At what time ...?	*Um wie viel Uhr ...?*	um vee feel oor ...
At ...	*Um ...*	um ...
am	*vormittags*	fawr·mi·taaks
pm (midday–6pm)	*nachmittags*	naakh·mi·taaks
pm (6pm–midnight)	*abends*	aa·bents
Monday	*Montag*	mawn·taak
Tuesday	*Dienstag*	deens·taak
Wednesday	*Mittwoch*	mit·vokh
Thursday	*Donnerstag*	do·ners·taak
Friday	*Freitag*	frai·taak
Saturday	*Samstag*	zams·taak
Sunday	*Sonntag*	zon·taak

January	Januar	yan·u·aar
February	Februar	fey·bru·aar
March	März	merts
April	April	a·pril
May	Mai	mai
June	Juni	yoo·ni
July	Juli	yoo·li
August	August	ow·gust
September	September	zep·tem·ber
October	Oktober	ok·taw·ber
November	November	no·vem·ber
December	Dezember	de·tsem·ber

What date is it today?
Der Wievielte ist heute?　　dair vee·feel·te ist hoy·te

It's (18 October).
Heute ist (der achtzehnte Oktober).　　hoy·te ist dair (akh·tseyn·te ok·taw·ber)

| since (May) | seit (Mai) | zait (mai) |
| until (June) | bis (Juni) | bis (yoo·ni) |

yesterday	gestern	ges·tern
today	heute	hoy·te
tonight	heute Abend	hoy·te aa·bent
tomorrow	morgen	mor·gen

last ...		
night	vergangene Nacht	fer·gang·e·ne nakht
week	letzte Woche	lets·te vo·khe
month	letzten Monat	lets·ten maw·nat
year	letztes Jahr	lets·tes yaar

next ...		
week	nächste Woche	neykhs·te vo·khe
month	nächsten Monat	neykhs·ten maw·nat
year	nächstes Jahr	neykhs·tes yaar

yesterday/	gestern/	ges·tern/
tomorrow ...	morgen ...	mor·gen ...
morning	Morgen	mor·gen
afternoon	Nachmittag	naakh·mi·taak
evening	Abend	aa·bent

weather

What's the weather like?	Wie ist das Wetter?	vee ist das *ve*·ter

It's ...		
cloudy	Es ist wolkig.	es ist *vol*·kikh
cold	Es ist kalt.	es ist kalt
hot	Es ist heiß.	es ist hais
raining	Es regnet.	es *reyg*·net
snowing	Es schneit.	es shnait
sunny	Es ist sonnig.	es ist *zo*·nikh
warm	Es ist warm.	es ist varm
windy	Es ist windig.	es ist *vin*·dikh

spring	Frühling m	*frew*·ling
summer	Sommer m	*zo*·mer
autumn	Herbst m	herpst
winter	Winter m	*vin*·ter

border crossing

I'm here ...	Ich bin hier ...	ikh bin heer ...
in transit	auf der Durchreise	owf dair *durkh*·rai·ze
on business	auf Geschäftsreise	owf ge·*shefts*·rai·ze
on holiday	im Urlaub	im *oor*·lowp

I'm here for ...	Ich bin hier für ...	ikh bin heer fewr ...
(10) days	(zehn) Tage	(tseyn) *taa*·ge
(three) weeks	(drei) Wochen	(drai) *vo*·khen
(two) months	(zwei) Monate	(tsvai) *maw*·na·te

I'm going to (Salzburg).
Ich gehe nach (Salzburg).   ikh *gey*·e nakh *zalts*·boorg

I'm staying at the (Hotel Park).
Ich wohne im (Hotel Park).   ikh *vaw*·ne im (ho·*tel* park)

I have nothing to declare.
Ich habe nichts zu verzollen.   ikh *haa*·be nikhts tsoo fer·*tso*·len

I have something to declare.
Ich habe etwas zu verzollen.   ikh *haa*·be *et*·vas tsoo fer·*tso*·len

That's (not) mine.
Das ist (nicht) meins.   das ist (nikht) mains

transport

tickets & luggage

Where can I buy a ticket?
Wo kann ich eine Fahrkarte kaufen? vaw kan ikh *ai*-ne *faar*-kar-te *kow*-fen

Do I need to book a seat?
Muss ich einen Platz mus ikh *ai*-nen plats
reservieren lassen? re-zer-*vee*-ren *la*-sen

One ...ticket to (Berlin), please.	*Einen ... nach (Berlin), bitte.*	*ai*-nen ... naakh (ber-*leen*) *bi*-te
one-way	*einfache Fahrkarte*	*ain*-fa-khe *faar*-kar-te
return	*Rückfahrkarte*	*rewk*-faar-kar-te

I'd like to ...	*Ich möchte meine*	ikh *meukh*-te *mai*-ne
my ticket, please.	*Fahrkarte bitte ...*	*faar*-kar-te *bi*-te ...
cancel	*zurückgeben*	tsu-*rewk*-gey-ben
change	*ändern lassen*	*en*-dern *la*-sen
collect	*abholen*	*ab*-ho-len
confirm	*bestätigen lassen*	be-*shtey*-ti-gen *la*-sen

I'd like a ...	*Ich hätte gern*	ikh *he*-te gern
seat, please.	*einen ...*	*ai*-nen ...
nonsmoking	*Nichtraucherplatz*	*nikht*-row-kher-plats
smoking	*Raucherplatz*	*row*-kher-plats

How much is it?
Was kostet das? vas *kos*-tet das

Is there air conditioning?
Gibt es eine Klimaanlage? gipt es *ai*-ne *klee*-ma-an-*laa*-ge

Is there a toilet?
Gibt es eine Toilette? gipt es *ai*-ne to-a-*le*-te

How long does the trip take?
Wie lange dauert die Fahrt? vee *lang*-e *dow*-ert dee faart

Is it a direct route?
Ist es eine direkte Verbindung? ist es *ai*-ne di-*rek*-te fer-*bin*-dung

I'd like a luggage locker.
Ich hätte gern ein Gepäckschließfach. ikh *he*-te gern ain ge-*pek*-shlees-fakh

My luggage has been ...	*Mein Gepäck ist ...*	main ge-*pek* ist ...
damaged	*beschädigt*	be-*shey*-dikht
lost	*verloren gegangen*	fer-*law*-ren ge-*gang*-en
stolen	*gestohlen worden*	ge-*shtaw*-len *vor*-den

getting around

Where does flight (D4) arrive?
Wo ist die Ankunft des Fluges (D4)?   vaw ist dee *an*-kunft des *floo*-ges (de feer)

Where does flight (D4) depart?
Wo ist die der Abflug des Fluges (D4)?   vaw ist dair *ab*-flug des *floo*-ges (de feer)

Where's the ...?	*Wo ist ...?*	vaw ist ...
arrivalls hall	*Ankunftshalle*	an-kunfts-*ha*-le
departures hall	*Abflughalle*	ab-flug-*ha*-le

Is this the ...	*Fährt ...*	fairt ...
to (Hamburg)?	*nach (Hamburg)?*	nakh (*ham*-burg)
boat	*das Boot*	das bawt
bus	*der Bus*	dair bus
plane	*das Flugzeug*	das *flook*-tsoyk
train	*der Zug*	dair tsook

What time's	*Wann fährt der*	van fairt dair
the ... bus?	*... Bus?*	... bus
first	*erste*	*ers*-te
last	*letzte*	*lets*-te
next	*nächste*	*neykhs*-te

At what time does it leave?
Wann fährt es ab?   van fairt es ap

At what time does it arrive?
Wann kommt es an?   van komt es an

How long will it be delayed?
Wie viel Verspätung wird es haben?   vee feel fer-*shpey*-tung virt es *haa*-ben

What station/stop is this?
Welcher Bahnhof/Halt ist das?   *vel*-kher *baan*-hawf/halt ist das

What's the next station/stop?
Welches ist der nächste   *vel*-khes ist dair *neykhs*-te
Bahnhof/Halt?   *baan*-hawf/halt

Does it stop at (Freiburg)?
Hält es in (Freiburg)?   helt *es* in (*frai*·boorg)

Please tell me when we get to (Kiel).
Könnten Sie mir bitte sagen,   *keun*·ten zee meer *bi*·te *zaa*·gen
wann wir in (Kiel) ankommen?   van veer in (keel) *an*·ko·men

How long do we stop here?
Wie lange halten wir hier?   vee *lan*·ge *hal*·ten veer heer

Is this seat available?
Ist dieser Platz frei?   ist *dee*·zer plats frai

That's my seat.
Dieses ist mein Platz.   *dee*·zes ist main plats

I'd like a taxi ...	*Ich hätte gern*	ikh *he*·te gern
	ein Taxi für ...	ain *tak*·si fewr ...
at (9am)	*(neun Uhr vormittags)*	(noyn oor *fawr*·mi·taaks)
now	*sofort*	zo·*fort*
tomorrow	*morgen*	*mor*·gen

Is this taxi available?
Ist dieses Taxi frei?   ist *dee*·zes *tak*·si frai

How much is it to ...?
Was kostet es bis ...?   vas *kos*·tet es bis ...

Please put the meter on.
Schalten Sie bitte den Taxameter ein.   *shal*·ten zee *bi*·te deyn tak·sa·*mey*·ter ain

Please take me to (this address).
Bitte bringen Sie mich zu   *bi*·te *bring*·en zee mikh tsoo
(dieser Adresse).   (*dee*·zer a·*dre*·se)

Please ...	*Bitte ...*	*bi*·te ...
slow down	*fahren Sie langsamer*	*faa*·ren zee *lang*·za·mer
stop here	*halten Sie hier*	*hal*·ten zee heer
wait here	*warten Sie hier*	*var*·ten zee heer

car, motorbike & bicycle hire

I'd like to hire a ...	Ich möchte ... mieten.	ikh *meukh*·te ... *mee*·ten
bicycle	ein Fahrrad	ain *faar*·raat
car	ein Auto	ain *ow*·to
motorbike	ein Motorrad	ain *maw*·tor·raat

with ...	mit ...	mit ...
a driver	Fahrer	*faa*·rer
air conditioning	Klimaanlage	*klee*·ma·an·*laa*·ge

How much for ... hire?	Wie viel kostet es pro ...?	vee feel *kos*·tet es praw ...
hourly	Stunde	*shtun*·de
daily	Tag	taak
weekly	Woche	*vo*·khe

air	Luft f	luft
oil	Öl n	eul
petrol	Benzin n	ben·*tseen*
tyres	Reifen m pl	*rai*·fen

I need a mechanic.
Ich brauche einen Mechaniker.   ikh *brow*·khe *ai*·nen me·*khaa*·ni·ker

I've run out of petrol.
Ich habe kein Benzin mehr.   ikh *haa*·be kain ben·*tseen* mair

I have a flat tyre.
Ich habe eine Reifenpanne.   ikh *haa*·be *ai*·ne *rai*·fen·pa·ne

directions

Where's the ...?	Wo ist ...?	vaw ist ...
bank	die Bank	dee bangk
city centre	die Innenstadt	*i*·nen·shtat
hotel	das Hotel	das ho·*tel*
market	der Markt	dair markt
police station	das Polizeirevier	das po·li·*tsai*·re·veer
post office	das Postamt	das *post*·amt
public toilet	die öffentliche Toilette	dee *eu*·fent·li·khe to·a·*le*·te
tourist office	das Fremdenverkehrsbüro	das *frem*·den·fer·kairs·bew·raw

Is this the road to (Frankfurt)?
Führt diese Straße — fewrt *dee·ze shtraa·se*
nach (Frankfurt)? — naakh (*frank·*foort)

Can you show me (on the map)?
Können Sie es mir — *keu·*nen zee es meer
(auf der Karte) zeigen? — (owf dair *kar·*te) *tsai·*gen

What's the address?
Wie ist die Adresse? — vee ist dee a·*dre·*se

How far is it?
Wie weit ist es? — vee *vait* ist es

How do I get there?
Wie kann ich da hinkommen? — vee kan ikh daa *hin·*ko·men

Turn ...	*Biegen Sie ... ab.*	*bee·*gen zee ... ap
at the corner	*an der Ecke*	an dair *e·*ke
at the traffic lights	*bei der Ampel*	bai dair *am·*pel
left/right	*links/rechts*	lingks/rekhts
It's ...	*Es ist ...*	es ist ...
behind ...	*hinter ...*	*hin·*ter ...
far away	*weit weg*	vait vek
here	*hier*	heer
in front of ...	*vor ...*	fawr ...
left	*links*	lingks
near (to ...)	*nahe (zu ...)*	*naa·*e (zoo ...)
next to ...	*neben ...*	*ney·*ben ...
on the corner	*an der Ecke*	an dair *e·*ke
opposite ...	*gegenüber ...*	*gey·*gen·*ew·*ber ...
right	*rechts*	rekhts
straight ahead	*geradeaus*	ge·raa·de·*ows*
there	*dort*	dort
north	*Norden* m	*nor·*den
south	*Süden* m	*zew·*den
east	*Osten* m	*os·*ten
west	*Westen* m	*ves·*ten
by bus	*mit dem Bus*	mit deym *bus*
by taxi	*mit dem Taxi*	mit deym *tak·*si
by train	*mit dem Zug*	mit deym *tsook*
on foot	*zu Fuß*	tsoo *foos*

signs

Eingang/Ausgang	*ain-gang/ows-gang*	**Entrance/Exit**
Offen/Geschlossen	*o-fen/ge-shlo-sen*	**Open/Closed**
Zimmer Frei	*tsi-mer frai*	**Rooms Available**
Ausgebucht	*ows-ge-bukht*	**No Vacancies**
Auskunft	*ows-kunft*	**Information**
Polizeirevier	*po-li-tsai-re-veer*	**Police Station**
Verboten	*fer-baw-ten*	**Prohibited**
Toiletten/WC	*to-a-le-ten/vee-tsee*	**Toilets**
Herren	*hair-en*	**Men**
Damen	*daa-men*	**Women**
Heiß/Kalt	*hais/kalt*	**Hot/Cold**

accommodation

finding accommodation

Where's a/an ...?	*Wo ist ...?*	*vaw ist ...*
camping ground	*ein Campingplatz*	*ain kem-ping-plats*
guesthouse	*eine Pension*	*ai-ne paang-zyawn*
hotel	*ein Hotel*	*ain ho-tel*
inn	*ein Gasthof*	*ain gast-hawf*
youth hostel	*eine Jugendherberge*	*ai-ne yoo-gent-her-ber-ge*

Can you recommend	*Können Sie etwas*	*keu-nen zee et-vas*
somewhere ...?	*... empfehlen?*	*... emp-fey-len*
cheap	*Billiges*	*bi-li-ges*
good	*Gutes*	*goo-tes*
luxurious	*Luxuriöses*	*luk-su-ri-eu-ses*
nearby	*in der Nähe*	*in dair ney-e*

I'd like to book a room, please.
  Ich möchte bitte ein   ikh meukh-te bi-te ain
  Zimmer reservieren.   tsi-mer re-zer-vee-ren

I have a reservation.
  Ich habe eine Reservierung.   ikh haa-be ai-ne re-zer-vee-rung

My name's ...
  Mein Name ist ...   main naa-me ist ...

Do you have a ... room?	Haben Sie ein ...?	haa·ben zee ain ...
single	Einzelzimmer	ain·tsel·tsi·mer
double	Doppelzimmer mit einem Doppelbett	do·pel·tsi·mer mit ai·nem do·pel·bet
twin	Doppelzimmer mit zwei Einzelbetten	do·pel·tsi·mer mit tsvai ain·tsel·be·ten

Can I pay by ...?	Nehmen Sie ...?	ney·men zee ...
credit card	Kreditkarten	kre·deet·kar·ten
travellers cheque	Reiseschecks	rai·ze·sheks

How much is it per ...?	Wie viel kostet es pro ...?	vee feel kos·tet es praw ...
night	Nacht	nakht
person	Person	per·zawn

I'd like to stay for (two) nights.
Ich möchte für (zwei)
Nächte bleiben.
ikh meukh·te fewr (tsvai)
nekh·te blai·ben

From (July 2) to (July 6).
Vom (zweiten Juli) bis zum
(sechsten Juli).
vom (tsvai·ten yoo·li) bis tsum
(zeks·ten yoo·li)

Can I see it?
Kann ich es sehen?
kan ikh es zey·en

Am I allowed to camp here?
Kann ich hier zelten?
kan ikh heer tsel·ten

Is there a camp site nearby?
Gibt es in der Nähe einen Zeltplatz?
gipt es in dair ney·e ai·nen tselt·plats

requests & queries

When/Where is breakfast served?
Wann/Wo gibt es Frühstück?
van/vaw gipt es frew·shtewk

Please wake me at (seven).
Bitte wecken Sie mich
um (sieben) Uhr.
bi·te ve·ken zee mikh
um (zee·ben) oor

Could I have my key, please?
Könnte ich bitte meinen Schlüssel
haben?
keun·te ikh bi·te mai·nen shlew·sel
haa·ben

Can I get another (blanket)?
Kann ich noch (eine Decke) bekommen?
kan ikh nokh (ai·ne de·ke) be·ko·men

72

Is there a/an ...?	Haben Sie ...?	haa·ben zee ...
elevator	einen Aufzug	ai·nen owf·tsook
safe	einen Safe	ai·nen sayf

The room is too ...	Es ist zu ...	es ist tsoo ...
expensive	teuer	toy·er
noisy	laut	lowt
small	klein	klain

The ... doesn't work.	... funktioniert nicht.	... fungk·tsyo·neert nikht
air conditioning	Die Klimaanlage	dee klee·ma·an·laa·ge
fan	Der Ventilator	dair ven·ti·laa·tor
toilet	Die Toilette	dee to·a·le·te

This ... isn't clean.	Dieses ... ist nicht sauber.	dee·zes ... ist nikht zow·ber
pillow	Kopfkissen	kopf·ki·sen
sheet	Bettlaken	bet·laa·ken
towel	Handtuch	hant·tookh

checking out

What time is checkout?
Wann muss ich auschecken? — van mus ikh *ows*·che·ken

Can I leave my luggage here?
Kann ich meine Taschen hier lassen? — kan ikh *mai*·ne *ta*·shen heer *la*·sen

Could I have	Könnte ich bitte ...	keun·te ikh bi·te ...
my ..., please?	haben?	haa·ben
deposit	meine Anzahlung	mai·ne an·tsaa·lung
passport	meinen Pass	mai·nen pas
valuables	meine Wertsachen	mai·ne vert·za·khen

communications & banking

the internet

Where's the local Internet café?
Wo ist hier ein Internet-Café? — vaw ist heer ain *in*·ter·net·ka·fey

How much is it per hour?
Was kostet es pro Stunde? — vas *kos*·tet es praw *shtun*·de

I'd like to ...	Ich möchte ...	ikh *meukh*·te ...
check my email	meine E-Mails checken	*mai*·ne *ee*·mayls *che*·ken
get Internet access	Internetzugang haben	*in*·ter·net·tsoo·gang *haa*·ben
use a printer	einen Drucker benutzen	*ai*·nen *dru*·ker be·*nu*·tsen
use a scanner	einen Scanner benutzen	*ai*·nen *ske*·ner be·*nu*·tsen

mobile/cell phone

I'd like a ...	Ich hätte gern ...	ikh *he*·te gern ...
mobile/cell phone for hire	ein Miethandy	ain *meet*·hen·di
SIM card for your network	eine SIM-Karte für Ihr Netz	*ai*·ne *zim*·kar·te fewr eer nets

What are the rates?
Wie hoch sind die Gebühren?   vee hawkh zint dee ge·*bew*·ren

telephone

What's your phone number?
Wie ist Ihre Telefonnummer?   vee ist *ee*·re te·le·*fawn*·nu·mer

The number is ...
Die Nummer ist ...   dee *nu*·mer ist ...

Where's the nearest public phone?
Wo ist das nächste öffentliche Telefon?   vaw ist das *neykhs*·te *eu*·fent·li·khe te·le·*fawn*

I'd like to buy a phonecard.
Ich möchte eine Telefonkarte kaufen.   ikh *meukh*·te *ai*·ne te·le·*fawn*·kar·te *kow*·fen

I want to ...	Ich möchte ...	ikh *meukh*·te ...
call (Singapore)	(nach Singapur) telefonieren	(naakh *zing*·a·poor) te·le·fo·*nee*·ren
make a local call	ein Ortsgespräch machen	ain *awrts*·ge·shpreykh *ma*·khen
reverse the charges	ein R-Gespräch führen	ain *air*·ge·shpreykh *few*·ren

How much does ... cost?	Wie viel kostet ...?	vee feel *kos*·tet ...
a (three)-minute	ein (drei)-minutiges	ain (*drai*)·mi·noo·ti·ges
call	Gespräch	ge·*shpreykh*
each extra	jede zusätzliche	*yey*·de tsoo·*zeyts*·li·khe
minute	Minute	mi·*noo*·te

It's (one euro) per (minute).
(Ein Euro) für (eine Minute).   (ain *oy*·ro) fewr (*ai*·ne mi·*noo*·te)

post office

I want to send a ...	Ich möchte ... senden.	ikh *meukh*·te ... *zen*·den
fax	ein Fax	ain faks
letter	einen Brief	*ai*·nen breef
parcel	ein Paket	ain pa·*keyt*
postcard	eine Postkarte	*ai*·ne *post*·kar·te

I want to buy a/an ...	Ich möchte ... kaufen.	ikh *meukh*·te ... *kow*·fen
envelope	einen Umschlag	*ai*·nen *um*·shlaak
stamp	eine Briefmarke	*ai*·ne *breef*·mar·ke

Please send it	Bitte schicken Sie das	*bi*·te *shi*·ken zee das
(to Australia) by ...	(nach Australien) per ...	(nakh ows·*traa*·li·en) per ...
airmail	Luftpost	*luft*·post
express mail	Expresspost	eks·*pres*·post
registered mail	Einschreiben	*ain*·shrai·ben
surface mail	Landbeförderung	*lant*·be·feur·de·rung

Is there any mail for me? *Ist Post für mich da?* ist post fewr mikh da

bank

Where's a/an ...?	Wo ist ...?	vaw ist ...
ATM	der Geldautomat	dair *gelt*·ow·to·maat
foreign exchange office	die Geldwechselstube	dee *gelt*·vek·sel·shtoo·be

I'd like to ...	Ich möchte ...	ikh *meukh*·te ...
Where can I ...?	Wo kann ich ...?	vaw kan ikh ...
arrange a transfer	einen Transfer tätigen	*ai*·nen trans·*fer* tey·ti·gen
cash a cheque	einen Scheck einlösen	*ai*·nen shek *ain*·leu·zen
change a travellers cheque	einen Reisescheck einlösen	*ai*·nen *rai*·ze·shek *ain*·leu·zen
change money	Geld umtauschen	gelt *um*·tow·shen
get a cash advance	eine Barauszahlung	*ai*·ne *baar*·ows·tsaa·lung
withdraw money	Geld abheben	gelt *ap*·hey·ben

What's the ...?	Wie ...?	vee ...
charge for that	hoch sind die Gebühren dafür	hawkh zint dee ge·*bew*·ren da·*fewr*
exchange rate	ist der Wechselkurs	ist dair *vek*·sel·kurs

It's ...	Das ...	das ...
(12) euros	kostet (zwölf) euro	*kos*·tet (zveulf) *oy*·ro
free	ist umsonst	ist um·*zonst*

What time does the bank open?
Wann macht die Bank auf? — van makht dee bangk owf

Has my money arrived yet?
Ist mein Geld schon angekommen? — ist main gelt shawn *an*·ge·ko·men

sightseeing

getting in

What time does it open/close?
Wann macht es auf/zu? — van makht es owf/tsoo

What's the admission charge?
Was kostet der Eintritt? — vas *kos*·tet dair *ain*·trit

Is there a discount for children/students?
Gibt es eine Ermäßigung für Kinder/Studenten? — gipt es *ai*·ne er·*mey*·si·gung fewr *kin*·der/shtu·*den*·ten

I'd like a ...	Ich hätte gern ...	ikh he-te gern ...
catalogue	einen Katalog	ai-nen ka-ta-lawg
guide	einen Reiseführer	ai-nen rai-ze-few-rer
local map	eine Karte von hier	ai-ne kar-te fon heer

I'd like to see ...	Ich möchte ... sehen.	ikh meukh-te ... zey-en
What's that?	Was ist das?	vas ist das
Can I take a photo?	Kann ich fotografieren?	kan ikh fo-to-gra-fee-ren

tours

When's the	Wann ist der/die	van ist dair/dee
next ...?	nächste ...? m/f	neykhs-te ...
day trip	Tagesausflug m	taa-ges-ows-flook
tour	Tour f	toor

Is ... included?	Ist ... inbegriffen?	ist ... in-be-gri-fen
accommodation	die Unterkunft	dee un-ter-kunft
the admission charge	der Eintritt	dair ain-trit
food	das Essen	das e-sen
transport	die Beförderung	dee be-feur-de-rung

How long is the tour?
Wie lange dauert die Führung?   vee lang-e dow-ert dee few-rung

What time should we be back?
Wann sollen wir zurück sein?   van zo-len veer tsu-rewk zain

sightseeing

castle	Burg f	burk
cathedral	Dom m	dawm
church	Kirche f	kir-khe
main square	Hauptplatz m	howpt-plats
monastery	Kloster n	klaws-ter
monument	Denkmal n	dengk-maal
museum	Museum n	mu-zey-um
old city	Altstadt f	alt-stat
palace	Schloss n	shlos
ruins	Ruinen f pl	ru-ee-nen
stadium	Stadion n	shtaa-di-on
statues	Statuen f pl	shtaa-tu-e

shopping

enquiries

Where's a ...?	Wo ist ...?	vaw ist ...
bank	die Bank	dee bangk
bookshop	die Buchhandlung	dee *bookh*·hand·lung
camera shop	das Fotogeschäft	das fo·to·ge·*sheft*
department store	das Warenhaus	das *vaa*·ren·hows
grocery store	der Lebensmittelladen	dair *ley*·bens·mi·tel·laa·den
market	der Markt	dair markt
newsagency	der Zeitungshändler	dair *tsai*·tungks·hen·dler
supermarket	der Supermarkt	dair *zoo*·per·markt

Where can I buy (a padlock)?
Wo kann ich (ein Vorhängeschloss) kaufen?
vaw kan ikh (ain *fawr*·heng·e·shlos) *kow*·fen

I'm looking for ...
Ich suche nach ...
ikh *zoo*·khe nakh ...

Can I look at it?
Können Sie es mir zeigen?
keu·nen zee es meer *tsai*·gen

Do you have any others?
Haben Sie noch andere?
haa·ben zee nokh *an*·de·re

Does it have a guarantee?
Gibt es darauf Garantie?
gipt es da·*rowf* ga·ran·*tee*

Can I have it sent overseas?
Kann ich es ins Ausland verschicken lassen?
kan ikh es ins *ows*·lant fer·*shi*·ken *la*·sen

Can I have my ... repaired?
Kann ich mein ... reparieren lassen?
kan ikh main ... re·pa·*ree*·ren *la*·sen

It's faulty.
Es ist fehlerhaft.
es ist *fey*·ler·haft

I'd like ..., please.	Ich möchte bitte ...	ikh *meukh*·te *bi*·te ...
a bag	eine Tüte	*ai*·ne *tew*·te
a refund	mein Geld	main gelt
	zurückhaben	tsu·*rewk*·haa·ben
to return this	dieses zurückgeben	*dee*·zes tsu·*rewk*·gey·ben

paying

How much is it?
Wie viel kostet das?
vee feel *kos*·tet das

Can you write down the price?
Können Sie den Preis aufschreiben?
keu·nen zee deyn prais *owf*·shrai·ben

That's too expensive.
Das ist zu teuer.
das ist tsoo *toy*·er

Can you lower the price?
Können Sie mit dem Preis heruntergehen?
keu·nen zee mit dem prais he·*run*·ter·gey·en

I'll give you (five) euros.
Ich gebe Ihnen (fünf) euro.
ikh *gey*·be *ee*·nen (fewnf) *oy*·ro

There's a mistake in the bill.
Da ist ein Fehler in der Rechnung.
daa ist ain *fey*·ler in dair *rekh*·nung

Do you accept ...?	Nehmen Sie ...?	*ney*·men zee ...
credit cards	Kreditkarten	kre·*deet*·kar·ten
debit cards	Debitkarten	*dey*·bit·kar·ten
travellers cheques	Reiseschecks	*rai*·ze·sheks

I'd like ..., please.	Ich möchte bitte ...	ikh *meukh*·te *bi*·te ...
a receipt	eine Quittung	*ai*·ne *kvi*·tung
my change	mein Wechselgeld	main *vek*·sel·gelt

clothes & shoes

Can I try it on?
Kann ich es anprobieren?
kan ikh es *an*·pro·bee·ren

My size is (40).
Ich habe Größe (vierzig).
ikh *haa*·be *greu*·se (*feer*·tsikh)

It doesn't fit.
Es passt nicht.
es past nikht

small	klein	klain
medium	mittelgroß	*mi*·tel·graws
large	groß	graws

books & music

I'd like a ...   *Ich hätte gern ...*   ikh *he*·te gern ...
  newspaper   *eine Zeitung*   *ai*·ne *tsai*·tung
  (in English)   *(auf Englisch)*   (owf *eng*·lish)
  pen   *einen Kugelschreiber*   *ai*·nen *koo*·gel·shrai·ber

Is there an English-language bookshop?
Gibt es einen Buchladen   gipt es *ai*·nen *bookh*·laa·den
für englische Bücher?   fewr *eng*·li·she *bew*·kher

I'm looking for something by (Herman Hesse).
Ich suche nach etwas von   ikh *zoo*·khe nakh *et*·vas fon
(Herman Hesse).   (*her*·man *he*·se)

Can I listen to this?
Kann ich mir das anhören?   kan ikh meer das *an*·heu·ren

photography

Can you ...?   *Können Sie ...?*   *keu*·nen zee ...
  burn a CD from   *eine CD von meiner*   *ai*·ne tse de von *mai*·ner
  my memory card   *Speicherkarte brennen*   *shpai*·kher·*kar*·te *bre*·nen
  develop this film   *diesen Film entwickeln*   *dee*·zen film ent·*vi*·keln
  load my film   *mir den Film einlegen*   meer deyn film *ain*·ley·gen

I need a ... film   *Ich brauche einen*   ikh *brow*·khe *ai*·nen
for this camera.   *... für diese Kamera.*   ... fewr *dee*·ze *ka*·me·ra
  APS   *APS-Film*   aa·pey·*es*·film
  B&W   *Schwarzweißfilm*   shvarts·*vais*·film
  colour   *Farbfilm*   *farp*·film
  slide   *Diafilm*   *dee*·a·film
  (200) speed   *(zweihundert)-*   (*tsvai*·hun·dert)·
        ASA-Film   *aa*·za·film

When will it be ready?   *Wann ist er fertig?*   van ist air *fer*·tikh

meeting people

greetings, goodbyes & introductions

Hello. (Austria)	*Servus.*	*zer*·vus
Hello. (Germany)	*Guten Tag.*	*goo*·ten taak
Hello. (Switzerland)	*Grüezi.*	*grew*·e·tsi
Hi.	*Hallo.*	*ha*·lo
Good night.	*Gute Nacht.*	*goo*·te nakht
Goodbye.	*Auf Wiedersehen.*	owf *vee*·der·zey·en
Bye.	*Tschüss/Tschau.*	chews/chow
See you later.	*Bis später.*	bis *shpey*·ter
Mr	*Herr*	her
Mrs	*Frau*	frow
Miss	*Fräulein*	*froy*·lain
How are you?	*Wie geht es Ihnen?*	vee geyt es *ee*·nen
Fine. And you?	*Danke, gut. Und Ihnen?*	*dang*·ke goot unt *ee*·nen
What's your name?	*Wie ist Ihr Name?*	vee ist eer *naa*·me
My name is ...	*Mein Name ist ...*	main *naa*·me ist ...
I'm pleased to meet you.	*Angenehm.*	*an*·ge·neym

This is my ...	*Das ist mein/meine ...* m/f	das ist main/*mai*·ne ...
brother	*Bruder*	*broo*·der
daughter	*Tochter*	*tokh*·ter
father	*Vater*	*faa*·ter
friend	*Freund/Freundin* m/f	froynt/*froyn*·din
husband	*Mann*	man
mother	*Mutter*	*mu*·ter
partner (intimate)	*Partner/Partnerin* m/f	*part*·ner/*part*·ne·rin
sister	*Schwester*	*shves*·ter
son	*Sohn*	zawn
wife	*Frau*	frow

Here's my ...	*Hier ist meine ...*	heer ist *mai*·ne ...
What's your...?	*Wie ist Ihre ...?*	vee ist *ee*·re ...
address	*Adresse*	a·*dre*·se
email address	*E-mail-Adresse*	ee·mayl·a·*dre*·se
fax number	*Faxnummer*	*faks*·nu·mer
phone number	*Telefonnummer*	te·le·*fawn*·nu·mer

occupations

What's your occupation?	*Als was arbeiten Sie?* pol	als vas *ar*-bai-ten zee
	Als was arbeitest du? inf	als vas *ar*-bai-test doo
I'm a/an ...	*Ich bin ein/eine ...* m/f	ikh bin ain/*ai*-ne ...
artist	*Künstler/Künstlerin* m/f	*kewnst*-ler/*kewnst*-le-rin
business person	*Geschäftsmann* m	ge-*shefts*-man
	Geschäftsfrau f	ge-*shefts*-frow
farmer	*Bauer/Bäuerin* m/f	*bow*-er/*boy*-e-rin
manual worker	*Arbeiter/Arbeiterin* m/f	*ar*-bai-ter/*ar*-bai-te-rin
office worker	*Büroangestellte* m&f	bew-*raw*-an-ge-shtel-te
scientist	*Wissenschaftler* m	*vi*-sen-shaft-ler
	Wissenschaftlerin f	*vi*-sen-shaft-le-rin
student	*Student/Studentin* m/f	shtu-*dent*/shtu-*den*-tin

background

Where are you from?	*Woher kommen Sie?* pol	*vaw*-hair *ko*-men zee
	Woher kommst du? inf	*vaw*-hair komst doo
I'm from ...	*Ich komme aus ...*	ikh *ko*-me ows ...
Australia	*Australien*	ows-*traa*-li-en
Canada	*Kanada*	*ka*-na-daa
England	*England*	*eng*-lant
New Zealand	*Neuseeland*	noy-*zey*-lant
the USA	*den USA*	deyn oo-es-*aa*
Are you married?	*Sind Sie verheiratet?* pol	zint zee fer-*hai*-ra-tet
	Bist du verheiratet? inf	bist doo fer-*hai*-ra-tet
I'm married.	*Ich bin verheiratet.*	ikh bin fer-*hai*-ra-tet
I'm single.	*Ich bin ledig.*	ikh bin *ley*-dikh

age

How old ...?	*Wie alt ...?*	vee alt ...
are you	*sind Sie* pol	zint zee
	bist du inf	bist doo
is your daughter	*ist Ihre Tochter* pol	ist *ee*-re *tokh*-ter
is your son	*ist Ihr Sohn* pol	ist eer zawn
I'm ... years old.	*Ich bin ... Jahre alt.*	ikh bin ... *yaa*-re alt
He/She is ... years old.	*Er/Sie ist ... Jahre alt.*	air/zee ist ... *yaa*-re alt

feelings

I'm (not) ...	*Ich bin (nicht) ...*	ikh bin (nikht) ...
Are you ...?	*Sind Sie ...?* pol	zint zee ...
	Bist du ...? inf	bist doo ...
happy	*glücklich*	*glewk*-likh
sad	*traurig*	*trow*-rikh
I'm (not) ...	*Ich habe (kein) ...*	ikh *haa*-be (kain) ...
Are you ...?	*Haben Sie ...?* pol	*haa*-ben zee ...
	Hast du ...? inf	hast doo ...
hungry	*Hunger*	*hung*-er
thirsty	*Durst*	durst
I'm (not) ...	*Mir ist (nicht) ...*	meer ist (nikht) ...
Are you ...?	*Ist Ihnen/dir ...?* pol/inf	ist *ee*-nen/deer ...
cold	*kalt*	kalt
hot	*heiß*	hais

entertainment

going out

Where can I find ...?	*Wo sind die ...?*	vaw zint dee ...
clubs	*Klubs*	klups
gay venues	*Schwulen- und Lesbenkneipen*	*shvoo*-len unt *les*-ben-*knai*-pen
pubs	*Kneipen*	*knai*-pen
I feel like going to a/the ...	*Ich hätte Lust, ... zu gehen.*	ikh *he*-te lust ... tsoo *gey*-en
concert	*zum Konzert*	tsoom kon-*tsert*
movies	*ins Kino*	ins *kee*-no
party	*zu eine Party*	tsoo *ai*-ne *par*-ti
restaurant	*in ein Restaurant*	in ain res-to-*rang*
theatre	*ins Theater*	ins te-*aa*-ter

interests

Do you like ...?	*Magst du ...?* inf	maakst doo ...
I (don't) like ...	*Ich mag (keine/* *keinen) ...* m/f	ikh maak (*kai*·ne/ *kai*·nen) ...
art	*Kunst* f	kunst
sport	*Sport* m	shport
I (don't) like ...	*Ich ... (nicht) gern.*	ikh ... (nikht) gern
cooking	*koche*	*ko*·khe
reading	*lese*	*ley*·ze
travelling	*reise*	*rai*·ze
Do you like to dance?		
Tanzt du gern? inf		tantst doo gern
Do you like music?		
Hörst du gern Musik? inf		heurst doo gern mu·*zeek*

food & drink

finding a place to eat

Can you recommend a ...?	*Können Sie ... empfehlen?*	*keu*·nen zee ... emp·*fey*·len
bar	*eine Kneipe*	*ai*·ne *knai*·pe
café	*ein Café*	ain ka·*fey*
restaurant	*ein Restaurant*	ain res·to·*rang*
I'd like ..., please.	*Ich hätte gern ..., bitte.*	ikh *he*·te gern ... *bi*·te
a table for (five)	*einen Tisch für (fünf) Personen*	*ai*·nen tish fewr (fewnf) per·*zaw*·nen
the (non)smoking section	*einen (Nicht-) rauchertisch*	*ai*·nen (*nikht*·) *row*·kher·tish

ordering food

breakfast	*Frühstück* n	*frew*·shtewk
lunch	*Mittagessen* n	*mi*·taak·e·sen
dinner	*Abendessen* n	*aa*·bent·e·sen
snack	*Snack* m	snek

What would you recommend?
Was empfehlen Sie? vas emp·*fey*·len zee

I'd like (the) ..., please. *Bitte bringen Sie ...* *bi*·te *bring*·en zee ...
bill	*die Rechnung*	dee *rekh*·nung
drink list	*die Getränkekarte*	dee ge·*treng*·ke·kar·te
menu	*die Speisekarte*	dee *shpai*·ze·kar·te
that dish	*dieses Gericht*	*dee*·zes ge·*rikht*

drinks

(cup of) coffee ...	*(eine Tasse) Kaffee ...*	(*ai*·ne *ta*·se) ka·*fey* ...
(cup of) tea ...	*(eine Tasse) Tee ...*	(*ai*·ne *ta*·se) tey ...
with milk	*mit Milch*	mit milkh
without sugar	*ohne Zucker*	*aw*·ne *tsu*·ker
(orange) juice	*(Orangen)Saft* m	(o·*rang*·zhen·)zaft
mineral water	*Mineralwasser* n	mi·ne·*raal*·va·ser
soft drink	*Softdrink* m	*soft*·dringk
(boiled) water	*(heißes) Wasser* n	(*hai*·ses) *va*·ser

in the bar

I'll have ...	*Ich hätte gern ...*	ikh *he*·te gern ...
I'll buy you a drink.	*Ich gebe dir einen aus.* inf	ikh *gey*·be deer *ai*·nen ows
What would you like?	*Was möchtest du?* inf	vas *meukh*·test doo
Cheers!	*Prost!*	prawst
brandy	*Weinbrand* m	*vain*·brant
cognac	*Kognak* m	*ko*·nyak
cocktail	*Cocktail* m	*kok*·tayl
a shot of (whisky)	*einen (Whisky)*	*ai*·nen (*vis*·ki)
a bottle of ...	*eine Flasche ...*	*ai*·ne *fla*·she ...
a glass of ...	*ein Glas ...*	ain glaas ...
red wine	*Rotwein*	*rawt*·vain
sparkling wine	*Sekt*	zekt
white wine	*Weißwein*	*vais*·vain
a ... of beer	*... Bier*	... beer
bottle	*eine Flasche*	*ai*·ne *fla*·she
glass	*ein Glas*	ain glaas

self-catering

What's the local speciality?
Was ist eine örtliche Spezialität?   vas ist *ai*·ne *eurt*·li·khe shpe·tsya·li·*teyt*

What's that?
Was ist das?   vas ist das

How much is (a kilo of cheese)?
Was kostet (ein Kilo Käse)?   vas *kos*·tet (ain *kee*·lo *key*·ze)

I'd like ...	*Ich möchte ...*	ikh *meukh*·te ...
(100) grams	*(hundert) Gramm*	(hun·dert) gram
(two) kilos	*(zwei) Kilo*	(tsvai) *kee*·lo
(three) pieces	*(drei) Stück*	(drai) shtewk
(six) slices	*(sechs) Scheiben*	(zeks) *shai*·ben

Less.	*Weniger.*	*vey*·ni·ger
Enough.	*Genug.*	ge·*nook*
More.	*Mehr.*	mair

special diets & allergies

Is there a vegetarian restaurant near here?
Gibt es ein vegetarisches   gipt es ain vege·*tar*·ish·shes
Restaurant hier in der Nähe?   res·to·*rang* heer in dair *ney*·e

Do you have vegetarian food?
Haben Sie vegetarisches Essen?   *haa*·ben zee ve·ge·*taa*·ri·shes *e*·sen

Could you prepare	*Können Sie ein Gericht*	*keu*·nen zee ain ge·*rikht*
a meal without ...?	*ohne ... zubereiten?*	*aw*·ne ... *tsoo*·be·rai·ten
butter	*Butter*	*bu*·ter
eggs	*Eiern*	*ai*·ern
meat stock	*Fleischbrühe*	*flaish*·brew·e

I'm allergic to ...	*Ich bin allergisch*	ikh bin a·*lair*·gish
	gegen ...	*gey*·gen ...
dairy produce	*Milchprodukte*	*milkh*·pro·duk·te
gluten	*Gluten*	*gloo*·ten
MSG	*Natrium-glutamat*	*naa*·tri·um·glu·ta·maat
nuts	*Nüsse*	*new*·se
seafood	*Meeresfrüchte*	*mair*·res·frewkh·te

emergencies

basics

Help!	*Hilfe!*	*hil*·fe
Stop!	*Halt!*	halt
Go away!	*Gehen Sie weg!*	*gey*·en zee vek
Thief!	*Dieb!*	deeb
Fire!	*Feuer!*	*foy*·er
Watch out!	*Vorsicht!*	for·*zikht*
Call ...!	*Rufen Sie ...!*	*roo*·fen zee ...
a doctor	*einen Arzt*	*ai*·nen artst
an ambulance	*einen Krankenwagen*	*ai*·nen *krang*·ken·vaa·gen
the police	*die Polizei*	dee po·li·*tsai*

It's an emergency!
Es ist ein Notfall!
es ist ain *nawt*·fal

Could you help me, please?
Könnten Sie mir bitte helfen?
keun·ten zee meer *bi*·te *hel*·fen

I have to use the telephone.
Ich muss das Telefon benutzen.
ikh mus das te·le·*fawn* be·*nu*·tsen

I'm lost.
Ich habe mich verirrt.
ikh *haa*·be mikh fer·*irt*

Where are the toilets?
Wo ist die Toilette?
vo ist dee to·a·*le*·te

police

Where's the police station?
Wo ist das Polizeirevier?
vaw ist das po·li·*tsai*·re·veer

I want to report an offence.
Ich möchte eine Straftat melden.
ikh *meukh*·te *ai*·ne *shtraaf*·taat *mel*·den

I have insurance.
Ich bin versichert.
ikh bin fer·*zi*·khert

I've been ...	*Ich bin ... worden.*	ikh bin ... *vor*·den
assaulted	*angegriffen*	*an*·ge·gri·fen
raped	*vergewaltigt*	fer·ge·*val*·tikht
robbed	*bestohlen*	be·*shtaw*·len

I've lost my...	Ich habe ... verloren.	ikh *haa*·be ... fer·*law*·ren
My ... was/	Man hat mir ...	man hat meer ...
were stolen.	gestohlen.	ge·*shtaw*·len
backpack	meinen Rucksack	*mai*·nen *ruk*·zak
bags	meine Reisetaschen	*mai*·ne *rai*·ze·ta·shen
credit card	meine Kreditkarte	*mai*·ne kre·*deet*·karte
handbag	meine Handtasche	*mai*·ne *hant*·ta·she
jewellery	meinen Schmuck	*mai*·nen shmuk
money	mein Geld	main gelt
passport	meinen Pass	*mai*·nen pas
travellers cheques	meine Reiseschecks	*mai*·ne *rai*·ze·sheks
wallet	meine Brieftasche	*mai*·ne *breef*·ta·she
I want to contact	Ich möchte mich mit	ikh *meukh*·te mikh mit
my ...	... in Verbindung setzen.	... in fer·*bin*·dung *ze*·tsen
consulate	meinem Konsulat	*mai*·nem kon·zu·*laat*
embassy	meiner Botschaft	*mai*·ner *bawt*·shaft

health

medical needs

Where's the nearest ...?	Wo ist der/die/das nächste ...? m/f/n	vaw ist dair/dee/das *neykhs*·te ...
dentist	Zahnarzt m	*tsaan*·artst
doctor	Arzt m	artst
hospital	Krankenhaus n	*krang*·ken·hows
(night) pharmacist	(Nacht)Apotheke f	(nakht·)a·po·*tey*·ke

I need a doctor (who speaks English).
Ich brauche einen Arzt
(der Englisch spricht).
ikh *brow*·khe *ai*·nen artst
(dair *eng*·lish shprikht)

Could I see a female doctor?
Könnte ich von einer
Ärztin behandelt werden?
keun·te ikh fon *ai*·ner
erts·tin be·*han*·delt *ver*·den

I've run out of my medication.
Ich habe keine
Medikamente mehr.
ikh *haa*·be *kai*·ne
me·di·ka·*men*·te mair

symptoms, conditions & allergies

| I'm sick. | Ich bin krank. | ikh bin krangk |
| It hurts here. | Es tut hier weh. | es toot heer *vey* |

I have (a) ...	Ich habe ...	ikh *haa*·be ...
asthma	Asthma	*ast*·ma
bronchitis	Bronchitis	bron·*khee*·tis
constipation	Verstopfung	fer·*shtop*·fung
cough	Husten	*hoos*·ten
diarrhoea	Durchfall	*durkh*·fal
fever	Fieber	*fee*·ber
headache	Kopfschmerzen	*kopf*·shmer·tsen
heart condition	Herzbeschwerden	*herts*·be·shver·den
nausea	Übelkeit	*ew*·bel·kait
pain	Schmerzen	*shmer*·tsen
sore throat	Halsschmerzen	*hals*·shmer·tsen
toothache	Zahnschmerzen	*tsaan*·shmer·tsen

I'm allergic to ...	Ich bin allergisch gegen ...	ikh bin a·*lair*·gish *gey*·gen ...
antibiotics	Antibiotika	an·ti·bi·*aw*·ti·ka
anti-inflammatories	entzündungs-hemmende Mittel	en·*tsewn*·dungks·he·men·de *mi*·tel
aspirin	Aspirin	as·pi·*reen*
bees	Bienen	*bee*·nen
codeine	Kodein	ko·de·*een*
penicillin	Penizillin	pe·ni·tsi·*leen*

antiseptic	Antiseptikum n	an·ti·*zep*·ti·kum
bandage	Verband m	fer·*bant*
condoms	Kondom n	kon·*dawm*
contraceptives	Verhütungsmittel n	fer·*hew*·tungks·mi·tel
diarrhoea medicine	Mittel gegen Durchfall n	*mi*·tel gey·gen durkh·fal
insect repellent	Insektenschutzmittel n	in·*zek*·ten·shuts·mi·tel
laxatives	Abführmittel n	*ap*·fewr·mi·tel
painkillers	Schmerzmittel n	*shmerts*·mi·tel
rehydration salts	Kochsalzlösung n	kokh·zalts·*leu*·zung
sleeping tablets	Schlaftabletten f pl	*shlaaf*·ta·ble·ten

english–german dictionary

German nouns in this dictionary have their gender indicated by ⓜ (masculine), ⓕ (feminine) or ⓝ (neuter). If it's a plural noun, you'll also see pl. Words are also marked as n (noun), a (adjective), v (verb), sg (singular), pl (plural), inf (informal) and pol (polite) where necessary.

A

accident *Unfall* ⓜ un-fal
accommodation *Unterkunft* ⓕ un-ter-kunft
adaptor *Adapter* ⓜ a-dap-ter
address *Adresse* ⓕ a-dre-se
after *nach* naakh
air-conditioned *mit Klimaanlage* ⓕ
  mit klee-ma-an-laa-ge
airplane *Flugzeug* ⓝ flook-tsoyk
airport *Flughafen* ⓜ flook-haa-fen
alcohol *Alkohol* ⓜ al-ko-hawl
all a *alle* a-le
allergy *Allergie* ⓕ a-lair-gee
ambulance *Krankenwagen* ⓜ krang-ken-vaa-gen
and *und* unt
ankle *Knöchel* ⓜ kneu-khel
arm *Arm* ⓜ arm
ashtray *Aschenbecher* ⓜ a-shen-be-kher
ATM *Geldautomat* ⓜ gelt-ow-to-maat
Austria *Österreich* ⓝ eus-ter-raikh

B

baby *Baby* ⓝ bay-bi
back (body) *Rücken* ⓜ rew-ken
backpack *Rucksack* ⓜ ruk-zak
bad *schlecht* shlekht
bag *Tasche* ⓕ ta-she
baggage claim *Gepäckausgabe* ⓕ ge-pek-ows-gaa-be
bank *Bank* ⓕ bangk
bar *Lokal* ⓝ lo-kaal
bathroom *Badezimmer* ⓝ baa-de-tsi-mer
battery *Batterie* ⓕ ba-te-ree
beautiful *schön* sheun
bed *Bett* ⓝ bet
beer *Bier* ⓝ beer
before *vor* fawr
behind *hinter* hin-ter
Belgium *Belgien* ⓝ bel-gi-en

bicycle *Fahrrad* ⓝ faar-raat
big *groß* graws
bill *Rechnung* ⓕ rekh-nung
black *schwarz* shvarts
blanket *Decke* ⓕ de-ke
blood group *Blutgruppe* ⓕ bloot-gru-pe
blue *blau* blow
book (make a reservation) v *buchen* boo-khen
bottle *Flasche* ⓕ fla-she
bottle opener *Flaschenöffner* ⓜ fla-shen-euf-ner
boy *Junge* ⓜ yung-e
brakes (car) *Bremsen* ⓕ pl brem-zen
breakfast *Frühstück* ⓝ frew-shtewk
broken (faulty) *kaputt* ka-put
bus *Bus* ⓜ bus
business *Geschäft* ⓝ ge-sheft
buy *kaufen* kow-fen

C

café *Café* ⓝ ka-fey
camera *Kamera* ⓕ ka-me-ra
camp site *Zeltplatz* ⓜ tselt-plats
cancel *stornieren* shtor-nee-ren
can opener *Dosenöffner* ⓜ daw-zen-euf-ner
car *Auto* ⓝ ow-to
cash *Bargeld* ⓝ baar-gelt
cash (a cheque) v *(einen Scheck) einlösen*
  (ai-nen shek) ain-leu-zen
cell phone *Handy* ⓝ hen-di
centre *Zentrum* ⓝ tsen-trum
change (money) v *wechseln* vek-seln
cheap *billig* bi-likh
check (bill) *Rechnung* ⓕ rekh-nung
check-in *Abfertigungsschalter* ⓜ
  ap-fer-ti-gungks-shal-ter
chest *Brustkorb* ⓜ brust-korp
child *Kind* ⓝ kint
cigarette *Zigarette* ⓕ tsi-ga-re-te
city *Stadt* ⓕ shtat
clean a *sauber* zow-ber

closed *geschlossen* ge-*shlo*-sen
coffee *Kaffee* ⓜ ka-fey
coins *Münzen* ⓕ pl *mewn*-tsen
cold a *kalt* kalt
collect call *R-Gespräch* ⓝ air-ge-shpreykh
come *kommen* ko-men
computer *Computer* ⓜ kom-*pyoo*-ter
condom *Kondom* ⓝ kon-*dawm*
contact lenses *Kontaktlinsen* ⓕ pl kon-*takt*-lin-zen
cook v *kochen* ko-khen
cost *Preis* ⓜ prais
credit card *Kreditkarte* ⓕ kre-*deet*-kar-te
cup *Tasse* ⓕ ta-se
currency exchange *Geldwechsel* ⓜ *gelt*-vek-sel
customs (immigration) *Zoll* ⓜ tsol

D

dangerous *gefährlich* ge-*fair*-likh
date (time) *Datum* ⓝ *daa*-tum
day *Tag* ⓜ taak
delay n *Verspätung* ⓕ fer-*shpey*-tung
dentist *Zahnarzt/Zahnärztin* ⓜ/ⓕ
   tsaan-artst/tsaan-*erts*-tin
depart *abfahren* ap-*faa*-ren
diaper *Windel* ⓕ *vin*-del
dictionary *Wörterbuch* ⓝ *veur*-ter-bookh
dinner *Abendessen* ⓝ *aa*-bent-e-sen
direct *direkt* di-*rekt*
dirty *schmutzig* *shmu*-tsikh
disabled *behindert* be-*hin*-dert
discount n *Rabatt* ⓜ ra-*bat*
doctor *Arzt/Ärztin* ⓜ/ⓕ *artst*/*erts*-tin
double bed *Doppelbett* ⓝ *do*-pel-bet
double room *Doppelzimmer mit einem Doppelbett* ⓝ
   do-pel-tsi-mer mit *ai*-nem *do*-pel-bet
drink *Getränk* ⓝ ge-*trengk*
drive v *fahren* *faa*-ren
drivers licence *Führerschein* ⓕ *few*-rer-shain
drugs (illicit) *Droge* ⓕ *draw*-ge
dummy (pacifier) *Schnuller* ⓜ *shnu*-ler

E

ear *Ohr* ⓝ awr
east *Osten* ⓜ *os*-ten
eat *essen* e-sen
economy class *Touristenklasse* ⓕ tu-*ris*-ten-kla-se
electricity *Elektrizität* ⓕ e-lek-tri-tsi-*teyt*
elevator *Lift* ⓜ lift

email *E-Mail* e-mayl
embassy *Botschaft* ⓕ *bawt*-shaft
emergency *Notfall* ⓜ *nawt*-fal
English (language) *Englisch* ⓝ *eng*-lish
entrance *Eingang* ⓜ *ain*-gang
evening *Abend* ⓜ *aa*-bent
exchange rate *Wechselkurs* ⓜ *vek*-sel-kurs
exit *Ausgang* ⓜ *ows*-gang
expensive *teuer* *toy*-er
express mail *Expresspost* ⓕ eks-*pres*-post
eye *Auge* ⓝ *ow*-ge

F

far *weit* vait
fast *schnell* shnel
father *Vater* ⓜ *faa*-ter
film (camera) *Film* ⓜ film
finger *Finger* ⓜ *fing*-er
first-aid kit *Verbandskasten* ⓜ fer-*bants*-kas-ten
first class *erste Klasse* ⓕ *ers*-te *kla*-se
fish *Fisch* ⓜ fish
food *Essen* ⓝ e-sen
foot *Fuß* ⓜ foos
fork *Gabel* ⓕ *gaa*-bel
free (of charge) *gratis* *graa*-tis
friend *Freund/Freundin* ⓜ/ⓕ froynt/*froyn*-din
fruit *Frucht* ⓕ frukht
full *voll* fol
funny *lustig* *lus*-tikh

G

German (language) *Deutsch* ⓝ doytsh
Germany *Deutschland* ⓝ *doytsh*-lant
gift *Geschenk* ⓝ ge-*shengk*
girl *Mädchen* ⓝ *meyt*-khen
glass (drinking) *Glas* ⓝ glaas
glasses *Brille* ⓕ *bri*-le
go *gehen* *gey*-en
good *gut* goot
green *grün* grewn
guide *Führer* ⓜ *few*-rer

H

half *Hälfte* ⓕ *helf*-te
hand *Hand* ⓕ hant
handbag *Handtasche* ⓕ *hant*-ta-she
happy *glücklich* *glewk*-likh

have *haben* haa-ben
he *er* air
head *Kopf* @ kopf
heart *Herz* @ herts
heat n *Hitze* ① hi-tse
heavy *schwer* shvair
help v *helfen* hel-fen
here *hier* heer
high *hoch* hawkh
highway *Autobahn* ① ow-to-baan
hike v *wandern* van-dern
holiday *Urlaub* @ oor-lowp
homosexual *homosexuell* haw-mo-zek-su-el
hospital *Krankenhaus* @ krang-ken-hows
hot *heiß* hais
hotel *Hotel* @ ho-tel
hungry *hungrig* hung-rikh
husband *Ehemann* @ ey-e-man

I

I *ich* ikh
identification (card) *Personalausweis* @
    per-zo-naal-ows-vais
ill *krank* krangk
important *wichtig* vikh-tikh
included *inbegriffen* in-be-gri-fen
injury *Verletzung* ① fer-le-tsung
insurance *Versicherung* ① fer-zi-khe-rung
Internet *Internet* @ in-ter-net
interpreter *Dolmetscher/Dolmetscherin* @/①
    dol-met-sher/dol-met-she-rin

J

jewellery *Schmuck* @ shmuk
job *Arbeitsstelle* ① ar-baits-shte-le

K

key *Schlüssel* @ shlew-sel
kilogram *Kilogramm* @ kee-lo-gram
kitchen *Küche* ① kew-khe
knife *Messer* @ me-ser

L

laundry (place) *Waschküche* ① vash-kew-khe
lawyer *Rechtsanwalt/Rechtsanwältin* @/①
    rekhts-an-valt/rekhts-an-vel-tin

left (direction) *links* lingks
left-luggage office *Gepäckaufbewahrung* ①
    ge-pek-owf-be-vaa-rung
leg *Bein* @ bain
lesbian *Lesbierin* ① les-bi-e-rin
less *weniger* vey-ni-ger
letter (mail) *Brief* @ breef
lift (elevator) *Lift* @ lift
light *Licht* @ likht
like v *mögen* meu-gen
lock *Schloss* @ shlos
long *lang* lang
lost *verloren* fer-law-ren
lost-property office *Fundbüro* @ funt-bew-raw
love v *lieben* lee-ben
luggage *Gepäck* @ ge-pek
lunch *Mittagessen* @ mi-taak-e-sen

M

mail *Post* ① post
man *Mann* @ man
map *Karte* ① kar-te
market *Markt* @ markt
matches *Streichhölzer* @ pl shtraikh-heul-tser
meat *Fleisch* @ flaish
medicine *Medizin* ① me-di-tseen
menu *Speisekarte* ① shpai-ze-kar-te
message *Mitteilung* ① mi-tai-lung
milk *Milch* ① milkh
minute *Minute* ① mi-noo-te
mobile phone *Handy* @ hen-di
money *Geld* @ gelt
month *Monat* @ maw-nat
morning *Morgen* @ mor-gen
mother *Mutter* ① mu-ter
motorcycle *Motorrad* @ maw-tor-raat
motorway *Autobahn* ① ow-to-baan
mouth *Mund* @ munt
music *Musik* ① mu-zeek

N

name *Name* @ naa-me
napkin *Serviette* ① zer-vye-te
nappy *Windel* ① vin-del
near *nahe* naa-e
neck *Hals* @ hals
new *neu* noy
news *Nachrichten* ① pl naakh-rikh-ten

newspaper *Zeitung* ⓕ *tsai*-tung
night *Nacht* ⓕ nakht
no *nein* nain
noisy *laut* lowt
nonsmoking *Nichtraucher* nikht-row-kher
north *Norden* ⓜ nor-den
nose *Nase* ⓕ naa-ze
now *jetzt* yetst
number *Zahl* ⓕ tsaal

O

oil (engine) *Öl* ⓝ eul
old *alt* alt
one-way ticket *einfache Fahrkarte* ⓕ
   ain-fa-khe faar-kar-te
open ⓐ *offen* o-fen
outside *draußen* drow-sen

P

package *Paket* ⓝ pa-keyt
paper *Papier* ⓝ pa-peer
park (car) ∨ *parken* par-ken
passport *(Reise)Pass* ⓜ (rai-ze-)pas
pay *bezahlen* be-tsaa-len
pen *Kugelschreiber* ⓜ koo-gel-shrai-ber
petrol *Benzin* ⓝ ben-tseen
pharmacy *Apotheke* ⓕ a-po-tey-ke
phonecard *Telefonkarte* ⓕ te-le-fawn-kar-te
photo *Foto* ⓝ faw-to
plate *Teller* ⓜ te-ler
police *Polizei* ⓕ po-li-tsai
postcard *Postkarte* ⓕ post-kar-te
post office *Postamt* ⓝ post-amt
pregnant *schwanger* shvang-er
price *Preis* ⓜ prais

Q

quiet *ruhig* roo-ikh

R

rain n *Regen* ⓜ rey-gen
razor *Rasierer* ⓜ ra-zee-rer
receipt *Quittung* ⓕ kvi-tung
red *rot* rawt
refund *Rückzahlung* ⓕ rewk-tsaa-lung
registered mail *Einschreiben* ⓝ ain-shrai-ben

rent ∨ *mieten* mee-ten
repair ∨ *reparieren* re-pa-ree-ren
reservation *Reservierung* ⓕ re-zer-vee-rung
restaurant *Restaurant* ⓝ res-to-raang
return ∨ *zurückkommen* tsu-rewk-ko-men
return ticket *Rückfahrkarte* ⓕ rewk-faar-kar-te
right (direction) *rechts* rekhts
road *Straße* ⓕ shtraa-se
room *Zimmer* ⓝ tsi-mer

S

safe ⓐ *sicher* zi-kher
sanitary napkin *Damenbinden* ⓕ pl daa-men-bin-den
seat *Platz* ⓜ plats
send *senden* zen-den
service station *Tankstelle* ⓕ tangk-shte-le
sex *Sex* ⓜ seks
shampoo *Shampoo* ⓝ sham-poo
share (a dorm) *teilen (mit)* tai-len (mit)
shaving cream *Rasiercreme* ⓕ ra-zeer-kreym
she *sie* zee
sheet (bed) *Bettlaken* ⓝ bet-laa-ken
shirt *Hemd* ⓝ hemt
shoes *Schuhe* ⓜ pl shoo-e
shop n *Geschäft* ⓝ ge-sheft
short *kurz* kurts
shower *Dusche* ⓕ doo-she
single room *Einzelzimmer* ⓝ ain-tsel-tsi-mer
skin *Haut* ⓕ howt
skirt *Rock* ⓜ rok
sleep ∨ *schlafen* shlaa-fen
slowly *langsam* lang-zaam
small *klein* klain
smoke (cigarettes) ∨ *rauchen* row-khen
soap *Seife* ⓕ zai-fe
some *einige* ai-ni-ge
soon *bald* balt
south *Süden* ⓜ zew-den
souvenir shop *Souvenirladen* ⓜ zu-ve-neer-laa-den
speak *sprechen* shpre-khen
spoon *Löffel* ⓜ leu-fel
stamp *Briefmarke* ⓕ breef-mar-ke
stand-by ticket *Standby-Ticket* ⓝ stend-bai-ti-ket
station (train) *Bahnhof* ⓜ baan-hawf
stomach *Magen* ⓜ maa-gen
stop ∨ *anhalten* an-hal-ten
stop (bus) *Bushaltestelle* ⓕ bus-hal-te-shte-le
street *Straße* ⓕ shtraa-se

student *Student/Studentin* ⓜ/ⓕ
  shtu-*dent*/shtu-*den*-tin
sun *Sonne* ⓕ *zo*-ne
sunscreen *Sonnencreme* ⓕ *zo*-nen-kreym
swim v *schwimmen* *shvi*-men
Switzerland *Schweiz* ⓕ shvaits

T

tampons *Tampons* ⓜ pl *tam*-pons
taxi *Taxi* ⓝ *tak*-si
teaspoon *Teelöffel* ⓜ *tey*-leu-fel
teeth *Zähne* ⓝ pl *tsey*-ne
telephone *Telefon* ⓝ te-le-*fawn*
television *Fernseher* ⓜ *fern*-zey-er
temperature (weather) *Temperatur* ⓕ tem-pe-ra-*toor*
tent *Zelt* ⓝ tselt
that (one) *jene* *yey*-ne
they *sie* zee
thirsty *durstig* *durs*-tikh
this (one) *diese* *dee*-ze
throat *Kehle* ⓕ *key*-le
ticket (transport) *Fahrkarte* ⓕ *faar*-kar-te
ticket (sightseeing) *Eintrittskarte* ⓕ *ain*-trits-kar-te
time *Zeit* ⓕ tsait
tired *müde* *mew*-de
tissues *Papiertaschentücher* ⓝ pl
  pa-*peer*-ta-shen-tew-kher
today *heute* *hoy*-te
toilet *Toilette* ⓕ to-a-*le*-te
tomorrow *morgen* *mor*-gen
tonight *heute Abend* *hoy*-te *aa*-bent
toothbrush *Zahnbürste* ⓕ *tsaan*-bewrs-te
toothpaste *Zahnpasta* ⓕ *tsaan*-pas-ta
torch (flashlight) *Taschenlampe* ⓕ *ta*-shen-lam-pe
tour *Tour* ⓕ toor
tourist office *Fremdenverkehrsbüro* ⓝ
  frem-den-fer-kairs-bew-raw
towel *Handtuch* ⓝ *hant*-tookh
train *Zug* ⓜ tsook
translate *übersetzen* ew-ber-*ze*-tsen
travel agency *Reisebüro* ⓝ *rai*-ze-bew-raw
travellers cheque *Reisescheck* ⓜ *rai*-ze-shek
trousers *Hose* ⓕ *haw*-ze
twin beds *zwei Einzelbetten* ⓝ pl tsvai *ain*-tsel-be-ten
tyre *Reifen* ⓜ *rai*-fen

U

underwear *Unterwäsche* ⓕ *un*-ter-ve-she
urgent *dringend* *dring*-ent

V

vacant *frei* frai
vacation *Ferien* pl *fair*-i-en
vegetable *Gemüse* ⓝ ge-*mew*-ze
vegetarian a *vegetarisch* ve-ge-*taa*-rish
visa *Visum* ⓝ *vee*-zum

W

waiter *Kellner/Kellnerin* ⓜ/ⓕ *kel*-ner/*kel*-ne-rin
walk v *gehen* *gey*-en
wallet *Brieftasche* ⓕ *breef*-ta-she
warm a *warm* varm
wash (something) *waschen* *va*-shen
watch *Uhr* ⓕ oor
water *Wasser* ⓝ *va*-ser
we *wir* veer
weekend *Wochenende* ⓝ *vo*-khen-en-de
west *Westen* ⓝ *ves*-ten
wheelchair *Rollstuhl* ⓜ *rol*-shtool
when *wann* van
where *wo* vaw
white *weiß* vais
who *wer* vair
why *warum* va-*rum*
wife *Ehefrau* ⓕ *ey*-e-frow
window *Fenster* ⓝ *fens*-ter
wine *Wein* ⓝ vain
with *mit* mit
without *ohne* *aw*-ne
woman *Frau* ⓕ frow
write *schreiben* *shrai*-ben

Y

yellow *gelb* gelp
yes *ja* yaa
yesterday *gestern* *ges*-tern
you sg inf *du* doo
you sg pol *Sie* zee
you pl *Sie* zee

Greek

greek alphabet				
Α α *al*-pha	Β β *vi*-ta	Γ γ *gha*-ma	Δ δ *dhel*-ta	Ε ε *ep*-si-lon
Ζ ζ *zi*-ta	Η η *i*-ta	Θ θ *thi*-ta	Ι ι *yio*-ta	Κ κ *ka*-pa
Λ λ *lam*-dha	Μ μ mi	Ν ν ni	Ξ ξ ksi	Ο ο *o*-mi-kron
Π π pi	Ρ ρ ro	Σ σ/ς* *sigh*-ma	Τ τ taf	Υ υ *ip*-si-lon
Φ φ fi	Χ χ hi	Ψ ψ psi	Ω ω o-*me*-gha	

* The letter Σ has two forms for the lower case – σ and ς. The second one is used at the end of words.

■ greek

introduction

Aristotle, Plato, Homer, Sappho and Herodotus can't all be wrong in their choice of language – if you've ever come across arcane concepts such as 'democracy', exotic disciplines like 'trigonometry' or a little-known neurosis termed 'the Oedipus complex', then you'll have some inkling of the widespread influence of Greek (Ελληνικά e·li·ni·ka). With just a little Modern Greek under your belt, you'll have a richer understanding of this language's impact on contemporary Western culture.

Modern Greek is a separate branch of the Indo-European language family, with Ancient Greek its only (extinct) relative. The first records of written Ancient Greek date from the 14th to the 12th centuries BC. By the 9th century BC, the Greeks had adapted the Phoenician alphabet to include vowels – the first alphabet to do so – and the script in use today came to its final form some time in the 5th century BC. The Greek script was the foundation for both the Cyrillic and the Latin alphabet.

Although written Greek has been remarkably stable over the millennia, the spoken language has evolved considerably. In the 5th century, the dialect spoken around Athens (known as 'Attic') became the dominant speech as a result of the city-state's cultural and political prestige. Attic gained even greater influence as the medium of administration for the vast empire of Alexander the Great, and remained the official language of the Eastern Roman Empire and the Orthodox Church after the demise of the Hellenistic world. Once the Ottoman Turks took Constantinople in 1453, the Attic dialect lost its official function. In the meantime, the common language, known as Koine (Κοινή ki·ni), continued to evolve, absorbing vocabulary from Turkish, Italian, Albanian and other Balkan languages.

When an independent Greece returned to the world stage in 1832, it needed to choose a national language. Purists advocated a slightly modernised version of Attic known as Καθαρεύουσα ka·tha·re·vu·sa (from the Greek word for 'clean'), which no longer resembled the spoken language. However, Koine had strong support as it was spoken and understood by the majority of Greeks, and in the end it gained official recognition, although it was banned during the military dictatorship (1967–74).

Today, Greek is the official language of Greece and a co-official language of Cyprus, and has over 13 million speakers worldwide. Start your Greek adventure with this chapter – and if you're having one of those days when you're dying to say 'It's all Greek to me!', remember that in your shoes, a Greek speaker would say: Αυτά για μένα είναι Κινέζικα af·ta yia me·na i·ne ki·ne·zi·ka (This is Chinese to me)!

pronunciation

vowel sounds

Greek vowels are pronounced separately even when they're written in sequence, eg ζώο *zo·o* (animal). You'll see though, in the table below, that some letter combinations correspond to a single sound – ουρά (queue) is pronounced u·*ra*. When a word ending in a vowel is followed by another word that starts with the same or a similar vowel sound, one vowel is usually omitted and the two words are pronounced as if they were one – Σε ευχαριστώ se ef·kha·ris·*to* becomes Σ' ευχαριστώ sef·kha·ris·*to* (Thank you). Note that the apostrophe (') is used in written Greek to show that two words are joined together.

symbol	english equivalent	greek example	transliteration
a	father	αλλά	a·*la*
e	bet	πλένομαι	*ple*·no·me
i	hit	πίσω, πόλη, υποφέρω, είδος, οικογένεια, υιός	*pi*·so, *po*·li, i·po·*fe*·ro, *i*·dhos, i·ko·ye·ni·a, i·*os*
ia	nostalgia	ζητιάνος	zi·*tia*·nos
io	ratio	πιο	pio
o	pot	πόνος, πίσω	*po*·nos, *pi*·so
u	put	ουρά	u·*ra*

word stress

Stress can fall on any of the last three syllables. In our pronunciation guides, the stressed syllable is always in italics, but in written Greek, the stressed syllable is always indicated by an accent over the vowel, eg καλά ka·*la* (good). If a vowel is represented by two letters, it's written on the second letter, eg ζητιάνος zi·*tia*·nos (beggar). If the accent is marked on the first of these two letters, they should be read separately, eg Μάιος *ma*·i·os (May). Where two vowels occur together but are not stressed, a diaeresis (¨) is used to indicate that they should be pronounced separately, eg λαϊκός la·i·*kos* (popular).

consonant sounds

Most Greek consonant sounds are also found in English – only the guttural gh and kh might need a bit of practice. Double consonants are only pronounced once – άλλος a-los (other). However, you'll notice that sometimes two Greek letters in combination form one single consonant sound – the combination of the letters μ and π makes the sound b, and the combination of the letters ν and τ makes the sound d.

symbol	english equivalent	greek example	transliteration
b	bed	μπαρ	bar
d	dog	ντομάτα	do-*ma*-ta
dh	that	δεν	dhen
dz	adds	τζάμι	dza-*mí*
f	fat	φως, αυτή	fos, af-*tí*
g	go	γκαρσόν	gar-*son*
gh	guttural sound, between 'goat' and 'loch'	γάτα	*gha*-ta
h	hat	χέρι	*he*-ri
k	kit	καλά	ka-*la*
kh	loch (guttural sound)	χαλί	kha-*lí*
l	let	λάδι	*la*-dhi
m	man	μαζί	ma-*zi*
n	not	ναός	na-*os*
ng	ring	ελέγχω	e-*leng*-kho
p	pet	πάνω	*pa*-no
r	red (trilled)	ράβω	*ra*-vo
s	sun	στυλό	sti-*lo*
t	top	τι	ti
th	thin	θέα	*the*-a
ts	hats	τσέπη	*tse*-pi
v	very	βίζα, αύριο	*vi*-za, *av*-ri-o
y	yes	γέρος	*ye*-ros
z	zero	ζέστη	*ze*-sti

tools

language difficulties

Do you speak English?
Μιλάς Αγγλικά;   mi·*las* ang·gli·*ka*

Do you understand?
Καταλαβαίνεις;   ka·ta·la·*ve*·nis

I understand.
Καταλαβαίνω.   ka·ta·la·*ve*·no

I don't understand.
Δεν καταλαβαίνω.   dhen ka·ta·la·*ve*·no

What does (μώλος) mean?
Τι σημαίνει (μώλος);   ti si·*me*·ni (*mo*·los)

How do you ...?	Πώς ...;	pos ...
pronounce this	προφέρεις αυτό	pro·*fe*·ris af·*to*
write (Madhuri)	γράφουν (Μαδουρή)	*ghra*·foun (ma·dhu·*ri*)

Could you	Θα μπορούσες	tha bo·*ru*·ses
please ...?	παρακαλώ να ...;	pa·ra·ka·*lo* na ...
repeat that	το επαναλάβεις	to e·pa·na·*la*·vis
speak more slowly	μιλάς πιο σιγά	mi·*las* pio si·*gha*
write it down	το γράψεις	to *ghrap*·sis

essentials

Yes.	Ναι.	ne
No.	Όχι.	*o*·hi
Please.	Παρακαλώ.	pa·ra·ka·*lo*
Thank you (very much).	Ευχαριστώ (πολύ).	ef·kha·ri·*sto* (po·*li*)
You're welcome.	Παρακαλώ.	pa·ra·ka·*lo*
Excuse me.	Με συγχωρείτε.	me sing·kho·*ri*·te
Sorry.	Συγνώμη.	si·*ghno*·mi

numbers

0	μυδέν	mi-dhen		15	δεκαπέντε	dhe-ka-pe-de
1	ένας/μία/ένα m/f/n	e-nas/mi-a/e-na		16	δεκαέξι	dhe-ka-ek-si
2	δύο	dhi-o		17	δεκαεφτά	dhe-ka-ef-ta
3	τρεις m&f	tris		18	δεκαοχτώ	dhe-ka-okh-to
	τρία n	tri-a		19	δεκαεννέα	dhe-ka-e-ne-a
4	τέσσερις m&f	te-se-ris		20	είκοσι	i-ko-si
	τέσσερα n	te-se-ra		21	είκοσι	i-ko-si
5	πέντε	pe-de			ένας/μία/	e-nas/mi-a/
6	έξι	ek-si			ένα m/f/n	e-na
7	εφτά	ef-ta		22	είκοσι δύο	i-ko-si dhi-o
8	οχτώ	okh-to		30	τριάντα	tri-a-da
9	εννέα	e-ne-a		40	σαράντα	sa-ra-da
10	δέκα	dhe-ka		50	πενήντα	pe-ni-da
11	έντεκα	e-de-ka		60	εξήντα	ek-si-da
12	δώδεκα	dho-dhe-ka		70	εβδομήντα	ev-dho-mi-da
13	δεκατρείς m&f	dhe-ka-tris		80	ογδόντα	ogh-dho-da
	δεκατρία n	dhe-ka-tri-a		90	ενενήντα	e-ne-ni-da
14	δεκατέσσερις m&f	dhe-ka-te-se-ris		100	εκατό	e-ka-to
	δεκατέσσερα n	dhe-ka-te-se-ra		1000	χίλια	hi-lia

time & dates

What time is it?	Τι ώρα είναι;	ti o-ra i-ne
It's one o'clock.	Είναι (μία) η ώρα.	i-ne (mi-a) i o-ra
It's (10) o'clock.	Είναι (δέκα) η ώρα.	i-ne (dhe-ka) i o-ra
Quarter past (10).	(Δέκα) και τέταρτο.	(dhe-ka) ke te-tar-to
Half past (10).	(Δέκα) και μισή.	(dhe-ka) ke mi-si
Quarter to (10).	(Δέκα) παρά τέταρτο.	(dhe-ka) pa-ra te-tar-to
At what time ...?	Τι ώρα ...;	ti o-ra ...
At ...	Στις ...	stis ...
Monday	Δευτέρα	dhef-te-ra
Tuesday	Τρίτη	tri-ti
Wednesday	Τετάρτη	te-tar-ti
Thursday	Πέμπτη	pem-ti
Friday	Παρασκευή	pa-ra-ske-vi
Saturday	Σάββατο	sa-va-to
Sunday	Κυριακή	ki-ria-ki

January	Ιανουάριος	i·a·nu·*a*·ri·os
February	Φεβρουάριος	fev·ru·*a*·ri·os
March	Μάρτιος	*mar*·ti·os
April	Απρίλιος	a·*pri*·li·os
May	Μάιος	*ma*·i·os
June	Ιούνιος	i·*u*·ni·os
July	Ιούλιος	i·*u*·li·os
August	Αύγουστος	*av*·ghu·stos
September	Σεπτέμβριος	sep·*tem*·vri·os
October	Οκτώβριος	ok·*tov*·ri·os
November	Νοέμβριος	no·*em*·vri·os
December	Δεκέμβριος	dhe·*kem*·vri·os

What date is it today?

Τι ημερομηνία είναι σήμερα; ti i·me·ro·mi·*ni*·a *i*·ne *si*·me·ra

It's (18 October).

Είναι (δεκαοχτώ Οκτωβρίου). *i*·ne (dhe·ka·okh·*to* ok·tov·*ri*·u)

| since (May) | από (το Μάιο) | a·*po* (to *ma*·i·o) |
| until (June) | μέχρι (τον Ιούνιο) | *meh*·ri (ton i·*u*·ni·o) |

yesterday	χτες	khtes
today	σήμερα	*si*·me·ra
tonight	απόψε	a·*pop*·se
tomorrow	αύριο	*av*·ri·o

last ...		
night	την περασμένη νύχτα	tin pe·raz·*me*·ni *nikh*·ta
week	την περασμένη εβδομάδα	tin pe·raz·*me*·ni ev·dho·*ma*·dha
month	τον περασμένο μήνα	ton pe·raz·*me*·no *mi*·na
year	τον περασμένο χρόνο	ton pe·raz·*me*·no *khro*·no

next ...		
week	την επόμενη εβδομάδα	tin e·*po*·me·ni ev·dho·*ma*·dha
month	τον επόμενο μήνα	ton e·*po*·me·no *mi*·na
year	τον επόμενο χρόνο	ton e·*po*·me·no *khro*·no

yesterday/	χτες/	khtes/
tomorrow ...	αύριο το ...	*av*·ri·o to ...
morning	πρωί	pro·*i*
afternoon	απόγευμα	a·*po*·yev·ma
evening	βράδι	*vra*·dhi

weather

What's the weather like?	Πως είναι ο καιρός;	pos *i*-ne o ke-*ros*
It's ...		
cloudy	Είναι συννεφιά.	*i*-ne si-ne-*fia*
cold	Κάνει κρύο.	*ka*-ni *kri*-o
hot	Κάνει πολλή ζέστη.	*ka*-ni po-*li* ze-sti
raining	Βρέχει.	*vre*-hi
snowing	Χιονίζει.	hio-*ni*-zi
sunny	Είναι λιακάδα.	*i*-ne lia-*ka*-dha
warm	Κάνει ζέστη.	*ka*-ni ze-sti
windy	Φυσάει.	fi-*sa*-i
spring	άνοιξη f	*a*-nik-si
summer	καλοκαίρι n	ka-lo-*ke*-ri
autumn	φθινόπωρο n	fthi-*no*-po-ro
winter	χειμώνας m	hi-*mo*-nas

border crossing

I'm here ...	Είμαι εδώ ...	*i*-me e-*dho* ...
in transit	τράνζιτ	*tran*-zit
on business	για δουλειά	yia dhu-*lia*
on holiday	σε διακοπές	se dhia-ko-*pes*
I'm here for (three) ...	Είμαι εδώ για (τρεις) ...	*i*-me e-*dho* yia (tris) ...
days	μέρες	*me*-res
weeks	εβδομάδες	ev-dho-*ma*-dhes
months	μήνες	*mi*-nes

I'm going to (Limassol).
Πηγαίνω στη (Λεμεσό).   pi-*ye*-no sti (le-me-*so*)

I'm staying at the (Xenia).
Μένω στο (Ξενία).   *me*-no sto (kse-*ni*-a)

I have nothing to declare.
Δεν έχω τίποτε να δηλώσω.   dhen e-*kho* *ti*-po-te na dhi-*lo*-so

I have something to declare.
Έχω κάτι να δηλώσω.   e-*kho* *ka*-ti na dhi-*lo*-so

That's (not) mine.
Αυτό (δεν) είναι δικό μου.   af-*to* (dhen) *i*-ne dhi-*ko* mu

transport

tickets & luggage

Where can I buy a ticket?	Που αγοράζω εισιτήριο;	pu a·gho·ra·zo i·si·ti·ri·o
Do I need to book a seat?	Χρειάζεται να κλείσω θέση;	khri·a·ze·te na kli·so the·si
One ... ticket	Ενα εισιτήριο ...	e·na i·si·ti·ri·o ...
to (Patras), please.	για την (Πάτρα), παρακαλώ.	yia tin (pa·tra) pa·ra·ka·lo
one-way	απλό	a·plo
return	με επιστροφή	me e·pi·stro·fi
I'd like to ... my ticket, please.	Θα ήθελα να ... το εισιτήριό μου, παρακαλώ.	tha i·the·la na ... to i·si·ti·ri·o mu pa·ra·ka·lo
cancel	ακυρώσω	a·ki·ro·so
change	αλλάξω	a·lak·so
confirm	επικυρώσω	e·pi·ki·ro·so
I'd like a ... seat.	Θα ήθελα μια θέση ...	tha i·the·la mia the·si ...
nonsmoking	στους μη καπνίζοντες	stus mi kap·ni·zo·des
smoking	στους καπνίζοντες	stus kap·ni·zo·des

How much is it?
Πόσο κάνει;
po·so ka·ni

Is there air conditioning?
Υπάρχει έρκοντίσιον;
i·par·hi e·kon·di·si·on

Is there a toilet?
Υπάρχει τουαλέτα;
i·par·hi tu·a·le·ta

How long does the trip take?
Πόσο διαρκεί το ταξίδι;
po·so dhi·ar·ki to tak·si·dhi

Is it a direct route?
Πηγαίνει κατ'ευθείαν;
pi·ye·ni ka·tef·thi·an

Where can I find a luggage locker?
Που μπορώ να βρω τη φύλαξη
αντικειμένων;
pu bo·ro na vro ti fi·lak·si
a·di·ki·me·non

My luggage has been ...	Οι αποσκευές μου έχουν ...	i a·pos·ke·ves mu e·khun ...
damaged	πάθει ζημιά	pa·thi zi·mia
lost	χαθεί	kha·thi
stolen	κλαπεί	kla·pi

getting around

Where does flight (10) arrive/depart?
Που προσγειώνεται/
απογειώνεται η πτήση (δέκα);
pu pros·yi·o·ne·te/
a·po·yi·o·ne·te i pti·si (dhe·ka)

Where's (the) ...?	Που είναι ...;	pu i·ne ...
arrivals hall	η αίθουσα των αφίξεων	i e·thu·sa tona·fik·se·on
departures hall	η αίθουσα των	i e·thu·sa ton
	ανα χωρήσεων	a·na kho·ri·se·on
duty-free shop	τα αφορολόγητα	ta a·fo·ro·lo·yi·ta
gate (nine)	η θύρα (εννέα)	i thi·ra (e·ne·a)

Is this the ...	Είναι αυτό το ...	i·ne af·to to ...
to (Athens)?	για την (Αθήνα);	yia tin (a·thi·na)
boat	πλοίο	pli·o
bus	λεωφορείο	le·o·fo·ri·o
ferry	φέρυ	fe·ri
plane	αεροπλάνο	a·e·ro·pla·no
train	τρένο	tre·no

What time's the	Πότε είναι το ...	po·te i·ne to ...
... (bus)?	(λεωφορείο);	(le·o·fo·ri·o)
first	πρώτο	pro·to
last	τελευταίο	te·lef·te·o
next	επόμενο	e·po·me·no

At what time does it arrive/depart?
Τι ώρα φτάνει/φεύγει;
ti o·ra fta·ni/fev·yi

What time does it get to (Thessaloniki)?
Τι ώρα φτάνει στη (Θεσσαλονίκη);
ti o·ra fta·ni sti (the·sa·lo·ni·ki)

How long will it be delayed?
Πόση ώρα θα καθυστερήσει;
po·si o·ra tha ka·thi·ste·ri·si

What station is this?
Ποιος σταθμός είναι αυτός;
pios stath·mos i·ne af·tos

What stop is this?
Ποια στάση είναι αυτή;
pia sta·si i·ne af·ti

What's the next station?
Ποιος είναι ο επόμενος σταθμός;
pios i·ne o e·po·me·nos stath·mos

What's the next stop?
Ποια είναι η επόμενη στάση;
pia i·ne i e·po·me·ni sta·si

Does it stop at (Iraklio)?
Σταματάει στο (Ηράκλειο);
sta·ma·*ta*·i sto (i·*ra*·kli·o)

Please tell me when we get to (Thessaloniki).
Παρακαλώ πέστε μου όταν
φτάσουμε στη (Θεσσαλονίκη).
pa·ra·ka·*lo* pe·ste mu o·tan
fta·su·me sti (the·sa·lo·*ni*·ki)

How long do we stop here?
Πόση ώρα θα σταματήσουμε εδώ;
po·si o·ra tha sta·ma·*ti*·su·me e·*dho*

Is this seat available?
Είναι αυτή η θέση ελεύθερη;
i·ne af·*ti* i *the*·si e·*lef*·the·ri

That's my seat.
Αυτή η θέση είναι δική μου.
af·*ti* i *the*·si i·ne dhi·*ki* mu

I'd like a taxi ... Θα ήθελα ένα ταξί ... tha i·*the*·la e·na tak·*si* ...
at (9am) στις (εννέα stis (e·*ne*·a
 πριν το μεσημέρι) prin to me·si·*me*·ri)
now τώρα *to*·ra
tomorrow αύριο *av*·ri·o

Is this taxi available?
Είναι αυτό το ταξί ελεύθερο;
i·ne af·*to* to tak·*si* e·*lef*·the·ro

How much is it to ...?
Πόσο κάνει για ...;
po·so *ka*·ni yia ...

Please put the meter on.
Παρακαλώ βάλε το ταξίμετρο.
pa·ra·ka·*lo va*·le to tak·*si*·me·tro

Please take me to (this address).
Παρακαλώ πάρε με σε
(αυτή τη διεύθυνση).
pa·ra·ka·*lo pa*·re me se
(af·*ti* ti dhi·*ef*·thin·si)

Please ... Παρακαλώ ... pa·ra·ka·*lo* ...
slow down πήγαινε πιο σιγά *pi*·ye·ne pio si·*gha*
stop here σταμάτα εδώ sta·*ma*·ta e·*dho*
wait here περίμενε εδώ pe·*ri*·me·ne e·*dho*

car, motorbike & bicycle hire

I'd like to Θα ήθελα να tha i·*the*·la na
hire a ... ενοικιάσω ένα ... e·ni·ki·*a*·so e·na ...
bicycle ποδήλατο po·*dhi*·la·to
car αυτοκίνητο af·to·*ki*·ni·to
motorbike μοτοσικλέτα mo·to·si·*kle*·ta

with ...	με ...	me ...
a driver	οδηγό	o·dhi·gho
air conditioning	έρκοντίσιον	e·kon·di·si·on

How much for ... hire?	Πόσο νοικάζεται την ...;	po·so ni·kia·ze·te tin ...
hourly	ώρα	o·ra
daily	ημέρα	i·me·ra
weekly	εβδομάδα	ev·dho·ma·dha

air	αέρας m	a·e·ras
oil	λάδι αυτοκινήτου n	la·dhi af·to·ki·ni·tu
petrol	βενζίνα f	ven·zi·na
tyres	λάστιχα n	la·sti·kha

I need a mechanic.	Χρειάζομαι μηχανικό.	khri·a·zo·me mi·kha·ni·ko
I've run out of petrol.	Μου τελείωσε η βενζίνα.	mu te·li·o·se i ven·zi·na
I have a flat tyre.	Μ'έπιασε λάστιχο.	me·pia·se la·sti·kho

directions

Where's the ...?	Που είναι ...;	pu i·ne ...
bank	η τράπεζα	i tra·pe·za
city centre	το κέντρο της πόλης	to ke·dro tis po·lis
hotel	το ξενοδοχείο	to kse·no·dho·hi·o
market	η αγορά	i a·gho·ra
police station	ο αστυνομικός σταθμός	o a·sti·no·mi·kos stath·mos
post office	το ταχυδρομείο	to ta·hi·dhro·mi·o
public toilet	τα δημόσια αποχωρητήρια	ta dhi·mo·si·a a·po·kho·ri·ti·ria
tourist office	το τουριστικό γραφείο	to tu·ri·sti·ko ghra·fi·o

Is this the road to (Lamia)?
Είναι αυτός ο δρόμος για (τη Λαμία);   i·ne af·tos o dhro·mos yia (ti la·mi·a)

Can you show me (on the map)?
Μπορείς να μου δείξεις (στο χάρτη);   bo·ris na mu dhik·sis (sto khar·ti)

What's the address?
Ποια είναι η διεύθυνση;   pia i·ne i dhi·ef·thin·si

How far is it?
Πόσο μακριά είναι;   po·so ma·kri·a i·ne

How do I get there?
Πως πηγαίνω εκεί;   pos pi·ye·no e·ki

Turn ...	Στρίψε ...	strip·se ...
at the corner	στη γωνία	sti gho·ni·a
at the traffic lights	στα φανάρια	sta fa·na·ria
left/right	αριστερά/δεξιά	a·ris·te·ra/dhek·si·a

It's ...	Είναι ...	i·ne ...
behind ...	πίσω ...	pi·so ...
far away	μακριά	ma·kri·a
here	εδώ	e·dho
in front of ...	μπροστά από ...	bros·ta a·po ...
near ...	κοντά ...	ko·da ...
next to ...	δίπλα από ...	dhip·la a·po ...
on the corner	στη γωνία	sti gho·ni·a
opposite ...	απέναντι ...	a·pe·na·di ...
straight ahead	κατ'ευθείαν	ka·tef·thi·an
there	εκεί	e·ki

by bus	με λεωφορείο	me le·o·fo·ri·o
by boat	με πλοίο	me pli·o
by taxi	με ταξί	me tak·si
by train	με τρένο	me tre·no
on foot	με πόδια	me po·dhia

north	βόρια	vo·ri·a
south	νότια	no·ti·a
east	ανατολικά	a·na·to·li·ka
west	δυτικά	dhi·ti·ka

signs

Είσοδος/Έξοδος	i·so·dhos/ek·so·dhos	Entrance/Exit
Ανοικτός/Κλειστός	a·nik·tos/kli·stos	Open/Closed
Ελεύθερα Δωμάτια	e·lef·the·ra dho·ma·ti·a	Rooms Available
Πλήρες	pli·res	No Vacancies
Πληροφορίες	pli·ro·fo·ri·es	Information
Αστυνομικός Σταθμός	a·sti·no·mi·kos stath·mos	Police Station
Απαγορεύεται	a·pa·gho·re·ve·te	Prohibited
Τουαλέτες	tu·a·le·tes	Toilets
Ανδρών	an·dhron	Men
Γυναικών	yi·ne·kon	Women
Ζεστό/Κρύο	zes·to/khri·o	Hot/Cold

accommodation

finding accommodation

Where's a ...?	Που είναι ...;	pu *i*·ne ...
camping ground	χώρος για κάμπινγκ	*kho*·ros yia *kam*·ping
guesthouse	ξενώνας	kse·*no*·nas
hotel	ξενοδοχείο	kse·no·dho·*hi*·o
youth hostel	γιουθ χόστελ	yiuth *kho*·stel
Can you recommend	Μπορείτε να συστήσετε	bo·*ri*·te na si·*sti*·se·te
somewhere ...?	κάπου ...;	*ka*·pu ...
cheap	φτηνό	fti·*no*
good	καλό	ka·*lo*
nearby	κοντινό	ko·di·*no*

I'd like to book a room, please.
Θα ήθελα να κλείσω ένα
δωμάτιο, παρακαλώ.
tha *i*·the·la na *kli*·so *e*·na
dho·*ma*·ti·o pa·ra·ka·*lo*

I have a reservation.
Έχω κάνει κάποια κράτηση.
e·kho *ka*·ni *ka*·pia *kra*·ti·si

My name's ...
Με λένε ...
me *le*·ne ...

Do you have a ... room?	Έχετε ένα ... δωμάτιο;	*e*·he·te *e*·na ... dho·*ma*·ti·o
single	μονό	mo·*no*
double	διπλό	dhi·*plo*
twin	δίκλινο	*dhi*·kli·no
How much is it per ...?	Πόσο είναι για κάθε ...;	*po*·so *i*·ne yia *ka*·the ...
night	νύχτα	*nikh*·ta
person	άτομο	*a*·to·mo
Can I pay ...?	Μπορώ να πληρώσω με ...;	bo·*ro* na pli·*ro*·so me ...
by credit card	πιστωτική κάρτα	pi·sto·ti·*ki kar*·ta
with a travellers	ταξιδιωτική	tak·si·dhio·ti·*ki*
cheque	επιταγή	e·pi·ta·*yi*

For (three) nights/weeks.

Για (τρεις) νύχτες/εβδομάδες.   yia (tris) *nikh*·tes/ev·dho·*ma*·dhes

From (2 July) to (6 July).

Από (τις δύο Ιουλίου)   a·*po* (tis *dhi*·o i·u·*li*·u)

μέχρι (τις έξι Ιουλίου).   *me*·khri (tis *ek*·si i·u·*li*·u)

Can I see it?

Μπορώ να το δω;   bo·*ro* na to dho

Am I allowed to camp here?

Μπορώ να κατασκηνώσω εδώ;   bo·*ro* na ka·ta·ski·*no*·so e·*dho*

Where can I find a camp site?

Που μπορώ να βρω το   pu bo·*ro* na vro to

χώρο του κάμπινγκ;   *kho*·ro tu *kam*·ping

requests & queries

When/Where is breakfast served?

Πότε/Που σερβίρεται το πρόγευμα;   *po*·te/pu ser·*vi*·re·te to *pro*·yev·ma

Please wake me at (seven).

Παρακαλώ ξύπνησέ με στις (εφτά).   pa·ra·ka·*lo ksip*·ni·se me stis (ef·*ta*)

Could I have my key, please?

Μπορώ να έχω το κλειδί μου   bo·*ro* na *e*·kho to kli·*dhi* mu

παρακαλώ;   pa·ra·ka·*lo*

Can I get another (blanket)?

Μπορώ να έχω και άλλη (κουβέρτα);   bo·*ro* na *e*·kho ke *a*·li (ku·*ver*·ta)

This (towel) isn't clean.

Αυτή (η πετσέτα) δεν είναι καθαρό.   af·*ti* (i pet·*se*·ta) dhen *i*·ne ka·tha·*ri*

Is there a/an ...?	Έχετε ...;	*e*·he·te ...
elevator	ασανσέρ	a·san·*ser*
safe	χρηματοκιβώτιο	khri·ma·to·ki·*vo*·ti·o

The room is too ...	Είναι πάρα πολύ ...	*i*·ne *pa*·ra po·*li* ...
expensive	ακριβό	a·kri·*vo*
noisy	θορυβώδες	tho·ri·*vo*·dhes
small	μικρό	mi·*kro*

The ... doesn't work.	... δεν λειτουργεί.	... dhen li·tur·*ghi*
air conditioning	Το έρκοντίσιον	to er·kon·*di*·si·on
fan	Ο ανεμιστήρας	o a·ne·mi·*sti*·ras
toilet	Η τουαλέτα	i tu·a·*le*·ta

checking out

What time is checkout?
Τι ώρα είναι η αναχώρηση; ti *o*·ra *i*·ne i a·na·*kho*·ri·si

Can I leave my luggage here?
Μπορώ να αφήσω τις βαλίτσες μου εδώ; bo·*ro* na a·*fi*·so tis va·*lit*·ses mu e·*dho*

Could I have my ..., please?	Μπορώ να έχω ... μου παρακλώ;	bo·*ro* na e·kho ... mu pa·ra·ka·*lo*
deposit	την προκαταβολή	tin pro·ka·ta·vo·*li*
passport	το διαβατήριό	to dhia·va·*ti*·rio
valuables	τα κοσμήματά	ta koz·*mi*·ma·ta

communications & banking

the internet

Where's the local Internet cafe?
Που είναι το τοπικό
καφενείο με διαδίκτυο; pu *i*·ne to to·pi·*ko*
ka·fe·*ni*·o me dhi·a·*dhik*·ti·o

How much is it per hour?
Πόσο κοστίζει κάθε ώρα; *po*·so ko·*sti*·zi *ka*·the *o*·ra

I'd like to ...	Θα ήθελα να ...	tha *i*·the·la na ...
check my email	ελέγξω την ηλεκτρονική αλληλογραφία μου	e·*leng*·so tin i·lek·tro·ni·*ki* a·li·lo·ghra·*fi*·a mu
get Internet access	έχω πρόσβαση στο διαδίκτυο	e·kho *pros*·va·si sto dhi·a·*dhik*·ti·o
use a printer	χρησιμοποιήσω έναν εκτυπωτή	khri·si·mo·pi·*i*·so e·nan ek·ti·po·*ti*
use a scanner	χρησιμοποιήσω ένα σκάνερ	khri·si·mo·pi·*i*·so e·na *ska*·ner

mobile/cell phone

I'd like a ...	Θα ήθελα ...	tha *i*·the·la ...
mobile/cell phone for hire	να νοικιάσω ένα κινητό τηλέφωνο	na ni·*kia*·so e·na ki·ni·*to* ti·*le*·fo·no
SIM card for	μια κάρτα SIM	mia *kar*·ta sim
your network	για το δίκτυό σας	yia to *dhik*·tio sas
What are the rates?	Ποιες είναι οι τιμές;	pies *i*·ne i ti·*mes*

telephone

What's your phone number?
Τι αριθμό τηλεφώνου έχεις;
ti a·*rith*·mo ti·le·*fo*·nu e·his

The number is ...
Ο αριθμός είναι ...
o a·*rith*·mos *i*·ne ...

Where's the nearest public phone?
Που είναι το πιο κοντινό
δημόσιο τηλέφωνο;
pu *i*·ne to pio ko·di·*no*
dhi·*mo*·si·o ti·*le*·fo·no

I'd like to buy a phonecard.
Θέλω να αγοράσω μια
τηλεφωνική κάρτα.
the·lo na a·gho·*ra*·so mia
ti·le·fo·ni·*ki kar*·ta

I want to ...	Θέλω να ...	*the*·lo na ...
call (Singapore)	τηλεφωνήσω (στη Σιγγαπούρη)	ti·le·fo·*ni*·so (sti sing·ga·*pu*·ri)
make a local call	κάνω ένα τοπικό τηλέφωνο	*ka*·no e·na to·pi·*ko* ti·*le*·fo·no
reverse the charges	αντιστρέψω τα έξοδα	a·di·*strep*·so ta *ek*·so·dha

How much does ... cost?	Πόσο κοστίζει ...;	*po*·so ko·*sti*·zi ...
a (three)- minute call	ένα τηλεφώνημα (τριών) λεπτών	e·na ti·le·*fo*·ni·ma (tri·*on*) lep·*ton*
each extra minute	κάθε έξτρα λεπτό	*ka*·the *eks*·tra lep·*to*

It's (40c) per (30) seconds.
(Σαράντα λεπτα) για (τριάντα)
δευτερόλεπτα.
(sa·*ra*·da lep·*ta*) yia (tri·*a*·da)
dhef·te·*ro*·lep·ta

post office

I want to send a ...	Θέλω να στείλω ...	the-lo na stí-lo ...
fax	ένα φαξ	e-na faks
letter	ένα γράμμα	e-na ghra-ma
parcel	ένα δέμα	e-na dhe-ma
postcard	μια κάρτα	mia kar-ta

I want to buy a/an ...	Θέλω να αγοράσω ένα ...	the-lo na a-gho-ra-so e-na ...
envelope	φάκελο	fa-ke-lo
stamp	γραμματόσημο	ghra-ma-to-si-mo

Please send it (to Australia) by ...	Παρακαλώ στείλτε το ... (στην Αυστραλία).	pa-ra-ka-lo stil-te to ... (stin af-stra-li-a)
airmail	αεροπορικώς	a-e-ro-po-ri-kos
express mail	εξπρές	eks-pres
registered mail	συστημένο	si-sti-me-no
surface mail	δια ξηράς	dhia ksi-ras

Is there any mail for me?
Υπάρχουν γράμματα για μένα;   i-par-khun ghra-ma-ta yia me-na

bank

Where's a/an ...?	Που είναι ...;	pu i-ne ...
ATM	μια αυτόματη μηχανή χρημάτων	mia af-to-ma-ti mi-kha-ni khri-ma-ton
foreign exchange office	ένα γραφείο αλλαγής χρημάτων	e-na ghra-fi-o a-la-yis khri-ma-ton

I'd like to ...	Θα ήθελα να ...	tha i-the-la na ...
Where can I ...?	Που μπορώ να ...;	pu bo-ro na ...
arrange a transfer	τακτοποιήσω μια μεταβίβαση	tak-to-pi-i-so mia me-ta-vi-va-si
cash a cheque	εξαργυρώσω μια επιταγή	ek-sar-yi-ro-so mia e-pi-ta-yi
change a travellers cheque	αλλάξω μια ταξιδιωτική επιταγή	a-lak-so mia tak-si-dhio-ti-ki e-pi-ta-yi
change money	αλλάξω χρήματα	a-lak-so khri-ma-ta
get a cash advance	κάνω μια ανάληψη σε μετρητά	ka-no mia a-na-lip-si se me-tri-ta
withdraw money	αποσύρω χρήματα	a-po-si-ro khri-ma-ta

What's the ...?	Ποια είναι ... ;	pia *i*·ne ...
charge for that	η χρέωση για αυτό	i *khre*·o·si yia af·*to*
exchange rate	η τιμή συναλλάγματος	i ti·*mi* si·na·*lagh*·ma·tos

It's (12) ...	Κάνει (δώδεκα) ...	*ka*·ni (*dho*·dhe·ka) ...
Cyprus pounds	λίρες Κύπρου	*li*·res *ki*·pru
euros	ευρώ	ev·*ro*

It's free.
Είναι δωρεάν. *i*·ne dho·re·*an*

What time does the bank open?
Τι ώρα ανοίγει η τράπεζα; ti o·ra a·*ni*·yi i *tra*·pe·za

Has my money arrived yet?
Έχουν φτάσει τα χρήματά μου; *e*·khun *fta*·si ta *khri*·ma·*ta* mu

sightseeing

getting in

What time does it open/close?
Τι ώρα ανοίγει/κλείνει; ti o·ra a·*ni*·yi/*kli*·ni

What's the admission charge?
Πόσο κοστίζει η είσοδος; *po*·so ko·*sti*·zi i *i*·so·dhos

Is there a discount for students/children?		
Υπάρχει έκπτωση για		i·*par*·hi *ek*·pto·si yia
σπουδαστές/παιδιά;		spu·dha·*stes*/pe·*dhia*

I'd like a ...	Θα ήθελα ...	tha *i*·the·la ...
catalogue	ένα κατάλογο	*e*·na ka·*ta*·lo·gho
guide	έναν οδηγό	*e*·nan o·dhi·*gho*
local map	ένα τοπικό χάρτη	*e*·na to·pi·*ko* *khar*·ti

I'd like to see ...	Θα ήθελα να δω ...	tha *i*·the·la na dho ...
What's that?	Τι είναι εκείνο;	ti *i*·ne e·*ki*·no
Can I take a photo?	Μπορώ να πάρω μια	bo·*ro* na *pa*·ro mia
	φωτογραφία;	fo·to·ghra·*fi*·a

tours

When's the next tour?
Πότε είναι η επόμενη περιήγηση;   *po*·te *i*·ne i e·*po*·me·ni pe·ri·*i*·yi·si

When's the next ...? Πότε είναι το επόμενο ...;   *po*·te *i*·ne to e·*po*·me·no ...
boat trip ταξίδι με τη βάρκα   tak·*si*·dhi me ti *var*·ka
day trip ημερήσιο ταξίδι   i·me·*ri*·si·o tak·*si*·dhi

Is ... included? Συμπεριλαμβάνεται ...;   si·be·ri·lam·*va*·ne·te ...
accommodation κατάλυμα   ka·*ta*·li·ma
the admission charge τιμή εισόδου   ti·*mi i*·so·dhu
food φαγητό   fa·yi·*to*
transport μεταφορά   me·ta·fo·*ra*

How long is the tour?
Πόση ώρα διαρκεί η περιήγηση;   *po*·si *o*·ra dhi·ar·*ki* i pe·ri·*i*·yi·si

What time should we be back?
Τι ώρα πρέπει να επιστρέψουμε;   ti *o*·ra *pre*·pi na e·pi·*strep*·su·me

sightseeing

amphitheatre	αμφιθέατρο n	am·fi·*the*·a·tro
castle	κάστρο n	*ka*·stro
cathedral	μητρόπολη f	mi·*tro*·po·li
church	εκκλησία f	e·kli·*si*·a
fresco	φρέσκο n	*fres*·ko
labyrinth	λαβύρινθος m	la·*vi*·rin·thos
main square	κεντρική πλατεία f	ken·dhri·*ki* pla·*ti*·a
monastery	μοναστήρι n	mo·na·*sti*·ri
monument	μνημείο n	mni·*mi*·o
mosaic	μωσαϊκό n	mo·sa·i·*ko*
museum	μουσείο n	mu·*si*·o
old city	αρχαία πόλι	ar·*khe*·a *po*·li
palace	παλάτι n	pa·*la*·ti
ruins	ερρίπια n pl	e·*ri*·pi·a
sculpture	γλυπτική f	ghlip·ti·*ki*
stadium	στάδιο n	*sta*·dhi·o
statue	άγαλμα n	*a*·ghal·ma
temple	ναός m	na·*os*

shopping

enquiries

Where's a ...?	Που είναι ...;	pu *i*·ne ...
bank	μια τράπεζα	mia *tra*·pe·za
bookshop	ένα βιβλιοπωλείο	e·na viv·li·o·po·*li*·o
camera shop	ένα κατάστημα φωτογραφικών ειδών	e·na ka·*ta*·sti·ma fo·to·ghra·fi·*kon* i·*dhon*
department store	ένα κατάστημα	e·na ka·*ta*·sti·ma
grocery store	ένα οπωροπωλείο	e·na o·po·ro·po·*li*·o
kiosk	ένα περίπτερο	e·na pe·*rip*·te·ro
market	μια αγορά	mia a·gho·*ra*
newsagency	το εφημεριδοπωλείο	to e·fi·me·ri·dho·po·*li*·o
supermarket	ένα σούπερμάρκετ	e·na *su*·per·*mar*·ket

Where can I buy (a padlock)?
Που μπορώ να αγοράσω
(μια κλειδαριά);
pu bo·*ro* na a·gho·*ra*·so
(mia kli·dha·*ria*)

I'd like to buy ...
Θα ήθελα να αγοράσω ...
tha *i*·the·la na a·gho·*ra*·so ...

Can I look at it?
Μπορώ να το κοιτάξω;
bo·*ro* na to ki·*tak*·so

Do you have any others?
Έχετε άλλα;
e·he·te *a*·la

Does it have a guarantee?
Έχει εγγύηση;
e·hi e·*gi*·i·si

Can I have it sent overseas?
Μπορείς να το στείλεις
στο εξωτερικό;
bo·*ris* na to *sti*·lis
sto ek·so·te·ri·*ko*

Can I have ... repaired?
Μπορώ να επισκευάσω εδώ ...;
bo·*ro* na e·pi·ske·*va*·so e·*dho* ...

Can I have a bag, please?
Μπορώ να έχω μια τσάντα, παρακαλώ;
bo·*ro* na e·kho mia *tsa*·da pa·ra·ka·*lo*

It's faulty.
Είναι ελαττωματικό.
i·ne e·la·to·ma·ti·*ko*

I'd like ..., please.	Θα ήθελα ..., παρακαλώ.	tha *i*·the·la ... pa·ra·ka·*lo*
a refund	επιστροφή χρημάτων	e·pi·stro·*fi* khri·*ma*·ton
to return this	να επιστρέψω αυτό	na e·pi·*strep*·so af·*to*

paying

How much is it?
Πόσο κάνει; *po·so ka·ni*

Can you write down the price?
Μπορείς να γράψεις την τιμή; bo·*ris* na *ghrap*·sis tin ti·*mi*

That's too expensive.
Είναι πάρα πολύ ακριβό. *i*·ne *pa*·ra po·*li* a·kri·*vo*

Can you lower the price?
Μπορείς να κατεβάσεις την τιμή; bo·*ris* na ka·te·*va*·sis tin ti·*mi*

I'll give you (five) euros.
Θα σου δώσω (πέντε) ευρώ. tha su *dho*·so (*pe*·de) ev·*ro*

I'll give you (five) Cyprus pounds.
Θα σου δώσω (πέντε) λίρες Κύπρου. tha su *dho*·so (*pe*·de) *li*·res *ki*·pru

There's a mistake in the bill.
Υπάρχει κάποιο λάθος i·*par*·hi *ka*·pio *la*·thos
στο λογαριασμό. sto lo·gha·riaz·*mo*

Do you accept ...?	Δέχεστε ...;	*dhe*·he·ste ...
credit cards	πιστωτικές κάρτες	pi·sto·ti·*kes kar*·tes
debit cards	χρεωτικές κάρτες	khre·o·ti·*kes kar*·tes
travellers cheques	ταξιδιωτικές	tak·si·dhio·ti·*kes*
	επιταγές	e·pi·ta·*yes*

I'd like my change, please.
Θα ήθελα τα ρέστα μου, παρακαλώ. tha *i*·the·la ta *re*·sta mu pa·ra·ka·*lo*

Can I have a receipt, please?
Μπορώ να έχω μια bo·*ro* na e·kho mia
απόδειξη, παρακαλώ; a·*po*·dhik·si pa·ra·ka·*lo*

clothes & shoes

Can I try it on?	Μπορώ να το προβάρω;	bo·*ro* na to pro·*va*·ro
My size is (40).	Το νούμερό μου είναι	to *nu*·me·ro mu *i*·ne
	(σαράντα).	(sa·*ra*·da)
It doesn't fit.	Δε μου κάνει.	dhe mu *ka*·ni
small	μικρό	mi·*kro*
medium	μεσαίο	me·*se*·o
large	μεγάλο	me·*gha*·lo

books & music

I'd like a ...	Θα ήθελα ...	tha *i*·the·la ...
newspaper	μια εφημερίδα	mia e·fi·me·*ri*·dha
(in English)	(στα Αγγλικά)	(sta ang·gli·*ka*)
pen	ένα στυλό	e·na sti·*lo*

Is there an English-language bookshop?
Υπάρχει ένα βιβλιοπωλείο   i·*par*·hi e·na viv·li·o·po·*li*·o
Αγγλικής γλώσσας;   ang·gli·*kis* ghlo·sas

I'm looking for something by (Anna Vissi).
Ψάχνω για κάτι (της Αννας Βίσση).   *psakh*·no yia ka·ti (tis *a*·nas *vi*·si)

Can I listen to this?
Μπορώ να το ακούσω;   bo·*ro* na to a·*ku*·so

photography

Can you ...?	Μπορείς να ...;	bo·*ris* na ...
develop this	εμφανίσεις αυτό	em·fa·*ni*·sis af·*to*
film	το φιλμ	to film
load my film	βάλεις το φιλμ	*va*·lis to film
	στη μηχανή μου	sti mi·kha·*ni* mu
transfer photos	μεταφέρεις	me·ta·*fe*·ris
from my	φωτογραφίες από	fo·to·ghra·*fi*·es a·*po*
camera to CD	την φωτογραφική	ti fo·to·ghra·fi·*ki*
	μου μηχανή στο CD	mu mi·kha·*ni* sto si·*di*

I need a/an ... film	Χρειάζομαι φιλμ ...	khri·*a*·zo·me film ...
for this camera.	για αυτή τη μηχανή.	yia af·*ti* ti mi·kha·*ni*
APS	APS	e·i·pi·es
B&W	μαυρόασπρο	mav·*ro*·a·spro
colour	έγχρωμο	*eng*·khro·mo
slide	σλάιντ	*sla*·id
(200) speed	ταχύτητα (διακοσίων)	ta·*hi*·ti·ta (dhia·ko·*si*·on)

When will it be ready?
Πότε θα είναι έτοιμο;   *po*·te tha *i*·ne *e*·ti·mo

meeting people

greetings, goodbyes & introductions

Hello/Hi.	Γεια σου.	yia su
Good night.	Καληνύχτα.	ka·li·*nikh*·ta
Goodbye/Bye.	Αντίο.	a·*di*·o
Mr	Κύριε	*ki*·ri·e
Mrs	Κυρία	ki·*ri*·a
Miss	Δις	dhes·pi·*nis*
How are you?	Τι κάνεις;	ti *ka*·nis
Fine. And you?	Καλά. Εσύ;	ka·*la* e·*si*
What's your name?	Πως σε λένε;	pos se *le*·ne
My name is ...	Με λένε ...	me *le*·ne ...
I'm pleased to meet you.	Χαίρω πολύ.	*he*·ro po·*li*
This is my ...	Από εδώ ... μου.	a·*po* e·*dho* ... mu
boyfriend	ο φίλος	o *fi*·los
brother	ο αδερφός	o a·dher·*fos*
daughter	η κόρη	i *ko*·ri
father	ο πατέρας	o pa·*te*·ras
friend	ο φίλος/η φίλη m/f	o *fi*·los/i *fi*·li
girlfriend	η φιλενάδα	i fi·le·*na*·dha
husband	ο σύζυγός	o *si*·zi·ghos
mother	η μητέρα	i mi·*te*·ra
partner (intimate)	ο/η σύντροφός m/f	o/i si·dro·*fos*
sister	η αδερφή	i a·dher·*fi*
son	ο γιος	o yios
wife	η σύζυγός	i *si*·zi·ghos
Here's my ...	Εδώ είναι ... μου.	e·*dho* i·ne ... mu
What's your ...?	Ποιο είναι ... σου;	pio *i*·ne ... su
email address	το ημέιλ	to i·*me*·il
fax number	το φαξ	to faks
phone number	το τηλέφωνό	to ti·*le*·fo·no

Here's my address.
Εδώ είναι η διεύθυνσή μου.   e·*dho* i·ne i dhi·*ef*·thin·si mu

What's your address?
Ποια είναι η δική σου διεύθυνση;   pia *i*·ne i dhi·*ki* su dhi·*ef*·thin·si

occupations

What's your occupation?	Τι δουλειά κάνεις;	ti dhu-*lia ka*-nis
I'm a/an ...	Είμαι/Δουλεύω ...	*i*-me/dhou-*lev*-o ...
businessperson	επιχειρηματίας m&f	e-pi-hi-ri-ma-*ti*-as
farmer	γεωργός m&f	ye-or-*ghos*
manual worker	εργάτης/εργάτρια m/f	er-*gha*-tis/er-*gha*-tri-a
office worker	σε γραφείο	se ghra-*phi*-o
scientist	επιστήμονας m&f	e-pi-*sti*-mo-nas
tradesperson	έμπορος m&f	*e*-bo-ros

background

Where are you from?	Από που είσαι;	a-*po* pu *i*-se
I'm from ...	Είμαι από ...	*i*-me a-*po* ...
Australia	την Αυστραλία	tin af-stra-*li*-a
Canada	τον Καναδά	ton ka-na-*dha*
England	την Αγγλία	tin ang-*gli*-a
New Zealand	την Νέα Ζηλανδία	tin *ne*-a zi-lan-*dhi*-a
the USA	την Αμερική	tin A-me-ri-*ki*
Are you married?	Είσαι παντρεμένος/ παντρεμένη; m/f	*i*-se pa-dre-*me*-nos/ pa-dre-*me*-ni
I'm married.	Είμαι παντρεμένος/ παντρεμένη. m/f	*i*-me pa-dre-*me*-nos/ pa-dre-*me*-ni
I'm single.	Είμαι ανύπαντρος/ ανύπαντρη. m/f	*i*-me a-*ni*-pa-dros/ a-*ni*-pa-dri

age

How old ...?	Πόσο χρονών ...;	*po*-so khro-*non* ...
are you	είσαι	*i*-se
is your daughter	είναι η κόρη σου	*i*-ne i *ko*-ri su
is your son	είναι ο γιος σου	*i*-ne o yios su
I'm ... years old.	Είμαι ... χρονών.	*i*-me ... khro-*non*
He/She is ... years old.	Αυτός/αυτή είναι ... χρονών.	af-*tos*/af-*ti i*-ne ... khro-*non*

feelings

I'm (not) ...	(Δεν) Είμαι ...	(dhen) *i*-me ...
Are you ...?	Είσαι ...;	*i*-se ...
happy	ευτυχισμένος m	ef-ti-hiz-*me*-nos
	ευτυχισμένη f	ef-ti-hiz-*me*-ni
hot	ζεστός/ζεστή m/f	ze-*stos*/ze-*sti*
hungry	πεινασμένος m	pi-naz-*me*-nos
	πεινασμένη f	pi-naz-*me*-ni
sad	στενοχωρημένος m	ste-no-kho-ri-*me*-nos
	στενοχωρημένη f	ste-no-kho-ri-*me*-ni
thirsty	διψασμένος m	dhip-saz-*me*-nos
	διψασμένη f	dhip-saz-*me*-ni

entertainment

going out

Where can I find ...?	Που μπορώ να βρω ...;	pu bo-*ro* na vro ...
clubs	κλαμπ	klab
gay venues	Χώρους συνάντησης	*kho*-rus si-*na*-di-sis
	για γκέη	yia *ge*-i
pubs	μπυραρίες	bi-ra-*ri*-es
I feel like going	Έχω όρεξη να	*e*-kho *o*-rek-si na
to a/the ...	πάω σε ...	*pa*-o se ...
concert	κονσέρτο	kon-*ser*-to
the movies	φιλμ	film
party	πάρτυ	*par*-ti
restaurant	εστιατόριο	e-sti-a-*to*-ri-o
theatre	θέατρο	*the*-a-tro

interests

Do you like ...?	Σου αρέσει ...;	su a-*re*-si ...
I (don't) like ...	(Δεν) μου αρέσει ...	(dhen) mu a-*re*-si ...
cooking	η μαγειρική	i ma-yi-ri-*ki*
reading	το διάβασμα	to *dhia*-vaz-ma

Do you like ...?	Σου αρέσουν ...;	su a·re·sun ...
I (don't) like ...	(Δεν) μου αρέσουν τα ...	(dhen) mu a·re·sun ta ...
art	καλλιτεχνικά	ka·li·tekh·ni·ka
movies	φιλμ	film
nightclubs	νάιτ κλαμπ	na·it klab
sport	σπορ	spor

Do you like to ...?	Σου αρέσει να ...;	sou a·re·si na ...
dance	χορεύεις	kho·re·vis
go to concerts	πηγαίνεις σε κονσέρτα	pi·ye·nis se kon·ser·ta
listen to music	ακούς μουσική	a·kus mu·si·ki

food & drink

finding a place to eat

Can you recommend a ...?	Μπορείς να συστήσεις ...;	bo·ris na si·sti·sis ...
bar	ένα μπαρ	e·na bar
café	μία καφετέρια	mi·a ka·fe·te·ria
restaurant	ένα εστιατόριο	e·stia·to·ri·o

I'd like ..., please.	Θα ήθελα ..., παρακαλώ.	tha i·thela ... pa·ra·ka·lo
a table for (five)	ένα τραπέζι για (πέντε)	e·na tra·pe·zi yia (pe·de)
the (non)smoking section	στους (μη) καπνίζοντες	stus (mi) kap·ni·zo·des

ordering food

breakfast	πρόγευμα n	pro·yev·ma
lunch	γεύμα n	yev·ma
dinner	δείπνο n	dhip·no
snack	μεζεδάκι n	me·ze·dha·ki

What would you recommend?
Τι θα συνιστούσες;   ti tha si·ni·stu·ses

I'd like (a/the) ..., please.	θα ήθελα ..., παρακαλώ.	tha *i*·the·la ... pa·ra·ka·*lo*
bill	το λογαριασμό	to lo·gha·riaz·*mo*
drink list	τον κατάλογο	ton ka·*ta*·lo·gho
	με τα ποτά	me ta po·*ta*
menu	το μενού	to me·*nu*
that dish	εκείνο το φαγητό	e·*ki*·no to fa·yi·*to*

drinks

(cup of) coffee ...	(ένα φλυτζάνι) καφέ ...	(e·na fli·*dza*·ni) ka·*fe* ...
(cup of) tea ...	(ένα φλυτζάνι) τσάι ...	(e·na fli·*dza*·ni) *tsa*·i ...
with milk	με γάλα	me *gha*·la
without sugar	χωρίς ζάχαρη	kho·*ris* za·kha·ri
(orange) juice	χυμός (πορτοκάλι) m	hi·*mos* (por·to·*ka*·li)
soft drink	αναψυκτικό n	a·nap·sik·ti·*ko*
... water	... νερό	... ne·*ro*
hot	ζεστό	ze·*sto*
(sparkling) mineral	(γαζόζα) μεταλλικό	(gha·zo·za) me·ta·li·*ko*

in the bar

I'll have ...	θα πάρω ...	tha *pa*·ro ...
I'll buy you a drink.	θα σε κεράσω εγώ.	tha se ke·*ra*·so e·*gho*
What would you like?	Τι θα ήθελες;	ti tha *i*·the·les
Cheers!	Εις υγείαν!	is i·*yi*·an
brandy	μπράντι n	*bran*·di
champagne	σαμπάνια f	sam·*pa*·nia
a glass/bottle of	ένα ποτήρι/μπουκάλι	e·na po·*ti*·ri/bu·*ka*·li
beer	μπύρα	*bi*·ra
ouzo	ούζο n	*u*·zo
a shot of (whisky)	ένα (ουίσκι)	e·na (u·*i*·ski)
a glass/bottle of ... wine	ένα ποτήρι/μπουκάλι ... κρασί	e·na po·*ti*·ri/bu·*ka*·li ... kra·*si*
red	κόκκινο	*ko*·ki·no
sparkling	σαμπάνια	sam·*pa*·nia
white	άσπρο	*a*·spro

self-catering

What's the local speciality?
Ποιες είναι οι τοπικές λιχουδιές; pies *i*·ne i to·pi·*kes* li·khu·*dhies*

What's that?
Τι είναι εκείνο; ti *i*·ne e·*ki*·no

How much is (a kilo of cheese)?
Πόσο κάνει (ένα κιλό τυρί); *po*·so *ka*·ni (*e*·na ki·*lo* ti·*ri*)

I'd like ...	Θα ήθελα ...	tha *i*·the·la ...
(100) grams	(εκατό) γραμμάρια	(e·ka·*to*) ghra·*ma*·ria
(two) kilos	(δύο) κιλά	(*dhi*·o) ki·*la*
(three) pieces	(τρία) κομμάτια	(*tri*·a) ko·*ma*·tia
(six) slices	(έξι) φέτες	(*ek*·si) *fe*·tes

Less.	Πιο λίγο.	pio *li*·gho
Enough.	Αρκετά.	ar·ke·*ta*
More.	Πιο πολύ.	pio po·*li*

special diets & allergies

Is there a vegetarian restaurant near here?
Υπάρχει ένα εστιατόριο χορτοφάγων i·*par*·hi *e*·na e·sti·a·*to*·ri·o hor·to·*fa*·ghon
εδώ κοντά; e·*dho* ko·*da*

Do you have vegetarian food?
Έχετε φαγητό για χορτοφάγους; *e*·he·te fa·yi·*to* yia khor·to·*fa*·ghus

I don't eat ...	Δεν τρώγω ...	dhen *tro*·gho ...
butter	βούτυρο	*vu*·ti·ro
eggs	αβγά	av·*gha*
meat stock	ζουμί από κρέας	zu·*mi* a·*po* *kre*·as

I'm allergic to ...	Είμαι αλλεργικός/	*i*·me a·ler·yi·*kos*
	αλλεργική ... m/f	a·ler·yi·*ki* ...
dairy produce	στα γαλακτικά	sta gha·lak·ti·*ka*
gluten	στη γλουτένη	sti ghlu·*te*·ni
MSG	στο MSG	sto em es dzi
nuts	στους ξηρούς καρπούς	stus ksi·*rus* kar·*pus*
seafood	στα θαλασσινά	sta tha·la·si·*na*

emergencies

basics

Help!	Βοήθεια!	vo·i·thia
Stop!	Σταμάτα!	sta·ma·ta
Go away!	Φύγε!	fi·ye
Thief!	Κλέφτης!	klef·tis
Fire!	Φωτιά!	fo·tia
Watch out!	Πρόσεχε!	pro·se·he
Call ...!	Κάλεσε ...!	ka·le·se ...
an ambulance	το ασθενοφόρο	to as·the·no·fo·ro
the doctor	ένα γιατρό	e·na yia·tro
the police	την αστυνομία	tin a·sti·no·mi·a

It's an emergency.
Είναι μια έκτακτη ανάγκη. — i·ne mia ek·tak·ti a·na·gi

Could you help me, please?
Μπορείς να βοηθήσεις, παρακαλώ; — bo·ris na vo·i·thi·sis pa·ra·ka·lo

Can I make a phone call?
Μπορώ να κάνω ένα τηλεφώνημα; — bo·ro na ka·no e·na ti·le·fo·ni·ma

I'm lost.
Εχω χαθεί. — e·kho kha·thi

Where are the toilets?
Που είναι η τουαλέτα; — pu i·ne i tu·a·le·ta

police

Where's the police station?
Που είναι ο αστυνομικός σταθμός; — pu i·ne o a·sti·no·mi·kos stath·mos

I want to report an offence.
Θέλω να αναφέρω μια παρανομία. — the·lo na a·na·fe·ro mia pa·ra·no·mi·a

I have insurance.
Εχω ασφάλεια. — e·kho as·fa·li·a

I've been ...	Με έχουν ...	me e·khun ...
assaulted	κακοποιήσει	ka·ko·pi·i·si
raped	βιάσει	vi·a·si
robbed	ληστέψει	li·step·si

I've lost my ...	Εχασα ... μου.	e·kha·sa ... mu
My ... was/were stolen.	Εκλεψαν ... μου.	e·klep·san ... mu
backpack	το σακίδιό	to sa·ki·dhio
bags	τις βαλίτσες	tis va·lits·es
credit card	την πιστωτική κάρτα	tin pi·sto·ti·ki kar·ta
handbag	την τσάντα	tin tsa·da
jewellery	τα κοσμήματά	ta koz·mi·ma·ta
money	τα χρήματά	ta khri·ma·ta
passport	το διαβατήριό	to dhia·va·ti·rio
travellers cheques	τις ταξιδιωτικές επιταγές	tis tak·si·dhio·ti·kes e·pi·ta·yes
wallet	το πορτοφόλι	to por·to·fo·li
I want to contact my ...	Θέλω να έρθω σε επαφή με ... μου.	the·lo na er·tho se e·pa·fi me ... mu
consulate	τηνπρεσβεία	tin prez·vi·a
embassy	το προξενείο	to pro·ksee·ni·o

health

medical needs

Where's the nearest ...?	Που είναι ο πιο κοντινός ...;	pu i·ne o pio ko·di·nos ...
dentist	οδοντίατρος	o·dho·di·a·tros
doctor	γιατρός	yia·tros
Where's the nearest ...?	Που είναι το πιο κοντινό...;	pu i·ne to pio ko·di·no ...
hospital	νοσοκομείο	no·so·ko·mi·o
(night) pharmacy	(νυχτερινό) φαρμακείο	(nikh·te·ri·no) far·ma·ki·o

I need a doctor (who speaks English).
Χρειάζομαι ένα γιατρό (που να μιλάει αγγλικά).
khri·a·zo·me e·na yia·tro (pu na mi·la·i ang·gli·ka)

Could I see a female doctor?
Μπορώ να δω μια γυναίκα γιατρό;
bo·ro na dho mia yi·ne·ka yia·tro

I've run out of my medication.
Μου έχουν τελειώσει τα φάρμακά μου.
mu e·khun te·li·o·si ta far·ma·ka mu

symptoms, conditions & allergies

I'm sick.	Είμαι άρρωστος/άρρωστη m/f	i·me a·ro·stos/a·ro·sti
It hurts here.	Πονάει εδώ.	po·na·i e·dho
I have (a/an) ...	Εχω ...	e·kho ...

asthma	άσθμα n	as·thma
bronchitis	βροχίτιδα f	vro·hi·ti·dha
constipation	δυσκοιλιότητα f	dhis·ki·li·o·ti·ta
cough	βήχα m	vi·kha
diarrhoea	διάρροια f	dhi·a·ri·a
fever	πυρετό m	pi·re·to
headache	πονοκέφαλο m	po·no·ke·fa·lo
heart condition	καρδιακή	kar·dhi·a·ki
	κατάσταση f	ka·ta·sta·si
nausea	ναυτία f	naf·ti·a
pain	πόνο m	po·no
sore throat	πονόλαιμο m	po·no·le·mo
toothache	πονόδοντο	po·no·dho·do

| I'm allergic to ... | Είμαι αλλεργικός/ | i·me a·ler·yi·kos |
| | αλλεργική ... m/f | a·ler·yi·ki ... |

antibiotics	στα αντιβιωτικά	sta a·di·vi·o·ti·ka
anti-inflammatories	στα αντιφλεγμονώδη	sta a·di·flegh·mo·no·dhi
aspirin	στην ασπιρίνη	stin as·pi·ri·ni
bees	στις μέλισσες	stis me·li·ses
codeine	στην κωδεΐνη	stin ko·dhe·i·ni
penicillin	στην πενικιλλίνη	stin pe·ni·ki·li·ni

antiseptic	αντισηπτικό n	a·di·sip·ti·ko
bandage	επίδεσμος m	e·pi·dhez·mos
condoms	προφυλακτικά n	pro·fi·lak·ti·ka
contraceptives	αντισυλληπτικά n pl	a·di·si·lip·ti·ka
diarrhoea medicine	φάρμακο διάροιας	far·ma·ko dhiar·ghias
insect repellent	εντομοαπωθητικό n	e·do·mo·a·po·thi·ti·ko
laxatives	καθαρτικό n	ka·thar·ti·ko
painkillers	παυσίπονα	paf·si·po·na
rehydration salts	ενυδρωτικά άλατα n pl	en·i·dhro·ti·ka a·la·ta
sleeping tablets	υπνωτικά χάπια n pl	ip·no·ti·ka kha·pia

english–greek dictionary

Greek nouns in this dictionary have their gender indicated by ⓜ (masculine), ① (feminine) or ⓝ (neuter). If it's a plural noun you'll also see pl. Adjectives are given in the masculine form only. Words are also marked as n (noun), a (adjective), v (verb), sg (singular), pl (plural), inf (informal) and pol (polite) where necessary.

A

accident ατύχημα ⓝ a-ti-hi-ma
accommodation κατάλυμα ⓝ ka-ta-li-ma
adaptor μετασχηματιστής ⓜ me-ta-shi-ma-ti-stis
address διεύθυνση ① dhi-ef-thin-si
aeroplane αεροπλάνο ⓝ a-e-ro-pla-no
after μετά me-ta
air-conditioned με έρκοντίσιον mer-kon-di-si-on
airport αεροδρόμιο ⓝ a-e-ro-dhro-mi-o
alcohol αλκοόλ ⓝ al-ko-ol
all όλοι ⓟ o-li
allergy αλλεργία ① a-ler-yi-a
ambulance νοσοκομειακό ⓝ no-so-ko-mi-a-ko
and και ke
ankle αστράγαλος ⓜ a-stra-gha-los
arm χέρι ⓝ he-ri
ashtray σταχτοθήκη ① stakh-to-thi-ki
ATM αυτόματη μηχανή χρημάτων ①
af-to-ma-ti mi-kha-ni khri-ma-ton

B

baby μωρό ⓝ mo-ro
back (body) πλάτη ① pla-ti
backpack σακίδιο ⓝ sa-ki-dhi-o
bad κακός ka-kos
bag σάκος ⓜ sa-kos
baggage claim παραλαβή αποσκευών ①
pa-ra-la-vi a-po-ske-von
bank τράπεζα ① tra-pe-za
bar μπαρ ⓝ bar
bathroom μπάνιο ⓝ ba-nio
battery μπαταρία ① ba-ta-ri-a
beautiful όμορφος o-mor-fos
bed κρεβάτι ⓝ kre-va-ti
beer μπύρα ① bi-ra
before πριν prin
behind πίσω pi-so
bicycle ποδήλατο ⓝ po-dhi-la-to
big μεγάλος me-gha-los

bill λογαριασμός ⓜ lo-gha-riaz-mos
black a μαύρος mav-ros
blanket κουβέρτα ① ku-ver-ta
blood group ομάδα αίματος ① o-ma-dha e-ma-tos
blue a μπλε ble
boat βάρκα ① var-ka
book (make a reservation) v κλείσω θέση kli-so the-si
bottle μπουκάλι ⓝ bu-ka-li
bottle opener ανοιχτήρι ⓝ a-nikh-ti-ri
boy αγόρι ⓝ a-gho-ri
brakes (car) φρένα ⓝ pl fre-na
breakfast πρωινό ⓝ pro-i-no
broken (faulty) ελαττωματικός e-la-to-ma-ti-kos
bus λεωφορείο ⓝ le-o-fo-ri-o
business επιχείρηση ① e-pi-hi-ri-si
buy αγοράζω a-gho-ra-zo

C

café καφετέρια ① ka-fe-te-ria
camera φωτογραφική μηχανή ①
fo-to-ghra-fi-ki mi-kha-ni
camp site χώρος για κάμπινγκ ⓜ kho-ros yia kam-ping
cancel ακυρώνω a-ki-ro-no
can opener ανοιχτήρι ⓝ a-nikh-ti-ri
car αυτοκίνητο ⓝ af-to-ki-ni-to
cash μετρητά ⓝ pl me-tri-ta
cash (a cheque) v εξαργυρώνω ek-sar-yi-ro-no
cell phone κινητό ⓝ ki-ni-to
centre κέντρο ⓝ ke-dro
change (money) v αλλάζω a-la-zo
cheap a φτηνός fti-nos
check (bill) λογαριασμός ⓜ lo-gha-riaz-mos
check-in ρεσεψιόν ① re-sep-sion
chest στήθος ⓝ sti-thos
child παιδί ⓝ pe-dhi
cigarette τσιγάρο ⓝ tsi-gha-ro
city πόλι ① po-li
clean a καθαρός ka-tha-ros
closed κλεισμένος kliz-me-nos
coffee καφές ⓜ ka-fes
coins κέρματα ⓝ pl ker-ma-ta
cold a κρυωμένος kri-o-me-nos

collect call κλήση με αντιστροφή της επιβάρυνσης ⓕ
kli-si me a-dis-tro-*fi* tis e-pi-*va*-rin-sis
come έρχομαι er-kho-me
computer κομπιούτερ ⓝ kom-*piu*-ter
condom προφυλακτικό ⓝ pro-fi-lak-ti-*ko*
contact lenses φακοί επαφής ⓜ pl fa-*ki* e-pa-*fis*
cook v μαγειρεύω ma-yi-*re*-vo
cost τιμή ⓕ ti-*mi*
credit card πιστωτική κάρτα ⓕ pi-sto-ti-*ki kar*-ta
cup φλιτζάνι ⓝ fli-*dza*-ni
currency exchange τιμή συναλλάγματος ⓕ
ti-*mi* si-na-*lagh*-ma-tos
customs (immigration) τελωνείο ⓝ te-lo-*ni*-o
Cypriot (nationality) Κύπριος/Κύπρια ⓜ/ⓕ
ki-pri-os/*ki*-pri-a
Cypriot a κυπριακός/κυπριακή ⓜ/ⓕ
ki-pri-a-*kos*/ki-pri-a-*ki*
Cyprus Κύπρος ⓕ *ki*-pros

D

dangerous επικίνδυνος e-pi-*kin*-dhi-nos
date (time) ημερομηνία ⓕ i-me-ro-*mi-ni*-a
day ημέρα ⓕ i-*me*-ra
delay καθυστέρηση ⓕ ka-thi-*ste*-ri-si
dentist οδοντίατρος ⓜ & ⓕ o-dho-*di*-a-tros
depart αναχωρώ a-na-kho-*ro*
diaper πάνα ⓕ *pa*-na
dictionary λεξικό ⓝ lek-si-*ko*
dinner δείπνο ⓝ *dhip*-no
direct άμεσος *a*-me-sos
dirty βρώμικος *vro*-mi-kos
disabled ανάπηρος a-*na*-pi-ros
discount έκπτωση ⓕ *ek*-pto-si
doctor γιατρός ⓜ & ⓕ yia-*tros*
double bed διπλό κρεβάτι ⓝ dhi-*plo* kre-*va*-ti
double room διπλό δωμάτιο ⓝ dhi-*plo* dho-*ma*-ti-o
drink ποτό ⓝ po-*to*
drive v οδηγώ o-dhi-*gho*
drivers licence άδεια οδήγησης ⓕ *a*-dhi-a o-*dhi*-yi-sis
drugs (illicit) ναρκωτικό ⓝ nar-ko-ti-*ko*
dummy (pacifier) πιπίλα ⓕ pi-*pi*-la

E

ear αφτί ⓝ af-*ti*
east ανατολή ⓕ a-na-to-*li*
eat τρώγω *tro*-gho
economy class τουριστική θέση ⓕ tu-ri-sti-*ki the*-si
electricity ηλεκτρισμός ⓜ i-lek-triz-*mos*

elevator ασανσέρ ⓝ a-san-*ser*
email ημέιλ ⓝ *i*-me-il
embassy πρεσβεία ⓕ pre-*zvi*-a
emergency έκτακτη ανάγκη ⓕ *ek*-tak-ti a-*na*-gi
English (language) Αγγλικά ⓝ ang-gli-*ka*
entrance είσοδος ⓕ *i*-so-dhos
evening βράδι ⓝ *vra*-dhi
exchange rate τιμή συναλλάγματος ⓕ
ti-*mi* si-na-*lagh*-ma-tos
exit έξοδος ⓕ *ek*-so-dhos
expensive ακριβός a-kri-*vos*
express mail επείγον ταχυδρομείο ⓝ
e-*pi*-ghon ta-hi-dhro-*mi*-o
eye μάτι ⓝ *ma*-ti

F

far μακριά ma-kri-*a*
fast γρήγορος *ghri*-gho-ros
father πατέρας ⓜ pa-*te*-ras
film (camera) φιλμ ⓝ film
finger δάκτυλο ⓝ *dhak*-ti-lo
first-aid kit κυτίο πρώτων βοηθειών ⓝ
ki-*ti*-o pro-ton vo-i-thi-*on*
first class πρώτη τάξη ⓕ *pro*-ti *tak*-si
fish ψάρι ⓝ *psa*-ri
food φαγητό ⓝ fa-yi-*to*
foot πόδι ⓝ *po*-dhi
fork πιρούνι ⓝ pi-*ru*-ni
free (of charge) δωρεάν dho-re-*an*
friend φίλος/φίλη ⓜ/ⓕ *fi*-los/*fi*-li
fruit φρούτα ⓝ pl *fru*-ta
full γεμάτο ye-*ma*-to
funny αστείος a-*sti*-os

G

gift δώρο ⓝ *dho*-ro
girl κορίτσι ⓝ ko-*rit*-si
glass (drinking) ποτήρι ⓝ po-*ti*-ri
glasses γιαλιά ⓝ yia-*lia*
go πηγαίνω pi-*ye*-no
good καλός ka-*los*
Greece Ελλάδα ⓕ e-*la*-dha
Greek (language) Ελληνικά ⓝ e-li-ni-*ka*
Greek (nationality) Έλληνες ⓜ pl e-*li*-nes
green πράσινος *pra*-si-nos
guide οδηγός ⓜ & ⓕ o-dhi-*ghos*

H

half μισό ⓝ mi-*so*
hand χέρι ⓝ *he*-ri
handbag τσάντα ⓕ *tsa*-da
happy ευτυχισμένος ef-ti-hiz-*me*-nos
have έχω e-kho
he αυτός ⓜ af-*tos*
head κεφάλι ⓝ ke-*fa*-li
heart καρδιά ⓕ kar-*dhia*
heat ζέστη ⓕ ze-sti
heavy βαρύς va-*ris*
help ν βοηθώ vo-i-*tho*
here εδώ e-*dho*
high ψηλός psi-*los*
highway δημόσιος δρόμος ⓜ dhi-mo-si-os *dhro*-mos
hike ν πεζοπορώ pe-zo-po-*ro*
holiday διακοπές ⓕ dhia-ko-*pes*
homosexual ομοφυλόφιλος ⓜ o-mo-fi-lo-fi-los
hospital νοσοκομείο ⓝ no-so-ko-*mi*-o
hot ζεστός ze-*stos*
hotel ξενοδοχείο ⓝ kse-no-dho-*hi*-o
hungry πεινασμένος pi-naz-*me*-nos
husband σύζυγος ⓜ *si*-zi-ghos

I

I εγώ e-*gho*
identification (card) ταυτότητα ⓕ taf-*to*-ti-ta
ill άρρωστος *a*-ro-stos
important σπουδαίος spu-*dhe*-os
included συμπεριλαμβανομένου si-be-ri-lam-va-no-*me*-nu
injury πληγή ⓕ pli-*yi*
insurance ασφάλεια as-*fa*-li-a
Internet διαδίκτυο ⓝ dhi-*a-dhik*-ti-o
interpreter διερμηνέας ⓜ&ⓕ dhi-er-mi-*ne*-as

J

jewellery κοσμήματα ⓝ pl koz-*mi*-ma-ta
job δουλειά ⓕ *dhu*-lia

K

key κλειδί ⓝ kli-*dhi*
kilogram χιλιόγραμμο ⓝ hi-*lio*-gra-mo
kitchen κουζίνα ⓕ ku-*zi*-na
knife μαχαίρι ⓝ ma-*he*-ri

L

laundry (place) πλυντήριο ⓝ pli-*di*-ri-o
lawyer δικηγόρος ⓜ&ⓕ dhi-ki-gho-ros
left (direction) αριστερός ⓜ a-ri-ste-*ros*
left-luggage office γραφείο φύλαξη αποσκευών ⓝ gra-*fi*-o fi-lak-si a-po-ske-*von*
leg πόδι ⓝ po-dhi
lesbian λεσβία ⓕ les-*vi*-a
less λιγότερο li-gho-te-ro
letter (mail) γράμμα ⓝ *ghra*-ma
lift (elevator) ασανσέρ ⓝ a-san-*ser*
light φως ⓝ fos
like ν μου αρέσει mu a-*re*-si
lock κλειδαριά ⓕ kli-dha-*ria*
long μακρύς ma-*kris*
lost χαμένος kha-*me*-nos
lost-property office γραφείο απωλεσθέντων αντικειμένων ⓝ gra-*fi*-o a-po-les-the-don a-di-ki-*me*-non
love ν αγαπώ a-gha-po
luggage αποσκευές ⓕ pl a-po-ske-*ves*
lunch μεσημεριανό φαγητό ⓝ me-si-me-ria-no fa-yi-to

M

mail (letters) αλληλογραφία ⓕ a-li-lo-ghra-*fi*-a
mail (postal system) ταχυδρομείο ⓝ ta-hi-dhro-*mi*-o
man άντρας ⓜ *a*-dras
map χάρτης ⓜ *khar*-tis
market αγορά ⓕ a-gho-*ra*
matches σπίρτα ⓝ pl *spir*-ta
meat κρέας ⓝ *kre*-as
medicine φάρμακο ⓝ *far*-ma-ko
menu μενού ⓝ me-*nu*
message μήνυμα ⓝ *mi*-ni-ma
milk γάλα ⓝ *gha*-la
minute λεπτό ⓝ lep-*to*
mobile phone κινητό ⓝ ki-ni-*to*
money χρήματα ⓝ *khri*-ma-ta
month μήνας ⓜ *mi*-nas
morning πρωί ⓝ pro-*i*
mother μητέρα ⓕ mi-*te*-ra
motorcycle μοτοσυκλέτα ⓕ mo-to-si-*kle*-ta
motorway αυτοκινητόδρομος ⓜ af-to-ki-ni-*to*-dhro-mos
mouth στόμα ⓝ *sto*-ma
music μουσική ⓕ mu-si-*ki*

N

name όνομα ⓝ *o*-no-ma
napkin πετσετάκι ⓝ pet-se-*ta*-ki
nappy πάνα ⓕ *pa*-na

near κοντά ko-*da*

neck λαιμός ⓜ le-*mos*

new νέος *ne*-os

news νέα ⓝ *ne*-a

newspaper εφημερίδα ⓕ e-fi-me-*ri*-dha

night νύχτα ⓕ *nikh*-ta

no όχι *o*-hi

noisy a θορυβώδης thor-i-*vo*-dhis

nonsmoking μη καπνίζοντες mi kap-*ni*-zo-des

north βοράς ⓜ vo-*ras*

nose μύτη ⓕ *mi*-ti

now τώρα *to*-ra

number αριθμός ⓜ a-rith-*mos*

O

oil (engine) λάδι αυτοκινήτου ⓝ *la*-dhi af-to-ki-*ni*-tu

old παλιός pa-*lios*

one-way ticket απλό εισιτήριο ⓝ a-*plo* i-si-*ti*-ri-o

open a ανοιχτός a-nikh-*tos*

outside έξω *ek*-so

P

package πακέτο ⓝ pa-*ke*-to

paper χαρτί ⓝ khar-*ti*

park (car) v παρκάρω par-*ka*-ro

passport διαβατήριο ⓝ dhia-va-*ti*-ri-o

pay v πληρώνω pli-*ro*-no

pen στυλό ⓝ sti-*lo*

petrol πετρέλαιο ⓝ pe-*tre*-le-o

pharmacy φαρμακείο ⓝ far-ma-*ki*-o

phonecard τηλεκάρτα ⓕ ti-le-*kar*-ta

photo φωτογραφία ⓕ fo-to-gra-*fi*-a

plate πιάτο ⓝ *pia*-to

police αστυνομία ⓕ a-sti-no-*mi*-a

postcard κάρτα ⓕ *kar*-ta

post office ταχυδρομείο ⓝ ta-hi-dhro-*mi*-o

pregnant έγκυος *e*-gi-os

price τιμή ⓕ ti-*mi*

Q

quiet ήσυχος *i*-si-khos

R

rain βροχή vro-*hi*

razor ξυριστική μηχανή ⓕ ksi-ri-sti-*ki* mi-kha-*ni*

receipt απόδειξη ⓕ a-*po*-dhik-si

red κόκκινο *ko*-ki-no

refund n επιστροφή χρημάτων ⓕ e-pi-stro-*fi* khri-*ma*-ton

registered mail συστημένο sis-ti-*me*-no

rent v ενοικιάζω e-ni-ki-*a*-zo

repair v επισκευάζω e-pi-ske-*va*-zo

reservation κράτηση ⓕ *kra*-ti-si

restaurant εστιατόριο ⓝ e-sti-a-*to*-ri-o

return v επιστρέφω e-pi-*stre*-fo

return ticket εισιτήριο μετ' επιστροφής ⓝ i-si-*ti*-ri-o me-te-pis-tro-*fis*

right (direction) δεξιός dhek-si-*os*

road δρόμος ⓜ *dhro*-mos

room δωμάτιο ⓝ dho-*ma*-ti-o

S

safe a ασφαλής as-fa-*lis*

sanitary napkin πετσετάκι υγείας ⓝ pet-se-*ta*-ki i-*yi*-as

seat θέση ⓕ *the*-si

send στέλνω *stel*-no

service station βενζινάδικο ⓝ ven-zi-*na*-dhi-ko

sex σεξ ⓝ seks

shampoo σαμπουάν ⓝ sam-pu-*an*

share (a dorm) μοιράζομαι mi-*ra*-zo-me

shaving cream κρέμα ξυρίσματος ⓕ *kre*-ma ksi-riz-ma-tos

she αυτή af-*ti*

sheet (bed) σεντόνι ⓝ se-*do*-ni

shirt πουκάμισο ⓝ pu-*ka*-mi-so

shoes παπούτσια ⓝ pl pa-*put*-si-a

shop μαγαζί ⓝ ma-gha-*zi*

short κοντός ko-*dos*

shower ντους ⓝ duz

single room μονό δωμάτιο ⓝ mo-*no* dho-*ma*-tio

skin δέρμα ⓝ *dher*-ma

skirt φούστα ⓕ *fu*-sta

sleep v κοιμάμαι ki-*ma*-me

slowly αργά ar-*gha*

small μικρός mi-*kros*

smoke (cigarettes) v καπνίζω kap-*ni*-zo

soap σαπούνι ⓝ sa-*pu*-ni

some μερικοί me-ri-*ki*

soon σύντομα *si*-do-ma

south νότος ⓜ *no*-tos

souvenir shop κατάστημα για σουβενίρ ⓝ ka-*ta*-sti-ma yia su-ve-*nir*

speak μιλάω mi-*la*-o

spoon κουτάλι ⓝ ku-*ta*-li

stamp γραμματόσημο ⓝ ghra-ma-*to*-si-mo

stand-by ticket εισιτήριο σταντ μπάι ⓝ i-si-*ti*-ri-o stand *ba*-i

station (train) σταθμός ⓜ stath-*mos*

stomach στομάχι ⓝ sto-*ma*-hi

stop v σταματάω sta-ma-*ta*-o

stop (bus) στάση ⓕ *sta*-si

street οδός ⓕ o-*dhos*

student σπουδαστής/σπουδάστρια ⓜ/ⓕ spu-dha-*stis*/spu-*dha*-stri-a

sun ήλιος ⓜ *i*-li-os

sunscreen αντηλιακό ⓝ a-di-i-li-a-*ko*

swim v κολυμπώ ko-li-*bo*

T

tampon ταμπόν ⓝ ta-*bon*

taxi ταξί ⓝ tak-*si*

teaspoon κουτάλι τσαγιού ⓝ ku-*ta*-li tsa-*yiu*

teeth δόντια ⓝ *dho*-dia

telephone τηλέφωνο ⓝ ti-*le*-fo-no

television τηλεόραση ⓕ ti-le-*o*-ra-si

temperature (weather) θερμοκρασία ⓕ ther-mo-kra-*si*-a

tent τέντα ⓕ *te*-da

that (one) εκείνο e-*ki*-no

they αυτοί af-*ti*

thirsty διψασμένος dhip-saz-*me*-nos

this (one) αυτός ⓜ af-*tos*

throat λαιμός ⓜ le-*mos*

ticket εισιτήριο ⓝ i-si-*ti*-ri-o

time ώρα ⓕ *o*-ra

tired κουρασμένος ku-raz-*me*-nos

tissues χαρτομάντηλα ⓝ pl khar-to-*ma*-di-la

today σήμερα *si*-me-ra

toilet τουαλέτα ⓕ tu-a-*le*-ta

tomorrow αύριο *av*-ri-o

tonight απόψε a-*pop*-se

toothbrush οδοντόβουρτσα ⓕ o-dho-*do*-vur-tsa

toothpaste οδοντόπαστα ⓕ o-dho-*do*-pa-sta

torch (flashlight) φακός ⓜ fa-*kos*

tour περιήγηση ⓕ pe-*ri*-i-yi-si

tourist office τουριστικό γραφείο ⓝ tu-ri-sti-*ko* ghra-*fi*-o

towel πετσέτα ⓕ pet-*se*-ta

train τρένο ⓝ *tre*-no

translate v μεταφράζω me-ta-*fra*-zo

travel agency ταξιδιωτικό γραφείο ⓝ tak-si-dhi-o-ti-*ko* ghra-*fi*-o

travellers cheque ταξιδιωτική επιταγή ⓕ tak-si-dhi-o-ti-*ki* e-pi-ta-*yi*

trousers παντελόνι ⓝ pa-de-*lo*-ni

twin beds δίκλινο δωμάτιο ⓝ *dhi*-kli-no dho-*ma*-ti-o

tyre λάστιχο ⓝ *la*-sti-kho

U

underwear εσώρουχα ⓝ pl e-*so*-ru-kha

urgent επείγον e-*pi*-ghon

V

vacant ελεύθερος e-*lef*-the-ros

vacation διακοπές ⓕ dhia-ko-*pes*

vegetable λαχανικά ⓝ pl la-kha-ni-*ka*

vegetarian n χορτοφάγος ⓜ&ⓕ khor-to-*fa*-ghos

visa βίζα ⓕ *vi*-za

W

waiter γκαρσόν ⓝ gar-*son*

walk v περπατάω per-pa-*ta*-o

wallet πορτοφόλι ⓝ por-to-*fo*-li

warm a ζεστός ze-*stos*

wash (something) v πλένω *ple*-no

watch ρολόι ⓝ ro-*lo*-i

water νερό ⓝ ne-*ro*

we εμείς e-*mis*

weekend Σαββατοκύριακο ⓝ sa-va-to-*ki*-ria-ko

west δύση ⓕ *dhi*-si

wheelchair αναπηρική καρέκλα ⓕ a-na-pi-ri-*ki* ka-*re*-kla

when όταν o-*tan*

where πού pu

white άσπρο as-pros

who ποιος pios

why γιατί yia-*ti*

wife σύζυγος ⓕ *si*-zi-ghos

window παράθυρο ⓝ pa-*ra*-thi-ro

wine κρασί ⓝ kra-*si*

with με me

without χωρίς kho-*ris*

woman γυναίκα ⓕ yi-*ne*-ka

write v γράφω *ghra*-fo

Y

yellow a κίτρινος *ki*-tri-nos

yes ναι ne

yesterday χτες khtes

you sg inf εσύ e-*si*

you sg pol & pl εσείς e-*sis*

Hungarian

hungarian alphabet

A a o	Á á a	B b bey	C c tsey	Cs cs chey	D d dey	Dz dz dzey	Dzs dzs jey
E e e	É é ey	F f ef	G g gey	Gy gy dyey	H h ha	I i i	Í í ee
J j yey	K k ka	L l el	Ly ly ey	M m em	N n en	Ny ny en′	O o aw
Ó ó āw	Ö ö eu	Ő ő eū	P p pey	Q q ku	R r er	S s esh	Sz sz es
T t tey	Ty ty tyey	U u u	Ú ú ū	Ü ü ew	Ű ű ēw	V v vey	W w du·plo·vey
X x iks	Y y ip·sil·awn	Z z zey	Zs zs zhey				

hungarian

MAGYAR

introduction

Hungarian (*magyar* mo-dyor) is a unique language. Though distantly related to Finnish, it has no significant similarities to any other language in the world. If you have some background in European languages you'll be surprised at just how different Hungarian is. English actually has more in common with Russian and Sinhala (from Sri Lanka) than it does with Hungarian – even though words like *goulash*, *paprika* and *vampire* came to English from this language.

So how did such an unusual language end up in the heart of the European continent? The answer lies somewhere beyond the Ural mountains in western Siberia, where the nomadic ancestors of today's Hungarian speakers began a slow migration west about 2000 years ago. At some point in the journey the group began to split. One group turned towards Finland, while the other continued towards the Carpathian Basin, arriving in the late 9th century. Calling themselves Magyars (derived from the Finno-Ugric words for 'speak' and 'man') they cultivated and developed the occupied lands. By AD 1000 the Kingdom of Hungary was officially established. Along the way Hungarian acquired words from languages like Latin, Persian, Turkish and Bulgarian, yet overall changed remarkably little.

With more than 14.5 million speakers worldwide, Hungarian is nowadays the official language of Hungary and a minority language in the parts of Eastern Europe which belonged to the Austro-Hungarian Empire before WWI – Slovakia, Croatia, the northern Serbian province of Vojvodina and parts of Austria, Romania and the Ukraine.

Hungarian is a language rich in grammar and expression. These characteristics can be both alluring and intimidating. Word order in Hungarian is fairly free, and it has been argued that this stimulates creative or experimental thinking. Some believe that the flexibility of the tongue, combined with Hungary's linguistic isolation, has encouraged the culture's strong tradition of poetry and literature. For the same reason, however, the language is resistant to translation and much of the nation's literary heritage is still unavailable to English speakers. Another theory holds that Hungary's extraordinary number of great scientists is also attributable to the language's versatile nature. Still, Hungarian needn't be intimidating and you won't need to look very far to discover the beauty of the language. You may even find yourself unlocking the poet or scientist within!

pronunciation

The Hungarian language may seem daunting with its long words and many accent marks, but it's surprisingly easy to pronounce. Like English, Hungarian isn't always written the way it's pronounced, but just stick to the coloured phonetic guides that accompany each phrase or word and you can't go wrong.

vowel sounds

Hungarian vowels sounds are similar to those found in the English words listed in the table below. The symbol ¯ over a vowel, like ā, means you say it as a long vowel sound.

symbol	english equivalent	hungarian example	transliteration
a	father	*hátizsák*	*ha·ti·zhak*
aw	law (but short)	*kor*	*kawr*
e	bet	*zsebkés*	*zheb·keysh*
ee	see	*cím*	*tseem*
eu	her	*zöld*	*zeuld*
ew	ee pronounced with rounded lips	*csütörtök*	*chew·teur·teuk*
ey	hey	*én*	*eyn*
i	bit	*rizs*	*rizh*
o	pot	*gazda*	*goz·do*
oy	toy	*megfojt, komoly*	*meg·foyt, kaw·moy*
u	put	*utas*	*u·tosh*

word stress

Accent marks over vowels don't influence word stress, which always falls on the first syllable of the word. The stressed syllables in our coloured pronunciation guides are always in italics.

consonant sounds

Always pronounce y like the 'y' in 'yes'. We've also used the ' symbol to show this y sound when it's attached to n, d, and t and at the end of a syllable. You'll also see double consonants like bb, dd or tt – draw them out a little longer than you would in English.

symbol	english equivalent	hungarian example	transliteration
b	bed	*bajusz*	*bo·yus*
ch	cheat	*család*	*cho·lad*
d	dog	*dervis*	*der·vish*
dy	during	*magyar*	*mo·dyor*
f	fat	*farok*	*fo·rawk*
g	go	*gallér, igen*	*gol·leyr, i·gen*
h	hat	*hát*	*hat*
j	joke	*dzsem, hogy*	*jem, hawj*
k	kit	*kacsa*	*ko·cho*
l	lot	*lakat*	*lo·kot*
m	man	*most*	*mawsht*
n	not	*nem*	*nem*
p	pet	*pamut*	*po·mut*
r	run (rolled)	*piros*	*pi·rawsh*
s	sun	*kolbász*	*kawl·bas*
sh	shot	*tojást*	*taw·yasht*
t	top	*tag*	*tog*
ty	tutor	*kártya*	*kar·tyo*
ts	hats	*koncert*	*kawn·tsert*
v	very	*vajon*	*vo·yawn*
y	yes	*hajó, melyik*	*ho·yāw, me·yik*
z	zero	*zab*	*zob*
zh	pleasure	*zsemle*	*zhem·le*
'	a slight y sound	*poggyász, hány*	*pawd'·dyas, han'*

tools

language difficulties

Do you speak English?
Beszél/Beszélsz angolul? pol/inf
be·seyl/be·seyls on·gaw·lul

Do you understand?
Érti/Érted? pol/inf
eyr·ti/eyr·ted

I (don't) understand.
(Nem) Értem.
(nem) eyr·tem

What does (*lángos*) mean?
Mit jelent az, hogy (lángos)?
mit ye·lent oz hawj (*lan·gawsh*)

How do you ...?	*Hogyan ...?*	haw·dyon ...
pronounce this	*mondja ki ezt*	mawnd·yo ki ezt
write (*útlevél*)	*írja azt, hogy (útlevél)*	eer·yo ozt hawj (*üt·le·veyl*)

Could you please ...?	*..., kérem.*	... key·rem
repeat that	*Megismételné ezt*	meg·ish·mey·tel·ney ezt
speak more slowly	*Tudna lassabban beszélni*	tud·no losh·shob·bon be·seyl·ni
write it down	*Leírná*	le·eer·na

essentials

Yes.	*Igen.*	i·gen
No.	*Nem.*	nem
Please.	*Kérem/Kérlek.* pol/inf	key·rem/keyr·lek
Thank you (very much).	*(Nagyon) Köszönöm.*	(no·dyawn) keu·seu·neum
You're welcome.	*Szívesen.*	see·ve·shen
Excuse me.	*Elnézést kérek.*	el·ney·zeysht key·rek
Sorry.	*Sajnálom.*	shoy·na·lawm

numbers

0	nulla	*nul·lo*		16	tizenhat	*ti·zen·hot*
1	egy	*ej*		17	tizenhét	*ti·zen·heyt*
2	kettő	*ket·tēū*		18	tizennyolc	*ti·zen·nyawlts*
3	három	*ha·rawm*		19	tizenkilenc	*ti·zen·ki·lents*
4	négy	*neyj*		20	húsz	*hūs*
5	öt	*eut*		21	huszonegy	*hu·sawn·ej*
6	hat	*hot*		22	huszonkettő	*hu·sawn·ket·tēū*
7	hét	*heyt*		30	harminc	*hor·mints*
8	nyolc	*nyawlts*		40	negyven	*nej·ven*
9	kilenc	*ki·lents*		50	ötven	*eut·ven*
10	tíz	*teez*		60	hatvan	*hot·von*
11	tizenegy	*ti·zen·ej*		70	hetven	*het·ven*
12	tizenkettő	*ti·zen·ket·tēū*		80	nyolcvan	*nyawlts·von*
13	tizenhárom	*ti·zen·ha·rawm*		90	kilencven	*ki·lents·ven*
14	tizennégy	*ti·zen·neyj*		100	száz	*saz*
15	tizenöt	*ti·zen·eut*		1000	ezer	*e·zer*

time & dates

What time is it?	*Hány óra?*	han' *āw·ra*
It's one o'clock.	*(Egy) óra van.*	(ej) *āw·ra von*
It's (10) o'clock.	*(Tíz) óra van.*	(teez) *āw·ra von*
Quarter past (10).	*Negyed (tizenegy).*	ne·dyed (*ti·zen·ej*)
Half past (10).	*Fél (tizenegy).*	feyl (*ti·zen·ej*)
Quarter to (11).	*Háromnegyed (tizenegy).*	ha·rawm·ne·dyed (*ti·zen·ej*)
At what time ...?	*Hány órakor ...?*	han' *āw·ro·kawr* ...
At ...	*...kor.*	...·kawr
am (morning)	*délelőtt*	*deyl·e·lēūtt*
pm (afternoon)	*délután*	*deyl·u·tan*
pm (evening)	*este*	*esh·te*
Monday	*hétfő*	*heyt·fēū*
Tuesday	*kedd*	kedd
Wednesday	*szerda*	*ser·do*
Thursday	*csütörtök*	*chew·teur·teuk*
Friday	*péntek*	*peyn·tek*
Saturday	*szombat*	*sawm·bot*
Sunday	*vasárnap*	*vo·shar·nop*

January	január	yo·nu·ar
February	február	feb·ru·ar
March	március	mar·tsi·ush
April	április	ap·ri·lish
May	május	ma·yush
June	június	yü·ni·ush
July	július	yü·li·ush
August	augusztus	o·u·gus·tush
September	szeptember	sep·tem·ber
October	október	awk·tāw·ber
November	november	naw·vem·ber
December	december	de·tsem·ber

What date is it today?

Hányadika van ma? ha·nyo·di·ko von mo

It's (18 October).

(Október tizennyolcadika) van. (awk·tāw·ber ti·zen·nyawl·tso·di·ko) von

| since (May) | (május) óta | (ma·yush) āw·to |
| until (June) | (június)ig | (yü·ni·ush)·ig |

yesterday	tegnap	teg·nop
last night	tegnap éjjel	hawl·nop ey·yel
today	ma	mo
tonight	ma este	mo esh·te
tomorrow	holnap	hawl·nop

last/next ...	a múlt/a jövő ...	o múlt/o yeu·vēū ...
week	héten	hey·ten
month	hónapban	hāw·nop·bon
year	évben	eyv·ben

yesterday/tomorrow ...	tegnap/holnap ...	teg·nop/hawl·nop ...
morning	reggel	reg·gel
afternoon	délután	deyl·u·tan
evening	este	esh·te

weather

What's the weather like?	*Milyen az idő?*	mi·yen oz i·dēū
It's ...		
cloudy	*Az idő felhős.*	oz i·dēū fel·hēūsh
cold	*Az idő hideg.*	oz i·dēū hi·deg
hot	*Az idő nagyon meleg.*	oz i·dēū no·dyawn me·leg
raining	*Esik az eső.*	e·shik oz e·shēū
snowing	*Esik a hó.*	e·shik o hāw
sunny	*Az idő napos.*	oz i·dēū no·pawsh
warm	*Az idő meleg.*	oz i·dēū me·leg
windy	*Az idő szeles.*	oz i·dēū se·lesh
spring	*tavasz*	to·vos
summer	*nyár*	nyar
autumn	*ősz*	ēūs
winter	*tél*	teyl

border crossing

I'm ...	*... vagyok.*	... vo·dyawk
in transit	*Átutazóban*	at·u·to·zāw·bon
on business	*Üzleti úton*	ewz·le·ti ū·tawn
on holiday	*Szabadságon*	so·bod·sha·gawn
I'm here for ...	*... vagyok itt.*	... vo·dyawk itt
(10) days	*(Tíz) napig*	(teez) no·pig
(two) months	*(Két) hónapig*	(keyt) hāw·no·pig
(three) weeks	*(Három) hétig*	(ha·rawm) hey·tig

I'm going to (Szeged).
(Szeged)re megyek. — (se·ged)·re me·dyek

I'm staying at (the Gellért Hotel).
A (Gellért)ben fogok lakni. — o (gel·leyrt)·ben faw·gawk lok·ni

I have nothing to declare.
Nincs elvámolnivalóm. — ninch el·va·mawl·ni·vo·lāwm

I have something to declare.
Van valami elvámolnivalóm. — von vo·lo·mi el·va·mawl·ni·vo·lāwm

That's (not) mine.
Az (nem) az enyém. — oz (nem) oz e·nyeym

transport

tickets & luggage

Where can I buy a ticket?
Hol kapok jegyet?   hawl *ko*·pawk *ye*·dyet

Do I need to book a seat?
Kell helyjegyet váltanom?   kell *he*·ye·dyet *val*·ta·nawm

One ... ticket to (Eger), please.	*Egy ... jegy (Eger)be.*	ej ... yej (*e*·ger)·be
one-way	*csak oda*	chok *aw*·do
return	*oda-vissza*	*aw*·do·*vis*·so

I'd like to ... my ticket, please.	*Szeretném ... a jegyemet.*	se·ret·neym ... o *ye*·dye·met
cancel	*törölni*	*teu*·reul·ni
change	*megváltoztatni*	*meg*·val·tawz·tot·ni
collect	*átvenni*	*at*·ven·ni
confirm	*megerősíteni*	*meg*·e·rēū·shee·te·ni

I'd like a ... seat, please.	*... helyet szeretnék.*	... *he*·yet se·ret·neyk
nonsmoking	*Nemdohányzó*	nem·daw·han'·zāw
smoking	*Dohányzó*	daw·han'·zāw

How much is it?
Mennyibe kerül?   men'·nyi·be *ke*·rewl

Is there air conditioning?
Van légkondicionálás?   von *leyg*·kawn·di·tsi·aw·na·lash

Is there a toilet?
Van vécé?   von *vey*·tsey

How long does the trip take?
Mennyi ideig tart az út?   men'·nyi *i*·de·ig tort oz ūt

Is it a direct route?
Ez közvetlen járat?   ez *keuz*·vet·len *ya*·rot

My luggage has been ...	*A poggyászom ...*	o *pawd'*·dya·sawm ...
damaged	*megsérült*	*meg*·shey·rewlt
lost	*elveszett*	*el*·ve·sett

My luggage has been stolen.
  Ellopták a poggyászomat.   el·lawp·tak o *pawd'*·dya·saw·mot

Where can I find a luggage locker?
  Hol találok egy poggyász-   hawl *to*·la·lawk ej *pawd'*·dyas·
  megőrző automatát?   meg·eūr·zēū *o*·u·taw·mo·tat

getting around

Where does flight (BA15) arrive?
  Hova érkezik a (BA tizenötös)   haw·vo eyr·ke·zik a (bey o *ti*·zen·eu·teush)
  számú járat?   sa·mū *ya*·rot

Where does flight (BA26) depart?
  Honnan indul a (BA huszonhatos)   hawn·non *in*·dul a (bey o *hu*·sawn·ho·tawsh)
  számú járat?   sa·mū *ya*·rot

Where's (the) ...?	*Hol van ...?*	hawl von ...
arrivals hall	*az érkezési csarnok*	oz eyr·ke·zey·shi *chor*·nawk
departures hall	*az indulási csarnok*	oz in·du·la·shi *chor*·nawk
duty-free shop	*a vámmentes üzlet*	o *vam*·men·tesh *ewz*·let
gate (five)	*az (ötös) kapu*	oz (*eu*·teush) *ko*·pu

Which ... goes	*Melyik ... megy*	*me*·yik ... mej
to (Budapest)?	*(Budapest)re?*	(*bu*·do·pesht)·re
boat	*hajó*	*ho*·yāw
bus	*busz*	bus
plane	*repülőgép*	re·pew·lēū·geyp
train	*vonat*	*vaw*·not

What time's the	*Mikor megy ... (busz)?*	*mi*·kawr mej ... (bus)
... (bus)?		
first	*az első*	oz *el*·shēū
last	*az utolsó*	oz *u*·tawl·shāw
next	*a következő*	o *keu*·vet·ke·zēū

At what time does it arrive/leave?
  Mikor érkezik/indul?   *mi*·kawr eyr·kez·ik/*in*·dul

How long will it be delayed?
  Mennyit késik?   men'·nyit key·shik

What station/stop is this?
  Ez milyen állomás/megálló?   ez *mi*·yen *al*·law·mash/*meg*·al·lāw

What's the next station/stop?
Mi a következő állomás/megálló?   mi o *keu*·vet·ke·zēū *al*·law·mash/*meg*·al·lāw

Does it stop at (Visegrád)?
Megáll (Visegrád)on?   *meg*·all (*vi*·she·grad)·on

Please tell me when we get to (Eger).
Kérem, szóljon, amikor   *key*·rem *sāwl*·yawn o·mi·kawr
(Eger)be érünk.   (e·ger)·be *ey*·rewnk

How long do we stop here?
Mennyi ideig állunk itt?   *men*'·nyi i·de·ig *al*·lunk itt

Is this seat available?
Szabad ez a hely?   *so*·bod ez o *he*·y

That's my seat.
Az az én helyem.   oz oz eyn *he*·yem

I'd like a taxi ...   *Szeretnék egy taxit ...*   se·ret·neyk ej *tok*·sit ...
  at (9am)   *(reggel kilenc)re*   (*reg*·gel *ki*·lents)·re
  now   *most*   mawsht
  tomorrow   *holnapra*   *hawl*·nop·ro

Is this taxi available?
Szabad ez a taxi?   *so*·bod ez o *tok*·si

How much is it to ...?
Mennyibe kerül ...ba?   *men*'·nyi·be *ke*·rewl ...·bo

Please put the meter on.
Kérem, kapcsolja be az órát.   *key*·rem *kop*·chawl·yo be oz *āw*·rat

Please take me to (this address).
Kérem, vigyen el (erre a címre).   *kay*·rem *vi*·dyen el (*er*·re o *tseem*·re)

Please ...   *Kérem, ...*   *key*·rem ...
  slow down   *lassítson*   *losh*·sheet·shawn
  stop here   *álljon meg itt*   *all*·yawn meg itt
  here   *várjon itt*   *var*·yawn itt

car, motorbike & bicycle hire

I'd like to hire a ...   *Szeretnék egy ... bérelni.*   se·ret·neyk ej ... *bey*·rel·ni
  bicycle   *biciklit*   *bi*·tsik·lit
  car   *autót*   *o*·u·tāwt
  motorbike   *motort*   *maw*·tawrt

with a driver	sofőrrel	shaw·feûr·rel
with air conditioning	lég-kondicionálóval	leyg·kawn·di·tsi·aw·na·lāw·vol
with antifreeze	fagyállóval	fod'·al·lāw·vol
with snow chains	hólánccal	hāw·lant'·tsol

How much	Mennyibe kerül	men'·nyi·be ke·rewl
for ... hire?	a kölcsönzés ...?	o keul·cheun·zeysh ...
hourly	óránként	āw·ran·keynt
daily	egy napra	ej nop·ro
weekly	egy hétre	ej heyt·re

air	levegő	le·ve·gēü
oil	olaj	aw·lo·y
petrol	benzin	ben·zin
tyres	gumi	gu·mi

I need a mechanic.
Szükségem van egy   sewk·shey·gem von ej
autószerelőre.   o·u·tāw·se·re·lēū·re

I've run out of petrol.
Kifogyott a benzinem.   ki·faw·dyawtt o ben·zi·nem

I have a flat tyre.
Defektem van.   de·fek·tem von

directions

Where's the ...?	Hol van a ...?	hawl von o ...
bank	bank	bonk
city centre	városközpont	va·rawsh·keuz·pawnt
hotel	szálloda	sal·law·do
market	piac	pi·ots
police station	rendőrség	rend·ēūr·sheyg
post office	postahivatal	pawsh·to·hi·vo·tol
public toilet	nyilvános vécé	nyil·va·nawsh vey·tsey
tourist office	turistairoda	tu·rish·to·i·raw·do

Is this the road to (Sopron)?
Ez az út vezet (Sopron)ba?   ez oz ūt ve·zet (shawp·rawn)·bo

Can you show me (on the map)?
Meg tudja mutatni nekem   meg tud'·yo mu·tot·ni ne·kem
(a térképen)?   (o teyr·key·pen)

What's the address?
Mi a cím? mi o tseem

How far is it?
Milyen messze van? mi·yen mes·se von

How do I get there?
Hogyan jutok oda? haw·dyon yu·tawk aw·do

Turn ...	Forduljon ...	fawr·dul·yawn ...
at the corner	a saroknál	o sho·rawk·nal
at the traffic lights	a közlekedési lámpánál	o keuz·le·ke·dey·shi lam·pa·nal
left/right	balra/jobbra	bol·ro/yawbb·ro

It's ...	... van.	... von
behind ...	... mögött	... meu·geutt
far away	Messze	mes·se
here	Itt	itt
in front of ...	... előtt	... e·lēūtt
left	Balra	bol·ro
near ...	... közelében	... keu·ze·ley·ben
next to ...	... mellett	... mel·lett
on the corner	A sarkon	o shor·kawn
opposite ...	... val szemben	... vol sem·ben
right	Jobbra	yawbb·ro
straight ahead	Egyenesen előttünk	e·dye·ne·shen e·lēūt·tewnk
there	Ott	ott

by bus	busszal	bus·sol
by taxi	taxival	tok·si·vol
by train	vonattal	vaw·not·tol
on foot	gyalog	dyo·lawg

north	észak	ey·sok
south	dél	deyl
east	kelet	ke·let
west	nyugat	nyu·got

signs

Bejárat/Kijárat	be·ya·rot/ki·ya·rot	Entrance/Exit
Nyitva/Zárva	nyit·vo/zar·vo	Open/Closed
Van Üres Szoba	von ew·resh saw·bo	Rooms Available
Minden Szoba Foglalt	min·den saw·bo fawg·lolt	No Vacancies
Információ	in·fawr·ma·tsi·āw	Information
Rendőrség	rend·ēūr·sheyg	Police Station
Tilos	ti·lawsh	Prohibited
Mosdó	mawsh·dāw	Toilets
Férfiak	feyr·fi·ok	Men
Nők	nēūk	Women
Meleg/Hideg	me·leg/hi·deg	Hot/Cold

accommodation

finding accommodation

Where's a ...?	Hol van egy ...?	hawl von ej ...
camping ground	kemping	kem·ping
guesthouse	panzió	pon·zi·āw
hotel	szálloda	sal·law·do
youth hostel	ifjúsági szálló	if·yū·sha·gi sal·lāw
Can you recommend somewhere ...?	Tud ajánlani egy ... helyet?	tud o·yan·lo·ni ej ... he·yet
cheap	olcsó	awl·chāw
good	jó	yāw
nearby	közeli	keu·ze·li
I'd like to book a room, please.	Szeretnék egy szobát foglalni.	se·ret·neyk ej saw·bat fawg·lol·ni
I have a reservation.	Van foglalásom.	von fawg·lo·la·shawm
My name's ...	A nevem ...	o ne·vem ...
Do you have a ... room?	Van Önnek kiadó egy ... szobája?	von eun·nek ki·o·dāw ed' ... saw·ba·yo
single	egyágyas	ej·a·dyosh
double	dupláágyas	dup·la·a·dyosh
twin	kétágyas	keyt·a·dyosh

How much is it per ...?	Mennyibe kerül egy ...?	men·nyi·be ke·rewl ej ...
night	éjszakára	ey·so·ka·ro
person	főre	feū·re

Can I pay by ...?	Fizethetek ...?	fi·zet·he·tek ...
credit card	hitelkártyával	hi·tel·kar·tya·vol
travellers cheque	utazási csekkel	u·to·za·shi chek·kel

I'd like to stay for (three) nights.
(Három) éjszakára. (ha·rawm) ey·so·ka·ro

From (July 2) to (July 6).
(Július kettő)től (július hat)ig. (yū·li·ush ket·tēū)·tēül (yū·li·ush hot)·ig

Can I see it?
Megnézhetem? meg·neyz·he·tem

Am I allowed to camp here?
Táborozhatok itt? ta·baw·rawz·ho·tawk itt

Where can I find the camping ground?
Hol találom a kempinget? hawl to·la·lawm o kem·pin·get

requests & queries

When/Where is breakfast served?
Mikor/Hol van a reggeli? mi·kawr/hawl von o reg·ge·li

Please wake me at (seven).
Kérem, ébresszen fel (hét)kor. key·rem eyb·res·sen fel (heyt)·kawr

Could I have my key, please?
Megkaphatnám a kulcsomat, kérem? meg·kop·hot·nam o kul·chaw·mot key·rem

Can I get another (blanket)?
Kaphatok egy másik (takaró)t? kop·ho·tawk ej ma·shik (to·ko·rāw)t

Is there a/an ...?	Van Önöknél ...?	von eu·neuk·neyl ...
elevator	lift	lift
safe	széf	seyf

The room is too ...	Túl ...	tūl ...
expensive	drága	dra·go
noisy	zajos	zo·yawsh
small	kicsi	ki·chi

The ... doesn't work.	A ... nem működik.	o ... nem *mēw*·keu·dik
air conditioning	légkondicionáló	*leyg*·kawn·di·tsi·aw·na·lāw
fan	ventilátor	*ven*·ti·la·tawr
toilet	vécé	*vey*·tsey

This ... isn't clean.	Ez a ... nem tiszta.	ez o ... nem *tis*·to
sheet	lepedő	*le*·pe·dēū
towel	törülköző	*teu*·rewl·keu·zēū

checking out

What time is checkout?
Mikor kell kijelentkezni?   mi·kawr kell *ki*·ye·lent·kez·ni

Can I leave my luggage here?
Itt hagyhatom a csomagjaimat?   itt *hoj*·ho·tawm o *chaw*·mog·yo·i·mot

Could I have my ..., please?	Visszakaphatnám ..., kérem?	vis·so·kop·hot·nam ... *key*·rem
deposit	a letétemet	o *le*·tey·te·met
passport	az útlevelemet	oz *üt*·le·ve·le·met
valuables	az értékeimet	oz *eyr*·tey·ke·i·met

communications & banking

the internet

Where's the local Internet café?
Hol van a legközelebbi internet kávézó?   hawl von o *leg*·keu·ze·leb·bi *in*·ter·net *ka*·vey·zāw

How much is it per hour?
Mennyibe kerül óránként?   men'·nyi·be ke·rewl *āw*·ran·keynt

I'd like to check my email.
Szeretném megnézni az e-mailjeimet.   se·ret·neym meg·neyz·ni oz *ee*·meyl·ye·i·met

I'd like to ...	Szeretnék ...	se·ret·neyk ...
get Internet access	rámenni az internetre	*ra*·men·ni oz *in*·ter·net·re
use a printer	használni egy nyomtatót	*hos*·nal·ni ej *nyawm*·to·tāwt
use a scanner	használni egy szkennert	*hos*·nal·ni ej *sken*·nert

mobile/cell phone

I'd like a ...	*Szeretnék egy ...*	se·ret·neyk ej ...
mobile/cell phone	*mobiltelefont*	maw·bil·te·le·fawnt
for hire	*bérelni*	bey·rel·ni
SIM card	*SIM-kártyát*	sim·kar·tyat
for your network	*ennek a hálózatnak*	en·nek o ha·lāw·zot·nok

What are the rates?	*Milyen díjak vannak?*	mi·yen dee·yok von·nok

telephone

What's your phone number?
Mi a telefonszáma/
telefonszámod? pol/inf
mi o *te·le·fawn·sa·ma/*
te·le·fawn·sa·mawd

The number is ...
A szám ...
o sam ...

Where's the nearest public phone?
Hol a legközelebbi
nyilvános telefon?
hawl o *leg·keu·ze·leb·bi*
nyil·va·nawsh te·le·fawn

I'd like to buy a phonecard.
Szeretnék telefonkártyát venni.
se·ret·neyk te·le·fawn·kar·tyat ven·ni

I want to make a reverse-charge call.
'R' beszélgetést szeretnék kérni.
er·be·seyl·ge·teysht se·ret·neyk keyr·ni

I want to ...	*Szeretnék ...*	se·ret·neyk ...
call (Singapore)	*(Szingapúr)ba*	(sin·go·pūr)·bo
	telefonálni	te·le·faw·nal·ni
make a local call	*helyi telefon-*	he·yi te·le·fawn·
	beszélgetést	be·seyl·ge·teysht
	folytatni	faw·y·tot·ni

How much	*Mennyibe*	men'·nyi·be
does ... cost?	*kerül ...?*	ke·rewl ...?
a (three)-minute	*egy (három)perces*	ej (ha·rawm)·per·tsesh
call	*beszélgetés*	be·seyl·ge·teysh
each extra minute	*minden további perc*	min·den taw·vab·bi perts

(30) forints per (30) seconds.
(Harminc) másodpercenként
(harminc) forint.
(hor·mints) ma·shawd·per·tsen·keynt
(hor·mints) faw·rint.

post office

I want to send a ...	... szeretnék küldeni.	... se·ret·neyk kewl·de·ni
fax	Faxot	fok·sawt
letter	Levelet	le·ve·let
parcel	Csomagot	chaw·mo·gawt
postcard	Képeslapot	key·pesh·lo·pawt

I want to buy a/an...	... szeretnék venni.	... se·ret·neyk ven·ni
envelope	Borítékot	baw·ree·tey·kawt
stamp	Bélyeget	bey·ye·get

Please send it to (Australia) by ...	Kérem, küldje ... (Ausztráliá)ba.	key·rem kewld·ye ... (o·ust·ra·li·a)·bo
airmail	légipostán	ley·gi·pawsh·tan
express mail	expresszel	eks·press·zel
registered mail	ajánlottan	o·yan·law·tton
surface mail	simán	shi·man

Is there any mail for me?	Van levelem?	von le·ve·lem

bank

Where's a/an ...?	Hol van egy ...?	hawl von ej ...
ATM	bankautomata	bonk·o·u·taw·mo·to
foreign exchange office	valutaváltó ügynökség	vo·lu·to·val·tāw ewj·neuk·sheyg

I'd like to ...	Szeretnék ...	se·ret·neyk ...
Where can I ...?	Hol tudok ...?	hawl tu·dawk ...
arrange a transfer	pénzt átutalni	peynzt at·u·tol·ni
cash a cheque	beváltani egy csekket	be·val·to·ni ej chek·ket
change a travellers cheque	beváltani egy utazási csekket	be·val·to·ni ej u·to·za·shi chek·ket
change money	pénzt váltani	peynzt val·to·ni
get a cash advance	készpénzelőleget felvenni	keys·peynz·e·lēū·le·get fel·ven·ni
withdraw money	pénzt kivenni	peynzt ki·ven·ni

What's the ...?	Mennyi ...?	men'·nyi ...
charge for that	a díj	o dee·y
exchange rate	a valutaárfolyam	o vo·lu·to·ar·faw·yom

It's (100) euros.	(Száz) euró.	(saz) e·u·raw
It's (500) forints.	(Ötszáz) forint.	(eut·saz) faw·rint
It's free.	Ingyen van.	in·dyen von

What time does the bank open?
Mikor nyit a bank?   mi·kawr nyit o bonk

Has my money arrived yet?
Megérkezett már a pénzem?   meg·eyr·ke·zett mar o peyn·zem

sightseeing

getting in

What time does it open/close?
Mikor nyit/zár?   mi·kawr nyit/zar

What's the admission charge?
Mennyibe kerül a belépőjegy?   men'·nyi·be ke·rewl o be·ley·pēü·yej

Is there a discount for students/children?
Van kedvezmény diákok/   von ked·vez·meyn' di·a·kawk/
gyerekek számára?   dye·re·kek sa·ma·ro

I'd like a ...	Szeretnék egy ...	se·ret·neyk ej ...
catalogue	katalógust	ko·to·lāw·gusht
guide	idegenvezetőt	i·de·gen·ve·ze·tēüt
local map	itteni térképet	it·te·ni teyr·key·pet

I'd like to see ...	Szeretnék látni ...	se·ret·neyk lat·ni ...
What's that?	Az mi?	oz mi
Can I take a photo?	Fényképezhetek?	feyn'·key·pez·he·tek

tours

When's the next ...?	Mikor van a következő ...?	mi·kawr von o keu·vet·ke·zēü ...
day trip	egynapos kirándulás	ej·no·pawsh ki·ran·du·lash
tour	túra	tū·ro

sightseeing

castle	*vár*	var
cathedral	*székesegyház*	sey-kesh-ej-haz
church	*templom*	temp-lawm
main square	*fő tér*	fēū ter
monastery	*kolostor*	kaw-lawsh-tawr
monument	*emlékmű*	em-leyk-mēw
museum	*múzeum*	mū-ze-um
old city	*óváros*	āw-va-rawsh
palace	*palota*	po-law-to
ruins	*romok*	raw-mawk
stadium	*stadion*	shto-di-awn
statues	*szobrok*	saw-brawk

Is ... included?	*Benne van az árban ...?*	ben-ne von oz ar-bon ...
accommodation	*a szállás*	o sal-lash
the admission charge	*a belépőjegy*	o be-ley-pēū-yej
food	*az ennivaló*	oz en-ni-vo-lāw
transport	*a közlekedés*	o keuz-le-ke-deysh

How long is the tour?
Mennyi ideig tart a túra? men'-nyi i-de-ig tort o tū-ra

What time should we be back?
Mikorra érünk vissza? mi-kawr-ro ey-rewnk vis-so

shopping

enquiries

Where's a ...?	*Hol van egy ...?*	hawl von ej ...
bank	*bank*	bonk
bookshop	*könyvesbolt*	keun'-vesh-bawlt
camera shop	*fényképezőgép-bolt*	feyn'-key-pe-zēū-geyp-bawlt
department store	*áruház*	a-ru-haz
grocery store	*élelmiszerbolt*	ey-lel-mi-ser-bawlt
market	*piac*	pi-ots
newsagency	*újságárus*	ū-y-shag-a-rush
supermarket	*élelmiszeráruház*	ey-lel-mi-ser-a-ru-haz

Where can I buy (a padlock)?
   Hol tudok venni (egy lakatot)?   hawl *tu*·dawk *ven*·ni (ej *lo*·ko·tawt)

I'm looking for ...
   Keresem a ...   *ke*·re·shem o ...

Can I look at it?
   Megnézhetem?   meg·neyz·he·tem

Do you have any others?
   Van másmilyen is?   von *mash*·mi·yen ish

Does it have a guarantee?
   Van rajta garancia?   von *ro*·y·to *go*·ron·tsi·o

Can I have it sent overseas?
   El lehet küldetni külföldre?   el *le*·het *kewl*·det·ni *kewl*·feuld·re

Can I have my ... repaired?
   Megjavíttathatnám itt ...?   meg·yo·veet·tot·hot·nam itt ...

It's faulty.
   Hibás.   *hi*·bash

I'd like ..., please.	*..., kérem.*	... *key*·rem
a bag	*Kaphatnék egy zacskót*	*kop*·hot·neyk ej *zoch*·kawt
a refund	*Vissza szeretném*	*vis*·so se·ret·neym
	kapni a pénzemet	*kop*·ni o *peyn*·ze·met
to return this	*Szeretném*	se·ret·neym
	visszaadni ezt	*vis*·so·od·ni ezt

paying

How much is it?
   Mennyibe kerül?   *men'*·nyi·be *ke*·rewl

Could you write down the price?
   Le tudná írni az árat?   le *tud*·na *eer*·ni oz *a*·rot

That's too expensive.
   Ez túl drága.   ez tül *dra*·go

Do you have something cheaper?
   Van valami olcsóbb?   von *vo*·lo·mi *awl*·chäwbb

I'll give you (500 forints).
   Adok Önnek (ötszáz forintot).   *o*·dawk *eun*·nek (*eut*·saz *faw*·rin·tawt)

There's a mistake in the bill.
   Valami nem stimmel a számlával.   *vo*·lo·mi nem *shtim*·mel o *sam*·la·vol

Do you accept ...?	Elfogadnak ...?	el·faw·god·nok ...
credit cards	hitelkártyát	hi·tel·kar·tyat
debit cards	bankkártyát	bonk·kar·tyat
travellers cheques	utazási csekket	u·to·za·shi chek·ket

I'd like ..., please.	..., kérem.	... key·rem
a receipt	Kaphatnék egy nyugtát	kop·hot·neyk ej nyug·tat
my change	Szeretném megkapni	se·ret·neym meg·kop·ni
	a visszajáró pénzt	o vis·so·ya·rāw peynzt

clothes & shoes

Can I try it on?	Felpróbálhatom?	fel·prāw·bal·ho·tawm
My size is (40).	A méretem	o mey·re·tem
	(negyvenes).	(nej·ve·nesh)
It doesn't fit.	Nem jó.	nem yāw

small	kicsi	ki·chi
medium	közepes	keu·ze·pesh
large	nagy	noj

books & music

I'd like a ...	Szeretnék egy ...	se·ret·neyk ej ...
newspaper	(angol)	(on·gawl)
(in English)	újságot	üy·sha·gawt
pen	tollat	tawl·lot

Is there an English-language bookshop?
| Van valahol egy angol | von vo·lo·hawl ej on·gawl |
| nyelvű könyvesbolt? | nyel·vēw keun'·vesh·bawlt |

I'm looking for something by (Zsuzsa Koncz).
| (Koncz Zsuzsá)tól | (konts zhu·zha)·tāwl |
| keresek valamit. | ke·re·shek vo·lo·mit |

Can I listen to this?
| Meghallgathatom ezt? | meg·holl·got·ho·tawm ezt |

photography

Can you transfer photos from my camera to CD?
Át tudják vinni a képeket   at *tud*·yak *vin*·ni o *key*·pe·ket
a fényképezőgépemről CD-re?   o *feyn'*·key·pe·zēū·gey·pem·rēūl *tsey*·dey·re

Can you develop this film?
Elő tudják hívni ezt a filmet?   e·lēū *tud*·yak *heev*·ni ezt o *fil*·met

Can you load my film?
Bele tudják tenni a filmet   be·le *tud*·yak *ten*·ni o *fil*·met
a gépembe?   o *gey*·pem·be

I need a ... film
for this camera.   *... filmet szeretnék.*   ... *fil*·met se·ret·neyk
   B&W   *Fekete-fehér*   fe·ke·te·*fe*·heyr
   colour   *Színes*   *see*·nesh
   slide   *Dia*   *di*·o
   (200) speed   *(Kétszáz)as*   (keyt·saz)·osh
     fényérzékenységű   feyn'·eyr·zey·ken'·shey·gēw

When will it be ready?   *Mikor lesz kész?*   *mi*·kawr les keys

meeting people

greetings, goodbyes & introductions

Hello.	*Szervusz/Szervusztok.* sg/pl	ser·vus/ser·vus·tawk
Hi.	*Szia/Sziasztok.* sg/pl	si·o/si·os·tawk
Good night.	*Jó éjszakát.*	yāw ey·y·so·kat
Goodbye.	*Viszlát.*	vis·lat
Bye.	*Szia/Sziasztok.* sg/pl	si·o/si·os·tawk
Mr	*Úr*	ūr
Mrs	*Asszony*	os·sawn'
Miss	*Kisasszony*	kish·os·sawn'
How are you?	*Hogy van/vagy?* pol/inf	hawj von/voj
Fine. And you?	*Jól. És Ön/te?* pol/inf	yāwl eysh eun/te
What's your name?	*Mi a neve/neved?* pol/inf	mi o *ne*·ve/ne·ved
My name is ...	*A nevem ...*	o *ne*·vem ...
I'm pleased to meet you.	*Örvendek.*	eur·ven·dek

This is my ...	*Ez ...*	ez ...
boyfriend	*a barátom*	o bo·ra·tawm
brother (older)	*a bátyám*	o ba·tyam
brother (younger)	*az öcsém*	oz eu·cheym
daughter	*a lányom*	o la·nyawm
father	*az apám*	oz o·pam
friend	*a barátom/barátnőm* m/f	o bo·ra·tawm/bo·rat·nēūm
girlfriend	*a barátnőm*	o bo·rat·nēūm
husband	*a férjem*	o feyr·yem
mother	*az anyám*	oz o·nyam
partner (intimate)	*a barátom/barátnőm* m/f	o bo·ra·tawm/bo·rat·nēūm
sister (older)	*a nővérem*	o nēū·vey·rem
sister (younger)	*a húgom*	o hū·gawm
son	*a fiam*	o fi·om
wife	*a feleségem*	o fe·le·shey·gem

Here's my ...	*Itt van ...*	itt von ...
address	*a címem*	o tsee·mem
email address	*az e-mail címem*	oz ee·meyl tsee·mem
fax number	*a faxszámom*	o foks·sa·mawm
phone number	*a telefonszámom*	o te·le·fawn·sa·mawm

What's your ...?	*Mi ...?*	mi ...
address	*a címe*	o tsee·me
email address	*az e-mail címe*	oz ee·meyl tsee·me
fax number	*a faxszáma*	o foks·sa·ma
phone number	*a telefonszáma*	o te·le·fawn·sa·ma

occupations

What's your occupation?	*Mi a foglalkozása/ foglalkozásod?* pol/inf	mi a fawg·lol·kaw·za·sho/ fawg·lol·kaw·za·shawd
I'm a/an ...	*... vagyok.*	... vo·dyawk
artist	*Művész*	mēw·veys
businessperson	*Üzletember* m	ewz·let·em·ber
	Üzletasszony f	ewz·let·os·sawn'
farmer	*Gazda*	goz·do
office worker	*Irodai dolgozó*	i·raw·do·i dawl·gaw·zāw
scientist	*Természettudós*	ter·mey·set·tu·dāwsh
student	*Diák*	di·ak
tradesperson	*Kereskedő*	ke·resh·ke·dēū

background

Where are you from?	Ön honnan jön? pol	eun *hawn*·non yeun
	Te honnan jössz? inf	te *hawn*·non yeuss
I'm from …	Én … jövök.	eyn … *yeu*·veuk
Australia	Ausztráliából	o·ust·ra·li·a·bāwl
Canada	Kanadából	ko·no·da·bāwl
England	Angliából	ong·li·a·bāwl
New Zealand	Új-Zélandból	ú·y·zey·lond·bāwl
the USA	USAból	u·sho·bāwl
Are you married? m	Nős?	nēūsh
Are you married? f	Férjnél van?	feyr·y·neyl von
I'm …	… vagyok.	… vo·dyawk
married	Nős/Férjnél m/f	nēūsh/feyr·y·neyl
single	Egyedülálló	e·dye·dewl·al·lāw

age

How old are you?	Hány éves? pol	han' *ey*·vesh
	Hány éves vagy? inf	han' *ey*·vesh voj
How old are your children?	Hány évesek a gyerekei/gyerekeid? pol/inf	han' *ey*·ve·shek o dye·re·ke·i/dye·re·ke·id
I'm … years old.	… éves vagyok.	… *ey*·vesh vo·dyawk
He/She is … years old.	… éves.	… *ey*·vesh

feelings

Are you …?	… vagy?	… voj
happy	Boldog	bawl·dawg
hungry	Éhes	ey·hesh
sad	Szomorú	saw·maw·rū
thirsty	Szomjas	sawm·yosh
I'm …	… vagyok.	… vo·dyawk
I'm not …	Nem vagyok …	nem vo·dyawk …
happy	boldog	bawl·dawg
hungry	éhes	ey·hesh
sad	szomorú	saw·maw·rū
thirsty	szomjas	sawm·yosh

Are you cold?	Fázik/Fázol? pol/inf	fa·zik/fa·zawl
I'm (not) cold.	(Nem) Fázom.	(nem) fa·zawm
Are you hot?	Melege/Meleged van? pol/inf	me·le·ge/me·le·ged von
I'm hot.	Melegem van.	me·le·gem von
I'm not hot.	Nincs melegem.	ninch me·le·gem

entertainment

going out

Where can I find ...?	Hol találok ...?	hawl to·la·lawk ...
clubs	klubokat	klu·baw·kot
gay venues	meleg	me·leg
	szórakozóhelyeket	sāw·ro·kaw·zāw·he·ye·ket
pubs	pubokat	po·baw·kot
I feel like going	Szeretnék	se·ret·neyk
to a/the ...	elmenni egy ...	el·men·ni ej ...
concert	koncertre	kawn·tsert·re
movies	moziba	maw·zi·bo
party	partira	por·ti·ro
restaurant	étterembe	eyt·te·rem·be
theatre	színházba	seen·haz·bo

interests

Do you like ...?	Szereted ...?	se·re·ted ...
I (don't) like ...	(Nem) Szeretem ...	(nem) se·re·tem ...
art	a művészetet	o mēw·vey·se·tet
movies	a filmeket	o fil·me·ket
sport	a sportot	o shpawr·tawt
Do you like ...?	Szeretsz ...?	se·rets ...
I (don't) like ...	(Nem) Szeretek ...	(nem) se·re·tek ...
cooking	főzni	fēūz·ni
nightclubs	diszkóba járni	dis·kāw·bo yar·ni
reading	olvasni	awl·vosh·ni
shopping	vásárolni	va·sha·rawl·ni
travelling	utazni	u·toz·ni

Do you ...?		
dance	*Táncolsz?*	*tan*-tsawls
go to concerts	*Jársz koncertre?*	yars *kawn*-tsert-re
listen to music	*Hallgatsz zenét?*	*holl*-gots *ze*-neyt

food & drink

finding a place to eat

Can you recommend a ...?	*Tud/Tudsz ajánlani egy ...?* pol/inf	tud/tuds *o*-yan-lo-ni ej ...
bar	*bárt*	bart
café	*kávézót*	*ka*-vey-zāwt
restaurant	*éttermet*	*eyt*-ter-met
I'd like ...	*Szeretnék ...*	*se*-ret-neyk ...
a table for (five)	*egy asztalt (öt)*	ej *os*-tolt (eut)
	személyre	*se*-mey-re
the (non)smoking section	*a (nem)dohányzó részben ülni*	o (nem)*daw*-han'-zāw *reys*-ben *ewl*-ni

ordering food

breakfast	*reggeli*	*reg*-ge-li
lunch	*ebéd*	*e*-beyd
dinner	*vacsora*	*vo*-chaw-ro
snack	*snack*	snekk
today's special	*napi ajánlat*	*no*-pi oy-an-lot

How long is the wait?
Mennyi ideig kell várni? — men'-nyi *i*-de-ig kell *vaar*-ni

What would you recommend?
Mit ajánlana? — mit *o*-yan-lo-no

I'd like (the) ...	*... szeretném.*	*... se*-ret-neym
bill	*A számlát*	o *sam*-lat
drink list	*Az itallapot*	oz *i*-tol-lo-pawt
menu	*Az étlapot*	oz *eyt*-lo-pawt
that dish	*Azt az ételt*	ozt oz *ey*-telt

drinks

(cup of) coffee ...	(csésze) kávé ...	(chey-se) ka-vey ...
(cup of) tea ...	(csésze) tea ...	(chey-se) te-o ...
with milk	tejjel	ey-yel
without sugar	cukor nélkül	tsu-kawr neyl-kewl
... mineral water	... ásványvíz	... ash-van'-veez
sparkling	szénsavas	seyn-sho-vosh
still	szénsavmentes	seyn-shov-men-tesh
orange juice	narancslé	no-ronch-ley
soft drink	üdítőital	ew-dee-tēū-i-tal
(boiled) water	(forralt) víz	(fawr-rolt) veez

in the bar

I'll have ...	... kérek.	... key-rek
I'll buy you a drink.	Fizetek neked egy italt.	fi-ze-tek ne-ked ej i-tolt
What would you like?	Mit kérsz?	mit keyrs
Cheers! (to one person)	Egészségedre!	e-geys-shey-ged-re
Cheers! (to more than one person)	Egészségetekre!	e-geys-shey-ge-tek-re
brandy	brandy	bren-di
champagne	pezsgő	pezh-gēū
cocktail	koktél	kawk-teyl
a bottle/glass of (beer)	egy üveg/pohár (sör)	ej ew-veg/paw-har (sheur)
a shot of (whisky)	egy kupica (whisky)	ej ku-pi-tso (vís-ki)
a bottle/glass of ... wine	egy üveg/pohár ... bor	ej ew-veg/paw-har ... bawr
red	vörös	veu-reush
sparkling	pezsgő	pezh-gēū
white	fehér	fe-heyr

self-catering

What's the local speciality?
Mi az itteni specialitás? mi oz *it*·te·ni *shpe*·tsi·o·li·tash

What's that?
Az mi? oz mi

How much is (a kilo of cheese)?
Mennyibe kerül (egy kiló sajt)? men'·nyi·be *ke*·rewl (ej *ki*·lāw shoyt)

I'd like ...	*Kérek ...*	*key*·rek ...
200 grams	*húsz dekát*	hüs *de*·kat
a kilo	*egy kilót*	ej *ki*·lāwt
a piece	*egy darabot*	ej *do*·ro·bawt
a slice	*egy szeletet*	ej *se*·le·tet
Less.	*Kevésbé.*	*ke*·veysh·bey
Enough.	*Elég.*	e·leyg
More.	*Több.*	teubb

special diets & allergies

Is there a vegetarian restaurant near here?
Van a közelben von o *keu*·zel·ben
vegetáriánus étterem? ve·ge·ta·ri·a·nush *eyt*·te·rem

Do you have vegetarian food?
Vannak Önöknél von·nok *eu*·neuk·neyl
vegetáriánus ételek? ve·ge·ta·ri·a·nush *ey*·te·lek

Could you prepare	*Tudna készíteni*	*tud*·no *key*·see·te·ni
a meal without ...?	*egy ételt ... nélkül?*	ej *ey*·telt ... *neyl*·kewl
butter	*vaj*	vo·y
eggs	*tojás*	*taw*·yash
meat stock	*húsleveskocka*	*hūsh*·le·vesh·kawts·ko
I'm allergic to ...	*Allergiás vagyok a ...*	*ol*·ler·gi·ash *vo*·dyawk o ...
dairy produce	*tejtermékekre*	*te*·y·ter·mey·kek·re
gluten	*sikérre*	*shi*·keyr·re
MSG	*monoszódium*	*maw*·naw·sāw·di·um
	glutamátra	*glu*·to·mat·ro
nuts	*diófélékre*	*di*·āw·fey·leyk·re
seafood	*tenger gyümölcseire*	*ten*·ger yew·meul·che·i·re

emergencies

basics

Help!	Segítség!	she·geet·sheyg
Stop!	Álljon meg!	all·yawn meg
Go away!	Menjen innen!	men·yen in·nen
Thief!	Tolvaj!	tawl·voy
Fire!	Tűz!	tēwz
Watch out!	Vigyázzon!	vi·dyaz·zawn
Call a doctor!	Hívjon orvost!	heev·yawn awr·vawsht
Call an ambulance!	Hívja a mentőket!	heev·yo o men·tēū·ket
Call the police!	Hívja a rendőrséget!	heev·yo o rend·ēūr·shey·get

It's an emergency!
Sürgős esetről van szó.   shewr·gēūsh e·shet·rēūl von sāw

Could you help me, please?
Tudna segíteni?   tud·no she·gee·te·ni

Can I use your phone?
Használhatom a telefonját?   hos·nal·ho·tawm o te·le·fawn·yat

I'm lost.
Eltévedtem.   el·tey·ved·tem

Where are the toilets?
Hol a vécé?   hawl o vey·tsey

police

Where's the police station?
Hol a rendőrség?   hawl o rend·ēūr·sheyg

I want to report an offence.
Bűncselekményt szeretnék   bēwn·che·lek·meynyt se·ret·neyk
bejelenteni.   be·ye·len·te·ni

I have insurance.
Van biztosításom.   von biz·taw·shee·ta·shawm

I've been ...
assaulted	Megtámadtak.	meg·ta·mod·tok
raped	Megerőszakoltak.	meg·e·rēū·so·kawl·tok
robbed	Kiraboltak.	ki·ro·bawl·tok

I've lost my ...	Elvesztettem ...	el-ves-tet-tem ...
My ... was/were stolen.	Ellopták ...	el-lawp-tak ...
backpack	a hátizsákomat	o ha-ti-zha-kaw-mot
bags	a csomagjaimat	o chaw-mog-yo-i-mot
credit card	a hitelkártyámat	o hi-tel-kar-tya-mot
handbag	a kézitáskámat	o key-zi-tash-ka-mot
jewellery	az ékszereimet	oz eyk-se-re-i-met
money	a pénzemet	o peyn-ze-met
passport	az útlevelemet	oz üt-le-ve-le-met
travellers cheques	az utazási csekkjeimet	oz u-to-za-shi chekk-ye-i-met
wallet	a tárcámat	o tar-tsa-mot

I want to contact my embassy/consulate.

Kapcsolatba akarok lépni a követségemmel/ konzulátusommal.

kop-chaw-lot-bo o-ko-rawk leyp-ni o keu-vet-shey-gem-mel/ kawn-zu-la-tu-shawm-mol

health

medical needs

Where's the nearest ...?	Hol a legközelebbi ...?	hawl o leg-keu-ze-leb-bi ...
dentist	fogorvos	fawg-awr-vawsh
doctor	orvos	awr-vawsh
hospital	kórház	kawr-haz
(night) pharmacist	(éjszaka nyitvatartó) gyógyszertár	(ey-so-ko nyit-vo-tor-täw) dyäwj-ser-tar

I need a doctor (who speaks English).

(Angolul beszélő) Orvosra van szükségem.

(on-gaw-lul be-sey-lēū) awr-vawsh-ro von sewk-shey-gem

Could I see a female doctor?

Beszélhetnék egy orvosnővel?

be-seyl-het-neyk ej awr-vawsh-nēū-vel

I've run out of my medication.

Elfogyott az orvosságom.

el-faw-dyawtt oz awr-vawsh-sha-gawm

symptoms, conditions & allergies

I'm sick.	Rosszul vagyok.	raws·sul vo·dyawk
It hurts here.	Itt fáj.	itt fa·y

I have a ...		
cough	Köhögök.	keu·heu·geuk
headache	Fáj a fejem.	fa·y o fe·yem
sore throat	Fáj a torkom.	fa·y o tawr·kawm
toothache	Fáj a fogam.	fa·y o faw·gom

I have (a) ...	... van.	... von
asthma	Asztmám	ost·mam
bronchitis	Hörghurutom	heurg·hu·rut·awm
constipation	Székrekedésem	seyk·re·ke·dey·shem
diarrhoea	Hasmenésem	hosh·me·ney·shem
fever	Lázam	la·zom
heart condition	Szívbetegségem	seev·be·teg·sheyg·em
nausea	Hányingerem	han'·in·ge·rem
pain	Fájdalmam	fay·dol·mom

I'm allergic to ...	Allergiás vagyok ...	ol·ler·gi·ash vo·dyawk ...
antibiotics	az antibiotikumokra	oz on·ti·bi·aw·ti·ku·mawk·ro
anti-inflammatories	a gyulladásgátlókra	o dyul·lo·dash·gat·läwk·ro
aspirin	az aszpirinre	oz os·pi·rin·re
bees	a méhekre	o mey·hek·re
codeine	a kodeinre	o ko·de·in·re
penicillin	a penicillinre	o pe·ni·tsil·lin·re

antiseptic n	fertőzésgátló	fer·tēū·zeysh·gat·läw
bandage	kötés	keu·teysh
condoms	óvszer	āwv·ser
contraceptives	fogamzásgátló	faw·gom·zash·gat·läw
diarrhoea medicine	hasmenés gyógyszer	hosh·men·eysh dyäwd'·ser
insect repellent	rovarirtó	raw·vor·ir·täw
laxatives	hashajtó	hosh·ho·y·täw
painkillers	fájdalomcsillapító	fa·y·do·lawm·chil·lo·pee·täw
rehydration salts	folyadékpótló sók	faw·yo·deyk·päwt·läw shäwk
sleeping tablets	altató	ol·to·täw

english–hungarian dictionary

In this dictionary, words are marked as n (noun), a (adjective), v (verb), sg (singular), pl (plural), inf (informal) or pol (polite) where necessary.

A

accident *baleset* bol-e-shet
accommodation *szállás* sal-lash
adaptor *adapter* o-dop-ter
address n *cím* tseem
after *után* u-tan
air-conditioned *légkondicionált* leyg-kawn-di-tsi-aw-nalt
airplane *repülőgép* re-pew-lêü-geyp
airport *repülőtér* re-pew-lêü-teyr
alcohol *alkohol* ol-kaw-hawl
all *minden* min-den
allergy *allergia* ol-ler-gi-o
ambulance *mentő* men-têü
and *és* eysh
ankle *boka* baw-ko
arm *kar* kor
ashtray *hamutartó* ho-mu-tor-tāw
ATM *bankautomata* bonk-o-u-taw-mo-to

B

baby *baba* bo-bo
back (body) *hát* hat
backpack *hátizsák* ha-ti-zhak
bad *rossz* rawss
bag *táska* tash-ko
baggage claim *poggyászkiadó* pawd'-dyas-ki-o-dāw
bank *bank* bonk
bar *bár* bar
bathroom *fürdőszoba* fewr-dêü-saw-bo
battery *elem* e-lem
beautiful *szép* seyp
bed *ágy* aj
beer *sör* sheur
before *előtt* e-lêütt
behind *mögött* meu-geutt
bicycle *bicikli* bi-tsik-li
big *nagy* noj
bill *számla* sam-lo
black *fekete* fe-ke-te

blanket *takaró* to-ko-rāw
blood group *vércsoport* veyr-chaw-pawrt
blue *kék* keyk
boat (big) *hajó* ho-yāw
boat (small) *csónak* chāw-nok
book (make a reservation) v *lefoglal* le-fawg-lol
bottle *üveg* ew-veg
bottle opener *sörnyitó* sheur-nyi-tāw
boy *fiú* fi-ü
brake (car) *fék* feyk
breakfast *reggeli* reg-ge-li
broken (faulty) *hibás* hi-bash
bus *busz* bus
business *üzlet* ewz-let
buy *vesz* ves

C

café *kávézó* ka-vey-zāw
camera *fényképezőgép* feyn'-key-pe-zêü-geyp
camp site *táborhely* ta-bawr-he-y
cancel *töröl* teu-reul
can opener *konzervnyitó* kawn-zerv-nyi-tāw
car *autó* o-u-tāw
cash n *készpénz* keys-peynz
cash (a cheque) v *bevált csekket* be-valt chek-ket
cell phone *mobil telefon* maw-bil te-le-fawn
centre n *központ* keuz-pawnt
change (money) v *pénzt vált* peynzt valt
cheap *olcsó* awl-chāw
check (bill) *számla* sam-lo
check-in n *bejelentkezés* be-ye-lent-ke-zeysh
chest *mellkas* mell-kosh
child *gyerek* dye-rek
cigarette *cigaretta* tsi-go-ret-to
city *város* va-rawsh
clean a *tiszta* tis-to
closed *zárva* zar-vo
coffee *kávé* ka-vey
coins *pénzérmék* peynz-eyr-meyk
cold a *hideg* hi-deg
collect call *'R' beszélgetés* er-be-seyl-ge-teysh
come *jön* yeun

computer *számítógép* sa-mee-täw-geyp
condom *óvszer* äwv-ser
contact lenses *kontaktlencse* kawn-tokt-len-che
cook v *főz* féüz
cost n *ár* ar
credit card *hitelkártya* hi-tel-kar-tyo
cup *csésze* chey-se
currency exchange *valutaátváltás* vo-lu-to-at-val-tash
customs (immigration) *vám* vam

D

dangerous *veszélyes* ve-sey-yesh
date (time) *dátum* da-tum
day *nap* nop
delay n *késés* key-sheysh
dentist *fogorvos* fawg-awr-vawsh
depart *elutazik* el-u-to-zik
diaper *pelenka* pe-len-ko
dictionary *szótár* sáw-tar
dinner *vacsora* vo-chaw-ro
direct *közvetlen* keuz-vet-len
dirty *piszkos* pis-kawsh
disabled *mozgássérült* mawz-gash-shey-rewlt
discount n *árengedmény* ar-en-ged-meyn'
doctor *orvos* awr-vawsh
double bed *dupla ágy* dup-lo aj
double room *duplaágyas szoba* dup-lo-a-dyosh saw-bo
drink n *ital* i-tol
drive v *vezet* ve-zet
drivers licence *jogosítvány* yaw-gaw-sheet-van'
drug (illicit) *kábítószerek* ka-bee-táw-se-rek
dummy (pacifier) *cumi* tsu-mi

E

ear *fül* fewl
east *kelet* ke-let
eat *eszik* e-sik
economy class *turistaosztály* tu-rish-to-aws-ta-y
electricity *villany* vil-lon'
elevator *lift* lift
email *e-mail* ee-meyl
embassy *nagykövetség* noj-keu-vet-sheyg
emergency *vészhelyzet* veys-he-y-zet
English (language) *angol* on-gawl
entrance *bejárat* be-ya-rot
evening *este* esh-te
exchange rate *átváltási árfolyam* at-val-ta-shi ar-faw-yom

exit n *kijárat* ki-ya-rot
expensive *drága* dra-go
express mail *expressz posta* eks-press pawsh-to
eye *szem* sem

F

far *messze* mes-se
fast *gyors* dyawrsh
father *apa* o-po
film (camera) *film* film
finger *ujj* u-y
first-aid kit *elsősegély-láda* el-shéü-she-gey-la-do
first class *első osztály* el-shéü aws-ta-y
fish n *hal* hol
food *ennivaló* en-ni-vo-láw
foot *lábfej* lab-fe-y
fork *villa* vil-lo
free (of charge) *ingyenes* in-dye-nesh
friend (female) *barátnő* bo-rat-néü
friend (male) *barát* bo-rat
fruit *gyümölcs* dyew-meulch
full *tele* te-le
funny *mulatságos* mu-lot-sha-gawsh

G

gift *ajándék* o-yan-deyk
girl *lány* lan'
glass (drinking) *üveg* ew-veg
glasses *szemüveg* sem-ew-veg
go *megy* mej
good *jó* yáw
green *zöld* zeuld
guide n *idegenvezető* i-de-gen-ve-ze-téü

H

half n *fél* feyl
hand *kéz* keyz
handbag *kézitáska* key-zi-tash-ko
happy *boldog* bawl-dawg
have *van neki* von ne-ki
he *ő* éü
head *fej* fe-y
heart *szív* seev
heat n *forróság* fawr-ráw-shag
heavy *nehéz* ne-heyz
help v *segít* she-geet
here *itt* itt

high *magas* mo-gosh
highway *országút* awr-sag-út
hike v *kirándul* ki-ran-dul
holiday *szabadság* so-bod-shag
homosexual n *homoszexuális* haw-maw-sek-su-a-lish
hospital *kórház* kawr-haz
hot *forró* fawr-ràw
hotel *szálloda* sal-law-do
Hungarian (language) *magyar* mo-dyor
Hungary *Magyarország* mo-dyor-awr-sag
hungry *éhes* ey-hesh
husband *férj* feyr-y

I

I *én* eyn
identification (card) *személyi igazolvány*
  se-mey-yi i-go-zawl-van'
ill *beteg* be-teg
important *fontos* fawn-tawsh
included *beleértve* be-le-eyrt-ve
injury *sérülés* shey-rew-leysh
insurance *biztosítás* biz-taw-shee-tash
Internet *Internet* in-ter-net
interpreter *tolmács* tawl-mach

J

jewellery *ékszerek* eyk-se-rek
job *állás* al-lash

K

key *kulcs* kulch
kilogram *kilogramm* ki-làw-gromm
kitchen *konyha* kawn'-ho
knife *kés* keysh

L

laundry (place) *mosoda* maw-shaw-do
lawyer *jogász* yaw-gas
left (direction) *balra* bol-ro
left-luggage office *csomagmegőrző*
  chaw-mog-meg-eür-zëü
leg *láb* lab
lesbian n *leszbikus* les-bi-kush
less *kevésbé* ke-veysh-bey
letter (mail) *levél* le-veyl
lift (elevator) *lift* lift

light n *fény* feyn'
like v *szeret* se-ret
lock n *zár* zar
long *hosszú* haws-sü
lost *elveszett* el-ve-sett
lost-property office *talált tárgyak hivatala*
  to-lalt tar-dyok hi-vo-to-lo
love v *szeret* se-ret
luggage *poggyász* pawd'-dyas
lunch *ebéd* e-beyd

M

mail n *posta* pawsh-to
man *férfi* feyr-fi
map *térkép* teyr-keyp
market *piac* pi-ots
matches *gyufa* dyu-fo
meat *hús* hüsh
medicine *orvosság* awr-vawsh-shag
menu *étlap* eyt-lop
message *üzenet* ew-ze-net
milk *tej* te-y
minute *perc* perts
mobile phone *mobil telefon* maw-bil te-le-fawn
money *pénz* peynz
month *hónap* hàw-nop
morning *reggel* reg-gel
mother *anya* o-nyo
motorcycle *motorbicikli* maw-tawr-bi-tsik-li
motorway *autópálya* o-u-tàw-pa-yo
mouth *száj* sa-y
music *zene* ze-ne

N

name *keresztnév* ke-rest-neyv
napkin *szalvéta* sol-vey-to
nappy *pelenka* pe-len-ko
near *közelében* keu-ze-ley-ben
neck *nyak* nyok
new *új* ü-y
news *hírek* hee-rek
newspaper *újság* ü-y-shag
night *éjszaka* ey-so-ko
no *nem* nem
noisy *zajos* zo-yawsh
nonsmoking *nemdohányzó* nem-daw-han'-zäw
north *észak* ey-sok
nose *orr* awrr
now *most* mawsht
number *szám* sam

O

oil (engine) olaj aw-lo-y
old (person/thing) öreg/régi eu-reg/rey-gi
one-way ticket csak oda jegy chok aw-do yej
open a nyitva nyit-vo
outside kint kint

P

package csomag chaw-mog
paper papír po-peer
park (a car) v parkol por-kawl
passport útlevél üt-le-veyl
pay fizet fi-zet
pen golyóstoll gaw-yawsh-tawll
petrol benzin ben-zin
pharmacy gyógyszertár dyäw-ser-tar
phonecard telefonkártya te-le-fawn-kar-tyo
photo fénykép feyn'-keyp
plate tányér ta-nyeyr
police rendőrség rend-ëür-sheyg
postcard levelezőlap le-ve-le-zëü-lop
post office postahivatal pawsh-to-hi-vo-tol
pregnant terhes ter-hesh
price ár ar

Q

quiet csendes chen-desh

R

rain n eső e-shëü
razor borotva baw-rawt-vo
receipt n nyugta nyug-to
red piros pi-rawsh
refund n visszatérítés vis-so-tey-ree-teysh
registered mail ajánlott levél o-yan-lawtt le-veyl
rent v bérel bey-rel
repair v megjavít meg-yo-veet
reservation foglalás fawg-lo-lash
restaurant étterem eyt-te-rem
return v visszatér vis-so-teyr
return ticket oda-vissza jegy aw-do-vis-so yej
right (direction) jobbra yawbb-ro
road út üt
room szoba saw-bo

S

safe a biztonságos biz-tawn-sha-gawsh
sanitary napkin egészségügyi törlőkendő
e-geys-sheyg-ew-dyi teur-lëü-ken-dëü
seat ülés ew-leysh
send küld kewld
service station benzinkút ben-zin-küt
sex szex seks
shampoo sampon shom-pawn
share (a dorm) v ben/ban lakik -ben/-ban lo-kik
shaving cream borotvakrém baw-rawt-vo-kreym
she ő ëü
sheet (bed) lepedő le-pe-dëü
shirt ing ing
shoes cipők tsi-pëük
shop n üzlet ewz-let
short alacsony o-lo-chawn'
shower zuhany zu-hon'
single room egyágyas szoba ej-a-dyosh saw-bo
skin bőr bëür
skirt szoknya sawk-nyo
sleep v alszik ol-sik
slowly lassan losh-shon
small kicsi ki-chi
smoke (cigarettes) v dohányzik daw-han'-zïk
soap szappan sop-pon
some néhány ney-han'
soon hamarosan ho-mo-raw-shon
south dél deyl
souvenir shop ajándékbolt o-yan-deyk-bawlt
speak beszél be-seyl
spoon kanál ko-nal
stamp n bélyeg bey-yeg
stand-by ticket készenléti jegy key-sen-ley-ti yej
station (train) állomás al-law-mash
stomach gyomor dyaw-mawr
stop v abbahagy ob-bo-hoj
stop (bus) n megálló meg-al-läw
street utca ut-tso
student diák di-ak
sun nap nop
sunscreen napolaj nop-aw-lo-y
swim v úszik ü-sik

T

tampons tampon tom-pawn
taxi taxi tok-si
teaspoon tedskanál te-ash-ko-nal
teeth fogak faw-gok
telephone n telefon te-le-fawn

television *televízió* te-le-vee-zi-áw
temperature (weather) *hőmérséklet*
   hēū-meyr-sheyk-let
tent *sátor* sha-tawr
that (one) *az* oz
they *ők* ēūk
thirsty *szomjas* sawm-yosh
this (one) *ez* ez
throat *torok* taw-rawk
ticket *jegy* yej
time *idő* i-dēū
tired *fáradt* fa-rott
tissues *szövetek* seu-ve-tek
today *ma* mo
toilet *vécé* vey-tsey
tomorrow *holnap* hawl-nop
tonight *ma este* mo esh-te
toothbrush *fogkefe* fawg-ke-fe
toothpaste *fogkrém* fawg-kreym
torch (flashlight) *zseblámpa* zheb-lam-po
tour n *túra* tū-ro
tourist office *turistairoda* tu-rish-to-i-raw-do
towel *törülköző* teu-rewl-keu-zēū
train *vonat* vaw-not
translate *fordít* fawr-deet
travel agency *utazási iroda* u-to-za-shi i-raw-do
travellers cheque *utazási csekk* u-to-za-shi chekk
trousers *nadrág* nod-rag
twin beds *két ágy* keyt aj
tyre *autógumi* o-u-tāw-gu-mi

U

underwear *alsónemű* ol-shāw-ne-mèw
urgent *sürgős* shewr-gēūsh

V

vacant *üres* ew-resh
vacation *vakáció* vo-ka-tsi-āw

vegetable n *zöldség* zeuld-sheyg
vegetarian a *vegetáriánus* ve-ge-ta-ri-a-nush
visa *vízum* vee-zum

W

waiter *pincér* pin-tseyr
walk v *sétál* shey-tal
wallet *tárcá* tar-tsa-mot
warm a *meleg* me-leg
wash (something) *megmos* meg-mawsh
watch n *óra* āw-ro
water *víz* veez
we *mi* mi
weekend *hétvége* heyt-vey-ge
west *nyugat* nyu-got
wheelchair *rokkantkocsi* rawk-kont-kaw-chi
when *mikor* mi-kawr
where *hol* hawl
white *fehér* fe-heyr
who *ki* ki
why *miért* mi-eyrt
wife *feleség* fe-le-sheyg
window *ablak* ob-lok
wine *bor* bawr
with *-val/-vel* -vol/-vel
without *nélkül* neyl-kewl
woman *nő* nēū
write *ír* eer

Y

yellow *sárga* shar-go
yes *igen* i-gen
yesterday *tegnap* teg-nop
you sg inf *te* te
you pl inf *ti* ti
you sg pol *Ön* eun
you pl pol *Önök* eu-neuk

Italian

italian alphabet

A a a	*B b* bee	*C c* chee	*D d* dee	*E e* e
F f e·fe	*G g* jee	*H h* a·ka	*I i* ee	*L l* e·le
M m e·me	*N n* e·ne	*O o* o	*P p* pee	*Q q* koo
R r e·re	*S s* e·se	*T t* tee	*U u* oo	*V v* voo
Z z tse·ta				

italian

ITALIANO

introduction

All you need for *la dolce vita* is to be able to tell your *Moschino* from your *macchiato* and your *Fellini* from your *fettuccine*. Happily, you'll find Italian (*italiano* ee-ta-*lya*-no) an easy language to start speaking as well as a beautiful one to listen to. When even a simple sentence sounds like an aria it can be difficult to resist striking up a conversation – and thanks to widespread migration and the huge popularity of Italian culture and cuisine, you're probably familiar with words like *ciao*, *pasta* and *bella* already.

There are also many similarities between Italian and English which smooth the way for language learners. Italian is a Romance language – a descendent of Latin, the language of the Romans (as are French, Spanish, Portuguese and Romanian), and English has been heavily influenced by Latin, particularly via contact with French.

Up until the 19th century, Italy was a collection of autonomous states, rather than a nation-state. As a result, Italian has many regional dialects, including Sardinian and Sicilian. Some dialects are so different from standard Italian as to be considered distinct languages in their own right. It wasn't until the 19th century that the Tuscan dialect – the language of Dante, Boccaccio and Petrarch – became the standard language of the nation, and the official language of schools, media and administration. 'Standard Italian' is the variety that will take you from the top of the boot to the very toe – all the language in this phrasebook is in standard Italian.

The majority of the approximately 65 million people who speak Italian live, of course, in Italy. However, the language also has official status in San Marino, Vatican City, parts of Switzerland, Slovenia and the Istrian peninsula of Croatia. Italian was the official language of Malta during the period of the Knights of St John (1530–1798) and afterwards shared that status with English during the British rule. Only in 1934 was Italian withdrawn and substituted with the native Maltese language. Today, Maltese people are generally fluent in Italian. It might surprise you to learn that Italian is also spoken in the African nation of Eritrea, which was a colony of Italy from 1880 until 1941. Most Eritreans nowadays speak Italian only as a second language. Italian is widely used in Albania, Monaco and France, and spoken by large communities of immigrants worldwide. This chapter is designed to help you on your adventures in the Italian-speaking world – so, as the Italians would say, *In bocca al lupo!* een bo-ka-*loo*-po (lit: in the mouth of the wolf) – good luck!

pronunciation

vowel sounds

Italian vowel sounds are generally shorter than those in English. They also tend not to run together to form vowel sound combinations (diphthongs), though it can often sound as if they do to English speakers.

symbol	english equivalent	italian example	transliteration
a	father	*pane*	*pa·*ne
ai	aisle	*mai*	mai
ay	say	*vorrei*	vo·*ray*
e	bet	*letto*	*le·*to
ee	see	*vino*	*vee·*no
o	pot	*molo*	*mo·*lo
oo	zoo	*frutta*	*froo·*ta
oy	toy	*poi*	poy
ow	how	*ciao, autobus*	chow, *ow·*to·boos

word stress

In Italian, you generally emphasise the second-last syllable of a word. When a written word has an accent marked on a vowel, though, the stress is on that syllable. The stressed syllable is always italicised in our pronunciation guides. The characteristic sing-song quality of an Italian sentence is created by pronouncing the syllables evenly and rhythmically, then swinging down on the last word.

consonant sounds

In addition to the sounds described on the next page, Italian consonants can also have a stronger, more emphatic pronunciation. The actual sounds are basically the same, though meaning can be altered between a normal consonant sound and this double consonant sound. The phonetic guides in this book don't distinguish between the two forms. Refer to the written Italian beside each phonetic guide as the cue –

if the word is written with a double consonant, use the stronger form. Even if you never distinguish them, you'll always be understood in context. Here are some examples where this 'double consonant' effect can make a difference:

sonno	son·no	**sleep**	*sono*	so·no	**I am**
pappa	pap·pa	**baby food**	*sono*	pa·pa	**pope**
			papa		

symbol	english equivalent	italian example	transliteration
b	**b**ed	*bello*	*be·lo*
ch	**ch**eat	*centro*	*chen·tro*
d	**d**og	*denaro*	*de·na·ro*
dz	a**dd**s	*mezzo, zaino*	*me·dzo, dzai·no*
f	**f**at	*fare*	*fa·re*
g	**g**o	*gomma*	*go·ma*
j	**j**oke	*cugino*	*ku·jee·no*
k	**k**it	*cambio, quanto*	*kam·byo, kwan·to*
l	**l**ot	*linea*	*lee·ne·a*
ly	mi**lli**on	*figlia*	*fee·lya*
m	**m**an	*madre*	*ma·dre*
n	**n**ot	*numero*	*noo·me·ro*
ny	ca**ny**on	*bagno*	*ba·nyo*
p	**p**et	*pronto*	*pron·to*
r	**r**ed (stronger and rolled)	*ristorante*	*ree·sto·ran·te*
s	**s**un	*sera*	*se·ra*
sh	**sh**ot	*sciare*	*shya·re*
t	**t**op	*teatro*	*te·a·tro*
ts	hi**ts**	*grazie, sicurezza*	*gra·tsye, see·koo·re·tsa*
v	**v**ery	*viaggio*	*vya·jo*
w	**w**in	*uomo*	*wo·mo*
y	**y**es	*italiano*	*ee·ta·lya·no*
z	**z**ero	*casa*	*ka·za*

tools

language difficulties

Do you speak English?
Parla inglese? par·la een·*gle*·ze

Do you understand?
Capisce? ka·*pee*·she

I (don't) understand.
(Non) capisco. (non) ka·*pee*·sko

What does (*giorno*) mean?
Che cosa vuol dire (giorno)? ke *ko*·za vwol *dee*·re (*jor*·no)

How do you ...? *Come si ...?* *ko*·me see ...
  pronounce this *pronuncia questo* pro·*noon*·cha *kwe*·sto
  write (*arrivederci*) *scrive (arrivederci)* *skree*·ve (a·ree·ve·*der*·chee)

Could you please ...? *Può ... per favore?* pwo ... per fa·*vo*·re
  repeat that *ripeterlo* ree·*pe*·ter·lo
  speak more *parlare più* par·*la*·re pyoo
    slowly *lentamente* len·ta·*men*·te
  write it down *scriverlo* *skree*·ver·lo

essentials

Yes.	*Sì.*	see
No.	*No.*	no
Please.	*Per favore.*	per fa·*vo*·re
Thank you (very much).	*Grazie (mille).*	*gra*·tsye (*mee*·le)
You're welcome.	*Prego.*	*pre*·go
Excuse me.	*Mi scusi.* pol	mee *skoo*·zee
	Scusami. inf	*skoo*·za·mee
Sorry.	*Mi dispiace.*	mee dees·*pya*·che

numbers

0	zero	*dze*·ro	16	sedici	*se*·dee·chee
1	uno	*oo*·no	17	diciassette	dee·cha·*se*·te
2	due	*doo*·e	18	diciotto	dee·*cho*·to
3	tre	tre	19	diciannove	dee·cha·*no*·ve
4	quattro	*kwa*·tro	20	venti	*ven*·tee
5	cinque	*cheen*·kwe	21	ventuno	ven·*too*·no
6	sei	say	22	ventidue	ven·tee·*doo*·e
7	sette	*se*·te	30	trenta	*tren*·ta
8	otto	*o*·to	40	quaranta	kwa·*ran*·ta
9	nove	*no*·ve	50	cinquanta	cheen·*kwan*·ta
10	dieci	*dye*·chee	60	sessanta	se·*san*·ta
11	undici	*oon*·dee·chee	70	settanta	se·*tan*·ta
12	dodici	*do*·dee·chee	80	ottanta	o·*tan*·ta
13	tredici	*tre*·dee·chee	90	novanta	no·*van*·ta
14	quattordici	kwa·*tor*·dee·chee	100	cento	*chen*·to
15	quindici	*kween*·dee·chee	1000	mille	*mee*·le

time & dates

What time is it?	*Che ora è?*	ke *o*·ra e
It's one o'clock.	*È l'una.*	e *loo*·na
It's (two) o'clock.	*Sono le (due).*	*so*·no le (*doo*·e)
Quarter past (one).	*(L'una) e un quarto.*	(*loo*·na) e oon *kwar*·to
Half past (one).	*(L'una) e mezza.*	(*loo*·na) e *me*·dza
Quarter to (eight).	*(Le otto) meno un quarto.*	(le *o*·to) *me*·no oon *kwar*·to
At what time ...?	*A che ora ...?*	a ke *o*·ra ...
At ...	*Alle ...*	*a*·le ...
am	*di mattina*	dee ma·*tee*·na
pm	*di pomeriggio*	dee po·me·*ree*·jo
Monday	*lunedì*	loo·ne·*dee*
Tuesday	*martedì*	mar·te·*dee*
Wednesday	*mercoledì*	mer·ko·le·*dee*
Thursday	*giovedì*	jo·ve·*dee*
Friday	*venerdì*	ve·ner·*dee*
Saturday	*sabato*	*sa*·ba·to
Sunday	*domenica*	do·*me*·nee·ka

January	*gennaio*	je-*na*-yo
February	*febbraio*	fe-*bra*-yo
March	*marzo*	*mar*-tso
April	*aprile*	a-*pree*-le
May	*maggio*	*ma*-jo
June	*giugno*	*joo*-nyo
July	*luglio*	*loo*-lyo
August	*agosto*	a-*gos*-to
September	*settembre*	se-*tem*-bre
October	*ottobre*	o-*to*-bre
November	*novembre*	no-*vem*-bre
December	*dicembre*	dee-*chem*-bre

What date is it today?
   Che giorno è oggi?   ke *jor*-no e *o*-jee

It's (15 December).
   È (il quindici) dicembre.   e (eel *kween*-dee-chee) dee-*chem*-bre

| since (May) | *da (maggio)* | da (*ma*-jo) |
| until (June) | *fino a (giugno)* | *fee*-no a (*joo*-nyo) |

yesterday	*ieri*	*ye*-ree
today	*oggi*	*o*-jee
tonight	*stasera*	sta-*se*-ra
tomorrow	*domani*	do-*ma*-nee

last ...		
night	*ieri notte*	*ye*-ree *no*-te
week	*la settimana scorsa*	la se-tee-*ma*-na *skor*-sa
month	*il mese scorso*	eel *me*-ze *skor*-so
year	*l'anno scorso*	*la*-no *skor*-so

next ...		
week	*la settimana prossima*	la se-tee-*ma*-na *pro*-see-ma
month	*il mese prossimo*	eel *me*-ze *pro*-see-mo
year	*l'anno prossimo*	*la*-no *pro*-see-mo

yesterday/tomorrow ...	*ieri/domani ...*	*ye*-ree/do-*ma*-nee ...
morning	*mattina*	ma-*tee*-na
afternoon	*pomeriggio*	po-me-*ree*-jo
evening	*sera*	*se*-ra

weather

What's the weather like?	Che tempo fa?	ke *tem*·po fa

It's ...
cloudy	È nuvoloso.	e noo·vo·*lo*·zo
cold	Fa freddo.	fa *fre*·do
hot	Fa caldo.	fa *kal*·do
raining	Piove.	*pyo*·ve
snowing	Nevica.	ne·*vee*·ka
sunny	È soleggiato.	e so·le·*ja*·to
warm	Fa bel tempo.	fa bel *tem*·po
windy	Tira vento.	*tee*·ra *ven*·to

spring	primavera f	pree·ma·*ve*·ra
summer	estate f	es·*ta*·te
autumn	autunno m	ow·*too*·no
winter	inverno m	een·*ver*·no

border crossing

I'm here ...	Sono qui ...	*so*·no kwee ...
in transit	in transito	een *tran*·see·to
on business	per affari	per a·*fa*·ree
on holiday	in vacanza	een va·*kan*·tsa

I'm here for ...	Sono qui per ...	*so*·no kwee per ...
(10) days	(dieci) giorni	(*dye*·chee) *jor*·nee
(three) weeks	(tre) settimane	(tre) se·tee·*ma*·ne
(two) months	(due) mesi	(*doo*·e) *me*·zee

I'm going to (Perugia).
Vado a (Perugia). · *va*·do a (pe·*roo*·ja)

I'm staying at the (Minerva Hotel).
Alloggio al (Minerva). · a·*lo*·jo al (mee·*ner*·va)

I have nothing to declare.
Non ho niente da dichiarare. · non o *nyen*·te da dee·kya·*ra*·re

I have something to declare.
Ho delle cose da dichiarare. · o *de*·le *ko*·ze da dee·kya·*ra*·re

That's (not) mine. m/f
(Non) è mio/mia. · (non) e *mee*·o/*mee*·a

tools – ITALIAN

279

transport

tickets & luggage

Where can I buy a ticket?
Dove posso comprare un biglietto?   do·ve po·so kom·pra·re oon bee·lye·to

Do I need to book a seat?
Bisogna prenotare un posto?   bee·zo·nya pre·no·ta·re oon pos·to

One ... ticket (to Rome), please.	*Un biglietto ... (per Roma), per favore.*	oon bee·lye·to ... (per ro·ma) per fa·vo·re
one-way	*di sola andata*	dee so·la an·da·ta
return	*di andata e ritorno*	dee an·da·ta e ree·tor·no
I'd like to ... my ticket, please.	*Vorrei ... il mio biglietto, per favore.*	vo·ray ... eel mee·o bee·lye·to per fa·vo·re
cancel	*cancellare*	kan·che·la·re
change	*cambiare*	kam·bya·re
collect	*ritirare*	ree·tee·ra·re
confirm	*confermare*	kon·fer·ma·re
I'd like a ... seat, please.	*Vorrei un posto ..., per favore.*	vo·ray oon pos·to ... per fa·vo·re
nonsmoking	*per non fumatori*	per non foo·ma·to·ree
smoking	*per fumatori*	per foo·ma·to·ree

How much is it?
Quant'è?   kwan·te

Is there air conditioning?
C'è l'aria condizionata?   che la·rya kon·dee·tsyo·na·ta

Is there a toilet?
C'è un gabinetto?   che oon ga·bee·ne·to

How long does the trip take?
Quanto ci vuole?   kwan·to chee vwo·le

Is it a direct route?
È un itinerario diretto?   e oo·nee·tee·ne·ra·ryo dee·re·to

I'd like a luggage locker.
Vorrei un armadietto per il bagaglio.   vo·ray oon ar·ma·dye·to per eel ba·ga·lyo

My luggage	Il mio bagaglio	eel *mee*-o ba-*ga*-lyo
has been ...	è stato ...	e *sta*-to ...
damaged	danneggiato	da-ne-*ja*-to
lost	perso	*per*-so
stolen	rubato	roo-*ba*-to

getting around

Where does flight (004) arrive?
Dove arriva il volo (004)? do-ve a-*ree*-va eel *vo*-lo (*dze*-ro *dze*-ro *kwa*-tro)

Where does flight (004) depart?
Da dove parte il volo (004)? da *do*-ve *par*-te eel *vo*-lo (*dze*-ro *dze*-ro *kwa*-tro)

Where's the ...?	Dove sono ...?	*do*-ve *so*-no ...
arrivalls hall	gli arrivi	lyee a-*ree*-vee
departures hall	le partenze	le par-*ten*-dze

Is this the ...	È questo/questa ...	e *kwes*-to/*kwes*-ta ...
to (Venice)?	per (Venezia)? m/f	per (ve-*ne*-tsya)
boat	la nave f	la *na*-ve
bus	l'autobus m	*low*-to-boos
plane	l'aereo m	la-*e*-re-o
train	il treno m	eel *tre*-no

What time's	A che ora passa	a ke *o*-ra *pa*-sa
the ... bus?	... autobus?	... *ow*-to-boos
first	il primo	eel *pree*-mo
last	l'ultimo	*lool*-tee-mo
next	il prossimo	eel *pro*-see-mo

At what time does it arrive/leave?
A che ora arriva/parte? a ke *o*-ra a-*ree*-va/*par*-te

How long will it be delayed?
Di quanto ritarderà? dee *kwan*-to ree-tar-de-*ra*

What station/stop is this?
Che stazione/fermata è questa? ke sta-*tsyo*-ne/fer-*ma*-ta e *kwe*-sta

What's the next station/stop?
Qual'è la prossima stazione/ fermata? kwa-*le* la *pro*-see-ma sta-*tsyo*-ne/ fer-*ma*-ta

Does it stop at (Milan)?
Si ferma a (Milano)? see *fer*-ma a (mee-*la*-no)

Please tell me when we get to (Taranto).
Mi dica per favore quando arriviamo a (Taranto).
mee *dee*·ka per fa·*vo*·re *kwan*·do a·ree·*vya*·mo a (ta·*ran*·to)

How long do we stop here?
Per quanto tempo ci fermiamo qui?
per *kwan*·to *tem*·po chee fer·*mya*·mo kwee

Is this seat available?
È libero questo posto?
e *lee*·be·ro *kwe*·sto *pos*·to

That's my seat.
Quel posto è mio.
kwel *pos*·to e *mee*·o

I'd like a taxi …	*Vorrei un tassì …*	vo·*ray* oon ta·*see* …
at (9am)	*alle (nove di mattina)*	*a*·le (*no*·ve dee ma·*tee*·na)
now	*adesso*	a·*de*·so
tomorrow	*domani*	do·*ma*·nee

Is this taxi available?
È libero questo tassì?
e *lee*·be·ro *kwe*·sto ta·*see*

How much is it to …?
Quant'è per …?
kwan·*te* per …

Please put the meter on.
Usi il tassametro, per favore.
oo·zee eel ta·sa·*me*·tro per fa·*vo*·re

Please take me to (this address).
Mi porti a (questo indirizzo), per piacere.
mee *por*·tee a (*kwe*·sto een·dee·*ree*·tso) per pya·*che*·re

Please …	*…, per favore.*	… per fa·*vo*·re
slow down	*Rallenti*	ra·*len*·tee
stop here	*Si fermi qui*	see *fer*·mee kwee
wait here	*Mi aspetti qui*	mee as·*pe*·tee kwee

car, motorbike & bicycle hire

I'd like to hire a/an …	*Vorrei noleggiare …*	vo·*ray* no·le·*ja*·re …
bicycle	*una bicicletta*	*oo*·na bee·chee·*kle*·ta
car	*una macchina*	*oo*·na *ma*·kee·na
motorbike	*una moto*	*oo*·na *mo*·to
with …	*con …*	kon …
a driver	*un'autista*	oo·now·*tee*·sta
air conditioning	*aria condizionata*	*a*·rya kon·dee·tsyo·*na*·ta

How much for ... hire?	*Quanto costa ...?*	kwan·to kos·ta ...
hourly	*all'ora*	a·lo·ra
daily	*al giorno*	al jor·no
weekly	*alla settimana*	a·la se·tee·ma·na

air	*aria* f	a·rya
oil	*olio* m	o·lyo
petrol	*benzina* f	ben·dzee·na
tyres	*gomme* f pl	go·me

I need a mechanic.
Ho bisogno di un meccanico.   o bee·zo·nyo dee oon me·ka·nee·ko

I've run out of petrol.
Ho esaurito la benzina.   o e·zow·ree·to la ben·dzee·na

I have a flat tyre.
Ho una gomma bucata.   o oo·na go·ma boo·ka·ta

directions

Where's the ...?	*Dov'è ...?*	do·ve ...
bank	*la banca*	la ban·ka
city centre	*il centro città*	eel chen·tro chee·ta
hotel	*l'albergo*	lal·ber·go
market	*il mercato*	eel mer·ka·to
police station	*il posto di polizia*	eel pos·to dee po·lee·tsee·a
post office	*l'ufficio postale*	loo·fee·cho pos·ta·le
public toilet	*il gabinetto*	eel ga·bee·ne·to
	pubblico	poo·blee·ko
tourist office	*l'ufficio del turismo*	loo·fee·cho del too·reez·mo

Is this the road to (Milan)?
Questa strada porta a (Milano)?   kwe·sta stra·da por·ta a (mee·la·no)

Can you show me (on the map)?
Può mostrarmi (sulla pianta)?   pwo mos·trar·mee (soo·la pyan·ta)

What's the address?
Qual è l'indirizzo?   kwa·le leen·dee·ree·tso

How far is it?
Quant'è distante?   kwan·te dees·tan·te

How do I get there?
Come ci si arriva?   ko·me chee see a·ree·va

Turn ...	Giri ...	jee·ree ...
at the corner	all'angolo	a·lan·go·lo
at the traffic lights	al semaforo	al se·ma·fo·ro
left/right	a sinistra/destra	a see·nee·stra/de·stra

It's ...	È ...	e ...
behind ...	dietro ...	dye·tro ...
far away	lontano	lon·ta·no
here	qui	kwee
in front of ...	davanti a ...	da·van·tee a ...
left	a sinistra	a see·nee·stra
near (to ...)	vicino (a ...)	vee·chee·no (a ...)
next to ...	accanto a ...	a·kan·to a ...
on the corner	all'angolo	a lan·go·lo
opposite ...	di fronte a ...	dee fron·te a ...
right	a destra	a de·stra
straight ahead	sempre diritto	sem·pre dee·ree·to
there	là	la

by bus	con l'autobus	kon low·to·boos
by taxi	con il tassì	ko·neel ta·see
by train	con il treno	ko·neel tre·no
on foot	a piedi	a pye·dee

north	nord m	nord
south	sud m	sood
east	est m	est
west	ovest m	o·vest

signs

Entrata/Uscita	en·tra·ta/oo·shee·ta	Entrance/Exit
Aperto/Chiuso	a·per·to/kyoo·zo	Open/Closed
Camere Libere	ka·me·re lee·be·re	Rooms Available
Completo	kom·ple·to	No Vacancies
Informazioni	een·for·ma·tsyo·nee	Information
Posto di Polizia	pos·to dee po·lee·tsee·a	Police Station
Proibito	pro·ee·bee·to	Prohibited
Gabinetti	ga·bee·ne·tee	Toilets
Uomini	wo·mee·nee	Men
Donne	do·ne	Women
Caldo/Freddo	kal·do/fre·do	Hot/Cold

accommodation

finding accommodation

Where's a/an ...?	Dov'è ...?	do·ve ...
camping ground	un campeggio	oon kam·pe·jo
guesthouse	una pensione	oo·na pen·syo·ne
inn	una locanda	oo·na lo·kan·da
hotel	un albergo	oo·nal·ber·go
youth hostel	un ostello della gioventù	oo·nos·te·lo de·la jo·ven·too

Can you recommend somewhere ...?	Può consigliare qualche posto ...?	pwo kon·see·lya·re kwal·ke pos·to ...
cheap	economico	e·ko·no·mee·ko
good	buono	bwo·no
nearby	vicino	vee·chee·no

I'd like to book a room, please.
Vorrei prenotare una camera, per favore.
vo·ray pre·no·ta·re oo·na ka·me·ra per fa·vo·re

I have a reservation.
Ho una prenotazione.
o oo·na pre·no·ta·tsyo·ne

My name's ...
Mi chiamo ...
mee kya·mo ...

Do you have a ... room?	Avete una camera ...?	a·ve·te oo·na ka·me·ra ...
single	singola	seen·go·la
double	doppia con letto matrimoniale	do·pya kon le·to ma·tree·mo·nya·le
twin	doppia a due letti	do·pya a doo·e le·tee

How much is it per ...?	Quanto costa per ...?	kwan·to kos·ta per ...
night	una notte	oo·na no·te
person	persona	per·so·na

Can I pay by ...?	Posso pagare con ...?	po·so pa·ga·re kon ...
credit card	la carta di credito	la kar·ta dee kre·dee·to
travellers cheque	un assegno di viaggio	oo·na·se·nyo dee vee·a·jo

I'd like to stay for (two) nights.
Vorrei rimanere (due) notti.   vo·*ray* ree·ma·*ne*·re (*doo*·e) *no*·tee

From (July 2) to (July 6).
Dal (due luglio) al (sei luglio).   dal (*doo*·e *loo*·lyo) al (say *loo*·lyo)

Can I see it?
Posso vederla?   *po*·so ve·*der*·la

Am I allowed to camp here?
Si può campeggiare qui?   see pwo kam·pe·*ja*·re kwee

Is there a camp site nearby?
C'è un campeggio qui vicino?   che oon kam·*pe*·jo kwee vee·*chee*·no

requests & queries

When's breakfast served?
A che ora è la prima colazione?   a ke *o*·ra e la *pree*·ma ko·la·*tsyo*·ne

Where's breakfast served?
Dove si prende la prima colazione?   *do*·ve see *pren*·de la *pree*·ma ko·la·*tsyo*·ne

Please wake me at (seven).
Mi svegli alle (sette), per favore.   mee *sve*·lyee *a*·le (*se*·te) per fa·*vo*·re

Could I have my key, please?
Posso avere la chiave, per favore?   *po*·so a·*ve*·re la *kya*·ve per fa·*vo*·re

Can I get another (blanket)?
Può darmi un altra (coperta)?   pwo *dar*·mee oo·*nal*·tra (ko·*per*·ta)

This (sheet) isn't clean.
Questo (lenzuolo) non è pulito.   *kwe*·sto (len·*tzwo*·lo) non e poo·*lee*·to

Is there a/an ...?	*C'è ...?*	che ...
elevator	*un ascensore*	oo·na·shen·*so*·re
safe	*una cassaforte*	oo·na ka·sa·*for*·te
The room is too ...	*La camera è troppo ...*	la *ka*·me·ra e *tro*·po ...
expensive	*cara*	*ka*·ra
noisy	*rumorosa*	roo·mo·*ro*·za
small	*piccola*	*pee*·ko·la
The ... doesn't work.	*... non funziona.*	... non foon·*tsyo*·na
air conditioning	*L'aria condizionata*	*la*·rya kon·dee·tsyo·*na*·ta
fan	*Il ventilatore*	eel ven·tee·la·*to*·re
toilet	*Il gabinetto*	eel ga·bee·*ne*·to

checking out

What time is checkout?
A che ora si deve lasciar   a ke o·ra see *de*·ve la·*shar*
libera la camera?   *lee*·be·ra la *ka*·me·ra

Can I leave my luggage here?
Posso lasciare ili mio bagaglio qui?   *po*·so la·*sha*·re eel *mee*·o ba·*ga*·lyo kwee

Could I have my ..., please?	*Posso avere ..., per favore?*	*po*·so a·*ve*·re ... per fa·*vo*·re
deposit	*la caparra*	la ka·*pa*·ra
passport	*il mio passaporto*	eel *mee*·o pa·sa·*por*·to
valuables	*i miei oggetti di valore*	ee myay o·*je*·tee dee va·*lo*·re

communications & banking

the internet

Where's the local Internet café?
Dove si trova l'Internet point?   *do*·ve see *tro*·va *leen*·ter·net poynt

How much is it per hour?
Quanto costa all'ora?   *kwan*·to *kos*·ta a·*lo*·ra

I'd like to ...	*Vorrei ...*	vo·*ray* ...
check my email	*controllare le mie email*	kon·tro·*la*·re le *mee*·e e·mayl
get Internet access	*usare Internet*	oo·*za*·re *een*·ter·net
use a printer	*usare una stampante*	oo·*za*·re *oo*·na stam·*pan*·te
use a scanner	*scandire*	skan·*dee*·re

mobile/cell phone

I'd like a ...	*Vorrei ...*	vo·*ray* ...
mobile/cell phone for hire	*un cellulare da noleggiare*	oon che·loo·*la*·re da no·le·*ja*·re
SIM card for your network	*un SIM card per la rete telefonica*	oon seem kard per la *re*·te te·le·*fo*·nee·ka

What are the rates?   *Quali sono le tariffe?*   *kwa*·lee *so*·no le ta·*ree*·fe

telephone

What's your phone number?
Qual'è il Suo/tuo numero kwa-*le* eel *soo*-o/*too*-o *noo*-me-ro
di telefono? pol/inf dee te-*le*-fo-no

The number is ...
Il numero è ... eel *noo*-me-ro e ...

Where's the nearest public phone?
Dov'è il telefono pubblico do-*ve* eel te-*le*-fo-no *poo*-blee-ko
più vicino? pyoo vee-*chee*-no

I'd like to buy a phonecard.
Vorrei comprare una vo-*ray* kom-*pra*-re *oo*-na
scheda telefonica. *ske*-da te-le-*fo*-nee-ka

I want to ...	*Vorrei ...*	vo-*ray* ...
call (Singapore)	*fare una chiamata*	*fa*-re *oo*-na kya-*ma*-ta
	a (Singapore)	a (seen-ga-*po*-re)
make a local call	*fare una chiamata*	*fa*-re *oo*-na kya-*ma*-ta
	locale	lo-*ka*-le
reverse the charges	*fare una chiamata a*	*fa*-re *oo*-na kya-*ma*-ta a
	carico del destinatario	ka-ree-ko del des-tee-na-*ta*-ryo

How much does ... cost?	*Quanto costa ...?*	kwan-to *kos*-ta ...
a (three)-minute	*una telefonata*	*oo*-na te-le-fo-*na*-ta
call	*di (tre) minuti*	dee (tre) mee-*noo*-tee
each extra minute	*ogni minuto in più*	*o*-nyee mee-*noo*-to een pyoo

It's (one euro) per (minute).
(Un euro) per (un minuto). (oon e-*oo*-ro) per (oon mee-*noo*-to)

post office

I want to send a ...	*Vorrei mandare ...*	vo-*ray* man-*da*-re ...
fax	*un fax*	oon faks
letter	*una lettera*	*oo*-na *le*-te-ra
parcel	*un pacchetto*	oon pa-*ke*-to
postcard	*una cartolina*	*oo*-na kar-to-*lee*-na

I want to buy ...	*Vorrei comprare ...*	vo-*ray* kom-*pra*-re ...
an envelope	*una busta*	*oo*-na *boo*-sta
stamps	*dei francobolli*	day fran-ko-*bo*-lee

Please send it	*Lo mandi ... (in*	lo *man*·dee ... (een
(to Australia) by ...	*Australia), per favore.*	ow·*stra*·lya) per fa·*vo*·re
airmail	*via aerea*	vee·a a·*e*·re·a
express mail	*posta prioritaria*	*pos*·ta pryo·ree·*ta*·rya
registered mail	*posta raccomandata*	*pos*·ta ra·ko·man·*da*·ta
surface mail	*posta ordinaria*	*pos*·ta or·dee·*na*·rya

Is there any mail for me? *C'è posta per me?*   che *pos*·ta per me

bank

Where's a/an ...?	*Dov'è ... più vicino?*	do·*ve* ... pyoo vee·*chee*·no
ATM	*il Bancomat*	eel *ban*·ko·mat
foreign exchange office	*il cambio*	eel *kam*·byo

I'd like to ...	*Vorrei ...*	vo·*ray* ...
Where can I ...?	*Dove posso ...?*	*do*·ve *po*·so ...
arrange a transfer	*trasferire soldi*	tras·fe·*ree*·re *sol*·dee
cash a cheque	*riscuotere*	ree·*skwo*·te·re
	un assegno	oo·na·*se*·nyo
change a travellers cheque	*cambiare un assegno di viaggio*	kam·*bya*·re oo·na·*se*·nyo dee vee·*a*·jo
change money	*cambiare denaro*	kam·*bya*·re de·*na*·ro
get a cash advance	*prelevare con carta di credito*	pre·le·*va*·re kon *kar*·ta dee *kre*·dee·to
withdraw money	*fare un prelievo*	*fa*·re oon pre·*lye*·vo

What's the ...?	*Quant'è ...?*	kwan·*te* ...
commission	*la commissione*	la ko·mee·*syo*·ne
exchange rate	*il cambio*	eel *kam*·byo

It's ...	*È ...*	e ...
(12) euros	*(dodici) euro*	(*do*·dee·chee) e·*oo*·ro
free	*gratuito*	gra·too·*ee*·to

What's the charge for that?
Quanto costa?   kwan·to *kos*·ta

What time does the bank open?
A che ora apre la banca?   a ke *o*·ra *a*·pre la *ban*·ka

Has my money arrived yet?
È arrivato il mio denaro?   e a·ree·*va*·to eel *mee*·o de·*na*·ro

sightseeing

getting in

What time does it open/close?
A che ora apre/chiude?
a ke *o*·ra *a*·pre/*kyoo*·de

What's the admission charge?
Quant'è il prezzo d'ingresso?
kwan·*te* eel *pre*·tso deen·*gre*·so

Is there a discount for children/students?
*C'è uno sconto per
bambini/studenti?*
che *oo*·no *skon*·to per
bam·*bee*·nee/stoo·*den*·tee

I'd like a ...
Vorrei ...
vo·*ray* ...

catalogue
un catalogo
oon ka·*ta*·lo·go

guide
una guida
oo·na *gwee*·da

local map
*una cartina
della zona*
oo·na kar·*tee*·na
de·la *dzo*·na

I'd like to see ...
Vorrei vedere ...
vo·*ray* ve·*de*·re ...

What's that?
Cos'è?
ko·*ze*

Can I take a photo?
Posso fare una foto?
po·so *fa*·re *oo*·na *fo*·to

tours

**When's the
next ...?**
*A che ora parte la
prossima ...?*
a ke *o*·ra *par*·te la
pro·see·ma ...

day trip
*escursione
in giornata*
es·koor·*syo*·ne
een jor·*na*·ta

tour
gita turistica
jee·ta too·ree·*stee*·ka

Is ... included?
È incluso ...?
e een·*kloo*·zo ...

accommodation
l'alloggio
la·*lo*·jo

the admission charge
il prezzo d'ingresso
eel *pre*·tso deen·*gre*·so

food
il vitto
eel *vee*·to

transport
il trasporto
eel tras·*por*·to

How long is the tour?
Quanto dura la gita?
kwan·to *doo*·ra la *jee*·ta

What time should we be back?
A che ora dovremmo ritornare?
a ke *o*·ra dov·*re*·mo ree·tor·*na*·re

sightseeing

castle	castello m	kas-te-lo
cathedral	duomo m	dwo-mo
church	chiesa f	kye-za
main square	piazza principale f	pya-tsa preen-chee-pa-le
monastery	monastero m	mo-nas-te-ro
monument	monumento m	mo-noo-men-to
museum	museo m	moo-ze-o
old city	centro storico m	chen-tro sto-ree-ko
palace	palazzo m	pa-la-tso
ruins	rovine f pl	ro-vee-ne
stadium	stadio m	sta-dyo
statues	statue f pl	sta-too-e

shopping

enquiries

Where's a ...?	Dov'è ...?	do-ve ...
bank	la banca	la ban-ka
bookshop	la libreria	la lee-bre-ree-a
camera shop	il fotografo	eel fo-to-gra-fo
department store	il grande magazzino	eel gran-de ma-ga-dzee-no
grocery store	la drogheria	la dro-ge-ree-a
market	il mercato	eel mer-ka-to
newsagency	l'edicola	le-dee-ko-la
supermarket	il supermercato	eel soo-per-mer-ka-to

Where can I buy (a padlock)?

Dove posso comprare (un lucchetto)?   do-ve po-so kom-pra-re (oon loo-ke-to)

I'm looking for ...

Sto cercando ...   sto cher-kan-do ...

Can I look at it?
Posso dare un'occhiata? po·so da·re oo·no·kya·ta

Do you have any others?
Ne avete altri? ne a·ve·te al·tree

Does it have a guarantee?
Ha la garanzia? a la ga·ran·tsee·a

Can I have it sent overseas?
Può spedirlo all'estero? pwo spe·deer·lo a·les·te·ro

Can I have my ... repaired?
Posso far aggiustare ... qui? po·so far a·joo·sta·re ... kwee

It's faulty.
È difettoso. e dee·fe·to·zo

I'd like (a) ..., please.	*Vorrei ..., per favore.*	vo·ray ... per fa·vo·re
bag	*un sacchetto*	oon sa·ke·to
refund	*un rimborso*	oon reem·bor·so
to return this	*restituire questo*	res·tee·twee·re kwe·sto

paying

How much is it?
Quant'è? kwan·te

Can you write down the price?
Può scrivere il prezzo? pwo skree·ve·re eel pre·tso

That's too expensive.
È troppo caro. e tro·po ka·ro

Can you lower the price?
Può farmi lo sconto? pwo far·mee lo skon·to

I'll give you (five) euros.
Le offro (cinque) euro. le o·fro (cheen·kwe) e·oo·ro

There's a mistake in the bill.
C'è un errore nel conto. che oon e·ro·re nel kon·to

Do you accept ...?	*Accettate ...?*	a·che·ta·te ...
credit cards	*la carta di credito*	la kar·ta dee kre·dee·to
debit cards	*la carta di debito*	la kar·ta dee de·bee·to
travellers cheques	*gli assegni di viaggio*	lyee a·se·nyee dee vee·a·jo

I'd like …, please.	Vorrei …, per favore.	vo-*ray* … per fa-*vo*-re
a receipt	*una ricevuta*	*oo*-na ree-che-*voo*-ta
my change	*il mio resto*	eel *mee*-o *res*-to

clothes & shoes

Can I try it on?	Potrei provarmelo?	po-*tray* pro-*var*-me-lo
My size is (40).	Sono una taglia (quaranta).	*so*-no *oo*-na *ta*-lya (kwa-*ran*-ta)
It doesn't fit.	Non va bene.	non va *be*-ne

small	*piccola*	*pee*-ko-la
medium	*media*	*me*-dya
large	*forte*	*for*-te

books & music

I'd like a …	Vorrei …	vo-*ray* …
newspaper	*un giornale*	oon jor-*na*-le
(in English)	*(in inglese)*	(een een-*gle*-ze)
pen	*una penna*	*oo*-na *pe*-na

Is there an English-language bookshop?

| *C'è una libreria specializzata* | che *oo*-na lee-bre-*ree*-a spe-cha-lee-*dza*-ta |
| *in lingua inglese?* | een *leen*-gwa een-*gle*-ze |

I'm looking for something by (Alberto Moravia).

| *Sto cercando qualcosa di* | sto cher-*kan*-do kwal-*ko*-za dee |
| *(Alberto Moravia).* | (al-*ber*-to mo-*ra*-vee-a) |

Can I listen to this?

| *Potrei ascoltarlo?* | po-*tray* as-kol-*tar*-lo |

photography

Can you …?	Potrebbe …?	po-*tre*-be …
burn a CD from	*masterizzare un*	mas-te-ree-*tsa*-re oon
my memory card	*CD dalla mia*	chee dee *da*-la *mee*-a
	memory card	*me*-mo-ree kard
develop this	*sviluppare*	svee-loo-*pa*-re
film	*questo rullino*	*kwe*-sto roo-*lee*-no
load my film	*inserire il*	een-se-*ree*-re eel
	mio rullino	*mee*-o roo-*lee*-no

I need a/an ... film for this camera.	Vorrei un rullino ... per questa macchina fotografica.	vo·ray oon roo·lee·no ... per kwe·sta ma·kee·na fo·to·gra·fee·ka
APS	da APS	da a·pee·e·se
B&W	in bianco e nero	een byan·ko e ne·ro
colour	a colori	a ko·lo·ree
slide	per diapositive	per dee·a·po·zee·tee·ve
(200) speed	da (duecento) ASA	da (doo·e chen·to) a·za
When will it be ready?	Quando sarà pronto?	kwan·do sa·ra pron·to

meeting people

greetings, goodbyes & introductions

Hello.	Buongiorno.	bwon·jor·no
Hi.	Ciao.	chow
Good night.	Buonanotte.	bwo·na·no·te
Goodbye.	Arrivederci.	a·ree·ve·der·chee
Bye.	Ciao.	chow
See you later.	A più tardi.	a pyoo tar·dee
Mr	Signore	see·nyo·re
Mrs	Signora	see·nyo·ra
Miss	Signorina	see·nyo·ree·na
How are you?	Come sta? pol	ko·me sta
	Come stai? inf	ko·me stai
Fine. And you?	Bene. E Lei? pol	be·ne e lay
	Bene. E tu? inf	be·ne e too
What's your name?	Come si chiama? pol	ko·me see kya·ma
	Come ti chiami? inf	ko·me tee kya·mee
My name is ...	Mi chiamo ...	mee kya·mo ...
I'm pleased to meet you.	Piacere.	pya·che·re

This is my ...	Le/Ti presento ... pol/inf	le/tee pre-*zen*-to ...
boyfriend	mio ragazzo	*mee*-o ra-*ga*-tso
brother	mio fratello	*mee*-o fra-*te*-lo
daughter	mia figlia	*mee*-a *fee*-lya
father	mio padre	*mee*-o *pa*-dre
friend	il mio amico m	eel *mee*-o a-*mee*-ko
	la mia amica f	la *mee*-a a-*mee*-ka
girlfriend	mia ragazza	*mee*-a ra-*ga*-tsa
husband	mio marito	*mee*-o ma-*ree*-to
mother	mia madre	*mee*-a *ma*-dre
partner (intimate)	il mio compagno m	eel *mee*-o kom-*pa*-nyo
	la mia compagna f	la *mee*-a kom-*pa*-nya
sister	mia sorella	*mee*-a so-*re*-la
son	mio figlio	*mee*-o *fee*-lyo
wife	mia moglie	*mee*-a *mo*-lye

Here's my ...	Ecco il mio ...	e-ko eel *mee*-o ...
What's your ...?	Qual'è il	kwa-*le* eel
	Suo/tuo ...? pol/inf	*soo*-o/*too*-o ...
address	indirizzo	een-dee-*ree*-tso
email address	indirizzo di email	een-dee-*ree*-tso dee e-mayl
fax number	numero di fax	*noo*-me-ro dee faks
phone number	numero di telefono	*noo*-me-ro dee te-*le*-fo-no

occupations

What's your occupation?	Che lavoro fa/fai? pol/inf	ke la-*vo*-ro fa/fai
I'm a/an ...	Sono ...	*so*-no ...
artist	artista m&f	ar-*tees*-ta
business person	uomo/donna	*wo*-mo/*do*-na
	d'affari m/f	da-*fa*-ree
farmer	agricoltore m	a-gree-kol-*to*-re
	agricoltrice f	a-gree-kol-*tree*-che
manual worker	manovale m&f	ma-no-*va*-le
office worker	impiegato/a m/f	eem-pye-*ga*-to/a
scientist	scienziato/a m/f	shen-tsee-*a*-to/a
student	studente m	stoo-*den*-te
	studentessa f	stoo-den-*te*-sa
tradesperson	operaio/a m/f	o-pe-*ra*-yo/a

background

Where are you from?	*Da dove viene/vieni?* pol/inf	da *do*·ve *vye*·ne/*vye*·nee
I'm from ...	*Vengo ...*	*ven*·go ...
Australia	*dall'Australia*	dal·ow·*stra*·lya
Canada	*dal Canada*	dal *ka*·na·da
England	*dall'Inghilterra*	da·leen·geel·*te*·ra
New Zealand	*dalla Nuova Zelanda*	*da*·la *nwo*·va ze·*lan*·da
the USA	*dagli Stati Uniti*	*da*·lyee sta·tee oo·*nee*·tee
Are you married?	*È sposato/a?* m/f pol	e spo·*za*·to/a
	Sei sposato/a? m/f inf	say spo·*za*·to/a
I'm married.	*Sono sposato/a.* m/f	so·no spo·*za*·to/a
I'm single.	*Sono celibe/nubile.* m/f	che·lee·be/*noo*·bee·le

age

How old ...?	*Quanti anni ...?*	kwan·tee *a*·nee ...
are you	*ha/hai* pol/inf	a/ai
is your daughter	*ha Sua/tua*	a *soo*·a/*too*·a
	figlia pol/inf	*fee*·lya
is your son	*ha Suo/tuo*	a *soo*·o/*too*·o
	figlio pol/inf	*fee*·lyo
I'm ... years old.	*Ho ... anni.*	o ... *a*·nee
He/She is ... years old.	*Ha ... anni.*	a ... *a*·nee

feelings

I'm (not) ...	*(Non) Ho ...*	(non) o ...
Are you ...?	*Ha/Hai ...?* pol/inf	a/ai ...
cold	*freddo*	*fre*·do
hot	*caldo*	*kal*·do
hungry	*fame*	*fa*·me
thirsty	*sete*	*se*·te
I'm (not) ...	*(Non) Sono ...*	(non) *so*·no ...
Are you ...?	*È/Sei ...?* pol/inf	e/say ...
happy	*felice*	fe·*lee*·che
sad	*triste*	*tree*·ste

entertainment

going out

Where can I find ...?	*Dove sono ...?*	*do*·ve *so*·no ...
clubs	*dei clubs*	day kloob
gay venues	*dei locali gay*	day lo·*ka*·lee ge
pubs	*dei pub*	day pab
I feel like going	*Ho voglia*	o *vo*·lya
to a/the ...	*d'andare ...*	dan·*da*·re ...
concert	*a un concerto*	a oon kon·*cher*·to
movies	*al cinema*	al *chee*·nee·ma
party	*a una festa*	a *oo*·na *fes*·ta
restaurant	*in un ristorante*	een oon rees·to·*ran*·te
theatre	*a teatro*	a te·*a*·tro

interests

Do you like ...?	*Ti piace/*	tee *pya*·che/
	piacciono ...? sg/pl	pya·*cho*·no ...
I (don't) like ...	*(Non) Mi piace/*	(non) mee *pya*·che/
	piacciono ... sg/pl	pya·*cho*·no ...
art	*l'arte* sg	*lar*·te
cooking	*cucinare* sg	koo·chee·*na*·re
movies	*i film* pl	ee feelm
nightclubs	*le discoteche* pl	le dees·ko·*te*·ke
reading	*leggere* sg	*le*·je·re
shopping	*lo shopping* sg	lo *sho*·ping
sport	*lo sport* sg	lo sport
travelling	*viaggiare* sg	vee·a·*ja*·re
Do you like to ...?	*Ti piace ...?*	tee *pya*·che ...
dance	*ballare*	ba·*la*·re
go to concerts	*andare ai concerti*	an·*da*·re ai kon·*cher*·tee
listen to music	*ascoltare la musica*	as·kol·*ta*·re la *moo*·zee·ka

food & drink

finding a place to eat

Can you recommend a ...?	Potrebbe consigliare un ...?	po·tre·be kon·see·lya·re oon ...
bar	locale	lo·ka·le
café	bar	bar
restaurant	ristorante	rees·to·ran·te
I'd like ..., please.	Vorrei ..., per favore.	vo·ray ... per fa·vo·re
a table for	un tavolo per	oon ta·vo·lo per
(four)	(quattro)	(kwa·tro)
the (non)smoking section	(non) fumatori	(non) foo·ma·to·ree

ordering food

breakfast	prima colazione f	pree·ma ko·la·tsyo·ne
lunch	pranzo m	pran·dzo
dinner	cena f	che·na
snack	spuntino m	spoon·tee·no

What would you recommend?
Cosa mi consiglia?   ko·za mee kon·see·lya

I'd like (the) ..., please.	Vorrei ..., per favore.	vo·ray ... per fa·vo·re
bill	il conto	eel kon·to
drink list	la lista delle bevande	la lee·sta de·le be·van·de
menu	il menù	eel me·noo
that dish	questo piatto	kwe·sto pya·to

drinks

(cup of) coffee ...	(un) caffè ...	(oon) ka·fe ...
(cup of) tea ...	(un) tè ...	(oon) te ...
with milk	con latte	kon *la*·te
without sugar	senza zucchero	sen·tsa tsoo·ke·ro
orange juice (bottled)	succo d'arancia m	soo·ko da·*ran*·cha
orange juice (fresh)	spremuta d'arancia f	spre·*moo*·ta da·*ran*·cha
soft drink	bibita f	bee·bee·ta
... water	acqua ...	*a*·kwa ...
boiled	bollita	bo·*lee*·ta
mineral	minerale	mee·ne·*ra*·le
sparkling mineral	frizzante	free·*tsan*·te
still mineral	naturale	na·too·*ra*·le

in the bar

I'll have ...	Prendo ...	*pren*·do ...
I'll buy you a drink.	Ti offro da bere. inf	tee *of*·ro da *be*·re
What would you like?	Cosa prendi?	*ko*·za *pren*·dee
Cheers!	Salute!	sa·*loo*·te
brandy	cognac m	*ko*·nyak
champagne	champagne m	sham·*pa*·nye
cocktail	cocktail m	*kok*·tayl
a shot of (whisky)	un sorso di (whisky)	oon *sor*·so dee (*wee*·skee)
a ... of beer	... di birra	... dee *bee*·ra
bottle	una bottiglia	*oo*·na bo·*tee*·lya
glass	un bicchiere	oon bee·*kye*·re
a bottle of ...	una bottiglia di	*oo*·na bo·*tee*·lya dee
wine	vino ...	*vee*·no ...
a glass of ...	un bicchiere di	oon bee·*kye*·re dee
wine	vino ...	*vee*·no ...
red	rosso	*ro*·so
sparkling	spumante	spoo·*man*·te
white	bianco	*byan*·ko

self-catering

What's the local speciality?
Qual'è la specialità   kwa·*le* la spe·cha·lee·*ta*
di questa regione?   dee *kwe*·sta re·*jo*·ne

What's that?
Cos'è?   ko·*ze*

How much is (a kilo of cheese)?
Quanto costa (un chilo   *kwan*·to *kos*·ta (oon *kee*·lo
di formaggio)?   dee for·*ma*·jo)

I'd like ...	*Vorrei ...*	vo·*ray* ...
100 grams	*un etto*	oo·*ne*·to
(two) kilos	*(due) chili*	(*doo*·e) *kee*·lee
(three) pieces	*(tre) pezzi*	(tre) *pe*·tsee
(six) slices	*(sei) fette*	(say) *fe*·te
Less.	*Meno.*	*me*·no
Enough.	*Basta.*	*bas*·ta
More.	*Più.*	pyoo

special diets & allergies

Is there a vegetarian restaurant near here?
C'è un ristorante vegetariano   che oon rees·to·*ran*·te ve·je·ta·*rya*·no
qui vicino?   kwee vee·*chee*·no

Do you have vegetarian food?
Avete piatti vegetariani?   a·*ve*·te *pya*·tee ve·je·ta·*rya*·nee

Could you prepare	*Potreste preparare*	po·*tres*·te pre·pa·*ra*·re
a meal without ...?	*un pasto senza ...?*	oon *pas*·to *sen*·tsa ...
butter	*burro*	*boo*·ro
eggs	*uova*	*wo*·va
meat stock	*brodo di carne*	*bro*·do dee *kar*·ne

I'm allergic to ...	*Sono allergico/a ...* m/f	*so*·no a·*ler*·jee·ko/a ...
dairy produce	*ai latticini*	ai la·tee·*chee*·nee
gluten	*al glutine*	al *gloo*·tee·ne
MSG	*al glutammato*	al glu·ta·*ma*·to
	monosodico	mo·no·so·dee·ko
nuts	*alle noci*	*a*·le *no*·chee
seafood	*ai frutti di mare*	ai *froo*·tee dee *ma*·re

emergencies

basics

Help!	*Aiuto!*	ai·*yoo*·to
Stop!	*Fermi!*	*fer*·mee
Go away!	*Vai via!*	vai *vee*·a
Thief!	*Ladro!*	*la*·dro
Fire!	*Al fuoco!*	al *fwo*·ko
Watch out!	*Attenzione!*	a·ten·*tsyo*·ne
Call ...!	*Chiami ...!*	*kya*·mee ...
a doctor	*un medico*	oon *me*·dee·ko
an ambulance	*un'ambulanza*	o·nam·boo·*lan*·tsa
the police	*la polizia*	la po·lee·*tsee*·a

It's an emergency!
È un'emergenza!   e oo·ne·mer·*jen*·tsa

Could you help me, please?
Mi può aiutare, per favore?   mee pwo ai·yoo·*ta*·re per fa·*vo*·re

I have to use the telephone.
Devo fare una telefonata.   *de*·vo *fa*·re *oo*·na te·le·fo·*na*·ta

I'm lost.
Mi sono perso/a. m/f   mee *so*·no *per*·so/a

Where are the toilets?
Dove sono i gabinetti?   *do*·ve *so*·no ee ga·bee·ne·tee

police

Where's the police station?
Dov'è il posto di polizia?   do·*ve* eel *pos*·to dee po·lee·*tsee*·a

I want to report an offence.
Voglio fare una denuncia.   *vo*·lyo *fa*·re *oo*·na de·*noon*·cha

I have insurance.
Ho l'assicurazione.   o la·see·koo·ra·*tsyo*·ne

I've been ...	*Sono stato/a ...* m/f	*so*·no *sta*·to/a ...
assaulted	*aggredito/a* m/f	a·gre·*dee*·to/a
raped	*violentato/a* m/f	vyo·len·*ta*·to/a
robbed	*derubato/a* m/f	roo·*ba*·to/a

I've lost my ...	Ho perso ...	o per-so ...
My ... was/were stolen.	Mi hanno rubato ...	mee a-no roo-ba-to ...
backpack	il mio zaino	eel mee-o dzai-no
bags	i miei bagagli	ee mee-ay ba-ga-lyee
credit card	la mia carta di credito	la mee-a kar-ta dee kre-dee-to
handbag	la mia borsa	la mee-a bor-sa
jewellery	i miei gioielli	ee mee-ay jo-ye-lee
money	i miei soldi	ee mee-ay sol-dee
passport	il mio passaporte	eel mee-o pa-sa-por-te
travellers cheques	i miei assegni di viaggio	ee mee-ay a-se-nyee dee vee-a-jo
wallet	portafoglio	por-ta-fo-lyo
I want to contact my ...	Vorrei contattare ...	vo-ray kon-ta-ta-re ...
consulate	il mio consolato	eel mee-o kon-so-la-to
embassy	la mia ambasciata	la mee-a am-ba-sha-ta

health

medical needs

Where's the nearest ...?	Dov'è ... più vicino/a? m/f	do-ve ... pyoo vee-chee-no/a
dentist	il dentista m	eel den-tee-sta
doctor	il medico m	eel me-dee-ko
hospital	l'ospedale m	los-pe-da-le
(night) pharmacist	la farmacia (di turno) f	la far-ma-chee-a (dee toor-no)

I need a doctor (who speaks English).

Ho bisogno di un medico (che parli inglese).

o bee-zo-nyo dee oon me-dee-ko (ke par-lee een-gle-ze)

Could I see a female doctor?

Posso vedere una dottoressa?

po-so ve-de-re oo-na do-to-re-sa

I've run out of my medication.

Ho finito la mia medicina.

o fee-nee-to la mee-a me-dee-chee-na

symptoms, conditions & allergies

| I'm sick. | Mi sento male. | mee sen·to ma·le |
| It hurts here. | Mi fa male qui. | mee fa ma·le kwee |

I have (a) ...	Ho ...	o ...
asthma	asma	as·ma
bronchitis	la bronchite	la bron·kee·te
constipation	la stitichezza	la stee·tee·ke·tsa
cough	la tosse	la to·se
diarrhoea	la diarrea	la dee·a·re·a
fever	la febbre	la fe·bre
headache	mal di testa	mal dee tes·ta
heart condition	un problema cardiaco	oon pro·ble·ma kar·dee·a·ko
nausea	la nausea	la now·ze·a
pain	un dolore	oon do·lo·re
sore throat	mal di gola	mal dee go·la
toothache	mal di denti	mal dee den·tee

I'm allergic to ...	Sono allergico/a ... m/f	so·no a·ler·jee·ko/a ...
antibiotics	agli	a·lyee
	antibiotici	an·tee·bee·o·tee·chee
anti-inflammatories	agli	a·lyee
	antinfiammatori	an·teen·fya·ma·to·ree
aspirin	all'aspirina	a·las·pee·ree·na
bees	alle api	a·le a·pee
codeine	alla codeina	a·la ko·de·ee·na
penicillin	alla penicillina	a·la pe·nee·chee·lee·na

antiseptic	antisettico m	an·tee·se·tee·ko
bandage	fascia f	fa·sha
condoms	preservativi m pl	pre·zer·va·tee·vee
contraceptives	contraccettivi m pl	kon·tra·che·tee·vee
diarrhoea medicine	antidissenterico m	an·tee·dee·sen·te·ree·ko
insect repellent	repellente per	re·pe·len·te per
	gli insetti m	lyee een·se·tee
laxatives	lassativi m pl	la·sa·tee·vee
painkillers	analgesico m	a·nal·je·ze·ko
rehydration salts	sali minerali m pl	sa·lee mee·ne·ra·lee
sleeping tablets	sonniferi m pl	so·nee·fe·ree

english–italian dictionary

Italian nouns in this dictionary, and adjectives affected by gender, have their gender indicated by ⓜ (masculine) or ⓕ (feminine). If it's a plural noun, you'll also see pl. Words are also marked as n (noun), a (adjective), v (verb), sg (singular), pl (plural), inf (informal) and pol (polite) where necessary.

A

accident *incidente* ⓜ een-chee-*den*-te
accommodation *alloggio* ⓜ a-*lo*-jo
adaptor *presa multipla* ⓕ *pre*-sa mool-*tee*-pla
address *indirizzo* ⓜ een-dee-*ree*-tso
after *dopo* *do*-po
air-conditioned *ad aria condizionata*
   ad *a*-rya kon-dee-*tsyo*-na-ta
airplane *aereo* ⓜ a-*e*-re-o
airport *aeroporto* ⓜ a-e-ro-*por*-to
alcohol *alcol* ⓜ *al*-kol
all a *tutto/a* *too*-to/a
allergy *allergia* ⓕ a-ler-*jee*-a
ambulance *ambulanza* ⓕ am-boo-*lan*-tsa
and e e
ankle *caviglia* ⓕ ka-*vee*-lya
arm *braccio* ⓜ *bra*-cho
ashtray *portacenere* ⓜ por-ta-*che*-ne-re
ATM *Bancomat* ⓜ *ban*-ko-mat

B

baby *bimbo/a* ⓜ/ⓕ *beem*-bo/a
back (body) *schiena* ⓕ *skye*-na
backpack *zaino* ⓜ *dzai*-no
bad *cattivo/a* ⓜ/ⓕ ka-*tee*-vo/a
bag *borsa* ⓕ *bor*-sa
baggage claim *ritiro bagagli* ⓜ ree-*tee*-ro ba-*ga*-lyee
bank *banca* ⓕ *ban*-ka
bar *locale* ⓜ lo-*ka*-le
bathroom *bagno* ⓜ *ba*-nyo
battery *pila* ⓕ *pee*-la
beautiful *bello/a* ⓜ/ⓕ *be*-lo/a
bed *letto* ⓜ *le*-to
beer *birra* ⓕ *bee*-ra
before *prima* *pree*-ma
behind *dietro* *dye*-tro
bicycle *bicicletta* ⓕ bee-chee-*kle*-ta
big *grande* *gran*-de
bill *conto* ⓜ *kon*-to

black *nero/a* ⓜ/ⓕ *ne*-ro/a
blanket *coperta* ⓕ ko-*per*-ta
blood group *gruppo sanguigno* ⓜ *groo*-po san-*gwee*-nyo
blue *azzurro/a* ⓜ/ⓕ a-*dzoo*-ro/a
boat *barca* ⓕ *bar*-ka
book (make a reservation) v *prenotare* pre-no-*ta*-re
bottle *bottiglia* ⓕ bo-*tee*-lya
bottle opener *apribottiglie* ⓕ a-pree-bo-*tee*-lye
boy *ragazzo* ⓜ ra-*ga*-tso
brakes (car) *freno* ⓜ *fre*-no
breakfast (prima) colazione ⓕ (*pree*-ma) ko-la-*tsyo*-ne
broken (faulty) *rotto/a* ⓜ/ⓕ *ro*-to/a
bus *autobus* ⓜ *ow*-to-boos
business *affari* ⓜ pl a-*fa*-ree
buy *comprare* kom-*pra*-re

C

café *bar* ⓜ bar
camera *macchina fotografica* ⓕ
   ma-kee-na fo-to-*gra*-fee-ka
camp site *campeggio* ⓜ kam-*pe*-jo
cancel *cancellare* kan-che-*la*-re
can opener *apriscatole* ⓜ a-pree-*ska*-to-le
car *macchina* ⓕ *ma*-kee-na
cash *soldi* ⓜ pl *sol*-dee
cash (a cheque) v *riscuotere un assegno*
   ree-*skwo*-te-re oon a-*se*-nyo
cell phone *telefono cellulare* ⓜ te-*le*-fo-no che-loo-*la*-re
centre *centro* ⓜ *chen*-tro
change (money) v *cambiare* kam-*bya*-re
cheap *economico/a* ⓜ/ⓕ e-ko-*no*-mee-ko/a
check (bill) *conto* ⓜ *kon*-to
check-in *registrazione* ⓕ re-jee-stra-*tsyo*-ne
chest *petto* ⓜ *pe*-to
child *bambino/a* ⓜ/ⓕ bam-*bee*-no/a
cigarette *sigaretta* ⓕ see-ga-*re*-ta
city *città* ⓕ chee-*ta*
clean a *pulito/a* ⓜ/ⓕ poo-*lee*-to/a
closed *chiuso/a* ⓜ/ⓕ *kyoo*-zo/a
coffee *caffè* ⓜ ka-*fe*
coins *monete* ⓕ pl mo-*ne*-te

cold a *freddo/a* ⓜ/ⓕ *fre*-do/a
collect call *chiamata a carico del destinatario* ⓕ
   kya-*ma*-ta a ka-*ree*-ko del des-tee-na-*ta*-ryo
come *venire* ve-*nee*-re
computer *computer* ⓜ kom-*pyoo*-ter
condom *preservativo* ⓜ pre-zer-va-*tee*-vo
contact lenses *lenti a contatto* ⓕ pl *len*-tee a kon-*ta*-to
cook v *cucinare* koo-chee-*na*-re
cost *prezzo* ⓜ *pre*-tso
credit card *carta di credito* ⓕ *kar*-ta dee *kre*-dee-to
cup *tazza* ⓕ *ta*-tsa
currency exchange *cambio valuta* ⓜ *kam*-byo va-*loo*-ta
customs (immigration) *dogana* ⓕ do-*ga*-na

D

dangerous *pericoloso/a* ⓜ/ⓕ pe-ree-ko-*lo*-zo/a
date (time) *data* ⓕ *da*-ta
day *giorno* ⓜ *jor*-no
delay *ritardo* ⓜ ree-*tar*-do
dentist *dentista* ⓜ/ⓕ den-*tee*-sta
depart *partire* par-*tee*-re
diaper *pannolino* ⓜ pa-no-*lee*-no
dictionary *vocabolario* ⓜ vo-ka-bo-*la*-ryo
dinner *cena* ⓕ *che*-na
direct *diretto/a* ⓜ/ⓕ dee-*re*-to/a
dirty *sporco/a* ⓜ/ⓕ *spor*-ko/a
disabled *disabile* dee-*za*-bee-le
discount *sconto* ⓜ *skon*-to
doctor *medico* ⓜ *me*-dee-ko
double bed *letto matrimoniale* ⓜ *le*-to ma-tree-mo-*nya*-le
double room *camera doppia* ⓕ *ka*-mer-a do-pya
drink *bevanda* ⓕ be-*van*-da
drive v *guidare* gwee-*da*-re
drivers licence *patente di guida* ⓕ pa-*ten*-te dee gwee-da
drugs (illicit) *droga* ⓕ *dro*-ga
dummy (pacifier) *ciucciotto* ⓜ choo-*cho*-to

E

ear *orecchio* ⓜ o-*re*-kyo
east *est* ⓜ est
eat *mangiare* man-*ja*-re
economy class *classe turistica* ⓕ *kla*-se too-ree-stee-ka
electricity *elettricità* ⓕ e-le-tree-*chee*-ta
elevator *ascensore* ⓜ a-shen-*so*-re
email *email* ⓕ e-mayl
embassy *ambasciata* ⓕ am-ba-*sha*-ta
emergency *emergenza* ⓕ e-mer-*jen*-tsa
English (language) *inglese* een-*gle*-ze

entrance *entrata* ⓕ en-*tra*-ta
evening *sera* ⓕ *se*-ra
exchange rate *tasso di cambio* ⓜ *ta*-so dee *kam*-byo
exit *uscita* ⓕ *ta*-so dee *kam*-byo
expensive *caro/a* ⓜ/ⓕ *ka*-ro/a
express mail *posta prioritaria* ⓕ *pos*-ta pree-o-ree-*ta*-rya
eye *occhio* ⓜ *o*-kyo

F

far *lontano/a* ⓜ/ⓕ lon-*ta*-no/a
fast *veloce* ve-*lo*-che
father *padre* ⓜ *pa*-dre
film (camera) *rullino* ⓜ roo-*lee*-no
finger *dito* ⓜ *dee*-to
first-aid kit *valigetta del pronto soccorso* ⓕ
   va-lee-*je*-ta del *pron*-to so-*kor*-so
first class *prima classe* ⓕ *pree*-ma *kla*-se
fish n *pesce* ⓜ *pe*-she
food *cibo* ⓜ *chee*-bo
foot *piede* ⓜ *pye*-de
fork *forchetta* ⓕ for-*ke*-ta
free (of charge) *gratuito/a* ⓜ/ⓕ gra-*too*-ee-to/a
friend *amico/a* ⓜ/ⓕ a-*mee*-ko/a
fruit *frutta* ⓕ *froo*-ta
full *pieno/a* ⓜ/ⓕ *pye*-no/a
funny *divertente* dee-ver-*ten*-te

G

gift *regalo* ⓜ re-*ga*-lo
girl *ragazza* ⓕ ra-*ga*-tsa
glass (drinking) *bicchiere* ⓜ bee-*kye*-re
glasses *occhiali* ⓜ pl o-*kya*-lee
go *andare* an-*da*-re
good *buono/a* ⓜ/ⓕ *bwo*-no/a
green *verde* *ver*-de
guide n *guida* ⓕ *gwee*-da

H

half *mezzo* ⓜ *me*-dzo
hand *mano* ⓕ *ma*-no
handbag *borsetta* ⓕ bor-*se*-ta
happy *felice* ⓜ/ⓕ fe-*lee*-che
have *avere* a-*ve*-re
he *lui* *loo*-ee
head *testa* ⓕ *tes*-ta
heart *cuore* ⓜ *kwo*-re
heat n *caldo* ⓜ *kal*-do

heavy *pesante* pe-*zan*-te
help v *aiutare* a-yoo-*ta*-re
here *qui* kwee
high *alto/a* ⓜ/ⓕ *al*-to/a
highway *autostrada* ⓕ *ow*-to-stra-da
hike v *fare un'escursione a piedi*
  fa-re oon es-koor-syo-ne a *pye*-de
holiday *vacanze* ⓕ pl va-*kan*-tse
homosexual n *omosessuale* ⓜ&ⓕ o-mo-se-swa-le
hospital *ospedale* ⓜ os-pe-*da*-le
hot *caldo/a* ⓜ/ⓕ *kal*-do/a
hotel *albergo* ⓜ al-*ber*-go
hungry *affamato/a* ⓜ/ⓕ a-fa-*ma*-to
husband *marito* ⓜ ma-*ree*-to

I

I *io* ee-o
identification (card) *carta d'identità* ⓕ
  kar-ta dee-den-*tee*-*ta*
ill *malato/a* ⓜ/ⓕ ma-*la*-to/a
important *importante* eem-por-*tan*-te
included *compreso/a* ⓜ/ⓕ kom-*pre*-zo/a
injury *ferita* ⓕ fe-*ree*-ta
insurance *assicurazione* ⓕ a-see-koo-ra-*tsyo*-ne
Internet *Internet* een-ter-net
interpreter *interprete* ⓜ/ⓕ een-*ter*-pre-te
Italy *Italia* ⓕ ee-*ta*-lya
Italian (language) *italiano* ee-ta-*lya*-no

J

jewellery *gioielli* ⓜ pl jo-*ye*-lee
job *lavoro* ⓜ la-*vo*-ro

K

key *chiave* ⓕ *kya*-ve
kilogram *chilo* ⓜ *kee*-lo
kitchen *cucina* ⓕ koo-*chee*-na
knife *coltello* ⓜ kol-*te*-lo

L

laundry (place) *lavanderia* ⓕ la-van-de-*ree*-a
lawyer *avvocato/a* ⓜ/ⓕ a-vo-*ka*-to/a
left (direction) *sinistra* see-*nee*-stra
left-luggage office *deposito bagagli* ⓜ
  de-*po*-zee-to ba-*ga*-lyee
leg *gamba* ⓕ *gam*-ba

lesbian n *lesbica* ⓕ *lez*-bee-ka
less *(di) meno* (dee) *me*-no
letter (mail) *lettera* ⓕ *le*-te-ra
lift (elevator) *ascensore* ⓜ a-shen-*so*-re
light *luce* ⓕ *loo*-che
like v *piacere* pya-*che*-re
lock *serratura* ⓕ se-ra-*too*-ra
long *lungo/a* ⓜ/ⓕ *loon*-go/a
lost *perso/a* ⓜ/ⓕ *per*-so/a
lost-property office *ufficio oggetti smarriti* ⓜ
  oo-*fee*-cho o-*je*-tee sma-*ree*-tee
love v *amare* a-*ma*-re
luggage *bagaglio* ⓜ ba-*ga*-lyo
lunch *pranzo* ⓜ *pran*-dzo

M

mail *posta* ⓕ *pos*-ta
man *uomo* ⓜ *wo*-mo
map *pianta* ⓕ *pyan*-ta
market *mercato* ⓜ mer-*ka*-to
matches *fiammiferi* ⓜ pl fya-*mee*-fe-ree
meat *carne* ⓕ *kar*-ne
medicine *medicina* ⓕ me-dee-*chee*-na
menu *menu* ⓜ me-*noo*
message *messaggio* ⓜ me-*sa*-jo
milk *latte* ⓜ *la*-te
minute *minuto* ⓜ mee-*noo*-to
mobile phone *telefono cellulare* ⓜ te-*le*-fo-no che-loo-*la*-re
money *denaro* ⓜ de-*na*-ro
month *mese* ⓜ *me*-ze
morning *mattina* ⓕ ma-*tee*-na
mother *madre* ⓕ *ma*-dre
motorcycle *moto* ⓕ *mo*-to
motorway *autostrada* ⓕ *ow*-to-stra-da
mouth *bocca* ⓕ *bo*-ka
music *musica* ⓕ *moo*-zee-ka

N

name *nome* ⓜ *no*-me
napkin *tovagliolo* ⓜ to-va-*lyo*-lo
nappy *pannolino* ⓜ pa-no-*lee*-no
near *vicino (a)* vee-*chee*-no (a)
neck *collo* ⓜ *ko*-lo
new *nuovo/a* ⓜ/ⓕ *nwo*-vo/a
news *notizie* ⓕ pl no-*tee*-tsye
newspaper *giornale* ⓜ jor-*na*-le
night *notte* ⓕ *no*-te
no *no* no no

noisy *rumoroso/a* ⓜ/ⓕ roo-mo-ro-zo/a
nonsmoking *non fumatore* non foo-ma-to-re
north *nord* ⓜ nord
nose *naso* ⓜ na-zo
now *adesso* a-de-so
number *numero* ⓜ noo-me-ro

O

oil (engine) *olio* ⓜ o-lyo
old *vecchio/a* ⓜ/ⓕ ve-kyo/a
one-way ticket *biglietto di solo andata*
    bee-lye-to dee so-lo an-da-ta
open a *aperto/a* ⓜ/ⓕ a-per-to/a
outside *fuori* fwo-ree

P

package *pacchetto* ⓜ pa-ke-to
paper *carta* ⓕ kar-ta
park (car) v *parcheggiare* par-ke-ja-re
passport *passaporto* ⓜ pa-sa-por-to
pay *pagare* pa-ga-re
pen *penna (a sfera)* ⓕ pe-na (a sfe-ra)
petrol *benzina* ⓕ ben-dzee-na
pharmacy *farmacia* ⓕ far-ma-chee-a
phonecard *scheda telefonica* ⓕ ske-da te-le-fo-nee-ka
photo *foto* ⓕ fo-to
plate *piatto* ⓜ pya-to
police *polizia* ⓕ po-lee-tsee-a
postcard *cartolina* ⓕ kar-to-lee-na
post office *ufficio postale* ⓜ oo-fee-cho pos-ta-le
pregnant *incinta* een-cheen-ta
price *prezzo* ⓜ pre-tso

Q

quiet *tranquillo/a* ⓜ/ⓕ tran-kwee-lo/a

R

rain n *pioggia* ⓕ pyo-ja
razor *rasoio* ⓜ ra-zo-yo
receipt *ricevuta* ⓕ ree-che-voo-ta
red *rosso/a* ⓜ/ⓕ ro-so/a
refund *rimborso* ⓜ reem-bor-so
registered mail *posta raccomandata* ⓕ
    pos-ta ra-ko-man-da-ta
rent v *prendere in affitto* pren-de-re een a-fee-to
repair v *riparare* ree-pa-ra-re

reservation *prenotazione* ⓕ pre-no-ta-tsyo-ne
restaurant *ristorante* ⓜ rees-to-ran-te
return v *ritornare* ree-tor-na-re
return ticket *biglietto di andata e ritorno*
    bee-lye-to dee an-da-ta e ree-tor-no
right (direction) *destra* de-stra
road *strada* ⓕ stra-da
room *camera* ⓕ ka-me-ra

S

safe a *sicuro/a* ⓜ/ⓕ see-koo-ro/a
sanitary napkins *assorbenti igienici* ⓜ pl
    as-or-ben-tee ee-je-nee-chee
seat *posto* ⓜ pos-to
send *mandare* man-da-re
service station *stazione di servizio* ⓕ
    sta-tsyo-ne dee ser-vee-tsyo
sex *sesso* ⓜ se-so
shampoo *shampoo* ⓜ sham-poo
share (a dorm) *condividere* kon-dee-vee-de-re
shaving cream *crema da barba* ⓕ kre-ma da bar-ba
she *lei* lay
sheet (bed) *lenzuolo* ⓜ len-tswo-lo
shirt *camicia* ⓕ ka-mee-cha
shoes *scarpe* ⓕ pl skar-pe
shop *negozio* ⓜ ne-go-tsyo
short *corto/a* ⓜ/ⓕ kor-to/a
shower *doccia* ⓕ do-cha
single room *camera singola* ⓕ ka-me-ra seen-go-la
skin *pelle* ⓕ pe-le
skirt *gonna* ⓕ go-na
sleep v *dormire* dor-mee-re
slowly *lentamente* len-ta-men-te
small *piccolo/a* ⓜ/ⓕ pee-ko-lo/a
smoke (cigarettes) v *fumare* foo-ma-re
soap *sapone* ⓜ sa-po-ne
some *alcuni/e* ⓜ/ⓕ pl al-koo-nee/al-koo-ne
soon *fra poco* fra po-ko
south *sud* ⓜ sood
souvenir shop *negozio di souvenir* ⓜ
    ne-go-tsyo dee soo-ve-neer
speak *parlare* par-la-re
spoon *cucchiaio* ⓜ koo-kya-yo
stamp *francobollo* ⓜ fran-ko-bo-lo
stand-by ticket *in lista d'attesa* een lee-sta da-te-za
station (train) *stazione* ⓕ sta-tsyo-ne
stomach *stomaco* ⓜ sto-ma-ko
stop v *fermare* fer-ma-re
stop (bus) *fermata* ⓕ fer-ma-ta

street *strada* ① *stra*-da

student *studente/studentessa* ⓜ/① stoo-den-te/stoo-den-te-sa

sun *sole* ⓜ *so*-le

sunscreen *crema solare* ① *kre*-ma so-*la*-re

swim v *nuotare* nwo-ta-re

Switzerland *Svizzera* ① *svee-tse*-ra

T

tampons *assorbenti interni* ⓜ pl
a-sor-ben-tee een-ter-nee

taxi *tassi* ⓜ ta-see

teaspoon *cucchiaino* ⓜ koo-kya-ee-no

teeth *denti* ⓜ pl *den*-tee

telephone *telefono* ⓜ te-*le*-fo-no

television *televisione* ① te-le-vee-zyo-ne

temperature (weather) *temperatura* ①
tem-pe-ra-*too*-ra

tent *tenda* ① *ten*-da

that (one) *quello/a* ⓜ/① *kwe*-lo/a

they *loro* *lo*-ro

thirsty *assetato/a* ⓜ/① a-se-*ta*-to

this (one) *questo/a* ⓜ/① *kwe*-sto/a

throat *gola* ① *go*-la

ticket *biglietto* ⓜ bee-*lye*-to

time *tempo* ⓜ *tem*-po

tired *stanco/a* ⓜ/① *stan*-ko/a

tissues *fazzolettini di carta* ⓜ pl
fa-tso-le-*tee*-nee dee *kar*-ta

today *oggi* o-jee

toilet *gabinetto* ⓜ ga-bee-*ne*-to

tomorrow *domani* do-*ma*-nee

tonight *stasera* sta-se-ra

toothbrush *spazzolino da denti* ⓜ
spa-tso-*lee*-no da *den*-tee

toothpaste *dentifricio* ⓜ den-tee-*free*-cho

torch (flashlight) *torcia elettrica* ① *tor*-cha e-*le*-tree-ka

tour *gita* ① *jee*-ta

tourist office *ufficio del turismo* ⓜ
oo-*fee*-cho del too-reez-mo

towel *asciugamano* ⓜ a-shoo-ga-*ma*-no

train *treno* ⓜ *tre*-no

translate *tradurre* tra-*doo*-re

travel agency *agenzia di viaggio* ①
a-jen-*tsee*-a dee *vee-a*-jo

travellers cheque *assegno di viaggio* ⓜ
a-se-nyo dee *vee-a*-jo

trousers *pantaloni* ⓜ pl pan-ta-*lo*-nee

twin beds *due letti* doo-e *le*-tee

tyre *gomma* ① *go*-ma

U

underwear *biancheria intima* ⓜ byan-ke-*ree*-a *een*-tee-ma

urgent *urgente* ⓜ/① oor-*jen*-te

V

vacant *libero/a* ⓜ/① *lee*-be-ro/a

vacation *vacanza* ① va-*kan*-tsa

vegetable *verdura* ① ver-*doo*-ra

vegetarian a *vegetariano/a* ⓜ/① ve-je-ta-*rya*-no/a

visa *visto* ⓜ *vee*-sto

W

waiter *cameriere/a* ⓜ/① ka-mer-ye-re/a

walk v *camminare* ka-mee-*na*-re

wallet *portafoglio* ⓜ por-ta-fo-lyo

warm a *tiepido/a* ⓜ/① *tye*-pee-do/a

wash (something) *lavare* la-*va*-re

watch *orologio* ⓜ o-ro-*lo*-jo

water *acqua* ① *a*-kwa

we *noi* noy

weekend *fine settimana* ① *fee*-ne se-tee-*ma*-na

west *ovest* ⓜ o-vest

wheelchair *sedia a rotelle* ① *se*-dya a ro-*te*-le

when *quando* kwan-do

where *dove* *do*-ve

white *bianco/a* ⓜ/① *byan*-ko/a

who *chi* kee

why *perché* per-ke

wife *moglie* ① *mo*-lye

window *finestra* ① fee-*nes*-tra

wine *vino* ⓜ *vee*-no

with *con* kon

without *senza* sen-tsa

woman *donna* ① *do*-na

write *scrivere* *skree*-ve-re

Y

yellow *giallo/a* ⓜ/① *ja*-lo/a

yes *sì* see

yesterday *ieri* ye-ree

you sg inf *tu* too

you sg pol *Lei* lay

you pl *voi* voy

Polish

polish alphabet

A a a	*Ą ą* om/on	*B b* be	*C c* tse	*Ć ć* che	*D d* de
E e e	*Ę ę* em/en	*F f* ef	*G g* gye	*H h* kha	*I i* ee
J j yot	*K k* ka	*L l* el	*Ł ł* ew	*M m* em	*N n* en
Ń ń en′	*O o* o	*Ó ó* oo	*P p* pe	*R r* er	*S s* es
Ś ś esh	*T t* te	*U u* oo	*W w* woo	*Y y* i	*Z z* zet
Ż ż zhet	*Ż ż* zhyet				

polish

introduction

Ask most English speakers what they know about Polish (*polski* pol-skee), the language which donated the words *horde*, *mazurka* and *vodka* to English, and they will most likely dismiss it as an unpronounceable language. Who could pronounce an apparently vowel-less word like *szczyt* shchit (peak), for example? To be put off by this unfairly gained reputation, however, would be to miss out on a rich and rewarding language. The mother tongue of Copernicus, Chopin, Marie Curie and Pope John Paul II has a fascinating and turbulent past and symbolises the resilience of the Polish people in the face of domination and adversity.

The Polish tribes who occupied the basins of the Oder and Vistula rivers in the 6th century spoke a range of West Slavic dialects, which over time evolved into Polish. The closest living relatives of Polish are Czech and Slovak which also belong to the wider West Slavic family of languages. The language reached the apex of its influence during the era of the Polish Lithuanian Commonwealth (1569–1795). The Commonwealth covered a swath of territory from what are now Poland and Lithuania through Belarus, Ukraine and Latvia and part of Western Russia. Polish became a lingua franca throughout much of Central and Eastern Europe at this time due to the political, cultural, scientific and military might of this power.

When Poland was wiped off the map of Europe from 1795 to 1918 after three successive partitions in the second half of the 18th century (when it was carved up between Russia, Austria and Prussia), the language suffered attempts at both Germanisation and Russification. Later, after WWII, Poland became a satellite state of the Soviet Union and the language came under the renewed influence of Russian. Polish showed impressive resistance in the face of this oppression. The language not only survived these onslaughts but enriched itself by borrowing many words from both Russian and German. The works of Poland's greatest literary figures who wrote in exile – the Romantic poet Adam Mickiewicz and, during Communist rule, the Nobel Prize winner Czesław Miłosz – are testament to this fact.

Today, Poland is linguistically one of the most homogenous countries in Europe – over 95% of the population speaks Polish as their first language. There are significant Polish-speaking minorities in the western border areas of Ukraine, Belarus and in southern Lithuania, with smaller populations in other neighbouring countries.

pronunciation

vowel sounds

Polish vowels are generally prounounced short, giving them a 'clipped' quality.

symbol	english equivalent	polish example	transliteration
a	run	*tak*	tak
ai	aisle	*tutaj*	*too*·tai
e	bet	*bez*	bes
ee	see	*wino*	*vee*·no
ey	hey	*kolejka*	ko·*ley*·ka
i	bit	*czy*	chi
o	pot	*woda*	*vo*·da
oo	zoo	*zakupy, mój*	za·*koo*·pi, mooy
ow	how	*migdał*	*meeg*·dow
oy	toy	*ojciec*	*oy*·chets

Polish also has nasal vowels, pronounced as though you're trying to force the air out of your nose rather than your mouth. Nasal vowels are indicated in written Polish by the letters *ą* and *ę*. Depending upon the letters that follow these vowels, they're pronounced with either an 'm' or an 'n' sound following the vowel.

symbol	english equivalent	polish example	transliteration
em	like the 'e' in 'get' plus	*wstęp*	fstemp
en	nasal consonant sound	*mięso*	*myen*·so
om	like the 'o' in 'not' plus	*kąpiel*	*kom*·pyel
on	nasal consonant sound	*wąsy*	*von*·si

word stress

In Polish, stress almost always falls on the second-last syllable. In our coloured pronunciation guides, the stressed syllable is italicised.

consonant sounds

Most Polish consonant sounds are also found in English, with the exception of the kh sound (pronounced as in the Scottish word *loch*) and the rolled r sound.

symbol	english equivalent	polish example	transliteration
b	bed	*babka*	bap·ka
ch	cheat	*cień, czas, ćma*	chen', chas, chma
d	dog	*drobne*	drob·ne
f	fat	*fala*	fa·la
g	go	*garnek*	gar·nek
j	joke	*dzieci*	je·chee
k	kit	*kac*	kats
kh	loch	*chata, hałas*	kha·ta, kha·was
l	lot	*lato*	la·to
m	man	*malarz*	ma·lash
n	not	*nagle*	na·gle
p	pet	*palec*	pa·lets
r	run (rolled)	*róg*	roog
s	sun	*samolot*	sa·mo·lot
sh	shot	*siedem, śnieg, szlak*	shye·dem, shnyek, shlak
t	top	*targ*	tark
v	very	*widok*	vee·dok
w	win	*złoto*	zwo·to
y	yes	*zajęty*	za·yen·ti
z	zero	*zachód*	za·khoot
zh	pleasure	*zima, żart, rzeźba*	zhee·ma, zhart, zhezh·ba
'	a slight y sound	*kwiecień*	kfye·chen'

tools

language difficulties

Do you speak English?
Czy pan/pani mówi   chi pan/*pa*·nee *moo*·vee
po angielsku? m/f pol   po an·*gyel*·skoo

Do you understand?
Czy pan/pani rozumie? m/f pol   chi pan/*pa*·nee ro·*zoo*·mye

I (don't) understand.
(Nie) Rozumiem.   (nye) ro·*zoo*·myem

What does (nieczynne) mean?
Co to znaczy (nieczynne)?   tso to *zna*·chi (nye·*chi*·ne)

How do you ...?	*Jak się ...?*	yak shye ...
pronounce this	*to wymawia*	to vi·*mav*·ya
write (pierogi)	*pisze (pierogi)*	*pee*·she (pye·*ro*·gee)

Could you please ...?	*Proszę ...*	*pro*·she ...
repeat that	*to powtórzyć*	to pov·*too*·zhich
speak more	*mówić trochę*	*moo*·veech *tro*·khe
slowly	*wolniej*	*vol*·nyey
write it down	*to napisać*	to na·*pee*·sach

essentials

Yes.	*Tak.*	tak
No.	*Nie.*	nye
Please.	*Proszę.*	*pro*·she
Thank you (very much).	*Dziękuję (bardzo).*	jyen·*koo*·ye (*bar*·dzo)
You're welcome.	*Proszę.*	*pro*·she
Excuse me.	*Przepraszam.*	pshe·*pra*·sham
Sorry.	*Przepraszam.*	pshe·*pra*·sham

numbers

0	zero	ze·ro	15	piętnaście	pyent·nash·chye
1	jeden m	ye·den	16	szesnaście	shes·nash·chye
	jedna f	yed·na	17	siedemnaście	shye·dem·nash·chye
	jedno n	yed·no	18	osiemnaście	o·shem·nash·chye
2	dwa m	dva	19	dziewiętnaście	jye·vyet·nash·chye
	dwie f	dvye	20	dwadzieścia	dva·jyesh·chya
	dwoje n	dvo·ye	21	dwadzieścia	dva·jyesh·chya
3	trzy	tshi		jeden	ye·den
4	cztery	chte·ri	22	dwadzieścia	dva·jyesh·chya
5	pięć	pyench		dwa	dva
6	sześć	sheshch	30	trzydzieści	tshi·jyesh·chee
7	siedem	shye·dem	40	czterdzieści	chter·jyesh·chee
8	osiem	o·shyem	50	pięćdziesiąt	pyen·jye·shont
9	dziewięć	jye·vyench	60	sześćdziesiąt	shesh·jye·shont
10	dziesięć	jye·shench	70	siedemdziesiąt	shye·dem·jye·shont
11	jedenaście	ye·de·nash·chye	80	osiemdziesiąt	o·shem·jye·shont
12	dwanaście	dva·nash·chye	90	dziewięćdziesiąt	jye·vyen·jye·shont
13	trzynaście	tshi·nash·chye	100	sto	sto
14	czternaście	chter·nash·chye	1000	tysiąc	ti·shonts

time & dates

What time is it?	Która jest godzina?	ktoo·ra yest go·jee·na
It's one o'clock.	Pierwsza.	pyerf·sha
It's (10) o'clock.	Jest (dziesiąta).	yest (jye·shon·ta)
Quarter past (10).	Piętnaście po (dziesiątej).	pyent·nash·chye po (jye·shon·tey)
Half past (10).	Wpół do (jedenastej).	fpoow do (ye·de·nas·tey)
Quarter to (11).	Za piętnaście (jedenasta).	za pyent·nash·chye (ye·de·nas·ta)
At what time ...?	O której godzinie ...?	o ktoo·rey go·jee·nye ...
At ...	O ...	o ...
in the morning	rano	ra·no
in the afternooon	po południu	po po·wood·nyoo
in the evening (6pm–10pm)	wieczorem	vye·cho·rem
at night (11pm–3am)	w nocy	v no·tsi

Monday	*poniedziałek*	po·nye·*jya*·wek
Tuesday	*wtorek*	*fto*·rek
Wednesday	*środa*	*shro*·da
Thursday	*czwartek*	*chfar*·tek
Friday	*piątek*	*pyon*·tek
Saturday	*sobota*	so·*bo*·ta
Sunday	*niedziela*	nye·*jye*·la
January	*styczeń*	*sti*·chen'
February	*luty*	*loo*·ti
March	*marzec*	*ma*·zhets
April	*kwiecień*	*kfye*·chyen'
May	*maj*	mai
June	*czerwiec*	*cher*·vyets
July	*lipiec*	*lee*·pyets
August	*sierpień*	*shyer*·pyen'
September	*wrzesień*	*vzhe*·shyen'
October	*październik*	pazh·*jyer*·neek
November	*listopad*	lees·*to*·pat
December	*grudzień*	*groo*·jyen'

What date is it today?	*Którego jest dzisiaj?*	ktoo·*re*·go yest *jee*·shai
It's (18 October).	*Jest (osiemnastego października).*	yest (o·shem·nas·*te*·go pazh·jyer·*nee*·ka)
last night	*wczoraj wieczorem*	*fcho*·rai vye·*cho*·rem
last/next ...	*w zeszłym/przyszłym ...*	v *zesh*·wim/*pshish*·wim ...
week	*tygodniu*	ti·*god*·nyoo
month	*miesiącu*	mye·*shon*·tsoo
year	*roku*	*ro*·koo
yesterday/	*wczoraj/*	*fcho*·rai/
tomorrow ...	*jutro ...*	*yoo*·tro ...
morning	*rano*	*ra*·no
afternoon	*po południu*	po po·*wood*·nyoo
evening	*wieczorem*	vye·*cho*·rem

weather

What's the weather like?	Jaka jest pogoda?	ya·ka yest po·go·da

It's ...

cloudy	Jest pochmurnie.	yest pokh·moor·nye
cold	Jest zimno.	yest zheem·no
hot	Jest gorąco.	yest go·ron·tso
raining	Pada deszcz.	pa·da deshch
snowing	Pada śnieg.	pa·da shnyeg
sunny	Jest słonecznie.	yest swo·nech·nye
warm	Jest ciepło.	yest chyep·wo
windy	Jest wietrznie.	yest vyetzh·nye

spring	wiosna f	vyos·na
summer	lato n	la·to
autumn	jesień f	ye·shyen'
winter	zima f	zhee·ma

border crossing

I'm ...

in transit	Jestem ...	yes·tem ...
	w tranzycie	v tran·zi·chye
on business	służbowo	swoozh·bo·vo
on holiday	na wakacjach	na va·kats·yakh

I'm here for ...

(10) days	Będę tu przez ...	ben·de too pshes ...
	(dziesięć) dni	(jye·shench) dnee
(three) weeks	(trzy) tygodnie	(tshi) ti·god·nye
(two) months	(dwa) miesiące	(dva) mye·shon·tse

I'm going to (Kraków).
Jadę do (Krakowa). ya·de do (kra·ko·va)

I'm staying at the (Pod Różą Hotel).
Zatrzymuję się w (hotelu 'pod Różą'). za·tshi·moo·ye shye v (ho·te·loo pod roo·zhom)

I have nothing to declare.
Nie mam nic do zgłoszenia. nye mam neets do zgwo·she·nya

I have something to declare.
Mam coś do zgłoszenia. mam tsosh do zgwo·she·nya

That's (not) mine.
To (nie) jest moje. to (nye) yest mo·ye

transport

tickets & luggage

Where can I buy a ticket?
Gdzie mogę kupić bilet?   gjye mo·ge koo·peech bee·let

Do I need to book a seat?
Czy muszę rezerwować?   chi moo·she re·zer·vo·vach

One ... ticket	*Proszę bilet ...*	pro·she bee·let ...
(to Katowice), please.	*(do Katowic).*	do (ka·to·veets)
one-way	*w jedną stronę*	v yed·nom stro·ne
return	*powrotny*	po·vro·tni

I'd like to ...	*Chcę ... mój bilet.*	khtse ... mooy bee·let
my ticket, please.		
cancel	*odwołać*	od·vo·wach
change	*zmienić*	zmye·neech
collect	*odebrać*	o·de·brach
confirm	*potwierdzić*	po·tvyer·jyeech

I'd like a ... seat,	*Proszę miejsce ...*	pro·she myeys·tse ...
please.		
nonsmoking	*dla niepalących*	dla nye·pa·lon·tsikh
smoking	*dla palących*	dla pa·lon·tsikh

How much is it?
Ile kosztuje?   ee·le kosh·too·ye

Is there air conditioning?
Czy jest tam klimatyzacja?   chi yest tam klee·ma·ti·za·tsya

Is there a toilet?
Czy jest tam toaleta?   chi yest tam to·a·le·ta

How long does the trip take?
Ile trwa podróż?   ee·le trfa po·droosh

Is it a direct route?
Czy to jest bezpośrednie połączenie?   chi to yest bes·po·shred·nye po·won·che·nye

Where can I find a luggage locker?
Gdzie jest schowek na bagaż?   gjye yest skho·vek na ba·gazh

My luggage	Mój bagaż	mooy *ba*-gazh
has been ...	został ...	*zos*-tow ...
damaged	uszkodzony	oosh-ko-*dzo*-ni
lost	zagubiony	za-goo-*byo*-ni
stolen	skradziony	skra-*jyo*-ni

getting around

Where does flight (LO125) arrive/depart?

Skąd przylatuje/odlatuje — skont pshi-la-*too*-ye/od-la-*too*-ye
lot (LO125)? — lot (el o sto dva-*jyesh*-chya pyench)

Where's (the) ...?	Gdzie jest ...?	*gjye* yest ...
arrivals hall	hala przylotów	*kha*-la pshi-*lo*-toof
departures hall	hala odlotów	*kha*-la od-*lo*-toof
duty-free shop	sklep wolnocłowy	sklep vol-no-*tswo*-vi
gate (five)	wejście	*veysh*-chye
	(numer pięć)	(*noo*-mer pyench)

Is this the ...	Czy to jest ...	chi to yest ...
to (Wrocław)?	do (Wrocławia)?	do (vrots-*wa*-vya)
bus	autobus	ow-*to*-boos
plane	samolot	sa-*mo*-lot
train	pociąg	*po*-chonk

When's the ... bus?	Kiedy jest ... autobus?	*kye*-di yest ... ow-*to*-boos
first	pierwszy	*pyerf*-shi
last	ostatni	os-*tat*-nee
next	następny	nas-*temp*-ni

At what time does it arrive/leave?

O której godzinie przyjeżdża/ — o *ktoo*-rey go-*jee*-nye pshi-*yezh*-ja/
odjeżdża? — ot-*yezh*-ja

How long will it be delayed?

Jakie będzie opóźnienie? — *ya*-kye *ben*-jye o-poozh-*nye*-nye

What's the next station?

Jaka jest następna stacja? — *ya*-ka yest nas-*temp*-na *sta*-tsya

What's the next stop?

Jaki jest następny przystanek? — *ya*-kee yest nas-*tem*-pni pshi-*sta*-nek

Does it stop at (Kalisz)?
Czy on się zatrzymuje w (Kaliszu)? chi on shye za·tshi·moo·ye f (ka·lee·shoo)

Please tell me when we get to (Krynica).
Proszę mi powiedzieć gdy pro·she mee po·vye·jyech gdi
dojedziemy do (Krynicy). do·ye·jye·mi do (kri·nee·tsi)

How long do we stop here?
Na jak długo się tu zatrzymamy? na yak dwoo·go shye too za·tshi·ma·mi

Is this seat available?
Czy to miejsce jest wolne? chi to myeys·tse yest vol·ne

That's my seat.
To jest moje miejsce. to yest mo·ye myeys·tse

I'd like a taxi ...	*Chcę zamówić*	khtse za·moo·veech
	taksówkę na ...	tak·soof·ke na ...
now	*teraz*	*te·*ras
tomorrow	*jutro*	*yoo·*tro
at (9am)	*(dziewiątą rano)*	(jye·*vyon·*tom *ra·*no)

Is this taxi available?
Czy ta taksówka jest wolna? chi ta tak·soof·ka yest vol·na

How much is it to (Szczecin)?
Ile kosztuje do (Szczecina)? ee·le kosh·too·ye (do shche·chee·na)

Please put the meter on.
Proszę włączyć taksometr. pro·she vwon·chich tak·so·metr

Please take me to (this address).
Proszę mnie zawieźć pod (ten adres). pro·she mnye za·vyeshch pod (ten ad·res)

Please ...	*Proszę ...*	*pro·*she ...
slow down	*zwolnić*	*zvol·*neech
stop here	*się tu zatrzymać*	shye too za·*tshi·*mach
wait here	*tu zaczekać*	too za·*che·*kach

car, motorbike & bicycle hire

I'd like to hire a ...	*Chcę wypożyczyć ...*	khtse vi·po·*zhi·*chich ...
bicycle	*rower*	*ro·*ver
car	*samochód*	sa·*mo·*khoot
motorbike	*motocykl*	mo·*to·*tsikl

with ...	z ...	z ...
air conditioning	klimatyzacją	klee·ma·ti·za·tsyom
a driver	kierowcą	kye·rof·tsom
antifreeze	płynem nie	pwi·nem nye
	zamarzającym	za·mar·za·yon·tsim
snow chains	łańcuchami	wan'·tsoo·kha·mee
	śnieżnymi	shnezh·ni·mee
How much for	Ile kosztuje	ee·le kosh·too·ye
... hire?	wypożyczenie na ...?	vi·po·zhi·che·nye na ...
hourly	godzinę	go·jee·ne
daily	dzień	jyen'
weekly	tydzień	ti·jyen'
air	powietrze n	po·vye·tshe
oil	olej m	o·ley
petrol	benzyna f	ben·zi·na
tyre	opona f	o·po·na

I need a mechanic.
Potrzebuję mechanika. po·tshe·boo·ye me·kha·nee·ka

I've run out of petrol.
Zabrakło mi benzyny. za·bra·kwo mee ben·zi·ni

I have a flat tyre.
Złapałem/Złapałam gumę. m/f zwa·pa·wem/zwa·pa·wam goo·me

directions

Where's the ...?	Gdzie jest ...?	gjye yest ...
bank	bank	bank
city centre	centrum miasta	tsen·troom myas·ta
hotel	hotel	ho·tel
market	targ	tark
police station	komisariat	ko·mee·sar·yat
	policji	po·leets·yee
post office	urząd pocztowy	oo·zhond poch·to·vi
public toilet	toaleta publiczna	to·a·le·ta poo·bleech·na
tourist office	biuro turystyczne	byoo·ro too·ris·tich·ne

Is this the road to (Malbork)?
Czy to jest droga do (Malborka)? chi to yest dro·ga do (mal·bor·ka)

Can you show me (on the map)?
Czy może pan/pani
mi pokazać (na mapie)? m/f

chi *mo*-zhe pan/*pa*-nee
mee po-*ka*-zach (na *ma*-pye)

What's the address?
Jaki jest adres?

ya-kee yest *ad*-res

How far is it?
Jak daleko to jest?

yak da-*le*-ko to yest

How do I get there?
Jak tam mogę się dostać?

yak tam *mo*-ge shye *dos*-tach

Turn ...	*Proszę skręcić ...*	*pro*-she *skren*-cheech ...
at the corner	*na rogu*	na *ro*-goo
at the traffic lights	*na światłach*	na *shfyat*-wakh
left/right	*w lewo/prawo*	v *le*-vo/*pra*-vo
It's ...	*To jest ...*	to yest ...
behind ...	*za ...*	za ...
far away	*daleko*	da-*le*-ko
here	*tu*	too
in front of ...	*przed ...*	pshet ...
left	*po lewej*	po *le*-vey
near	*blisko*	*blees*-ko
next to ...	*obok ...*	*o*-bok ...
on the corner	*na rogu*	na *ro*-goo
opposite ...	*naprzeciwko ...*	nap-she-*cheef*-ko ...
right	*po prawej*	po *pra*-vey
straight ahead	*na wprost*	na fprost
there	*tam*	tam
by bus	*autobusem*	ow-to-*boo*-sem
by taxi	*taksówką*	tak-*soof*-kom
by train	*pociągiem*	po-*chon*-gyem
on foot	*pieszo*	*pye*-sho
north	*północ*	*poow*-nots
south	*południe*	po-*wood*-nye
east	*wschód*	fskhoot
west	*zachód*	*za*-khoot

Wjazd/Wyjazd	vyazd/vi-yazd	Entrance/Exit
Otwarte/Zamknięte	ot-far-te/zamk-nyen-te	Open/Closed
Wolne pokoje	vol-ne po-ko-ye	Rooms Available
Brak wolnych miejsc	brak vol-nikh myeysts	No Vacancies
Informacja	een-for-ma-tsya	Information
Komisariat policji	ko-mee-sar-yat po-lee-tsyee	Police Station
Zabroniony	za-bro-nyo-ni	Prohibited
Toalety	to-a-le-ti	Toilets
Męskie	mens-kye	Men
Damskie	dams-kye	Women
Zimna/Gorąca	zheem-na/go-ron-tsa	Hot/Cold

accommodation

finding accommodation

Where's a ...?	Gdzie jest ...?	gjye yest ...
camping ground	kamping	kam-peeng
guesthouse	pokoje gościnne	po-ko-ye gosh-chee-ne
hotel	hotel	ho-tel
youth hostel	schronisko	skhro-nees-ko
	młodzieżowe	mwo-jye-zho-ve

Can you recommend	Czy może pan/pani	chi mo-zhe pan/pa-nee
somewhere ...?	polecić coś ...? m/f	po-le-cheech tsosh ...
cheap	taniego	ta-nye-go
good	dobrego	do-bre-go
nearby	coś w pobliżu	tsosh f po-blee-zhoo

I'd like to book a room, please.
Chcę zarezerwować pokój.   khtse za-re-zer-vo-vach po-kooy

I have a reservation.
Mam rezerwację.   mam re-zer-va-tsye

My name's ...
Nazywam się ...   na-zi-vam shye ...

Do you have a . . . room?	*Czy jest pokój . . . ?*	chi yest *po*-kooy . . .
single	*jednoosobowy*	yed-no-o-so-*bo*-vi
double	*z podwójnym*	z pod-*vooy*-nim
	łóżkiem	*woozh*-kyem
twin	*z dwoma łóżkami*	z *dvo*-ma wozh-*ka*-mee

How much is it per . . . ?	*Ile kosztuje za . . . ?*	*ee*-le kosh-*too*-ye za . . .
night	*noc*	nots
person	*osobę*	o-*so*-be

Can I pay . . . ?	*Czy mogę zapłacić . . . ?*	chi *mo*-ge za-*pwa*-cheech . . .
by credit card	*kartą kredytową*	*kar*-tom kre-di-*to*-vom
with a travellers	*czekami*	che-*ka*-mee
cheque	*podróżnymi*	po-droozh-*ni*-mee

For (three) nights/weeks.
Na (trzy) noce/tygodnie. — na (tshi) *no*-tse/ti-*god*-nye

From (2 July) to (6 July).
Od (drugiego lipca) do (szóstego lipca). — od (droo-*gye*-go *leep*-tsa) do (shoos-*te*-go *leep*-tsa)

Can I see it?
Czy mogę go zobaczyć? — chi *mo*-ge go zo-*ba*-chich

Am I allowed to I camp here?
Czy mogę się tutaj rozbić? — chi *mo*-ge shye *too*-tai *roz*-beech

Where can I find the camping ground?
Gdzie jest pole kampingowe? — gjye yest *po*-le kam-peen-*go*-ve

requests & queries

When's breakfast served?
O której jest śniadanie? — o *ktoo*-rey yest shnya-*da*-nye

Where's breakfast served?
Gdzie jest śniadanie? — gjye yest shnya-*da*-nye

Please wake me at (seven).
Proszę obudzić mnie o (siódmej). — *pro*-she o-*boo*-jeech mnye o (*shyood*-mey)

Could I have my key, please?
Czy mogę prosić o klucz? — chi *mo*-ge *pro*-sheech o klooch

Can I get another (blanket)?
Czy mogę prosić o jeszcze jeden (koc)? — chi *mo*-ge *pro*-sheech o *yesh*-che *ye*-den (kots)

Is there an elevator/a safe?
Czy jest winda/sejf?　　　　　　chi yest *veen*·da/seyf

This (towel) isn't clean.
Ten (ręcznik) nie jest czysty.　　ten (*rench*·neek) nye yest *chis*·ti

It's too ...	*Jest zbyt ...*	yest zbit ...
expensive	*drogi*	*dro*·gee
noisy	*głośny*	*gwosh*·ni
small	*mały*	*ma*·wi

The ... doesn't work.	*... nie działa.*	... nye *jya*·wa
air conditioner	*Klimatyzator*	klee·ma·ti·*za*·tor
fan	*Wentylator*	ven·ti·*la*·tor
toilet	*Ubikacja*	oo·bee·*kats*·ya

checking out

What time is checkout?
O której godzinie　　　　　　　o *ktoo*·rey go·*jye*·nye
muszę się wymeldować?　　　　moo·she shye vi·mel·*do*·vach

Can I leave my luggage here?
Czy mogę tu zostawić　　　　　chi *mo*·ge too zo·*sta*·veech
moje bagaże?　　　　　　　　　*mo*·ye ba·*ga*·zhe

Could I have	*Czy mogę prosić*	chi *mo*·ge *pro*·sheech
my ..., please?	*o mój/moje ...?* sg/pl	o mooy/*mo*·ye ...
deposit	*depozyt* sg	de·*po*·zit
passport	*paszport* sg	*pash*·port
valuables	*kosztowności* pl	kosh·tov·*nosh*·chee

communications & banking

the internet

Where's the local Internet café?
Gdzie jest kawiarnia internetowa?　　gjye yest ka·*vyar*·nya een·ter·ne·*to*·va

How much is it per hour?
Ile kosztuje za godzinę?　　　　　　ee·le kosh·*too*·ye za go·*jee*·ne

I'd like to ...	Chciałem/Chciałam ... m/f	khchow-em/khchow-am ...
check my email	sprawdzić mój email	sprav-jeech mooy ee-mayl
get Internet access	podłączyć się do internetu	pod-won-chich shye do een-ter-ne-too
use a printer	użyć drukarki	oo-zhich droo-kar-kee
use a scanner	użyć skaner	oo-zhich ska-ner

mobile/cell phone

I'd like a ...	Chciałem/Chciałam ... m/f	khchow-em/khchow-am ...
mobile/cell phone for hire	wypożyczyć telefon komórkowy	vi-po-zhi-chich te-le-fon ko-moor-ko-vi
SIM card for your network	kartę SIM na waszą sieć	kar-te seem na va-shom shyech

What are the rates?	Jakie są stawki za rozmowy?	ya-kye som staf-kee za roz-mo-vi

telephone

What's your phone number?
Jaki jest pana/pani numer telefonu? m/f pol
ya-kee yest pa-na/pa-nee noo-mer te-le-fo-noo

The number is ...
Numer jest ...
noo-mer yest ...

Where's the nearest public phone?
Gdzie jest najbliższy telefon?
gjye yest nai-bleezh-shi te-le-fon

I'd like to buy a chip phonecard.
Chciałem/Chciałam kupić czipową kartę telefoniczną. m/f
khchow-em/khchow-am koo-peech chee-po-vom kar-te te-le-fo-neech-nom

I want to ...	Chciałem/Chciałam ... m/f	khchow-em/khchow-am ...
call (Singapore)	zadzwonić do (Singapuru)	zad-zvo-neech do (seen-ga-poo-roo)
make a local call	zadzwonić pod lokalny numer	zad-zvo-neech pod lo-kal-ni noo-mer
reverse the charges	zamówić rozmowę na koszt odbiorcy	za-moo-veech roz-mo-ve na kosht od-byor-tsi

How much does … cost?	Ile kosztuje …?	ee·le kosh·too·ye …
a (three)-minute call	rozmowa (trzy) minutowa	roz·mo·va (tshi) mee·noo·to·va
each extra minute	każda dodatkowa minuta	kazh·da do·dat·ko·va mee·noo·ta
(Two złotys) per (30) seconds.	(Dwa złote) za (trzydzieści) sekund.	(dva zwo·te) za (tshi·jyesh·chee) se·koond

post office

I want to send a …	Chciałem/Chciałam wysłać … m/f	khchow·em/khchow·am vis·wach …
fax	faks	faks
letter	list	leest
parcel	paczkę	pach·ke
postcard	pocztówkę	poch·toof·ke
I want to buy a/an …	Chciałem/Chciałam kupić … m/f	khchow·em/khchow·am koo·peech …
envelope	kopertę	ko·per·te
stamp	znaczek	zna·chek
Please send it (to Australia) by …	Proszę wysłać to … (do Australii).	pro·she vis·wach to … (do aus·tra·lyee)
airmail	pocztą lotniczą	poch·tom lot·nee·chom
express mail	pocztą ekspresową	poch·tom eks·pre·so·vom
registered mail	pocztą poleconą	poch·tom po·le·tso·nom
surface mail	pocztą lądową	poch·tom lon·do·vom
Is there any mail for me?	Czy jest dla mnie jakaś korespondencja?	chi yest dla mnye ya·kash ko·res·pon·den·tsya

bank

Where's a/an …?	Gdzie jest …?	gjye yest …
ATM	bankomat	ban·ko·mat
foreign exchange office	kantor walut	kan·tor va·loot

I'd like to ...	Chciałem/Chciałam ... m/f	khchow·em/khchow·am ...
Where can I ...?	Gdzie mogę ...?	gjye mo·ge ...
cash a cheque	wymienić czek	vi·mye·neech chek
	na gotówkę	na go·toof·ke
change a travellers cheque	wymienić czek	vi·mye·neech chek
	podróżny	po·droozh·ni
change money	wymienić	vi·mye·neech
	pieniądze	pye·nyon·dze
get a cash advance	dostać zaliczkę	dos·tach za·leech·ke
	na moją kartę	na mo·yom kar·te
	kredytową	kre·di·to·vom
withdraw money	wypłacić	vi·pwa·cheech
	pieniądze	pye·nyon·dze

What's the ...?	Jaki/Jaka jest ...? m/f	ya·kee/ya·ka yest ...
charge for that	prowizja f	pro·veez·ya
exchange rate	kurs wymiany m	koors vi·mya·ni

It's (12) złotys.
To kosztuje (dwanaście) złotych.   to kosh·too·ye (dva·nash·chye) zwo·tikh

It's free.
Jest bezpłatny.   yest bes·pwat·ni

What time does the bank open?
W jakich godzinach   v ya·keekh go·jee·nakh
jest bank otwarty?   yest bank ot·far·ti

Has my money arrived yet?
Czy doszły już moje pieniądze?   chi dosh·wi yoosh mo·ye pye·nyon·dze

sightseeing

getting in

What time does it open/close?
O której godzinie jest   o ktoo·rey go·jee·nye yest
otwarte/zamknięte?   ot·far·te/zam·knyen·te

What's the admission charge?
Ile kosztuje wstęp?   ee·le kosh·too·ye fstemp

Is there a discount for students/children?

Czy jest zniżka dla studentów/dzieci? chi yest znee*zh*·ka dla stoo·*den*·toof/*jye*·chee

I'd like to see ...

Chciałem/Chciałam obejrzeć ... m/f khchow·em/khchow·am o·*bey*·zhech ...

What's that?

Co to jest? tso to yest

Can I take a photo?

Czy mogę zrobić zdjęcie? chi *mo*·ge *zro*·beech zdyen·chye

I'd like a ... Chciałem/Chciałam ... m/f khchow·em/khchow·am ...
catalogue broszurę bro·*shoo*·re
guide przewodnik pshe·*vod*·neek
local map mapę okolic *ma*·pe o·*ko*·leets

tours

When's the next ...? Kiedy jest następna ...? *kye*·di yest nas·*temp*·na ...
day trip wycieczka jednodniowa vi·*chyech*·ka yed·no·*dnyo*·va
tour tura *too*·ra

Is ... included? Czy ... wliczone/a? n&pl/f chi ... vlee·*cho*·ne/na
accommodation noclegi są pl nots·*le*·gee som
the admission charge opłata za wstęp jest f o·*pwa*·ta za fstemp yest
food wyżywienie jest n vi·zhi·*vye*·nye yest

Is transport included?

Czy transport jest wliczony? chi *trans*·port yest vlee·*cho*·ne

How long is the tour?

Jak długo trwa wycieczka? yak *dwoo*·go trfa vi·*chyech*·ka

What time should we be back?

O której godzinie powinniśmy wrócić? o *ktoo*·rey go·*jee*·nye po·vee·*neesh*·mi *vroo*·cheech

sightseeing

castle	*zamek* m	*za*-mek
cathedral	*katedra* f	ka-*te*-dra
church	*kościół* m	*kosh*-chyoow'
main square	*rynek główny* m	*ri*-nek *gwoov*-ni
monastery	*klasztor* m	*klash*-tor
monument	*pomnik* m	*pom*-neek
museum	*muzeum* n	moo-*ze*-oom
old city	*stare miasto* n	*sta*-re *myas*-to
palace	*pałac* m	*pa*-wats
ruins	*ruiny* f pl	roo-*ee*-ni
stadium	*stadion* m	*sta*-dyon
statue	*pomnik* m	*pom*-neek

shopping

enquiries

Where's a ...?	*Gdzie jest ...?*	gjye yest ...
bank	*bank*	bank
bookshop	*księgarnia*	kshyen-*gar*-nya
camera shop	*sklep fotograficzny*	sklep fo-to-gra-*feech*-ni
department store	*dom towarowy*	dom to-va-*ro*-vi
grocery store	*sklep spożywczy*	sklep spo-*zhiv*-chi
market	*targ*	tark
newsagency	*kiosk*	kyosk
supermarket	*supermarket*	soo-per-*mar*-ket

Where can I buy (a padlock)?
Gdzie mogę kupić (kłódkę)?   gjye *mo*-ge *koo*-peech (*kwoot*-ke)

I'm looking for ...
Szukam ...   *shoo*-kam

Can I look at it?
Czy mogę to zobaczyć?   chi *mo*-ge to zo-*ba*-chich

Do you have any others?
Czy są jakieś inne?   chi som *ya*-kyesh *ee*-ne

Does it have a guarantee?
Czy to ma gwarancję?   chi to ma gva-*ran*-tsye

Can I have it sent overseas?
Czy mogę to wysłać za granicę?   chi *mo*-ge to *vis*-wach za gra-*nee*-tse

Can I have my ... repaired?
Czy mogę tu oddać ... do naprawy?   chi *mo*-ge too ot-dach ... do na-*pra*-vi

It's faulty.
To jest wadliwe.   to yest vad-*lee*-ve

I'd like to return this, please.
Chciałem/Chciałam to zwrócić. m/f   *khchow*-em/*khchow*-am to *zvroo*-cheech

I'd like a ..., please.	*Proszę o ...*	*pro*-she o ...
bag	*torbę*	*tor*-be
refund	*zwrot pieniędzy*	zvrot pye-*nyen*-dzi

paying

How much is it?
Ile to kosztuje?   *ee*-le to kosh-*too*-ye

Can you write down the price?
Proszę napisać cenę.   *pro*-she na-*pee*-sach *tse*-ne

That's too expensive.
To jest za drogie.   to yest za *dro*-gye

What's your final price?
Jaka jest pana/pani   *ya*-ka yest pa-na/*pa*-nee
ostateczna cena? m/f   os-ta-*tech*-na *tse*-na

I'll give you (10 złotys).
Dam panu/pani (dziesięć złotych). m/f   dam pa-noo/*pa*-nee (*jye*-shench *zwo*-tikh)

There's a mistake in the bill.
Na czeku jest pomyłka.   na *che*-koo yest po-*miw*-ka

Do you accept ...?	*Czy mogę zapłacić ...?*	chi *mo*-ge za-*pwa*-cheech ...
credit cards	*kartą kredytową*	*kar*-tom kre-di-*to*-vom
debit cards	*kartą debetową*	*kar*-tom de-be-*to*-vom
travellers cheques	*czekami podróżnymi*	che-*ka*-mee pod-roozh-*ni*-mee

I'd like ..., please.	*Proszę o ...*	*pro*-she o ...
a receipt	*rachunek*	ra-*khoo*-nek
my change	*moją resztę*	*mo*-yom *resh*-te

clothes & shoes

Can I try it on?	Czy mogę przymierzyć?	chi *mo*·ge pshi·*mye*·zhich
My size is (40).	Noszę rozmiar	*no*·she *roz*·myar
	(czterdzieści).	(chter·*jyesh*·chee)
It doesn't fit.	Nie pasuje.	nye pa·*soo*·ye
large/medium/small	L/M/S	*el*·ke/*em*·ke/*es*·ke

books & music

I'd like a ...	Chciałem/Chciałam ... m/f	khchow·em/khchow·am ...
newspaper	gazetę (w języku	ga·*ze*·te (v yen·*zi*·koo
(in English)	angielskim)	an·*gyel*·skeem)
pen	długopis	dwoo·*go*·pees

Is there an English-language bookshop?
Czy jest tu księgarnia angielska?   chi yest too kshyen·*gar*·nya an·*gyel*·ska

I'm looking for something by (Górecki).
Szukam czegoś (Góreckiego).   *shoo*·kam *che*·gosh (goo·rets·*kye*·go)

Can I listen to this?
Czy mogę tego posłuchać?   chi *mo*·ge *te*·go pos·*woo*·khach

photography

Can you ...?	Czy może pan/pani ...? m/f	chi *mo*·zhe pan/*pa*·nee ...
develop this film	wywołać ten film	vi·*vo*·wach ten film
load my film	założyć film	za·*wo*·zhich film
transfer photos	skopiować zdjęcia	sko·*pyo*·vach *zdyen*·chya
from my camera	z mojego aparatu	z mo·*ye*·go a·pa·*ra*·too
to CD	na płytę kompaktową	na *pwi*·te kom·pak·*to*·vom

I need a/an ... film	Potrzebuję film ...	po·tshe·*boo*·ye film ...
for this camera.	do tego aparatu.	do *te*·go a·pa·*ra*·too
APS	APS	a pe es
B&W	panchromatyczny	pan·khro·ma·*tich*·ni
colour	kolorowy	ko·lo·*ro*·vi
slide	do slajdów	do *slai*·doof
(200) speed	(dwieście) ASA	(*dvyesh*·chye) *a*·sa

When will it be ready?   Na kiedy będzie gotowe?   na *kye*·di *ben*·jye go·*to*·ve

meeting people

greetings, goodbyes & introductions

Hello/Hi.	*Cześć.*	cheshch
Good night.	*Dobranoc.*	do·*bra*·nots
Goodbye.	*Do widzenia.*	do vee·*dze*·nya
Bye.	*Pa.*	pa
See you later.	*Do zobaczenia.*	do zo·ba·*che*·nya
Mr/Mrs/Miss	*Pan/Pani/Panna*	pan/*pa*·nee/*pa*·na
How are you?	*Jak pan/pani*	yak pan/*pa*·nee
	się miewa? m/f pol	shye *mye*·va
	Jak się masz? inf	yak shye mash
Fine. And you?	*Dobrze. A pan/pani?* m/f pol	*dob*·zhe a pan/*pa*·nee
	Dobrze. A ty? inf	*dob*·zhe a ti
What's your name?	*Jak się pan/pani*	yak shye pan/*pa*·nee
	nazywa? m/f pol	na·*zi*·va
	Jakie się nazywasz? inf	yak shye na·*zi*·vash
My name is ...	*Nazywam się ...*	na·*zi*·vam shye ...
I'm pleased to	*Miło mi pana/panią*	*mee*·wo mee *pa*·na/*pa*·nyom
meet you.	*poznać.* m/f pol	*po*·znach
	Miło mi ciebie poznać. inf	*mee*·wo mee *chye*·bye *po*·znach
This is my ...	*To jest mój/moja ...* m/f	to yest mooy/*mo*·ya ...
boyfriend	*chłopak*	*khwo*·pak
brother	*brat*	brat
daughter	*córka*	*tsoor*·ka
father	*ojciec*	*oy*·chyets
friend	*przyjaciel* m	pzhi·*ya*·chyel
	przyjaciółka f	pzhi·*ya*·chyoow·ka
girlfriend	*dziewczyna*	jyev·*chi*·na
husband	*mąż*	monzh
mother	*matka*	*mat*·ka
partner (intimate)	*partner/partnerka* m/f	*part*·ner/part·*ner*·ka
sister	*siostra*	*shyos*·tra
son	*syn*	sin
wife	*żona*	*zho*·na

Here's my ...	Tu jest mój ...	too yest mooy ...
What's your ...?	Jaki jest pana/	ya·kee yest pa·na/
	pani ...? m/f pol	pa·nee ...
(email) address	adres (emailowy)	ad·res (e·mai·lo·vi)
fax number	numer faksu	noo·mer fak·soo
phone number	numer telefonu	noo·mer te·le·fo·noo

occupations

What's your occupation?	Jaki jest pana/pani zawód? m/f pol	ya·kee yest pa·na/pa·nee za·vood
I'm a/an ...	Jestem ...	yes·tem ...
artist	artystą/artystką m/f	ar·tis·tom/ar·tist·kom
farmer	rolnikiem m&f	rol·nee·kyem
manual worker	pracownikiem fizycznym m&f	pra·tsov·nee·kyem fee·zich·nim
office worker	pracownikiem biurowym m&f	pra·tsov·nee·kyem byoo·ro·vim
scientist	naukowcem m&f	now·kov·tsem
tradesperson	rzemieślnikiem m&f	zhe·mye·shlnee·kyem

background

Where are you from?	Skąd pan/pani jest? m/f pol	skont pan/pa·nee yest
I'm from ...	Jestem z ...	yes·tem z ...
Australia	Australii	ow·stra·lyee
Canada	Kanady	ka·na·di
England	Anglii	ang·lee
New Zealand	Nowej Zelandii	no·vey ze·lan·dyee
the USA	USA	oo es a

Are you married? (to a man)
Czy jest pan żonaty? pol — chi yest pan zho·na·ti

Are you married? (to a woman)
Czy jest pani zamężna? pol — chi yest pa·nee za·menzh·na

I'm married.
Jestem żonaty/zamężna. m/f — yes·tem zho·na·ti/za·menzh·na

I'm single.
Jestem nieżonaty/niezamężna. m/f — nye·zho·na·ti/nye·za·menzh·na

age

How old is your ...?	Ile lat ma pana/ pani ...? m/f pol	ee·le lat ma pa·na/ pa·nee ...
daughter	córka	tsoor·ka
son	syn	sin
How old are you?	Ile pan/pani ma lat? m/f pol	ee·le pan/pa·nee ma lat
	Ile masz lat? inf	ee·le mash lat
I'm ... years old.	Mam ... lat.	mam ... lat
He/She is ... years old.	On/Ona ma ... lat.	on/o·na ma ... lat

feelings

I'm (not) ...	(Nie) Jestem ...	(nye) yes·tem ...
Are you ...?	Czy jest pan/pani ...? m/f pol	chi yest pan/pa·nee ...
cold	zmarznięty/a m/f	zmar·znyen·ti/a
happy	szczęśliwy/a m/f	shchen·shlee·vi/a
hungry	głodny/a m/f	gwod·ni/a
sad	smutny/a m/f	smoot·ni/a
thirsty	spragniony/a m/f	sprag·nyo·ni/a

entertainment

going out

Where can I find ...?	Gdzie mogę znaleźć ...?	gjye mo·ge zna·lezhch ...
clubs	kluby nocne	kloo·bi nots·ne
gay venues	kluby dla gejów	kloo·bi dla ge·yoof
pubs	puby	pa·bi
I feel like going to a/the ...	Mam ochotę pójść ...	mam o·kho·te pooyshch ...
concert	na koncert	na kon·tsert
movies	na film	na feelm
party	na imprezę	na eem·pre·ze
restaurant	do restauracji	do res·tow·ra·tsyee
theatre	na sztukę	na shtoo·ke

interests

Do you like ...?	*Czy lubisz ...?* inf	chi *loo*·beesh ...
I like ...	*Lubię ...*	*loo*·bye ...
cooking	*gotować*	go·*to*·vach
movies	*oglądać filmy*	o·*glon*·dach *feel*·mi
reading	*czytać*	*chi*·tach
sport	*sport*	sport
travelling	*podróżować*	po·droo·*zho*·vach
Do you like art?	*Czy lubisz sztukę?* inf	chi *loo*·beesh *shtoo*·ke
I like art.	*Lubię sztukę.*	*loo*·bye *shtoo*·ke
Do you ...?	*Czy ...?* inf	chi ...
dance	*tańczysz*	*tan'*·chish
go to concerts	*chodzisz na koncerty*	*kho*·jeesh na *kon*·tser·ti
listen to music	*słuchasz muzyki*	*swoo*·khash moo·*zi*·kee

food & drink

finding a place to eat

Can you recommend a ...?	*Czy może pan/pani polecić ...?* m/f	chi *mo*·zhe pan/*pa*·nee po·*le*·cheech ...
bar	*bar*	bar
café	*kawiarnię*	ka·*vyar*·nye
restaurant	*restaurację*	res·tow·*rats*·ye
I'd like ..., please.	*Proszę ...*	*pro*·she ...
a table for (five)	*o stolik na (pięć) osób*	o *sto*·leek na (pyench) o·soob
the (non)smoking section	*dla (nie)palących*	dla (nye·)pa·*lon*·tsikh

ordering food

breakfast	*śniadanie* n	shnya·*da*·nye
lunch	*obiad* m	o·byad
dinner	*kolacja* f	ko·*la*·tsya
snack	*przekąska* f	pshe·*kons*·ka

What would you recommend?

Co by pan polecił? m		tso bi pan po-*le*-cheew
Co by pani poleciła? f		tso bi *pa*-nee po-le-*chee*-wa

I'd like (the) ..., please. *Proszę ...*   *pro*-she ...

bill	*o rachunek*	o ra-*khoo*-nek
drink list	*o spis napojów*	o spees na-*po*-yoof
menu	*o jadłospis*	o ya-*dwo*-spees
that dish	*to danie*	to *da*-nye

drinks

(cup of) coffee ...	*(filiżanka) kawy ...*	(fee-lee-*zhan*-ka) *ka*-vi ...
(cup of) tea ...	*(filiżanka) herbaty ...*	(fee-lee-*zhan*-ka) her-*ba*-ti ...
with milk	*z mlekiem*	z *mle*-kyem
without sugar	*bez cukru*	bez *tsoo*-kroo
(orange) juice	*sok (pomarańczowy)* m	sok (po-ma-ran'-*cho*-vi)
soft drink	*napój* m	*na*-pooy
... water	*woda ...*	*vo*-da ...
hot	*gorąca*	go-*ron*-tsa
mineral	*mineralna*	mee-ne-*ral*-na

in the bar

I'll have ...	*Proszę ...*	*pro*-she ...
I'll buy you a drink.	*Kupię ci drinka.* inf	*koo*-pye chee *dreen*-ka
What would you like?	*Co zamówić dla ciebie?* inf	tso za-*moo*-veech dla *chye*-bye
Cheers!	*Na zdrowie!*	na *zdro*-vye
brandy	*brandy* m	*bren*-di
champagne	*szampan* m	*sham*-pan
a shot of (vodka)	*kieliszek (wódki)*	kye-*lee*-shek (*vood*-kee)
a bottle/glass of beer	*butelka/szklanka piwa*	boo-*tel*-ka/*shklan*-ka *pee*-va
a bottle/glass	*butelka/kieliszek*	boo-*tel*-ka/kye-*lee*-shek
of ... wine	*wina ...*	*vee*-na ...
red	*czerwonego*	cher-vo-*ne*-go
sparkling	*musującego*	moo-soo-yon-*tse*-go
white	*białego*	bya-*we*-go

self-catering

What's the local speciality?
Co jest miejscową   tso yest myeys-*tso*-vom
specjalnością?   spe-tsyal-*nosh*-chyom

What's that?
Co to jest?   tso to yest

How much (is a kilo of cheese)?
Ile kosztuje (kilogram sera)?   ee-le kosh-*too*-ye (kee-*lo*-gram *se*-ra)

I'd like ...	*Proszę ...*	*pro*-she ...
200 grams	*dwadzieścia deko*	dva-*jyesh*-chya *de*-ko
(two) kilos	*(dwa) kilo*	(dva) *kee*-lo
(three) pieces	*(trzy) kawałki*	(tshi) ka-*vow*-kee
(six) slices	*(sześć) plasterków*	(sheshch) plas-*ter*-koof

Less.	*Mniej.*	mney
Enough.	*Wystarczy.*	vis-*tar*-chi
More.	*Więcej.*	*vyen*-tsey

special diets & allergies

Is there a vegetarian restaurant near here?
Czy jest tu gdzieś restauracja   chi yest too gjyesh res-tow-*ra*-tsya
wegetariańska?   ve-ge-ta-*ryan'*-ska

Do you have vegetarian food?
Czy jest żywność wegetariańska?   chi yest *zhiv*-noshch ve-ge-tar-*yan'*-ska

Could you prepare	*Czy można przygotować*	chi *mo*-zhna pshi-go-*to*-vach
a meal without ...?	*jedzenie bez ...?*	ye-*dze*-nye bes ...
butter	*masła*	*mas*-wa
eggs	*jajek*	*yai*-ek
meat stock	*wywaru mięsnego*	vi-*va*-roo myens-*ne*-go

I'm allergic to ...	*Mam uczulenie na ...*	mam oo-choo-*le*-nye na ...
dairy produce	*produkty mleczne*	pro-*dook*-ti *mlech*-ne
gluten	*gluten*	*gloo*-ten
MSG	*glutaminian sodu*	gloo-ta-*mee*-nyan *so*-doo
nuts	*orzechy*	o-*zhe*-khi
seafood	*owoce morza*	o-*vo*-tse *mo*-zha

emergencies

basics

Help!	*Na pomoc!*	na *po*-mots
Stop!	*Stój!*	stooy
Go away!	*Odejdź!*	o-deyj
Thief!	*Złodziej!*	zwo-jyey
Fire!	*Pożar!*	po-zhar
Watch out!	*Uważaj!*	oo-*va*-zhai
Call ...!	*Zadzwoń po ...!*	zad-zvon' po ...
a doctor	*lekarza*	le-*ka*-zha
an ambulance	*karetkę*	ka-*ret*-ke
the police	*policję*	po-*lee*-tsye

It's an emergency.
To nagły wypadek.   to *nag*-wi vi-*pa*-dek

Could you help me, please?
Czy może pan/pani mi pomóc? m/f   chi *mo*-zhe pan/*pa*-nee mee po-*moots*

Can I use the telephone?
Czy mogę użyć telefon?   chi *mo*-ge oo-zhich te-*le*-fon

I'm lost.
Zgubiłem/Zgubiłam się. m/f   zgoo-*bee*-wem/zgoo-*bee*-wam shye

Where are the toilets?
Gdzie są toalety?   gjye som to-a-*le*-ti

police

Where's the police station?
Gdzie jest posterunek policji?   gje yest pos-te-*roo*-nek po-*lee*-tsyee

I want to report an offence.
Chciałem/Chciałam zgłosić przestępstwo. m/f   khchow-em/khchow-am zgwo-sheech pshe-*stemps*-tfo

I have insurance.
Mam ubezpieczenie.   mam oo-bes-pye-*che*-nye

I've been ...	Zostałem/Zostałam ... m/f	zo-*stow*-em/zo-*stow*-am ...
assaulted	napadnięty/a m/f	na-pad-*nyen*-ti/a
raped	zgwałcony/a m/f	zgvow-*tso*-ni/a
robbed	okradziony/a m/f	o-kra-*jyo*-ni/a

I've lost my ...	Zgubiłem/ Zgubiłam ... m/f	zgoo-*bee*-wem/ zgoo-*bee*-wam ...
backpack	plecak	*ple*-tsak
bag	torbę	*tor*-be
credit card	kartę kredytową	*kar*-te kre-di-*to*-vom
handbag	torebkę	to-*rep*-ke
jewellery	biżuterię	bee-zhoo-*ter*-ye
money	pieniądze	pye-*nyon*-dze
passport	paszport	*pash*-port
wallet	portfel	*port*-fel

I want to contact my ...	Chcę się skontaktować z ...	khtse shye skon-tak-*to*-vach z ...
consulate	moim konsulatem	*mo*-yeem kon-soo-*la*-tem
embassy	moją ambasadą	*mo*-yom am-ba-*sa*-dom

health

medical needs

Where's the nearest ...?	Gdzie jest najbliższy/a ...? m/f	gjye yest nai-*bleezh*-shi/a ...
dentist	dentysta m	den-*tis*-ta
doctor	lekarz m	*le*-kash
hospital	szpital m	*shpee*-tal
(night) pharmacist	apteka (nocna) f	ap-*te*-ka (*nots*-na)

I need a doctor (who speaks English).
Szukam lekarza (który mówi po angielsku).
shoo-kam le-*ka*-zha (*ktoo*-ri *moo*-vee po an-*gyel*-skoo)

Could I see a female doctor?
Czy mogę się widzieć z lekarzem kobietą?
chi *mo*-ge shye *vee*-jyech z le-*ka*-zhem ko-*bye*-tom

I've run out of my medication.
Skończyły mi się lekarstwa.
skon-*chi*-wi mee shye le-*kars*-tfa

symptoms, conditions & allergies

I'm sick.	Jestem chory/a. m/f	yes·tem kho·ri/a
It hurts here.	Tutaj boli.	too·tai bo·lee
I have (a) ...	Mam ...	mam ...

asthma	astma f	ast·ma
constipation	zatwardzenie n	zat·far·dze·nye
cough	kaszel m	ka·shel
diarrhoea	rozwolnienie n	roz·vol·nye·nye
fever	gorączka f	go·ronch·ka
headache	ból głowy m	bool gwo·vi
heart condition	stan serca m	stan ser·tsa
nausea	mdłości f pl	mdwosh·chee
pain	ból m	bool
sore throat	ból gardła m	bool gar·dwa
toothache	ból zęba m	bool zem·ba

I'm allergic to ...	Mam alergię na ...	mam a·ler·gye na ...
antibiotics	antybiotyki	an·ti·byo·ti·kee
anti-inflammatories	leki przeciwzapalne	le·kee pshe·cheef·za·pal·ne
aspirin	aspirynę	as·pee·ri·ne
bees	pszczoły	pshcho·wi
codeine	kodeinę	ko·de·ee·ne
penicillin	penicylinę	pe·nee·tsi·lee·ne

antiseptic	środki odkażające m pl	shrod·kee od·ka·zha·yon·tse
bandage	bandaż m	ban·dash
condoms	kondom m pl	kon·dom
contraceptives	środki	shrod·kee
	antykoncepcyjne m pl	an·ti·kon·tsep·tsiy·ne
diarrhoea medicine	rozwolnienie	ros·vol·nye·nye
insect repellent	środek na owady m	shro·dek na o·va·di
laxatives	środek	shro·dek
	przeczyszczający m	pshe·chish·cha·yon·tsi
painkillers	środki	shrod·kee
	przeciwbólowe m pl	pshe·cheef·boo·lo·ve
rehydration salts	sole fizjologiczne f pl	so·le fee·zyo·lo·geech·ne
sleeping tablets	pigułki nasenne f pl	pee·goow·kee na·se·ne

english–polish dictionary

Polish nouns in this dictionary have their gender indicated by ⓜ (masculine), ⓕ (feminine) or ⓝ (neuter). If it's a plural noun, you'll also see pl. Adjectives are given in the masculine form only. Words are also marked as a (adjective), v (verb), sg (singular), pl (plural), inf (informal) or pol (polite) where necessary.

A

accident *wypadek* ⓜ vi-*pa*-dek
accommodation *nocleg* ⓜ *nots*-leg
adaptor *zasilacz* ⓜ za-*shee*-lach
address *adres* ⓜ *a*-dres
after *po* • *za* po • za
air conditioning *klimatyzacja* ⓕ klee-ma-ti-*za*-tsya
airplane *samolot* ⓜ sa-*mo*-lot
airport *lotnisko* ⓝ lot-*nees*-ko
alcohol *alkohol* ⓜ al-ko-khol
all *wszystko* ⓕ*shist*-ko
allergy *alergia* ⓕ a-*ler*-gya
ambulance *karetka pogotowia* ⓕ ka-*ret*-ka po-go-to-*vya*
and *i* ee
ankle *kostka* ⓕ *kost*-ka
arm *ręka* ⓕ *ren*-ka
ashtray *popielniczka* ⓕ po-pyel-*neech*-ka
ATM *bankomat* ⓜ ban-ko-mat

B

baby *niemowlę* ⓝ nye-*mov*-le
back (body) *plecy* pl *ple*-tsi
backpack *plecak* ⓜ *ple*-tsak
bad *zły* zwi
bag *torba* ⓕ *tor*-ba
baggage claim *odbiór bagażu* ⓜ od-byoor ba-*ga*-zhoo
bank *bank* ⓜ bank
bar *bar* ⓜ bar
bathroom *łazienka* ⓕ wa-*zhyen*-ka
battery *bateria* ⓕ ba-*te*-rya
beautiful *piękny* pyen-kni
bed *łóżko* ⓝ *woozh*-ko
beer *piwo* ⓝ *pee*-vo
before *przed* pshet
behind *za* za
bicycle *rower* ⓜ *ro*-ver
big *duży* doo-zhi
bill *rachunek* ⓜ ra-*khoo*-nek
black *czarny* char-ni
blanket *koc* ⓜ kots

blood group *grupa krwi* ⓕ *groo*-pa krfee
blue *niebieski* nye-*byes*-kee
boat *łódź* ⓕ wooj
book (make a reservation) v *rezerwować* re-zer-*vo*-vach
bottle *butelka* ⓕ boo-*tel*-ka
bottle opener *otwieracz do butelek* ⓜ ot-*fye*-rach do boo-*te*-lek
boy *chłopiec* ⓜ khwo-pyets
brakes (car) *hamulce* ⓜ pl ha-*mool*-tse
breakfast *śniadanie* ⓝ shnya-*da*-nye
broken (faulty) *połamany* po-wa-*ma*-ni
bus *autobus* ⓜ ow-to-boos
business *firma* ⓕ *feer*-ma
buy *kupować* koo-po-vach

C

café *kawiarnia* ⓕ ka-*vyar*-nya
camera *aparat* ⓜ a-*pa*-rat
camp site *kamping* ⓜ *kam*-peeng
can opener *otwieracz do konserw* ⓜ ot-*fye*-rach do kon-serf
cancel *unieważniać* oo-nye-*vazh*-nyach
car *samochód* ⓜ sa-mo-*khoot*
cash *gotówka* ⓕ go-*toof*-ka
cash (a cheque) v *zrealizować czek* zre-a-lee-zo-vach chek
cell phone *telefon komórkowy* ⓜ te-*le*-fon ko-moor-*ko*-vi
centre *środek* ⓜ *shro*-dek
change (money) v *rozmieniać* roz-*mye*-nyach
cheap *tani* ta-nee
check (bill) *sprawdzenie* ⓝ sprav-*dze*-nye
check-in *zameldowanie* ⓝ za-mel-do-va-nye
chest *klatka piersiowa* ⓕ *klat*-ka pyer-*shyo*-va
child *dziecko* ⓝ *jye*-tsko
cigarette *papieros* ⓜ pa-*pye*-ros
city *miasto* ⓝ *myas*-to
clean a *czysty* chi-sti
closed *zamknięty* zam-*knyen*-ti
coffee *kawa* ⓕ *ka*-va
coins *monety* ⓕ pl mo-*ne*-ti
cold a *zimny* zheem-ni

42

collect call *rozmowa opłacona przez odbierającego* ①
roz-*mo*-va o-*pwa*-tso-na pshes od-bye-ra-yon-*tse*-go
come (by vehicle) *przyjść* pshiysh
come (on foot) *przychodzić* pshi-*kho*-jeech
computer *komputer* ⓜ kom-*poo*-ter
condom *kondom* ⓜ kan-dom
contact lenses *soczewki kontaktowe* ① pl
so-*chef*-kee kon-tak-*to*-ve
cook v *gotować* go-*to*-vach
cost *koszt* ⓜ kosht
credit card *karta kredytowa* ① *kar*-ta kre-di-*to*-va
cup *filiżanka* ① fee-lee-*zhan*-ka
currency exchange *kantor* ⓜ *kan*-tor
customs (immigration) *urząd celny* ⓜ
oo-zhont *tsel*-ni

D

dangerous *niebezpieczny* nye-bes-*pyech*-ni
date (time) *data* ① *da*-ta
day *dzień* ⓝ jyen'
delay *opóźnienie* o-poozh-*nye*-nye
dentist *dentysta* ⓜ den-*tis*-ta
depart *odjeżdżać* od-*yezh*-jach
diaper *pieluszka* ① pye-*loosh*-ka
dictionary *słownik* ⓜ *swov*-neek
dinner *kolacja* ① ko-*la*-tsya
direct *bezpośredni* bes-po-*shred*-nee
dirty *brudny* *brood*-ni
disabled *niepełnosprawny* nye-pew-no-*sprav*-ni
discount *zniżka* ① *zneesh*-ka
doctor *lekarz* ⓜ *le*-kash
double bed *łóżko małżeńskie* ⓝ
woozh-ko mow-*zhen'*-skye
double room *pokój dwuosobowy* ⓜ
po-kooy dvoo-o-so-*bo*-vi
drink *napój* ⓜ *na*-pooy
drive v *kierować* kye-*ro*-vach
drivers licence *prawo jazdy* ⓝ *pra*-vo *yaz*-di
drugs (illicit) *narkotyki* ⓜ pl nar-ko-*ti*-kee
dummy (pacifier) *smoczek* ⓜ *smo*-chek

E

ear *ucho* ⓝ *oo*-kho
east *wschód* ⓜ vskhood
eat *jeść* yeshch
economy class *klasa oszczędnościowa* ①
kla-sa osh-chend-nosh-*chyo*-va
electricity *elektryczność* ① e-lek-*trich*-noshch
elevator *winda* ① *veen*-da
email *email* ⓜ e-mail

embassy *ambasada* ① am-ba-*sa*-da
emergency *nagły przypadek* ⓜ *nag*-wi pshi-*pa*-dek
English (language) *angielski* an-*gyel*-skee
entrance *wejście* ⓝ *veysh*-chye
evening *wieczór* ⓜ *vye*-choor
exchange rate *kurs wymiany* ⓜ koors vi-*mya*-ni
exit *wyjście* ⓝ *viysh*-chye
expensive *drogi* *dro*-gee
express mail *list ekspresowy* ⓜ leest eks-pre-*so*-vi
eye *oko* ⓝ *o*-ko

F

far *daleki* da-*le*-kee
fast *szybki* *shib*-kee
father *ojciec* ⓜ *oy*-chyets
film (camera) *film* ⓝ feelm
finger *palec* ⓜ *pa*-lets
first-aid kit *apteczka pierwszej pomocy* ①
ap-*tech*-ka pyerf-shey po-*mo*-tsi
first class *pierwsza klasa* ① *pyerf*-sha *kla*-sa
fish *ryba* ① *ri*-ba
food *żywność* ① *zhiv*-noshch
foot *stopa* ① *sto*-pa
fork *widelec* ⓜ vee-*de*-lets
free (of charge) *bezpłatny* bes-*pwat*-ni
friend *przyjaciel/przyjaciółka* ⓜ / ①
pshi-ya-*chyel*/pshi-ya-*choow*-ka
fruit *owoc* ⓜ *o*-vots
full *pełny* pew-ni
funny *zabawny* za-*bav*-ni

G

gift *prezent* ⓜ *pre*-zent
girl *dziewczyna* ① jyev-*chi*-na
glass (drinking) *szklanka* ① *shklan*-ka
glasses *okulary* pl o-koo-*la*-ri
go (by vehicle) *jechać* ye-khach
go (on foot) *iść* eeshch
good *dobry* *do*-bri
green *zielony* zhye-*lo*-ni
guide *przewodnik* ⓜ pshe-*vod*-neek

H

half *połówka* ① po-*woof*-ka
hand *ręka* ① *ren*-ka
handbag *torebka* ① to-*rep*-ka
happy *szczęśliwy* shchen-*shlee*-vi
have *mieć* myech
he *on* on

head *głowa* ① gwo-va
heart *serce* ① ser-tse
heat *upał* ⑩ oo-pow
heavy *ciężki* ⑩ chyensh-kee
help v *pomagać* po-ma-gach
here *tutaj* too-tai
high *wysoki* vi-so-kee
highway *szosa* ① sho-sa
hike v *wędrować* ven-dro-vach
holiday *święto* ⑪ shvyen-to
homosexual n *homoseksualista* ⑩
ho-mo-sek-soo-a-*lees*-ta
hospital *szpital* ⑩ shpee-tal
hot *gorący* go-ron-tsi
hotel *hotel* ⑩ ho-tel
hungry *głodny* gwo-dni
husband *mąż* ⑩ monzh

I

I *ja* ya
identification (card) *dowód tożsamości* ⑩
do-vood tozh-sa-mosh-chee
ill *chory* kho-ri
important *ważny* vazh-ni
included *wliczony* vlee-cho-ni
injury *rana* ① ra-na
insurance *ubezpieczenie* ⑪ oo-bes-pye-che-nye
Internet *internet* ⑩ een-ter-net
interpreter *tłumacz/tłumaczka* ⑩/①
twoo-mach/twoo-mach-ka

J

jewellery *biżuteria* ① bee-zhoo-ter-ya
job *praca* ① pra-tsa

K

key *klucz* ⑩ klooch
kilogram *kilogram* ⑩ kee-lo-gram
kitchen *kuchnia* ① kookh-nya
knife *nóż* ⑩ noosh

L

laundry (place) *pralnia* ① pral-nya
lawyer *prawnik* ⑩ prav-neek
left (direction) *lewy* ⑩ le-vi
left-luggage office *przechowalnia bagażu* ①
pshe-kho-val-nya ba-ga-zhoo

leg *noga* ① no-ga
lesbian n *lesbijka* ① les-beey-ka
less *mniej* mnyey
letter (mail) *list* ⑩ leest
lift (elevator) *winda* ① veen-da
light *światło* ⑪ shvyat-wo
like v *lubić* loo-beech
lock *zamek* ⑩ za-mek
long *długi* dwoo-gee
lost *zgubiony* zgoo-byo-ni
lost-property office *biuro rzeczy znalezionych* ⑪
byoo-ro zhe-chi zna-le-zhyo-nikh
love v *kochać* ko-khach
luggage *bagaż* ⑩ ba-gash
lunch *lunch* ⑩ lanch

M

mail (letters) *list* ⑩ leest
mail (postal system) *poczta* ① poch-ta
man *mężczyzna* ⑩ menzh-chiz-na
map (of country) *mapa* ① ma-pa
map (of town) *plan* ⑩ plan
market *rynek* ⑩ ri-nek
matches *zapałki* ① pl za-pow-kee
meat *mięso* ⑪ myen-so
medicine *lekarstwo* ⑪ le-karst-fo
menu *jadłospis* ⑩ ya-dwo-spees
message *wiadomość* ① vya-do-moshch
milk *mleko* ⑪ mle-ko
minute *minuta* ① mee-noo-ta
mobile phone *telefon komórkowy* ⑩
te-le-fon ko-moor-ko-vi
money *pieniądze* ① pl pye-nyon-dze
month *miesiąc* ⑩ mye-shonts
morning *rano* ⑪ ra-no
mother *matka* ① mat-ka
motorcycle *motor* ⑩ mo-tor
motorway *autostrada* ① ow-to-stra-da
mouth *usta* pl oos-ta
music *muzyka* ① moo-zi-ka

N

name *imię* ⑪ ee-mye
napkin *serwetka* ① ser-vet-ka
nappy *pieluszka* ① pye-loosh-ka
near *bliski* blees-kee
neck *szyja* ① shi-ya
new *nowy* no-vi
news *wiadomości* ① pl vya-do-mosh-chee
newspaper *gazeta* ① ga-ze-ta
night *noc* ① nots

no *nie* nye
noisy *hałaśliwy* ha-wa-*shlee*-vi
nonsmoking *niepalący* nye-pa-*lon*-tsi
north *północ* ① *poow*-nots
nose *nos* ⓜ nos
now *teraz* *te*-ras
number *numer* ⓜ *noo*-mer

O

oil (engine) *olej* ⓜ o-ley
old *stary* *sta*-ri
one-way ticket *bilet w jedną stronę* ⓜ
  bee-let w *yed*-nom *stro*-ne
open a *otwarty* ot-*far*-ti
outside *na zewnątrz* na zev-nontsh

P

package *paczka* ① *pach*-ka
paper *papier* ⓜ *pa*-pyer
park (car) v *parkować* par-*ko*-vach
passport *paszport* ⓜ *pash*-port
pay *płacić* pwa-cheech
pen *długopis* ⓜ dwoo-go-pees
petrol *benzyna* ① ben-*zi*-na
pharmacy *apteka* ① ap-*te*-ka
phonecard *karta telefoniczna* ① *kar*-ta te-le-fo-*neech*-na
photo *zdjęcie* ① *zdyen*-chye
plate *talerz* ⓜ *ta*-lesh
Poland *Polska* ① *pol*-ska
police *policja* ① po-*lee*-tsya
Polish (language) *polski* ⓜ *pol*-skee
postcard *pocztówka* ① poch-*toof*-ka
post office *urząd pocztowy* ⓜ *oo*-zhond poch-*to*-vi
pregnant *w ciąży* v chyon-zhi
price *cena* ① *tse*-na

Q

quiet *cichy* chee-khi

R

rain *deszcz* ⓜ deshch
razor *brzytwa* ① *bzhit*-fa
receipt *rachunek* ① ra-*khoo*-nek
red *czerwony* cher-*vo*-ni
refund *zwrot pieniędzy* ⓜ zvrot pye-*nyen*-dzi
registered mail *list polecony* ⓜ leest po-le-*tso*-ni
rent v *wynająć* vi-*na*-yonch

repair v *naprawić* na-*pra*-veech
reservation *rezerwacja* ① re-zer-*va*-tsya
restaurant *restauracja* ① res-tow-*ra*-tsya
return v *wracać* vra-tsach
return ticket *bilet powrotny* ⓜ *bee*-let po-*vro*-tni
right (direction) *prawoskrętny* pra-vo-*skrent*-ni
road *droga* ① *dro*-ga
room *pokój* ⓜ *po*-kooy

S

safe a *bezpieczny* bes-*pyech*-ni
sanitary napkin *podpaski higieniczne* ① pl
  pod-*pas*-kee hee-gye-*neech*-ne
seat *miejsce* ⓜ *myeys*-tse
send *wysyłać* vi-*si*-wach
service station *stacja obsługi* ① *sta*-tsya ob-*swoo*-gee
sex *seks* ⓜ seks
shampoo *szampon* ⓜ *sham*-pon
share (a dorm) v *mieszkać z kimś* *myesh*-kach z keemsh
shaving cream *krem do golenia* ⓜ krem do go-*le*-nya
she *ona* o-na
sheet (bed) *prześcieradło* ① pshesh-chye-*ra*-dwo
shirt *koszula* ① ko-*shoo*-la
shoes *buty* ⓜ pl *boo*-ti
shop *sklep* ⓜ sklep
short *krótki* kroot-kee
shower *prysznic* ⓜ *prish*-neets
single room *pokój jednoosobowy* ⓜ
  po-kooy ye-dno-o-so-*bo*-vi
skin *skóra* ① *skoo*-ra
skirt *spódnica* ① spood-*nee*-tsa
sleep v *spać* spach
slowly *powoli* po-*vo*-lee
small *mały* *ma*-wi
smoke (cigarettes) v *palić* *pa*-leech
soap *mydło* ⓜ *mid*-wo
some *kilka* *keel*-ka
soon *wkrótce* *fkroot*-tse
south *południe* ① po-*wood*-nye
souvenir shop *sklep z pamiątkami* ⓜ
  sklep z pa-*myont*-ka-mi
speak *mówić* *moo*-veech
spoon *łyżka* ① *wish*-ka
stamp *znaczek* ⓜ *zna*-chek
stand-by ticket *bilet z listy rezerwowej* ⓜ
  bee-let z *lees*-ti re-zer-*vo*-vey
station (train) *stacja* ① *sta*-tsya
stomach *żołądek* ⓜ zho-*won*-dek
stop v *przestać* *pshes*-tach
stop (bus) *przystanek* ① pshi-*sta*-nek
street *ulica* ① oo-*lee*-tsa
student *student* ⓜ *stoo*-dent

sun *słońce* ⓝ *swon'*-tse
sunscreen *krem przeciwsłoneczny* ⓜ
  krem pshe-cheef-swo-nech-ni
swim v *pływać* pwi-vach

T

tampon *tampon* ⓜ *tam*-pon
taxi *taksówka* ① *tak-soof*-ka
teaspoon *łyżeczka* ① *wi-zhech*-ka
teeth *zęby* ⓜ pl *zem*-bi
telephone *telefon* ⓜ *te-le*-fon
television *telewizja* ① *te-le-veez*-ya
temperature (weather) *temperatura* ①
  tem-pe-ra-*too*-ra
tent *namiot* ⓜ *na*-myot
that (one) *który ktoo*-ri
they *oni o*-nee
thirsty *spragniony* sprag-*nyo*-ni
this (one) *ten* ten
throat *gardło gard*-wo
ticket *bilet bee*-let
time *czas* ⓜ chas
tired *zmęczony* zmen-*cho*-ni
tissues *chusteczki* ① pl khoos-*tech*-kee
today *dzisiaj* jee-*shyai*
toilet *toaleta* ① to-a-*le*-ta
tomorrow *jutro yoo*-tro
tonight *dzisiaj wieczorem* jee-*shyai* vye-*cho*-rem
toothbrush *szczotka do zębów* ① *shchot*-ka do *zem*-boof
toothpaste *pasta do zębów* ① *pas*-ta do *zem*-boof
torch (flashlight) *latarka* ① la-*tar*-ka
tour *wycieczka* ① vi-*chyech*-ka
tourist office *biuro turystyczne* ⓝ *byoo*-ro too-ris-*tich*-ne
towel *ręcznik* ⓜ *rench*-neek
train *pociąg* ⓜ *po*-chyonk
translate *przetłumaczyć* pshe-twoo-*ma*-chich
travel agency *biuro podróży* ⓝ *byoo*-ro po-*droo*-zhi
travellers cheques *czeki podróżne* ⓜ pl
  che-kee po-*droozh*-ne
trousers *spodnie* pl *spo*-dnye
twin beds *dwa łóżka* ⓝ pl dva *woosh*-ka
tyre *opona* ① *o-po*-na

U

underwear *bielizna* ① bye-*leez*-na
urgent *pilny peel*-ni

V

vacant *wolny vol*-ni
vacation *wakacje* pl va-*ka*-tsye
vegetable *warzywo* ⓝ va-*zhi*-vo
vegetarian a *wegetariański* ve-ge-tar-*yan'*-skee
visa *wiza* ① *vee*-za

W

waiter *kelner* ⓜ *kel*-ner
walk v *spacerować* spa-tse-*ro*-vach
wallet *portfel* ⓜ *port*-fel
warm a *ciepły chyep*-wi
Warsaw *Warszawa* ① var-*sha*-va
wash (something) *prać* prach
watch *zegarek* ⓜ ze-*ga*-rek
water *woda* ① *vo*-da
we *my* mi
weekend *weekend* ⓜ *wee*-kend
west *zachód* ⓜ za-*khood*
wheelchair *wózek inwalidzki* ⓜ
  voo-zek een-va-*leets*-kee
when *kiedy kye*-di
where *gdzie gjye*
white *biały bya*-wi
who *kto* kto
why *dlaczego* dla-*che*-go
wife *żona* ① *zho*-na
window *okno* ⓝ *ok*-no
wine *wino* ⓝ *vee*-no
with *z* z
without *bez* bes
woman *kobieta* ① ko-*bye*-ta
write *pisać pee*-sach

Y

yellow *żółty zhoow*-ti
yes *tak* tak
yesterday *wczoraj fcho*-rai
you sg inf *ty* ti
you sg pol *pan/pani* ⓜ/① pan/*pa*-nee
you pl inf *wy* vi
you pl pol *panowie/panie* ⓜ/① pa-*no*-vye/*pa*-nye
you pl pol *państwo* ⓜ&① *pan'*-stfo

Portuguese

portuguese alphabet

A a aa	*B b* be	*C c* se	*D d* de	*E e* e
F f e·fe	*G g* je	*H h* a·*gaah*	*I i* ee	*J j* *jo*·ta
K k ka·pa	*L l* e·le	*M m* e·me	*N n* e·ne	*O o* o
P p pe	*Q q* ke	*R r* e·rre	*S s* e·se	*T t* te
U u oo	*V v* ve	*W w* da·blyoo	*X x* sheesh	*Y y* *eeps*·lon
Z z ze				

portuguese

introduction

Portuguese (*português* poor-too-*gesh*), the language which produced words such as *albino*, *brocade* and *molasses*, comes from the Romance language family and is closely related to Spanish, French and Italian. Descended from the colloquial Latin spoken by Roman soldiers, it's now used by over 200 million people worldwide.

Linguists believe that before the Roman invasion of the Iberian Peninsula in 218 BC, the locals of modern-day Portugal spoke a Celtic language. That local language was supplanted by the vernacular form of Latin (sometimes called 'Romance') spoken by the occupying forces under the Romans' 500-year rule of the province of Lusitania (present-day Portugal and Spanish Galicia). During this period, Portuguese also absorbed elements of the languages of invading Germanic tribes. The greatest influence on today's Portuguese, however, was a result of the Moorish invasion of the peninsula in AD 711. Arabic was imposed as the official language of the region until the expulsion of the Moors in 1249, and although Romance was still spoken by the masses, the Moorish language left its mark on the vocabulary. From the 16th century on, there were only minor changes to the language, mostly influences from France and Spain. The earliest written documents were composed in the 12th century, and the Portuguese used in 1572 by Luís de Camões (author of the first great Portuguese classic, *Os Lusíadas*) was already identifiable as the language of José Saramago's Nobel Prize-winning works in the 20th century.

The global distribution of the Portuguese language began during the period know as *Os Descobrimentos* (the Discoveries), the golden era of Portugal's colonial expansion into Africa, Asia and South America. In the 15th and 16th centuries, the peninsular nation was a world power and had enormous economic, cultural and political influence. The empire's reach can be seen today in the number of countries besides Portugal where Portuguese still has the status of an official language – Brazil, Madeira and the Azores in the Atlantic Ocean off Europe, Cape Verde, São Tomé and Príncipe, Guinea-Bissau, Angola and Mozambique (all in Africa), and Macau and East Timor in Asia.

While there are differences between European Portuguese and that spoken elsewhere, you shouldn't have many problems being understood throughout the Portuguese-speaking world. As the Portuguese say, *Quem não arrisca, não petisca* keng nowng a-*rreesh*-ka, nowng pe-*teesh*-ka (If you don't take a risk, you won't eat delicacies).

pronunciation

vowel sounds

The vowel sounds in Portuguese are quite similar to those found in English. Most vowel sounds in Portuguese also have a nasal version with an effect similar to the silent '-ng' ending in English, as in *amanhã* aa-ma-*nyang* (tomorrow), for example. The letter 'n' or 'm' at the end of a syllable or a tilde (~) in written Portuguese indicate that the vowel is nasal.

symbol	english equivalent	portuguese example	transliteration
a	run	*maçã*	ma-*sang*
aa	father	*tomate*	too-*maa*-te
ai	aisle	*pai*	pai
ay	say	*lei*	lay
e	bet	*cedo*	*se*-doo
ee	see	*fino*	*fee*-noo
o	pot	*sobre*	*so*-bre
oh	oh	*couve*	*koh*-ve
oo	book	*gato*	*ga*-too
ow	how	*Austrália*	ow-*shtraa*-lya
oy	toy	*noite*	*noy*-te

word stress

In Portuguese, stress generally falls on the second-to-last syllable of a word, though there are exceptions. If a written vowel has a circumflex (ˆ) or an acute (´) or grave (`) accent marked on it, this cancels the general rule and the stress falls on that syllable. When a word ends in a written *i*, *im*, *l*, *r*, *u*, *um* or *z*, or is pronounced with a nasalised vowel, the stress falls on the last syllable. Don't worry too much about it when using phrases from this book though – the stressed syllable is always italicised in our coloured pronunciation guides.

consonant sounds

Most of the consonant sounds in Portuguese are also found in English, and even *r* (rr) will be familiar to many people (it's similar to the French 'r'). Note that the letter ç ('c' with a cedilla) is pronounced as s rather than k.

symbol	english equivalent	portuguese example	transliteration
b	bed	*beber*	be-*ber*
d	dog	*dedo*	*de*-doo
f	fat	*faca*	*faa*-ka
g	go	*gasolina*	ga-zoo-*lee*-na
k	kit	*cama*	*ka*-ma
l	lot	*lixo*	*lee*-shoo
ly	million	*muralhas*	moo-*raa*-lyash
m	man	*macaco*	ma-*kaa*-koo
n	not	*nada*	*naa*-da
ng	ring (indicates the nasalisation of the preceding vowel)	*ambos, uns, amanhã*	*ang*-boosh, oongsh, aa-ma-*nyang*
ny	canyon	*linha*	*lee*-nya
p	pet	*padre*	*paa*-dre
r	like 'tt' in 'butter' said fast	*hora*	*o*-ra
rr	run (throaty)	*relva*	*rrel*-va
s	sun	*criança*	kree-*ang*-sa
sh	shot	*chave*	*shaa*-ve
t	top	*tacho*	*taa*-shoo
v	very	*vago*	*vaa*-goo
w	win	*água*	*aa*-gwa
y	yes	*edifício*	ee-dee-*fee*-syoo
z	zero	*camisa*	ka-*mee*-za
zh	pleasure	*cerveja*	serr-*ve*-zha

tools

language difficulties

Do you speak English?
Fala inglês?   *faa·la eeng·glesh*

Do you understand?
Entende?   eng·*teng*·de

I (don't) understand.
(Não) Entendo.   (nowng) eng·*teng*·doo

What does (bem-vindo) mean?
O que quer dizer (bem-vindo)?   oo ke ker dee·*zer* (beng·*veeng*·doo)

How do you ...?	*Como é que se ...?*	*ko·moo* e ke se ...
pronounce this	*pronuncia isto*	proo·noong·*see*·a *esh*·too
write (ajuda)	*escreve (ajuda)*	*shkre*·ve (a·*zhoo*·da)

Could you please ...?	*Podia ..., por favor?*	poo·*dee*·a ... poor fa·*vor*
repeat that	*repetir isto*	rre·pe·*teer* eesh·too
speak more slowly	*falar mais devagar*	fa·*laar* maish de·va·*gaar*
write it down	*escrever isso*	*shkre*·ver ee·soo

essentials

Yes.	*Sim.*	seeng
No.	*Não.*	nowng
Please.	*Por favor.*	poor fa·*vor*
Thank you	*(Muito)*	(*mweeng*·too)
(very much).	*Obrigado/a.* m/f	o·bree·*gaa*·doo/a
You're welcome.	*De nada.*	de *naa*·da
Excuse me.	*Faz favor!*	faash fa·*vor*
Sorry.	*Desculpe.*	desh·*kool*·pe

PORTUGUÊS – tools

numbers

0	zero	ze·roo	16	dezasseis	de·za·saysh
1	um	oong	17	dezassete	de·za·se·te
2	dois	doysh	18	dezoito	de·zoy·too
3	três	tresh	19	dezanove	de·za·no·ve
4	quatro	kwaa·troo	20	vinte	veeng·te
5	cinco	seeng·koo	21	vinte e um	veeng·te e oong
6	seis	saysh	22	vinte e dois	veeng·te e doysh
7	sete	se·te	30	trinta	treeng·ta
8	oito	oy·too	40	quarenta	kwa·reng·ta
9	nove	no·ve	50	cinquenta	seeng·kweng·ta
10	dez	desh	60	sessenta	se·seng·ta
11	onze	ong·ze	70	setenta	se·teng·ta
12	doze	do·ze	80	oitenta	oy·teng·ta
13	treze	tre·ze	90	noventa	no·veng·ta
14	catorze	ka·tor·ze	100	cem	seng
15	quinze	keeng·ze	1000	mil	meel

time & dates

What time is it?	Que horas são?	kee o·rash sowng
It's one o'clock.	É uma hora.	e oo·ma o·ra
It's (10) o'clock.	São (dez) horas.	sowng (desh) o·rash
Quarter past (10).	(Dez) e quinze.	(desh) e keeng·ze
Half past (10).	(Dez) e meia.	(desh) e may·a
Quarter to (10).	Quinze para as (dez).	keeng·ze pa·ra ash (desh)
At what time ...?	A que horas ...?	a ke o·rash ...
At ...	Às ...	ash ...
in the morning	da manhã	da ma·nyang
in the afternoon	da tarde	da taar·de
in the evening	da noite	da noy·te
Monday	segunda-feira	se·goong·da·fay·ra
Tuesday	terça-feira	ter·sa·fay·ra
Wednesday	quarta-feira	kwaar·ta·fay·ra
Thursday	quinta-feira	keeng·ta·fay·ra
Friday	sexta-feira	saysh·ta·fay·ra
Saturday	sábado	saa·ba·doo
Sunday	domingo	doo·meeng·goo

January	*Janeiro*	zha-*nay*-roo
February	*Fevereiro*	fe-*vray*-roo
March	*Março*	maar-soo
April	*Abril*	a-*breel*
May	*Maio*	maa-yoo
June	*Junho*	zhoo-nyoo
July	*Julho*	zhoo-lyoo
August	*Agosto*	a-*gosh*-too
September	*Setembro*	se-*teng*-broo
October	*Outubro*	oh-*too*-broo
November	*Novembro*	no-*veng*-broo
December	*Dezembro*	de-*zeng*-broo

What date is it today?
   Qual é a data de hoje?   kwaal e a *daa*-ta de *o*-zhe

It's (18 October).
   Hoje é dia (dezoito de Outubro).   *o*-zhe e *dee*-a (de-*zoy*-too de oh-*too*-broo)

since (May)	*desde (Maio)*	desh-de (*maa*-yoo)
until (June)	*até (Junho)*	a-*te* (zhoo-nyoo)
last ...		
night	*a noite passada*	a *noy*-te pa-*saa*-da
week	*a semana passada*	a se-*ma*-na pa-*saa*-da
month	*o mês passado*	oo mesh pa-*saa*-doo
year	*o ano passado*	oo *a*-noo pa-*saa*-doo
next ...		
week	*na próxima semana*	na *pro*-see-ma se-*ma*-na
month	*no próximo mês*	noo *pro*-see-moo mesh
year	*no próximo ano*	noo *pro*-see-moo *a*-noo
yesterday/tomorrow ...	*ontem/amanhã ...*	ong-teng/aa-ma-*nyang* ...
morning	*de manhã*	de ma-*nyang*
afternoon	*à tarde*	aa *taar*-de
evening	*à noite*	aa *noy*-te

weather

What's the weather like?	Como está o tempo?	ko·moo shtaa oo teng·poo
It's ...	Está ...	shtaa ...
cloudy	enublado	e·noo·blaa·doo
cold	frio	free·oo
hot	muito quente	mweeng·too keng·te
raining	a chover	a shoo·ver
snowing	a nevar	a ne·vaar
sunny	sol	sol
warm	quente	keng·te
windy	ventoso	veng·to·zoo
spring	primavera f	pree·ma·ve·ra
summer	verão m	ve·rowng
autumn	outono m	oh·to·noo
winter	inverno m	eeng·ver·noo

border crossing

I'm here ...	Estou ...	shtoh ...
in transit	em trânsito	eng trang·zee·too
on business	em negócios	eng ne·go·syoosh
on holiday	de férias	de fe·ree·ash
I'm here for ...	Vou ficar por ...	voh fee·kaar poor ...
(10) days	(dez) dias	(desh) dee·ash
(three) weeks	(três) semanas	(tresh) se·ma·nash
(two) months	(dois) meses	(doysh) me·zesh

I'm going to (Elvas).
Vou para (Elvas).   voh pa·ra (el·vash)

I'm staying at the (Hotel Lisbon).
Estou no (Hotel Lisboa).   shtoh noo (o·tel leezh·bo·a)

I have nothing to declare.
Não tenho nada a declarar.   nowng ta·nyoo naa·da a de·kla·raar

I have something to declare.
Tenho algo a declarar.   ta·nyoo al·goo a de·kla·raar

That's (not) mine.
Isto (não) é meu.   eesh·too (nowng) e me·oo

transport

tickets & luggage

Where can I buy a ticket?
Onde é que eu compro o bilhete?   ong-de e ke e-oo kong-proo oo bee-*lye*-te

Do I need to book a seat?
Preciso de fazer reserva?   pre-*see*-zoo de fa-*zer* rre-*zer*-va

One ... ticket	*Um bilhete de ...*	oong bee-*lye*-te de ...
(to Braga), please.	*(para Braga), por favor.*	(pra *braa*-ga) poor fa-*vor*
one-way	*ida*	ee-da
return	*ida e volta*	ee-da ee *vol*-ta

I'd like to ...	*Queria ... o bilhete,*	ke-*ree*-a ... oo bee-*lye*-te
my ticket, please.	*por favor.*	poor fa-*vor*
cancel	*cancelar*	kang-se-*laar*
change	*trocar*	troo-*kaar*
collect	*cobrar*	koo-*braar*
confirm	*confirmar*	kong-feer-*maar*

I'd like a ... seat,	*Queria um lugar ...*	ke-*ree*-a oong loo-*gaar* ...
please.	*por favor.*	poor fa-*vor*
nonsmoking	*de não fumadores*	de nowng foo-ma-*do*-resh
smoking	*para fumadores*	pra foo-ma-*do*-resh

How much is it?
Quanto é?   kwang-too e

Is there air conditioning?
Tem ar condicionado?   teng aar kong-dee-syoo-*naa*-doo

Is there a toilet?
Tem casa de banho?   teng *kaa*-za de ba-nyoo

How long does the trip take?
Quanto tempo é que   kwang-too teng-poo e ke
leva a viagem?   *le*-va a vee-*aa*-zheng

Is it a direct route?
É uma rota directa?   e *oo*-ma rro-ta dee-*re*-ta

I'd like a luggage locker.
Queria o depósito de   ke-*ree*-a oo de-*po*-zee-too de
bagagens.   ba-*gaa*-zhengsh

My luggage	A minha	a mee-nya
has been ...	bagagem ...	ba-gaa-zheng ...
damaged	foi danificada	foy da-nee-fee-kaa-da
lost	perdeu-se	per-de-oo-se
stolen	foi roubada	foy rroh-baa-da

getting around

Where does flight (TP 615) arrive/depart?

De onde pára/parte o voo   de ong-de paa-ra/paar-te oo vo-oo
(TP 615)?   (te pe saysh-seng-toosh e keeng-ze)

Where's (the) ...?	Onde é ...?	ong-de e ...
arrivals hall	a porta de chegada	a por-ta de she-gaa-da
departures hall	a porta de partida	a por-ta de par-tee-da
duty-free shop	a loja duty-free	a lo-zha doo-tee-free
gate (12)	a porta (doze)	a por-ta (do-ze)

Is this the ...	Este é o ...	esh-te e oo ...
to (Lisbon)?	para (Lisboa)?	pra (leezh-bo-a)
boat	barco	baar-koo
bus	autocarro	ow-to-kaa-rroo
plane	avião	a-vee-owng
train	comboio	kong-boy-oo

What time's	Quando é que sai	kwang-doo e ke sai
the ... bus?	o ... autocarro?	oo ... ow-to-kaa-rroo
first	primeiro	pree-may-roo
last	último	ool-tee-moo
next	próximo	pro-see-moo

At what time does it arrive/leave?

A que horas chega/sai?   a ke o-rash she-ga/sai

How long will it be delayed?

Quanto tempo é que   kwang-too teng-poo e ke
vai chegar atrasado?   vai she-gaar a-tra-zaa-doo

What station/stop is this?

Qual estação/paragem é este?   kwaal shta-sowng/pa-raa-zheng e esh-te

What's the next station/stop?

Qual é a próxima estação/   kwaal e a pro-see-ma shta-sowng/
paragem?   pa-raa-zheng

Does it stop at (Amarante)?
Pára em (Amarante)? paa·ra eng (a·ma·rang·te)

Please tell me when we get to (Évora).
Por favor avise-me quando poor fa·vor a·vee·ze·me kwang·doo
chegarmos a (Évora). she·gaar·moosh a (e·voo·ra)

How long do we stop here?
Quanto tempo vamos kwang·too teng·poo va·moosh
ficar parados aqui? fee·kaar pa·raa·doosh a·kee

Is this seat available?
Este lugar está vago? esh·te loo·gaar shtaa va·goo

That's my seat.
Este é o meu lugar. esh·te e oo me·oo loo·gaar

I'd like a taxi … *Queria chamar* ke·ree·a sha·maar
  um táxi … oong taak·see …
  at (9am) *para as (nove* pra ash (no·ve
    da manhã) da ma·nyang)
  now *agora* a·go·ra
  tomorrow *amanhã* aa·ma·nyang

Is this taxi available?
Este táxi está livre? esh·te taak·see shtaa lee·vre

How much is it to …?
Quanto custa até ao …? kwang·too koosh·ta a·te ow …

Please put the meter on.
Por favor, ligue o taxímetro. poor fa·vor lee·ge oo taak·see·me·troo

Please take me to (this address).
Leve-me para (este endereço), le·ve·me pa·ra (esh·te eng·de·re·soo)
por favor. poor fa·vor

Please … *Por favor …* poor fa·vor …
  slow down *vá mais devagar* vaa maish de·va·gaar
  stop here *pare aqui* paa·re a·kee
  wait here *espere aqui* shpe·re a·kee

car, motorbike & bicycle hire

I'd like to hire a ...	Queria alugar ...	ke-ree-a a-loo-gaar ...
bicycle	uma bicicleta	oo-ma bee-see-kle-ta
car	um carro	oong kaa-rroo
motorbike	uma mota	oo-ma mo-ta

with ...	com ...	kong ...
a driver	motorista	moo-too-reesh-ta
air conditioning	ar condicionado	aar kong-dee-syoo-naa-doo

How much	Quanto custa para	kwang-too koosh-ta pa-ra
for ... hire?	alugar por...?	a-loo-gaar poor ...
hourly	hora	o-ra
daily	dia	dee-a
weekly	semana	se-ma-na

air	ar m	aar
oil	óleo m	o-le-oo
petrol	gasolina f	ga-zoo-lee-na
tyres	pneus m pl	pe-ne-oosh

I need a mechanic.
Preciso de um mecânico.   pre-see-zoo de oong me-kaa-nee-koo

I've run out of petrol.
Estou sem gasolina.   shtoh seng ga-zoo-lee-na

I have a flat tyre.
Tenho um furo no pneu.   ta-nyoo oong foo-roo noo pe-ne-oo

directions

Where's the ...?	Onde é ...?	ong-de e ...
bank	o banco	oo bang-koo
city centre	o centro da cidade	oo seng-troo da see-daa-de
hotel	o hotel	oo o-tel
market	o mercado	oo mer-kaa-doo
police station	a esquadra da polícia	a shkwaa-dra da poo-lee-sya
post office	o correio	oo koo-rray-oo
public toilet	a casa de banho pública	a kaa-za de ba-nyoo poo-blee-ka
tourist office	o escritório de turismo	oo shkree-to-ryoo de too-reezh-moo

Is this the road to (Sintra)?
Esta é a estrada para (Sintra)? esh·ta e a shtraa·da pa·ra (seeng·tra)

Can you show me (on the map)?
Pode-me mostrar (no mapa)? po·de·me moosh·traar (noo maa·pa)

How far is it?
A que distância fica? a ke deesh·tang·sya fee·ka

How do I get there?
Como é que eu chego lá? ko·moo e ke e·oo she·goo laa

Turn ...	Vire ...	vee·re ...
at the corner	na esquina	na shkee·na
at the traffic lights	nos semáforos	noosh se·maa·foo·roosh
left	à esquerda	aa shker·da
right	à direita	aa dee·ray·ta

It's ...	É ...	e ...
behind ...	atrás de ...	a·traash de ...
far away	longe	long·zhe
here	aqui	a·kee
in front of ...	em frente de ...	eng freng·te de ...
left	à esquerda	aa shker·da
near (to ...)	perto (de ...)	per·too (de ...)
next to ...	ao lado de ...	ow laa·doo de ...
on the corner	na esquina	na shkee·na
opposite ...	do lado	doo laa·doo
	oposto ...	oo·posh·too ...
right	à direita	aa dee·ray·ta
straight ahead	em frente	eng freng·te
there	lá	laa

by bus	de autocarro	de ow·to·kaa·rroo
by taxi	de táxi	de taak·see
by train	de comboio	de kong·boy·oo
on foot	a pé	a pe

north	norte	nor·te
south	sul	sool
east	leste	lesh·te
west	oeste	o·esh·te

Entrada/Saída	eng-*traa*-da/sa-*ee*-da	**Entrance/Exit**
Aberto/Fechado	a-*ber*-too/fe-*shaa*-doo	**Open/Closed**
Há Vaga	aa *vaa*-ga	**Rooms Available**
Não Há Vaga	nowng aa *vaa*-ga	**No Vacancies**
Informação	eeng-for-ma-*sowng*	**Information**
Esquadra da Polícia	shkwaa-dra da poo-*lee*-sya	**Police Station**
Proibido	pro-ee-*bee*-doo	**Prohibited**
Casa de Banho	*kaa*-za de ba-nyoo	**Toilets**
Homens	o-mengsh	**Men**
Mulheres	moo-*lye*-resh	**Women**
Quente/Frio	*keng*-te/*free*-oo	**Hot/Cold**

accommodation

finding accommodation

Where's a ...?	*Onde é que há ...?*	ong-de e ke aa ...
camping ground	*um parque de campismo*	oong *paar*-ke de kang-*peezh*-moo
guesthouse	*uma casa de hóspedes*	*oo*-ma *kaa*-za de *osh*-pe-desh
hotel	*um hotel*	oong o-*tel*
youth hostel	*uma pousada de juventude*	*oo*-ma poh-*zaa*-da de zhoo-veng-*too*-de

Can you recommend somewhere ...?	*Pode recomendar algum lugar ...?*	po-de rre-koo-meng-*daar* aal-*goong* loo-*gaar* ...
cheap	*barato*	ba-*raa*-too
good	*bom*	bong
nearby	*perto daqui*	*per*-too da-*kee*

I'd like to book a room, please.
Eu queria fazer uma reserva, por favor. — e-oo ke-*ree*-a fa-*zer* *oo*-ma rre-*zer*-va poor fa-*vor*

I have a reservation.
Eu tenho uma reserva. — e-oo *ta*-nyoo *oo*-ma rre-*zer*-va

My name's ...
O meu nome é ... — oo *me*-oo *no*-me e ...

Do you have a … room?	Tem um quarto …?	teng oong *kwaar*·too …
single	de solteiro	de sol·*tay*·roo
double	de casal	de ka·*zaal*
twin	duplo	doo·ploo

How much is it per …?	Quanto custa por …?	*kwang*·too *koosh*·ta poor …
night	noite	*noy*·te
person	pessoa	pe·*so*·a

Can I pay by …?	Posso pagar com …?	*po*·soo pa·*gaar* kong …
credit card	cartão de crédito	kar·*towng* de *kre*·dee·too
travellers cheque	traveller cheque	*tra*·ve·ler shek

I'd like to stay for (three) nights.
Para (três) noites.   pa·ra (tresh) *noy*·tesh

From (2 July) to (6 July).
De (dois de julho) até   de (doysh de *zhoo*·lyoo) a·te
(seis de julho).   (saysh de *zhoo*·lyoo)

Can I see it?
Posso ver?   *po*·soo ver

Am I allowed to camp here?
Posso acampar aqui?   *po*·soo a·kang·*paar* a·*kee*

Where can I find a camping ground?
Onde é o parque de campismo?   *ong*·de e oo *par*·ke de kang·*peesh*·moo

requests & queries

When/Where is breakfast served?
Quando/Onde é que servem   *kwang*·doo/*ong*·de e ke *ser*·veng
o pequeno almoço?   oo pe·*ke*·noo aal·*mo*·soo

Please wake me at (seven).
Por favor acorde-me às (sete).   poor fa·*vor* aa·*kor*·de·me aash (*se*·te)

Could I have my key, please?
Pode-me dar a minha chave,   *po*·de·me daar a *mee*·nya *shaa*·ve
por favor?   poor fa·*vor*

Can I get another (blanket)?
Pode-me dar mais um (cobertor)?   *po*·de·me daar maish oong (koo·ber·*tor*)

Is there a/an ...?	Tem ...?	teng ...
elevator	elevador	e·le·va·dor
safe	cofre	ko·fre

The room is too ...	É demasiado ...	e de·ma·zee·aa·doo ...
expensive	caro	kaa·roo
noisy	barulhento	ba·roo·lyeng·too
small	pequeno	pe·ke·noo

The ... doesn't work.	... não funciona.	... nowng foong·see·o·na
air conditioner	O ar condicionado	oo aar kong·dee·syoo·naa·doo
fan	A ventoínha	a veng·too·ee·na
toilet	A sanita	a sa·nee·ta

This ... isn't clean.	Esta ... está suja.	esh·ta ... shtaa soo·zha
pillow	almofada	aal·moo·faa·da
towel	toalha	twaa·lya

| This sheet isn't clean. | Este lençol está sujo. | esh·te leng·sol shtaa soo·zho |

checking out

What time is checkout?
A que horas é a partida?
a ke o·rash e a par·tee·da

Can I leave my luggage here?
Posso deixar as minhas
po·soo day·shaar ash mee·nyash
malas aqui?
maa·lash a·kee

Could I have	Pode-me devolver	po·de·me de·vol·ver
my ..., please?	..., por favor?	... poor fa·vor
deposit	o depósito	oo de·po·zee·too
passport	o passaporte	oo paa·sa·por·te
valuables	os objectos	oosh o·be·zhe·toosh
	de valor	de va·lor

communications & banking

the internet

Where's the local Internet café?
Onde fica um café da internet   ong-de *fee*-ka oong ka-*fe* da eeng-ter-*net*
nas redondezas?   nash rre-dong-*de*-zash

How much is it per hour?
Quanto custa por hora?   *kwang*-too *koosh*-ta pooro-ra

I'd like to ...	*Queria ...*	ke-*ree*-a ...
check my email	*ler o meu email*	ler oo *me*-oo ee-*mayl*
get Internet access	*ter acesso à internet*	ter a-*se*-soo aa eeng-ter-*net*
use a printer	*usar uma*	oo-*zaar* oo-ma
	impressora	eeng-pre-*so*-ra
use a scanner	*usar um*	oo-*zaar* oong
	digitalizador	dee-zhee-ta-lee-za-*dor*

mobile/cell phone

I'd like a ...	*Queria ...*	ke-*ree*-a ...
mobile/cell	*alugar um*	a-loo-*gaar* oong
phone for hire	*telemóvel*	te-le-*mo*-vel
SIM card for	*cartão SIM*	kar-*towng* seeng
your network	*para a sua rede*	*pa*-ra a *soo*-a rre-de

What are the rates?
Qual é o valor cobrado?   kwaal e oo va-*lor* koo-*braa*-doo

telephone

What's your phone number?
Qual é o seu número de telefone?   kwaal e oo *se*-oo *noo*-me-roo de te-le-*fo*-ne

The number is ...
O número é ...   oo *noo*-me-roo e ...

Where's the nearest public phone?
Onde fica o telefone   ong-de *fee*-ka o te-le-*fo*-ne
público mais perto?   poo-blee-koo maish *per*-too

I'd like to buy a phonecard.
Quero comprar um   ke-roo kong-*praar* oong
cartão telefónico.   kar-*towng* te-le-*fo*-nee-koo

I want to ...	Quero ...	ke·roo ...
call (Singapore)	telefonar (para Singapura)	te·le·foo·*naar* (*pa*·ra seeng·ga·*poo*·ra)
make a local call	fazer uma chamada local	fa·*zer* *oo*·ma sha·*maa*·da loo·*kaal*
reverse the charges	fazer uma chamada a cobrar	fa·*zer* *oo*·ma sha·*maa*·da a koo·*braar*

How much does ... cost?	Quanto custa ...?	kwang·too *koosh*·ta ...
a (three)-minute call	uma ligação de (três) minutos	*oo*·ma lee·ga·*sowng* de (tresh) mee·*noo*·toosh
each extra minute	cada minuto extra	*kaa*·da mee·*noo*·too *aysh*·tra

It's (30c) per (30) seconds.
(Trinta cêntimos) por (trinta) segundos.
(*treeng*·ta seng·tee·moosh) poor (*treeng*·ta) se·*goong*·doosh

post office

I want to send a ...	Quero enviar ...	ke·roo eng·vee·*aar* ...
fax	um fax	oong faks
letter	uma carta	*oo*·ma *kaar*·ta
parcel	uma encomenda	*oo*·ma eng·koo·*meng*·da
postcard	um postal	oong poosh·*taal*

I want to buy a/an ...	Quero comprar um ...	ke·*roo* kong·*praar* oong ...
envelope	envelope	eng·ve·*lo*·pe
stamp	selo	se·loo

Please send it (to Australia) by ...	Por favor envie isto (para Australia) por ...	poor fa·*vor* eng·vee·e *eesh*·too (*pa*·ra owsh·*traa*·lya) poor ...
airmail	via aérea	vee·a a·e·ree·a
express mail	correio azul	koo·*rray*·oo a·*zool*
registered mail	registado/a m/f	rre·zheesh·*taa*·doo/a
surface mail	via terrestre	vee·a te·*rresh*·tre

Is there any mail for me?
Há alguma correspondência para mim?
aa aal·*goo*·ma koo·rresh·pong·*deng*·sya *pa*·ra meeng

bank

English	Portuguese	Pronunciation
Where's a/an ...?	*Onde é que há ...?*	ong-de e ke aa ...
ATM	*um caixa automático*	oong *kai*-sha ow-too-*maa*-tee-koo
foreign exchange office	*um câmbio*	oong *kang*-byoo
I'd like to ...	*Queria ...*	ke-*ree*-a ...
Where can I ...?	*Onde é que posso ...?*	ong-de e ke *po*-soo ...
arrange a transfer	*fazer uma transferencia*	faa-*zer* oo-ma trans-fe-*reng*-sya
cash a cheque	*trocar um cheque*	troo-*kaar* oong *she*-ke
change a travellers cheque	*trocar traveller cheque*	troo-*kaar* tra-ve-ler shek
change money	*trocar dinheiro*	troo-*kaar* dee-*nyay*-roo
get a cash advance	*fazer um levantamento adiantado*	fa-*zer* oong le-vang-ta-*meng*-too a-dee-ang-*taa*-doo
withdraw money	*levantar dinheiro*	le-vang-*taar* dee-*nyay*-roo
What's the ...?	*Qual é ...?*	kwaal e ...
commission	*a comissão*	a koo-mee-*sowng*
charge for that	*o imposto*	oo eeng-*posh*-too
exchange rate	*o câmbio do dia*	oo *kang*-byoo doo *dee*-a
It's ...	*É ...*	e ...
(12) euros	*(doze) euros*	(*do*-ze) e-*oo*-roosh
free	*gratuito*	gra-*twee*-too

What time does the bank open?
A que horas é que abre o banco? a ke o-rash e ke *aa*-bre oo *bang*-koo

Has my money arrived yet?
O meu dinheiro já chegou? oo *me*-oo dee-*nyay*-roo zhaa she-*goh*

sightseeing

getting in

What time does it open/close?
A que horas abre/fecha?   a ke o-rash aa-bre/fe-sha

What's the admission charge?
Qual é o preço de entrada?   kwaal e oo pre-soo de eng-traa-da

Is there a discount for children/students?
Tem desconto para crianças/   teng desh-kong-too pa-ra kree-ang-sash/
estudantes?   shtoo-dang-tesh

I'd like a ...	*Queria um ...*	ke-ree-a oong ...
catalogue	*catálogo*	ka-taa-loo-goo
guide	*guia*	gee-a
local map	*mapa local*	maa-pa loo-kaal

I'd like to see ...	*Eu gostava de ver ...*	e-oo goosh-taa-va de ver ...
What's that?	*O que é aquilo?*	oo ke e a-kee-loo
Can I take a photo?	*Posso tirar uma*	po-soo tee-raar oo-ma
	fotografia?	foo-too-gra-fee-a

tours

When's the next ...?	*Quando é ...?*	kwang-doo e ...
day trip	*o próximo passeio*	oo pro-see-moo pa-say-oo
tour	*a próxima excursão*	a pro-see-ma shkoor-sowng

Is ... included?	*Inclui ...?*	eeng-kloo-ee ...
accommodation	*hospedagem*	osh-pe-daa-zheng
the admission charge	*preço de entrada*	pre-soo de eng-traa-da
food	*comida*	koo-mee-da
transport	*transporte*	trangsh-por-te

How long is the tour?
Quanto tempo dura   kwang-too teng-poo doo-ra
a excursão?   a shkoor-sowng

What time should we be back?
A que hora é que devemos   a ke o-ra e ke de-ve-moosh
estar de volta?   shtaar de vol-ta

sightseeing

castle	*castelo* m	kash·*te*·loo
cathedral	*catedral* f	ka·te·*draal*
church	*igreja* f	ee·*gre*·zha
main square	*praça principal* f	*praa*·sa preeng·see·*paal*
monastery	*mosteiro* m	moosh·*tay*·roo
monument	*monumento* m	moo·noo·*meng*·too
museum	*museu* m	moo·ze·oo
old city	*cidade antiga* f	see·*daa*·de ang·*tee*·ga
palace	*palácio* m	pa·*laa*·syoo
ruins	*ruínas* f pl	rroo·ee·nash
stadium	*estádio* m	*shtaa*·dyoo
statues	*estátuas* f pl	shtaa·too·ash

shopping

enquiries

Where's a ...?	*Onde é ...?*	*ong*·de e ...
bank	*o banco*	oo *bang*·koo
bookshop	*a livraria*	a lee·vra·*ree*·a
department store	*loja de departamentos*	*lo*·zha de de·par·ta·*meng*·toosh
grocery store	*a mercearia*	a mer·see·a·*ree*·a
market	*o mercado*	oo mer·*kaa*·doo
newsagency	*o quiosque*	oo kee·*osh*·ke
supermarket	*o supermercado*	oo soo·per·mer·*kaa*·doo

Where can I buy (a padlock)?
Onde é que posso comprar (um cadeado)?
ong·de e ke *po*·soo kong·*praar* (oong ka·de·*aa*·doo)

I'm looking for ...
Estou à procura de ...
shtoh aa proo·*koo*·ra de ...

Can I look at it?
Posso ver?
po·soo ver

Do you have any others?
Tem outros?
teng *oh*·troosh

Does it have a guarantee?
Tem garantia? — teng ga·rang·*tee*·a

Can I have it sent overseas?
Podem enviar para o — po·deng eng·vee·*aar pa*·ra oo
estrangeiro? — shtrang·*zhay*·roo

Can I have my ... repaired?
Vocês consertam ...? — vo·*sesh* kong·*ser*·tang ...

It's faulty.
Tem defeito. — teng de·*fay*·too

I'd like ..., please.	*Queria ..., por favor.*	ke·*ree*·a ... poor fa·*vor*
a bag	*um saco*	oong *saa*·koo
a refund	*ser reembolsado/a* m/f	ser rre·eng·bol·*saa*·doo/a
to return this	*devolver isto*	de·vol·*ver eesh*·too

paying

How much is it?
Quanto custa? — *kwang*·too *koosh*·ta

Can you write down the price?
Pode escrever o preço? — po·de shkre·*ver* oo *pre*·soo

That's too expensive.
Está muito caro. — shtaa *mweeng*·too *kaa*·roo

What's your lowest price?
Qual é o seu último preço? — kwaal e oo se·oo *ool*·tee·moo *pre*·soo

I'll give you (five) euros.
Dou-lhe (cinco) euros. — doh·lye (*seeng*·koo) e·*oo*·roosh

There's a mistake in the bill.
Há um erro na conta. — aa oong e·rroo na *kong*·ta

Do you accept ...?	*Aceitam ...?*	a·*say*·tang ...
credit cards	*cartão de crédito*	kar·*towng* de *kre*·dee·too
debit cards	*multibanco*	mool·tee·*bang*·koo
travellers cheques	*travellers cheques*	tra·ve·ler *she*·kesh

I'd like ..., please.	*Queria ..., por favor.*	ke·*ree*·a ... poor fa·*vor*
a receipt	*um recibo*	oong rre·*see*·boo
my change	*o troco*	oo *tro*·koo

clothes & shoes

Can I try it on?	Posso experimentar?	po·soo shpree·meng·taar
My size is (40).	O meu número é (quarenta).	oo me·oo noo·me·roo e (kwa·reng·ta)
It doesn't fit.	Não serve.	nowng ser·ve
small	pequeno/pequena m/f	pe·ke·noo/pe·ke·na
medium	meio/meia m/f	may·oo/may·a
large	grande m&f	grang·de

books & music

I'd like a ...	Queria comprar ...	ke·ree·a kong·praar ...
newspaper	um jornal	oong zhor·naal
(in English)	(em inglês)	(eng eeng·glesh)
pen	uma caneta	oo·ma ka·ne·ta

Is there an English-language bookshop?

Há uma livraria de língua inglesa?
aa oo·ma lee·vra·ree·a de leeng·gwa eeng·gle·za

I'm looking for something by (Fernando Pessoa).

Estou à procura de qualquer coisa do (Fernando Pessoa).
shtoh aa proo·koo·ra de kwaal·ker koy·za doo (fer·nang·doo pe·so·a)

Can I listen to this?

Posso ouvir?
po·soo oh·veer

photography

I need a/an ... film for this camera.	Preciso de filme ... para esta máquina.	pre·see·zoo de feel·me ... pa·ra esh·ta maa·kee·na
APS	sistema APS	seesh·te·ma aa pe e·se
B&W	a preto e branco	a pre·too e brang·koo
colour	a cores	a ko·resh
slide	de diapositivos	de dee·a·po·zee·tee·voosh
(200) ASA	de (duzentos) ASA	de (doo·zeng·toosh) aa·za

When will it be ready?	Quando fica pronto?	kwang·doo fee·ka prong·too

Can you ...?	Pode ...?	po·de ...
develop this film	revelar este filme	rre·ve·laar esh·te feel·me
load my film	carregar o filme	kaa·rre·gaar oo feel·me
transfer photos	transferir as	trangsh·fe·reer ash
from my camera	fotografias	foo·too·gra·fee·ash
to CD	da minha máquina	da mee·nya maa·kee·na
	para um CD	pa·ra oong se·de

meeting people

greetings, goodbyes & introductions

Hello/Hi.	Olá.	o·laa
Good night.	Boa noite.	bo·a noy·te
Goodbye/Bye.	Adeus.	a·de·oosh
See you later.	Até logo.	a·te lo·goo
Mr	Senhor	se·nyor
Mrs	Senhora	se·nyo·ra
Ms	Senhorita	se·nyo·ree·ta
How are you?	Como está?	ko·moo shtaa
Fine. And you?	Bem. E você?	beng e vo·se
What's your name?	Qual é o seu nome?	kwaal e oo se·oo no·me
My name is ...	O meu nome é ...	oo me·oo no·me e ...
I'm pleased to	Prazer em conhecê-lo/	pra·zer eng koo·nye·se·lo/
meet you.	conhecê-la. m/f	koo·nye·se·la
This is my ...	Este é o meu ... m	esh·te e oo me·oo ...
	Esta é a minha ... f	esh·ta e a mee·nya ...
brother	irmão	eer·mowng
daughter	filha	fee·lya
father	pai	pai
friend	amigo/a m/f	a·mee·goo/a
husband	marido	ma·ree·doo
mother	mãe	maing
partner (intimate)	companheiro/a m/f	kong·pa·nyay·roo/a
sister	irmã	eer·mang
son	filho	fee·lyoo
wife	esposa	shpo·za

Here's my ...	Aqui está o meu ...	a·*kee* shtaa oo *me*·oo ...
What's your ...?	Qual é o seu ...?	kwaal e oo *se*·oo ...
address	endereço	eng·de·*re*·soo
email address	email	ee·*mayl*
fax number	número de fax	*noo*·me·roo de faaks
phone number	número de telefone	*noo*·me·roo de te·le·*fo*·ne

occupations

What's your occupation?
Qual é a sua profissão?   kwaal e a *soo*·a proo·fee·*sowng*

I'm a/an ...	Sou ...	soh ...
artist	artista m&f	ar·*teesh*·ta
business person	homem/mulher de	*o*·meng/moo·*lyer* de
	negócios m/f	ne·*go*·syoosh
farmer	agricultor m&f	a·gree·kool·*tor*
manual worker	trabalhador m	tra·ba·lya·*dor*
	trabalhadora f	tra·ba·lya·*do*·ra
office worker	empregado/a	eng·pre·*gaa*·doo/a
	de escritório m/f	de shkree·*to*·ryoo
scientist	cientista m&f	see·eng·*teesh*·ta
student	estudante m&f	shtoo·*dang*·te
tradesperson	comerciante m&f	koo·mer·see·*aang*·te

background

Where are you from?	De onde é?	*dong*·de e
I'm from ...	Eu sou ...	e·oo soh ...
Australia	da Austrália	da owsh·*traa*·lya
Canada	do Canadá	doo ka·na·*daa*
England	da Inglaterra	da eeng·gla·*te*·rra
New Zealand	da Nova Zelândia	da *no*·va ze·*lang*·dya
the USA	dos Estados	doosh *shtaa*·doosh
	Unidos	oo·*nee*·doosh
Are you married?	É casado/a? m/f	e ka·*zaa*·doo/a
I'm ...	Eu sou ...	e·oo soh ...
married	casado/a m/f	ka·*zaa*·doo/a
single	solteiro/a m/f	sol·*tay*·roo/a

age

How old ...?	Quantos anos ...?	kwang-toosh a-noosh ...
are you	tem	teng
is your daughter	tem a sua filha	teng a soo-a fee-lya
is your son	tem o seu filho	teng oo se-oo fee-lyoo
I'm ... years old.	Tenho ... anos.	ta-nyoo ... a-noosh
He/She is ... years old.	Ele/Ela tem ... anos.	e-le/e-la teng ... a-noosh

feelings

I'm (not) ...	(Não) Estou ...	(nowng) shtoh ...
Are you ...?	Está ...	shtaa ...
cold	com frio	kong free-oo
happy	feliz	fe-leesh
hot	com calor	kong ka-lor
hungry	com fome	kong fo-me
OK	bem	beng
sad	triste	treesh-te
thirsty	com sede	kong se-de
tired	cansado/a m/f	kang-saa-doo/a

entertainment

going out

Where can I find ...?	Onde é que há ...?	ong-de e ke aa ...
clubs	discotecas	deesh-koo-te-kash
gay/lesbian	lugares de	loo-gaa-resh de
venues	gays/lésbicas	gaysh/lezh-bee-kash
pubs	bares	ba-resh
I feel like	Está-me a	shtaa-me a
going to a ...	apetecer ir a ...	a-pe-te-ser eer a ...
concert	um concerto	oong kong-ser-too
movies	um filme	oong feel-me
party	uma festa	oo-ma fesh-ta
restaurant	um restaurante	oong rresh-tow-rang-te
theatre	uma peça de teatro	oo-ma pe-sa de tee-aa-troo

interests

Do you like ...?	Gosta de ...?	gosh·ta de ...
I (don't) like ...	Eu (não) gosto de ...	e·oo (nowng) gosh·too de ...
art	arte	aar·te
cooking	cozinhar	koo·zee·nyaar
movies	ver filmes	ver feel·mesh
reading	ler	ler
sport	fazer desporto	fa·zer desh·por·too
travelling	viajar	vee·a·zhaar

Do you like to ...?	Costuma ...?	koosh·too·ma ...
dance	ir dançar	eer dang·saar
go to concerts	ir a concertos	eer a kong·ser·toosh
listen to music	ouvir música	oh·veer moo·zee·ka

food & drink

finding a place to eat

Can you recommend a ...?	Pode-me recomendar um ...?	po·de·me rre·koo·meng·daar oong ...
bar	bar	bar
café	café	ka·fe
restaurant	restaurante	rresh·tow·rang·te

I'd like ..., please.	Queria uma ..., por favor.	ke·ree·a oo·ma ... poor fa·vor
a table for (five)	mesa para (cinco)	me·za pa·ra (seeng·koo)
the (non)smoking section	mesa de (não) fumador	me·za de (nowng) foo·ma·dor

ordering food

breakfast	pequeno almoço m	pe·ke·noo aal·mo·soo
lunch	almoço m	aal·mo·soo
dinner	jantar m	zhang·taar
snack	lanche m	lang·she

What would you recommend?
O que é que recomenda? — oo ke e ke rre·koo·meng·da

I'd like (the) …, please.	Queria …, por favor.	ke-*ree*-a …poor fa-*vor*
bill	a conta	a *kong*-ta
drink list	a lista das bebidas	a *leesh*-ta dash be-*bee*-dash
menu	um menu	oong me-*noo*
that dish	aquele prato	a-*ke*-le *praa*-too

drinks

(cup of) coffee …	(chávena de) café …	(*shaa*-ve-na de) ka-*fe* …
(cup of) tea …	(chávena de) chá …	(*shaa*-ve-na de) shaa …
with milk	com leite	kong *lay*-te
without sugar	sem açúcar	seng a-*soo*-kar
(orange) juice	sumo (de laranja) m	*soo*-moo (de la-*rang*-zha)
soft drink	refrigerante m	rre-free-zhe-*rang*-te
… water	água …	*aa*-gwa …
hot	quente	*keng*-te
(sparkling) mineral	mineral (com gás)	mee-ne-*raal* (kong gaash)

in the bar

I'll have …	Eu queria …	e-oo ke-*ree*-a …
I'll buy you a drink.	Eu pago-lhe uma bebida.	e-oo *paa*-goo-lye *oo*-ma be-*bee*-da
What would you like?	O que é que quer?	oo ke e ke ker
Cheers!	À nossa!	aa *no*-sa

brandy	brandy f	*brang*-dee
cocktail	cocktail m	kok-*tayl*
a shot of (whisky)	um copinho de (uísque)	oong koo-*pee*-nyoo de (oo-*eesh*-kee)

a … of beer	… de cerveja	… de ser-*ve*-zha
bottle	uma garrafa	*oo*-ma ga-*rraa*-fa
glass	um copo	oong *ko*-poo

a bottle of … wine	uma garrafa de vinho …	*oo*-ma ga-*rraa*-fa de *vee*-nyoo …
a glass of … wine	um copo de vinho …	oong *ko*-poo de *vee*-nyoo …
red	tinto	*teeng*-too
sparkling	espumante	shpoo-*mang*-te
white	branco	*brang*-koo

self-catering

What's the local speciality?
Qual é a especialidade local? — kwaal e a shpe-see-a-lee-*daa*-de loo-*kaal*

What's that?
O que é aquilo? — oo ke e a-*kee*-loo

How much is (a kilo of cheese)?
Quanto é (um quilo de queijo)? — *kwang*-too e (oong *kee*-loo de *kay*-zhoo)

I'd like ...	*Eu queria ...*	e-oo ke-*ree*-a ...
(200) grams	*(duzentos) gramas*	(doo-*zeng*-toosh) *graa*-mash
(two) kilos	*(dois) quilos*	(doysh) *kee*-loosh
(three) pieces	*(três) peças*	(tresh) *pe*-sash
(six) slices	*(seis) fatias*	(saysh) fa-*tee*-ash

Less.	*Menos.*	*me*-noosh
Enough.	*Chega.*	*she*-ga
More.	*Mais.*	maish

special diets & allergies

Is there a vegetarian restaurant near here?
Há algum restaurante vegetariano perto daqui? — aa aal-*goong* rresh-tow-*rang*-te ve-zhe-ta-ree-*aa*-noo *per*-too da-*kee*

Do you have vegetarian food?
Tem comida vegetariana? — teng koo-*mee*-da ve-zhe-ta-ree-*aa*-na

Could you prepare a meal without ...?	*Pode preparar sem ...?*	*po*-de pre-pa-*raar* seng ...
butter	*manteiga*	mang-*tay*-ga
eggs	*ovos*	*o*-voosh
meat stock	*caldo de carne*	*kaal*-doo de *kaar*-ne

I'm allergic to ...	*Eu sou alérgico/a a ... m/f*	e-oo soh a-*ler*-zhee-koo/a a ...
dairy produce	*produtos lácteos*	pro-*doo*-toosh *laak*-tee-oosh
gluten	*glúten*	*gloo*-teng
MSG	*MSG*	e-me-e-se-*zhe*
nuts	*oleaginosas*	o-lee-a-zhee-*no*-zash
seafood	*marisco*	ma-*reesh*-koo

76

emergencies

basics

English	Portuguese	Pronunciation
Help!	Socorro!	soo-ko-rroo
Stop!	Stop!	stop
Go away!	Vá-se embora!	vaa-se eng-bo-ra
Thief!	Ladrão!	la-drowng
Fire!	Fogo!	fo-goo
Watch out!	Cuidado!	kwee-daa-doo
Call ...!	Chame ...!	shaa-me ...
a doctor	um médico	oong me-dee-koo
an ambulance	uma ambulância	oo-ma ang-boo-lang-sya
the police	a polícia	a poo-lee-sya

It's an emergency.
É uma emergência. e oo-ma ee-mer-zheng-sya

Could you help me, please?
Pode ajudar, por favor? po-de a-zhoo-daar poor fa-vor

Can I use the telephone?
Posso usar o seu telefone? po-soo oo-zaar oo se-oo te-le-fo-ne

I'm lost.
Estou perdido/a. m/f shtoh per-dee-doo/a

Where are the toilets?
Onde é a casa de banho? ong-de e a kaa-za de ba-nyoo

police

Where's the police station?
Onde é a esquadra da polícia? ong-de e a shkwaa-dra da poo-lee-sya

I want to report an offence.
Eu quero denunciar um crime. e-oo ke-roo de-noong-see-aar oong kree-me

I have insurance.
Eu estou coberto/a pelo seguro. m/f e-oo shtoh koo-ber-too/a pe-loo se-goo-roo

I've been assaulted.	Eu fui agredido/a. m/f	e-oo fwee a-gre-dee-doo/a
I've been raped.	Eu fui violado/a. m/f	e-oo fwee vee-oo-laa-doo/a
I've been robbed.	Eu fui roubado/a. m/f	e-oo fwee rroh-baa-doo/a

I've lost my ...	Eu perdi ...	e·oo per·dee
My ... was/were stolen.	Roubaram ...	rroh·baa·rang ...
backpack	a minha mochila	a meeng·nya moo·shee·la
bags	os meus sacos	oosh me·oosh saa·koosh
credit card	o meu cartão de crédito	oo me·oo kar·towng de kre·dee·too
handbag	a minha bolsa	a mee·nya bol·sa
jewellery	as minhas jóias	ash mee·nyash zhoy·ash
money	o meu dinheiro	oo me·oo dee·nyay·roo
passport	o meu passaporte	oo me·oo paa·sa·por·te
travellers cheques	os meus travellers cheques	oosh me·oosh tra·ve·ler she·kesh
wallet	a minha carteira	a mee·nya kar·tay·ra
I want to contact my ...	Eu quero contactar com ...	e·oo ke·roo kong·tak·taar kong ...
consulate	o meu consulado	oo me·oo kong·soo·laa·doo
embassy	a minha embaixada	a mee·nya eng·bai·shaa·da

health

medical needs

Where's the nearest ...?	Qual é ... mais perto?	kwaal e ... maish per·too
dentist	o dentista	oo deng·teesh·ta
doctor	o médico m	oo me·dee·koo
	a médica f	a me·dee·ka
hospital	o hospital	oo osh·pee·taal
(night) pharmacist	a farmácia (de serviço)	a far·maa·sya (de ser·vee·soo)

I need a doctor (who speaks English).
Eu preciso de um médico (que fale inglês).
e·oo pre·see·zoo de oong me·dee·koo (que faa·le eeng·glesh)

Could I see a female doctor?
Posso ser vista por uma médica?
po·soo ser veesh·ta poor oo·ma me·dee·ka

I've run out of my medication.
Os meus medicamentos acabaram.
oosh me·oosh me·dee·ka·meng·toosh a·ka·baa·rowng

symptoms, conditions & allergies

| I'm sick. | Estou doente. | shtoh doo-*eng*-te |
| It hurts here. | Dói-me aqui. | doy-me a-*kee* |

I have (a) …	Eu tenho …	e-oo ta-nyoo …
asthma	asma	*ash*-ma
bronchitis	bronquite	brong-*kee*-te
constipation	prisão de ventre	pree-*zowng* de *veng*-tre
cough	tosse	*to*-se
diarrhoea	diarreia	dee-a-*rray*-a
fever	febre	*fe*-bre
headache	dor de cabeça	dor de ka-*be*-sa
heart condition	problemas cardíacos	proo-*ble*-mash kar-*dee*-a-koosh
nausea	náusea	*now*-zee-a
pain	dor	dor
sore throat	dores de garganta	*do*-resh de gar-*gang*-ta
toothache	uma dor de dentes	*oo*-ma dor de *deng*-tesh

I'm allergic to …	Eu sou alérgico/a	e-oo soh a-*ler*-zhee-koo/a
	a … m/f	a …
antibiotics	antibióticos	ang-tee-bee-*o*-tee-koosh
anti-inflammatories	anti-inflamatórios	ang-tee-eeng-fla-ma-*to*-ryoosh
aspirin	aspirina	ash-pee-*ree*-na
bees	abelhas	a-*be*-lyash
codeine	codeína	ko-de-*ee*-na
penicillin	penicilina	pe-nee-see-*lee*-na

antiseptic	antiséptico m	ang-tee-*se*-tee-koo
bandage	ligadura f	lee-ga-*doo*-ra
condoms	preservativos m pl	pre-zer-va-*tee*-voosh
contraceptives	contraceptivos m pl	kong-tra-se-*tee*-voosh
diarrhoea medicine	remédio para diarreia m	re-*me*-dyo *pa*-ra dee-a-*rray*-a
insect repellent	repelente m	rre-pe-*leng*-te
laxatives	laxantes m pl	la-*shang*-tesh
painkillers	comprimidos para as dores m pl	kong-pree-*mee*-doosh *pa*-ra ash *do*-resh
rehydration salts	sais rehidratantes m pl	saish rre-ee-dra-*tang*-tesh
sleeping tablets	pílulas para dormir f pl	*pee*-loo-laash *pa*-ra door-*meer*

english–portuguese dictionary

Portuguese nouns and adjectives in this dictionary have their gender indicated with ⓜ (masculine) and ⓕ (feminine). If it's a plural noun, you'll also see see pl. Words are also marked as v (verb), n (noun), a (adjective), pl (plural), sg (singular), inf (informal) and pol (polite) where necessary.

A

accident *acidente* ⓜ a-see-*deng*-te
accommodation *hospedagem* ⓕ osh-pe-*daa*-zheng
adaptor *adaptador* ⓜ a-da-pe-ta-*dor*
address *endereço* ⓜ eng-de-re-soo
after *depois* de-*poysh*
air conditioned *com ar condicionado*
  kong aar kong-dee-syoo-*naa*-doo
airplane *avião* ⓜ a-vee-*owng*
airport *aeroporto* ⓜ a-e-ro-*por*-too
alcohol *alcoól* ⓜ al-ko-*ol*
all a *todo/a* ⓜ/ⓕ *to*-doo/a
allergy *alergia* ⓕ a-ler-*zhee*-a
ambulance *ambulância* ⓕ ang-boo-*lang*-sya
and *e* e
ankle *tornozelo* ⓜ toor-noo-ze-loo
arm *braço* ⓜ *braa*-soo
ashtray *cinzeiro* ⓜ seeng-*zay*-roo
ATM *caixa automática* ⓕ *kai*-sha ow-too-*maa*-tee-koo

B

baby *bebé* ⓜ&ⓕ be-*be*
back (body) *costas* ⓕ pl *kosh*-tash
backpack *mochila* ⓕ moo-*shee*-la
bad *mau/má* ⓜ/ⓕ *ma*-oo/maa
bag *saco* ⓜ *saa*-koo
baggage claim *balcão de bagagens* ⓜ
  bal-*kowng* de ba-*gaa*-zhengsh
bank *banco* ⓜ *bang*-koo
bar *bar* ⓜ *baar*
bathroom *casa de banho* ⓕ *kaa*-za de ba-*nyoo*
battery *pilha* ⓕ *pee*-lya
beautiful *bonito/a* ⓜ/ⓕ boo-*nee*-too/a
bed *cama* ⓕ *ka*-ma
beer *cerveja* ⓕ ser-ve-zha
before *antes* ang-*tesh*
behind *atrás* a-*traash*
bicycle *bicicleta* ⓕ bee-see-*kle*-ta
big *grande* ⓜ&ⓕ *grang*-de

bill *conta* ⓕ *kong*-ta
black *preto/a* ⓜ/ⓕ *pre*-too/a
blanket *cobertor* ⓜ koo-ber-*tor*
blood group *grupo sanguíneo* ⓜ
  groo-poo sang-*gwee*-nee-oo
blue *azul* a-*zool*
boat *barco* ⓜ *baar*-koo
book (make a reservation) v *reservar* rre-zer-*vaar*
bottle *garrafa* ⓕ ga-*rraa*-fa
bottle opener *saca-rolhas* ⓜ *saa*-ka-rro-lyash
boy *menino* ⓜ me-*nee*-noo
brake (car) *travão* ⓜ tra-*vowng*
breakfast *pequeno almoço* ⓜ pe-ke-noo aal-*mo*-soo
broken (faulty) *defeituoso/a* ⓜ/ⓕ de-fay-too-o-zoo/a
bus *autocarro* ⓜ ow-to-*kaa*-roo
business *negócios* ⓜ pl ne-go-syosh
buy *comprar* kong-*praar*

C

café *café* ⓜ ka-fe
camera *máquina fotográfica* ⓕ
  maa-kee-na foo-too-*graa*-fee-ka
camp site *parque de campismo* ⓜ
  paar-ke de kang-*peezh*-moo
cancel *cancelar* kang-se-*laar*
can opener *abre latas* ⓜ *aa*-bre *laa*-tash
car *carro* ⓜ *kaa*-rroo
cash *dinheiro* ⓜ dee-*nyay*-roo
cash (a cheque) v *levantar (um cheque)*
  le-vang-*taar* (oong she-ke)
cell phone *telemóvel* ⓜ te-le-*mo*-vel
centre *centro* ⓜ *seng*-troo
change (money) v *trocar* troo-*kaar*
cheap *barato/a* ba-*raa*-too/a
check (bill) *conta* ⓕ *kong*-ta
check-in *check-in* ⓜ shek-*eeng*
chest *peito* ⓜ *pay*-too
child *criança* ⓜ&ⓕ kree-*ang*-sa
cigarette *cigarro* ⓜ see-*gaa*-rroo
city *cidade* ⓕ see-*daa*-de
clean a *limpo/a* ⓜ/ⓕ *leeng*-poo/a

closed *fechado/a* ⓜ/ⓕ fe-*shaa*-doo/a
coffee *café* ⓜ ka-fe
coins *moedas* ⓕ pl moo-e-dash
cold a *frio/a* ⓜ/ⓕ *free*-oo/a
collect call *ligação a cobrar* ⓕ lee-ga-*sowng* a koo-*braar*
come *vir* veer
computer *computador* ⓜ kong-poo-ta-*dor*
condom *preservativo* ⓜ pre-zer-va-*tee*-voo
contact lenses *lentes de contacto* ⓜ pl
  leng-tesh de kong-*taak*-too
cook v *cozinhar* koo-zee-*nyaar*
cost *preço* ⓜ *pre*-soo
credit card *cartão de crédito* ⓜ kar-*towng* de *kre*-dee-too
cup *chávena* ⓕ *shaa*-ve-na
currency exchange *câmbio* ⓜ *kang*-byoo
customs (immigration) *alfândega* ⓕ aal-*fang*-de-ga

D

dangerous *perigoso/a* ⓜ/ⓕ pe-ree-go-*zoo*/a
date (time) *data* ⓕ *daa*-ta
day *dia* ⓜ *dee*-a
delay n *atraso* ⓜ a-*traa*-zoo
dentist *dentista* ⓜ&ⓕ deng-*teesh*-ta
depart *partir* par-*teer*
diaper *fralda* ⓕ *fraal*-da
dictionary *dicionário* ⓜ dee-syoo-*naa*-ryoo
dinner *jantar* ⓜ zhang-*taar*
direct *directo/a* ⓜ/ⓕ dee-*re*-too/a
dirty *sujo/a* ⓜ/ⓕ *soo*-zhoo/a
disabled *deficiente* de-fee-see-*eng*-te
discount *desconto* ⓜ desh-*kong*-too
doctor *médico/a* ⓜ/ⓕ *me*-dee-koo/a
double bed *cama de casal* ⓕ *ka*-ma de ka-*zaal*
double room *quarto de casal* ⓜ *kwaar*-too de ka-*zaal*
drink *bebida* ⓕ be-*bee*-da
drive v *conduzir* kong-doo-*zeer*
drivers licence *carta de condução* ⓕ
  kaar-ta de kong-doo-*sowng*
drugs (illicit) *droga* ⓕ *dro*-ga
dummy (pacifier) *chupeta* ⓕ shoo-*pe*-ta

E

ear *orelha* ⓕ o-*re*-lya
east *leste* *lesh*-te
eat *comer* koo-*mer*
economy class *classe económica* ⓕ
  klaa-se ee-ko-*no*-mee-ka
electricity *electricidade* ⓕ ee-le-tree-see-*daa*-de

elevator *elevador* ⓜ ee-le-va-*dor*
email *email* ⓜ ee-*mayl*
embassy *embaixada* ⓕ eng-bai-*shaa*-da
emergency *emergência* ⓕ ee-mer-*zheng*-sya
English (language) *inglês* ⓜ eeng-*glesh*
entrance *entrada* ⓕ eng-*traa*-da
evening *noite* ⓕ *noy*-te
exchange rate *taxa de câmbio* ⓕ *taa*-sha de *kang*-byoo
exit *saída* ⓕ sa-*ee*-da
expensive *caro/a* ⓜ/ⓕ *kaa*-roo/a
express mail *correio azul* ⓜ koo-*rray*-oo a-*zool*
eye *olho* ⓜ *o*-lyoo

F

far *longe* *long*-zhe
fast *rápido/a* ⓜ/ⓕ *rraa*-pee-doo/a
father *pai* ⓜ pai
film (camera) *filme* ⓜ *feel*-me
finger *dedo* ⓜ *de*-doo
first-aid kit *estojo de primeiros socorros* ⓜ
  shto-zhoo de pree-*may*-roosh so-*ko*-rroosh
first class *primeira classe* ⓕ pree-*may*-ra *klaa*-se
fish *peixe* ⓜ *pay*-she
food *comida* ⓕ koo-*mee*-da
foot *pé* ⓜ pe
fork *garfo* ⓜ *gaar*-foo
free (of charge) a *grátis* *graa*-teesh
friend *amigo/a* ⓜ/ⓕ a-*mee*-goo/a
fruit *fruta* ⓕ *froo*-ta
full *cheio/a* ⓜ/ⓕ *shay*-oo/a
funny *engraçado/a* ⓜ/ⓕ eng-gra-*saa*-doo/a

G

gift *presente* ⓜ pre-*zeng*-te
girl *menina* ⓕ me-*nee*-na
glass (drinking) *copo* ⓜ *ko*-poo
glasses *óculos* ⓜ pl *o*-koo-loosh
go *ir* eer
good *bom/boa* ⓜ/ⓕ bong/*bo*-a
green *verde* *ver*-de
guide n *guia* ⓕ *gee*-a

H

half *metade* ⓕ me-*taa*-de
hand *mão* ⓕ mowng
handbag *mala de mão* ⓕ *maa*-la de mowng
happy *feliz* ⓜ&ⓕ fe-*leesh*

have *ter* ter

he *ele* e-le
head *cabeça* ⓜ ka-*be*-sa
heart *coração* ⓜ koo-ra-*sowng*
heat *calor* ⓜ ka-*lor*
heavy *pesado/a* ⓜ/ⓕ pe-*zaa*-doo/a
help v *ajudar* a-zhoo-*daar*
here *aqui* a-*kee*
high *alto/a* ⓜ/ⓕ *aal*-too/aa
highway *autoestrada* ⓕ ow-to-*shtraa*-da
hike v *caminhar* ka-mee-*nyaar*
holiday *feriado* ⓜ fe-ree-*aa*-doo
homosexual n&a *homosexual* ⓜ&ⓕ
  o-mo-sek-soo-*aal*
hospital *hospital* ⓜ osh-pee-*taal*
hot *quente* keng-te
hotel *hotel* ⓜ o-*tel*
hungry *faminto/a* ⓜ/ⓕ fa-*meeng*-too/a
husband *marido* ⓜ ma-*ree*-doo

I

I *eu* e-oo
identification (card) *bilhete de identidade* ⓜ
  bee-*lye*-te de ee-deng-tee-*daa*-de
ill *doente* ⓜ&ⓕ doo-*eng*-te
important *importante* ⓜ&ⓕ eeng-por-*tang*-te
included *incluído/a* ⓜ/ⓕ eeng-kloo-*ee*-doo/a
injury *ferimento* ⓜ fe-ree-*meng*-too
insurance *seguro* ⓜ se-*goo*-roo
Internet *internet* ⓕ eeng-ter-*net*
interpreter *intérprete* ⓜ&ⓕ eeng-*ter*-pre-te

J

jewellery *ourivesaria* ⓕ oh-ree-ve-za-*ree*-a
job *emprego* ⓜ eng-*pre*-goo

K

key *chave* ⓕ *shaa*-ve
kilogram *quilograma* ⓜ kee-loo-*graa*-ma
kitchen *cozinha* ⓕ koo-*zee*-nya
knife *faca* ⓕ *faa*-ka

L

laundry (place) *lavandaria* ⓕ la-vang-da-*ree*-a
lawyer *advogado/a* ⓜ/ⓕ a-de-voo-*gaa*-doo/a
left (direction) *esquerda* ⓕ *shker*-da

left-luggage office *perdidos e achados* ⓜ pl
  per-*dee*-doosh ee aa-*shaa*-doosh
leg *perna* ⓕ *per*-na
lesbian n&a *lésbica* ⓕ *lezh*-bee-ka
less *menos* me-noosh
letter (mail) *carta* ⓕ *kaar*-ta
lift (elevator) *elevador* ⓜ ee-le-va-*dor*
light *luz* ⓕ loosh
like v *gostar* goosh-*taar*
lock *tranca* ⓕ *trang*-ka
long *longo/a* ⓜ/ⓕ *long*-goo/a
lost *perdido/a* ⓜ/ⓕ per-*dee*-doo/a
lost-property office *gabinete de perdidos e achados* ⓜ
  gaa-bee-*ne*-te de per-*dee*-doosh ee a-*shaa*-doosh
love v *amar* a-*maar*
luggage *bagagem* ⓕ ba-*gaa*-zheng
lunch *almoço* ⓜ *aal*-mo-soo

M

mail *correio* ⓜ koo-*rray*-oo
man *homem* ⓜ *o*-meng
map *mapa* ⓜ *maa*-pa
market *mercado* ⓜ mer-*kaa*-doo
matches *fósforos* ⓜ pl *fosh*-foo-roosh
meat *carne* ⓕ *kaar*-ne
medicine *medicamentos* ⓜ pl me-dee-ka-*meng*-toosh
menu *ementa* ⓕ ee-*meng*-ta
message *mensagem* ⓕ meng-*saa*-zheng
milk *leite* ⓜ *lay*-te
minute *minuto* ⓜ mee-*noo*-too
mobile phone *telemóvel* ⓜ te-le-*mo*-vel
money *dinheiro* ⓜ dee-*nyay*-roo
month *mês* ⓜ mesh
morning *manhã* ⓕ ma-*nyang*
mother *mãe* ⓕ maing
motorcycle *mota* ⓕ *mo*-ta
motorway *autoestrada* ⓕ ow-to-*shtraa*-da
mouth *boca* ⓕ *bo*-ka
music *música* ⓕ *moo*-zee-ka

N

name *nome* ⓜ *no*-me
napkin *guardanapo* ⓜ gwar-da-*naa*-poo
nappy *fralda* ⓕ *fraal*-da
near *perto* per-too
neck *pescoço* ⓜ pesh-*ko*-soo
new *novo/a* ⓜ/ⓕ *no*-voo/a
news *notícias* ⓕ pl noo-*tee*-syash

newspaper *jornal* ⓜ zhor-*naal*
night *noite* ⓕ *noy*-te
noisy *barulhento/a* ⓜ/ⓕ ba-roo-*lyeng*-too/a
nonsmoking *não-fumador* nowng-foo-ma-*dor*
north *norte* *nor*-te
nose *nariz* na-*reesh*
now *agora* a-*go*-ra
number *número* ⓜ *noo*-me-roo

O

oil (engine) *petróleo* pe-*tro*-lyoo
old *velho/a* ⓜ/ⓕ *ve*-lyoo/a
one-way ticket *bilhete de ida* bee-*lye*-te de *ee*-da
open a *aberto/a* ⓜ/ⓕ a-*ber*-too/a
outside *fora* *fo*-ra

P

package *embrulho* ⓜ eng-*broo*-lyoo
paper *papel* ⓜ pa-*pel*
park (car) v *estacionar* shta-syoo-*naar*
passport *passaporte* paa-sa-*por*-te
pay *pagar* pa-*gaar*
pen *caneta* ⓕ ka-*ne*-ta
petrol *gasolina* ⓕ ga-zoo-*lee*-na
pharmacy *farmácia* ⓕ far-*maa*-sya
phonecard *cartão telefónico* ⓜ
    kar-*towng* te-le-fo-*nee*-koo
photo *fotografia* ⓕ foo-too-gra-*fee*-a
plate *prato* ⓜ *praa*-too
police *polícia* ⓕ poo-*lee*-sya
Portugal *Portugal* poor-too-*gaal*
Portuguese (language) *português* ⓜ poor-too-*gesh*
postcard *postal* poosh-*taal*
post office *correio* ⓜ koo-*rray*-oo
pregnant *grávida* ⓕ *graa*-vee-da
price *preço* ⓜ *pre*-soo

Q

quiet *calado/a* ⓜ/ⓕ ka-*laa*-doo/a

R

rain *chuva* ⓕ *shoo*-va
razor *gilete* ⓕ zhee-*le*-te
receipt *recibo* ⓜ rre-*see*-boo
red *vermelho/a* ⓜ/ⓕ ver-*me*-lyoo/a

refund *reembolso* ⓜ rre-eng-*bol*-soo
registered mail *correio registado* ⓜ
    koo-*rray*-oo re-zhee-*shtaa*-doo
rent v *alugar* a-loo-*gaar*
repair v *consertar* kong-ser-*taar*
reservation *reserva* ⓕ rre-*zer*-va
restaurant *restaurante* ⓜ rresh-tow-*rang*-te
return v *voltar* vol-*taar*
return ticket *bilhete de ida e volta* ⓜ
    bee-*lye*-te de *ee*-da ee *vol*-ta
right (direction) *direita* ⓕ dee-*ray*-ta
road *estrada* ⓕ *shtraa*-da
room *quarto* ⓜ *kwaar*-too

S

safe a *seguro/a* ⓜ/ⓕ se-*goo*-roo/a
sanitary napkin *penso higiénico* ⓜ
    peng-soo ee-zhee-e-nee-koo
seat *assento* ⓜ a-*seng*-too
send *enviar* eng-vee-*aar*
service station *posto de gasolina* ⓜ
    posh-too de ga-zoo-*lee*-na
sex *sexo* ⓜ *sek*-soo
shampoo *champô* ⓜ shang-*poo*
share (a dorm) *partilhar* par-tee-*lyaar*
shaving cream *creme de barbear* ⓜ
    kre-me de bar-bee-*aar*
she n *ela* *e*-la
sheet (bed) *lençol* ⓜ leng-*sol*
shirt *camisa* ⓕ ka-*mee*-za
shoes *sapatos* ⓜ pl sa-*paa*-toosh
shop n *loja* ⓕ *lo*-zha
short *curto/a* ⓜ/ⓕ *koor*-too/a
shower n *chuveiro* ⓜ shoo-*vay*-roo
single room *quarto de solteiro* ⓜ
    kwaar-too de sol-*tay*-roo
skin *pele* ⓕ *pe*-le
skirt *saia* ⓕ *sai*-a
sleep v *dormir* door-*meer*
slowly *vagarosamente* va-ga-ro-za-*meng*-te
small *pequeno/a* ⓜ/ⓕ pe-ke-*noo*/a
smoke (cigarettes) v *fumar* foo-*maar*
soap *sabonete* ⓜ sa-boo-*ne*-te
some n *uns/umas* ⓜ/ⓕ pl oongsh/*oo*-mash
soon *em breve* eng *bre*-ve
south *sul* sool
souvenir shop *loja de lembranças* ⓕ
    lo-zha de leng-*brang*-sash
speak *falar* fa-*laar*

spoon colher ① koo-lyer
stamp selo ⓜ se-loo
stand-by ticket bilhete sem garantia ⓜ
  bee-lye-te seng ga-rang-tee-a
station (train) estação ① shta-sowng
stomach estômago ⓜ shto-ma-goo
stop v parar pa-raar
stop (bus) paragem ① pa-raa-zheng
street rua ① rroo-a
student estudante ⓜ&① shtoo-dang-te
sun sol ⓜ sol
sunscreen protecção anti-solar ①
  proo-te-sowng ang-tee-soo-laar
swim v nadar na-daar

T

tampons tampões ⓜ pl tang-powngsh
taxi táxi ⓜ taak-see
teaspoon colher de chá ① koo-lyer de shaa
teeth dentes ⓜ pl deng-tesh
telephone telefone ⓜ te-le-fo-ne
television televisão ① te-le-vee-zowng
temperature (weather) temperatura ①
  teng-pe-ra-too-ra
tent tenda ① teng-da
that (one) aquele/a ⓜ/① a-ke-le/a
they eles/elas ⓜ/① e-lesh/e-lash
thirsty sedento/a ⓜ/① se-deng-too/a
this (one) este/a ⓜ/① esh-te/a
throat garganta ① gar-gang-ta
ticket bilhete ⓜ bee-lye-te
time tempo ⓜ teng-poo
tired cansado/a ⓜ/① kang-saa-doo/a
tissues lenços de papel ⓜ pl leng-soosh de pa-pel
today hoje o-zhe
toilet casa de banho ① kaa-za de ba-nyoo
tomorrow amanhã aa-ma-nyang
tonight hoje à noite o-zhe aa noy-te
toothbrush escova de dentes ① shko-va de deng-tesh
toothpaste pasta de dentes ① paash-ta de deng-tesh
torch (flashlight) lanterna eléctrica ①
  lang-ter-na ee-le-tree-ka
tour n excursão ① shkoor-sowng
tourist office escritório de turismo ⓜ
  shkree-to-ryoo de too-reezh-moo
towel toalha ① twaa-lya
train comboio ⓜ kong-boy-oo
translate traduzir tra-doo-zeer

travel agency agência de viagens ①
  a-zheng-sya de vee-aa-zhengsh
travellers cheque travellers cheque ⓜ tra-ve-ler shek
trousers calças ① pl kaal-sash
twin beds camas gémeas ① pl ka-mash zhe-me-ash
tyre pneu ⓜ pe-ne-oo

U

underwear roupa interior ① rroh-pa eeng-te-ree-or
urgent urgente ⓜ&① oor-zheng-te

V

vacant vago/a ⓜ/① vaa-goo/a
vacation férias ① pl fe-ree-ash
vegetable legume ⓜ le-goo-me
vegetarian a vegetariano/a ⓜ/① ve-zhe-ta-ree-a-noo/a
visa visto ⓜ veesh-too

W

waiter criado/a de mesa ⓜ/① kree-aa-doo/a de me-za
walk v caminhar ka-mee-nyaar
wallet carteira ① kar-tay-ra
warm a morno/a ⓜ/① mor-noo/a
wash (something) lavar la-vaar
watch relógio ⓜ rre-lo-zhyoo
water água ① aa-gwa
we nós nosh
weekend fim-de-semana ⓜ feeng-de-se-ma-na
west oeste o-esh-te
wheelchair cadeira de rodas ① ka-day-ra de rro-dash
when quando kwang-doo
where onde ong-de
white branca/a ⓜ/① brang-koo/a
who quem keng
why porquê poor-ke
wife esposa ① shpo-za
window janela ① zha-ne-la
wine vinho ⓜ vee-nyoo
with com kong
without sem seng
woman mulher ① moo-lyer
write escrever shkre-ver

Y

yellow amarelo/a ⓜ/① a-ma-re-loo/a
yes sim seeng
yesterday ontem ong-teng
you inf sg/pl tu/vocês too/vo-sesh
you pol sg/pl você/vós vo-se/vosh

Romanian

romanian alphabet

A a a	*Ă ă* uh	*Â â* ew	*B b* be	*C c* che
D d de	*E e* e	*F f* ef	*G g* je	*H h* hash
I i ee	*Î î* ew	*J j* zhe	*K k* ka	*L l* el
M m em	*N n* en	*O o* o	*P p* pe	*R r* er
S s es	*Ş ş* shew	*T t* te	*Ţ ţ* tsew	*U u* oo
V v ve	*X x* eeks	*Y y* ee grek	*Z z* zed	

romanian

introduction

Romanian (*limba română leem*·ba ro·*mew*·nuh), 'a Latin island in a Slav sea', holds the intriguing status of being the only member of the Romance language family in Eastern Europe. As a descendant of Latin, it shares a common heritage with French, Italian, Spanish and Portuguese – but its evolution took a separate path, mainly due to its geographical isolation from Rome and the influence of Catholicism. The Slavic invasion of the Balkans and the historical circumstances which placed Romanians in the Orthodox cultural sphere added to Romanian's distinguishing characteristics. Greek, Turkish and Hungarian touches spiced up the mixture even more.

It's generally believed that the base for modern Romanian was the language of the Dacians, who in ancient times inhabited the Danubian lands near the Black Sea. After Dacia became a province of the Roman Empire in AD 106, its Romanisation was so thorough that most of vocabulary and grammar of Romanian today is of Latin origin. However, with the withdrawal of the Romans from the area by AD 275, their linguistic influence ceased, leaving behind in Romanian many aspects of Latin that no longer exist in other Romance languages (such as noun cases). The void was filled with the arrival of the Slavs in the Balkans in the 6th century. The interaction with Bulgarian and Serbian (reflected in many loanwords) was intensified from the 13th century, through the shared Byzantine culture and the influence of Old Church Slavonic, the liturgical language of the Orthodox Church until the 18th century.

The oldest written record in Romanian is a letter from 1521 to the mayor of Braşov, written in the Cyrillic alphabet. The Roman alphabet first came into use in the 17th century, along with Hungarian spelling conventions, but it only replaced the earlier script in the mid-19th century. It was gradually adapted to the sounds of Romanian with the creation of some additional letters and was officially recognised in 1859. During the Soviet rule, a Russian version of the Cyrillic alphabet was used in Moldova, but the Roman alphabet was reintroduced in 1989.

Today, Romanian is the official language of Romania and Moldova (where it's called Moldovan – *limba moldovenească leem*·ba mol·do·ve·ne·*as*·kuh), with about 24 million speakers, including the Romanian-speaking minorities in Hungary, Serbia and Ukraine. Considering the Latin origin of much of the English vocabulary and the phonetic nature of the Romanian alphabet, communicating in Romanian with this phrasebook should be *floare la ureche* flo·*a*·re la oo·*re*·ke (lit: 'flower at your ear') – a piece of cake!

pronunciation

vowel sounds

Romanian vowels form vowel combinations with adjacent vowels. At the beginning of a word, *e* and *i* are pronounced as if there were a faint y sound preceding them. At the end of a word, a single *i* is usually almost silent (and represented in our pronunciation guides with an apostrophe), while *ii* is pronounced as ee.

symbol	english equivalent	romanian example	transliteration
a	father	*pat*	pat
ai	aisle	*mai*	mai
e	bet	*sete*	*se*·te
ee	see	*bine*	*bee*·ne
ew	ee pronounced with rounded lips	*frîne*	*frew*·ne
i	bit	*ochi*	*o*·ki
o	pot	*opt*	opt
oh	oh	*cadou*	ka·*doh*
oo	zoo	*bun*	boon
ow	how	*restaurant*	res·*tow*·rant
oy	toy	*noi*	noy
uh	ago	*casă*	*ka*·suh
'	very short, unstressed i	*cinci*	cheench'

word stress

There's no general rule for stress in Romanian. It falls on different syllables in different words, and just has to be learned. You'll be fine if you just follow our coloured pronunciation guides, in which the stressed syllable is always in italics.

consonant sounds

Romanian consonant sounds all have equivalents in English. Note that the sounds w and y generally act as semi-vowels.

symbol	english equivalent	romanian example	transliteration
b	bed	*bilet*	bee·*let*
ch	cheat	*rece*	re·che
d	dog	*verde*	ver·de
f	fat	*frate*	*fra*·te
g	go	*negru*	ne·groo
h	hat	*hartă*	har·tuh
j	joke	*gest*	jest
k	kit	*cald*	kald
l	lot	*lapte*	*lap*·te
m	man	*maro*	ma·*ro*
n	not	*inel*	ee·*nel*
p	pet	*opus*	o·*poos*
r	run	*aprozar*	a·pro·*zar*
s	sun	*săpun*	suh·*poon*
sh	shot	*şah*	shah
t	top	*trist*	treest
ts	hats	*soţ*	sots
v	very	*vin*	veen
w	win	*două*	do·wuh
y	yes	*iată*	yaa·tuh
z	zero	*zero*	ze·ro
zh	pleasure	*dejun*	de·*zhoon*

tools

language difficulties

Do you speak English?
Vorbiți engleza?
vor·beets′ en·gle·za

Do you understand?
Înțelegeți?
ewn·tse·le·gets′

I (don't) understand.
Eu (nu) înțeleg.
ye·oo (noo) ewn·tse·leg

What does (*azi*) mean?
Ce înseamnă (azi)?
che ewn·se·am·nuh (a·zi)

How do you ...? *Cum ...?* koom ...
  pronounce this *se pronunță asta* se pro·noon·tsuh as·ta
  write (*mulțumesc*) *se scrie* se skree·ye
    (mulțumesc) (mool·tsoo·mesk)

Could you please ...? *Ați putea ...?* uhts′ poo·te·a ...
  repeat that *repeta* re·pe·ta
  speak more slowly *vorbi mai rar* vor·bee mai rar
  write it down *scrie* skree·ye

essentials

Yes.	*Da.*	da
No.	*Nu.*	noo
Please.	*Vă rog.*	vuh rog
Thank you (very much).	*Mulțumesc.*	mool·tsoo·mesk
You're welcome.	*Cu plăcere.*	koo pluh·che·re
Excuse me.	*Scuzați-mă.*	skoo·za·tsee·muh
Sorry.	*Îmi pare rău.*	ewm′ pa·re ruh·oo

numbers

0	*zero*	ze·ro		17	*şapte-sprezece*	shap·te·spre·ze·che
1	*unu*	oo·noo		18	*optsprezece*	opt·spre·ze·che
2	*doi*	doy		19	*nouă-sprezece*	no·wuh·spre·ze·che
3	*trei*	trey		20	*douăzeci*	do·wuh·ze·chi
4	*patru*	pa·troo		21	*douăzeci şi unu*	do·wuh·ze·chi shee oo·noo
5	*cinci*	cheench'		22	*douăzeci şi doi*	do·wuh·ze·chi shee doy
6	*şase*	sha·se		30	*treizeci*	trey·ze·chi
7	*şapte*	shap·te		40	*patruzeci*	pa·troo·ze·chi
8	*opt*	opt		50	*cincizeci*	cheench·ze·chi
9	*nouă*	no·wuh		60	*şaizeci*	shai·ze·chi
10	*zece*	ze·che		70	*şaptezeci*	shap·te·ze·chi
11	*unsprezece*	oon·spre·ze·che		80	*optzeci*	opt·ze·chi
12	*doisprezece*	doy·spre·ze·che		90	*nouăzeci*	no·wuh·ze·chi
13	*treisprezece*	trey·spre·ze·che		100	*o sută*	o soo·tuh
14	*paisprezece*	pai·spre·ze·che		1000	*o mie*	o mee·e
15	*cinci-sprezece*	cheench'·spre·ze·che				
16	*şai-sprezece*	shai·spre·ze·che				

time & dates

What time is it?	*Cât e ceasul?*	kewt ye che·a·sool
It's one o'clock.	*E ora unu.*	ye o·ra oo·noo
It's (two) o'clock.	*E ora (două).*	ye o·ra (do·wuh)
Quarter past (one).	*(Unu) şi un sfert.*	(oo·noo) shee oon sfert
Half past (one).	*(Unu) şi jumătate.*	(oo·noo) shee zhoo·muh·ta·te
Quarter to (eight).	*(Opt) fără un sfert.*	(opt) fuh·ruh oon sfert
At what time ...?	*La ce oră ...?*	la che o·ruh ...
At ...	*La ora ...*	la o·ra ...
am	*dimineaţa*	dee·mee·ne·a·tsa
pm (afternoon)	*după masa*	doo·puh ma·sa
pm (evening)	*seara*	se·a·ra

Monday	*luni*	*loo*·ni
Tuesday	*marţi*	*muhr*·tsi
Wednesday	*miercuri*	*myer*·koo·ri
Thursday	*joi*	zhoy
Friday	*vineri*	*vee*·ne·ri
Saturday	*sâmbătă*	*sewm*·buh·tuh
Sunday	*duminică*	doo·*mee*·nee·kuh

January	*ianuarie*	ya·*nwa*·rye
February	*februarie*	fe·*brwa*·rye
March	*martie*	*mar*·tye
April	*aprilie*	a·*pree*·lye
May	*mai*	mai
June	*iunie*	*yoo*·nye
July	*iulie*	*yoo*·lye
August	*august*	*ow*·goost
September	*septembrie*	sep·*tem*·brye
October	*octombrie*	ok·*tom*·brye
November	*noiembrie*	no·*yem*·brye
December	*decembrie*	de·*chem*·brye

What date is it today?
  Ce dată este astăzi? che *da*·tuh *yes*·te as·*tuh*·zi

It's (15 December).
  E (cincisprezece decembrie). ye (*cheench*·spre·ze·che de·*chem*·brye)

| since (May) | *din (mai)* | deen (mai) |
| until (June) | *până în (iunie)* | *pew*·nuh ewn (*yoo*·nye) |

last ...	... *trecut/trecută* m/f	... tre·*koot*/tre·*koo*·tuh
next ...	... *viitor/viitoare* m/f	... vee·ee·*tor*/vee·ee·to·*a*·re
night	*noaptea* f	*no*·ap·te·a
week	*săptămâna* f	suhp·tuh·*mew*·na
month	*luna* f	*loo*·na
year	*anul* m	*a*·nool

yesterday/tomorrow ...	*ieri/mâine ...*	*ye*·ri/mew·*ee*·ne ...
morning	*dimineaţă*	dee·mee·ne·*a*·tsuh
afternoon	*după amiază*	doo·puh a·*mya*·zuh
evening	*seară*	se·*a*·ruh

weather

What's the weather like?	Cum e afară?	koom ye a·fa·ruh
It's...	E ...	ye ...
cloudy	înnorat	ew·no·rat
cold	frig	freeg
hot	foarte cald	fo·ar·te kald
sunny	soare	so·a·re
warm	cald	kald

It's snowing.	Ninge.	neen·je
It's raining.	Plouă.	plo·wuh
It's windy.	Bate vântul.	ba·te vewn·tool

spring	primăvară f	pree·muh·va·ruh
summer	vară f	va·ruh
autumn	toamnă f	to·am·nuh
winter	iarnă f	yar·nuh

border crossing

I'm here ...	Sunt aici ...	soont a·eech ...
on business	cu afaceri	koo a·fa·che·ri
on holiday	în vacanţă	ewn va·kan·tsuh

I'm here for ...	Sunt aici pentru ...	soont a·eech pen·troo ...
(10) days	(zece) zile	(ze·che) zee·le
(two) months	(două) luni	(do·wuh) loo·ni
(three) weeks	(trei) săptămâni	(trey) suhp·tuh·mew·ni

I'm going to (Braşov).
Mă duc la (Braşov). muh dook la (bra·shov)

I'm staying at the (Park Hotel).
Stau la (Hotel Park). stow la (ho·tel park)

I have nothing to declare.
Nu am nimic de declarat. noo am nee·meek de de·kla·rat

I have something to declare.
Am ceva de declarat. am che·va de de·kla·rat

That's (not) mine.
Acesta (nu) e al meu. a·ches·ta (noo) ye al me·oo

transport

tickets & luggage

Where can I buy a ticket?
Unde pot cumpăra un bilet?   oon·de pot koom·puh·ra oon bee·let

Do I need to book a seat?
Trebuie să rezerv locul?   tre·boo·ye suh re·zerv lo·kool

One ... ticket (to Cluj), please.	*Un bilet ...* *(până la Cluj), vă rog.*	oon bee·let ... (pew·nuh la kloozh) vuh rog
one-way	*dus*	doos
return	*dus-întors*	doos ewn·tors

I'd like to ...	*Aş dori să-mi ...*	ash do·ree suhm' ...
my ticket, please.	*biletul, vă rog.*	bee·le·tool vuh rog
cancel	*anulez*	a·noo·lez
change	*schimb*	skeemb
collect	*jau*	yow
confirm	*confirm*	kon·feerm

I'd like a ... seat, please.	*Aş dori un loc la ...,* *vă rog.*	ash do·ree oon lok la ... vuh rog
nonsmoking	*nefumători*	ne·foo·muh·to·ri
smoking	*fumători*	foo·muh·to·ri

How much is it?
Cât costă?   kewt kos·tuh

Is there air conditioning?
Are aer condiţionat?   a·re a·er kon·dee·tsyo·nat

Is there a toilet?
Are toaletă?   a·re to·a·le·tuh

How long does the trip take?
Cât durează călătoria?   kewt doo·re·a·zuh kuh·luh·to·ree·a

Is it a direct route?
E o rută directă?   ye o roo·tuh dee·rek·tuh

I'd like a luggage locker.
Aş dori un dulap de încuiat bagajul.   ash do·ree oon doo·lap de ewn·koo·yat ba·ga·zhool

My luggage has been ...	Bagajul meu a fost ...	ba·ga·zhool me·oo a fost ...
damaged	deteriorat	de·te·ryo·rat
lost	pierdut	pyer·doot
stolen	furat	foo·rat

getting around

Where does flight (7) arrive/depart?

Unde soseşte/pleacă   oon·de so·sesh·te/ple·a·kuh
cursa (7)?   koor·sa (shap·te)

Where's (the) ...?	Unde este ...?	oon·de yes·te ...
arrivals hall	sala pentru sosiri	sa·la pen·troo so·see·ri
departures hall	sala pentru plecări	sa·la pen·troo ple·kuh·ri
duty-free shop	magazinul	ma·ga·zee·nool
	duty-free	dyoo·tee·free
gate (12)	poarta de îmbarcare	po·ar·ta de ewm·bar·ka·re
	(doisprezece)	(doy·spre·ze·che)

Is this the ... to (Cluj)?	Acesta e ... de (Cluj)?	a·ches·ta ye ... de (kloozh)
boat	vaporul	va·po·rool
bus	autobuzul	ow·to·boo·zool
plane	avionul	a·vyo·nool
train	trenul	tre·nool

What time's the	Când este ...	kewnd yes·te ...
... bus?	autobuz?	ow·to·booz
first	primul	pree·mool
last	ultimul	ool·tee·mool
next	următorul	oor·muh·to·rool

At what time does it arrive/leave?

La ce oră soseşte/pleacă?   la che o·ruh so·sesh·te/ple·a·kuh

How long will it be delayed?

Cât întârzie?   kewt ewn·tewr·zye

What station/stop is this?

Ce gară/staţie e aceasta?   che ga·ruh/sta·tsye ye a·che·as·ta

What's the next station/stop?

Care este următoarea   ca·re yes·te oor·muh·to·a·re·a
gară/staţie?   ga·ruh/sta·tsye

Does it stop at (Galaţi)?
Opreşte la (Galaţi)? · o·*presh*·te la (ga·*la*·tsi)

Please tell me when we get to (Iaşi).
Vă rog, când ajungem la (Iaşi)? · vuh rog kewnd a·*zhoon*·jem la (*ya*·shi)

How long do we stop here?
Cât stăm aici? · kewt stuhm a·*eech*

Is this seat available?
E liber locul? · ye *lee*·ber lo·*kool*

That's my seat.
Acesta e locul meu. · a·*ches*·ta ye lo·*kool* me·oo

I'd like a taxi ...	*Aş dori un taxi ...*	ash do·*ree* oon tak·*see* ...
at (9am)	*la ora (nouă dimineaţa)*	la o·ra (*no*·wuh dee·mee·*ne*·a·tsa)
now	*acum*	a·*koom*
tomorrow	*mâine*	mew·ee·ne

Is this taxi available?
E liber taxiul? · ye *lee*·ber tak·see·ool

How much is it to ...?
Cât costă până la ...? · kewt kos·tuh *pew*·nuh la ...

Please put the meter on.
Vă rog, daţi drumul la aparat. · vuh rog dats' *droo*·mool la a·pa·*rat*

Please take me to (this address).
Vă rog, duceţi-mă la (această adresă). · vuh rog doo·*chets*'·muh la (a·che·*as*·tuh a·*dre*·suh)

Please ...	*Vă rog, ...*	vuh rog ...
slow down	*încetiniţi*	ewn·che·tee·*neets*'
stop here	*opriţi aici*	o·*preets*' a·*eech*
wait here	*aşteptaţi aici*	ash·tep·*tats*' a·*eech*

car, motorbike & bicycle hire

I'd like to hire a ...	*Aş dori să închiriez o ...*	ash do·*ree* suh ewn·kee·*ryez* o ...
bicycle	*bicicletă*	bee·chee·*kle*·tuh
car	*maşină*	ma·*shee*·nuh
motorbike	*motocicletă*	mo·to·chee·*kle*·tuh

with ...	cu ...	koo ...
a driver	şofer	sho-*fer*
air conditioning	aer condiţionat	a-er kon-dee-tsyo-*nat*
antifreeze	antigel	an-tee-*jel*
snow chains	lanţuri pentru	lan-*tsoo*-ri *pen*-troo
	zăpadă	zuh-*pa*-duh

How much for ... hire?	Cât costă chiria pe ...?	kewt *kos*-tuh kee-*ree*-a pe ...
hourly	oră	o-ruh
daily	zi	zee
weekly	săptămână	suhp-tuh-*mew*-nuh

air	aer n	*a*-er
oil	ulei n	oo-*ley*
petrol	benzină f	ben-*zee*-nuh
tyres	cauciucuri n pl	kow-*choo*-koo-ri

I need a mechanic.
Am nevoie de un mecanic.　　　　am ne-*vo*-ye de oon me-*ka*-neek

I've run out of petrol.
Am rămas fără benzină.　　　　am ruh-*mas* fuh-ruh ben-*zee*-nuh

I have a flat tyre.
Am un cauciuc dezumflat.　　　　am oon kow-*chook* de-zoom-*flat*

directions

Where's the ...?	Unde este ...?	oon-de *yes*-te ...
bank	banca	*ban*-ka
city centre	centrul oraşului	*chen*-trool o-*ra*-shoo-looy
hotel	hotelul	ho-*te*-lool
market	piaţa	*pya*-tsa
police station	secţia de poliţie	*sek*-tsya de po-*lee*-tsye
post office	poşta	*posh*-ta
public toilet	toaleta publică	to-a-*le*-ta *poo*-blee-kuh
tourist office	biroul de	bee-*ro*-ool de
	informaţii	een-for-*ma*-tsee
	turistice	too-*rees*-tee-che

Is this the road to (Arad)?
Acesta e drumul spre (Arad)?
a·ches·ta ye droo·mool spre (a·rad)

Can you show me (on the map)?
Puteţi să-mi arătaţi
poo·te·tsi suh·mi a·ruh·tats'
(pe hartă)?
(pe har·tuh)

What's the address?
Care este adresa?
ka·re yes·te a·dre·sa

How far is it?
Cît e de departe?
kewt ye de de·par·te

How do I get there?
Cum ajung acolo?
koom a·zhoong a·ko·lo

Turn ...	Viraţi la ...	vee·rats' la ...
at the corner	colţ	kolts
at the traffic lights	semafor	se·ma·for
left/right	stînga/dreapta	stewn·ga/dre·ap·ta

It's ...	Este ...	yes·te ...
behind ...	în spatele ...	ewn spa·te·le ...
far away	departe	de·par·te
here	aici	a·eech
in front of ...	în faţa ...	ewn fa·tsa ...
left	la stânga	la stewn·ga
near (to ...)	aproape (de ...)	a·pro·a·pe (de ...)
next to ...	lângă ...	lewn·guh ...
on the corner	pe colţ	pe kolts
opposite ...	vis-à-vis de ...	vee·za·vee de ...
right	la dreapta	la dre·ap·ta
straight ahead	tot înainte	tot ew·na·een·te
there	acolo	a·ko·lo

by bus	cu autobuzul	koo ow·to·boo·zool
by taxi	cu taxiul	koo tak·see·ool
by train	cu trenul	koo tre·nool
on foot	pe jos	pe zhos

north	nord	nord
south	sud	sood
east	est	est
west	vest	vest

signs

Intrare	een·*tra*·re	Entrance
Ieşire	ye·*shee*·re	Exit
Deschis	des·*kees*	Open
Închis	ewn·*kees*	Closed
Camere libere	ka·me·re *lee*·be·re	Rooms Available
Ocupat	o·koo·*pat*	No Vacancies
Informaţii	een·for·*ma*·tsee	Information
Secţie de poliţie	sek·tsye de po·*lee*·tsye	Police Station
Interzis	een·ter·*zees*	Prohibited
Toalete	to·a·*le*·te	Toilets
Bărbaţi	buhr·*ba*·tsi	Men
Femei	fe·*mey*	Women
Cald/Rece	kald/*re*·che	Hot/Cold

accommodation

finding accommodation

Where's a ...?	Unde se află ...?	oon·de se *a*·fluh ...
camping ground	un teren de camping	oon te·*ren* de *kem*·peeng
guesthouse	o pensiune	o pen·*syoo*·ne
hotel	un hotel	oon ho·*tel*
youth hostel	un hostel	oon *hos*·tel

Can you recommend	Puteţi recomanda	poo·*te*·tsi re·ko·man·*da*
somewhere ...?	ceva ...?	che·*va* ...
cheap	ieftin	*yef*·teen
good	bun	boon
nearby	în apropiere	ewn a·pro·*pye*·re

I'd like to book a room, please.
Aş dori să rezerv o cameră, vă rog. ash do·*ree* suh re·*zerv* o *ka*·me·ruh vuh rog

I have a reservation.
Am o rezervaţie. am o re·zer·*va*·tsye

My name's ...
Numele meu este ... *noo*·me·le *me*·oo *yes*·te ...

Do you have a ... room?	*Aveți o cameră ...?*	a-*vets*'o *ka*-me-ruh ...
single	*de o persoană*	de o per-so-*a*-nuh
double	*dublă*	*doo*-bluh
twin	*dublă cu două*	*doo*-bluh koo do-*wuh*
	paturi separate	pa-*too*-ri se-pa-*ra*-te

How much is it per ...?	*Cît costă ...?*	kewt *kos*-tuh ...
night	*pe noapte*	pe no-*ap*-te
person	*de persoană*	de per-so-*a*-nuh

Can I pay ...?	*Pot plăti ...?*	pot pluh-*tee* ...
by credit card	*cu carte de credit*	koo *kar*-te de *kre*-deet
with a travellers	*cu un cec de*	koo oon chek de
cheque	*călătorie*	kuh-luh-to-*ree*-e

I'd like to stay for (two) nights.
Aș dori să stau (două) nopți.　　　ash doo-*ree* suh stow (*do*-wuh) *nop*-tsi

From (2 July) to (6 July).
Din (doi iulie) până în　　　deen (doy *yoo*-lye) *pew*-nuh ewn
(șase iulie).　　　(*sha*-se *yoo*-lye)

Can I see it?
Pot să văd?　　　pot suh vuhd

Am I allowed to camp here?
Pot să-mi pun cortul aici?　　　pot suhm' poon *kor*-tool a-*eech*

Is there a camp site nearby?
Există un loc de camping　　　eg-*zees*-tuh oon lok de *kem*-peeng
prin apropiere?　　　preen a-pro-*pye*-re

requests & queries

When/Where is breakfast served?
Când/Unde se servește　　　kewnd/*oon*-de se ser-*vesh*-te
micul dejun?　　　*mee*-kool de-*zhoon*

Please wake me at (seven).
Vă rog treziți-mă la (șapte).　　　vuh rog tre-*zee*-tsee-muh la (*shap*-te)

Could I have my key, please?
Puteţi să-mi daţi o cheie?   poo-*tets'* suhm' dats' o *ke*-ye

Can I get another (blanket)?
Puteţi să-mi daţi încă   poo-*tets'* suhm' dats' *ewn*-kuh
(o pătură)?   (o *puh*-too-ruh)

Is there a/an ...?	*Există ...?*	eg-*zees*-tuh ...
elevator	*lift*	leeft
safe	*seif*	seyf

The room is too ...	*Camera e prea ...*	*ka*-me-ra ye pre-*a* ...
expensive	*scumpă*	*skoom*-puh
noisy	*gălăgioasă*	guh-luhj-*yo*-a-suh
small	*mică*	*mee*-kuh

The ... doesn't work.	*Nu funcţionează ...*	noo foonk-tsyo-ne-*a*-zuh ...
air conditioning	*aerul condiţionat*	*a*-e-rool kon-dee-tsyo-*nat*
fan	*ventilatorul*	ven-tee-la-*to*-rool
toilet	*toaleta*	to-a-*le*-ta

This ... isn't clean.	*Acest ... nu este curat.*	a-*chest* ... noo *yes*-te koo-*rat*
sheet	*cearceaf*	che-ar-che-*af*
towel	*prosop*	pro-*sop*

This pillow isn't clean.
Această pernă   a-che-*as*-tuh *per*-nuh
nu este curată.   noo *yes*-te koo-*ra*-tuh

checking out

What time is checkout?
La ce oră trebuie   la che *o*-ruh *tre*-boo-ye
eliberată camera?   e-lee-be-*ra*-tuh *ka*-me-ra

Can I leave my luggage here?
Pot să-mi las bagajul aici?   pot suhm' las ba-*ga*-zhool a-*eech*

Could I have	*Vă rog, îmi puteţi*	vuh rog ewm' poo-*tets'*
my ..., please?	*înapoia ...?*	ew-na-po-*ya* ...
deposit	*aconto-ul*	a-*kon*-to-ool
passport	*paşaportul*	pa-sha-*por*-tool
valuables	*obiectele de valoare*	o-*byek*-te-le de va-lo-*a*-re

communications & banking

the internet

Where's the local Internet café?
Unde se află un internet café în apropiere?
oon·de se *a*·fluh oon een·ter·*net* ka·*fe* ewn a·pro·*pye*·re

How much is it per hour?
Cât costă pe oră?
kewt *kos*·tuh pe *o*·ruh

I'd like to ... | *Aş dori ...* | ash do·*ree* ...
check my email | *să-mi verific e-mailul* | suhm' ve·*ree*·feek ee·meyl·ool
get Internet access | *să accesez internetul* | suh ak·che·*sez* een·ter·ne·*tool*
use a printer | *să folosesc o imprimantă* | suh fo·lo·*sesk* o eem·pree·*man*·tuh
use a scanner | *să folosesc un scanner* | suh fo·lo·*sesk* oon *ske*·ner

mobile/cell phone

I'd like a ... | *Aş dori ...* | ash do·*ree* ...
mobile/cell phone for hire | *să închiriez un telefon mobil* | suh ewn·kee·*ryez* oon te·le·*fon* mo·*beel*
SIM card for your network | *un SIM card pentru reţeaua locală* | oon seem kard *pen*·troo re·tse·*a*·wa lo·*ka*·luh

What are the rates?
Care este tariful?
ka·re *yes*·te ta·*ree*·fool

telephone

What's your phone number?
Ce număr de telefon aveţi?
che *noo*·muhr de te·le·*fon* a·*vets'*

Where's the nearest public phone?
Unde se află cel mai apropiat telefon public?
oon·de se *a*·fluh chel mai a·pro·*pyat* te·le·*fon* poo·*bleek*

I'd like to buy a phonecard.
Aş dori să cumpăr o cartelă de telefon.
ash do·*ree* suh *koom*·puhr o kar·*te*·luh de te·le·*fon*

I want to ...	Aş dori ...	ash do·ree ...
call (Singapore)	să telefonez la (Singapore)	suh te·le·fo·nez la (seen·ga·po·re)
make a local call	să dau un telefon local	suh dow oon te·le·fon lo·kal
reverse the charges	o convorbire cu taxă inversă	o kon·vor·bee·re koo tak·suh een·ver·suh

How much does ... cost?	Cât costă ...?	kewt kos·tuh ...?
a (three)-minute call	o convorbire de (trei) minute	o kon·vor·bee·re de (trey) mee·noo·te
each extra minute	fiecare minut suplimentar	fye·ka·re mee·noot soo·plee·men·tar

| (10) lei per minute. | (Zece) lei pe minut. | (ze·che) ley pe mee·noot |

post office

I want to send a ...	Aş dori să trimit ...	ash do·ree suh tree·meet ...
letter	o scrisoare	o skree·so·a·re
parcel	un colet	oon ko·let
postcard	o carte poştală	o kar·te posh·ta·luh

I want to buy a/an ...	Aş dori să cumpăr un ...	ash do·ree suh koom·puhr oon ...
envelope	plic	pleek
stamp	timbru	teem·broo

Please send it (to Australia) by ...	Vă rog, expediaţi-l (în Australia) ...	vuh rog ek·spe·dya·tseel (ewn ows·tra·lya) ...
airmail	cu avionul	koo a·vyo·nool
express mail	expres	eks·pres
registered mail	recomandat	re·ko·man·dat
surface mail	cu vaporul	koo va·po·rool

| Is there any mail for me? | Am primit scrisori? | am pree·meet skree·so·ri |

bank

Where's a/an ...?	Unde se află un ...?	oon·de se a·fluh oon ...
ATM	bancomat	ban·ko·mat
foreign exchange office	birou de schimb valutar	bee·roh de skeemb va·loo·tar

I'd like to ...	Aș dori să ...	ash do-ree suh ...
Where can I ...?	Unde aș putea ...?	oon-de ash poo-te-a ...
arrange a transfer	efectua un transfer	e-fek-twa oon trans-fer
cash a cheque	încasa un cec	ewn-ka-sa oon chek
change a travellers cheque	schimba un cec de călătorie	skeem-ba oon chek de kuh-luh-to-ree-e
change money	schimba bani	skeem-ba ba-ni
get a cash advance	obține un imprumut financiar	ob-tsee-ne oon ewm-proo-moot fee-nan-chyar
withdraw money	retrage bani	re-tra-je ba-ni

What's the ...?	Care este ...?	ka-re yes-te ...
charge for that	taxa pentru	tak-sa pen-troo
commission	comision	ko-mee-syon
exchange rate	rata de schimb	ra-ta de skeemb

It's ...	Este ...	yes-te ...
(12) euros	(doisprezece) euro	(doy-spre-ze-che) e-oo-ro
(20) lei	(douăzeci) lei	(do-wuh-ze-chi) ley
free	gratis	gra-tees

What time does the bank open?
La ce oră se deschide banca? la che o-ruh se des-kee-de ban-ka

Has my money arrived yet?
Mi-au sosit banii? myow so-seet ba-nee

sightseeing

getting in

What time does it open/close?
La ce oră se deschide/închide? la che o-ruh se des-kee-de/ewn-kee-de

What's the admission charge?
Cât costă intrarea? kewt kos-tuh een-tra-re-a

Is there a discount for students/children?
Există reducere pentru studenți/copii? eg-zees-tuh re-doo-che-re pen-troo stoo-den-tsi/ko-pee

I'd like a ...	Aș dori ...	ash do-*ree* ...
catalogue	un catalog	oon ka·ta·*log*
guide	un ghid	oon geed
local map	o hartă a	o *har*·tuh a
	localității	lo·ka·lee·*tuh*·tsee

I'd like to see ...	Aș dori să văd ...	ash do-*ree* suh vuhd ...
What's that?	Ce-i asta?	chey *as*·ta
Can I take a photo?	Pot să fac o fotografie?	pot suh fak o fo·to·gra·*fye*

tours

When's the next ...?	Când este ...?	kewnd *yes*·te ...
day trip	următoarea	oor·muh·to·*a*·re·a
	excursie de zi	eks·*koor*·sye de zee
tour	următorul tur	oor·muh·*to*·rool toor

Is ... included?	Sunt incluse ...?	soont een·*kloo*·se ...
accommodation	cazarea	ka·*za*·re·a
the admission charge	taxa de intrare	*tak*·sa de een·*tra*·re
food	mâncarea	mewn·*ka*·re·a
transport	transportul	trans·*por*·tool

How long is the tour?
Cît durează turul? kewt doo·re·*a*·zuh *too*·rool

What time should we be back?
La ce oră e întoarcerea? la che *o*·ruh ye ewn·to·*ar*·che·re·a

sightseeing

castle	castel n	kas·*tel*
cathedral	catedrală f	ka·te·*dra*·luh
church	biserică f	bee·*se*·ree·kuh
main square	piața centrală f	*pya*·tsa chen·*tra*·luh
monastery	mănăstire f	muh·nuhs·*tee*·re
monument	monument n	mo·noo·*ment*
museum	muzeu n	moo·*ze*·oo
old city	orașul vechi n	o·*ra*·shool *ve*·ki
palace	palat n	pa·*lat*
ruins	ruine f pl	roo·*ee*·ne
statue	statuie f	sta·*too*·ye

shopping

enquiries

Where's a ... ?	Unde se află ...?	oon-de se a-fluh ...
bank	o bancă	o ban-kuh
bookshop	o librărie	o lee-bruh-ree-e
camera shop	un magazin foto	oon ma-ga-zeen fo-to
grocery store	un magazin alimentar	oon ma-ga-zeen a-lee-men-tar
department store	un magazin universal	oon ma-ga-zeen oo-nee-ver-sal
market	o piață	o pya-tsuh
newsagency	un stand de ziare	oon stand de zee-a-re
supermarket	un supermarket	oon soo-per-mar-ket

Where can I buy (a padlock)?
Unde pot cumpăra (un lacăt)? oon-de pot koom-puh-ra (oon la-kuht)

I'm looking for ...
Caut ... kowt ...

Can I look at it?
Pot să mă uit? pot suh muh ooyt

Do you have any others?
Mai aveți și altele? mai a-vets' shee al-te-le

Does it have a guarantee?
E cu garanție? ye koo ga-ran-tsee-e

Can I have it sent overseas?
Îl puteți expedia peste hotare? ewl poo-tets' eks-pe-dya pes-te ho-ta-re

Can I have my ... repaired?
Îmi puteți repara ...? ewm' poo-tets' re-pa-ra ...

It's faulty.
E defect. ye de-fekt

I'd like ..., please.	Vă rog, aș dori ...	vuh rog ash do-ree ...
a bag	o geantă	o je-an-tuh
a refund	o rambursare	o ram-boor-sa-re
to return this	să returnez asta	suh re-toor-nez as-ta

paying

How much is it?
Cât costă?
kewt *kos*·tuh

Can you write down the price?
Puteţi scrie preţul?
poo·*tets*' *skree*·e *pre*·tsool

That's too expensive.
E prea scump.
ye pre·*a* skoomp

What's your lowest price?
Care e preţul cel mai redus?
ka·re ye *pre*·tsool chel mai re·*doos*

I'll give you (five) euros.
Vă dau (cinci) euro.
vuh dow (cheench') *e*·oo·ro

I'll give you (50) lei.
Vă dau (cincizeci) lei.
vuh dow (cheench·*ze*·chi) ley

There's a mistake in the bill.
Chitanţa conţine o greşeală.
kee·*tan*·tsa kon·*tsee*·ne o gre·she·*a*·luh

Do you accept ...?	*Acceptaţi ...?*	ak·chep·*tats*' ...
credit cards	*cărţi de credit*	*kuhr*·tsi de *kre*·deet
debit cards	*cărţi de debit*	*kuhr*·tsi de *de*·beet
travellers cheques	*cecuri de*	*che*·koo·ri de
	călătorie	kuh·luh·to·*ree*·e

I'd like ..., please.	*Vă rog, daţi-mi ...*	vuh rog *da*·tsee·mi ...
a receipt	*chitanţa*	kee·*tan*·tsa
my change	*restul*	*res*·tool

clothes & shoes

Can I try it on?
Pot să probez?
pot suh pro·*bez*

My size is (40).
Port numărul (patruzeci).
port *noo*·muh·rool (pa·troo·ze·chi)

It doesn't fit.
Nu mi se potriveşte.
noo mee se po·tree·*vesh*·te

small	*mic*	meek
medium	*mijlociu*	meezh·lo·*chyoo*
large	*mare*	*ma*·re

books & music

I'd like a …	Aş dori …	ash do-*ree* …
newspaper	un ziar	oon zee-*ar*
(in English)	(în engleză)	(ewn en-*gle*-zuh)
pen	un pix	oon peeks

Is there an English-language bookshop?

Există o librărie cu cărţi   eg-*zees*-tuh o lee-bruh-*ree*-e koo *kuhr*-tsi
în limba engleză?   ewn *leem*-ba en-*gle*-zuh

I'm looking for something by (Enescu/Caragiale).

Caut ceva de (Enescu/Caragiale).   kowt che-*va* de (e-*nes*-koo/ka-raj-*ya*-le)

Can I listen to this?

Pot asculta asta?   pot as-kool-*ta as*-ta

photography

Can you …?	Îmi puteţi …?	ewm' poo-*tets'* …
burn a CD from	imprima un	eem-pree-*ma* oon
my memory card	CD după	see-dee doo-puh
	cardul de memorie	kar-dool de me-mo-*ree*-e
develop this film	developa acest film	de-ve-lo-pa a-*chest* feelm
load my film	încărca filmul	ewn-kuhr-*ka* feel-*mool*
	în aparat	ewn a-pa-*rat*

I need a/an … film	Am nevoie de un film …	am ne-*vo*-ye de oon feelm …
for this camera.	pentru acest aparat.	pen-troo a-*chest* a-pa-*rat*
APS	APS	a-pe-*se*
B&W	alb-negru	alb-*ne*-groo
colour	color	ko-*lor*
slide	diapozitiv	dee-a-po-zee-*teev*
(200) speed	de (două sute) ASA	de (*do*-wuh soo-te) *a*-sa

When will it be ready?	Când va fi gata?	kewnd va fee *ga*-ta

meeting people

greetings, goodbyes & introductions

Hello/Hi.	*Bună ziua/Bună.*	boo·nuh zee·wa/boo·nuh
Good night.	*Noapte bună.*	no·ap·te boo·nuh
Goodbye/Bye.	*La revedere/Pa.*	la re·ve·de·re/pa
Mr/Mrs	*Domnul/Doamna*	dom·nool/do·am·na
Miss	*Domnişoara*	dom·nee·sho·a·ra
How are you?	*Ce mai faceţi?*	che mai *fa*·chets'
Fine. And you?	*Bine.*	bee·ne
	Dumneavoastră?	doom·ne·a·vo·as·truh
What's your name?	*Cum vă numiţi?*	koom vuh noo·meets'
My name is …	*Numele meu este …*	noo·me·le me·oo yes·te …
I'm pleased to	*Încântat/*	ewn·kewn·tat/
meet you.	*Încântată*	ewn·kewn·ta·tuh
	de cunoştinţă. m/f	de koo·nosh·teen·tsuh

This is my …	*Vă prezint …*	vuh pre·zeent …
boyfriend	*prietenul meu*	pree·e·te·nool me·oo
brother	*fratele meu*	fra·te·le me·oo
daughter	*fiica mea*	fee·ee·ka me·a
father	*tatăl meu*	ta·tuhl me·oo
friend	*un prieten* m	oon pree·e·ten
	o prietenă f	o pree·e·te·nuh
girlfriend	*prietena mea*	pree·e·te·na me·a
husband	*soţul meu*	so·tsool me·oo
mother	*mama mea*	ma·ma me·a
partner (intimate)	*partenerul meu* m	par·te·ne·rool me·oo
	partenera mea f	par·te·ne·ra me·a
sister	*sora mea*	so·ra me·a
son	*fiul meu*	fee·ool me·oo
wife	*soţia mea*	so·tsee·a me·a

Here's my …	*Acesta/Aceasta este*	a·ches·ta/a·che·as·ta yes·te
	… meu/mea. m/f	… me·oo/me·a
What's your …?	*Care e …?*	ka·re ye …
(email) address	*adresa ta (de e-mail)*	a·dre·sa ta (de ee·meyl)
phone number	*numărul tău*	noo·muh·rool tuh·oo
	de telefon	de te·le·fon

occupations

What's your occupation?	Ce meserie aveți?	che me·se·ree·e a·vets'
I'm a/an ...	Sunt ...	soont ...
artist	artist m&f	ar·teest
businessperson	om de afaceri m&f	om de a·fa·che·ri
farmer	fermier m&f	fer·myer
office worker	funcționar m	foonk·tsyo·nar
	funcționară f	foonk·tsyo·na·ruh
scientist	om de știință m&f	om de shteen·tsuh
student	student/studentă m/f	stoo·dent/stoo·den·tuh
tradesperson	comerciant m&f	ko·mer·chyant

background

Where are you from?	De unde sunteți?	de oon·de soon·tets'
I'm from ...	Sunt din ...	soont deen ...
Australia	Australia	ows·tra·lya
Canada	Canada	ka·na·da
England	Anglia	ang·lya
New Zealand	Noua Zeelandă	no·wa ze·e·lan·duh
the USA	Statele Unite	sta·te·le oo·nee·te

Are you married?	Sunteți căsătorit/	soon·tets' kuh·suh·to·reet/
	căsătorită? m/f	kuh·suh·to·ree·tuh
I'm ...	Sunt ...	soont ...
married	căsătorit m	kuh·suh·to·reet
	căsătorită f	kuh·suh·to·ree·tuh
single	necăsătorit m	ne·kuh·suh·to·reet
	necăsătorită f	ne·kuh·suh·to·ree·tuh

age

How old ...?	Ce vârstă ...?	che vewr·stuh ...
are you	aveți	a·vets'
is your daughter	are fiica	a·re fee·ee·ka
	dumneavoastră	doom·ne·a·vo·as·truh
is your son	are fiul	a·re fee·ool
	dumneavoastră	doom·ne·a·vo·as·truh

I'm ... years old.		
Am ... ani.		am ... *a*·ni
He/She is ... years old.		
El/Ea are ... ani.		yel/ya *a*·re ... *a*·ni

feelings

I'm (not) ...	(Nu) Îmi este ...	(noo) *ew*·mi *yes*·te ...
Are you ...?	Vă este ...?	vuh *yes*·te ...
cold	frig	freeg
hot	cald	kald
hungry	foame	fo·*a*·me
thirsty	sete	*se*·te

I'm (not) ...	(Nu) Sunt ...	(noo) soont ...
Are you ...?	Sunteți ...?	*soon*·tets' ...
happy	fericit m	fe·ree·*cheet*
	fericită f	fe·ree·*chee*·tuh
OK	bine m&f	*bee*·ne
sad	trist/tristă m/f	treest/*trees*·tuh
tired	obosit/obosită m/f	o·bo·*seet*/o·bo·*see*·tuh

entertainment

going out

Where can I find ...?	Unde pot găsi ...?	*oon*·de pot guh·*see* ...
clubs	cluburi	*kloo*·boo·ri
gay venues	cluburi gay	*kloo*·boo·ri gey
pubs	localuri	lo·*ka*·loo·ri

I feel like going to a/the ...	Aș merge la ...	ash *mer*·je la ...
concert	un concert	oon kon·*chert*
movies	un film	oon feelm
party	o petrecere	o pe·*tre*·che·re
restaurant	un restaurant	oon res·tow·*rant*
theatre	un teatru	oon te·*a*·troo

interests

Do you like ...?	*Vă place ...?*	vuh *pla*-che ...
I (don't) like ...	*Mie (nu) îmi place ...*	mee-e (noo) ew-mi *pla*-che ...
art	*arta*	*ar*-ta
cooking	*bucătăria*	boo-kuh-tuh-*ree*-a
movies	*cinema-ul*	chee-ne-*ma*-ool
reading	*lectura*	lek-*too*-ra
shopping	*la cumpărături*	la koom-puh-ruh-*too*-ri
sport	*sportul*	*spor*-tool
travelling	*să călătoresc*	suh kuh-luh-to-*resk*
Do you like to ...?	*Vă place ...?*	vuh *pla*-che ...
dance	*dansul*	*dan*-sool
go to concerts	*mersul la concerte*	*mer*-sool la kon-*cher*-te
listen to music	*să ascultaţi muzică*	as-kool-*tats'* *moo*-zee-kuh

food & drink

finding a place to eat

Can you	*Îmi puteţi*	ew-mi poo-*tets'*
recommend a ...?	*recomanda ...?*	re-ko-man-*da* ...
bar	*un bar*	oon bar
café	*o cafenea*	o ka-fe-ne-*a*
restaurant	*un restaurant*	oon res-tow-*rant*
I'd like ..., please.	*Vă rog, aş dori ...*	vuh rog ash do-*ree* ...
a table for (four)	*o masă de (patru)*	o *ma*-suh de (*pa*-troo)
	persoane	per-so-*a*-ne
the (non)smoking	*la (ne)fumători*	la (*ne*-)foo-muh-*to*-ri
section		

ordering food

breakfast	*micul dejun* n	*mee*-kool de-*zhoon*
lunch	*dejun* n	de-*zhoon*
dinner	*cină* f	*chee*-nuh
snack	*gustare* f	goos-*ta*-re

12

What would you recommend?

Ce recomandați?		che re·ko·man·*dats'*

I'd like (the) ..., please.	*Vă rog, aș dori ...*	vuh rog ash do·*ree* ...
bill	*nota de plată*	*no*·ta de *pla*·tuh
drink list	*lista de băuturi*	*lees*·ta de buh·oo·*too*·ri
menu	*meniul*	me·*nee*·ool
that dish	*acel fel de mâncare*	a·*chel* fel de mewn·*ka*·re

drinks

(cup of) coffee ...	*(o ceașcă de) cafea ...*	(o che·*ash*·kuh de) ka·fe·*a* ...
(cup of) tea ...	*(o cană de) ceai ...*	(o *ka*·nuh de) che·*ai* ...
with milk	*cu lapte*	koo *lap*·te
without sugar	*fără zahăr*	*fuh*·ruh za·*huhr*
(orange) juice	*suc (de portocale)* n	sook (de por·to·*ka*·le)
soft drink	*băutură*	buh·oo·*too*·ruh
	nealcoolică f	ne·al·ko·o·*lee*·kuh
(boiled/mineral)	*apă (fiartă/* f	a·*puh* (*fyar*·tuh/
water	*minerală)* f	mee·ne·*ra*·luh)

in the bar

I'll have ...	*Aș dori ...*	ash do·*ree* ...
I'll buy you a drink.	*Vă ofer o băutură.*	vuh o·*fer* o buh·oo·*too*·ruh
What would you like?	*Ce v-ar plăcea?*	che var *pluh*·che·a
Cheers!	*Noroc!*	no·*rok*

brandy	*țuică* f	*tsooy*·kuh
cocktail	*cocteil* n	*kok*·teyl
a shot of (whisky)	*un (whisky) mic*	oon (*wee*·skee) meek

a ... of beer	*... de bere*	... de *be*·re
bottle	*o sticlă*	o *stee*·kluh
glass	*un pahar*	oon pa·*har*

a bottle of ... wine	*o sticlă de vin ...*	o *stee*·kluh de veen ...
a glass of ... wine	*un pahar de vin ...*	*oon* pa·*har* de veen ...
red	*roșu*	*ro*·shoo
sparkling	*spumos*	spoo·*mos*
white	*alb*	alb

self-catering

What's the local speciality?
Care e specialitatea locală?   ka-re ye spe-chya-lee-*ta*-te-a lo-*ka*-luh

What's that?
Ce-i aia?   chey *a*-ya

How much is (a kilo of cheese)?
Cât costă (kilogramul de brânză)?   kewt *kos*-tuh (kee-lo-*gra*-mool de *brewn*-zuh)

I'd like ...	*Aş dori ...*	ash do-*ree* ...
(100) grams	*(o sută) de grame*	(o *soo*-tuh) de *gra*-me
(two) kilos	*(două) kile*	(*do*-wuh) *kee*-le
(three) pieces	*(trei) bucăţi*	(trey) boo-*kuh*-tsi
(six) slices	*(şase) felii*	(*sha*-se) fe-*lee*

Less.	*Mai puţin.*	mai poo-*tseen*
Enough.	*Destul.*	des-*tool*
More.	*Mai mult.*	mai moolt

special diets & allergies

Is there a vegetarian restaurant near here?
Există pe aici un restaurant vegetarian?   eg-*zees*-tuh pe a-*eech* oon res-tow-*rant* ve-je-ta-*ryan*

Do you have vegetarian food?
Aveţi mâncare vegetariană?   a-*ve*-tsi mewn-*ka*-re ve-je-ta-*rya*-nuh

Could you prepare a meal without ...?	*Puteţi servi ceva fără ...?*	poo-*tets*' ser-*vee* che-va *fuh*-ruh ...
butter	*unt*	oont
eggs	*ouă*	*o*-wuh
meat stock	*zeamă de carne*	ze-*a*-muh de *kar*-ne

I'm allergic to ...	*Am alergie la ...*	am a-ler-*jee*-ye la ...
dairy produce	*produse lactate*	pro-*doo*-se lak-*ta*-te
gluten	*gluten*	gloo-*ten*
MSG	*MSG (monosodiu glutamat)*	em-es-*je* (mo-no-*so*-dyoo gloo-ta-*mat*)
nuts	*nuci şi alune*	*noo*-chi shee a-*loo*-ne
seafood	*peşte şi fructe de mare*	*pesh*-te shee *frook*-te de *ma*-re

emergencies

basics

Help!	*Ajutor!*	a·zhoo·*tor*
Stop!	*Stop!*	stop
Go away!	*Pleacă!*	ple·*a*·kuh
Thief!	*Hoţii!*	*ho*·tsee
Fire!	*Foc!*	fok
Watch out!	*Atenţie!*	a·*ten*·tsye

Call ...!	*Chemaţi ...!*	ke·*mats'* ...
a doctor	*un doctor*	oon *dok*·tor
an ambulance	*o ambulanţă*	o am·boo·*lan*·tsuh
the police	*poliţia*	po·*lee*·tsya

It's an emergency!
E un caz de urgenţă! ye oon kaz de oor·*jen*·tsuh

Could you help me, please?
Ajutaţi-mă, vă rog! a·zhoo·*ta*·tsee·muh vuh rog

I have to use the telephone.
Trebuie să dau un telefon. tre·*boo*·ye suh dow oon te·le·*fon*

I'm lost.
M-am rătăcit. mam ruh·tuh·*cheet*

Where are the toilets?
Unde este o toaletă? oon·*de yes*·te o to·a·*le*·tuh

police

Where's the police station?
Unde e secţia de poliţie? oon·de ye *sek*·tsya de po·*lee*·tsye

I want to report an offence.
Vreau să raportez o contravenţie. vre·*ow* suh ra·por·*tez* o kon·tra·*ven*·tsye

I have insurance.
Am asigurare. am a·see·goo·*ra*·re

I've been ...	*Am fost ...*	am fost ...
assaulted	*atacat/atacată* m/f	a·ta·*kat*/a·ta·*ka*·tuh
raped	*violat/violată* m/f	vee·o·*lat*/vee·o·*la*·tuh
robbed	*jefuit/jefuită* m/f	zhe·foo·*eet*/zhe·foo·*ee*·tuh

I've lost my ...	Mi-am pierdut ...	myam pyer·doot ...
My ... was/were stolen.	Mi s-a/s-au furat ... sg/pl	mee sa/sow foo·rat ...
bags	valizele pl	va·lee·ze·le
credit card	cartea de credit sg	kar·te·a de kre·deet
handbag	geanta sg	je·an·ta
jewellery	bijuteriile pl	bee·zhoo·te·ree·ee·le
passport	paşaportul sg	pa·sha·por·tool
travellers cheques	cecurile de călătorie pl	che·koo·ree·le de kuh·luh·to·ree·e
wallet	portofelul sg	por·to·fe·lool

I want to contact my consulate/embassy.

Aş dori să contactez consulatul/ambasada.

ash do·ree suh kon·tak·tez kon·soo·la·tool/am·ba·sa·da

health

medical needs

Where's the nearest ...?	Unde se află cel mai apropiat ...?	oon·de se a·fluh chel mai a·pro·pyat ...
dentist	dentist	den·teest
doctor	doctor	dok·tor
hospital	spital	spee·tal

Where's the nearest (night) pharmacist?

Unde se află cea mai apropiată farmacie (cu program non-stop)?

oon·de se a·fluh che·a mai a·pro·pya·tuh far·ma·chee·e (koo pro·gram non stop)

I need a doctor (who speaks English).

Am nevoie de un doctor (care să vorbească engleza).

am ne·vo·ye de oon dok·tor (ka·re suh vor·be·as·kuh en·gle·za)

Could I see a female doctor?

Pot fi consultată de o doctoriţă?

pot fee kon·sool·ta·tuh de o dok·to·ree·tsuh

I've run out of my medication.

Mi s-a terminat doctoria prescrisă.

mee sa ter·mee·nat dok·to·ree·a pre·skree·suh

symptoms, conditions & allergies

| I'm sick. | Mă simt rău. | muh seemt ruh·oo |
| It hurts here. | Mă doare aici. | muh do·a·re a·eech |

I have (a) ...	Sufăr de ...	soo·fuhr de ...
asthma	astm	astm
bronchitis	bronşită	bron·shee·tuh
constipation	constipaţie	kon·stee·pa·tsye
cough	tuse	too·se
diarrhoea	diaree	dee·a·re·e
fever	febră	fe·bruh
headache	durere de cap	doo·re·re de kap
heart condition	inimă	ee·nee·muh
nausea	greaţă	gre·a·tsuh
pain	dureri	doo·re·ri
sore throat	durere în gât	doo·re·re ewn gewt
toothache	durere de dinţi	doo·re·re de deen·tsi

I'm allergic to ...	Am alergie la ...	am a·ler·jee·ye la ...
antibiotics	antibiotice	an·tee·byo·tee·che
anti-inflammatories	anti-inflamatorii	an·tee·een·fla·ma·to·ree
aspirin	aspirină	as·pee·ree·nuh
bees	albine	al·bee·ne
codeine	codeină	ko·de·ee·nuh
penicillin	penicilină	pe·nee·chee·lee·nuh

antiseptic	antiseptic n	an·tee·sep·teek
bandage	bandaj n	ban·dazh
condoms	prezervative n pl	pre·zer·va·tee·ve
contraceptives	contraceptive n pl	kon·tra·chep·tee·ve
diarrhoea medicine	medicament	me·dee·ka·ment
	împotriva	ewm·po·tree·va
	diareei n	dee·a·re·ey
insect repellent	loţiune	lo·tsyoo·ne
	împotriva	ewm·po·tree·va
	insectelor f	een·sek·te·lor
laxatives	laxative n pl	lak·sa·tee·ve
painkillers	analgezice n pl	a·nal·je·zee·che
rehydration salts	săruri rehidratante f pl	suh·roo·ri re·hee·dra·tan·te
sleeping tablets	somnifere n pl	som·nee·fe·re

english–romanian dictionary

Romanian nouns in this dictionary have their gender indicated by ⓜ (masculine), ⓕ (feminine) or ⓝ (neuter). If it's a plural noun, you'll also see pl. Note that neuter nouns take feminine adjectives in the plural and masculine adjectives in the singular. Words are also marked as a (adjective), v (verb), sg (singular), pl (plural), inf (informal) or pol (polite) where necessary.

A

accident *accident* ⓝ ak-*chee*-dent
accommodation *cazare* ⓕ ka-*za*-re
adaptor *adaptor* ⓝ a-dap-*tor*
address *adresă* ⓕ a-*dre*-suh
after *după* doo-puh
air-conditioned *cu aer condiționat* koo a-er kon-dee-tsyo-*nat*
airplane *avion* ⓝ a-*vyon*
airport *aeroport* ⓝ a-e-ro-*port*
alcohol *alcool* ⓝ al-ko-*ol*
all *tot/toată* ⓜ/ⓕ tot/to-*a*-tă
allergy *alergie* ⓕ a-ler-*jee*-e
ambulance *ambulanță* ⓕ am-boo-*lan*-tsuh
and *și* shee
ankle *glezna* ⓕ *glez*-na
arm *braț* ⓝ brats
ashtray *scrumieră* ⓕ skroo-*mye*-ruh
ATM *bancomat* ⓝ ban-ko-*mat*

B

baby *bebeluș* ⓜ be-be-*loosh*
back (body) *spatele* ⓝ *spa*-te-le
backpack *rucsac* ⓝ *rook*-sak
bad *rău/rea* ⓜ/ⓕ ruh-oo/re-*a*
bag *geantă* ⓕ je-an-tuh
baggage claim *bandă de bagaje* ⓕ *ban*-duh de ba-*ga*-zhe
bank *bancă* ⓕ *ban*-kuh
bar *bar* ⓝ bar
bathroom *baie* ⓕ *ba*-ye
battery *baterie* ⓕ ba-te-*ree*-e
beautiful *frumos/frumoasă* ⓜ/ⓕ froo-*mos*/froo-mo-*a*-suh
bed *pat* ⓝ pat
beer *bere* ⓕ *be*-re
before *înainte* ewn-a-*een*-te
behind *înapoi* ewn-na-*poy*
bicycle *bicicletă* ⓕ bee-chee-*kle*-tuh
big *mare* ⓜ&ⓕ *ma*-re
bill *plată* ⓕ *pla*-tuh
black *negru/neagră* ⓜ/ⓕ *ne*-groo/ne-*a*-gruh
blanket *pătură* ⓕ *puh*-too-ruh

blood group *grupa sanguină* ⓕ *groo*-pa san-*gooy*-nuh
blue *albastru/albastră* ⓜ/ⓕ al-*bas*-troo/al-*bas*-truh
boat *barcă* ⓕ *bar*-kuh
book (make a reservation) v *rezerva* re-*zer*-va
bottle *sticlă* ⓕ *stee*-kluh
bottle opener *tirbușon* ⓝ teer-boo-*shon*
boy *băiat* ⓜ buh-*yat*
brakes (car) *frâne* ⓕ pl *frew*-ne
breakfast *micul dejun* ⓜ *mee*-kool de-*zhoon*
broken (faulty) *defect/defectă* ⓜ/ⓕ de-*fekt*/de-*fek*-tuh
bus *autobuz* ⓝ ow-to-*booz*
business *afacere* ⓕ a-*fa*-che-re
buy v *cumpăra* koom-puh-*ra*

C

café *cafenea* ⓕ ka-fe-ne-*a*
camera *aparat foto* ⓝ a-pa-*rat fo*-to
camp site *loc de camping* ⓝ lok de *kem*-peeng
cancel v *anula* a-noo-*la*
can opener *deschizător de conserve* ⓝ des-kee-zuh-*tor* de kon-*ser*-ve
car *mașină* ⓕ ma-*shee*-nuh
cash *bani cash* ⓜ pl *ba*-ni kesh
cash (a cheque) v *încasa (un cec)* ewn-ka-*sa* (oon check)
cell phone *celular* ⓝ che-loo-*lar*
centre *centru* ⓝ *chen*-troo
change (money) v *schimba (bani)* skeem-*ba* (*ba*-ni)
cheap *ieftin/ieftină* ⓜ/ⓕ *yef*-teen/*yef*-tee-nuh
check (bill) *nota de plată* ⓕ *no*-ta de *pla*-tuh
chest *cufăr* ⓝ *koo*-fuhr
child *copil* ⓜ ko-*peel*
cigarette *țigaretă* ⓕ tsee-ga-*re*-tuh
city *oraș* ⓝ o-*rash*
clean *curat/curată* ⓜ/ⓕ koo-*rat*/koo-*ra*-tuh
closed *închis/închisă* ⓜ/ⓕ ewn-*kees*/ewn-*kee*-suh
coffee *cafea* ⓕ ka-fe-*a*
coins *monezi* ⓕ pl mo-*ne*-zi
cold a *rece* ⓜ&ⓕ *re*-che

collect call *telefon cu taxă inversă* ⓝ
te-le-fon koo tak-suh een-ver-suh
come *veni* ve-nee
computer *calculator* ⓝ kal-koo-la-tor
condom *prezervativ* ⓝ pre-zer-va-teev
contact lenses *lentile de contact* ⓕ pl
len-tee-le de kon-takt
cook ∨ *găti* guh-tee
cost *cost* ⓝ kost
credit card *carte de credit* ⓕ kar-te de kre-deet
cup *cană* ⓕ ka-nuh
currency exchange *schimb valutar* ⓝ
skeemb va-loo-tar
customs (immigration) *vamă* ⓕ va-muh

D

dangerous *periculos/periculoasă* ⓜ/ⓕ
pe-ree-koo-los/pe-ree-koo-lo-a-suh
date (time) *data* ⓕ da-ta
day *ziua* ⓕ zee-wa
delay *întârziere* ⓕ ewn-tewr-zye-re
dentist *dentist* ⓝ den-teest
depart *pleca* ple-ka
diaper *scutec* ⓝ skoo-tek
dictionary *dicționar* ⓝ deek-tsyo-nar
dinner *cină* ⓕ chee-nuh
direct *direct/directă* ⓜ/ⓕ dee-rekt/dee-rek-tuh
dirty *murdar/murdară* ⓜ/ⓕ moor-dar/moor-da-ruh
disabled *invalid/invalidă* ⓜ/ⓕ
een-va-leed/een-va-lee-duh
discount *reducere* ⓕ re-doo-che-re
doctor *doctor* ⓝ dok-tor
double bed *pat dublu* ⓝ pat doo-bloo
double room *cameră dublă* ⓕ ka-me-ruh doo-bluh
drink *băutură* ⓕ buh-oo-too-ruh
drive ∨ *conduce* kon-doo-che
drivers licence *carnet de conducere* ⓝ
kar-net de kon-doo-che-re
drugs (illicit) *droguri* ⓝ pl dro-goo-ri
dummy (pacifier) *suzetă* ⓕ soo-ze-tuh

E

ear *ureche* ⓕ oo-re-ke
east *est* est
eat ∨ *mânca* mewn-ka
economy class *clasa economy* ⓕ kla-sa e-ko-no-mee
electricity *electricitate* ⓕ e-lek-tree-chee-ta-te
elevator *lift* ⓝ leeft
email *e-mail* ⓝ ee-meyl
embassy *ambasadă* ⓕ am-ba-sa-duh
emergency *urgență* ⓕ en-gle-za
English (language) *engleza* ⓕ en-gle-za
entrance *intrare* ⓕ een-tra-re

evening *seară* ⓕ se-a-ruh
exchange rate *rata de schimb* ⓕ ra-ta de skeemb
exit *ieșire* ⓕ ye-shee-re
expensive *scump/scumpă* ⓜ/ⓕ skoomp/skoom-puh
express mail *poștă expres* ⓕ posh-tuh eks-pres
eye *ochi* ⓝ o-ki

F

far *departe* de-par-te
fast *repede* re-pe-de
father *tată* ⓜ ta-tuh
film (camera) *film* ⓝ feelm
finger *deget* ⓝ de-jet
first-aid kit *trusă de prim ajutor* ⓕ
troo-suh de preem a-zhoo-tor
first class *clasa întâi* ⓕ kla-sa ewn-tew-ee
fish *pește* ⓜ pesh-te
food *mâncare* ⓕ mewn-ka-re
foot *picior* ⓝ pee-chyor
fork *furculiță* ⓕ foor-koo-lee-tsuh
free (of charge) *gratis* gra-tees
friend *prieten/prietenă* ⓜ/ⓕ pree-e-ten/pree-e-te-nuh
fruit *fructe* ⓝ pl frook-te
full *plin/plină* ⓜ/ⓕ pleen/plee-nuh
funny *nostim/nostimă* ⓜ/ⓕ nos-teem/nos-tee-muh

G

gift *cadou* ⓝ ka-doh
girl *fată* ⓕ fa-tuh
glass (drinking) *pahar* ⓝ pa-har
glasses *ochelari* ⓝ pl o-ke-la-ri
go *merge* mer-je
good *bun/bună* ⓜ/ⓕ boon/boo-nuh
green *verde* ⓜ&ⓕ ver-de
guide *ghid* ⓝ geed

H

half *jumătate* ⓕ zhoo-muh-ta-te
hand *mână* ⓕ mew-nuh
handbag *poșetă* ⓕ po-she-tuh
happy *bucuros/bucuroasă* ⓜ/ⓕ
boo-koo-ros/boo-koo-ro-a-suh
have *avea* a-ve-a
he *el* yel
head *cap* ⓝ kap
heart *inimă* ⓕ ee-nee-muh
heat *căldură* ⓕ kuhl-doo-ruh
heavy *greu/grea* ⓜ/ⓕ gre-oo/gre-a
help ∨ *ajuta* a-zhoo-ta
here *aici* a-eech'

high *înalt/înaltă* ⓜ/ⓕ *ew-nalt/ew-nal-tuh*
highway *şosea* ⓕ *sho-se-a*
hike v *merge pe jos* *mer-je pe zhos*
holiday *vacanţă* ⓕ *va-kan-tsuh*
homosexual *homosexual* ⓜ *ho-mo-sek-swal*
hospital *spital* ⓝ *spee-tal*
hot *fierbinte* ⓜ/ⓕ *fyer-been-te*
hotel *hotel* ⓝ *ho-tel*
hungry *înfometat/înfometată* ⓜ/ⓕ
    ewn-fo-me-tat/ewn-fo-me-ta-tuh
husband *soţ* ⓜ *sots*

I

I *eu* *ye-oo*
identification (card) *buletin de identitate* ⓝ
    boo-le-teen de ee-den-tee-ta-te
ill *bolnav/bolnavă* ⓜ/ⓕ *bol-nav/ bol-na-vuh*
important *important/importantă* ⓜ/ⓕ
    eem-por-tant/eem-por-tan-tuh
included *inclus/inclusă* ⓜ/ⓕ *een-kloos/een-kloo-suh*
injury *rană* ⓕ *ra-nuh*
insurance *asigurare* ⓕ *a-see-goo-ra-re*
Internet *internet* ⓝ *een-ter-net*
interpreter *interpret* ⓜ *een-ter-pret*

J

jewellery *bijuterii* ⓕ pl *bee-zhoo-te-ree*
job *serviciu* ⓝ *ser-vee-chyoo*

K

key *cheie* ⓕ *ke-ye*
kilogram *kilogram* ⓝ *kee-lo-gram*
kitchen *bucătărie* ⓕ *boo-kuh-tuh-ree-e*
knife *cuţit* ⓝ *koo-tseet*

L

laundry (place) *spălătorie* ⓕ *spuh-luh-to-ree-e*
lawyer *avocat* ⓜ *a-vo-kat*
left (direction) *la stânga* *la stewn-ga*
left-luggage office *birou pentru păstrarea bagajelor*
    ⓝ *bee-roh pen-troo puhs-tra-re-a ba-ga-zhe-lor*
leg *picior* ⓝ *pee-chyor*
lesbian *lesbiană* ⓕ *les-bya-nuh*
less *mai puţin* *mai poo-tseen*
letter (mail) *scrisoare* ⓕ *skree-so-a-re*
lift (elevator) *lift* ⓝ *leeft*
light *lumină* ⓕ *loo-mee-nuh*

like v *place* *pla-che*
lock *lacăt* ⓝ *la-kuht*
long *lung/lungă* ⓜ/ⓕ *loong/loon-guh*
lost *pierdut/pierdută* ⓜ/ⓕ *pyer-doot/pyer-doo-tuh*
lost-property office *birou bagaje pierdute* ⓝ
    bee-roh ba-ga-zhe pyer-doo-te
love v *iubi* *yoo-bee*
luggage *bagaje* ⓝ pl *ba-ga-zhe*
lunch *dejun* ⓝ *de-zhoon*

M

mail *poştă* ⓕ *posh-tuh*
man *bărbat* ⓜ *buhr-bat*
map *hartă* ⓕ *har-tuh*
market *piaţă* ⓕ *pya-tsuh*
matches *chibrituri* ⓝ pl *kee-bree-too-ri*
meat *carne* ⓕ *kar-ne*
medicine *doctorie* ⓕ *dok-to-ree-e*
menu *meniu* ⓝ *me-nyoo*
message *mesaj* ⓝ *me-sazh*
milk *lapte* ⓝ *lap-te*
minute *minut* ⓝ *mee-noot*
mobile phone *telefon mobil* ⓝ *te-le-fon mo-beel*
Moldova *Moldova* *mol-do-va*
money *bani* ⓝ pl *ba-ni*
month *lună* ⓕ *loo-nuh*
morning *dimineaţă* ⓕ *dee-mee-ne-a-tsuh*
mother *mamă* ⓕ *ma-muh*
motorcycle *motocicletă* ⓕ *mo-to-chee-kle-tuh*
motorway *autostradă* ⓕ *ow-to-stra-duh*
mouth *gură* ⓕ *goo-ruh*
music *muzică* ⓕ *moo-zee-kuh*

N

name *nume* ⓝ *noo-me*
napkin *şerveţel* ⓝ *sher-ve-tsel*
nappy *scutec* ⓝ *skoo-tek*
near *aproape* *a-pro-a-pe*
neck *gâtul* ⓝ *gew-tool*
new *nou/nouă* ⓜ/ⓕ *noh/no-wuh*
news *ştiri* ⓕ pl *shtee-ri*
newspaper *ziar* ⓝ *zee-ar*
night *noapte* ⓕ *no-ap-te*
no *nu* *noo*
noisy *zgomotos/zgomotoasă* ⓜ/ⓕ
    zgo-mo-tos/zgo-mo-to-a-suh
nonsmoking section *la nefumători* *la ne-foo-muh-to-ri*
north *nord* *nord*
nose *nas* ⓝ *nas*
now *acum* *a-koom*
number *număr* ⓝ *noo-muhr*

O

oil (engine) *ulei de motor* ⓝ oo-*ley* de mo-*tor*
old *vechi/veche* ⓜ/ⓕ *ve*-ki/*ve*-ke
one-way ticket *bilet dus* ⓝ *bee*-let doos
open a *deschis/deschisă* ⓜ/ⓕ des-*kees*/des-*kee*-suh
outside *afară* a-*fa*-ruh

P

package *pachet* ⓝ pa-*ket*
paper *hârtie* ⓕ hewr-*tee*-e
park (car) v *parca* par-*ka*
passport *paşaport* ⓝ pa-sha-*port*
pay v *plăti* pluh-*tee*
pen *pix* ⓝ peeks
petrol *benzină* ⓕ ben-*zee*-nuh
pharmacy *farmacie* ⓕ far-ma-*chee*-e
phonecard *cartelă de telefon* ⓕ kar-*te*-luh de te-le-*fon*
photo *fotografie* ⓕ fo-to-gra-*fee*-e
plate *farfurie* ⓕ far-foo-*ree*-e
police *poliţie* ⓕ po-*lee*-tsye
postcard *carte poştală* ⓕ *kar*-te posh-*ta*-luh
post office *oficiu poştal* ⓝ o-*fee*-chyoo posh-*tal*
pregnant *însărcinată* ⓕ ewn-suhr-chee-*na*-tuh
price *preţ* ⓝ prets

Q

quiet *liniştit/liniştită* ⓜ/ⓕ lee-neesh-*teet*/lee-neesh-tee-*tuh*

R

rain *ploaie* ⓕ plo-*a*-ye
razor *aparat de ras* ⓝ a-pa-*rat* de ras
receipt *chitanţă* ⓕ kee-*tan*-tsuh
red *roşu/roşie* ⓜ/ⓕ ro-*shoo*/ro-*shee*-e
refund *rambursare* ⓕ ram-boor-*sa*-re
registered mail *poştă înregistrată* ⓕ *posh*-tuh ewn-re-jees-*tra*-tuh
rent v *închiria* ewn-kee-*rya*
repair v *repara* re-pa-*ra*
reservation *rezervaţie* ⓕ re-zer-*va*-tsye
restaurant *restaurant* ⓝ res-tow-*rant*
return v se *întoarce* se ewn-to-*ar*-che
return ticket *bilet dus-întors* ⓝ *bee*-let doos-ewn-*tors*
right (direction) *la dreapta* la dre-*ap*-ta
road *şosea* ⓕ sho-se-*a*
Romania *România* ro-mew-*nee*-a

Romanian (language) *limba română* *leem*-ba ro-mew-*nuh*
Romanian a *românesc/românească* ⓜ/ⓕ ro-mew-*nesk*/ro-mew-ne-*as*-kuh
room *cameră* ⓕ *ka*-me-ruh

S

safe a *protejat/protejată* ⓜ/ⓕ pro-te-*zhat*/pro-te-zha-*tuh*
sanitary napkin *absorbante* ⓕ ab-sor-*ban*-te
seat *loc* ⓝ lok
send v *trimite* tree-*mee*-te
service station *staţie de benzină* ⓕ *sta*-tsye de ben-*zee*-nuh
sex *sex* ⓝ seks
shampoo *şampon* ⓝ sham-*pon*
share (a dorm) *împărţi* ewm-*puhr*-tsee
shaving cream *cremă de ras* ⓕ *kre*-muh de ras
she *ea* ya
sheet (bed) *cearceaf* ⓝ che-ar-*che*-af
shirt *cămaşă* ⓕ kuh-*ma*-shuh
shoes *pantofi* ⓝ pl pan-*to*-fi
shop *magazin* ⓝ ma-ga-*zeen*
short *scurt/scurtă* ⓜ/ⓕ skoort/*skoor*-tuh
shower *duş* ⓝ doosh
single room *cameră de o persoană* ⓕ *ka*-me-ruh de o per-so-*a*-nuh
skin *piele* ⓕ *pye*-le
skirt *fustă* ⓕ *foos*-tuh
sleep v *dormi* dor-*mee*
slowly *încet* ewn-*chet*
small *mic/mică* ⓜ/ⓕ meek/*mee*-kuh
smoke (cigarettes) v *fuma* foo-*ma*
soap *săpun* ⓝ suh-*poon*
some *nişte* ⓜ&ⓕ *neesh*-te
soon *curând* koo-*rewnd*
south *sud* sood
souvenir shop *magazin de suveniruri* ⓝ ma-ga-*zeen* de soo-ve-nee-*roo*-ri
speak *vorbi* vor-*bee*
spoon *lingură* ⓕ *leen*-goo-ruh
stamp *timbru* ⓝ *teem*-broo
stand-by ticket *bilet neconfirmat* ⓝ *bee*-let ne-kon-feer-*mat*
station (train) *gară* ⓕ *ga*-ruh
stomach *stomac* ⓝ sto-*mak*
stop v *opri* o-*pree*
stop (bus) *staţie de autobuz* ⓕ *sta*-tsye de ow-to-*booz*
street *stradă* ⓕ *stra*-duh

student *student/studentă* ⓜ/ⓕ
stoo-dent/stoo-den-tuh
sun *soare* ⓝ so-a-re
sunscreen *loţiune contra soarelui* ⓕ
lo-tsyoo-ne kon-tra so-a-re-looy
swim v *înota* ew-no-ta

T

tampons *tampoane* ⓝ pl tam-po-a-ne
taxi *taxi* ⓝ tak-see
teaspoon *linguriţă* ⓕ leen-goo-ree-tsa
teeth *dinţi* ⓜ pl deen-tsi
telephone *telefon* ⓝ te-le-fon
television (set) *televizor* ⓝ te-le-vee-zor
temperature (weather) *temperatură* ⓕ
tem-pe-ra-too-ruh
tent *cort* ⓕ kort
that (one) *acela/aceea* ⓜ/ⓕ a-che-la/a-che-ya
they *ei/ele* yey/ye-le
thirsty *însetat/însetată* ⓜ/ⓕ ewn-se-tat/ewn-se-ta-tuh
this (one) *acesta/aceasta* ⓜ/ⓕ a-ches-ta/a-che-as-ta
throat *în gât* ⓝ ewn gewt
ticket *bilet* ⓝ bee-let
time *ora* ⓕ o-ra
tired *obosit/obosită* ⓜ/ⓕ o-bo-seet/o-bo-see-tuh
tissues *şerveţele* ⓝ pl sher-ve-tse-le
today *azi* a-zi
toilet *toaletă* ⓕ to-a-le-tuh
tomorrow *mâine* mew-ee-ne
tonight *diseară* dee-se-a-ruh
toothbrush *periuţă de dinţi* ⓕ
pe-ree-oo-tsuh de deen-tsi
toothpaste *pastă de dinţi* ⓕ pas-tuh de deen-tsi
torch (flashlight) *lanternă* ⓕ lan-ter-nuh
tour *tur* ⓝ toor
tourist office *birou de informaţii turistice* ⓝ
bi-roh de in-for-ma-tsee too-rees-tee-che
towel *prosop* ⓝ pro-sop
train *tren* ⓝ tren
translate *traduce* tra-doo-che
travel agency *agenţie de voiaj* ⓕ
a-jen-tsee-e de vo-yazh
travellers cheque *cecuri de călătorie* ⓝ pl
che-koo-ri de kuh-luh-to-ree-e
trousers *pantaloni* ⓝ pl pan-ta-lo-ni
twin beds *cameră cu două paturi separate* ⓕ
ka-me-ruh koo do-wuh pa-too-ri se-pa-ra-te
tyre *cauciuc* ⓝ kow-chook

U

underwear *lenjerie de corp* ⓕ len-zhe-ree-e de korp
urgent *urgent/urgentă* ⓜ/ⓕ oor-jent/oor-jen-tuh

V

vacant *liber/liberă* ⓜ/ⓕ lee-ber/lee-be-ruh
vacation *vacanţă* ⓕ va-kan-tsuh
vegetable *legumă* ⓕ le-goo-muh
vegetarian a *vegetarian/vegetariana* ⓜ/ⓕ
ve-je-ta-ryan/ve-je-ta-rya-nuh
visa *viză* ⓕ vee-zuh

W

waiter *chelner* ⓜ kel-ner
walk v *merge pe jos* mer-je pe zhos
wallet *portofel* ⓝ por-to-fel
warm a *cald/caldă* ⓜ/ⓕ kald/kal-duh
wash (something) v *spăla* spuh-la
watch *ceas* ⓝ che-as
water *apă* ⓕ a-puh
we *noi* noy
weekend *weekend* ⓝ wee-kend
west *vest* vest
wheelchair *scaun cu rotile* ⓝ skown koo ro-tee-le
when *când* kewnd
where *unde* oon-de
white *alb/albă* ⓜ/ⓕ alb/al-buh
who *cine* chee-ne
why *de ce* de che
wife *nevastă* ⓕ ne-vas-tuh
window *fereastră* ⓕ fe-re-as-truh
wine *vin* ⓝ veen
with *cu* koo
without *fără* fuh-ruh
woman *femeie* ⓕ fe-me-ye
write v *scrie* skree-ye

Y

yellow *galben/galbenă* ⓜ/ⓕ gal-ben/gal-be-nuh
yes *da* da
yesterday *ieri* ye-ri
you sg inf *tu* too
you pl inf *voi* voy
you sg&pl pol *dumneavoastră* doom-ne-a-vo-as-truh

Russian

russian alphabet

А а a	Б б be	В в ve	Г г ge	Д д de
Е е ye	Ё ё yo	Ж ж zhe	З з ze	И и ee
Й й ee-*krat*-ka-ye	К к ka	Л л el	М м em	Н н en
О о o	П п pe	Р р er	С с es	Т т te
У у u	Ф ф ef	Х х kha	Ц ц tse	Ч ч che
Ш ш sha	Щ щ shcha	Ъ ъ *tvyor*-di znak	Ы ы ih	Ь ь *myakh*-ki znak
Э э e	Ю ю yu	Я я ya		

■ russian

PYCCKИЙ

introduction

Words such as *apparatchik*, *tsar* and *vodka* come from Russian (русский *rus*-kee) – the language which unites the largest nation in the world, the 'riddle wrapped in a mystery inside an enigma' spread over two continents and 11 time zones. The official language of the Russian Federation, Russian is also used as a second language in the former republics of the USSR and is widely spoken throughout Eastern Europe. With a total of more than 270 million speakers, it's the fifth most spoken language in the world.

Russian belongs to the East Slavic group of languages, together with Belarusian and Ukrainian. These languages were initially considered so similar that they were classified as one language – Old Russian. Russian was recognised as a distinct, modern language in the 10th century, when the Cyrillic alphabet was adopted along with Orthodox Christianity by way of Old Church Slavonic. This South Slavic language was used principally in religious literature, while written secular texts were much closer to the spoken East Slavic language. For centuries these two forms of Old Russian coexisted, and it was a third, 'middle' style which emerged in the 18th century as the basis of modern Russian. Pushkin, the nation's first great poet, was essentially writing in the Russian of today when he published *Eugene Onegin* in 1831. The alphabet was radically simplified at two major turning points in Russian history – as part of Peter the Great's reforms at the turn of the 17th century, and after the October Revolution in 1917.

For a language spoken across such a vast geographical area, Russian is surprisingly uniform, and the regional differences don't get in the way of communication. The language was standardised by the centralised education system in the USSR, which spread literacy and enforced 'literary' Russian. In practical terms, Russian is divided into the northern and the southern dialects; Moscow's dialect has some features of both. From the 16th century onward Muscovite Russian was the standard tongue, even after Peter the Great's court had moved to St Petersburg.

Some admirers of Russian literature have claimed that the русская душа *rus*-ka-ya du-*sha* (Russian soul) of Dostoevsky, Chekhov and Tolstoy simply can't be understood, or at least fully appreciated, in translation. All exaggeration aside, the Russian language boasts a rich vocabulary and highly colourful expressions. This linguistic flamboyance has thankfully resisted the influence of dour communist style and the 'socrealist' literature of the 20th century, as you'll soon find out on your travels!

pronunciation

Russian is often considered difficult to learn because of its script, but this is merely prejudice – some Cyrillic letters look and sound the same as their English peers, and the others aren't difficult to learn. Contrary to popular caricatures of the 'harsh' Russian accent, the language has a pleasant, soft sound characterised by several 'lisping' consonants. Most of the sounds in Russian are also found in English, and those that are unfamiliar aren't difficult to master. Use the coloured pronunciation guides to become familiar with them, and then read from the Cyrillic alphabet when you feel more confident.

There are remarkably few variations in modern Russian pronunciation and vocabulary. This phrasebook is written in standard Russian as it's spoken around Moscow, and you're sure to be understood by Russian speakers everywhere.

vowel sounds

symbol	english equivalent	russian example	transliteration
a	father	да	da
ai	aisle	май	mai
e	bet	это	e·ta
ee	see	мир	meer
ey	hey	бассейн	bas·yeyn
i	bit	мыло	mi·la
o	pot	дом	dom
oy	toy	сырой	si·roy
u	put	ужин	u·zheen

word stress

Russian stress is free (it can fall on any syllable) and mobile (it can change in different forms of the same word). Each word has only one stressed syllable, which you'll need to learn as you go. In the meantime, follow our pronunciation guides, which have the stressed syllable marked in italics.

consonant sounds

Most Russian consonants are similar to English sounds, so they won't cause you too much difficulty. The 'soft' sign ь and the 'hard' sign ъ don't have a sound of their own, but show in writing whether the consonant before them is pronounced 'soft' (with a slight y sound after it) or 'hard' (as it's written). In our pronunciation guides, the soft sign is represented with an apostrophe (') – as in бедность *byed*-nast' – but the hard sign isn't included as it's very rarely used.

symbol	english equivalent	russian example	transliteration
b	bed	брат	brat
ch	cheat	чай	chai
d	dog	вода	va-*da*
f	fat	кофе	*ko*-fee
g	go	город	*go*-rat
k	kit	сок	sok
kh	loch	смех	smyekh
l	lot	лифт	leeft
m	man	место	*mye*-sta
n	not	нога	na-*ga*
p	pet	письмо	pees-*mo*
r	run (rolled)	река	ree-*ka*
s	sun	снег	snyek
sh	shot	душа	du-*sha*
t	top	так	tak
ts	hats	отец	at-*yets*
v	very	врач	vrach
y	yes	мой	moy
z	zoo	звук	zvuk
zh	pleasure	жизнь	zhizn'
'	a slight y sound	власть	vlast'

pronunciation произношение

tools

language difficulties

Do you speak English?
Вы говорите по-английски?   vi ga·va·*reet*·ye pa·an·*glee*·skee

Do you understand?
Вы понимаете?   vi pa·nee·*ma*·eet·ye

I (don't) understand.
Я (не) понимаю.   ya (nye) pa·nee·*ma*·yu

What does (пуп) mean?
Что обозначает слово (пуп)?   shto a·baz·na·*cha*·eet *slo*·va (pup)

How do you say ... in Russian?
Как будет ... по-русски?   kak bu·deet ... pa·*ru*·skee

How do you ...?	Как ...?	kak ...
pronounce this	это произносится	e·ta pra·eez·*no*·seet·sa
write (Путин)	пишется (Путин)	*pee*·shit·sa (*pu*·teen)

Could you please ...?	..., пожалуйста.	... pa·*zhal*·sta
repeat that	Повторите	paf·ta·*reet*·ye
speak more	Говорите	ga·va·*reet*·ye
slowly	помеделенее	pa·meed·leen·*ye*·ye
write it down	Запишите	za·pee·*shit*·ye

essentials

Yes.	Да.	da
No.	Нет.	nyet
Please.	Пожалуйста.	pa·*zhal*·sta
Thank you	Спасибо	spa·*see*·ba
(very much).	(большое).	(bal'·*sho*·ye)
You're welcome.	Пожалуйста.	pa·*zhal*·sta
Excuse me.	Извините, пожалуйста.	eez·vee·*neet*·ye pa·*zhal*·sta
Sorry.	Извините, пожалуйста.	eez·vee·*neet*·ye pa·*zhal*·sta

numbers

0	ноль	nol'	15	пятнадцать	peet·*nat*·sat'
1	один m	a·*deen*	16	шестнадцать	shist·*nat*·sat'
	одна f	ad·*na*	17	семнадцать	seem·*nat*·sat'
	одно n	ad·*no*	18	восемнадцать	va·seem·*nat*·sat'
2	два m&n	dva	19	девятнадцать	dee·veet·*nat*·sat'
	две f	dvye	20	двадцать	*dvat*·sat'
3	три	tree	21	двадцать	*dvat*·sat'
4	четыре	chee·*ti*·ree		один	a·*deen*
5	пять	pyat'	22	двадцать два	*dvat*·sat' dva
6	шесть	shest'	30	тридцать	*treet*·sat'
7	семь	syem'	40	сорок	*so*·rak
8	восемь	*vo*·seem'	50	пятьдесят	pee·dees·*yat*
9	девять	*dye*·veet'	60	шестдесят	shis·dees·*yat*
10	десять	*dye*·seet'	70	семьдесят	syem'·dee·seet
11	одиннадцать	a·*dee*·nat·sat'	80	восемьдесят	*vo*·seem'·dee·seet
12	двенадцать	dvee·*nat*·sat'	90	девяносто	dee·vee·*no*·sta
13	тринадцать	tree·*nat*·sat'	100	сто	sto
14	четырнадцать	chee·*tir*·nat·sat'	1000	тысяча	*ti*·see·cha

time & dates

What time is it?	Который час?	ka·*to*·ri chas
It's one o'clock.	Час.	chas
It's (two/three/four) o'clock.	(Два/Три/Четыре) часа.	(dva/tree/chee·*ti*·ree) chee·*sa*
It's (10) o'clock.	(Десять) часов.	(*dye*·veet') chee·*sof*
Quarter past (10).	(Десять) пятнадцать.	(*dye*·seet') peet·*nat*·sat'
Half past (10).	(Десять) тридцать.	(*dye*·seet') *treet*·sat'
Twenty to (11).	(Десять) сорок. (lit: ten forty)	(*dye*·seet') *so*·rak
At what time ...?	В котором часу ...?	f ka·*to*·ram chee·*su* ...
At ...	В ... часов.	v ... chee·*sof*
in the morning	утра	ut·*ra*
in the afternoon	дня	dnya
in the evening	вечера	*vye*·chee·ra

Monday	понедельник	pa-nee-dyel'-neek
Tuesday	вторник	ftor-neek
Wednesday	среда	sree-da
Thursday	четверг	cheet-vyerk
Friday	пятница	pyat-neet-sa
Saturday	суббота	su-bo-ta
Sunday	воскресенье	vas-krees-yen'-ye
January	январь	yeen-var'
February	февраль	feev-ral'
March	март	mart
April	апрель	ap-ryel'
May	май	mai
June	июнь	ee-yun'
July	июль	ee-yul'
August	август	av-gust
September	сентябрь	seent-yabr'
October	октябрь	akt-yabr'
November	ноябрь	na-yabr'
December	декабрь	dee-kabr'
What date is it today?	Какое сегодня число?	ka-ko-ye see-vod-nya chees-lo
It's (1 May).	(Первое мая).	(pyer-va-ye ma-ya)
since (May)	с (мая)	s (ma-ya)
until (June)	до (июня)	da (ee-yun-ya)
last ...		
night	вчера вечером	fchee-ra vye-chee-ram
week	на прошлой неделе	na prosh-ley need-yel-ye
month	в прошлом месяце	f prosh-lam mye-seet-se
year	в прошлом году	f prosh-lam ga-du
next ...		
week	на следующей неделе	na slye-du-yu-shee need-yel-ye
month	в следующем месяце	f slye-du-yu-sheem mye-seet-se
year	в следующем году	f slye-du-yu-sheem ga-doo
yesterday/tomorrow ...	вчера/завтра ...	fchee-ra/zaf-tra ...
morning	утром	ut-ram
afternoon	днём	dnyom
evening	вечером	vye-chee-ram

weather

What's the weather like?	Какая погода?	ka-*ka*-ya pa-*go*-da

It's ...

cloudy	Облачно.	*ob*-lach-na
cold	Холодно.	*kho*-lad-na
hot	Жарко.	*zhar*-ka
raining	Идёт дождь.	eed-*yot* dozhd'
snowing	Идёт снег.	eed-*yot* snyek
sunny	Солнечно.	*sol*-neech-na
warm	Тепло.	tee-*plo*
windy	Ветрено.	*vye*-tree-na

spring	весна f	vees-*na*
summer	лето n	*lye*-ta
autumn	осень f	*o*-seen'
winter	зима f	zee-*ma*

border crossing

I'm here ...	Я здесь ...	ya zdyes' ...
for study	учусь	u-*chus'*
on business	по бизнесу	pa *beez*-nee-su
on holiday	в отпуске	v *ot*-pus-kye

I'm here for ...	Я здесь ...	ya zdyes' ...
(10) days	(десять) дней	(*dye*-seet') dnyey
(three) weeks	(три) недели	(tree) need-*ye*-lee
(two) months	(два) месяца	(dva) *mye*-seet-sa

I'm going to (Akademgorodok).
Я еду в (Академгородок).   ya *ye*-du v (a-ka-deem-ga-ra-*dok*)

I'm staying at (the Kosmos).
Я останавливаюсь в (Космосе).   ya as-ta-*nav*-lee-va-yus' v (*kos*-mas-ye)

I have nothing to declare.
Мне нечего декларировать.   mnye *nye*-chee-va dee-kla-*ree*-ra-vat'

I have something to declare.
Мне нужно что-то задекларировать.   mnye *nuzh*-na *shto*-ta za-dee-kla-*ree*-ra-vat'

That's (not) mine.
Это (не) моё.   *e*-ta (nye) ma-*yo*

transport

tickets & luggage

Where can I buy a ticket?
Где можно купить билет?
gdye *mozh*·na ku·*peet'* beel·*yet*

Do I need to book a seat?
Мне нужно зарезервировать
место?
mnye *nuzh*·na za·re·zer·*vee*·ra·vat'
myes·ta

One ... ticket (to	Билет ...	beel·*yet* ...
Novgorod), please.	(на Новгород).	(na *nov*·ga·rat)
one-way	в один конец	v a·*deen* kan·*yets*
return	в оба конца	v *o*·ba kant·*sa*

I'd like to ...	Я бы хотел/хотела	ya bi khat·*yel*/khat·*ye*·la
my ticket, please.	... билет, пожалуйста. m/f	... beel·*yet* pa·*zhal*·sta
cancel	отменить	at·mee·*neet'*
change	поменять	pa·meen·*yat'*
collect	забрать	zab·*rat'*
confirm	подтвердить	pat·veer·*deet'*

I'd like a (non)smoking seat, please.
Я бы хотел/хотела место в
отделении для (не)курящих,
пожалуйста. m/f
ya bi khat·*yel*/khat·*ye*·la *mye*·sta v
a·*deel*·ye·nee·ee dlya (nee·)kur·*ya*·sheekh
pa·*zhal*·sta

How much is it?
Сколько стоит?
skol'·ka *sto*·eet

Is there air conditioning?
Есть кондиционер?
yest' kan·deet·si·an·*yer*

Is there a toilet?
Есть туалет?
yest' tu·al·*yet*

How long does the trip take?
Сколько времени
уйдёт на эту поездку?
skol'·ka *vrye*·mee·nee
uyd·*yot* na e·tu pa·*yest*·ku

Is it a direct route?
Это прямой рейс?
e·ta pree·*moy* ryeys

Where's the luggage locker?
Где камера-автомат?
gdye *ka*·mee·ra·af·ta·*mat*

My luggage has been ...	Мой багаж ...	moy ba-*gash* ...
damaged	повредили	pa-vree-*dee*-lee
lost	пропал	pra-*pal*
stolen	украли	u-*kra*-lee

getting around

Where does flight (M2) arrive?
Куда прибывает самолёт (M2)? ku-*da* pree-bi-*va*-et sa-ma-*lyot* (em dva)

Where does flight (M2) depart?
Откуда отправляется самолёт (M2)? at-ku-da at-prav-*lya*-eet-sa sa-ma-*lyot* (em dva)

Which gate for (Omsk)?
Какой выход на посадку до (Омска)? ka-*koy* vi-khat na pa-*sat*-ku da (*om*-ska)

Where's (the) ...?	Где ...?	gdye ...
arrivals hall	зал прибытий	zal pree-*bi*-tee-ye
departures hall	зал отправлений	zal at-prav-*lye*-nee
duty-free shop	товары без пошлины	ta-*va*-ri byes *posh*-lee-ni
gate (three)	выход на посадку (три)	*vi*-khat na pa-*sat*-ku (tree)

Is this the ... to (Moscow)?	Этот ... идёт в (Москву)?	e-tat ... eed-*yot* v (mask-*vu*)
boat	параход	pa-ra-*khot*
bus	автобус	af-*to*-bus
plane	самолёт	sa-mal-*yot*
train	поезд	*po*-yeest

What time's the ... bus?	Когда будет ... автобус?	kag-*da* bu-deet ... af-*to*-bus
first	первый	*pyer*-vi
last	последний	pas-*lyed*-nee
next	следующий	*slye*-du-yu-shee

At what time does it arrive/leave?
Когда он прибывает/отправляется? kag-*da* on pree-bi-*va*-et/ at-prav-*lya*-eet-sa

How long will it be delayed?
На сколько он опаздывает? na *skol*'-ka on a-*paz*-di-va-yet

What station/stop is this?
Какая эта станция/остановка? ka·ka·ya e·ta stant·si·ya/a·sta·nof·ka

What's the next station/stop?
Какая следующая ka·ka·ya slye·du·yu·sha·ya
станция/остановка? stant·si·ya/a·sta·nof·ka

Does it stop at (Solntsevo)?
Поезд останавливается po·yeest a·sta·nav·lee·va·yeet·sa
в (Солнцево)? v (sont·see·va)

Please tell me when we get to (Magadan).
Объявите, пожалуйста, когда ab·yee·veet·ye pa·zhal·sta kag·da
мы подъедем к (Магадану). mi pad·ye·deem k (ma·ga·da·nu)

How long do we stop here?
Сколько времени поезд skol'·ka vrye·mee·nee po·eest
стоит на этой станции? sta·eet na e·tay stant·see

Is this seat available?
Это место занято? e·ta mye·sta za·nee·ta

That's my seat.
Это моё место. e·ta ma·yo mye·sta

I'd like a taxi … Мне нужно такси … mnye nuzh·na tak·see …
  at (9am) в (девять часов утра) v (dye·veet' chee·sof u·tra)
  now сейчас see·chas
  tomorrow завтра zaf·tra

Is this taxi available?
Свободен? sva·bo·deen

How much is it to …?
Сколько стоит доехать до …? skol'·ka sto·eet da·ye·khat' da …

Please put the meter on.
Включите счётчик, пожалуйста! fklyu·cheet·ye shot·cheek pa·zhal·sta

Please take me to (this address).
До (этого адреса) не довезёте? da (e·ta·va a·dree·sa) nye da·veez·yot·ye

Please … …, пожалуйста! … pa·zhal·sta
  slow down Не так быстро nee tak bi·stra
  stop here Остановитесь здесь a·sta·na·veet·yes' zdyes'
  wait here Подождите здесь pa·dazh·deet·ye zdyes'

car, motorbike & bicycle hire

I'd like to hire a …	Я бы хотел/хотела	ya bi khat-yel/khat-ye-la
	взять … на прокат. m/f	vzyat' … na pra-kat
bicycle	велосипед	vee-la-seep-yet
car	машину	ma-shi-nu
motorbike	мотоцикл	ma-tat-sikl

with …	с …	s …
a driver	шофёром	shaf-yo-ram
air conditioning	кондиционером	kan-deet-si-an-ye-ram
antifreeze	антифриз	an-tee-freez
snow chains	снеговые цепи	snye-go-vi-ye tse-pee

How much for … hire?	Сколько стоит …прокат?	skol'-ka sto-eet … pra-kat
hourly	часовой	cha-sa-voy
daily	однодневный	ad-nad-nyev-ni
weekly	недельный	need-yel'-ni

air	воздух m	voz-dukh
oil	масло n	mas-la
petrol	бензин m	been-zeen
tyre	шина f	shi-na

I need a mechanic.
Мне нужен автомеханик. mnye nu-zhin af-ta-mee-kha-neek

I've run out of petrol.
У меня кончился бензин. u meen-ya kon-cheel-sa been-zeen

I have a flat tyre.
У меня лопнула шина. u meen-ya lop-nu-la shi-na

directions

Where's the …?	Где (здесь) …?	gdye (zdyes') …
bank	банк	bank
city centre	центр города	tsentr go-ra-da
hotel	гостиница	ga-stee-neet-sa
market	рынок	ri-nak
police station	полицейский участок	pa-leet-sey-skee u-cha-stak
post office	почта	poch-ta
public toilet	общественный туалет	ap-shest-vee-ni tu-al-yet

Is this the road to (Kursk)?
Эта дорога ведёт в (Курск)? — *e*·ta da·*ro*·ga veed·*yot* f (kursk)

Can you show me (on the map)?
Покажите мне, — pa·ka·*zhi*·tye mnye
пожалуйста (на карте). — pa·*zhal*·sta (na *kart*·ye)

What's the address?
Какой адрес? — ka·*koy a*·drees

Is it nearby/far away?
Близко/Далеко? — *blees*·ka/da·lee·*ko*

How do I get there?
Как туда попасть? — kak tu·*da* pa·*past'*

Turn …	Поверните …	pa·veer·*neet*·ye …
at the corner	за угол	*za*·u·gal
at the traffic lights	на светофоре	na svee·ta·*for*·ye
left/right	налево/направо	nal·*ye*·va/na·*pra*·va

It's …		
behind …	За …	za …
far away	Далеко.	da·lee·*ko*
here	Здесь.	zdyes'
in front of …	Перед …	*pye*·reet …
left	Налево.	nal·*ye*·va
near …	Около …	*o*·ka·la …
next to …	Рядом с …	*rya*·dam s …
on the corner	На углу.	na u·*glu*
opposite …	Напротив …	na·*pro*·teef …
straight ahead	Прямо.	*prya*·ma
right	Направо.	na·*pra*·va
there	Там.	tam

by bus	автобусом	af·*to*·bu·sam
by taxi	на такси	na tak·*see*
by train	электричкой	e·leek·*treech*·key
on foot	пешком	peesh·*kom*

north	север	*sye*·veer
south	юг	yuk
east	восток	va·*stok*
west	запад	*za*·pat

ВЪЕЗД/ВЫЕЗД	vyest/vi·yest	**Entrance/Exit**
ОТКРЫТО/ЗАКРЫТО	at·kri·ta/za·kri·ta	**Open/Closed**
СВОБОДНЫЕ МЕСТА	sva·bod·ni·ye mee·sta	**Rooms Available**
МЕСТ НЕТ	myest nyet	**No Vacancies**
ИНФОРМАЦИЯ	een·far·mat·si·ya	**Information**
ОТДЕЛЕНИЕ МИЛИЦИИ	a·deel·ye·nee·ye mee·leet·si	**Police Station**
ЗАПРЕЩЕНО	za·pree·shee·no	**Prohibited**
ТУАЛЕТ	tu·a·yet	**Toilets**
МУЖСКОЙ (М)	mush·skoy	**Men**
ЖЕНСКИЙ (Ж)	zhen·ski	**Women**
ГОРЯЧИЙ/ХОЛОДНЫЙ	ga·rya·chi/kha·lod·ni	**Hot/Cold**

accommodation

finding accommodation

Where's a ...?	Где ...?	gdye ...
camping ground	кемпинг	kyem·peeng
guesthouse	пансионат	pan·see·a·nat
hotel	гостиница	ga·stee·neet·sa
youth hostel	общежитие	ap·shee·zhi·tee·ye
Can you	Вы можете	vi mo·zhit·ye
recommend	порекомендовать	pa·ree·ka·meen·da·vat'
somewhere ...?	что-нибудь ...?	shto·nee·bud' ...
cheap	дешёвое	dee·sho·va·ye
good	хорошее	kha·ro·she·ye
luxurious	роскошное	ras·kosh·na·ye
nearby	близко отсюда	blees·ka at·syu·da

I'd like to book a room, please.
Я бы хотел/хотела
забронировать номер. m/f
ya bi khat·yel/khat·ye·la
za·bra·nee·ra·vat' no·meer

I have a reservation.
Я заказал/заказала номер. m/f
ya za·ka·zal/za·ka·za·la no·meer

My surname is ...
Моя фамилия ...
ma·ya fa·mee·lee·ya ...

Do you have a ... room?	У вас есть ...?	u vas yest' ...
single	одноместный номер	ad·nam·yes·ni no·meer
double	номер с двуспальней кроватью	no·meer z dvu·spaln·yey kra·vat·yu
twin	двухместный номер	dvukh·myes·ni no·meer

How much is it per/for ...?	Сколько стоит за ...?	skol'·ka sto·eet za ...
night	ночь	noch'
two people	двоих	dva·eekh

Can I pay ...?	Можно расплатиться ...?	mozh·na ras·pla·teet'·sa ...
by credit card	кредитной карточкой	kree·deet·nay kar·tach·kay
with a travellers cheque	дорожным чеком	da·rozh·nim che·kam

For (three) nights.
(Трое) суток. — (tro·ye) su·tak

From (5 July) to (8 July).
С (пятого июля) по (восьмое июля). — s (pya·ta·va ee·yul·ya) pa (vas'·mo·ye ee·yul·ya)

Can I see it?
Можно посмотреть? — mozh·na pas·mat·ryet'

Am I allowed to camp here?
Можно устроить стоянку здесь? — mozh·na u·stro·eet' sta·yan·ku zdyes'

Where can I find a camp site?
Где кемпинг? — gdye kyem·peenk

requests & queries

When/Where is breakfast served?
Когда/Где завтрак? — kag·da/gdye zaf·trak

Please wake me at (seven).
Позвоните мне, пожалуйста, в (семь) часов. — paz·va·neet·ye mnye pa·zhal·sta v (syem') chee·sof

Could I have my key, please?

Дайте, пожалуйста ключ *dayt*-ye pa-*zhal*-sta klyuch

от моего номера. at ma-*yee*-*vo* *no*-mee-ra

Can I get another (blanket)?

Дайте, пожалуйста ещё (одеяло). *dayt*-ye pa-*zhal*-sta yee-*sho* (a-dee-*ya*-la)

Is there an elevator/a safe?

У вас есть лифт/сейф? u vas yest' leeft/syeyf

The room is too ...	В комнате очень ...	f *kom*-nat-ye *o*-cheen' ...
cold	холодно	*kho*-lad-na
noisy	шумно	*shum*-na
small	тесно	*tyes*-na

The ... doesn't work.	... не работает.	... nye ra-*bo*-ta-yeet
air conditioner	Кондиционер	kan-deet-si-an-*yer*
heater	Отопление	a-tap-*lye*-nee-ye
toilet	Туалет	tu-al-*yet*

This ... isn't clean.	Эта ... грязная.	*e*-ta ... *gryaz*-na-ya
pillow	подушка	pa-*dush*-ka
sheet	простыня	pra-stin-*ya*

This towel isn't clean. Это полотенце грязное. *e*-ta pa-lat-*yent*-se *gryaz*-no-ye

checking out

What time is checkout?

Когда нужно освободить номер? kag-*da nuzh*-na as-va-ba-*deet' no*-meer

Can I leave my bags here?

Здесь можно оставлять багаж? zdyes' *mozh*-na a-stav-*lyat'* ba-*gash*

Could I have my ..., please?	Дайте, пожалуйста ...	*dayt*-ye pa-*zhal*-sta ...
deposit	мой аванс	moy a-*vans*
passport	мой паспорт	moy *pas*-part
valuables	мои ценности	ma-*ee tse*-nas-tee

communications & banking

the internet

Where's the local Internet café?
Где здесь интернет-кафе? · gdye zdyes' een·ter·net·ka·fe

How much is it per hour?
Сколько стоит час? · skol'·ka sto·eet chas

I'd like to ...	Я бы хотел/ хотела ... m/f	ya bi khat·yel/ khat·ye·la ...
check my email	проверить свой и-мэйл	prav·ye·reet' svoy ee·meyl
get Internet access	подключиться к интернету	pat·klyu·cheet'·sa k een·ter·ne·tu
use a printer	воспользоваться принтером	vas·pol'·za·vat'·sa een·ter·ne·tam
use a scanner	воспользоваться сканером	vas·pol'·za·vat'·sa skan·ye·ram

mobile/cell phone

I'd like a ...	Я бы хотел/ хотела ... m/f	ya bi khat·yel/ khat·ye·la ...
mobile/cell phone for hire	взять мобильный телефон напрокат	vzyat' ma·beel'·ni tee·lee·fon nap·ra·kat
SIM card for your network	СИМ-карту для вашей сети	seem·kar·tu dlya va·shey se·tee

What are the rates?
Какие тарифы? · ka·kee·ye ta·ree·fi

telephone

What's your phone number?
Можно ваш номер телефона? · mozh·na vash no·meer tee·lee·fo·na

The number is ...
Телефон ... · tee·lee·fon ...

Where's the nearest public phone?
Где ближайший телефон-автомат? · gdye blee·zhey·shee tee·lee·fon·af·ta·mat

I want to ...	Я бы хотел/	ya bi khat·yel/
	хотела ... m/f	khat·ye·la ...
call (Singapore)	позвонить	paz·va·neet'
	(в Сингапур)	(v seen·ga·por)
make a local call	сделать местный	sdye·lat' myest·ni
	звонок	zva·nok
reverse the charges	позвонить с оплатой	paz·va·neet's a·pla·tey
	вызываемого	vi·zi·va·yee·ma·va

How much does each minute cost?

| Сколько стоит минута? | skol'·ka sto·eet mee·nu·ta |

(Five) roubles per (30) seconds.

| (Пять) рублей за (тридцать) секунд. | (pyat') rub·lyey za (treet·sat') see·kunt |

I'd like to buy a phonecard.

| Я бы хотел/хотела купить | ya bi khat·yel/khat·ye·la ku·peet' |
| телефонную карточку. m/f | tee·lee·fo·nu·yu kar·tach·ku |

post office

I want to send a ...	Я хочу послать ...	ya kha·chu pas·lat' ...
fax	факс	faks
letter	письмо	pees'·mo
parcel	посылку	pa·sil·ku
postcard	открытку	at·krit·ku

I want to buy ...	Я хочу купить ...	yak ha·chu ku·peet' ...
an envelope	конверт	kan·vyert
a stamp	марку	mar·ku

Please send it	Пошлите, пожалуйста,	pash·leet·ye pa·zhal·sta
(to Australia) by ...	... в (Австралию).	... v (af·stra·lee·yu)
airmail	авиа почтой	a·vee·a poch·tay
express mail	экспресс почтой	eeks·pres poch·tay
registered mail	заказной почтой	za·kaz·noy poch·tay
surface mail	обычной почтой	a·bich·nay poch·tay

| Is there any mail for me? | Есть почта для меня? | yest' poch·ta dlya meen·ya |

bank

Where's a/an ...?	Где ...?	gdye ...
ATM	банкомат	ban·ka·*mat*
foreign exchange office	обмен валюты	ab·*myen* val·*yu*·ti
Where can I ...?	Где можно ...?	gdye *mozh*·na ...
I'd like to ...	Я бы хотел/	ya bi khat·*yel*/
	хотела ... m/f	khat·ye·la ...
arrange a transfer	сделать денежный перевод	*sdye*·lat' *dye*·neezh·ni pee·ree·*vod*
cash a cheque	обменять чек	ab·meen·*yat'* chek
change a travellers cheque	обменять дорожный чек	ab·meen·*yat'* da·*rozh*·ni chek
change money	поменять деньги	pa·meen·*yat'* *dyen'*·gee
get a cash advance	снять деньги по кредитной карточке	snyat' *dyen'*·gee pa kree·*deet*·ney *kar*·tach·kye
withdraw money	снять деньги	snyat' *dyen'*·gee

What's the charge for that?
Сколько нужно заплатить?   *skol'*·ka *nuzh*·na za·pla·*teet'*

What's the exchange rate?
Какой курс?   ka·*koy* kurs

It's (12) roubles.
Это будет (двенадцать) рублей.   *e*·ta *bu*·deet (dvee·*nat*·sat') rub·*lyey*

It's free.
Это будет бесплатно.   *e*·ta *bu*·deet bees·*plat*·na

What time does the bank open?
Когда открывается банк?   kag·*da* at·kri·*va*·yeet·sa bank

Has my money arrived yet?
Мои деньги уже пришли?   moy *dyen'*·gee u·*zhe* preesh·*lee*

sightseeing

getting in

What time does it open/close?
Когда открывается/
закрывается?
kag-da at-kri-va-yeet-sa/
za-kri-va-yeet-sa

What's the admission charge?
Сколько стоит входной билет?
skol'-ka sto-eet fkhad-noy beel-yet

Is there a discount for students/children?
Есть скидка для студентов/детей?
yest' skeet-ka dlya stud-yen-taf/deet-yey

I'd like a …	Я бы хотел/ хотела … m/f	*ya bi khat-yel/ khat-ye-la …*
catalogue	каталог	*ka-ta-lok*
guide	гида	*gee-da*
local map	карту города	*kar-tu go-ra-da*

I'd like to see …	Я бы хотел/хотела посетить … m/f	*ya bi khat-yel/khat-ye-la pa-see-teet' …*
What's that?	Что это?	*shto e-ta*
Can I take a photo?	Можно сфотографировать?	*mozh-na sfa-ta-gra-fee-ra-vat'*

tours

When's the next tour?
Когда следующая экскурсия?
kag-da slye-du-yu-sha-ya eks-kur-see-ya

How long is the tour?
Как долго продолжается
экскурсия?
kag dol-ga pra-dal-zha-yeet-sa
eks-kur-see-ya

What time should we be back?
Когда мы возвращаемся?
kag-da mi vaz-vra-sha-yeem-sa

Is … included?	Цена включает …?	*tse-na fklyu-cha-yeet …*
accommodation	помещение	*pa-mee-she-nee-ye*
the admission charge	входной билет	*fkhad-noy beel-yet*
food	обед	*ab-yet*
transport	транспорт	*tran-spart*

sightseeing

castle	замок m	za·mak
cathedral	собор m	sa·bor
church	церковь f	tser·kaf'
main square	главная площадь f	glav·na·ya plo·shat'
monastery	монастырь m	ma·na·stir
monument	памятник m	pam·yeet·neek
museum	музей m	muz·yey
old city	старый город m	sta·ri go·rat
palace	дворец m	dvar·yets
ruins	развалины f pl	raz·va·lee·ni
stadium	стадион m	sta·dee·on
statue	статуя f	sta·tu·ya

shopping

enquiries

Where's a ...?	Где ...?	gdye ...
bank	банк	bank
bookshop	книжный магазин	kneezh·ni ma·ga·zeen
camera shop	фотографический магазин	fo·to·gra·fee·chee·skee ma·ga·zeen
department store	универмаг	u·nee·veer·mak
grocery store	гастроном	gast·ra·nom
market	рынок	ri·nak
newsagency	газетный киоск	gaz·yet·ni kee·osk
supermarket	универсам	u·nee·veer·sam

Where can I buy ...?
Где можно купить ...?　　　　gdye mozh·na ku·peet' ...

Can I look at it?
Покажите, пожалуйста.　　　　pa·ka·zhit·ye pa·zhal·sta

Do you have any others?
У вас есть другие?　　　　u vas yest' dru·gee·ye

Does it have a guarantee?
Есть гарантия?　　　　yest' ga·ran·tee·ya

Can I have it sent overseas?
Вы можете переслать
это за границу?
vi *mo*·zhit·ye pee·rees·*lat'*
e·ta za gra·*neet*·su

Can you repair this?
Вы можете это починить?
vi *mo*·zhit·ye e·ta pa·chee·*neet'*

It's faulty.
Это браковано.
e·ta z bra·*ko*·va·na

I'd like ...
Я бы хотел/
хотела ... m/f
ya bi khat·*yel*/
khat·*ye*·la ...

a bag	пакет	pak·*yet*
a refund	получить	pa·lu·*cheet'*
	обратно деньги	ab·*rat*·na *dyen'*·gee
to return this	это возвратить	e·ta vaz·vra·*teet'*

paying

How much is it?
Сколько стоит?
skol'·ka *sto*·eet

Can you write down the price?
Запишите, пожалуйста, цену.
za·pee·*shit*·ye pa·*zhal*·sta *tse*·nu

That's too expensive.
Это очень дорого.
e·ta *o*·cheen' *do*·ra·ga

Can you lower the price?
Вы можете снизить цену?
vi *mo*·zhit·ye *snee*·zeet' *tse*·nu

I'll give you (100) roubles.
Я вам дам (сто) рублей.
ya vam dam (sto) rub·*lyey*

There's a mistake in the bill.
Меня обсчитали.
meen·*ya* ap·shee·*ta*·lee

Do you accept ...?
Вы принимаете
оплату ...?
vi pri·ni·*ma*·it·ye
a·*pla*·tu ...

credit cards	кредитной карточкой	kri·*dit*·ney *kar*·tach·key
debit cards	дебитной карточкой	*dye*·bit·ney *kar*·tach·key
travellers cheques	дорожным чеком	da·*rozh*·nihm *che*·kam

I'd like ...
Я бы хотел/
хотела ... m/f
ya bi khat·*yel*/
khat·*ye*·la ...

a receipt	квитанцию	kvee·*tant*·si·yu
my change	сдачу	*zda*·chu

clothes & shoes

Can I try it on?	Можно это примерить?	mozh·na e·ta preem·ye·reet'
My size is (40).	Мой размер (сорок).	moy raz·myer (so·rak)
It doesn't fit.	Это не подходит.	e·ta nye pat·kho·deet
small	маленький	ma·leen'·kee
medium	средний	sryed·nee
large	большой	bal'·shoy

books & music

I'd like a …	Я бы хотел/	ya bi khat·yel/
	хотела … m/f	khat·ye·la …
newspaper	газету	gaz·ye·tu
(in English)	(на английском)	(na an·glee·skam)
pen	ручку	ruch·ku

Is there an English-language bookshop?
Есть магазин английской книги?   yest' ma·ga·zeen an·glee·skey knee·gee

Can I listen to this?
Можно послушать?   mozh·na pas·lu·shat'

photography

Can you …?	Вы можете …?	vi mo·zhit·ye …
develop this film	проявить эту плёнку	pra·yee·veet' e·tu plyon·ku
load this film	вложить эту плёнку	vla·zhit' e·tu plyon·ku
transfer photos	перебросить	pee·ree·bro·seet'
from my camera	снимки с камеры	sneem·kee s kam·ye·ri
to CD	на компакт-диск	na kam·pakt·deesk
I need a … film	Мне нужна … плёнка	mnye nuzh·na … plyon·ka
for this camera.	на эту камеру.	na e·tu kam·ye·ru
B&W	чёрно-белая	chor·nab·ye·la·ya
colour	цветная	tsvet·na·ya
slide	слайд-овая	slaid·a·va·ya
(high) speed	(высоко-)	(vi·sa·ko·)
	чувствительная	chus·vee·teel'·na·ya

When will it be ready? Когда она будет готова?   kag·da a·na bu·deet ga·to·va

meeting people

greetings, goodbyes & introductions

Hello.	Здравствуйте.	*zdrast*·vuyt·ye
Hi.	Привет.	preev·*yet*
Goodbye/Bye.	До свидания/Пока.	da svee·*dan*·ya/pa·*ka*
See you later.	До скорой встречи.	da *sko*·rey fstrye·chee
Mr	господин	ga·spa·*deen*
Mrs/Miss	госпожа	ga·spa·*zha*
How are you?	Как дела?	kag dyee·*la*
Fine, thanks.	Спасибо, хорошо.	spa·*see*·ba kha·ra·*sho*
And you?	А у вас?	a u vas
What's your name?	Как вас зовут?	kak vaz za·*vut*
My name is ...	Меня зовут ...	meen·*ya* za·*vut* ...
I'm pleased to meet you.	Очень приятно.	*o*·cheen' pree·*yat*·na

This is my ...	Это ...	*e*·ta ...
boyfriend	мой парень	moy *pa*·reen
brother	мой брат	moy brat
daughter	моя дочка	ma·*ya doch*·ka
father	мой отец	moy at·*yets*
friend	мой друг m	moy druk
	моя подруга f	ma·ya pa·*dru*·ga
girlfriend	моя девушка	ma·*ya dye*·vush·ka
husband	мой муж	moy mush
mother	моя мать	ma·*ya* mat'
partner	мой парень m	moy *pa*·reen
(intimate)	моя девушка f	ma·*ya dye*·vush·ka
sister	моя сестра	ma·*ya* seest·*ra*
son	мой сын	moy sin
wife	моя жена	ma·*ya* zhi·*na*

Here's my ...	Вот мой ...	vot moy ...
What's your ...?	Можно ваш ...?	*mozh*·na vash ...
address	адрес	*a*·drees
email address	и-мейл	ee·*meyl*
fax number	номер факса	*no*·meer *fak*·sa
phone number	номер телефона	*no*·meer tee·lee·*fo*·na

occupations

What's your occupation?	Кем вы работаете?	kyem vi ra·bo·ta·yeet·ye
I'm a/an ...	Я ...	ya ...
artist	художник m	khu·dozh·neek
	художница f	khu·dozh·neet·sa
businessperson	бизнесмен	beez·nees·myen
farmer	фермер	fyer·meer
office worker	служащий m	slu·zha·shee
	служащая f	slu·zha·shee·ya
scientist	учёный/учёная m/f	u·cho·ni/u·cho·na·ya
student	студент m	stud·yent
	студентка f	stud·yent·ka
tradesperson	ремесленник	reem·yes·lee·neek

background

Where are you from?	Вы откуда?	vi at·ku·da
I'm from ...	Я из ...	ya eez ...
Australia	Австралии	af·stra·lee·ee
Canada	Канады	ka·na·di
England	Англии	an·glee·ee
New Zealand	Новой Зеландии	no·voy zee·lan·dee·ee
the USA	США	se·sha·a
Are you married?	Вы женаты? m	vi zhi·na·ti
	Вы замужем? f	vi za·mu·zhim
I'm married.	Я женат/замужем. m/f	ya zhi·nat/za·mu·zhim
I'm single.	Я холост/холоста. m/f	ya kho·last/kha·la·sta

age

How old ...?	Сколько ... лет?	skol'·ka ... lyet
are you	вам	vam
is your daughter	вашей дочке	va·shey doch·kye
is your son	вашему сыну	va·shi·mu si·nu
I'm ... years old.	Мне ... лет.	mnye ... lyet
He/She is ... years old.	Ему/Ей ... лет.	ye·mu/yey ... lyet

feelings

I'm (not) ...	Я (не) ...	ya (nye) ...
cold	замёрз m	zam-yors
	замёрзла f	zam-yorz-la
happy	счастлив m	shas-leef
	счастлива f	shas-lee-va
hot	умираю от жары	u-mee-ra-yu ad zha-ri
hungry	голоден m	go-la-deen
	голодна f	ga-lad-na
sad	грущу	gru-shu
thirsty	хочу пить	kha-chu peet'
What about you?	А вы?	a vih

entertainment

going out

Where can I find ...?	Где находятся ...?	gdye na-kho-deet-sa ...
clubs	клубы	klu-bi
gay venues	гей-клубы	gyey-klu-bi
pubs	пивные	peev-ni-ye
I feel like	Мне хочется	mnye kho-cheet-sa
going to a/the ...	пойти ...	pey-tee ...
concert	на концерт	na kant-sert
movies	в кино	v kee-no
party	на тусовку	na tu-sof-ku
restaurant	в ресторан	v ree-sta-ran
theatre	в театр	f tee-atr

interests

Do you like ...?	Вам нравится ...?	vam nra-veet-sa ...
I (don't) like ...	Мне (не) нравится ...	mnye (nye) nra-veet-sa ...
art	искусство	ees-kust-va
cooking	готовить	ga-to-veet'
movies	кино	kee-no
reading	читать	chee-tat'
sport	спорт	sport
travelling	путешествовать	pu-tee-shest-va-vat'

Do you like to ...?	Вы ...?	vi ...
dance	танцуете	tant-su-eet-ye
go to concerts	ходите на	kho-deet-ye na
	концерты	kant-ser-ti
listen to music	слушаете музыку	slu-sha-yeet-ye mu-zi-ku

food & drink

finding a place to eat

Can you	Вы можете	vi mo-zhit-ye
recommend a ...?	порекомендовать ...?	pa-ree-ka-meen-da-vat' ...
bar	бар	bar
café	кафе	ka-fe
restaurant	ресторан	ree-sta-ran

I'd like ...,	Я бы хотел/	ya bi khat-yel/
please.	хотела ... m/f	khat-ye-la ...
a table for (three)	столик на (троих)	sto-leek na (tra-eekh)
the nonsmoking	некурящий	nye-kur-yash-chee
section		
the smoking section	курящий	kur-yash-chee

ordering food

breakfast	завтрак m	zaf-trak
lunch	обед m	ab-yet
dinner	ужин m	u-zhin
snack	закуска f	za-kus-ka

What would you	Что вы	shto vi
recommend?	рекомендуете?	ree-ka-meen-du-eet-ye

I'd like (the) ...,	Я бы хотел/	ya bi khat-yel/
please.	хотела ... m/f	khat-ye-la ...
bill	счёт	shot
drink list	карту вин	kar-tu veen
menu	меню	meen-yu
that dish	это блюдо	e-ta blyu-da

drinks

cup of coffee/tea ...	чашка кофе/чаю ...	*chash*·ka *kof*·ye/*cha*·yu ...
with milk	с молоком	s ma·la·*kom*
without sugar	без сахару	byez *sa*·kha·ru
... water	... вода	... va·*da*
boiled	кипячёная	kee·pee·*cho*·na·ya
(sparkling) mineral	(шипучая)	(shi·*pu*·cha·ya)
	минеральная	mee·nee·*ral'*·na·ya
(orange) juice	(апельсиновый) сок m	(a·*peel'*·*see*·na·vi) sok
soft drink	безалкогольный	bye·zal·ka·*gol'*·ni
	напиток m	na·*pee*·tak

in the bar

I'll have ...	..., пожалуйста.	... pa·*zhal*·sta
I'll buy you a drink.	Я угощаю.	ya u·ga·*sha*·yu
What would you like?	Что вы хотите?	shto vi kha·*tee*·tye
Cheers!	Пей до дна!	pyey da dna
champagne	шампанское n	sham·*pan*·ska·ye
cocktail	коктейль m	kak·*teyl*
vodka	водка f	*vot*·ka
whisky	виски m	*vees*·kee
a ... of beer	... пива	... *pee*·va
bottle	бутылка	bu·*til*·ka
glass	стакан	sta·*kan*
a bottle/glass	бутылка/рюмка	bu·*til*·ka/*ryum*·ka
of ... wine	... вина	... vee·*na*
red	красного	*kras*·na·va
sparkling	шипучего	shi·*pu*·chee·va
white	белого	*bye*·la·va

self-catering

What's the local speciality?
Что типично местное?
shto tee-*peech*-na *myes*-na-ye

What's that?
Что это?
shto e-ta

How much (is a kilo of cheese)?
Сколько стоит (кило сыра)?
skol'-ka *sto*-eet (kee-*lo si*-ra)

I'd like ...	Дайте ...	*deyt*-ye ...
(200) grams	(двести) грамм	(*dvye*-stee) gram
(two) kilos	(два) кило	(dva) kee-*lo*
(three) pieces	(три) куска	(tree) kus-*ka*
(six) slices	(шесть) ломтика	(shest') *lom*-tee-ka

Less.	Меньше.	*myen'*-shi
Enough.	Достаточно.	da-*sta*-tach-na
More.	Немного.	neem-*no*-ga

special diets & allergies

Is there a vegetarian restaurant nearby?
Здесь есть вегетарианский
ресторан?
zdyes' yest' vee-gee-ta-ree-*an*-skee
ree-sta-*ran*

Do you have vegetarian food?
У вас есть овощные блюда?
u vas yest' a-vashch-*ni*-ye *blyu*-da

Could you prepare a meal without ...?	Вы могли бы приготовить блюдо без ...?	vi ma-*glee* bi pree-ga-*to*-veet' *blu*-da byez ...
butter	масла	*mas*-la
eggs	яиц	*ya*-eets
meat stock	мясного бульона	myas-*no*-va bu-*lo*-na

I'm allergic to ...	У меня аллергия на ...	u meen-*ya* a-leer-*gee*-ya na ...
dairy produce	молочные продукты	ma-*loch*-ni-ye pra-*duk*-ti
gluten	клейковину	klyey-ka-*vee*-nu
MSG	МНГ	em-en-*ge*
nuts	орехи	ar-*ye*-khee
seafood	морепродукты	mor-ye-pra-*duk*-ti

emergencies

basics

Help!	Помогите!	pa·ma·*gee*·tye
Stop!	Прекратите!	pree·kra·*tee*·tye
Go away!	Идите отсюда!	ee·*deet*·ye at·*syu*·da
Thief!	Вор!	vor
Fire!	Пожар!	pa·*zhar*
Watch out!	Осторожно!	a·sta·*rozh*·na

Call ...!	Вызовите ...!	*vi*·za·*veet*·ye ...
a doctor	врача	vra·*cha*
an ambulance	скорую помощь	*sko*·ru·yu *po*·mash'
the police	милицию	*vi*·za·*veet*·ye mee·*leet*·si·yu

It's an emergency.
Это срочно! — *e*·ta *sroch*·na

Could you help me, please?
Помогите, пожалуйста! — pa·ma·*geet*·ye pa·*zhal*·sta

Can I use your phone?
Можно воспользоваться телефоном? — *mozh*·na vas·*pol'*·za·vat'·sa tee·lee·*fo*·nam

Where are the toilets?
Где здесь туалет? — gdye zdyes' tu·al·*yet*

I'm lost.
Я потерялся/потерялась. m/f — ya pa·teer·*yal*·sa/pa·teer·*ya*·las'

police

Where's the police station?
Где милицейский участок? — gdye mee·leet·*sey*·skee u·*cha*·stak

I want to report an offence.
Я хочу заявить в милицию. — ya kha·*chu* za·ya·*veet'* v mee·*leet*·si·yu

I have insurance.
У меня есть страховка. — u meen·*ya* yest' stra·*khof*·ka

I've been ...	Меня ...	meen·*ya* ...
assaulted	побили	pa·*bee*·lee
raped	изнасиловали	eez·na·*see*·la·va·lee
robbed	ограбили	a·*gra*·bee·lee

I've lost my ...	Я потерял/	ya pa·teer·yal/
	потеряла ... m/f	pa·teer·ya·la ...
My ... was/were stolen.	У меня украли ...	u meen·ya u·kra·lee ...
backpack	рюкзак	ryug·zak
bags	багаж	ba·gash
credit card	кредитную	kree·deet·nu·yu
	карточку	kar·tach·ku
handbag	сумку	sum·ku
jewellery	драгоценности	dra·gat·se·na·stee
money	деньги	dyen'·gee
passport	паспорт	pas·part
travellers cheques	дорожные	da·rozh·ni·ye
	чеки	che·kee
wallet	бумажник	bu·mazh·neek
I want to contact	Я хочу обратиться	ya kha·chu a·bra·teet'·sa
my ...	в своё ...	f sva·yo ...
consulate	консульство	kan·sulst·vo
embassy	посольство	pa·solst·va

health

medical needs

Where's the nearest ...?	Где здесь ...?	gdye zdyes' ...
dentist	зубной врач	zub·noy vrach
doctor	врач	vrach
hospital	больница	bal'·neet·sa
(night) pharmacist	(ночная) аптека	(nach·na·ya) ap·tye·ka

I need a doctor (who speaks English).

Мне нужен врач,
(говорящий на
английском языке).

mnye nu·zhin vrach
(ga·var·ya·shee na
an·glee·skam ya·zik·ye)

Could I see a female doctor?

Можно записаться на
приём к женщине-врачу?

mozh·na za·pee·sat'·sa na
pree·yom k zhen·sheen·ye·vra·chu

I've run out of my medication.

У меня кончилось лекарство.

u meen·ya kon·chee·las' lee·karst·va

symptoms, conditions & allergies

I'm sick.	Я болею.	ya bal·*ye*·yu
It hurts here.	Здесь болит.	zdyes' ba·*leet*
I have (a) ...	У меня ...	u meen·*ya* ...
asthma	астма f	*ast*·ma
bronchitis	бронхит m	bran·*kheet*
constipation	запор m	za·*por*
cough	кашель m	*ka*·shel'
diarrhoea	понос m	pa·*nos*
fever	температура f	teem·pee·ra·*tu*·ra
headache	головная боль f	ga·lav·*na*·ya bol'
heart condition	болезнь сердца f	bal·*yezn' syerd*·tsa
nausea	тошнота f	tash·na·*ta*
pain	боль f	bol'
sore throat	болит горло n	ba·*leet gor*·la
toothache	зубная боль f	zub·*na*·ya bol
I'm allergic to ...	У меня аллергия на...	u meen·*ya* a·leer·*gee*·ya na ...
antibiotics	антибиотики	an·tee·bee·*o*·tee·kee
anti-	противо-	pra·tee·va·
inflammatories	воспалительные	va·spa·*lee*·teel'·ni·ye
	препараты	pree·pa·*ra*·ti
aspirin	аспирин	a·spee·*reen*
bees	пчелиный укус	pchee·*lee*·ni *u*·kus
codeine	кодеин	kad·ye·*een*
penicillin	пеницилин	pee·neet·*si*·leen
antiseptic	антисептик m	an·tees·*yep*·teek
bandage	бинт m	beent
condoms	презерватив m	pree·zeer·va·*teef*
contraceptives	противозачаточные	pra·tee·va·za·*cha*·tach·ni·ye
	средства n pl	*sryets*·tva
diarrhoea medicine	лекарство от поноса n	li·*karst*·va at pa·*no*·sa
insect repellent	средство от насекомых n	*sryets*·tva at na·see·*ko*·mikh
laxative	слабительное n	sla·*bee*·teel'·na·ye
painkillers	болеутоляющие n pl	bo·lee·u·tal·*ya*·yu·shee·ye
rehydration salts	нюхательная	*nyu*·kha·teel'·na·ya
	соль f	sol'
sleeping tablets	снотворные	snat·*vor*·ni·ye
	таблетки f pl	tab·*lyet*·kee

english–russian dictionary

Russian nouns in this dictionary have their gender indicated by ⓜ masculine, ⓕ feminine or ⓝ neuter. If it's a plural noun you'll also see pl. Adjectives are given in the masculine form only. Words are also marked as a (adjective), v (verb), sg (singular), pl (plural), inf (informal) or pol (polite) where necessary.

A

accident авария ⓕ *a-va-ree-ya*
accommodation помещение ⓝ *pa-mee-she-ee-ye*
adaptor адаптер ⓜ *a-dap-teer*
address адрес ⓜ *a-drees*
after после *pos-lye*
air conditioning кондиционирование ⓝ *kan-deet-si-a-nee-ra-va-nee-ye*
airplane самолёт ⓜ *sa-mal-yot*
airport аэропорт ⓜ *a-e-ra-port*
alcohol алкоголь ⓜ *al-ka-gol'*
all все *fsye*
allergy аллергия ⓕ *al-yer-gee-ya*
ambulance скорая помощь ⓕ *sko-ra-ya po-mash*
and и *ee*
ankle лодыжка ⓕ *la-dish-ka*
arm рука ⓕ *ru-ka*
ashtray пепельница ⓕ *pye-peel'-neet-sa*
ATM банкомат ⓜ *ban-ka-mat*

B

baby ребёнок ⓜ *reeb-yo-nak*
back (body) спина ⓕ *spee-na*
backpack рюкзак ⓜ *ryug-zak*
bad плохой *pla-khoy*
bag мешок ⓜ *mee-shok*
baggage claim выдача багажа ⓕ *vi-da-cha ba-ga-zha*
bank банк ⓜ *bank*
bar бар ⓜ *bar*
bathroom ванная ⓕ *va-na-ya*
battery батарея ⓕ *ba-tar-ye-ya*
beautiful красивый *kra-see-vi*
bed кровать ⓕ *kra-vat'*
beer пиво ⓝ *pee-va*
before до *do*
behind за *za*
bicycle велосипед ⓜ *vee-la-seep-yet*
big большой *bal'-shoy*
bill счёт ⓜ *shot*
black чёрный *chor-ni*
blanket одеяло ⓝ *a-dee-ya-la*
blood group группа крови ⓕ *gru-pa kro-vee*

blue (dark) синий *see-nee*
blue (light) голубой *ga-lu-boy*
boat лодка ⓕ *lot-ka*
book (make a reservation) v заказать *za-ka-zat'*
bottle бутылка ⓕ *bu-til-ka*
bottle opener (beer) открывалка ⓕ *at-kri-val-ka*
bottle opener (wine) штопор ⓜ *shto-par*
boy мальчик ⓜ *mal'-cheek*
brakes (car) тормоза ⓜ pl *tar-ma-za*
breakfast завтрак ⓜ *zaf-trak*
broken (faulty) ошибочный *a-shi-bach-ni*
bus автобус ⓜ *af-to-bus*
business бизнес ⓜ *beez-nees*
buy купить *ku-peet'*

C

café кафе ⓝ *ka-fe*
camera фотоаппарат ⓜ *fo-to-a-pa-rat*
camp site кемпинг ⓜ *kyem-peenk*
cancel отменить *at-mee-neet'*
can opener открывашка ⓕ *at-kri-vash-ka*
car машина ⓕ *ma-shi-na*
cash наличные ⓝ pl *na-leech-ni-ye*
cash (a cheque) v обменять *ab-meen-yat'*
cell phone мобильный телефон ⓜ *ma-beel'-ni tee-lee-fon*
centre центр ⓜ *tsentr*
change (money) v обменять *ab-meen-yat'*
cheap дешёвый *dee-sho-vi*
check (bill) счёт ⓜ *shot*
check-in регистрация ⓕ *ree-geest-rat-si-ya*
chest грудная клетка ⓕ *grud-na-ya klyet-ka*
child ребёнок ⓜ *reeb-yo-nak*
cigarette сигарета ⓕ *see-gar-ye-ta*
city город ⓜ *go-rat*
clean a чистый *chee-sti*
closed закрытый *za-kri-ti*
coffee кофе ⓜ *kof-ye*
coins монеты ⓕ pl *man-ye-ti*
cold a холодный *kha-lod-ni*
collect call звонок по коллекту ⓜ *zva-nok pa kal-yek-tu*
come прийти *pree-tee*
computer компьютер ⓜ *kam-pyu-teer*

DICTIONARY

condom презерватив ⓜ *pree-zeer-va-teef*
contact lenses контактные линзы ① pl
  kan-takt-ni-ye leen-zi
cook v готовить *ga-to-veet'*
cost цена ① *tse-na*
credit card кредитная карточка ①
  kri-deet-na-ya kar-tach-ka
cup чашка ① *chash-ka*
currency exchange обмен валюты ⓜ
  ab-myen val-yu-ti
customs (immigration) таможня ① *ta-mozh-nya*

D

dangerous опасный *a-pas-ni*
date (time) число ① *chees-lo*
day день ⓜ *dyen'*
delay задержка ① *zad-yersh-ka*
dentist зубной врач ⓜ *zub-noy vrach*
depart отправиться *at-pra-veet'-sa*
diaper подгузник ⓜ *pad-guz-neek*
dictionary словарь ⓜ *sla-var'*
dinner ужин ⓜ *u-zhin*
direct прямой *pree-moy*
dirty грязный *gryaz-ni*
disabled инвалид ⓜ *een-va-leet*
discount скидка ① *skeet-ka*
doctor врач ⓜ *vrach*
double bed двуспальная кровать ①
  dvu-spal'-na-ya kra-vat'
double room номер на двоих ⓜ *no-meer na*
  dva-eekh
drink напиток ⓜ *na-pee-tak*
drive v водить машину *va-deet' ma-shi-nu*
drivers licence водительские права ① pl
  va-dee-teel'-skee-ye pra-va
drugs (illicit) наркотики ① pl *nar-ko-tee-kee*
dummy (pacifier) соска ① *sos-ka*

E

ear ухо ⓝ *u-kha*
east восток ⓜ *va-stok*
eat есть *yest'*
economy class пассажирский класс ⓜ
  pa-sa-zhir-skee klas
electricity электричество ⓝ *e-leek-tree-cheest-va*
elevator лифт ⓜ *leeft*
email и-мейл ⓜ *ee-meyl*
embassy посольство ⓝ *pa-solst-va*
emergency авария ① *a-va-ree-ya*
English (language) английский *an-glee-skee*
entrance вход ⓜ *fkhot*

evening вечер ⓜ *vye-cheer*
exchange rate обменный курс ⓜ *ab-mye-ni kurs*
exit выход ⓜ *vi-khat*
expensive дорогой *da-ra-goy*
express mail экспресс почта ① *eks-pres poch-ta*
eyes глаза ① pl *gla-za*

F

far далеко *da-lee-ko*
fast быстрый *bist-ri*
father отец ⓜ *at-yets*
film (camera) плёнка ① *plyon-ka*
finger палец ⓜ *pa-leets*
first-aid kit санитарная сумка ①
  sa-nee-tar-na-ya sum-ka
first class в первом классе f *pyer-vam klas-ye*
fish рыба ① *ri-ba*
food еда ① *yee-da*
foot нога ① *na-ga*
fork вилка ① *veel-ka*
free (of charge) бесплатный *bees-plat-ni*
friend друг/подруга ⓜ/① *druk/pa-dru-ga*
fruit фрукты ① pl *fruk-ti*
full полный *pol-ni*
funny смешной *smeesh-noy*

G

gift подарок ⓜ *pa-da-rak*
girl (teenage) девушка ① *dye-vush-ka*
girl (pre-teen) девочка ① *dye-vach-ka*
glass (drinking) стакан ⓜ *sta-kan*
glasses очки ① pl *ach-kee*
go (on foot) идти *ee-tee*
go (by vehicle) ехать *ye-khat'*
good хороший *kha-ro-shi*
green зелёный *zeel-yo-ni*
guide гид ⓜ *geet*

H

half половина ① *pa-la-vee-na*
hand рука ① *ru-ka*
handbag сумочка ① *su-mach-ka*
happy счастливый *shees-lee-vi*
have y ... есть y ... *yest'*
he он *on*
head голова ① *ga-la-va*
heart сердце ⓝ *syerd-tsi*
heat жара ① *zha-ra*
heavy тяжёлый *tya-zho-li*
help v помочь *pa-moch'*

I

here здесь zdyes'
high высокий vi-so-kee
highway шоссе ⓝ sha-se
hike v ходить пешком kha-deet' peesh-kom
holiday каникулы ⓕ pl ka-nee-ku-li
homosexual гомосексуалист ⓜ
  go-mo-seek-su-a-leest
hospital больница ⓕ bol'-neet-sa
hot жаркий zhar-kee
hotel гостиница ⓕ ga-stee-neet-sa
hungry голоден go-la-deen
husband муж ⓜ mush

I

I я ya
identification (card) идентификационная карта ⓕ
  eed-yen-tee-fee-kat-si-o-na-ya kar-ta
ill болен bo-leen
important важный vazh-ni
included включая fklyu-cha-ya
injury травма ⓕ trav-ma
insurance страхование ⓝ stra-kha-va-nee-ye
Internet интернет ⓜ een-ter-net
interpreter переводчик ⓜ pee-ree-vot-cheek

J

jewellery ювелирные изделия ⓝ pl
  yu-vi-leer-ni-ye eez-dye-lee-ya
job работа ⓕ ra-bo-ta

K

key ключ ⓜ klyuch
kilogram килограмм ⓜ kee-la-gram
kitchen кухня ⓕ kukh-nya
knife нож ⓜ nosh

L

laundry (place) прачечная ⓕ pra-cheech-na-ya
lawyer адвокат ⓜ ad-va-kat
left (direction) левый lye-vi
left-luggage office камера хранения ⓕ
  ka-mee-ra khran-ye-nee-ya
leg нога ⓕ na-ga
lesbian лесбианка ⓕ lees-bee-an-ka
less меньше myen'-she
letter (mail) письмо ⓝ pees'-mo
lift (elevator) лифт ⓜ leeft
light свет ⓜ svyet

like v любить lyu-beet'
lock замок ⓜ za-mok
long длинный dlee-ni
lost пропавший pra-paf-shi
lost-property office бюро находок ⓝ
  byu-ro na-kho-dak
love v любить lyu-beet'
luggage багаж ⓜ ba-gash
lunch обед ⓜ ab-yet

M

mail почта ⓕ poch-ta
man мужчина ⓜ mush-chee-na
map карта ⓕ kar-ta
market рынок ⓜ ri-nak
matches спички ⓕ pl speech-kee
meat мясо ⓝ mya-sa
medicine лекарство ⓝ lee-karst-va
menu меню ⓝ meen-yu
message записка ⓕ za-pees-ka
milk молоко ⓝ ma-la-ko
minute минута ⓕ mee-nu-ta
mobile phone мобильный телефон ⓜ
  ma-beel'-ni tee-lee-fon
money деньги ⓕ pl dyen'-gee
month месяц ⓜ mye-seets
morning утро ⓝ u-tra
mother мать ⓕ mat'
motorcycle мотоцикл ⓜ ma-tat-sikl
motorway шоссе ⓝ sha-se
mouth рот ⓜ rot
music музыка ⓕ mu-zi-ka

N

name (personal) имя ⓝ eem-ya
name (of object) название ⓝ na-zva-nee-ye
napkin салфетка ⓕ salf-yet-ka
nappy подгузник ⓜ pad-guz-neek
near близко blees-ka
neck шея ⓕ she-ya
new новый no-vi
news новости ⓕ pl no-va-stee
newspaper газета ⓕ gaz-ye-ta
night ночь ⓕ noch'
no нет nyet
noisy шумный shum-ni
nonsmoking некурящий nee-kur-ya-shee
north север ⓜ sye-veer
nose нос ⓜ nos
now сейчас see-chas
number номер ⓜ no-meer

O

oil (engine) масло ⑩ *mas*-la
old старый *sta*-ri ⑩
one-way ticket билет в один конец ⑩
  beel-*yet* v a-*deen* kan-*yets*
open a открытый at-*kri*-ti
outside снаружи sna-*ru*-zhi

P

package посылка ① pa-*sil*-ka
paper бумага ① bu-*ma*-ga
park (a car) v поставить (машину)
  pa-*sta*-veet' (ma-*shi*-nu)
passport паспорт ⑩ *pas*-part
pay заплатить za-pla-*teet'*
pen ручка ① *ruch*-ka
petrol бензин ⑩ been-*zeen*
pharmacy аптека ① apt-*ye*-ka
phonecard телефонная карточка ①
  tee-lee-*fo*-na-ya *kar*-tach-ka
photo снимок ⑩ *snee*-mak
plate тарелка ① tar-*yel*-ka
police милиция ① mee-*leet*-si-ya
postcard открытка ① at-*krit*-ka
post office почта ① *poch*-ta
pregnant беременная beer-*ye*-mee-na-ya
price цена ① tse-*na*

Q

quiet тихий *ti*-khee

R

rain дождь ⑩ dozht'
razor бритва ① *breet*-va
receipt квитанция ① kvee-*tan*-tsi-ya
red красный *kras*-ni
refund возвращение денег ⑩
  vaz-vra-*she*-nee-ye *dye*-neek
registered mail заказной ① za-kaz-*noy*
rent v арендовать a-reen-da-*vat'*
repair v починить pa-chee-*neet'*
reservation заказ ⑩ za-*kas*
restaurant ресторан ⑩ rees-ta-*ran*
return v вернуться veer-*nut'*-sa
return ticket обратный билет ⑩ a-*brat*-ni beel-*yet*
right (direction) правый *pra*-vi
road дорога ① da-*ro*-ga
room (hotel) номер ⑩ *no*-meer
room (house) комната ① *kom*-na-ta
Russia Россия ⑩ ra-*see*-ya

S

Russian (language) русский ⑩ *rus*-kee
Russian a русский/русская ⑩/① *rus*-kee/*rus*-ka-ya

safe a безопасный beez-a-*pas*-ni
sanitary napkin гигиеническая салфетка ①
  gee-gee-ee-*nee*-chee-ska-ya salf-*yet*-ka
seat место ⑩ *myes*-ta
send послать pas-*lat'*
service station заправочная станция ①
  za-*pra*-vach-na-ya *stant*-si-ya
sex секс ⑩ syeks
shampoo шампунь ⑩ sham-*pun'*
share (a dorm) жить в одной комнате
  zhit' v ad-*noy* kom-nat-ye
shaving cream крем для бритья ⑩
  kryem dlya breet-*ya*
she она a-*na*
sheet (bed) простыня ① pra-stin-*ya*
shirt рубашка ① ru-*bash*-ka
shoes туфли ① pl *tuf*-lee
shop магазин ⑩ ma-ga-*zeen*
short короткий ka-*rot*-kee
shower душ ⑩ dush
single room одноместный номер ⑩
  ad-na-*mes*-ni *no*-meer
skin кожа ① *ko*-zha
skirt юбка ① *yup*-ka
sleep v спать spat'
slowly медленно *myed*-lee-na
small маленький *ma*-leen'-kee
smoke (cigarettes) v курить ku-*reet'*
soap мыло ⑩ *mi*-la
some несколько *nye*-skal'-ka
soon скоро *sko*-ra
south юг ⑩ yuk
souvenir shop сувенирный магазин ⑩
  su-vee-*neer*-ni ma-ga-*zeen*
speak говорить ga-va-*reet'*
spoon ложка ① *losh*-ka
stamp марка ① *mar*-ka
stand-by ticket стенд-бай билет ⑩
  styend-*bai* beel-*yet*
station (train) станция ① *stant*-see-ya
stomach желудок ⑩ zhi-*lu*-dak
stop v перестать pee-ree-*stat'*
stop (bus) остановка ① a-sta-*nof*-ka
street улица ① *u*-lee-tsa
student студент/студентка ⑩/①
  stud-*yent*/stud-*yent*-ka
sun солнце ⑩ *solnt*-se
sunscreen солнцезащитный крем ⑩
  sont-se-za-*sheet*-ni kryem
swim v плавать *pla*-vat'

T

tampons тампон ⓜ tam-*pon*
taxi такси ⓜ tak-*see*
teaspoon чайная ложка ⓕ *chey*-na-ya *losh*-ka
teeth зубы ⓜ pl *zu*-bi
telephone телефон ⓜ tee-lee-*fon*
television телевизор ⓜ tee-lee-*vee*-zar
temperature (weather) температура ⓕ teem-pee-ra-*tu*-ra
tent палатка ⓕ pa-*lat*-ka
that (one) то to
they они a-*nee*
thirsty (be) хочется пить *kho*-cheet-sa peet'
this (one) это *e*-ta
throat горло ⓝ *gor*-la
ticket билет ⓜ beel-*yet*
time время ⓝ *vryem*-ya
tired устал u-*stal*
tissues салфетки ⓕ pl salf-*yet*-kee
today сегодня see-*vod*-nya
toilet туалет ⓜ tu-al-*yet*
tomorrow завтра *zaf*-tra
tonight сегодня вечером see-*vod*-nya *vye*-chee-ram
toothbrush зубная щётка ⓕ zub-*na*-ya *shot*-ka
toothpaste зубная паста ⓕ zub-*na*-ya *pa*-sta
torch (flashlight) фонарик ⓜ fa-*na*-reek
tour экскурсия ⓕ eks-*kur*-see-ya
tourist office туристическое бюро ⓝ tu-rees-*tee*-chee-ska-ye byu-*ro*
towel полотенце ⓝ pa-lat-*yent*-se
train поезд ⓜ *po*-eest
translate перевести pee-ree-vee-*stee*
travel agency бюро путешествий ⓝ byu-*ro* pu-tee-*shest*-vee
travellers cheque дорожный чек ⓜ da-*rozh*-ni chek
trousers брюки ⓜ pl *bryu*-kee
twin beds две односпальные кровати dvye ad-na-*spal*-ni-ye kra-*va*-tee
tyre шина ⓕ *shi*-na

U

underwear бельё ⓝ beel-*yo*
urgent срочный *sroch*-ni

V

vacant свободный sva-*bod*-ni
vacation каникулы ⓕ pl ka-*nee*-ku-li
vegetable овощ ⓜ *o*-vash
vegetarian вегетарианец/вегетарианка ⓜ/ⓕ vee-gee-ta-ree-*a*-neets/vee-gee-ta-ree-*an*-ka
visa виза ⓕ *vee*-za

W

waiter официант/официантка ⓜ/ⓕ a-feet-si-*ant*/a-feet-si-*ant*-ka
walk v гулять gul-*yat'*
wallet кошелёк ⓜ ka-she-*lyok*
warm a тёплый *typo*-li
wash (something) выстирать *vi*-stee-rat'
watch часы ⓜ pl chee-*si*
water вода ⓕ *va*-da
we мы mi
weekend выходные ⓜ pl vi-khad-*ni*-ye
west запад ⓜ *za*-pat
wheelchair инвалидная коляска ⓕ een-va-*leed*-na-ya kal-*yas*-ka
when когда kag-*da*
where где gdye
white белый *bye*-li
who кто kto
why почему pa-chee-*mu*
wife жена ⓕ *zhi*-na
window окно ⓝ *ak*-no
wine вино ⓝ vee-*no*
with с s
without без byez
woman женщина ⓕ *zhen*-shee-na
write написать na-pee-*sat'*

Y

yellow жёлтый *zhol*-ti
yes да da
yesterday вчера fchee-*ra*
you sg inf ты ti
you sg pol & pl вы vi

Spanish

spanish alphabet

A a a	*B b* be	*C c* the	*Ch ch* che	*D d* de
E e e	*F f* e·fe	*G g* khe	*H h* a·che	*I i* ee
J j kho·ta	*K k* ka	*L l* e·le	*LL ll* e·lye	*M m* e·me
N n e·ne	*Ñ ñ* e·nye	*O o* o	*P p* pe	*Q q* koo
R r e·re	*S s* e·se	*T t* te	*U u* oo	*V v* oo·ve
W w oo·ve do·vle	*X x* e·kees	*Y y* ee·grye·ga	*Z z* the·ta	

spanish

ESPAÑOL

introduction

The lively and picturesque language of Cervantes' *Don Quijote* and Almodóvar's movies, Spanish (*español* es·pa·nyol), or Castilian (*castellano* kas·te·lya·no), as it's also called in Spain, has over 390 million speakers worldwide. Outside Spain, it's the language of most of Latin America and the West Indies and is also spoken in the Philippines and Guam, in some areas of the African coast and in the US.

Spanish belongs to the Romance group of languages – the descendents of Latin – together with French, Italian, Portuguese and Romanian. It's derived from Vulgar Latin, which Roman soldiers and merchants brought to the Iberian Peninsula during the period of Roman conquest (3rd to 1st century BC). By 19 BC Spain had become totally Romanised and Latin became the language of the peninsula in the four centuries that followed. Thanks to the Arabic invasion in AD 711 and the Arabs' continuing presence in Spain during the next eight centuries, Spanish has also been strongly influenced by Arabic, although mostly in the vocabulary. Today's Castilian is spoken in the north, centre and south of Spain. Completing the colourful linguistic profile of the country, Basque (*euskera* e·oos·ke·ra), Catalan (*catalán* ka·ta·lan) and Galician (*gallego* ga·lye·go) are also official languages in Spain, though Castilian covers by far the largest territory.

Besides the shared vocabulary of Latin origin that English and Spanish have in common, there's also a large corpus of words from the indigenous American languages that have entered English via Spanish. After Columbus' discovery of the New World in 1492, America's indigenous languages had a considerable impact on Spanish, especially in words to do with flora, fauna and topography (such as *tobacco*, *chocolate*, *coyote*, *canyon*, to name only a few).

Even if you're not familiar with the sound of Spanish through, say, the voices of José Carreras or Julio Iglesias, you'll be easily seduced by this melodic language and have fun trying to roll your rr's like the locals. You may have heard the popular legend about one of the Spanish kings having a slight speech impediment which prompted all of Spain to mimic his lisp. Unfortunately, this charming explanation of the lisping 's' is only a myth – it's actually due to the way Spanish evolved from Latin and has nothing to do with lisping monarchs at all. So, when you hear someone say *gracias* gra·thyas, they're no more lisping than when you say 'thank you' in English.

pronunciation

vowel sounds

Vowels are pronounced short and fairly closed. The sound remains level, and each vowel is pronounced as an individual unit. There are, however, a number of cases where two vowel sounds become very closely combined (so-called diphthongs).

symbol	english equivalent	spanish example	transliteration
a	run	*agua*	*a*·gwa
ai	aisle	*bailar*	bai·*lar*
ay	say	*seis*	says
e	bet	*número*	noo·me·ro
ee	see	*día*	dee·a
o	pot	*ojo*	o·kho
oo	zoo	*gusto*	goo·sto
ow	how	*autobús*	ow·to·*boos*
oy	toy	*hoy*	oy

word stress

Spanish words have stress, which means you emphasise one syllable of a word over another. Here's a rule of thumb: when a written word ends in *n*, *s* or a vowel, the stress falls on the second-last syllable. Otherwise, the final syllable is stressed. If you see an accent mark over a syllable, it cancels out this rule and you just stress that syllable instead. You needn't worry about this though, as the stressed syllables are always italicised in our pronunciation guides .

consonant sounds

Remember that in Spanish the letter *h* is never pronounced. The Spanish *v* sounds more like a *b*, said with the lips pressed together. When ending a word, *d* is pronounced soft, like a th, or it's so slight it doesn't get pronounced at all. Finally, try to roll your *r*'s, especially at the start of a word and in words with *rr*.

symbol	english equivalent	spanish example	transliteration
b	bed	*barco*	*bar*·ko
ch	cheat	*chica*	*chee*·ka
d	dog	*dinero*	dee·*ne*·ro
f	fat	*fiesta*	*fye*·sta
g	go	*gato*	*ga*·to
k	kit	*cabeza*, *queso*	ka·*be*·tha, *ke*·so
kh	loch (harsh and guttural)	*jardín*, *gente*	khar·*deen*, *khen*·te
l	lot	*lago*	*la*·go
ly	million	*llamada*	lya·*ma*·da
m	man	*mañana*	ma·*nya*·na
n	not	*nuevo*	*nwe*·vo
ny	canyon	*señora*	se·*nyo*·ra
p	pet	*padre*	*pa*·dre
r	like 'tt' in 'butter' said fast	*hora*	*o*·ra
rr	run (but stronger and rolled)	*ritmo*, *burro*	*rreet*·mo, *boo*·rro
s	sun	*semana*	se·*ma*·na
t	top	*tienda*	*tyen*·da
th	thin	*Barcelona*, *manzana*	bar·the·*lo*·na, man·*tha*·na
v	soft 'b', between 'v' and 'b'	*abrir*	a·*vreer*
w	win	*guardia*	*gwar*·dya
y	yes	*viaje*	*vya*·khe

tools

language difficulties

Do you speak English?
¿Habla inglés? — *ab*·la een·*gles*

Do you understand?
¿Me entiende? — me en·*tyen*·de

I (don't) understand.
(No) Entiendo. — (no) een·*tyen*·do

What does (*cuenta*) mean?
¿Qué significa (cuenta)? — ke seeg·nee·*fee*·ka (*kwen*·ta)

How do you ...? — *¿Cómo se ...?* — *ko*·mo se ...
  pronounce this — *pronuncia esta* — pro·*noon*·thya *es*·ta
  word — *palabra* — pa·*lab*·ra
  write (*ciudad*) — *escribe (ciudad)* — es·*kree*·be (thee·oo·*da*)

Could you — *¿Puede ...,* — *pwe*·de ...
please ...? — *por favor?* — por fa·*vor*
  repeat that — *repetir* — rre·pe·*teer*
  speak more slowly — *hablar más despacio* — ab·*lar* mas des·*pa*·thyo
  write it down — *escribirlo* — es·kree·*beer*·lo

essentials

Yes.	*Sí.*	see
No.	*No.*	no
Please.	*Por favor.*	por fa·*vor*
Thank you (very much).	*(Muchas) Gracias.*	(*moo*·chas) *gra*·thyas
You're welcome.	*De nada.*	de *na*·da
Excuse me.	*Perdón/Discúlpeme.*	per·*don*/dees·*kool*·pe·me
Sorry.	*Lo siento.*	lo *syen*·to

numbers

0	cero	the·ro	16	dieciséis	dye·thee·seys
1	uno	oo·no	17	diecisiete	dye·thee·sye·te
2	dos	dos	18	dieciocho	dye·thee·o·cho
3	tres	tres	19	diecinueve	dye·thee·nwe·ve
4	cuatro	kwa·tro	20	veinte	veyn·te
5	cinco	theen·ko	21	veintiuno	veyn·tee·oo·no
6	seis	seys	22	veintidós	veyn·tee·dos
7	siete	sye·te	30	treinta	treyn·ta
8	ocho	o·cho	40	cuarenta	kwa·ren·ta
9	nueve	nwe·ve	50	cincuenta	theen·kwen·ta
10	diez	dyeth	60	sesenta	se·sen·ta
11	once	on·the	70	setenta	se·ten·ta
12	doce	do·the	80	ochenta	o·chen·ta
13	trece	tre·the	90	noventa	no·ven·ta
14	catorce	ka·tor·the	100	cien	thyen
15	quince	keen·the	1000	mil	mil

time & dates

What time is it?	¿Qué hora es?	ke o·ra es
It's one o'clock.	Es la una.	es la oo·na
It's (10) o'clock.	Son (las diez).	son (las dyeth)
Quarter past (one).	Es (la una) y cuarto.	es (la oo·na) ee kwar·to
Half past (one).	Es (la una) y media.	es (la oo·na) ee me·dya
Quarter to (one).	Es (la una) menos cuarto.	es (la oo·na) me·nos kwar·to
At what time ...?	¿A qué hora ...?	a ke o·ra ...
At ...	A las ...	a las ...
am	de la mañana	de la ma·nya·na
pm	de la tarde	de la tar·de
Monday	lunes	loo·nes
Tuesday	martes	mar·tes
Wednesday	miércoles	myer·ko·les
Thursday	jueves	khwe·ves
Friday	viernes	vyer·nes
Saturday	sábado	sa·ba·do
Sunday	domingo	do·meen·go

January	*enero*	e-*ne*-ro
February	*febrero*	fe-*bre*-ro
March	*marzo*	*mar*-tho
April	*abril*	a-*breel*
May	*mayo*	*ma*-yo
June	*junio*	*khoo*-nyo
July	*julio*	*khoo*-lyo
August	*agosto*	a-*gos*-to
September	*septiembre*	sep-*tyem*-bre
October	*octubre*	ok-*too*-bre
November	*noviembre*	no-*vyem*-bre
December	*diciembre*	dee-*thyem*-bre

What date is it today?
　¿Qué día es hoy?　　　　　　　　ke *dee*-a es oy

It's (18 October).
　Es (el dieciocho de octubre).　　es (el dye-thee-*o*-cho de ok-*too*-bre)

| **since (May)** | *desde (mayo)* | *des*-de (*ma*-yo) |
| **until (June)** | *hasta (junio)* | *as*-ta (*khoo*-nyo) |

last ...		
night	*anoche*	a-*no*-che
week	*la semana pasada*	la se-*ma*-na pa-*sa*-da
month	*el mes pasado*	el mes pa-*sa*-do
year	*el año pasado*	el *a*-nyo pa-*sa*-do

next ...	*... que viene*	*... ke *vye*-ne
week	*la semana*	la se-*ma*-na
month	*el mes*	el mes
year	*el año*	el *a*-nyo

yesterday/tomorrow ...	*ayer/mañana por la ...*	a-*yer*/ma-*nya*-na por la ...
morning	*mañana*	ma-*nya*-na
afternoon	*tarde*	*tar*-de
evening	*noche*	*no*-che

weather

What's the weather like?	*¿Qué tiempo hace?*	ke *tyem*·po *a*·the

It's ...		
cloudy	*Está nublado.*	es·*ta* noo·*bla*·do
cold	*Hace frío.*	*a*·the *free*·o
hot	*Hace calor.*	*a*·the ka·*lor*
raining	*Está lloviendo.*	es·*ta* lyo·*vyen*·do
snowing	*Está nevando.*	es·*ta* ne·*van*·do
sunny	*Hace sol.*	*a*·the sol
warm	*Hace calor.*	*a*·the ka·*lor*
windy	*Hace viento.*	*a*·the *vyen*·to

spring	*primavera* f	pree·ma·*ve*·ra
summer	*verano* m	ve·*ra*·no
autumn	*otoño* m	o·*to*·nyo
winter	*invierno* m	een·*vyer*·no

border crossing

I'm here ...	*Estoy aquí ...*	es·*toy* a·*kee* ...
in transit	*en tránsito*	en *tran*·see·to
on business	*de negocios*	de ne·*go*·thyos
on holiday	*de vacaciones*	de va·ka·*thyo*·nes

I'm here for ...	*Estoy aquí por ...*	es·*toy* a·*kee* por ...
(10) days	*(diez) días*	(dyeth) *dee*·as
(three) weeks	*(tres) semanas*	(tres) se·*ma*·nas
(two) months	*(dos) meses*	(dos) *me*·ses

I'm going to (Salamanca).
Voy a (Salamanca). voy a (sa·la·*man*·ka)

I'm staying at the (Flores Hotel).
Me estoy alojando en (hotel Flores). me es·*toy* a·lo·*khan*·do en (o·*tel* flo·res)

I have nothing to declare.
No tengo nada que declarar. no *ten*·go *na*·da ke dek·la·*rar*

I have something to declare.
Quisiera declarar algo. kee·*sye*·ra dek·la·*rar* *al*·go

That's (not) mine.
Eso (no) es mío. eso (no) es *mee*·o

transport

tickets & luggage

Where can I buy a ticket?
¿Dónde puedo comprar un billete?   don·de pwe·do kom·prar oon bee·lye·te

Do I need to book a seat?
¿Tengo que reservar?   ten·go ke rre·ser·var

One ... ticket to	*Un billete ... a*	oon bee·lye·te ... a
(Barcelona), please.	*(Barcelona), por favor.*	(bar·the·lo·na) por fa·vor
one-way	*sencillo*	sen·thee·lyo a
return	*de ida y vuelta*	de ee·da ee vwel·ta

I'd like to ...	*Me gustaría ...*	me goos·ta·ree·a ...
my ticket.	*mi billete.*	mee bee·lye·te
cancel	*cancelar*	kan·the·lar
change	*cambiar*	kam·byar
confirm	*confirmar*	kon·feer·mar

I'd like a ... seat.	*Quisiera un asiento ...*	kee·sye·ra oon a·syen·to ...
nonsmoking	*de no fumadores*	de no foo·ma·do·res
smoking	*de fumadores*	de foo·ma·do·res

How much is it?
¿Cuánto cuesta?   kwan·to kwes·ta

Is there air conditioning?
¿Hay aire acondicionado?   ai ai·re a·kon·dee·thyo·na·do

Is there a toilet?
¿Hay servicios?   ai ser·vee·thyos

How long does the trip take?
¿Cuánto se tarda?   kwan·to se tar·da

Is it a direct route?
¿Es un viaje directo?   es oon vya·khe dee·rek·to

I'd like a luggage locker.
Quisiera un casillero de consigna.   kee·sye·ra oon ka·see·lye·ro de kon·seeg·na

My luggage	Mis maletas	mees ma·*le*·tas
has been ...	han sido ...	an *see*·do ...
damaged	dañadas	da·*nya*·das
lost	perdidas	per·*dee*·das
stolen	robadas	rro·*ba*·das

getting around

Where does flight (G10) arrive/depart?
¿Dónde llega/sale el vuelo (G10)?   don·de *lye*·ga/*sa*·le el *vwe*·lo (khe dyeth)

Where's the ...?	¿Dónde está...?	don·de es·*ta* ...
arrivals hall	el hall de partidas	el hol de par·*tee*·das
departures hall	el hall de llegadas	el hol de lye·*ga*·das
duty-free shop	la tienda libre de	la *tyen*·da *lee*·bre de
	impuestos	eem·*pwe*·stos
gate (12)	la puerta (doce)	la *pwer*·ta (*do*·the)

Is this the ...	¿Es el ... para	es el ... *pa*·ra
to (Valencia)?	(Valencia)?	(va·*len*·thya)
boat	barco	*bar*·ko
bus	autobús	ow·to·*boos*
plane	avión	a·*vyon*
train	tren	tren

What time's	¿A qué hora es el	a ke *o*·ra es el
the ... bus?	... autobús?	... ow·to·*boos*
first	primer	pree·*mer*
last	último	*ool*·tee·mo
next	próximo	*prok*·see·mo

At what time does it arrive/leave?
¿A qué hora llega/sale?   a ke *o*·ra *lye*·ga/*sa*·le

How long will it be delayed?
¿Cuánto tiempo se retrasará?   *kwan*·to *tyem*·po se rre·tra·sa·*ra*

What station/stop is this?
¿Cuál es esta estación/parada?   kwal es *es*·ta es·ta·*thyon*/pa·*ra*·da

What's the next station/stop?
¿Cuál es la próxima   kwal es la *prok*·see·ma
estación/parada?   es·ta·*thyon*/pa·*ra*·da

Does it stop at (Aranjuez)?
¿Para en (Aranjuez)?   pa·ra en (a·ran·khweth)

Please tell me when we get to (Seville).
¿Puede avisarme   pwe·de a·vee·sar·me
cuando lleguemos a (Sevilla)?   kwan·do lye·ge·mos a (se·vee·lya)

How long do we stop here?
¿Cuánto tiempo vamos a parar aquí?   kwan·to tyem·po va·mos a pa·rar a·kee

Is this seat available?
¿Está libre este asiento?   es·ta lee·bre es·te a·syen·to

That's my seat.
Ése es mi asiento.   e·se es mee a·syen·to

I'd like a taxi ...	*Quisiera un taxi ...*	kee·sye·ra oon tak·see ...
at (9am)	*a (las nueve*	a (las nwe·ve
	de la mañana)	de la ma·nya·na)
now	*ahora*	a·o·ra
tomorrow	*mañana*	ma·nya·na

Is this taxi available?
¿Está libre este taxi?   es·ta lee·bre es·te tak·see

How much is it to ...?
¿Cuánto cuesta ir a ...?   kwan·to kwes·ta eer a ...

Please put the meter on.
Por favor, ponga el taxímetro.   por fa·vor pon·ga el tak·see·me·tro

Please take me to (this address).
Por favor, lléveme a (esta dirección).   por fa·vor lye·ve·me a (es·ta dee·rek·thyon)

Please ...	*Por favor ...*	por fa·vor ...
slow down	*vaya más despacio*	va·ya mas des·pa·thyo
stop here	*pare aquí*	pa·re a·kee
wait here	*espere aquí*	es·pe·re a·kee

car, motorbike & bicycle hire

I'd like to hire a ...	*Quisiera alquilar ...*	kee·sye·ra al·kee·lar ...
bicycle	*una bicicleta*	oo·na bee·thee·kle·ta
car	*un coche*	oon ko·che
motorbike	*una moto*	oo·na mo·to

with ...	con ...	kon ...
a driver	chófer	cho·fer
air conditioning	aire acondicionado	ai·re a·kon·dee·thyo·na·do
antifreeze	anticongelante	an·tee·kon·khe·lan·te
snow chains	cadenas de nieve	ka·de·nas de nye·ve

How much for	¿Cuánto cuesta	kwan·to kwes·ta
... hire?	el alquiler por ...?	el al·kee·ler por ...
hourly	hora	o·ra
daily	día	dee·a
weekly	semana	se·ma·na

air	aire m	ai·re
oil	aceite m	a·they·te
petrol	gasolina f	ga·so·lee·na
tyres	neumáticos f pl	ne·oo·ma·tee·kos

I need a mechanic.
Necesito un mecánico.   ne·the·see·to oon me·ka·nee·ko

I've run out of petrol.
Me he quedado sin gasolina.   me e ke·da·do seen ga·so·lee·na

I have a flat tyre.
Tengo un pinchazo.   ten·go oon peen·cha·tho

directions

Where's the ...?	¿Dónde está/	don·de es·ta/
	están ...? sg/pl	es·tan ...
bank	el banco sg	el ban·ko
city centre	el centro de la ciudad sg	el then·tro de la theew·da
hotel	el hotel sg	el o·tel
market	el mercado sg	el mer·ka·do
police station	la comisaría sg	la ko·mee·sa·ree·a
post office	el correos sg	el ko·rre·os
public toilet	los servicios pl	los ser·vee·thyos
tourist office	la oficina de	la o·fee·thee·na de
	turismo sg	too·rees·mo

Is this the road to (Valladolid)?
¿Se va a (Valladolid) por esta carretera?
se va a (va·lya·do·lee) por es·ta ka·rre·te·ra

Can you show me (on the map)?
¿Me lo puede indicar (en el mapa)?
me lo pwe·de een·dee·kar (en el ma·pa)

What's the address?
¿Cuál es la dirección?
kwal es la dee·rek·thyon

How far is it?
¿A cuánta distancia está?
a kwan·ta dees·tan·thya es·ta

How do I get there?
¿Cómo se llega ahí?
ko·mo se lye·ga a·ee

Turn ...	*Doble ...*	do·ble ...
at the corner	*en la esquina*	en la es·kee·na
at the traffic lights	*en el semáforo*	en el se·ma·fo·ro
left	*a la izquierda*	a la eeth·kyer·da
right	*a la iderecha*	a la de·re·cha

It's ...	*Está ...*	es·ta ...
behind ...	*detrás de ...*	de·tras de ...
far away	*lejos*	le·khos
here	*aquí*	a·kee
in front of ...	*enfrente de ...*	en·fren·te de ...
left	*por la izquierda*	por la eeth·kyer·da
near (to ...)	*cerca (de ...)*	ther·ka (de ...)
next to ...	*al lado de ...*	al la·do de ...
opposite ...	*frente a ...*	fren·te a ...
right	*por la derecha*	por la de·re·cha
straight ahead	*todo recto*	to·do rrek·to
there	*ahí*	a·ee

by bus	*por autobús*	por ow·to·boos
by taxi	*por taxi*	por tak·see
by train	*por tren*	por tren
on foot	*a pie*	a pye

north	*norte* m	nor·te
south	*sur* m	soor
east	*este* m	es·te
west	*oeste* m	o·es·te

signs

Acceso/Salida	ak·*the*·so/sa·*lee*·da	Entrance/Exit
Abierto/Cerrado	a·*byer*·to/the·*rra*·do	Open/Closed
Hay Lugar	ai loo·*gar*	Rooms Available
No Hay Lugar	no ai loo·*gar*	No Vacancies
Información	een·for·ma·*thyon*	Information
Comisaría	ko·mee·sa·*ree*·a	Police Station
de Policía	de po·lee·*thee*·a	
Prohibido	pro·ee·*bee*·do	Prohibited
Servicios	ser·*vee*·thyos	Toilets
Caballeros	ka·ba·*lye*·ros	Men
Señoras	se·*nyo*·ras	Women
Caliente/Frío	ka·*lyen*·te/*free*·o	Hot/Cold

accommodation

finding accommodation

Where's a ...?	¿Dónde hay ...?	*don*·de ai ...
camping ground	*un terreno de cámping*	oon te·*rre*·no de *kam*·peeng
guesthouse	*una pensión*	*oo*·na pen·*syon*
hotel	*un hotel*	oon o·*tel*
youth hostel	*un albergue juvenil*	oon al·*ber*·ge khoo·ve·*neel*

Can you recommend	¿Puede recomendar	*pwe*·de rre·ko·men·*dar*
somewhere ...?	*algún sitio ...?*	al·*goon* see·tio ...
cheap	*barato*	ba·*ra*·to
good	*bueno*	*bwe*·no
nearby	*cercano*	ther·*ka*·no

I'd like to book a room, please.
Quisiera reservar una habitación.   kee·*sye*·ra rre·ser·var *oo*·na a·bee·ta·*thyon*

I have a reservation.
He hecho una reserva.   e *e*·cho *oo*·na rre·*ser*·va

My name's ...
Me llamo ...   me *lya*·mo ...

Do you have a ... room?	**¿Tiene una habitación ...?**	tye·ne oo·na a·bee·ta·thyon ...
single	individual	een·dee·vee·dwal
double	doble	do·ble
twin	con dos camas	kon dos ka·mas

How much is it per ...?	**¿Cuánto cuesta por ...?**	kwan·to kwes·ta por ...
night	noche	no·che
person	persona	per·so·na

Can I pay by ...?	**¿Puedo pagar con ...?**	pwe·do pa·gar con ...
credit card	tarjeta de crédito	tar·khe·ta de kre·dee·to
travellers cheque	cheque de viajero	che·ke de vya·khe·ro

I'd like to stay for (three) nights/weeks.
Quisiera quedarme por (tres)
noches/semanas.
kee·sye·ra ke·dar·me por (tres)
no·ches/se·ma·nas

From (July 2) to (July 6).
Desde (el dos de julio)
hasta (el seis de julio).
des·de (el dos de khoo·lyo)
as·ta (el seys de khoo·lyo)

Can I see it?
¿Puedo verla?
pwe·do ver·la

Am I allowed to camp here?
¿Se puede acampar aquí?
se pwe·de a·kam·par a·kee

Is there a camp site nearby?
¿Hay un terreno de cámping
cercano?
ai oon te·rre·no de kam·peeng
ther·ka·no

requests & queries

When/Where's breakfast served?
¿Cuándo/Dónde se sirve el desayuno?
kwan·do/don·de se seer·ve el de·sa·yoo·no

Please wake me at (seven).
Por favor, despiérteme a (las siete).
por fa·vor des·pyer·te·me a (las sye·te)

Could I have my key, please?
¿Me puede dar la llave, por favor?
me pwe·de dar la lya·ve por fa·vor

Can I get another (blanket)?
¿Puede darme otra (manta)?
pwe·de dar·me ot·ra (man·ta)

Is there a/an ...?	¿Hay ...?	ai ...
elevator	ascensor	as·then·sor
safe	una caja fuerte	oo·na ka·kha fwer·te
The room is too ...	Es demasiado ...	es de·ma·sya·do ...
expensive	cara	ka·ra
noisy	ruidosa	rrwee·do·sa
small	pequeña	pe·ke·nya
The ... doesn't work.	No funciona ...	no foon·thyo·na ...
air conditioning	el aire	el ai·re
	acondicionado	a·kon·dee·thyo·na·do
fan	el ventilador	el ven·tee·la·dor
toilet	el retrete	el rre·tre·te
This ... isn't clean.	Esta ... no está limpia.	es·ta ... no es·ta leem·pya
pillow	almohada	al·mwa·da
sheet	sábana	sa·ba·na
towel	toalla	to·a·lya

checking out

What time is checkout?
  ¿A qué hora hay que dejar   a ke o·ra ai ke de·khar
  libre la habitación?   lee·bre la a·bee·ta·thyon

Can I leave my luggage here?
  ¿Puedo dejar las maletas aquí?   pwe·do de·khar las ma·le·tas a·kee

Could I have ..., please?	¿Me puede dar ..., por favor?	me pwe·de dar ... por fa·vor
my deposit	mi depósito	mee de·po·see·to
my passport	mi pasaporte	mee pa·sa·por·te
my valuables	mis objetos de valor	mees ob·khe·tos de va·lor

communications & banking

the internet

Where's the local Internet café?
¿Dónde hay un cibercafé cercano?   don·de ai oon thee·ber·ka·fe ther·ka·no

How much is it per hour?
¿Cuánto cuesta por hora?   kwan·to kwes·ta por o·ra

I'd like to ...	Quisiera ...	kee·sye·ra ...
check my email	revisar mi correo electrónico	rre·vee·sar mee ko·re·o e·lek·tro·nee·ko
get Internet access	usar el Internet	oo·sar el een·ter·net
use a printer	usar una impresora	oo·sar oo·na eem·pre·so·ra
use a scanner	usar un escáner	oo·sar oon es·ka·ner

mobile/cell phone

I'd like a ...	Quisiera ...	kee·sye·ra ...
mobile/cell phone for hire	un móvil para alquilar	oon mo·veel pa·ra al·kee·lar
SIM card for your network	una tarjeta SIM para su red	oo·na tar·khe·ta seem pa·ra soo rred

What are the rates?
¿Cuál es la tarifa?   kwal es la ta·ree·fa

telephone

What's your phone number?
¿Cuál es su/tu número de teléfono? pol/inf   kwal es soo/too noo·me·ro de te·le·fo·no

The number is ...
El número es ...   el noo·me·ro es ...

Where's the nearest public phone?
¿Dónde hay una cabina telefónica?   don·de ai oo·na ka·bee·na te·le·fo·nee·ka

I'd like to buy a phonecard.
Quiero comprar una tarjeta telefónica.   kye·ro kom·prar oo·na tar·khe·ta te·le·fo·nee·ka

I want to ...	Quiero ...	kye-ro ...
call (Singapore)	hacer una llamada (a Singapur)	a-ther oo-na lya-ma-da (a seen-ga-poor)
make a local call	hacer una llamada local	a-ther oo-na lya-ma-da lo-kal
reverse the charges	hacer una llamada a cobro revertido	a-ther oo-na lya-ma-da a ko-bro rre-ver-tee-do

How much does ... cost?	¿Cuánto cuesta ...?	kwan-to kwes-ta ...
a (three)-minute call	una llamada de (tres) minutos	oo-na lya-ma-da de (tres) mee-noo-tos
each extra minute	cada minuto extra	ka-da mee-noo-to ek-stra

It's (one euro) per (minute).
(Un euro) por (un minuto).   (oon e-oo-ro) por (oon mee-noo-to)

post office

I want to send a ...	Quisiera enviar ...	kee-sye-ra en-vee-ar ...
fax	un fax	oon faks
letter	una carta	oo-na kar-ta
parcel	un paquete	oon pa-ke-te
postcard	una postal	oo-na pos-tal

I want to buy ...	Quisiera comprar ...	kee-sye-ra kom-prar ...
an envelope	un sobre	oon so-bre
stamps	sellos	se-lyos

Please send it (to Australia) by ...	Por favor, mándelo (a Australia) por ...	por fa-vor man-de-lo (a ows-tra-lya) por ...
airmail	vía aérea	vee-a a-e-re-a
express mail	correo urgente	ko-rre-o oor-khen-te
registered mail	correo certificado	ko-rre-o ther-tee-fee-ka-do
surface mail	vía terrestre	vee-a te-rres-tre

Is there any mail for me?
¿Hay alguna carta para mí?   ai al-goo-na kar-ta pa-ra mee

bank

Where's a/an ...?	*¿Dónde hay ...?*	*don*·de ai ...
ATM	un cajero automático	oon ka·*khe*·ro ow·to·*ma*·tee·ko o
foreign exchange office	una oficina de cambio	*oo*·na o·fee·*thee*·na de *kam*·byo
I'd like to ...	*Me gustaría ...*	me *goos*·ta·*ree*·a ...
cash a cheque	cambiar un cheque	kam·*byar* oon *che*·ke
change a travellers cheque	cobrar un cheque de viajero	ko·*brar* oon *che*·ke de vee·a·*khe*·ro
change money	cambiar dinero	kam·*byar* dee·*ne*·ro
get a cash advance	obtener un adelanto	ob·te·*ner* oon a·de·*lan*·to
withdraw money	sacar dinero	sa·*kar* dee·*ne*·ro
What's the ...?	*¿Cuál es ...?*	kwal es ...
commission	la comisión	la ko·mee·*syon*
exchange rate	el tipo de cambio	el *tee*·po de *kam*·byo
It's (12) euros.	*Es (doce) euros.*	es (*do*·the) *e*·oo·ros
It's free.	*Es gratis.*	es *gra*·tees

What's the charge for that?
¿Cuánto hay que pagar por eso?   *kwan*·to ai ke pa·*gar* por *e*·so

What time does the bank open?
¿A qué hora abre el banco?   a ke *o*·ra *a*·bre el *ban*·ko

Has my money arrived yet?
¿Ya ha llegado mi dinero?   ya a lye·*ga*·do mee dee·*ne*·ro

sightseeing

getting in

What time does it open/close?
¿A qué hora abren/cierran?   a ke *o*·ra ab·ren/*thye*·rran

What's the admission charge?
¿Cuánto cuesta la entrada?   *kwan*·to *kwes*·ta la en·*tra*·da

Is there a discount for children/students?
¿Hay descuentos para niños/estudiantes?   ai des·*kwen*·tos *pa*·ra *nee*·nyos/es·too·*dyan*·tes

I'd like a ...	*Quisiera ...*	kee-*sye*-ra ...
catalogue	*un catálogo*	oon ka-*ta*-lo-go
guide	*una guía*	*oo*-na *gee*-a
(local) map	*un mapa (de la zona)*	oon *ma*-pa (de la *tho*-na)
I'd like to see ...	*Me gustaría ver ...*	me goos-ta-*ree*-a ver ...
What's that?	*¿Qué es eso?*	ke es *e*-so
Can I take a photo?	*¿Puedo tomar un foto?*	*pwe*-do to-*mar* un *fo*-to

tours

When's the next day trip?
¿Cuándo es la próxima   *kwan*-do es la *prok*-see-ma
excursión de un día?   eks-koor-*syon* de oon *dee*-a

When's the next tour?
¿Cuándo es el próximo recorrido?   *kwan*-do es ela *prok*-see-mo rre-ko-*rre*-do

Is ... included?	*¿Incluye ...?*	een-*kloo*-ye ...
accommodation	*alojamiento*	a-lo-kha-*myen*-to
the admission charge	*entrada*	en-*tra*-da
food	*comida*	ko-*mee*-da
transport	*transporte*	trans-*por*-te

How long is the tour?
¿Cuánto dura el recorrido?   *kwan*-to *doo*-ra el rre-ko-*rre*-do

What time should we be back?
¿A qué hora tenemos que volver?   a ke *o*-ra te-*ne*-mos ke vol-*ver*

sightseeing

castle	*castillo* m	kas-*tee*-lyo
cathedral	*catedral* f	ka-te-*dral*
church	*iglesia* f	ee-*gle*-sya
main square	*plaza mayor* f	*pla*-tha ma-*yor*
monastery	*monasterio* m	mo-na-*ste*-ryo
monument	*monumento* m	mo-noo-*men*-to
museum	*museo* m	moo-*se*-o
old city	*casco antiguo* m	*kas*-ko an-*tee*-gwo
palace	*palacio* m	pa-*la*-thyo
ruins	*ruinas* f pl	*rrwee*-nas
stadium	*estadio* m	es-*ta*-dyo
statues	*estatuas* f pl	es-*ta*-twas

shopping

enquiries

Where's a ...?	¿Dónde está ...?	don-de es-ta ...
bank	el banco	el ban-ko
bookshop	la librería	la lee-bre-ree-a
camera shop	la tienda de fotografía	la tyen-da de fo-to-gra-fee-a
department store	el centro comercial	el then-tro ko-mer-thyal
grocery store	la tienda de comestibles	la tyen-da de ko-mes-tee-bles
market	el mercado	el mer-ka-do
newsagency	el quiosco	el kyos-ko
supermarket	el supermercado	el soo-per-mer-ka-do

Where can I buy (a padlock)?
¿Dónde puedo comprar (un candado)?
don-de pwe-do kom-prar (oon kan-da-do)

I'm looking for ...
Estoy buscando ...
es-toy boos-kan-do ...

Can I look at it?
¿Puedo verlo?
pwe-do ver-lo

Do you have any others?
¿Tiene otros?
tye-ne o-tros

Does it have a guarantee?
¿Tiene garantía?
tye-ne ga-ran-tee-a

Can I have it sent overseas?
¿Pueden enviarlo por correo a otro país?
pwe-den en-vee-ar-lo por ko-rre-o a o-tro pa-ees

Can I have my ... repaired?
¿Puede reparar mi ... aquí?
pwe-de rre-pa-rar mee ... a-kee

It's faulty.
Es defectuoso.
es de-fek-too-o-so

I'd like ..., please.	Quisiera ..., por favor.	kee·sye·ra ... por fa·vor
a bag	una bolsa	oo·na bol·sa
a refund	que me devuelva	ke me de·vwel·va
	el dinero	el dee·ne·ro
to return this	devolver esto	de·vol·ver es·to

paying

How much is it?
¿Cuánto cuesta esto?   kwan·to kwes·ta es·to

Can you write down the price?
¿Puede escribir el precio?   pwe·de es·kree·beer el pre·thyo

That's too expensive.
Es muy caro.   es mooy ka·ro

What's your lowest price?
¿Cuál es su precio más bajo?   kwal es soo pre·thyo mas ba·kho

I'll give you (five) euros.
Te daré (cinco) euros.   te da·re (theen·ko) e·oo·ros

There's a mistake in the bill.
Hay un error en la cuenta.   ai oon e·rror en la kwen·ta

Do you accept ...?	¿Aceptan ...?	a·thep·tan ...
credit cards	tarjetas de crédito	tar·khe·tas de kre·dee·to
debit cards	tarjetas de débito	tar·khe·tas de de·bee·to
travellers cheques	cheques de viajero	che·kes de vya·khe·ro

I'd like ..., please.	Quisiera ..., por favor.	kee·sye·ra ... por fa·vor
a receipt	un recibo	oon rre·thee·bo
my change	mi cambio	mee kam·byo

clothes & shoes

Can I try it on?
¿Me lo puedo probar?   me lo pwe·do pro·bar

My size is (40).
Uso la talla (cuarenta).   oo·so la ta·lya (kwa·ren·ta)

It doesn't fit.
No me queda bien.   no me ke·da byen

small	pequeño/a m/f	pe·ke·nyo/a
medium	mediano/a m/f	me·dya·no/a
large	grande m&f	gran·de

books & music

I'd like a ...	Quisiera un ...	kee-sye-ra oon ...
newspaper	periódico	pe-ryo-dee-ko
(in English)	(en inglés)	(en een-gles)
pen	bolígrafo	bo-lee-gra-fo

Is there an English-language bookshop?
¿Hay alguna librería en inglés?   ai al-goo-na lee-bre-ree-a en een-gles

I'm looking for something by (Enrique Iglesias).
Estoy buscando algo de   es-toy boos-kan-do al-go de
(Enrique Iglesias).   (en-ree-ke ee-gle-syas)

Can I listen to this?
¿Puedo escuchar esto aquí?   pwe-do es-koo-char es-to a-kee

photography

Can you ...?	¿Puede usted ...?	pwe-de oos-ted ...
burn a CD from	copiar un disco	ko-pyar oon dees-ko
my memory card	compacto de esta	kom-pak-to de es-ta
	tarjeta de memoria	tar-khe-ta de me-mo-rya
develop this film	revelar este carrete	rre-ve-lar es-te ka-rre-te
load my film	cargar el carrete	kar-gar el ka-rre-te

I need a ... film	Necesito película ...	ne-the-see-to pe-lee-koo-la ...
for this camera.	para esta cámara.	pa-ra es-ta ka-ma-ra
APS	APS	a pe e-se
B&W	en blanco y negro	en blan-ko y ne-gro
colour	en color	en ko-lor
slide	para diapositivas	pa-ra dya-po-see-tee-vas
(200) speed	de sensibilidad	de sen-see-bee-lee-da
	(doscientos)	(dos-thyen-tos)

When will it be ready?   ¿Cuándo estará listo?   kwan-do es-ta-ra lees-to

meeting people

greetings, goodbyes & introductions

Hello/Hi.	*Hola.*	*o·*la
Good night.	*Buenas noches.*	*bwe·*nas *no·*ches
Goodbye/Bye.	*Adiós.*	a·*dyos*
See you later.	*Hasta luego.*	*as·*ta *lwe·*go
Mr	*Señor*	se·*nyor*
Mrs	*Señora*	se·*nyo·*ra
Miss	*Señorita*	se·nyo·*ree·*ta
How are you?	*¿Qué tal?*	ke tal
Fine, thanks.	*Bien, gracias.*	byen *gra·*thyas
And you?	*¿Y Usted/tú?* pol/inf	ee oos·*te/*too
What's your name?	*¿Cómo se llama Usted?* pol	*ko·*mo se *lya·*ma oos·*te*
	¿Cómo te llamas? inf	*ko·*mo te *lya·*mas
My name is ...	*Me llamo ...*	me *lya·*mo ...
I'm pleased to meet you.	*Mucho gusto.*	*moo·*cho *goos·*to
This is my ...	*Éste/Ésta es mi ...* m/f	*es·*te/a es mee ...
boyfriend	*novio*	*no·*vyo
brother	*hermano*	er·*ma·*no
daughter	*hija*	*ee·*kho
father	*padre*	*pa·*dre
friend	*amigo/a* m/f	a·*mee·*go/a
girlfriend	*novia*	*no·*vya
husband	*marido*	ma·*ree·*do
mother	*madre*	*ma·*dre
partner (intimate)	*pareja*	pa·*re·*kha
sister	*hermana*	er·*ma·*na
son	*hijo*	*ee·*kho
wife	*esposa*	es·*po·*sa
Here's my ...	*Éste/Ésta es mi ...* m/f	*es·*te/a es mee ...
What's your ...?	*¿Cuál es su/tu ...?* pol/inf	kwal es soo/too ...
address	*dirección* f	dee·rek·*thyon*
email address	*dirección de email* f	dee·rek·*thyon* de *ee·*mayl
fax number	*número de fax* m	*noo·*me·ro de faks
phone number	*número de teléfono* m	*noo·*me·ro de te·*le·*fo·no

occupations

What's your occupation?	¿A qué se dedica Usted? pol	a ke se de·dee·ka oos·te
	¿A qué te dedicas? inf	a ke te de·dee·kas
I'm a/an ...	Soy un/una ... m/f	soy oon/oo·na ...
artist	artista m&f	ar·tees·ta
business person	comerciante m&f	ko·mer·thyan·te
farmer	agricultor m	a·gree·kool·tor
	agricultora f	a·gree·kool·to·ra
manual worker	obrero/a m/f	o·bre·ro/a
office worker	oficinista m&f	o·fee·thee·nees·ta
scientist	científico/a m/f	thyen·tee·fee·ko/a
student	estudiante m&f	es·too·dyan·te
tradesperson	artesano/a m/f	ar·te·sa·no/a

background

Where are you from?	¿De dónde es Usted? pol	de don·de es oos·te
	¿De dónde eres? inf	de don·de e·res
I'm from ...	Soy de ...	soy de ...
Australia	Australia	ow·stra·lya
Canada	Canadá	ka·na·da
England	Inglaterra	een·gla·te·rra
New Zealand	Nueva Zelanda	nwe·va the·lan·da
the USA	los Estados Unidos	los es·ta·dos oo·nee·dos
Are you married?	¿Estás casado/a? m/f	es·tas ka·sa·do/a
I'm married.	Estoy casado/a. m/f	es·toy ka·sa·do/a
I'm single.	Soy soltero/a. m/f	soy sol·te·ro/a

age

How old ...?	¿Cuántos años ...?	kwan·tos a·nyos ...
are you	tienes inf	tye·nes
is your daughter	tiene su hija pol	tye·ne soo ee·kha
is your son	tiene su hijo pol	tye·ne soo ee·kho
I'm ... years old.	Tengo ... años.	ten·go ... a·nyos
He/She is ... years old.	Tiene ... años.	tye·ne ... a·nyos

feelings

I'm (not) ...	(No) Tengo ...	(no) ten·go ...
Are you ...?	¿Tiene Usted ...? pol	tye·ne oos·te ...
	¿Tienes ...? inf	tye·nes ...
cold	frío	free·o
hot	calor	ka·lor
hungry	hambre	am·bre
thirsty	sed	se

I'm (not) ...	(No) Estoy ...	(no) es·toy ...
Are you ...?	¿Está Usted ...? pol	es·ta oos·te ...
	¿Estás ...? inf	es·tas ...
happy	feliz m&f	fe·leeth
OK	bien m&f	byen
sad	triste m&f	trees·te
tired	cansado/a m/f	kan·sa·do/a

entertainment

going out

Where can I find ...?	¿Dónde hay ...?	don·de ai ...
clubs	clubs nocturnos	kloobs nok·toor·nos
gay venues	lugares gay	loo·ga·res gai
pubs	bares	ba·res

I feel like going to a/the ...	Tengo ganas de ir ...	ten·go ga·nas de eer ...
concert	a un concierto	a oon kon·thyer·to
movies	al cine	al thee·ne
party	a una fiesta	a oo·na fyes·ta
restaurant	a un restaurante	a oon rres·tow·ran·te
theatre	al teatro	al te·a·tro

interests

Do you like ...	¿Le/Te gusta ...? pol/inf	le/te goos·ta ...
I (don't) like ...	(No) Me gusta ...	(no) me goos·ta ...
art	el arte	el ar·te
movies	el cine	el thee·ne
reading	leer	le·er
sport	el deporte	el de·por·te
travelling	viajar	vya·khar

Do you like to ...?	¿Le/Te gusta ...? pol/inf	le/te goos·ta ...
dance	ir a bailar	eer a bai·lar
go to concerts	ir a conciertos	eer a kon·thyer·tos
listen to music	escuchar música	es·koo·char moo·see·ka

food & drink

finding a place to eat

Can you recommend a ...?	¿Puede recomendar un ...?	pwe·de rre·ko·men·dar oon ...
bar	bar	bar
café	café	ka·fe
restaurant	restaurante	rres·tow·ran·te

I'd like ..., please.	Quisiera ..., por favor.	kee·sye·ra ... por fa·vor
a table for (two)	una mesa para (dos)	oo·na me·sa pa·ra (dos)
the (non)smoking section	(no) fumadores	(no) foo·ma·do·res

ordering food

breakfast	desayuno m	de·sa·yoo·no
lunch	comida f	ko·mee·da
dinner	almuerzo m	al·mwer·tho
snack	tentempié m	ten·tem·pye

What would you recommend?

¿Qué recomienda? ke rre·ko·myen·da

I'd like (the) ...	Quisiera ..., por favor.	kee-sye-ra ... por fa-vor
bill	la cuenta	la kwen-ta
drink list	la lista de bebidas	la lees-ta de be-bee-das
menu	el menú	el me-noo
that dish	ese plato	e-se pla-to

drinks

(cup of) coffee ...	(taza de) café ...	(ta-tha de) ka-fe ...
(cup of) tea ...	(taza de) té ...	(ta-tha de) te ...
with milk	con leche	kon le-che
without sugar	sin azúcar	seen a-thoo-kar

| (orange) juice | zumo de (naranja) m | zoo-mo de (na-ran-kha) |
| soft drink | refresco m | rre-fres-ko |

... water	agua ...	a-gwa ...
boiled	hervida	er-vee-da
(sparkling) mineral	mineral (con gas)	mee-ne-ral (kon gas)

in the bar

I'll have ...	Para mí ...	pa-ra mee ...
I'll buy you a drink.	Te invito a una copa. inf	le/te een-vee-to a oo-na ko-pa
What would you like?	¿Qué quieres tomar? inf	ke kye-res to-mar
Cheers!	¡Salud!	sa-loo

brandy	coñac m	ko-nyak
cocktail	combinado m	kom-bee-na-do
red-wine punch	sangría f	san-gree-a
a shot of (whisky)	chupito de (güisqui)	choo-pee-to de (gwees-kee)

a ... of beer	una ... de cerveza	oo-na ... de ther-ve-tha
bottle	botella	bo-te-lya
glass	caña	ka-nya

a bottle/glass of	una botella/copa	oo-na bo-te-lya/ko-pa
... wine	de vino ...	de vee-no ...
red	tinto	teen-to
sparkling	espumoso	es-poo-mo-so
white	blanco	blan-ko

self-catering

What's the local speciality?
   ¿Cuál es la especialidad de la zona?   kwal es la es·pe·thya·lee·*da* de la *tho*·na

What's that?
   ¿Qué es eso?   ke es e·so

How much is (a kilo of cheese)?
   ¿Cuánto vale (un kilo de queso)?   kwan·to va·le (oon kee·lo de ke·so)

I'd like ...	*Póngame ...*	*pon*·ga·me ...
(200) grams	*(doscientos) gramos*	(dos·*thyen*·tos) *gra*·mos
(two) kilos	*(dos) kilos*	(dos) *kee*·los
(three) pieces	*(tres) piezas*	(tres) *pye*·thas
(six) slices	*(seis) lonchas*	(seys) *lon*·chas

Less.	*Menos.*	*me*·nos
Enough.	*Basta.*	*ba*·sta
More.	*Más.*	mas

special diets & allergies

Is there a vegetarian restaurant near here?
   ¿Hay un restaurante   ai oon rres·tow·*ran*·te
   vegetariano por aquí?   ve·khe·ta·*rya*·no por a·*kee*

Do you have vegetarian food?
   ¿Tienen comida vegetariana?   tye·nen ko·*mee*·da ve·khe·ta·*rya*·na

Could you prepare a	*¿Me puede preparar*	me *pwe*·de pre·pa·*rar*
meal without ...?	*una comida sin ...?*	*oo*·na ko·*mee*·da seen ...
butter	*mantequilla*	man·te·*kee*·lya
eggs	*huevos*	*we*·vos
meat stock	*caldo de carne*	*kal*·do de *kar*·ne

I'm allergic to ...	*Soy alérgico/a ...* m/f	soy a·*ler*·khee·ko/a ...
dairy produce	*a los productos*	a los pro·*dook*·tos
	lácteos	*lak*·te·os
gluten	*al gluten*	al *gloo*·ten
MSG	*al glutamato*	al gloo·ta·*ma*·to
	monosódico	mo·no·*so*·dee·ko
nuts	*a las nueces*	a las *nwe*·thes
seafood	*a los mariscos*	a los ma·*rees*·kos

emergencies

basics

Help!	¡Socorro!	so·ko·ro
Stop!	¡Pare!	pa·re
Go away!	¡Váyase!	va·ya·se
Thief!	¡Ladrón!	lad·ron
Fire!	¡Fuego!	fwe·go
Watch out!	¡Cuidado!	kwee·da·do

Call ...!	¡Llame a ...!	lya·me a ...
a doctor	un médico	oon me·dee·ko
an ambulance	una ambulancia	oo·na am·boo·lan·thya
the police	la policía	la po·lee·thee·a

It's an emergency.
Es una emergencia.
es oo·na e·mer·khen·thya

Could you help me, please?
¿Me puede ayudar, por favor?
me pwe·de a·yoo·dar por fa·vor

I have to use the telephone.
Necesito usar el teléfono.
ne·the·see·to oo·sar el te·le·fo·no

I'm lost.
Estoy perdido/a. m/f
es·toy per·dee·do/a

Where are the toilets?
¿Dónde están los servicios?
don·de es·tan los ser·vee·thyos

police

Where's the police station?
¿Dónde está la comisaría?
don·de es·ta la ko·mee·sa·ree·a

I want to report an offence.
Quiero denunciar un delito.
kye·ro de·noon·thyar oon de·lee·to

I have insurance.
Tengo seguro.
ten·go se·goo·ro

I've been assaulted.	He sido asaltado/a. m/f	e see·do a·sal·ta·do/a
I've been raped.	He sido violado/a. m/f	e see·do vee·o·la·do/a
I've been robbed.	Me han robado.	me an rro·ba·do

I've lost my ...	He perdido ...	e per·dee·do ...
backpack	mi mochila	mee mo·chee·la
bags	mis maletas	mees ma·le·tas
credit card	mi tarjeta de crédito	mee tar·khe·ta de kre·dee·to
handbag	mi bolso	mee bol·so
jewellery	mis joyas	mees kho·yas
money	mi dinero	mee dee·ne·ro
passport	mi pasaporte	mee pa·sa·por·te
travellers cheques	mis cheques de viajero	mees che·kes de vya·khe·ro
wallet	mi cartera	mee kar·te·ra

I want to contact my ...	Quiero ponerme en contacto con mi ...	kye·ro po·ner·me en kon·tak·to kon mee ...
consulate	consulado	kon·soo·la·do
embassy	embajada	em·ba·kha·da

health

medical needs

Where's the nearest ...?	¿Dónde está el ... más cercano?	don·de es·ta el ... mas ther·ka·no
dentist	dentista	den·tees·ta
doctor	médico	me·dee·ko
hospital	hospital	os·pee·tal

Where's the nearest (night) pharmacist?
¿Dónde está la farmacia
(de guardia) más cercana?
don·de es·ta la far·ma·thya
(de gwar·dya) mas ther·ka·na

I need a doctor (who speaks English).
Necesito un médico
(que hable inglés).
ne·the·see·to oon me·dee·ko
(ke a·ble een·gles)

Could I see a female doctor?
¿Puede examinarme una
médica?
pwe·de ek·sa·mee·nar·me oo·na
me·dee·ka

I've run out of my medication.
Se me terminaron los
medicamentos.
se me ter·mee·na·ron los
me·dee·ka·men·tos

symptoms, conditions & allergies

| I'm sick. | Estoy enfermo/a. m/f | es·*toy* en·*fer*·mo/a |
| It hurts here. | Me duele aquí. | me dwe·le a·*kee* |

I have (a) ...	Tengo...	*ten*·go ...
asthma	asma	*as*·ma
bronchitis	bronquitis	bron·*kee*·tees
constipation	estreñimiento	es·tre·nyee·*myen*·to
cough	tos	tos
diarrhoea	diarrea	dya·*rre*·a
fever	fiebre	*fye*·bre
headache	dolor de cabeza	do·*lor* de ka·*be*·tha
heart condition	una condición	*oo*·na kon·dee·*thyon*
	cardíaca	kar·*dee*·a·ka
nausea	náusea	*now*·se·a
pain	dolor	do·*lor*
sore throat	dolor de garganta	do·*lor* de gar·*gan*·ta
toothache	dolor de muelas	do·*lor* de *mwe*·las

I'm allergic to ...	Soy alérgico/a a ... m/f	soy a·*ler*·khee·ko/a a ...
antibiotics	los antibióticos	los an·tee·*byo*·tee·kos
anti-	los anti-	los *an*·tee·
inflammatories	inflamatorios	een·fla·ma·*to*·ryos
aspirin	la aspirina	la as·pee·*ree*·na
bees	las abejas	las a·*be*·khas
codeine	la codeina	la ko·de·*ee*·na
penicillin	la penicilina	la pe·nee·thee·*lee*·na

antiseptic	antiséptico m	an·tee·*sep*·tee·ko
bandage	vendaje m	ven·*da*·khe
condoms	condones m pl	kon·*do*·nes
contraceptives	anticonceptivos m pl	an·tee·kon·thep·*tee*·vos
diarrhoea medicine	medicina para diarrea f	me·dee·*thee*·na *pa*·ra dya·*rre*·a
insect repellent	repelente de insectos m	re·pe·*len*·te de een·*sek*·tos
laxatives	laxantes m pl	lak·*san*·tes
painkillers	analgésicos m pl	a·nal·*khe*·see·kos
rehydration salts	sales rehidratantes f pl	*sa*·les re·eed·ra·*tan*·tes
sleeping tablets	pastillas para dormir f pl	pas·*tee*·lyas *pa*·ra dor·*meer*

english–spanish dictionary

Spanish nouns in this dictionary, and adjectives affected by gender, have their gender indicated by ⓜ (masculine) or ⓕ (feminine). If it's a plural noun, you'll also see pl. Words are also marked as v (verb), n (noun), a (adjective), pl (plural), sg (singular), inf (informal) and pol (polite) where necessary.

A

accident *accidente* ⓜ ak-thee-*den*-te
accommodation *alojamiento* ⓜ a-lo-kha-*myen*-to
adaptor *adaptador* ⓜ a-dap-ta-*dor*
address *dirección* ⓕ dee-rek-*thyon*
after *después de* des-*pwes* de
air-conditioned *con aire acondicionado* kon *ai*-re a-kon-dee-thyo-*na*-do
airplane *avión* ⓜ a-*vyon*
airport *aeropuerto* ⓜ ay-ro-*pwer*-to
alcohol *alcohol* ⓜ al-*col*
all a *todo/a* *to*-do/a
allergy *alergia* ⓕ a-*ler*-khya
ambulance *ambulancia* ⓕ am-boo-*lan*-thya
ankle *tobillo* ⓜ to-*bee*-lyo
and *y* ee
arm *brazo* ⓜ *bra*-tho
ashtray *cenicero* ⓜ the-nee-*the*-ro
ATM *cajero automático* ka-*khe*-ro ow-to-*ma*-tee-ko

B

baby *bebé* ⓜ be-*be*
back (body) *espalda* ⓕ es-*pal*-da
backpack *mochila* ⓕ mo-*chee*-la
bad *malo/a* ⓜ/ⓕ *ma*-lo/a
bag *bolso* ⓜ *bol*-so
baggage claim *recogida de equipajes* ⓕ rre-ko-*khee*-da de e-kee-*pa*-khes
bank *banco* ⓜ *ban*-ko
bar *bar* ⓜ bar
bathroom *baño* ⓜ *ba*-nyo
battery (general) *pila* ⓕ *pee*-la
battery (car) *batería* ⓕ ba-te-*ree*-a
beautiful *hermoso/a* ⓜ/ⓕ er-*mo*-so/a
bed *cama* ⓕ *ka*-ma
beer *cerveza* ⓕ ther-*ve*-tha
before *antes* *an*-tes
behind *detrás de* de-*tras* de
bicycle *bicicleta* ⓕ bee-thee-*kle*-ta

big *grande* *gran*-de
bill *cuenta* ⓕ *kwen*-ta
black *negro/a* ⓜ/ⓕ *ne*-gro/a
blanket *manta* ⓕ *man*-ta
blood group *grupo sanguíneo* ⓜ *groo*-po san-*gee*-neo
blue *azul* a-*thool*
boat *barco* ⓜ *bar*-ko
book (make a reservation) v *reservar* rre-ser-*var*
bottle *botella* ⓕ bo-*te*-lya
bottle opener *abrebotellas* ⓜ a-bre-bo-*te*-lyas
boy *chico* ⓜ *chee*-ko
brakes (car) *frenos* ⓜ pl *fre*-nos
breakfast *desayuno* ⓜ des-a-*yoo*-no
broken (faulty) *roto/a* ⓜ/ⓕ *ro*-to/a
bus *autobús* ⓜ ow-to-*boos*
business *negocios* ⓜ pl ne-*go*-thyos
buy *comprar* kom-*prar*

C

café *café* ⓜ ka-*fe*
camera *cámara (fotográfica)* ⓕ *ka*-ma-ra (fo-to-*gra*-fee-ka)
camp site *cámping* ⓜ *kam*-peen
cancel *cancelar* kan-the-*lar*
can opener *abrelatas* ⓜ a-bre-*la*-tas
car *coche* ⓜ *ko*-che
cash in effectivo *dinero en efectivo* ⓜ dee-*ne*-ro en e-fek-*tee*-vo
cash (a cheque) v *cambiar (un cheque)* kam-*byar* (oon *che*-ke)
cell phone *teléfono móvil* ⓜ te-*le*-fo-no *mo*-veel
centre *centro* ⓜ *then*-tro
change (money) v *cambiar* kam-*byar*
cheap *barato/a* ⓜ/ⓕ ba-*ra*-to/a
check (bill) *cuenta* ⓕ *kwen*-ta
check-in *facturación de equipajes* ⓕ fak-too-ra-*thyon* de e-kee-*pa*-khes
chest *pecho* ⓜ *pe*-cho
child *niño/a* ⓜ/ⓕ *nee*-nyo/a
cigarette *cigarrillo* ⓜ thee-ga-*ree*-lyo
city *ciudad* ⓕ *theew*-*da*
clean a *limpio/a* ⓜ/ⓕ *leem*-pyo/a

closed *cerrado/a* ⓜ/ⓕ the-*rra*-do/a
coffee *café* ⓜ ka-*fe*
coins *monedas* ⓕ pl mo-*ne*-das
cold a *frío/a* ⓜ/ⓕ *free*-o/a
collect call *llamada a cobro revertido* ⓕ
lya-*ma*-da a ko-bro rev-er-*tee*-do
come *venir* ve-*neer*
computer *ordenador* ⓜ or-de-na-*dor*
condom *condones* ⓜ pl kon-*do*-nes
contact lenses *lentes de contacto* ⓜ pl
len-tes de kon-*tak*-to
cook v *cocinar* ko-thee-*nar*
cost *precio* ⓜ *pre*-thyo
credit card *tarjeta de crédito* ⓕ
tar-*khe*-ta de *kre*-dee-to
cup *taza* ⓕ *ta*-tha
currency exchange *cambio de dinero* ⓜ
kam-byo de dee-*ne*-ro
customs (immigration) *aduana* ⓕ a-*dwa*-na

D

dangerous *peligroso/a* ⓜ/ⓕ pe-lee-*gro*-so/a
date (time) *fecha* ⓕ *fe*-cha
day *día* ⓜ *dee*-a
delay *demora* ⓕ de-*mo*-ra
dentist *dentista* ⓜ/ⓕ den-*tees*-ta
depart *salir de* sa-*leer* de
diaper *pañal* ⓜ pa-*nyal*
dictionary *diccionario* ⓜ deek-thyo-*na*-ryo
dinner *cena* ⓕ *the*-na
direct *directo/a* ⓜ/ⓕ dee-*rek*-to/a
dirty *sucio/a* ⓜ/ⓕ *soo*-thyo/a
disabled *minusválido/a* ⓜ/ⓕ mee-noos-*va*-lee-do/a
discount *descuento* ⓜ des-*kwen*-to
doctor *doctor/doctora* ⓜ/ⓕ dok-*tor*/dok-*to*-ra
double bed *cama de matrimonio* ⓕ
ka-ma de ma-tree-*mo*-nyo
double room *habitación doble* ⓕ a-bee-ta-*thyon* *do*-ble
drink *bebida* ⓕ be-*bee*-da
drive v *conducir* kon-doo-*theer*
drivers licence *carnet de conducir* ⓜ
kar-*ne* de kon-doo-*theer*
drugs (illicit) *droga* ⓕ *dro*-ga
dummy (pacifier) *chupete* ⓜ choo-*pe*-te

E

ear *oreja* ⓕ o-*re*-kha
east *este* *es*-te
eat *comer* ko-*mer*

economy class *clase turística* ⓕ *kla*-se too-*rees*-tee-ka
electricity *electricidad* ⓕ e-lek-tree-thee-*da*
elevator *ascensor* ⓜ as-then-*sor*
email *correo electrónico* ⓜ ko-rre-o e-lek-*tro*-nee-ko
embassy *embajada* ⓕ em-ba-*kha*-da
emergency *emergencia* ⓕ e-mer-*khen*-thya
English (language) *inglés* ⓜ een-*gles*
entrance *entrada* ⓕ en-*tra*-da
evening *noche* ⓕ *no*-che
exchange rate *tipo de cambio* ⓜ *tee*-po de *kam*-byo
exit *salida* ⓕ sa-*lee*-da
expensive *caro/a* ⓜ/ⓕ *ka*-ro/a
express mail *correo urgente* ⓜ ko-rre-o oor-*khen*-te
eye *ojo* ⓜ *o*-kho

F

far *lejos* *le*-khos
fast *rápido/a* ⓜ/ⓕ *rra*-pee-do/a
father *padre* ⓜ *pa*-dre
film (camera) *carrete* ⓜ ka-*rre*-te
finger *dedo* *de*-do
first-aid kit *maletín de primeros auxilios* ⓜ
ma-le-*teen* de pree-*me*-ros ow-*ksee*-lyos
first class *de primera clase* de pree-*me*-ra *kla*-se
fish *pez* ⓜ peth
food *comida* ⓕ ko-*mee*-da
foot *pie* ⓜ pye
fork *tenedor* ⓜ te-ne-*dor*
free (of charge) *gratis* *gra*-tees
friend *amigo/a* ⓜ/ⓕ a-*mee*-go/a
fruit *fruta* ⓕ *froo*-ta
full *lleno/a* ⓜ/ⓕ *lye*-no/a
funny *gracioso/a* ⓜ/ⓕ gra-*thyo*-so/a

G

gift *regalo* ⓜ rre-*ga*-lo
girl *chica* ⓕ *chee*-ka
glass (drinking) *vaso* ⓜ *va*-so
glasses *gafas* ⓕ pl *ga*-fas
go *ir* eer
good *bueno/a* ⓜ/ⓕ *bwe*-no/a
green *verde* *ver*-de
guide n *guía* ⓜ/ⓕ *gee*-a

H

half *mitad* ⓕ mee-*tad*
hand *mano* ⓕ *ma*-no
handbag *bolso* ⓜ *bol*-so

happy *feliz* fe-*leeth*
have *tener* te-*ner*
he *él* el
head *cabeza* ⓕ ka-*be*-tha
heart *corazón* ⓜ ko-ra-*thon*
heat *calor* ⓜ ka-*lor*
heavy *pesado/a* ⓜ/ⓕ pe-*sa*-do/a
help v *ayudar* a-yoo-*dar*
here *aquí* a-*kee*
high *alto/a* ⓜ/ⓕ *al*-to/a
highway *autovía* ⓕ ow-to-*vee*-a
hike v *ir de excursión* eer de eks-koor-*syon*
holiday *vacaciones* ⓕ pl va-ka-*thyo*-nes
homosexual *homosexual* ⓜ/ⓕ o-mo-se-*kswal*
hospital *hospital* ⓜ os-pee-*tal*
hot *caliente* ka-*lyen*-te
hotel *hotel* ⓜ o-*tel*
hungry *hambriento/a* ⓜ/ⓕ am-bree-*en*-to/a
husband *marido* ⓜ ma-*ree*-do

I

I *yo* yo
identification (card) *carnet de identidad* ⓜ kar-*net* de ee-den-tee-*da*
ill *enfermo/a* ⓜ/ⓕ en-*fer*-mo/a
important *importante* eem-por-*tan*-te
included *incluido* een-kloo-*ee*-do
injury *herida* ⓕ e-*ree*-da
insurance *seguro* ⓜ se-*goo*-ro
Internet *Internet* ⓜ een-ter-*net*
interpreter *intérprete* ⓜ/ⓕ een-*ter*-pre-te

J

jewellery *joyas* ⓕ pl *kho*-yas
job *trabajo* ⓜ tra-*ba*-kho

K

key *llave* ⓕ *lya*-ve
kilogram *kilogramo* ⓜ kee-lo-*gra*-mo
kitchen *cocina* ⓕ ko-*thee*-na
knife *cuchillo* ⓜ koo-*chee*-lyo

L

laundry (place) *lavadero* ⓜ la-va-*de*-ro
lawyer *abogado/a* ⓜ/ⓕ a-bo-*ga*-do/a
left (direction) *izquierda* ⓕ eeth-*kyer*-da

left-luggage office *consigna* ⓕ kon-*seeg*-na
leg *pierna* ⓕ *pyer*-na
lesbian *lesbiana* ⓕ les-bee-*a*-na
less *menos* me-nos
letter (mail) *carta* ⓕ *kar*-ta
lift (elevator) *ascensor* ⓜ as-then-*sor*
light *luz* ⓕ looth
like v *gustar* goos-*tar*
lock *cerradura* ⓕ the-rra-*doo*-ra
long *largo/a* ⓜ/ⓕ *lar*-go/a
lost *perdido/a* ⓜ/ⓕ per-*dee*-do/a
lost-property office *oficina de objetos perdidos* ⓕ o-fee-*thee*-na de ob-*khe*-tos per-*dee*-dos
love v *querer* ke-*rer*
luggage *equipaje* ⓜ e-kee-*pa*-khe
lunch *almuerzo* ⓜ al-*mwer*-tho

M

mail *correo* ⓜ ko-*rre*-o
man *hombre* ⓜ *om*-bre
map *mapa* ⓜ *ma*-pa
market *mercado* ⓜ mer-*ka*-do
matches *cerillas* ⓕ pl the-*ree*-lyas
meat *carne* ⓕ *kar*-ne
medicine *medicina* ⓕ me-dee-*thee*-na
menu *menú* ⓜ me-*noo*
message *mensaje* ⓜ men-*sa*-khe
milk *leche* ⓕ *le*-che
minute *minuto* ⓜ mee-*noo*-to
mobile phone *teléfono móvil* ⓜ te-*le*-fo-no *mo*-veel
money *dinero* ⓜ dee-*ne*-ro
month *mes* ⓜ mes
morning *mañana* ⓕ ma-*nya*-na
mother *madre* ⓕ *ma*-dre
motorcycle *motocicleta* ⓕ mo-to-thee-*kle*-ta
motorway *autovía* ⓕ ow-to-*vee*-a
mouth *boca* ⓕ *bo*-ka
music *música* ⓕ *moo*-see-ka

N

name *nombre* ⓜ *nom*-bre
napkin *servilleta* ⓕ ser-vee-*lye*-ta
nappy *pañal* ⓜ pa-*nyal*
near *cerca* *ther*-ka
neck *cuello* ⓜ *kwe*-lyo
new *nuevo/a* ⓜ/ⓕ *nwe*-vo/a
news *noticias* ⓕ pl no-*tee*-thyas
newspaper *periódico* ⓜ pe-*ryo*-dee-ko

night *noche* ① *no*-che
no *no* no
noisy *ruidoso/a* ⑩/① rrwee-*do*-so/a
nonsmoking *no fumadores* no foo-ma-*do*-res
north *norte* ⑩ *nor*-te
nose *nariz* ① na-*reeth*
now *ahora* a-o-ra
number *número* ⑩ *noo*-me-ro

O

oil (engine) *aceite* ⑩ a-*they*-te
old *viejo/a* ⑩/① *vye*-kho/a
one-way ticket *billete sencillo* ⑩ bee-*lye*-te sen-*thee*-lyo
open a *abierto/a* ⑩/① a-*byer*-to/a
outside *exterior* ⑩ eks-te-*ryor*

P

package *paquete* ⑩ pa-*ke*-te
paper *papel* ⑩ pa-*pel*
park (car) v *estacionar* es-ta-thyo-*nar*
passport *pasaporte* ⑩ pa-sa-*por*-te
pay *pagar* pa-*gar*
pen *bolígrafo* ⑩ bo-*lee*-gra-fo
petrol *gasolina* ① ga-so-*lee*-na
pharmacy *farmacia* ① far-*ma*-thya
phonecard *tarjeta de teléfono* ① tar-*khe*-ta de te-*le*-fo-no
photo *foto* ① *fo*-to
plate *plato* ⑩ *pla*-to
police *policía* ① po-lee-*thee*-a
postcard *postal* ① pos-*tal*
post office *correos* ⑩ ko-*rre*-os
pregnant *embarazada* ① em-ba-ra-*tha*-da
price *precio* ⑩ *pre*-thyo

Q

quiet *tranquilo/a* ⑩/① tran-*kee*-lo/a

R

rain *lluvia* ① *lyoo*-vya
razor *afeitadora* ① a-fey-ta-*do*-ra
receipt *recibo* ⑩ rre-*thee*-bo
red *rojo/a* ⑩/① *rro*-kho/a
refund *reembolso* ⑩ rre-em-*bol*-so
registered mail *correo certificado* ⑩ ko-*rre*-o ther-tee-fee-*ka*-do

rent v *alquilar* al-kee-*lar*
repair v *reparar* rre-pa-*rar*
reservation *reserva* ① rre-*ser*-va
restaurant *restaurante* ⑩ rres-tow-*ran*-te
return v *volver* vol-*ver*
return ticket *billete de ida y vuelta* ⑩ bee-*lye*-te de ee-da ee *vwel*-ta
right (direction) *derecha* de-*re*-cha
road *carretera* ① ka-rre-*te*-ra
room *habitación* ① a-bee-ta-*thyon*

S

safe a *seguro/a* ⑩/① se-*goo*-ro/a
sanitary napkin *compresas* ① pl kom-*pre*-sas
seat *asiento* ⑩ a-*syen*-to
send *enviar* en-vee-*ar*
service station *gasolinera* ① ga-so-lee-*ne*-ra
sex *sexo* ⑩ *se*-kso
shampoo *champú* ⑩ cham-*poo*
share (a dorm) *compartir* kom-par-*teer*
shaving cream *espuma de afeitar* ① es-*poo*-ma de a-fey-*tar*
she *ella* ① *e*-lya
sheet (bed) *sábana* ① *sa*-ba-na
shirt *camisa* ① ka-*mee*-sa
shoes *zapatos* ⑩ pl tha-*pa*-tos
shop *tienda* ① *tyen*-da
short *corto/a* ⑩/① *kor*-to/a
shower *ducha* ① *doo*-cha
single room *habitación individual* ① a-bee-ta-*thyon* een-dee-vee-*dwal*
skin *piel* ① pyel
skirt *falda* ① *fal*-da
sleep v *dormir* dor-*meer*
slowly *despacio* des-*pa*-thyo
small *pequeño/a* ⑩/① pe-*ke*-nyo/a
smoke (cigarettes) v *fumar* foo-*mar*
soap *jabón* ⑩ kha-*bon*
some *alguno/a* ⑩/① al-*goo*-no/a
soon *pronto* *pron*-to
south *sur* ⑩ soor
souvenir shop *tienda de recuerdos* ① *tyen*-da de re-*kwer*-dos
Spain *España* ① es-*pa*-nya
Spanish (language) *español/castellano* ⑩ es-pa-*nyol*/kas-te-*lya*-no
speak *hablar* a-*blar*
spoon *cuchara* ① koo-*cha*-ra
stamp *sello* ⑩ *se*-lyo

english–spanish

stand-by ticket *billete de lista de espera* ⓜ
bee-*lye*-te de *lees*-ta de es-*pe*-ra

station (train) *estación* ① es-ta-*thyon*

stomach *estómago* ⓜ es-*to*-ma-go

stop v *parar* pa-*rar*

stop (bus) *parada* ① pa-*ra*-da

street *calle* ① *ka*-lye

student *estudiante* ① es-too-*dyan*-te

sun *sol* ⓜ sol

sunscreen *crema solar* ① *kre*-ma so-*lar*

swim v *nadar* na-*dar*

T

tampons *tampones* ⓜ pl tam-*po*-nes

taxi *taxi* ⓜ *tak*-see

teaspoon *cucharita* ① koo-cha-*ree*-ta

teeth *dientes* ⓜ pl *dyen*-tes

telephone *teléfono* ⓜ te-*le*-fo-no

television *televisión* ① te-le-vee-*syon*

temperature (weather) *temperatura* ①
tem-pe-ra-*too*-ra

tent *tienda (de campaña)* ① *tyen*-da (de kam-*pa*-nya)

that (one) *ése/a* ⓜ/① *e*-se/a

they *ellos/ellas* ⓜ/① *e*-lyos/e-lyas

thirsty *sediento/a* ⓜ/① se-*dee*-en-to/a

this (one) *éste/a* ⓜ/① *es*-te/a

throat *garganta* ① gar-*gan*-ta

ticket *billete* ⓜ bee-*lye*-te

time *tiempo* ⓜ *tyem*-po

tired *cansado/a* ⓜ/① kan-*sa*-do/a

tissues *pañuelos de papel* ⓜ pl pa-*nywe*-los de pa-*pel*

today *hoy* oy

toilet *servicio* ⓜ ser-*vee*-thyo

tomorrow *mañana* ma-*nya*-na

tonight *esta noche* es-ta *no*-che

toothbrush *cepillo de dientes* ⓜ the-*pee*-lyo de *dyen*-tes

toothpaste *pasta dentífrica* ① *pas*-ta den-*tee*-free-ka

torch (flashlight) *linterna* ① leen-*ter*-na

tour *excursión* ① eks-koor-*syon*

tourist office *oficina de turismo* ①
o-fee-*thee*-na de too-*rees*-mo

towel *toalla* ① to-*a*-lya

train *tren* ⓜ tren

translate *traducir* tra-doo-*theer*

travel agency *agencia de viajes* ①
a-*khen*-thya de *vya*-khes

travellers cheque *cheque de viajero* ⓜ
che-ke de *vya*-khe-ro

trousers *pantalones* ⓜ pl pan-ta-*lo*-nes

twin beds *dos camas* ① pl dos *ka*-mas

tyre *neumático* ⓜ ne-oo-*ma*-tee-ko

U

underwear *ropa interior* ① *rro*-pa een-te-*ryor*

urgent *urgente* oor-*khen*-te

V

vacant *vacante* va-*kan*-te

vacation *vacaciones* ① pl va-ka-*thyo*-nes

vegetable *verdura* ① ver-*doo*-ra

vegetarian a *vegetariano/a* ⓜ/① ve-khe-ta-*rya*-no/a

visa *visado* ⓜ vee-*sa*-do

W

waiter *camarero/a* ⓜ/① ka-ma-*re*-ro/a

walk v *caminar* ka-mee-*nar*

wallet *cartera* ① kar-*te*-ra

warm a *templado/a* ⓜ/① tem-*pla*-do/a

wash (something) *lavar* la-*var*

watch *reloj de pulsera* ① rre-*lokh* de pool-*se*-ra

water *agua* ⓜ *a*-gwa

we *nosotros/nosotras* ⓜ/① no-*so*-tros/ no-*so*-tras

weekend *fin de semana* ⓜ feen de se-*ma*-na

west *oeste* ⓜ o-*es*-te

wheelchair *silla de ruedas* ① *see*-lya de *rrwe*-das

when *cuando* kwan-do

where *donde* don-de

white *blanco/a* ⓜ/① *blan*-ko/a

who *quien* kyen

why *por qué* por ke

wife *esposa* ① es-*po*-sa

window *ventana* ① ven-*ta*-na

wine *vino* ⓜ *vee*-no

with *con* kon

without *sin* seen

woman *mujer* ① moo-*kher*

write *escribir* es-kree-*beer*

Y

yellow *amarillo/a* ⓜ/① a-ma-*ree*-lyo/a

yes *sí* see

yesterday *ayer* a-yer

you sg inf/pol *tú/Usted* too/oos-te

you pl *vosotros/vosotras* ⓜ/① vo-*so*-tros/vo-*so*-tras

Swedish

swedish alphabet

A a aa	*B b* bey	*C c* sey	*D d* dey	*E e* ey
F f ef	*G g* gey	*H h* hoh	*I i* ee	*J j* yoy
K k koh	*L l* el	*M m* em	*N n* en	*O o* oh
P p pey	*Q q* ku	*R r* er	*S s* es	*T t* tey
U u u	*V v* vey	*W w* *do*-belt vey	*X x* eks	*Y y* ew
Z z set	*Å å* aw	*Ä ä* e	*Ö ö* eu	

swedish

SVENSKA

introduction

The Swedish language (*svenska* sven·ska) gave us *ombudsman* and *smorgasbord*, which just confirms the image of the Swedes as a nation that's good at making the most of life in more ways than one. As a member of the Germanic language family, Swedish shares common roots with English and German. German, in particular, has influenced Swedish in the form of numerous loanwords. However, the closest relatives of Swedish are, of course, the other Scandinavian languages, Danish and Norwegian – all of them descendants of Old Norse, which started branching out from the 9th century and the Viking age.

The oldest inscriptions in Old Norse, dating from the same period, used the runic alphabet and were written on stone or wood. The missionaries who introduced Christianity in the 12th century brought the Roman alphabet (and the custom of writing on parchment) to the emerging Scandinavian languages, but some modification was necessary to represent the specific vowel sounds, so additional letters were eventually developed. The turning point in the evolution of Swedish coincided with the achievement of independence from Danish rule in 1526, when the first translation of the New Testament appeared. The modern literary language was shaped after the first Swedish translation of the whole Bible, known as *Gustav Vasas Bibel* as it was published under the patronage of King Gustav Vasa in 1541.

The standard language or *Rikssvenska* reek·sven·ska (lit: kingdom-Swedish) is based on the central dialects from the area around Stockholm. Some of the rural dialects that are spoken across the country are quite diverse – for example, *Skånska* skawn·ska, spoken in the southern province of Skåne, has flatter vowel sounds (and sounds a lot more like Danish), whereas *Dalmål* daal·mawl, spoken in the central region of Dalarna, has a very up-and-down sound.

Interestingly, Swedish doesn't have official status in Sweden itself, but it does in neighbouring Finland. This is easily explained though – Swedish is the national language of Sweden, spoken by the majority of residents (around 8.5 million), and it simply wasn't felt necessary to enforce its use by law. Finland, on the other hand, was part of Sweden from the mid-14th century until 1809, and Swedish was the language of administration. Today, it shares official status with Finnish and is a mandatory subject in schools, but it's the first language for only about 300,000 people or 6% of Finland's population. PS: any traveller to Sweden should know that the Swedish Chef from the Muppets doesn't really speak Swedish at all.

pronunciation

vowel sounds

Swedish vowel sounds can be either short or long – generally the stressed vowels are long, except when they are followed by double consonants, in which case they are short. The vowels in unstressed syllables are also short.

symbol	english equivalent	swedish example	transliteration
a	run	*glass*	glas
aa	father	*glas*	glaas
ai	aisle	*kaj*	kai
aw	saw	*gå*	gaw
e	bet	*vän*	ven
air	hair	*gärna*	yair·na
ee	see	*hit*	heet
eu	nurse	*söt*	seut
ew	ee pronounced with rounded lips	*nytt*	newt
ey	as in 'bet', but longer	*heta*	hey·ta
i	hit	*hitta*	hi·ta
o	pot	*kopp*	kop
oh	oh	*bott*	boht
oo	zoo	*kul*	kool
u	put	*buss*	bus

consonant sounds

Most Swedish consonants sounds are similar to their English counterparts. One exception is the fh sound (a breathy sound pronounced with rounded lips, like saying 'f' and 'w' at the same time), but with a little practice, you'll soon get it right.

symbol	english equivalent	swedish example	transliteration
b	bed	*bil*	beel
ch	cheat	*tjur*	choor
d	dog	*dyr*	dewr
f	fat	*filt*	filt
fh	f pronounced with rounded lips	*sjuk*	fhook
g	go	*gård*	gawrd
h	hat	*hård*	hawrd
k	kit	*kung*	kung
l	lot	*land*	land
m	man	*man*	man
n	not	*nej*	ney
ng	ring	*sång*	sawng
p	pet	*penna*	pe·na
r	red	*rosa*	roh·sa
s	sun	*sol*	sohl
sh	shot	*första*	feush·ta
t	top	*tröja*	tror·ya
v	very	*vit*	veet
y	yes	*jag*	yaag

word stress

In Swedish, stress usually falls on the first syllable in a word, but sometimes it falls on two syllables. It's important to get the stress right, as it can change the meaning of words (eg *anden an*·den 'duck' versus *anden an*·den 'spirit'). Words borrowed from other languages are often stressed on the last syllable (eg *bibliotek* bib·li·o·*tek* 'library'). In this chapter, the stressed syllables are always in italics.

tools

language difficulties

Do you speak English?
Talar du engelska? taa·lar doo eng·el·ska

Do you understand?
Förstår du? feur·shtawr doo

I (don't) understand.
Jag förstår (inte). yaa feur·shtawr (in·te)

What does (snus) mean?
Vad betyder (snus)? vaad be·tew·der (snoos)

How do you ...? *Hur ...?* hoor ...
  pronounce this *uttalar man detta* ut·taa·lar man de·ta
  write (spårvagn) *skrivar man* skree·var man
    (spårvagn) (spawr·vangn)

Could you please ...? *Kan du vara snäll och ...?* kan doo vaa·ra snel o ...
  repeat that *upprepa det* up·rey·pa det
  speak more *tala lite* taa·la lee·te
  slowly *långsammare* lawng·sa·ma·re
  write it down *skriva ner det* skree·va neyr de

essentials		
Yes.	*Ja.*	yaa
No.	*Nej.*	ney
Please.	*Tack.*	tak
Thank you (very much).	*Tack (så mycket).*	tak (saw mew·ke)
You're welcome.	*Varsågod.*	var·sha·gohd
Excuse me.	*Ursäkta mig.*	oor·shek·ta mey
Sorry.	*Förlåt.*	feur·lawt

numbers

0	*noll*	nol		16	*sexton*	seks-ton	
1	*ett*	et		17	*sjutton*	fhu-ton	
2	*två*	tvaw		18	*arton*	ar-ton	
3	*tre*	trey		19	*nitton*	ni-ton	
4	*fyra*	few-ra		20	*tjugo*	shoo-go	
5	*fem*	fem		21	*tjugoett*	shoo-go-et	
6	*sex*	seks		22	*tjugotvå*	shoo-go-tvaw	
7	*sju*	fhoo		30	*trettio*	tre-tee	
8	*åtta*	o-ta		40	*fyrtio*	fewr-tee	
9	*nio*	nee-oh		50	*femtio*	fem-tee	
10	*tio*	tee-oh		60	*sextio*	seks-tee	
11	*elva*	el-va		70	*sjuttio*	fhu-tee	
12	*tolv*	tolv		80	*åttio*	o-tee	
13	*tretton*	tre-ton		90	*nittio*	ni-tee	
14	*fjorton*	fyor-ton		100	*ett hundra*	et hun-dra	
15	*femton*	fem-ton		1000	*ett tusen*	et too-sen	

time & dates

What time is it?	*Hur mycket är klockan?*	hur *mew*-ke air *klo*-kan
It's one o'clock.	*Klockan är en.*	*klo*-kan air *eyn*
It's (two) o'clock.	*Klockan är (två).*	*klo*-kan air (*tvaw*)
Quarter past (one).	*Kvart över (en).*	kvart *eu*-ver (*eyn*)
Half past (one).	*Halv (två).* (lit: half two)	halv (*tvaw*)
Quarter to (nine).	*Kvart i (nio).*	kvart ee (*nee*-oh)
At what time ...?	*Hur dags ...?*	hur daks ...
At (10) o'clock.	*Klockan (tio).*	*klo*-kan (*tee*-oh)
am	*förmiddagen (f m)*	feur-mi-daa-gen
pm	*eftermiddagen (e m)*	ef-ter-mi-daa-gen
Monday	*måndag*	mawn-daa
Tuesday	*tisdag*	tees-taa
Wednesday	*onsdag*	ohns-daa
Thursday	*torsdag*	torsh-daa
Friday	*fredag*	frey-daa
Saturday	*lördag*	leur-daa
Sunday	*söndag*	seun-daa

January	januari	ya·nu·*aa*·ree
February	februari	fe·bru·*aa*·ree
March	mars	mars
April	april	a·*preel*
May	maj	mai
June	juni	*yoo*·nee
July	juli	*yoo*·lee
August	augusti	aw·*gus*·tee
September	september	sep·*tem*·ber
October	oktober	ok·*toh*·ber
November	november	noh·*vem*·ber
December	december	dey·*sem*·ber

What date is it today?
> *Vilket datum är det idag?* vil·ket *daa*·tum air de ee·*daag*

It's (15 December).
> *Det är (femtonde December).* de air (*fem*·ton·de dey·*sem*·ber)

| since (May) | sedan (maj) | seyn (mai) |
| until (June) | till (juni) | til (*yoo*·nee) |

last ...		
night	igår kväll	ee·*gawr* kvel
week	förra veckan	*feu*·ra *ve*·kan
month	förra månaden	*feu*·ra *maw*·na·den
year	förra året	*feu*·ra *aw*·ret

next ...	nästa ...	*nes*·ta ...
week	vecka	*ve*·ka
month	månad	*maw*·nad
year	år	awr

yesterday ...	igår ...	ee·*gawr* ...
morning	morse	*mor*·she
afternoon	eftermiddag	*ef*·ter·mi·daag
evening	kväll	kvel

tomorrow ...	imorgon ...	ee·*mor*·ron ...
morning	bitti	*bi*·ti
afternoon	eftermiddag	*ef*·ter·mi·daag
evening	kväll	kvel

weather

What's the weather like?	*Hur är vädret?*	hur air *vey*·dret

It's...		
cold	*Det är kallt.*	de air kalt
cloudy	*Det är molnigt.*	de air *mol*·nit
hot	*Det är het.*	de air heyt
raining	*Det regnar.*	de *reng*·nar
snowing	*Det snöar.*	de *sneu*·ar
sunny	*Solen skiner.*	*soh*·len *fhee*·ner
warm	*Det är varmt.*	de air varmt
windy	*Det blåser.*	de *blaw*·ser

spring	*vår*	vawr
summer	*sommar*	*so*·mar
autumn	*höst*	heust
winter	*vinter*	*vin*·ter

border crossing

I'm here ...	*Jag är ...*	yaa air ...
in transit	*i transit*	i *tran*·sit
on business	*på affärsresa*	paw a·*fairsh*·rey·sa
on holiday	*på semester*	paw se·*mes*·ter

I'm here for ...	*Jag stannar här ...*	yaa *sta*·nar hair ...
(10) days	*(tio) dagar*	(*tee*·oh) *daa*·gar
(three) weeks	*(tre) veckor*	(trey) *ve*·kor
(two) months	*(två) månader*	(tvaw) *maw*·na·der

I'm going to (Trelleborg).
Jag resar till (Trelleborg).   yaa *rey*·sa til (tre·le·*bory*)

I'm staying at the (Grand Hotel).
Jag bor på (Grand Hotell).   yaa bor paw (grand hoh·*tel*)

I have nothing to declare.
Jag har ingenting att förtulla.   yaa har *ing*·en·ting at feur·*tu*·la

I have something to declare.
Jag har något att förtulla.   yaa har *naw*·got at feur·*tu*·la

That's (not) mine.
Det är (inte) min.   de air (*in*·te) min

transport

tickets & luggage

Where can I buy a ticket?
Var kan jag köpa en biljett?   *var* kan yaa *sheu*·pa eyn bil·*yet*

Do I need to book a seat?
Måste man boka?   *maw*·ste man *boh*·ka

One ... ticket (to Stockholm), please.	*Jag skulle vilja ha en ... (till Stockholm).*	yaa *sku*·le *vil*·ya haa eyn ... (til *stok*·holm)
one-way	*enkelbiljett*	*en*·kel·bil·*yet*
return	*returbiljett*	re·*toor*·bil·*yet*

I'd like to ... my ticket, please.	*Jag vill gärna ... min biljett.*	yaa vil *yair*·na ... min bil·*yet*
cancel	*upphäva*	*up*·hey·va
change	*ändra*	*en*·dra
collect	*hämta*	*hem*·ta
confirm	*bekräfta*	be·*kref*·ta

I'd like a ... seat, please.	*Jag vill gärna ha en ... plads.*	yaa vil *yair*·na haa eyn ... plads
nonsmoking	*icke-rökande*	*i*·ke·reu·kan·de
smoking	*rökande*	*reu*·kan·de

How much is it?
Hur mycket kostar det?   hoor *mew*·ke *kos*·tar de

Is there air conditioning?
Finns det luft-konditionering?   fins de *luft*·kon·di·fho·*ney*·ring

Is there a toilet?
Finns det en toalett?   fins de eyn toh·aa·*let*

How long does the trip take?
Hur länge undgår resan?   hoor *leng*·e *und*·gawr *rey*·san

Is it a direct route?
Är det en direktförbindelse?   air de eyn dee·*rekt*·feur·bin·del·se

I'd like a luggage locker.
Jag vill gärna få ett låsbara skåp till mit bagage.   yaa vil *yair*·na faw et *laws*·ba·ra skawp til mit ba·*gaash*

My luggage has been ...	*Mit bagage är blivit ...*	mit ba-*gaash* air *blee*·vit ...
damaged	*skadat*	*skaa*·dat
lost	*förlorat*	feur·*loh*·rat
stolen	*stulit*	*stoo*·lit

getting around

Where does flight (SK403) arrive/depart?
Var ankommer/avgår flyg (SK403)?
var *an*·ko·mar/*aav*·gawr flewg (es koh *few*·ra nol trey)

Where's (the) ...?	*Var finns ...?*	var fins ...
arrivals hall	*ankomsthallen*	*an*·komst·ha·len
departures hall	*avgångshallen*	*aav*·gawngs·ha·len
duty-free shop	*en duty-free affär*	eyn *dyoo*·tee-*free* a·*fair*
gate (12)	*gate (tolv)*	gayt (tolv)

Is this the ... to (Stockholm)?	*Är den här ... till (Stockholm)?*	air den hair ... til (*stok*·holm)
boat	*båten*	*baw*·ten
bus	*bussen*	*bu*·sen

Is this the ... to (Stockholm)?	*Är det här ... till (Stockholm)?*	air de hair ... til (*stok*·holm)
plane	*planet*	*plaa*·net
train	*tåget*	*taw*·get

What time's the ... bus?	*När går ...?*	nair gawr ...
first	*första bussen*	*feursh*·ta *bu*·sen
last	*sista bussen*	*sis*·ta *bu*·sen
next	*nästa buss*	*nes*·ta bus

At what time does it arrive/leave?
Hur dags anländer/avgår den?
hoor daks an·*len*·der/*aav*·gawr deyn

How long will it be delayed?
Hur mycket är det försenat?
hoor *mew*·ket air dey feur·*shey*·nat

What station/stop is this?
Vilken station/hållplats är denna?
vil·ken sta·*fhohn/hawl*·plats air *dey*·na

What's the next station/stop?
Vilken är nästa station/hållplats?
vil·ken air *nes*·ta sta·*fhohn/hawl*·plats

Does it stop at (Lund)?
Stannar den på (Lund)?
sta·nar deyn paw (lund)

Please tell me when we get to (Linköping).
Kan du säga till när vi kommer till (Linköping)?
kan doo *say*·ya *til* nair vee *ko*·mer til (*lin*·sheu·ping)

How long do we stop here?
Hur länge stannar vi här?
hoor *leng*·e *sta*·nar vee hair

Is this seat available?
Är denna plads ledig?
air *dey*·na plats *ley*·dig

That's my seat.
Det är min plads.
de air *min* plats

I'd like a taxi ... | *Jag vill gärna få en taxi ...* | yaa vil *yair*·na faw eyn *tak*·see ...
at (9am) | *klockan (nio på morgonen)* | *klo*·kan (*nee*·oh paw *mo*·ro·nen)
now | *nu* | noo
tomorrow | *imorgon* | ee·*mo*·ron

Is this taxi available?
Är denna taxi ledig?
air *dey*·na *tak*·see *ley*·di

How much is it to ...?
Vad kostar det till ...?
vaad *kos*·tar de til ...

Please put the meter on.
Kan du kör på taxametern?
kan doo sheur paw tak·sa·*mey*·tern

Please take me to (this address).
Kan du köra mig till (denna address)?
kan doo *sheu*·ra mey til (*dey*·na a·*dres*)

Please ... | *Kan du ...?* | kan doo ...
slow down | *sakta ner* | *sak*·ta *neyr*
stop here | *stanna här* | *sta*·na *hair*
wait here | *vänta här* | *ven*·ta *hair*

car, motorbike & bicycle hire

I'd like to hire a ... | *Jag vill hyra en ...* | yaa vil *hew*·ra eyn ...
bicycle | *cykel* | *sew*·kel
car | *bil* | beel
motorbike | *motorcykel* | *moh*·tor·sew·kel

with ...	*med ...*	meyd ...
a driver	*chaufför*	fho·*feur*
air conditioning	*luft-konditionering*	luft·kon·di·fho·*ney*·ring
antifreeze	*kylarvätska*	shew·lar·vet·ska
snow chains	*snökedja*	sneu·she·dya

How much for ...	*Hur mycket kostar*	hoor mew·ke *kos*·tar
hire?	*det ...?*	de ...
hourly	*per timma*	peyr *ti*·ma
daily	*per dag*	peyr *daag*
weekly	*per vecka*	peyr *ve*·ka

air	*luft*	luft
oil	*olja*	ol·ya
petrol	*bensin*	ben·*seen*
tyres	*däck* n	dek

I need a mechanic.
Jag behöver en mekaniker.
yaa be·*heu*·ver eyn me·*kaa*·ni·ker

I've run out of petrol.
Jag har ingen bensin kvar.
yaa har *ing*·en ben·*seen* kvar

I have a flat tyre.
Jag har fått punktering.
yaa har fawt punk·*tey*·ring

directions

Where's the ...?	*Var ligger ...?*	var li·ger ...
bank	*banken*	*ban*·ken
city centre	*centrum*	*sen*·trum
hotel	*hotellet*	hoh·*te*·let
market	*salutorget*	*saa*·loo·*tor*·yet
police station	*polisen*	poh·*lee*·sen
post office	*posten*	*pos*·ten
public toilet	*en offentlig toalett*	eyn o·*feynt*·lig toh·aa·*let*
tourist office	*turistinformationen*	too·*rist*·in·for·ma·*fhoh*·nen

Is this the road to (Göteborg)?		
Går den här vägen till (Göteborg)?		gawr den hair *vey*-gen til (yeu-te-*bory*)

Can you show me (on the map)?		
Kan du visa mig (på kartan)?		kan doo *vee*-sa mey (paw *kar*-tan)

What's the address?		
Vilken adress är det?		*vil*-ken a-*dres* air de

How far is it?		
Hur långt är det?		hoor *lawngt* air de

How do I get there?		
Hur kommer man dit?		hoor *ko*-mar man *deet*

Turn ...	*Sväng ...*	sveng ...
at the corner	*vid hörnet*	veed *heur*-net
at the traffic lights	*vid trafikljuset*	veed tra-*feek*-yoo-set
left/right	*till vänster/höger*	til *ven*-ster/*heu*-ger

It's ...	*Det är ...*	de air ...
behind ...	*bakom ...*	*baa*-kom ...
far away	*långt*	lawngt
here	*här*	hair
in front of ...	*framför ...*	*fram*-feur ...
left	*till vänster*	til *ven*-ster
near (to ...)	*nära (på ...)*	*nair*-ra (paw ...)
next to ...	*bredvid ...*	breyd-*veed* ...
on the corner	*vid hörnet*	veed *heur*-net
opposite ...	*mitt emot ...*	mit ey-*moht* ...
right	*till höger*	til *heu*-ger
straight ahead	*rakt fram*	raakt fram
there	*där*	dair

by boat	*med båt*	me *bawt*
by bus	*med buss*	me *bus*
by taxi	*med taxi*	me *tak*-see
by train	*med tåg*	me *tawg*
on foot	*till fods*	til fohts

north	*nord*	nord
south	*syd*	sewd
east	*öst*	eust
west	*väst*	vest

signs

Ingång/Utgång	in-gawng/oot-gawng	Entrance/Exit
Öppet/Stängt	eu-pet/stengt	Open/Closed
Lediga Rum	ley-di-ga rum	Rooms Available
Fullt/Inga Lediga Rum	fult/ing-a ley-di-ga rum	No Vacancies
Information	in-for-ma-fhohn	Information
Polisstation	poh-lees-sta-fhohn	Police Station
Förbjudet	feur-byoo-det	Prohibited
Toaletter	toh-aa-le-ter	Toilets
Herrar	her-ar	Men
Damer	daa-mer	Women
Varm/Kall	varm/kal	Hot/Cold

accommodation

finding accommodation

Where's a ...?	Var finns det ...?	var fins de ...
camping ground	en campingplats	eyn kam-ping-plats
guesthouse	ett gästhus	et yest-hoos
hotel	ett hotell	et hoh-tel
youth hostel	ett vandrarhem	et van-drar-hem

Can you recommend	Kan ni rekommendera	kan nee re-ko-men-dey-ra
somewhere ...?	något ...?	naw-got ...
cheap	billigt	bi-lit
good	bra	braa
nearby	i närheten	ee nair-hey-ten

I'd like to book a room, please.
Jag skulle vilja boka ett rum.   yaa sku-le vil-ya boh-ka et rum

I have a reservation.
Jag har bokat.   yaa har boh-kat

My name's ...
Jag heter ...   yaa hey-ter ...

Do you have a ... room?	*Har ni ...?*	har nee ...
single	*ett enkeltrum*	et *en*-kelt-rum
double	*ett dubbeltrum*	et *du*-belt-rum
twin	*ett rum med två sängar*	et rum me tvaw *seng*-ar

How much is it per ...?	*Hur mycket kostar det per ...?*	hoor *mew*-ket *kos*-tar de peyr ...
night	*natt*	nat
person	*person*	*peyr*-shohn

Can I pay by ...?	*Tar ni ...?*	taar nee ...
credit card	*kreditkort*	kre-*deet*-kort
travellers cheque	*resecheckar*	*rey*-se-she-kar

I'd like to stay for (two) nights.
Jag tänker stanna (två) dagar.
yaa *ten*-kar *sta*-na (tvaw) *daa*-gar

From (July 2) to (July 6).
Från (annan Juli) till (sjätte Juli).
frawn (*a*-nen *yoo*-lee) til (*fhe*-te *yoo*-lee)

Can I see it?
Kan jag få se rummet?
kan yaa *faw* se *ru*-met

Am I allowed to camp here?
Får jag campa här?
fawr yaa *kam*-pa hair

Is there a campsite nearby?
Finns det någon campingplats i närheten?
fins de nawn *kam*-ping-*plats* ee *nair*-hey-ten

requests & queries

When/Where is breakfast served?
När/Var serveras frukost?
nair/var ser-*vey*-ras *froo*-kost

Please wake me at (seven).
Kan ni väcka mig klockan (sju).
kan nee *ve*-ka mey *klo*-kan (fhoo)

Could I have my key, please?
Jag vill gärna ha min nyckel.
yaa vil *yair*-na haa min *new*-kel

Can I get another (blanket)?
Kan jag få en (filt) till?
kan yaa fawr eyn (filt) *till*

Is there an elevator/a safe?
Finns det en hiss/förvaringsbox?
fins de eyn his/feur-*vaa*-rings-boks

14

The room is too ...	Rummet är för ...	ru·met air feur ...
expensive	dyrt	dewrt
noisy	bullrigt	bul·rit
small	litet	lee·tet

The ... doesn't work.	... funkar inte.	... fun·kar in·te
air conditioning	Luftkonditioneringen	luft·kon·di·fho·ney·ring·en
fan	Fläkten	flek·ten
toilet	Toaletten	toh·aa·le·ten

This ... isn't clean.	Denna ... är inte ren.	dey·na ... air in·te reyn
pillow	kudde	ku·de
sheet	lakan	laa·kan
towel	handduk	han·duk

checking out

What time is checkout?
Hur dags måste man checka ut?   hoor daks *maw*·ste man *she*·ka ut

Can I leave my luggage here?
Kan jag lämna min bagage här?   kan yaa *lem*·na min ba·*gaash* hair

Could I have my ..., please?	Kan jag få ...?	kan yaa fawr ...
deposit	min depositionsavgift	min de·poh·si·*fhohns*·aav·yift
passport	mitt pass	mit pas
valuables	mina värdesaker	*mee*·na *vair*·de·saa·ker

communications & banking

the internet

Where's the local Internet café?
Var finns det lokala Internet kaféet?   var fins de loh·*kaa*·la *in*·ter·net ka·*fey*·et

How much is it per hour?
Hur mycket kostar det per timma?   hoor *mew*·ke *kos*·tar de par *ti*·ma

I'd like to ...	*Jag skulle vilja ...*	yaa *sku*·le *vil*·ya ...
check my email	*kolla min e-post*	*ko*·la min *ey*·post
get Internet access	*koppla upp mig till Internetet*	*kop*·la *up* mey til *in*·ter·ne·tet
use a printer	*använda en printer*	*an*·ven·da eyn *prin*·ter
use a scanner	*använda en scanner*	*an*·ven·da eyn *ska*·ner

mobile/cell phone

I'd like a ...	*Jag skulle vilja ha ...*	yaa *sku*·le *vil*·ya haa ...
mobile/cell phone	*en mobil telefon*	eyn moh·*beel* te·le·*fohn*
for hire	*till hyra*	til *hew*·ra
SIM card for your network	*ett sim-kort till detta nätverk*	et *sim*·kort til *de*·ta *neyt*·verk

| What are the rates? | *Vad är prisarna?* | vaad air *pree*·sar·na |

telephone

What's your phone number?
Vad är ditt telefonnummer?　　　vaad air dit te·le·*fohn*·nu·mer

The number is ...
Numret är ...　　　*num*·ret air ...

Where's the nearest public phone?
Var ligger närmaste publiktelefon?　　　var *li*·ger *nair*·ma·ste pub·*leek*·te·le·*fohn*

I'd like to buy a phonecard.
Jag skulle vilja ha ett telefonkort.　　　yaa *sku*·le *vil*·ya haa et te·le·*fohn*·kort

I want to ...	*Jag skulle vilja ...*	yaa *sku*·le *vil*·ya ...
call (Singapore)	*ringa till (Singapore)*	*ring*·a til (*sing*·a·poor)
make a local call	*ringa lokalt*	*ring*·a loh·*kaalt*
reverse the charges	*göra ett ba-samtal*	*yeu*·ra et *be*·aa·sam·taal

How much does ... cost?	*Hur mycket kostar ...?*	hoor *mew*·ke *kos*·tar ...
a (three)-minute call	*ett (tre)minuter-samtal*	et (trey)·mi·noo·te·*sham*·taal
each extra minute	*varje extra minut*	*var*·ye *eks*·tra mi·*noot*

It's (three) kronor per minute.
(Tre) kronor per minut.　　　(tre) *kroh*·nor par mi·*noot*

post office

I want to send a ...	*Jag skulle vilja skicka ett ...*	yaa *sku*·le *vil*·ya *fhi*·ka et ...
fax	*fax*	faks
letter	*brev*	breyv
parcel	*paket*	pa·*keyt*
postcard	*vykort*	vew·kort

I want to buy ...	*Jag skulle vilja ha ...*	yaa *sku*·le *vil*·ya *haa* ...
an envelope	*kuvert*	koo·*ver*
stamps	*frimärken*	*free*·mair·ken

Please send it	*Var snäll och skicka den*	var snel o *fhi*·ka deyn
(to Australia) by ...	*(till Australien) ...*	(til o·*straa*·lyen) ...
airmail	*med flygpost*	me *flewg*·post
express mail	*express*	eks·*pres*
registered mail	*som rekommenderat*	som re·ko·men·*dey*·rat
	brev	breyv
surface mail	*som ytpost*	som *ewt*·post

| Is there any mail for me? | *Finns det post til mig?* | fins de post til mey |

bank

Where's a/an ...?	*Var finns det en ...?*	var fins de eyn ...
ATM	*bankomat*	ban·koh·*maat*
foreign exchange office	*utländsk valuta*	*oot*·lensk va·*loo*·ta

I'd like to ...	*Jag skulle vilja ...*	yaa *sku*·le *vil*·ya ...
arrange a transfer	*överföra pengar*	eu·ver·*fer*·ra *peng*·ar
cash a cheque	*lösa in en check*	*leu*·sa in eyn shek
change a travellers cheque	*växla resecheckar*	*veks*·la *rey*·se·she·kar
change money	*växla pengar*	*veks*·la *peng*·ar
get a cash advance	*ta ut kontant på*	taa oot kon·*tant* paw
	mitt bankkort	mit *bank*·kort
withdraw money	*dra ut pengar*	draa oot *peng*·ar

What's the ...?	*Vad är ...?*	vaad air ...
charge for that	*belastningen för det*	be·*last*·ning·en feur de
exchange rate	*växelkursen*	*vek*·sel·koor·shen

It's ...	*Det är ...*	de air ...
(25) kronor	*(tjugofem) kronor*	(shoo·go·*fem*) *kroh*·nor
free	*gratis*	*graa*·tis

What time does the bank open?
Hur dags öppnar banken? — hoor daks *eup*·nar *ban*·ken

Has my money arrived yet?
Är mina pengar kommit än? — air *mee*·na *peng*·ar *ko*·mit en

sightseeing

getting in

What time does it open/close?
Hur dags öppnar/stänger de? — hoor daks *eup*·nar/*steng*·ar dom

What's the admission charge?
Hur mycket kostar det i inträde? — hoor *mew*·ke *kos*·tar de i *in*·trey·de

Is there a discount for children/students?
Finns det barnrabatt/studentrabatt? — fins de *barn*·ra·bat/stoo·*dent*·ra·bat

I'd like a ...	*Jag skulle vilja ha en ...*	yaa *sku*·le *vil*·ya *haa* eyn ...
catalogue	*katalog*	ka·ta·*lohg*
guide	*resehandbok*	*rey*·se·hand·bohk
local map	*lokal karta*	loh·*kaal* *kar*·ta

I'd like to see ...	*Jag skulle vilja se ...*	yaa *sku*·le *vil*·ya se ...
What's that?	*Vad är det?*	vaad air *de*
Can I take a photo?	*Får jag fotografera?*	fawr yaa foh·toh·gra·*fey*·ra

tours

When's the next ...?	*När avgår nästa ...?*	nair *aav*·gawr *nes*·ta ...
day trip	*dagsturen*	*daks*·too·ren
tour	*turen*	*too*·ren

Is ... included?	*Inkluderas ...*	in·kloo·*dey*·ras ...
accommodation	*logi*	lo·*shee*
the admission charge	*inträden*	*in*·trey·den
food	*mat*	maat
transport	*transport*	tran·*sport*

How long is the tour?
Hur länge undgår turen?   hoor *leng*·e *oon*·gawr *too*·ren

What time should we be back?
Hur dags kommer vi tillbaka?   hoor *daks ko*·mar vee til·*baa*·ka

sightseeing

castle	*slott* n	slot
cathedral	*domkyrka*	*dom*·shewr·ka
church	*kyrka*	*shewr*·ka
main square	*stortorget* n	*stor*·tor·yet
monastery	*kloster* n	*klos*·ter
monument	*monument* n	mo·noo·*ment*
museum	*museum/museet* n	moo·*sey*·oom/moo·*sey*·et
old city	*gamla stan*	*gam*·la staan
palace	*palats*	pa·*lats*
ruins	*ruiner*	roo·*ee*·ner
stadium	*idrottsplats*	*i*·drots·plats
statues	*statyer*	sta·*tew*·er

shopping

enquiries

Where's a ...?	*Var finns det ...?*	var finns de ...
bank	*en bank*	eyn bank
bookshop	*en bokhandel*	eyn *bohk*·han·del
camera shop	*en fotoaffär*	eyn *fo*·toh·a·fair
department store	*ett varuhus*	et *va*·roo·hus
grocery store	*en livsmedelsaffär*	eyn *leevs*·mey·dels·a·fair
market	*en torghandel*	eyn *tory*·han·del
newsagency	*en pressbyrå*	eyn *pres*·bew·raw
supermarket	*ett snabbköp*	et *snab*·sheup

Where can I buy a (padlock)?
Var kan jag köpa ett (hänglås)?　　var kan yaa *sheu*·pa et (*heng*·laws)

I'm looking for …
Jag letar efter …　　yaa *ley*·tar *ef*·ter …

Can I look at it?
Får jag se den?　　fawr yaa se deyn

Do you have any others?
Har ni några andra?　　har nee *naw*·ra *an*·dra

Does it have a guarantee?
Har den garanti?　　har deyn ga·ran·*tee*

Can I have it sent overseas?
Kan jag få den skickat utomlands?　　kan yaa fawr deyn *fhi*·kat *oo*·tom·lants

Can I have (my backpack) repaired?
Kan jag får (min ryggsäck) reparerad?　　kan yaa fawr (min *rewg*·sek) re·pa·*rey*·rad

It's faulty.
Den är felaktig.　　deyn air *fey*·lak·ti

I'd like …, please.	*Jag vill gärna …*	yaa vil *yair*·na …
a bag	*ha en kasse*	ha eyn *ka*·se
a refund	*få en återbäring*	faw eyn *aw*·ter·bai·ring
to return this	*återlämna denna*	*aw*·ter·lem·na *dey*·na

paying

How much is it?
Hur mycket kostar det?　　hoor *mew*·ke *kos*·tar de

Can you write down the price?
Kan du skriva ner priset?　　kan du *skree*·va neyr *pree*·set

That's too expensive.
Det är för dyrt.　　de air feur *dewrt*

What's your lowest price?
Vad är dit lägste pris?　　vaad air dit *leyg*·ste prees

I'll give you (50) kronor.
Jag ger dig (femtio) kronor.　　yaa yer dey (*fem*·ti) *kroh*·nor

There's a mistake in the bill.
Det är ett fel på räkningen.　　de air et *fel* paw *reyk*·ning·en

Do you accept ...?	*Tar ni ...?*	tar nee ...
credit cards	*kreditkort*	kre-*deet*-kort
debit cards	*betalkort*	be-*taal*-kort
travellers cheques	*resecheckar*	*rey*-se-she-kar

I'd like ..., please.	*Jag vill gärna ha ...*	yaa vil *yair*-na ha ...
a receipt	*ett kvitto*	et *kvi*-to
my change	*min växel*	min *vek*-sel

clothes & shoes

Can I try it on?	*Får jag pröva den?*	fawr yaa *preu*-va deyn
My size is (40).	*Min storlek är (fyrtio).*	min *stor*-leyk air (*fewr*-tee)
It doesn't fit.	*Den passar inte.*	deyn *pa*-sar *in*-te

small	*liten*	*lee*-ten
medium	*medelstor*	*mey*-del-stor
large	*stor*	stor

books & music

I'd like a ...	*Jag skulle vilja ha en ...*	yaa *sku*-le *vil*-ya haa eyn ...
newspaper (in English)	*(engelsk) tidning*	(*eng*-elsk) *teed*-ning
pen	*penna*	*pe*-na

Is there an English-language bookshop?
Finns det an bokhandel   fins de eyn *bohk*-han-del
med böcker på engelska?   me *beu*-ker paa *eng*-el-ska

I'm looking for something by (Henning Mankell).
Jag letar efter något av   yaa *ley*-tar *ef*-ter nawt aav
(Henning Mankell).   (*he*-ning *man*-kel)

Can I listen to this?
Kan jag få höra denna?   kan yaa faw *heu*-ra *dey*-na

photography

Could you ...?	Kan du ...?	kan doo ...
burn a CD from	bränna en CD från	bre·na eyn se·de frawn
my memory card	min memory kort	min me·mo·ree kort
develop this film	framkalla denna	fram·ka·la dey·na
	filmen	fil·men
load my film	ladda film i min	la·da film i min
	kamera	kaa·me·ra

I need a ... film	Jag skulle vilja ha en ...	yaa sku·le vil·ya haa eyn ...
for this camera.	till den här kameran.	til deyn hair kaa·me·ra
APS	APS-film	aa·pe·es·film
B&W	svart-vit film	svart·vit film
colour	färg film	fairg film
slide	dia-film	dee·a·film
(200) speed	(tvåhundra)-film	(tvaw·hund·ra)·film

| When will it be ready? | När är den klar? | nair air deyn klaar |

meeting people

greetings, goodbyes & introductions

Hello.	Hej.	hey
Hi.	Hejså.	hey·saw
Good night.	Godnatt.	goh·nat
Goodbye.	Adjö./Hej då.	aa·yeu/hey daw
See you later.	Vi ses senare.	vee seys sey·na·re

Mr	herr	her
Mrs	fru	froo
Miss	fröken	freu·ken

How are you?	Hur står det till?	hoor stawr de til
Fine, thanks. And you?	Bra, tack. Och dig?	braa tak o dey
What's your name?	Vad heter du?	vaad hey·ter doo
My name is ...	Jag heter ...	yaa hey·ter ...
I'm pleased to meet you.	Trevligt att träffas.	treyv·lit at tre·fas

This is my ...	Detta är min ...	de·ta air min ...
boyfriend	pojkvän	poyk·ven
brother	bror	bror
daughter	dotter	do·ter
father	far	far
friend	vän/väninna m/f	ven/ve·ni·na
girlfriend	flickvän	flik·ven
husband	man	man
mother	mor	mor
partner (intimate)	partner	part·ner
sister	syster	sews·ter
son	son	sohn
wife	fru	froo

Here's my ...	Här är min ...	hair air min ...
What's your ...?	Vad är din ...?	vaad air din ...
address	adress	a·dres
email address	e-post adress	ey·post a·dres

Here's my ...	Här är mitt ...	hair air mit ...
What's your ...?	Vad är ditt ...?	vaad air dit ...
fax number	fax-nummer	faks·nu·mer
phone number	telefonnummer	te·le·fohn·nu·mer

occupations

What's your occupation?	Vad har du för yrke?	vaad har doo feur ewr·ke
I'm a/an ...	Jag är ...	yaa air ...
artist	konstnär	konst·nair
business person	affärsman	a·fairsh·man
office worker	kontorist	kon·to·rist
scientist	naturvetare	na·toor·vey·ta·re
tradesperson	detaljhandlare	de·taly·hand·la·re

background

Where are you from?	Varifrån kommer du?	var·ee·frawn ko·mer doo
I'm from ...	Jag kommer från ...	yaa ko·mer frawn ...
Australia	Australien	o·straa·lyen
Canada	Kanada	ka·na·da
England	England	eng·land
New Zealand	Nya Zealand	new·a sey·land
the USA	USA	oo·es·aa
Are you married?	Är du gift?	air doo yift
I'm married.	Jag är gift.	yaa air yift
I'm single.	Jag är ogift.	yaa air oh·yift

age

How old ...?	Hur gammal ...?	hoor ga·mal ...
are you	är du	air doo
is your daughter	är din dotter	air din do·ter
is your son	är din son	air din sohn

I'm ... years old.
Jag är ... år gammal.   yaa air ... awr ga·mal

He/She is ... years old.
Han/Hon är ... år gammal.   han/hon air ... awr ga·mal

feelings

I'm (not) ...	Jag är (inte) ...	yaa air (in·te) ...
Are you ...?	Är du ...?	air doo ...
happy	glad	glaad
hot	varm	varm
hungry	hungrig	hung·greeg
sad	ledsen	le·sen
thirsty	törstig	teur·shteeg
tired	trött	treut

Are you cold?	Fryser du?	frew·ser doo
I'm (not) cold.	Jag fryser (inte).	yaa frew·ser (in·te)
Are you OK?	Mår du bra?	mawr doo braa
I'm (not) OK.	Jag mår (inte) bra.	yaa mawr (in·te) braa

entertainment

going out

Where can I find ...?	Var finns ...?	var fins ...
clubs	klubbarna	klu·bar·na
gay venues	gayklubbarna	gay·klu·bar·na
pubs	pubbarna	pu·bar·na

I feel like going to a/the ...	Jag vil gärna gå på ...	yaa vil yair·na gaw paw ...
concert	konsert	kon·seyr
movies	bio	bee·oh
party	fest	fest
restaurant	restaurang	res·taw·rang
theatre	teater	tee·ay·ter

interests

Do you like ...?	Tycker du om ...?	tew·ker doo om ...
I (don't) like ...	Jag tycker (inte) om ...	yaa tew·ker (in·te) om ...
art	konst	konst
cooking	att laga mat	at laa·ga maat
movies	film	film
nightclubs	natklubbar	nat·klu·bar
reading	att läsa	at ley·sa
shopping	att shoppa	at sho·pa
sport	sport	sport
travelling	att resa	at rey·sa

Do you like to ...?	Tycker du om att ...?	tew·ker doo om at ...
dance	dansa	dan·sa
go to concerts	gå på konsert	gaw paw kon·seyr
listen to music	lyssna på musik	lews·na paw moo·seek

food & drink

finding a place to eat

Can you recommend a ...?	Kan du anbefalla en ...?	kan doo an·be·fa·la eyn ...
bar	bar	bar
café	kafé	ka·fey
restaurant	restaurang	res·taw·rang

I'd like ..., please.	..., tack.	... tak
a table for (four)	Ett bord för (fyra)	et bord feur (few·ra)
the nonsmoking section	Rökfria avdelningen	reuk·free·a aav·del·ning·en
the smoking section	Rökavdelningen	reuk·aav·del·ning·en

ordering food

breakfast	frukost	froo·kost
lunch	lunch	lunsh
dinner	middag	mi·daa
snack	mellanmål n	me·lan·mawl
today's special	dagens rätt	daa·gens ret

What would you recommend?
Vad skulle ni anbefalla?   vaad sku·le nee an·be·fa·la

I'd like (the) ...	Jag skulle vilja ha ...	yaa sku·le vil·ya haa ...
bill	räkningen	reyk·ning·en
drink list	drickslistan	driks·lis·tan
menu	menyn	me·newn
that dish	den maträtt	deyn maat·ret

drinks

(cup of) coffee ...	*(en kopp) kaffe ...*	*(eyn kop) ka·fe ...*
(cup of) tea ...	*(en kopp) te ...*	*(eyn kop) tey ...*
with milk	*med mjölk*	me myeulk
without sugar	*utan socker*	oo·taan so·ker
(orange) juice	*(apelsin)juice*	(a·pel·seen·)djoos
soft drink	*läsk*	lesk
boiled water	*kokt vatten* n	kohkt va·ten
mineral water	*mineralvatten* n	mi·ne·raal·va·ten
water	*vatten* n	va·ten

in the bar

I'll have ...
Jag vill ha ...   yaa vil haa ...

I'll buy you a drink.
Jag köper dig en drink.   yaa *sheu·*per dey eyn *drink*

What would you like?
Vad vill du ha?   vaad vil doo *haa*

Cheers!
Skål!   skawl

brandy	*brandy*	bran·dee
cocktail	*cocktail*	kok·tayl
cognac	*cognac*	kon·yak
a shot of (whisky)	*2 cl (whiskey)*	tvaw sen·ti·ley·ter (*vis·*kee)
a ... of beer	*... öl*	... eul
bottle	*en flaska*	eyn *flas·*ka
glass	*ett glass*	et glaas
a bottle of ...	*en flaska ...*	eyn *flas·*ka ...
a glass of ...	*ett glas ...*	et glaas ...
red wine	*rödvin*	reud·veen
sparkling wine	*mousserande vin*	moo·*sey·*ran·de veen
white wine	*vitt vin*	vit veen

self-catering

What's the local speciality?
Vad är den lokala specialiteten?   vaad air deyn loh·*kaa*·la spe·si·a·li·*tey*·ten

What's that?
Vad är det?   vaad air de

How much is (a kilo of cheese)?
Hur mycket kostar (en kilo ost)?   hoor *mew*·ke *kos*·tar (eyn *shee*·loh ohst)

I'd like ...	*Jag vil ha ...*	yaa vil ha ...
(100) grams	*(hundra) gram*	(*hun*·dra) gram
(two) kilos	*(två) kilo*	(*tvaw*) *shee*·loh
(three) pieces	*(tre) styck*	(*trey*) stewk
(six) slices	*(sex) skivor*	(*seks*) *fhee*·vor

Less.	*Mindre.*	*min*·dre
Enough.	*Det räcker.*	de *re*·ker
More.	*Mera.*	*mey*·ra

special diets & allergies

Is there a vegetarian restaurant near here?
Finns det en vegetarisk   fins de eyn ve·ge·*taa*·risk
restaurang i närheten?   res·taw·*rang* ee *nair*·hey·ten

Do you have vegetarian food?
Har ni vegetarisk mat?   har nee ve·ge·*taa*·risk maat

Could you prepare	*Kan ni laga*	kan nee *laa*·ga
a meal without ...?	*en maträtt utan ...?*	eyn *maat*·ret *oo*·tan ...
butter	*smör*	smeur
eggs	*ägg*	eg
meat stock	*köttspad*	*sheut*·spaad

I'm allergic to ...	*Jag är allergisk mot ...*	yaa air al·*leyr*·gisk moht ...
dairy produce	*mejeriprodukter*	me·ye·*ree*·pro·*dook*·ter
gluten	*gluten*	*gloo*·ten
MSG	*MSG*	em·es·*gee*
nuts	*nötter*	*neu*·ter
seafood	*fisk och skaldjur*	fisk o *skaal*·yoor

emergencies

basics

Help!	*Hjälp!*	yelp
Stop!	*Stanna!*	*sta*·na
Go away!	*Försvinn!*	feur·*shvin*
Thief!	*Ta fast tjuven!*	ta fast *shoo*·ven
Fire!	*Elden är lös!*	*el*·den air *leus*
Watch out!	*Se upp!*	se up

Call ...!	*Ring ...!*	ring ...
a doctor	*efter en doktor*	*ef*·ter en *dok*·tor
an ambulance	*efter en ambulans*	*ef*·ter en am·boo·*lans*
the police	*polisen*	poh·*lee*·sen

It's an emergency!
Det är ett nödsituation!   de air et *neud*·si·too·a·fhohn

Could you help me, please?
Kan du hjälpa mig?   kan doo *yel*·pa mai

I have to use the telephone.
Jag måste använda telefonen.   yaa *maws*·te *an*·ven·da te·le·*foh*·nen

I'm lost.
Jag har gått vilse.   yaa har got *vil*·se

Where are the toilets?
Var är toaletten?   var air toh·aa·*le*·ten

police

Where's the police station?
Var är polisstationen?   var air poh·*lees*·sta·*fhoh*·nen

I want to report an offence.
Jag vill anmäla ett brott.   yaa vil *an*·mey·la et brot

I have insurance.
Jag har försäkring.   yaa har feur·*shey*·kring

I've been assaulted.
Jag är blivit utsatt för övervåld.   yaa air *blee*·vit *ut*·sat feur *eu*·ver·vawld

I've been ...	Jag har blivit ...	yaa har *blee*·vit ...
raped	*våldtagen*	*vol*·taa·gen
robbed	*rånad*	*raw*·nad

I've lost my ...	Jag har förlorat ...	yaa har feur·*loh*·rat ...
backpack	*min ryggsäck*	min *rewk*·sek
bags	*mina väskor*	*mee*·na *ves*·kor
credit card	*min kreditkort*	min kre·*deet*·kort
handbag	*min handväska*	min *hand*·ves·ka
jewellery	*mina smycken*	*mee*·na *smew*·ken
money	*mina pengar*	*mee*·na *peng*·ar
passport	*mitt pass*	mit pas
travellers cheques	*mina resecheckar*	*mee*·na *rey*·se·she·kar
wallet	*min plånbok*	min *plawn*·bohk

I want to contact my ...	Jag vill kontakta ...	yaa vil kon·*tak*·ta ...
consulate	*mitt konsulat*	mit kon·soo·*laat*
embassy	*min ambassad*	min am·ba·*saad*

health

medical needs

Where's the nearest ...?	Var är närmaste ...?	var air *nair*·ma·ste ...
dentist	*tandläkaren*	*tand*·ley·ka·ren
doctor	*doktorn*	*dok*·torn
hospital	*sjukhuset*	*fhook*·hu·set
(night) pharmacist	*(natt)apoteket*	*(nat*·)a·poh·*te*·ket

I need a doctor (who speaks English).
Jag behöver en läkare   yaa be·*heu*·ver eyn *ley*·ka·re
(som talar engelska).   (som *taa*·lar *eng*·el·ska)

Could I see a female doctor?
Kan jag få träffa en kvinnlig läkare?   kan yaa faw *tre*·fa eyn *kvin*·li *ley*·ka·re

I've run out of my medication.
Jag har ingen medikament kvar.   yaa har *ing*·en me·di·ka·*ment* kvar

symptoms, conditions & allergies

I'm sick.	Jag är sjuk.	yaa air fhook
It hurts here.	Det gör ont här.	de yeur ont hair
I have nausea.	Jag mår illa.	yaa mawr i-la

I have (a) ...	Jag har ...	yaa haa ...
asthma	astma	ast-maa
bronchitis	bronkit	bron-keet
constipation	förstoppning	feur-shtop-ning
cough	en hosta	eyn hoh-sta
diarrhoea	diarré	dee-a-rey
fever	feber	fey-ber
headache	huvudvärk	hoo-vud-vairk
heart condition	en hjärttillstånd	eyn yairt-til-stawnd
pain	ont	ont
sore throat	ont i halsen	ont ee hal-sen
toothache	tandvärk	tand-verk

I'm allergic to ...	Jag är allergisk mot ...	yaa air a-leyr-gisk moht ...
antibiotics	antibiotika	an-tee-bee-oh-ti-ka
anti-inflammatories	anti-inflammatoriska medel	an-tee-in-fla-ma-toh-ri-ska mey-del
aspirin	magnecyl	mag-ne-sewl
bees	bin	been
codeine	kodein	koh-deen
penicillin	penicillin	pe-ne-si-leen

antiseptic	antiseptiskt medel n	an-tee-sep-tiskt mey-del
bandage	förband n	feur-band
condoms	kondomer	kon-doh-mer
diarrhoea medicine	medel mot diarré n	mey-del moht dee-a-rey
insect repellent	insektsmedel n	in-sekts-mey-del
laxatives	laxermedel n	lak-ser-mey-del
painkillers	smärtstillande medel n	smairt-sti-lan-de mey-del
rehydration salts	vätskeersätt-ningsmedel n	vet-ske-er-set-nings-mey-del
sleeping tablets	sovmedel n	sohv-mey-del

english–swedish dictionary

In this dictionary, words are marked as n (noun), a (adjective), v (verb), sg (singular), pl (plural), inf (informal) and pol (polite) where necessary. Note that Swedish nouns are either masculine, feminine or neuter. Masculine and feminine forms (known as 'common gender') take the indefinite article *en* (a) while the neuter forms take the article *ett* (a). Every Swedish noun needs to be learned with its indefinite article (*en* or *ett*). We've only indicated the neuter nouns with ⑩ after the Swedish word. Note also that the ending 't' is added to adjectives for the neuter form (ie when they accompany masculine singular nouns). In some cases both forms of the adjective (ie ⑩&⑥ form and ⑥ form) are spelled out in full and separated with a slash.

A

accident *olycka* oh-lew-ka
accommodation *husrum* ⑩ *hus*-rum
adaptor *adapter* a-*dap*-ter
address n *adress* a-*dres*
after *efter* ef-ter
air-conditioned *luftkonditionerad/luftkonditionerat*
 luft-kon-di-fho-*ney*-rad/*luft*-kon-di-fho-*ney*-rat
airplane *flygplan* ⑩ *flewg*-plaan
airport *flygplats* *flewg*-plats
alcohol *alkohol* al-ko-*hohl*
all *alla* a-la
all (everything) n *allt* alt
allergy *allergi* a-ler-*gee*
ambulance *ambulans* am-bu-*lans*
and *och* ok
ankle *vrist* vrist
arm *arm* arm
ashtray *askfat* ⑩ *ask*-faat
ATM *bankomat* bang-koh-*maat*

B

baby *baby* *bey*-bee
back (body) *rygg* rewg
backpack *ryggsäck* *rewg*-sek
bad *dårlig(t)* *dawr*-lig/*dawr*-lit
bag *väska* *ves*-ka
baggage claim *bagageavhämtning*
 ba-*gaash*-aav-*hemt*-ning
bank *bank* bank
bar *bar* baar
bathroom *badrum* ⑩ *baad*-rum
battery *batteri* ⑩ ba-te-*ree*
beautiful *vacker(t)* va-ker(t)
bed *säng* seng

beer *öl* ⑩ eul
before *framför* fram-*feur*
behind *bakom* baa-kom
bicycle *cykel* sew-kel
big *stor(t)* stawr(t)
bill *räkning* reyk-ning
black *svart* svart
blanket *filt* filt
blood group *blodgrupp* blohd-grup
blue *blå(tt)* blaw/blot
boat *båt* bawt
book (make a reservation) v *boka* boh-ka
bottle *flaska* flas-ka
bottle opener *flasköppnare* flask-eup-na-re
boy *pojke* poy-ke
brakes (car) *bromsar* brom-sar
breakfast *frukost* froo-kost
broken (faulty) *sönder* seun-der
bus *buss* bus
(do) business *handla* hand-la
buy *köpa* sheu-pa

C

café *kafé* ⑩ ka-*fey*
camera *kamera* kaa-me-ra
camp site *campingplats* kam-ping-plats
cancel *upphäva* up-hey-va
can opener *burköppnare* burk-eup-na-re
car *bil* beel
cash n *kontant* kon-*tant*
cash (a cheque) v *lösa in (en check)* leu-sa in (eyn shek)
cell phone *mobiltelefon* moh-*beel*-te-le-fohn
centre *center* ⑩ sen-ter
change (money) v *växla (pengar)* veyk-sla (peng-ar)
cheap *billig(t)* bi-lig/bi-lit
check (bill) *räkning* reyk-ning

check-in *incheckning* in-chek-ning
chest *bröst* ⓝ breust
child *barn* ⓝ barn
cigarette *cigarett* si-ga-ret
city *storstad* stawr-staad
clean a *ren(t)* reyn(t)
closed *stängd/stängt* stengd/stengt
coffee *kaffe* ⓝ ka-fe
coins *mynt* ⓝ mewnt
cold a *kylig(t)* shew-lig/shew-lit
collect call *ba-samtal* ⓝ be-aa-sam-taal
come *komma* ko-ma
computer *dator* daa-tor
condom *kondom* kon-dohm
contact lenses *kontaktlinser* kon-takt-lin-ser
cook v *laga mat* laa-ga maat
cost n *kostnad* kost-nad
credit card *kreditkort* ⓝ kre-deet-kort
cup *kopp* kop
currency exchange *växel* veyk-sel
customs (immigration) *tullen* tu-len

D

dangerous *farlig(t)* far-lig/far-lit
date (time) *datum* ⓝ daa-tum
day *dag* daag
delay *dröjsmål* ⓝ dreuys-mawl
dentist *tandläkare* tand-ley-ka-re
depart *avresa* aav-rey-sa
diaper *blöja* bleu-ya
dictionary *ordbok* ord-bohk
dinner *middag* mi-daag
direct *direkt* dee-rekt
dirty *smutsig(t)* smut-sig/smut-sit
disabled *handikappad* han-dee-ka-pad
discount n *rabatt* ra-bat
doctor *läkare* ley-ka-re
double bed *dubbelsäng* du-bel-seng
double room *dubbelt rum* ⓝ du-belt rum
drink n *dricka* dri-ka
drive v *köra* sheu-ra
drivers licence *körkort* ⓝ sheur-kort
drug (illicit) *narkotika* nar-koh-ti-ka
dummy (pacifier) *napp* nap

E

ear *öra* eu-ra
east *öst* eust

eat *äta* ey-ta
economy class *ekonomiklass* e-ko-noh-mee-klas
electricity *elektricitet* ey-lek-tri-si-teyt
elevator *hiss* his
email *e-post* ey-post
embassy *ambassad* am-ba-saad
emergency *nödsituation* ⓝ neud-si-too-a-fhohn
English (language) *engelska* eng-el-ska
entrance *ingång* in-gawng
evening *kväll* kvel
exchange rate *växelkurs* veyk-sel-kursh
exit n *utgång* oot-gawng
expensive *dyr(t)* dewr(t)
express mail *expresspost* eks-pres-post
eye *öga* ⓝ eu-ga

F

far *långt* lawngt
fast *snabb(t)* snab(t)
father *far* faar
film (camera) *film* film
finger *finger* ⓝ fing-er
first-aid kit *förbandslåda* feur-bants-law-da
first class *första klass* feu-shta klas
fish n *fisk* fisk
food *mat* maat
foot *fot* foht
fork *gaffel* ga-fel
free (of charge) *gratis* graa-tis
friend *vän/vännina* ⓜ/ⓕ ven/ve-ni-na
fruit *frukt* frukt
full *fylld/fyllt* fewld/fewlt
funny *rolig(t)* roh-lig/roh-lit

G

gift *gåva* gaw-va
girl *flicka* fli-ka
glass (drinking) *glas* ⓝ glaas
glasses *glasögon* ⓝ glaa-seu-gon
go *åka* aw-ka
good *bra* braa
green *grön(t)* greun(t)
guide n *guide* gaid

H

half n *halv* halv
hand *hand* hand

handbag *handväska* *hand*·vey·ska
happy *glad* glaad
have *ha* haa
he *han* han
head *huvud* ⓝ *hoo*·vud
heart *hjärta* *yair*·ta
heat n *hetta* *he*·ta
heavy *tung(t)* tung(t)
help v *hjälp* yelp
here *här* hair
high *hög(t)* heug(t)
highway *huvudväg* *hoo*·vud·veyg
hike v *fotvandra* *foht*·van·dra
holiday *semester* se·*mes*·ter
homosexual n&a *homosexuell* hoh·moh·sek·soo·*el*
hospital *sjukhus* ⓝ *fhook*·hoos
hot *varm(t)* varm(t)
hotel *hotell* ⓝ hoh·*tel*
hungry *hungrig(t)* *hung*·grig/*hung*·grit
husband *man* man

I

I *jag* yaag
identification (card) *identitetskort* ⓝ ee·den·ti·*teyts*·kort
ill *sjuk(t)* fhook(t)
important *viktig(t)* *vik*·tig/*vik*·tit
included *inklusiv* in·kloo·*seev*
injury *skada* *skaa*·da
insurance *försäkring* feu·*shey*·kring
Internet *Internet* ⓝ *in*·ter·net
interpreter *tolk* tolk

J

jewellery *smycke* ⓝ *smew*·ke
job *arbete* ⓝ *aar*·bey·te

K

key *nyckel* *new*·kel
kilogram *kilo(gram)* ⓝ *shee*·loh(·gram)
kitchen *kök* ⓝ sheuk
knife *kniv* kneev

L

laundry (place) *tvättstuga* *tvet*·stoo·ga
lawyer *advokat* ad·voh·*kaat*
left (direction) *vänster* *ven*·ster
left-luggage office *resgodsinlämning* *reys*·gohds·in·lem·ning
leg *ben* ⓝ beyn
lesbian a *lesbisk* *lez*·bisk
less *mindre* *min*·dre
letter (mail) *brev* ⓝ breyv
lift (elevator) *hiss* his
light *ljus* ⓝ yoos
like v *tycka om* *tew*·ka om
lock n *lås* laws
long *lång(t)* lawng(t)
(be) lost (of a person) *vilse* *vil*·se
(be) lost (of property) *borta* *bor*·ta
lost-property office *hittegodsexpedition* *hi*·te·gohds·eks·pe·di·*fhohn*
love v *älska* *el*·ska
luggage *bagage* ⓝ ba·*gaash*
lunch *lunch* lunsh

M

mail n *post* post
man *man* man
map *karta* *kar*·ta
market *marknad/torg* ⓝ *mark*·naad/tory
matches *tändstickor* *ten*·sti·kor
meat *kött* ⓝ sheut
medicine *medicin* me·di·*seen*
menu *meny/matsedel* me·*new*/*maat*·sey·del
message *bud* ⓝ bood
milk *mjölk* myeulk
minute *minut* mi·*noot*
mobile phone *mobiltelefon* moh·*beel*·te·le·fohn
money *pengar* *peng*·ar
month *månad* *maw*·nad
morning *morgon* *mor*·gon
mother *mor* mawr
motorcycle *motorcykel* *moh*·tor·sew·kel
motorway *motorväg* *moh*·tor·veyg
mouth *mun* mun
music *musik* moo·*seek*

N

name *namn* ⓝ namn
napkin *servett* seyr·*vet*
nappy *blöja* *bleu*·ya
near *nära* *nair*·a

neck *hals* hals
new *ny(tt)* new(t)
news *nyheter* new-hey-ter
newspaper *tidning* teed-ning
night *natt* nat
no *nej* ney
noisy *bullrig(t)* bul-rig/bul-rit
nonsmoking *icke-rökande* i-ke-reu-kan-de
north *nord* nord
nose *näsa* ney-sa
now *nu* noo
number *nummer* ⓝ nu-mer

O

oil (engine) *olja* ol-ya
old *gammal(t)* ga-mal(t)
one-way ticket *enkelbiljett* en-kel-bil-yet
open a *öppen/öppet* eu-pen/eu-pet
outside *utanför* oo-tan-feur

P

package *paket* ⓝ pa-keyt
paper *papper* ⓝ pa-per
park (car) v *parkera* par-key-ra
passport *pass* ⓝ pas
pay *betala* be-taa-la
pen *penna* pe-na
petrol *bensin* ben-seen
pharmacy *apotek* ⓝ a-poh-teyk
phonecard *telefonkort* ⓝ tel-le-fohn-kort
photo *foto* ⓝ foh-toh
plate *tallrik* tal-reek
police *polis* poh-lees
postcard *postkort* ⓝ post-kort
post office *posten* pos-ten
pregnant *gravid* gra-veed
price *pris* prees

Q

quiet *stilla* stil-la

R

rain n *regn* rengn
razor *rakhyvel* raak-hew-vel
receipt *kvitto* ⓝ kvi-toh

red *röd/rött* reud/reut
refund n *återbäring* aw-ter-bair-ing
registered mail *värdeförsändelse*
   vair-de-feu-shen-del-se
rent v *hyra* hew-ra
repair v *reparera* re-pa-rey-ra
reservation *beställning* be-stel-ning
restaurant *restaurang* res-taw-rang
return v *återvända* aw-ter-ven-da
return ticket *returbiljett* rey-toor-bil-yet
right (direction) *höger* heu-ger
road *väg* veyg
room *rum* ⓝ rum

S

safe a *trygg(t)* trewg(t)
sanitary napkin *dambinda* daam-bin-da
seat *sittplats* sit-plats
send *skicka* fhi-ka
service station *bensinstation* ben-seen-sta-fhohn
sex *samlag* ⓝ sam-laag
shampoo *schampo* ⓝ fham-poo
share (a dorm) *dela* dey-la
shaving cream *rakkräm* raak-kreym
she *hon* hoon
sheet (bed) *lakan* ⓝ laa-kan
shirt *skjorta* fhor-ta
shoes *skor* skor
shop n *affär* a-fair
short *kort* kort
shower n *dusch* doosh
single room *enkelt rum* ⓝ en-kelt rum
skin *hud* hood
skirt *kjol* shohl
sleep v *sova* soh-va
slowly *sakta* sak-ta
small *liten/litet* lee-ten/lee-tet
smoke (cigarettes) v *röka* reu-ka
soap *tvål* tvawl
some *någon/något* naw-gon/naw-got
soon *snart* snart
south *syd* sewd
souvenir shop *souvenir affär* su-ve-neer a-fair
speak *tala* taa-la
spoon *sked* fheyd
stamp *frimärke* ⓝ free-mair-ke
stand-by ticket *standbybiljett* stand-bai-bil-yet
station (train) *(järnvägs)station* (yairn-veyks-)sta-fhohn

stomach *mage* maa-ge
stop v *stanna/hålla* sta-na/haw-la
stop (bus) n *(buss)hållplats* (bus-)hawl-plats
street *gata* gaa-ta
student *studerande* stoo-dey-ran-de
sun *sol* sohl
sunscreen *solkräm* sohl-kreym
Sweden *Sverige* sve-rya
Swedish (language) *svenska* sven-ska
Swedish a *svensk(t)* svensk(t)
swim v *simma* si-ma

T

tampons *tampong* tam-pong
taxi *taxi* tak-see
teaspoon *tesked* tey-fheyd
teeth *tänder* te-ner
telephone n *telefon* te-le-fohn
television *TV* tey-vey
temperature (weather) *temperatur* tem-pe-ra-toor
tent *tält* n telt
that (one) *den* m & f/*det* n deyn/dey
they *dem* dom
thirsty *törstig(t)* teush-tig/teush-tit
this (one) *den här* m & f/*det här* n den hair/dey hair
throat *strupe* stroo-pe
ticket *biljett* bil-yet
time *tid* teed
tired *trött* treut
tissues *näsdukar* neys-doo-kar
today *i dag* i daag
toilet *toalett* toh-aa-let
tomorrow *imorgon* ee-mor-ron
tonight *i kväll* ee kvel
toothbrush *tandbörste* tand-beu-shte
toothpaste *tandkräm* tand-kreym
torch (flashlight) *ficklampa* fik-lam-pa
tour n *tur* toor
tourist office *turistbyrå* too-rist-bew-raw
towel *badduk* baad-dook
train *tåg* n tawg
translate *översätta* eu-ve-se-ta
travel agency *resebyrå* rey-se-bew-raw
travellers cheque *resecheck* rey-se-shek
trousers *byxor* bewk-sor
twin beds *två sängar* tvaw seng-ar
tyre *däck* n dek

U

underwear *underkläder* un-der-kley-der
urgent *angelägen/angeläget*
  an-ye-ley-gen/an-ye-ley-get

V

vacant *ledig(t)* ley-dig/ley-dit
vacation *semester* se-mes-ter
vegetable n *grönsak* greun-saak
vegetarian a *vegetarian* ve-ge-taa-ree-aan
visa *visum* n vee-sum

W

waiter *servitör* ser-vi-teur
Waiter! *Vaktmästern!* vakt-mes-tern
walk v *gå* gaw
wallet *plånbok* plawn-bohk
warm a *varm(t)* varm(t)
wash (something) *tvätta* tve-ta
watch n *klocka* klo-ka
water *vatten* n va-ten
we *vi* vee
weekend *helg* hely
west *väst* vest
wheelchair *rullstol* rul-stohl
when *när* nair
where *var* var
white *vit(t)* veet/vit
who *vem* vem
why *varför* var-feur
wife *fru* froo
window *fönster* feun-ster
wine *vin* n veen
with *med* meyd
without *utan* oo-taan
woman *kvinna* kvi-na
write *skriva* skree-va

Y

yellow *gul(t)* gul(t)
yes *ja* yaa
yesterday *igår* i-gawr
you sg inf *du* doo
you sg pol & pl *ni* nee

Turkish

A a a	*B b* be	*C c* je	*Ç ç* che	*D d* de
E e e	*F f* fe	*G g* ge	*Ğ ğ* yu-*moo*-shak ge	*H h* he
I ı uh	*İ i* ee	*J j* zhe	*K k* ke	*L l* le
M m me	*N n* ne	*O o* o	*Ö ö* er	*P p* pe
R r re	*S s* se	*Ş ş* she	*T t* te	*U u* oo
Ü ü ew	*V v* ve	*Y y* ye	*Z z* ze	

■ turkish

TÜRKÇE

introduction

Turkish (*Türkçe* tewrk-che) – the language which traces its roots as far back as 3500 BC, has travelled through Central Asia, Persia, North Africa and Europe and been written in both Arabic and Latin script – has left us words like *yogurt*, *horde*, *sequin* and *bridge* (the game) along the way. But how did it transform itself from a nomad's tongue spoken in Mongolia into the language of modern Turkey, with a prestigious interlude as the diplomatic language of the Ottoman Empire?

The first evidence of the Turkish language, which is a member of the Ural-Altaic language family, was found on stone monuments from the 8th century BC, in what's now Outer Mongolia. In the 11th century, the Seljuq clan invaded Asia Minor (Anatolia) and imposed their language on the peoples they ruled. Over time, Arabic and Persian vocabulary was adopted to express artistic and philosophical concepts and Arabic script began to be used. By the 14th century, another clan – the Ottomans – was busy establishing the empire that was to control Eurasia for centuries. In their wake, they left the Turkish language. There were then two levels of Turkish – ornate Ottoman Turkish, with flowery Persian phrases and Arabic honorifics (words showing respect), used for diplomacy, business and art, and the language of the common Turks, which still used 'native' Turkish vocabulary and structures.

When the Ottoman Empire fell in 1922, the military hero, amateur linguist and historian Kemal Atatürk came to power and led the new Republic of Turkey. With the backing of a strong language reform movement, he devised a phonetic Latin script that reflected Turkish sounds more accurately than Arabic script. On 1 November 1928, the new writing system was unveiled: within two months, it was illegal to write Turkish in the old script. In 1932 Atatürk created the *Türk Dil Kurumu* (Turkish Language Society) and gave it the brief of simplifying the Turkish language to its 'pure' form of centuries before. The vocabulary and structure was completely overhauled. As a consequence, Turkish has changed so drastically that even Atatürk's own speeches are barely comprehensible to today's speakers of *öztürkçe* ('pure Turkish').

With 70 million speakers worldwide, Turkish is the official language of Turkey and the Turkish Republic of Northern Cyprus (recognised as a nation only by the Turkish government). Elsewhere, the language is also called *Osmanlı* os-man-luh, and is spoken by large populations in Germany, Bulgaria, Macedonia, Greece and the '-stans' of Central Asia. So start practising and you might soon be complimented with *Ağzına sağlık!* a-zuh-na sa-luhk (lit: health to your mouth) – 'Well said!'

pronunciation

vowel sounds

Most Turkish vowel sounds can be found in English, although in Turkish they're generally shorter and slightly harsher. When you see a double vowel, such as *saat* sa-*at* (hour), you need to pronounce both vowels.

symbol	english equivalent	turkish example	transliteration
a	run	*abide*	a-bee-*de*
ai	aisle	*hayvan*	hai-*van*
ay	say	*ney*	nay
e	bet	*ekmek*	ek-*mek*
ee	see	*ile*	ee-*le*
eu	nurse	*özel*	eu-*zel*
ew	ee pronounced with rounded lips	*üye*	ew-*ye*
o	pot	*oda*	o-*da*
oo	zoo	*uçak*	oo-*chak*
uh	ago	*ıslak*	uhs-*lak*

word stress

In Turkish, the stress generally falls on the last syllable of the word. Most two-syllable placenames, however, are stressed on the first syllable (eg *Kıbrıs* kuhb-ruhs), and in three-syllable placenames the stress is usually on the second syllable (eg *İstanbul* ees-*tan*-bool). Another common exception occurs when a verb has a form of the negative marker *me* (*me* me, *ma* ma, *mı* muh, *mi* mee, *mu* moo, or *mü* mew) added to it. In those cases, the stress goes onto the syllable before the marker – eg *gelmiyorlar* gel-*mee*-yor-lar (they're not coming). You don't need to worry too much about this, as the stressed syllable is always in italics in our coloured pronunciation guides.

consonant sounds

Most Turkish consonants sound the same as in English, so they're straightforward to pronounce. The exception is the Turkish r, which is always rolled. Note also that ğ is a silent letter which extends the vowel before it – it acts like the 'gh' combination in 'weigh', and is never pronounced.

symbol	english equivalent	turkish example	transliteration
b	bed	*bira*	bee-ra
ch	cheat	*çanta*	chan-ta
d	dog	*deniz*	de-neez
f	fat	*fabrika*	fab-ree-ka
g	go	*gar*	gar
h	hat	*hala*	ha-la
j	joke	*cadde*	jad-de
k	kit	*kadın*	ka-duhn
l	lot	*lider*	lee-der
m	man	*maç*	mach
n	not	*nefis*	ne-fees
p	pet	*paket*	pa-ket
r	red (rolled)	*rehber*	reh-ber
s	sun	*saat*	sa-at
sh	shot	*şarkı*	shar-kuh
t	top	*tas*	tas
v	van (but softer, between 'v' and 'w')	*vadi*	va-dee
y	yes	*yarım*	ya-ruhm
z	zero	*zarf*	zarf
zh	pleasure	*jambon*	zham-bon

language difficulties

Do you speak English?
İngilizce konuşuyor musunuz?   een-gee-*leez*-je ko-noo-*shoo*-yor moo-soo-*nooz*

Do you understand?
Anlıyor musun?   an-*luh*-yor moo-*soon*

I understand.
Anlıyorum.   an-*luh*-yo-room

I don't understand.
Anlamıyorum.   an-*la*-muh-yo-room

What does (*kitap*) mean?
(Kitap) ne demektir?   (kee-*tap*) ne de-*mek*-teer

How do you pronounce this?
Bunu nasıl telaffuz edersiniz?   boo-*noo* na-*suhl* te-laf-*fooz* e-*der*-see-neez

How do you write (*yabancı*)?
(Yabancı) kelimesini   (ya-ban-*juh*) ke-lee-me-see-*nee*
nasıl yazarsınız?   na-*suhl* ya-*zar*-suh-nuhz

Could you please ...?	Lütfen ...?	lewt-fen ...
repeat that	tekrarlar mısınız	tek-*rar*-lar muh-suh-*nuhz*
speak more	daha yavaş	da-*ha* ya-vash
slowly	konuşur musunuz	ko-noo-*shoor* moo-soo-*nooz*
write it down	yazar mısınız	ya-*zar* muh-suh-*nuhz*

essentials

Yes.	*Evet.*	e-*vet*
No.	*Hayır.*	*ha*-yuhr
Please.	*Lütfen.*	*lewt*-fen
Thank you	*(Çok) Teşekkür*	(chok) te-shek-*kewr*
(very much). pol	*ederim.*	e-*de*-reem
Thanks. inf	*Teşekkürler.*	te-shek-*kewr*-ler
You're welcome.	*Birşey değil.*	beer-*shay* de-*eel*
Excuse me.	*Bakar mısınız?*	ba-*kar* muh-suh-*nuhz*
Sorry.	*Özür dilerim.*	eu-*zewr* dee-*le*-reem

numbers

0	*sıfır*	suh-*fuhr*	16	*onaltı*	on-al-*tuh*
1	*bir*	beer	17	*onyedi*	on-ye-dee
2	*iki*	ee-*kee*	18	*onsekiz*	on-se-*keez*
3	*üç*	ewch	19	*ondokuz*	on-do-*kooz*
4	*dört*	deurt	20	*yirmi*	yeer-*mee*
5	*beş*	besh	21	*yirmibir*	yeer-mee-beer
6	*altı*	al-*tuh*	22	*yirmiiki*	yeer-mee-ee-*kee*
7	*yedi*	ye-*dee*	30	*otuz*	o-*tooz*
8	*sekiz*	se-*keez*	40	*kırk*	kuhrk
9	*dokuz*	do-*kooz*	50	*elli*	el-*lee*
10	*on*	on	60	*altmış*	alt-*muhsh*
11	*onbir*	on-beer	70	*yetmiş*	yet-*meesh*
12	*oniki*	on-ee-*kee*	80	*seksen*	sek-*sen*
13	*onüç*	on-ewch	90	*doksan*	dok-*san*
14	*ondört*	on-deurt	100	*yüz*	yewz
15	*onbeş*	on-besh	1000	*bin*	been

time & dates

What time is it?	*Saat kaç?*	sa-*at* kach
It's one o'clock.	*Saat bir.*	sa-*at* beer
It's (10) o'clock.	*Saat (on).*	sa-*at* (on)
Quarter past (10).	*(Onu) çeyrek geçiyor.*	(o-*noo*) chay-*rek* ge-*chee*-yor
Half past (10).	*(On) buçuk.*	(on) boo-*chook*
Quarter to (11).	*(Onbire) çeyrek var.*	(on-bee-*re*) chay-*rek* var
At what time ...?	*Saat kaçta ...?*	sa-*at* kach-*ta* ...
At ...	*Saat ...*	sa-*at* ...
am (morning)	*sabah*	sa-*bah*
pm (afternoon)	*öğleden sonra*	er-le-*den* son-ra
pm (evening)	*gece*	ge-*je*
Monday	*Pazartesi*	pa-*zar*-te-see
Tuesday	*Salı*	sa-*luh*
Wednesday	*Çarşamba*	char-sham-*ba*
Thursday	*Perşembe*	per-shem-*be*
Friday	*Cuma*	joo-*ma*
Saturday	*Cumartesi*	joo-*mar*-te-see
Sunday	*Pazar*	pa-*zar*

January	Ocak	o·jak
February	Şubat	shoo·bat
March	Mart	mart
April	Nisan	nee·san
May	Mayıs	ma·yuhs
June	Haziran	ha·zee·ran
July	Temmuz	tem·mooz
August	Ağustos	a·oos·tos
September	Eylül	ay·lewl
October	Ekim	e·keem
November	Kasım	ka·suhm
December	Aralık	a·ra·luhk

What date is it today?

Bugün ayın kaçı?   boo·gewn a·yuhn ka·chuh

It's (18 October).

(Onsekiz Ekim).   (on·se·keez e·keem)

since (May)	*(Mayıs'tan) beri*	(ma·yuhs·tan) be·ree
until (June)	*(Haziran'a) kadar*	(ha·zee·ra·na) ka·dar
yesterday	*dün*	dewn
today	*bugün*	boo·gewn
tonight	*bu gece*	boo ge·je
tomorrow	*yarın*	ya·ruhn
last/next ...	*geçen/gelecek ...*	ge·chen/ge·le·jek ...
night	*gece*	ge·je
week	*hafta*	haf·ta
month	*ay*	ai
year	*yıl*	yuhl
yesterday/tomorrow ...	*dün/yarın ...*	dewn/ya·ruhn ...
morning	*sabah*	sa·bah
afternoon	*öğleden sonra*	eu·le·den son·ra
evening	*akşam*	ak·sham

544

weather

What's the weather like?	*Hava nasıl?*	ha·*va* na·suhl
It's ...	*Hava ...*	ha·va ...
cloudy	*bulutlu*	boo·loot·*loo*
cold	*soğuk*	so·*ook*
hot	*sıcak*	suh·*jak*
raining	*yağmurlu*	ya·moor·*loo*
snowing	*kar yağışlı*	kar ya·uhsh·*luh*
sunny	*güneşli*	gew·nesh·*lee*
warm	*ılık*	uh·*luhk*
windy	*rüzgarlı*	rewz·gar·*luh*
spring	*ilkbahar*	eelk·ba·har
summer	*yaz*	yaz
autumn	*sonbahar*	son·ba·har
winter	*kış*	kuhsh

border crossing

I'm here ...	*Ben ...*	ben ...
in transit	*transit yolcuyum*	tran·*seet* yol·joo·yoom
on business	*iş gezisindeyim*	eesh ge·zee·seen·de·yeem
on holiday	*tatildeyim*	ta·teel·de·yeem
I'm here for ...	*Ben ... buradayım.*	ben ... boo·ra·da·yuhm
(10) days	*(on) günlüğüne*	(on) gewn·lew·ew·ne
(three) weeks	*(üç) haftalığına*	(ewch) haf·ta·luh·uh·na
(two) months	*(iki) aylığına*	(ee·kee) ai·luh·uh·na

I'm going to (Sarıyer).
(Sarıyer'e) gidiyorum. (sa·ruh·ye·re) gee·dee·yo·room

I'm staying at the (Divan).
(Divan'da) kalıyorum. (dee·van·da) ka·luh·yo·room

I have nothing to declare.
Beyan edecek hiçbir şeyim yok. be·yan e·de·*jek* heech·beer she·yeem yok

I have something to declare.
Beyan edecek bir şeyim var. be·yan e·de·*jek* beer she·yeem var

That's (not) mine.
Bu benim (değil). boo be·*neem* (de·*eel*)

transport

tickets & luggage

Where can I buy a ticket?
Nereden bilet alabilirim?   ne·re·den bee·*let* a·*la*·bee·lee·reem

Do I need to book a seat?
Yer ayırtmam gerekli mi?   yer a·*yuhrt*·mam ge·rek·*lee* mee

One ... ticket to	*(Bostancı'ya)* ...	(bos·*tan*·juh·ya) ...
(Bostancı), please.	*lütfen.*	*lewt*·fen
one-way	*bir gidiş bileti*	beer gee·*deesh* bee·le·*tee*
return	*gidiş-dönüş*	gee·deesh·deu·*newsh*
	bir bilet	beer bee·*let*

I'd like to ... my	*Biletimi ...*	bee·le·tee·*mee* ...
ticket, please.	*istiyorum.*	ees·*tee*·yo·room
cancel	*iptal ettirmek*	eep·*tal* et·teer·*mek*
change	*değiştirmek*	de·eesh·teer·*mek*
collect	*almak*	al·*mak*
confirm	*onaylatmak*	o·nai·lat·*mak*

I'd like a ... seat,	*... bir yer istiyorum.*	... beer yer ees·*tee*·yo·room
please.		
nonsmoking	*Sigara içilmeyen*	see·*ga*·ra ee·*cheel*·me·yen
	kısımda	kuh·suhm·*da*
smoking	*Sigara içilen*	see·*ga*·ra ee·*chee*·len
	kısımda	kuh·suhm·*da*

How much is it?
Şu ne kadar?   shoo ne ka·*dar*

Is there air conditioning?
Klima var mı?   *klee*·ma var muh

Is there a toilet?
Tuvalet var mı?   too·va·*let* var muh

How long does the trip take?
Yolculuk ne kadar sürer?   yol·joo·*look* ne ka·*dar* sew·*rer*

Is it a direct route?
Direk güzergah mı?   dee·*rek* gew·zer·*gah* muh

Where's the luggage locker?
Emanet dolabı nerede?   e·ma·*net* do·la·*buh* ne·re·de

My luggage has been ...	*Bagajım ...*	ba·ga·*zhuhm* ...
damaged	*zarar gördü*	za·*rar* geu·*dew*
lost	*kayboldu*	kai·bol·*doo*
stolen	*çalındı*	cha·luhn·*duh*

getting around

Where does flight (TK0060) arrive?

(TK0060) sefer	(te·ka suh·*fuhr* suh·*fuhr* alt·*muhsh*)
sayılı uçak nereye iniyor?	se·*fer* sa·*yuh·luh* oo·*chak* ne·re·ye ee·*nee·yor*

Where does flight (TK0060) depart?

(TK0060) sefer	(te·ka suh·*fuhr* suh·*fuhr* alt·*muhsh*)
sayılı uçak nereden kalkıyor?	se·*fer* sa·*yuh·luh* oo·*chak* ne·re·den kal·*kuh·yor*

Where's (the) ...?	... *nerede?*	... ne·re·de
arrivals hall	*Gelen yolcu bölümü*	ge·*len* yol·*joo* beu·lew·*mew*
departures hall	*Giden yolcu bölümü*	gee·*den* yol·*joo* beu·lew·*mew*
duty-free shop	*Gümrüksüz*	gewm·rewk·*sewz*
	satış mağazası	sa·*tuhsh* ma·a·za·*suh*
gate (12)	*(Oniki) numaralı*	(on·ee·*kee*) noo·ma·ra·*luh*
	kapı	ka·*puh*

Is this the ... to (Sirkeci)?	*(Sirkeci'ye) giden*	(*seer*·ke·jee·ye) gee·*den*
	... *bu mu?*	... boo moo
boat	*vapur*	va·*poor*
bus	*otobüs*	o·to·*bews*
plane	*uçak*	oo·*chak*
train	*tren*	tren

What time's the ... bus?	... *otobüs*	... o·to·*bews*
	ne zaman?	ne za·*man*
first	*İlk*	eelk
last	*Son*	son
next	*Sonraki*	son·ra·*kee*

At what time does it arrive/leave?

Ne zaman varır/kalkacak?	ne za·*man* va·*ruhr*/kal·ka·*jak*

How long will it be delayed?

Ne kadar gecikecek?	ne ka·*dar* ge·jee·ke·*jek*

What station/stop is this?
   Bu hangi istasyon/durak?   boo *han*-gee ees-tas-*yon*/doo-*rak*

What's the next station/stop?
   Sonraki istasyon/durak hangisi?   son-ra-*kee* ees-tas-*yon*/doo-*rak han*-gee-*see*

Does it stop at (Kadıköy)?
   (Kadıköy'de) durur mu?   (ka-*duh*-kay-de) doo-*roor* moo

Please tell me when we get to (Beşiktaş).
   (Beşiktaş'a) vardığımızda   (be-*sheek*-ta-sha) var-duh-uh-muhz-*da*
   lütfen bana söyleyin.   *lewt*-fen ba-*na* say-le-yeen

How long do we stop here?
   Burada ne kadar duracağız?   boo-ra-*da* ne ka-*dar* doo-ra-*ja*-uhz

Is this seat available?
   Bu koltuk boş mu?   boo kol-*took* bosh moo

That's my seat.
   Burası benim yerim.   boo-ra-*suh* be-*neem* ye-*reem*

I'd like a taxi ...   *... bir taksi istiyorum.*   ... beer tak-*see* ees-*tee*-yo-room
   at (9am)   *(Sabah dokuzda)*   (sa-*bah* do-kooz-*da*)
   now   *Hemen*   he-men
   tomorrow   *Yarın*   ya-ruhn

Is this taxi available?
   Bu taksi boş mu?   boo tak-*see* bosh moo

How much is it to ...?
   ... ne kadar?   ... ne ka-*dar*

Please put the meter on.
   Lütfen taksimetreyi   *lewt*-fen tak-*see*-met-re-yee
   çalıştırın.   cha-luhsh-*tuh*-ruhn

Please take me to (this address).
   Lütfen beni (bu adrese) götürün.   *lewt*-fen be-*nee* (boo ad-re-*se*) geu-*tew*-rewn

Please ...   *Lütfen ...*   *lewt*-fen ...
   slow down   *yavaşlayın*   ya-vash-*la*-yuhn
   stop here   *burada durun*   boo-ra-*da* doo-roon
   wait here   *burada bekleyin*   boo-ra-*da* bek-le-yeen

car, motorbike & bicycle hire

I'd like to hire a ...	Bir ... kiralamak istiyorum.	beer ... kee-ra-la-mak ees-tee-yo-room
bicycle	bisiklet	bee-seek-let
car	araba	a-ra-ba
motorbike	motosiklet	mo-to-seek-let

with ...		
a driver	şoförlü	sho-feur-lew
air conditioning	klimalı	klee-ma-luh

How much for ... hire?	... kirası ne kadar?	... kee-ra-suh ne ka-dar
hourly	Saatlık	sa-at-luhk
daily	Günlük	gewn-lewk
weekly	Haftalık	haf-ta-luhk

air	hava	ha-va
oil	yağ	ya
petrol	benzin	ben-zeen
tyres	lastikler	las-teek-ler

I need a mechanic.
Tamirciye ihtiyacım var.　　　　ta-meer-jee-ye eeh-tee-ya-juhm var

I've run out of petrol.
Benzinim bitti.　　　　ben-zee-neem beet-tee

I have a flat tyre.
Lastiğim patladı.　　　　las-tee-eem pat-la-duh

directions

Where's the ...?	... nerede?	... ne-re-de
bank	Banka	ban-ka
city centre	Şehir merkezi	she-heer mer-ke-zee
hotel	Otel	o-tel
market	Pazar yeri	pa-zar ye-ree
police station	Polis karakolu	po-lees ka-ra-ko-loo
post office	Postane	pos-ta-ne
public toilet	Umumi tuvalet	oo-moo-mee too-va-let
tourist office	Turizm bürosu	too-reezm bew-ro-soo

Is this the road to (Taksim)?
(Taksim'e) giden yol bu mu? — (tak·see·me) gee·*den* yol boo moo

Can you show me (on the map)?
Bana (haritada) — ba·*na* (ha·ree·ta·*da*)
gösterebilir misiniz? — geus·te·re·bee·leer mee·seen·*neez*

What's the address?
Adresi nedir? — ad·re·*see ne*·deer

How far is it?
Ne kadar uzakta? — ne ka·*dar* oo·zak·*ta*

How do I get there?
Oraya nasıl gidebilirim? — o·ra·*ya* na·suhl gee·de·bee·lee·reem

Turn ...	... dön.	... deun
at the corner	Köşeden	keu·she·*den*
at the traffic lights	Trafik	tra·*feek*
	ışıklarından	uh·shuhk·la·ruhn·*dan*
left/right	Sola/Sağa	so·*la*/sa·*a*

It's ...		
behind ...	... arkasında.	... ar·ka·suhn·*da*
far away	Uzak.	oo·*zak*
here	Burada.	boo·ra·*da*
in front of ...	... önünde.	... eu·newn·*de*
left	Solda.	sol·*da*
near ...	... yakınında.	... ya·kuh·nuhn·*da*
next to ...	... yanında.	... ya·nuhn·*da*
on the corner	Köşede.	keu·she·*de*
opposite ...	... karşısında.	... kar·shuh·suhn·*da*
right	Sağda.	sa·*da*
straight ahead	Tam karşıda.	tam kar·shuh·*da*
there	Şurada.	shoo·ra·*da*

by bus	otobüslü	o·to·bews·*lew*
by taxi	taksili	tak·see·*lee*
by train	trenli	tren·*lee*
on foot	yürüyerek	yew·rew·ye·rek

north	kuzey	koo·*zay*
south	güney	gew·*nay*
east	doğu	do·*oo*
west	batı	ba·*tuh*

signs

Giriş/Çıkış	gee·reesh/chuh·kuhsh	Entrance/Exit
Açık/Kapalı	a·chuhk/ka·pa·luh	Open/Closed
Boş Oda	bosh o·da	Rooms Available
Boş Yer Yok	bosh yer yok	No Vacancies
Danışma	da·nuhsh·ma	Information
Polis Karakolu	po·lees ka·ra·ko·loo	Police Station
Yasak	ya·sak	Prohibited
Tuvaletler	too·va·let·ler	Toilets
Erkek	er·kek	Men
Kadın	ka·duhn	Women
Sıcak/Soğuk	suh·jak/so·ook	Hot/Cold

accommodation

finding accommodation

Where's a ...?	Buralarda nerede ... var?	boo·ra·lar·da ne·re·de ... var
camping ground	kamp yeri	kamp ye·ree
guesthouse	misafirhane	mee·sa·feer·ha·ne
hotel	otel	o·tel
youth hostel	gençlik hosteli	gench·leek hos·te·lee

Can you recommend somewhere ...?	... bir yer tavsiye edebilir misiniz?	... beer yer tav·see·ye e·de·bee·leer mee·see·neez
cheap	Ucuz	oo·jooz
good	İyi	ee·yee
nearby	Yakın	ya·kuhn

I'd like to book a room, please.
Bir oda ayırtmak beer o·da a·yuhrt·mak
istiyorum lütfen. ees·tee·yo·room lewt·fen

I have a reservation.
Rezervasyonum var. re·zer·vas·yo·noom var

My name's ...
Benim ismim ... be·neem ees·meem ...

Do you have a ... room?	... odanız var mı?	... o-da-*nuhz* var muh
single	*Tek kişilik*	tek kee-shee-*leek*
double	*İki kişilik*	ee-*kee* kee-shee-*leek*
twin	*Çift yataklı*	cheeft ya-tak-*luh*

How much is it per ...?	... ne kadar?	... ne ka-*dar*
night	*Geceliği*	ge-je-lee-*ee*
person	*Kişi başına*	kee-shee ba-shuh-*na*

Can I pay by ...?	... ile ödeyebilir miyim?	... *ee-le* eu-de-ye-be-*leer* mee-*yeem*
credit card	*Kredi kartı*	kre-dee kar-*tuh*
travellers cheque	*Seyahat çeki*	se-ya-*hat* che-kee

I'd like to stay for (three) nights.
Kalmak istiyorum (üç) geceliğine. kal-*mak* ees-tee-yo-room (ewch) ge-je-lee-ee-ne

From (2 July) to (6 July).
(İki Temmuz'dan) (ee-*kee* tem-mooz-*dan*)
(altı Temmuz'a) kadar. (al-*tuh* tem-moo-*za*) ka-*dar*

Can I see it?
Görebilir miyim. geu-re-bee-*leer* mee-*yeem*

Am I allowed to camp here?
Burada kamp yapabilir miyim? boo-ra-*da* kamp ya-*pa*-bee-leer mee-*yeem*

Where can I find a camping ground?
Kamp alanı nerede? kamp a-la-*nuh* ne-re-de

requests & queries

When/Where is breakfast served?
Kahvaltı ne zaman/ kah-val-*tuh* ne za-*man*/
nerede veriliyor? ne-re-de ve-ree-lee-yor

Please wake me at (seven).
Lütfen beni (yedide) kaldırın. lewt-fen be-*nee* (ye-dee-*de*) kal-*duh*-ruhn

Could I have my key, please?
Anahtarımı alabilir miyim? a-nah-ta-ruh-*muh* a-*la*-bee-leer mee-*yeem*

Can I get another (blanket)?
Başka bir (battaniye) bash-*ka* beer (bat-*ta*-nee-ye)
alabilir miyim? a-*la*-bee-leer mee-*yeem*

Is there an elevator/a safe?
Asansör/Kasanız var mı? a-san-*seur*/ka-sa-*nuhz* var muh

The room is too …	Çok …	chok …
expensive	pahalı	pa·ha·luh
noisy	gürültülü	gew·rewl·tew·lew
small	küçük	kew·chewk

The … doesn't work.	… çalışmıyor.	… cha·luhsh·muh·yor
air conditioning	Klima	klee·ma
fan	Fan	fan
toilet	Tuvalet	too·va·let

This … isn't clean.	Bu … temiz değil.	boo … te·meez de·eel
pillow	yastık	yas·tuhk
sheet	çarşaf	char·shaf
towel	havlu	hav·loo

checking out

What time is checkout?
Çıkış ne zaman?   chuh·kuhsh ne za·man

Can I leave my luggage here?
Eşyalarımı burada   esh·ya·la·ruh·muh boo·ra·da
bırakabilir miyim?   buh·ra·ka·bee·leer mee·yeem

Could I have my …, please?	… alabilir miyim lütfen?	… a·la·bee·leer mee·yeem lewt·fen
deposit	Depozitomu	de·po·zee·to·moo
passport	Pasaportumu	pa·sa·por·too·moo
valuables	Değerli eşyalarımı	de·er·lee esh·ya·la·ruh·muh

communications & banking

the internet

Where's the local Internet café?
En yakın internet kafe nerede?   en ya·kuhn een·ter·net ka·fe ne·re·de

How much is it per hour?
Saati ne kadar?   sa·a·tee ne ka·dar

I'd like to ...	... istiyorum.	... ees-tee-yo-room
check my email	E-postama bakmak	e-pos-ta-ma bak-mak
get Internet access	İnternete girmek	een-ter-ne-te geer-mek
use a printer	Printeri kullanmak	preen-te-ree kool-lan-mak
use a scanner	Tarayıcıyı	ta-ra-yuh-juh-yuh

mobile/cell phone

I'd like a ...	... istiyorum.	... ees-tee-yo-room
mobile/cell	Cep telefonu	jep te-le-fo-noo
phone for hire	kiralamak	kee-ra-la-mak
SIM card for	Buradaki şebeke	boo-ra-da-kee she-be-ke
your network	için SİM kart	ee-cheen seem kart

What are the rates?	Ücret tarifesi nedir?	ewj-ret ta-ree-fe-see ne-deer

telephone

What's your phone number?
Telefon numaranız nedir?
te-le-fon noo-ma-ra-nuhz ne-deer

The number is ...
Telefon numarası ...
te-le-fon noo-ma-ra-suh ...

Where's the nearest public phone?
En yakın telefon
en ya-kuhn te-le-fon
kulübesi nerede?
koo-lew-be-see ne-re-de

I'd like to buy a phonecard.
Telefon kartı almak istiyorum.
te-le-fon kar-tuh al-mak ees-tee-yo-room

I want to ...	... istiyorum.	... ees-tee-yo-room
call (Singapore)	(Singapur'u)	(seen-ga-poo-roo)
	aramak	a-ra-mak
make a local	Yerel bir görüşme	ye-rel beer geu-rewsh-me
call	yapmak	yap-mak
reverse the	Ödemeli görüşme	eu-de-me-lee ger-rewsh-me
charges	yapmak	yap-mak

How much does ... cost?	... ne kadar eder?	... ne ka-dar e-der
a (three)-minute call	(Üç) dakikalık konuşma	(ewch) da-kee-ka-luhk ko-noosh-ma
each extra minute	Her ekstra dakika	her eks-tra da-kee-ka

It's (10) yeni kuruş per minute.
Bir dakikası (on) yeni kuruş.   beer da-kee-ka-*suh* (on) ye-*nee* koo-*roosh*

post office

I want to send a ...	Bir ... göndermek istiyorum.	beer ... geun-der-mek ees-tee-yo-room
fax	faks	faks
letter	mektup	mek-toop
parcel	paket	pa-ket
postcard	kartpostal	kart-pos-tal

I want to buy a/an ...	... satın almak istiyorum.	... sa-tuhn al-mak ees-tee-yo-room
envelope	Zarf	zarf
stamp	Pul	pool

Please send it (to Australia) by ...	Lütfen ... (Avustralya'ya) gönderin.	lewt-fen ... (a-voos-tral-ya-ya) geun-de-reen
airmail	hava yoluyla	ha-va yo-looy-la
express mail	ekspres posta	eks-pres pos-ta
registered mail	taahhütlü posta	ta-ah-hewt-lew pos-ta
surface mail	deniz yoluyla	de-neez yo-looy-la

Is there any mail for me?	Bana posta var mı?	ba-na pos-ta var muh

bank

Where's a/an ...?	... nerede var?	... ne-re-de var
ATM	Bankamatik	ban-ka-ma-teek
foreign exchange office	Döviz bürosu	deu-veez bew-ro-soo

I'd like to ...	... istiyorum.	... ees-tee-yo-room
cash a cheque	Çek bozdurmak	chek boz-door-mak
change a travellers cheque	Seyahat çeki bozdurmak	se-ya-hat che-kee boz-door-mak
change money	Para bozdurmak	pa-ra boz-door-mak
get a cash advance	Avans çekmek	a-vans chek-mek
withdraw money	Para çekmek	pa-ra chek-mek

What's the ...?	... nedir?	... ne-deer
charge for that	Ücreti	ewj-re-tee
commission	Komisyon	ko-mees-yon
exchange rate	Döviz kuru	deu-veez koo-roo

It's ...		
(12) euros	(Oniki) euro.	(on-ee-kee) yoo-ro
(25) lira	(Yirmibeş) lira.	(yeer-mee-besh) lee-ra
free	Ücretsiz.	ewj-ret-seez

What time does the bank open?
Banka ne zaman açılıyor?   ban-ka ne za-man a-chuh-luh-yor

Has my money arrived yet?
Param geldi mi?   pa-ram gel-dee mee

sightseeing

getting in

What time does it open/close?
Saat kaçta açılır/kapanır?   sa-at kach-ta a-chuh-luhr/ka-pa-nuhr

What's the admission charge?
Giriş ücreti nedir?   gee-reesh ewj-re-tee ne-deer

Is there a discount for children/students?
Çocuk/Öğrenci indirimi var mı?   cho-jook/eu-ren-jee een-dee-ree-mee var muh

I'd like a ...	... istiyorum.	... ees-tee-yo-room
catalogue	Katalog	ka-ta-log
guide	Rehber	reh-ber
local map	Yerel Harita	ye-rel ha-ree-ta

I'd like to see ...	... görmek istiyorum.	... geur·mek ees·tee·yo·room
What's that?	Bu nedir?	boo ne·deer
Can I take a photo?	Bir fotoğrafınızı	beer fo·to·ra·fuh·nuh·zuh
	çekebilir miyim?	che·ke·bee·leer mee·yeem

tours

When's the next ...?	Sonraki ... ne zaman?	son·ra·kee ... ne za·man
day trip	gündüz turu	gewn·dewz too·roo
tour	tur	toor

Is ... included?	... dahil mi?	... da·heel mee
accommodation	Kalacak yer	ka·la·jak yer
the admission charge	Giriş	gee·reesh
food	Yemek	ye·mek
transport	Ulaşım	oo·la·shuhm

How long is the tour?
Tur ne kadar sürer?   toor ne ka·dar sew·rer

What time should we be back?
Saat kaçta dönmeliyiz?   sa·at kach·ta deun·me·lee·yeez

sightseeing

castle	kale	ka·le
church	kilise	kee·lee·se
main square	meydan	may·dan
monument	anıt	a·nuht
mosque	cami	ja·mee
museum	müze	mew·ze
old city	eski şehir	es·kee she·heer
palace	saray	sa·rai
ruins	harabeler	ha·ra·be·ler
stadium	stadyum	stad·yoom
statue	heykel	hay·kel
Turkish bath	hamam	ha·mam

shopping

enquiries

Where's a ...?	... *nerede?*	... ne·re·de
bank	*Banka*	ban·ka
bookshop	*Kitapçı*	kee·tap·chuh
camera shop	*Fotoğrafçı*	fo·to·raf·chuh
department store	*Büyük mağaza*	bew·yewk ma·a·za
grocery store	*Bakkal*	bak·kal
market	*Pazar yeri*	pa·zar ye·ree
newsagency	*Gazete bayii*	ga·ze·te ba·yee·ee
supermarket	*Süpermarket*	sew·per·mar·ket

Where can I buy (a padlock)?
Nereden (asma kilit)　　　　ne·re·den (as·ma kee·leet)
alabilirim?　　　　　　　　　　a·la·bee·lee·reem

I'm looking for ...
... istiyorum.　　　　　　　　... ees·tee·yo·room

Can I look at it?
Bakabilir miyim?　　　　　　ba·ka·bee·leer mee·yeem

Do you have any others?
Başka var mı?　　　　　　　bash·ka var muh

Does it have a guarantee?
Garantisi var mı?　　　　　　ga·ran·tee·see var muh

Can I have it sent overseas?
Yurt dışına gönderebilir　　　yoort duh·shuh·na geun·de·re·bee·leer
misiniz?　　　　　　　　　　mee·see·neez

Can I have my ... repaired?
... burada tamir ettirebilir　　... boo·ra·da ta·meer et·tee·re·bee·leer
miyim?　　　　　　　　　　mee·yeem

It's faulty.
Arızalı.　　　　　　　　　　a·ruh·za·luh

I'd like ..., please.	... *istiyorum lütfen.*	... ees·tee·yo·room lewt·fen
a bag	*Çanta*	chan·ta
a refund	*Para iadesi*	pa·ra ee·a·de·see
to return this	*Bunu iade etmek*	boo·noo ee·a·de et·mek

paying

How much is it?
Ne kadar?
ne ka-*dar*

Can you write down the price?
Fiyatı yazabilir misiniz?
fee-ya-*tuh* ya-*za*-bee-leer mee-see-*neez*

That's too expensive.
Bu çok pahalı.
boo chok pa-ha-*luh*

Is that your lowest price?
Son fiyatınız bu mu?
son fee-ya-tuh-*nuhz* boo moo

I'll give you (30) lira.
(Otuz) lira veririm.
(o-*tooz*) lee-*ra* ve-ree-reem

There's a mistake in the bill.
Hesapta bir yanlışlık var.
he-sap-*ta* beer yan-luhsh-*luhk* var

Do you accept ...?
... kabul ediyor musunuz?
... ka-*bool* e-dee-yor moo-soo-*nooz*

    credit cards — *Kredi kartı* — kre-dee kar-*tuh*
    debit cards — *Banka kartı* — ban-ka kar-*tuh*
    travellers cheques — *Seyahat çeki* — se-ya-*hat* che-kee

I'd like ..., please.
... istiyorum lütfen.
... ees-*tee*-yo-room *lewt*-fen

    a receipt — *Makbuz* — mak-*booz*
    my change — *Paramın üstünü* — pa-ra-*muhn* ews-tew-*new*

clothes & shoes

Can I try it on?
Deneyebilir miyim?
de-ne-ye-bee-leer mee-*yeem*

My size is (42).
(Kırkiki) beden giyiyorum.
(kuhrk-ee-kee) be-*den* gee-*yee*-yo-room

It doesn't fit.
Olmuyor.
ol-*moo*-yor

small — *küçük* — kew-*chewk*
medium — *orta* — or-*ta*
large — *büyük* — bew-*yewk*

books & music

I'd like a …	… istiyorum.	… ees-*tee*-yo-room
newspaper (in English)	*(İngilizce) bir gazete*	(een-gee-*leez*-je) beer ga-ze-te
pen	*Tükenmez kalem*	tew-ken-*mez* ka-*lem*

Is there an English-language bookshop?
İngilizce yayın satan bir dükkan var mı?
een-gee-*leez*-je ya-*yuhn* sa-*tan* beer dewk-*kan* var muh

I'm looking for something by (Yaşar Kemal).
(Yaşar Kemal'in) albümlerine bakmak istiyorum.
(ya-*shar* ke-mal-*een*) al-bewm-le-ree-*ne* bak-*mak* ees-*tee*-yo-room

Can I listen to this?
Bunu dinleyebilir miyim?
boo-*noo* deen-le-ye-bee-leer mee-*yeem*

photography

Can you …?	… misiniz?	… mee-see-*neez*
develop this film	*Bu filmi basabilir*	boo feel-*mee* ba-*sa*-bee-leer
load my film	*Filmi makineye takabilir*	feel-*mee* ma-kee-ne-*ye* ta-*ka*-bee-leer
transfer photos from my camera to CD	*Kameramdaki fotoğrafları CD'ye aktarabilir*	ka-me-ram-da-*kee* fo-to-raf-la-*ruh* see-*dee*-ye ak-ta-*ra*-bee-leer

I need a/an … film for this camera.	*Bu kamera için … film istiyorum.*	boo ka-me-*ra* ee-*cheen* … feelm ees-*tee*-yo-room
APS	*APS*	a-pe-*se*
B&W	*siyah-beyaz*	see-*yah*-be-yaz
colour	*renkli*	renk-*lee*
slide	*slayt*	slayt
(200) speed	*(ikiyüz) hızlı*	(ee-kee-*yewz*) huhz-*luh*

When will it be ready? *Ne zaman hazır olur?* ne za-*man* ha-*zuhr* o-*loor*

meeting people

greetings, goodbyes & introductions

Hello.	Merhaba.	mer·ha·ba
Hi.	Selam.	se·lam
Good night.	İyi geceler.	ee·yee ge·je·ler
Goodbye.	Hoşçakal. inf	hosh·cha·kal
(by person leaving)	Hoşçakalın. pol	hosh·cha·ka·luhn
Goodbye.	Güle güle.	gew·le gew·le
(by person staying)		
See you later.	Sonra görüşürüz.	son·ra ger·rew·shew·rewz
Mr	Bay	bai
Mrs/Miss	Bayan	ba·yan
How are you?	Nasılsın? inf	na·suhl·suhn
	Nasılsınız? pol	na·suhl·suh·nuhz
Fine. And you?	İyiyim. Ya sen/siz? inf/pol	ee·yee·yeem ya sen/seez
What's your name?	Adınız ne? inf	a·duh·nuhz ne
	Adınız nedir? pol	a·duh·nuhz ne·deer
My name is ...	Benim adım ...	be·neem a·duhm ...
I'm pleased to	Tanıştığımıza	ta·nuhsh·tuh·uh·muh·za
meet you.	sevindim.	se·veen·deem
This is my ...	Bu benim ...	boo be·neem ...
brother	kardeşim	kar·de·sheem
daughter	kızım	kuh·zuhm
father	babayım	ba·ba·yuhm
friend	arkadaşım	ar·ka·da·shuhm
husband	kocam	ko·jam
mother	anneyim	an·ne·yeem
partner (intimate)	partnerim	part·ne·reem
sister	kız kardeşim	kuhz kar·de·sheem
son	oğlum	o·loom
wife	karım	ka·ruhm
Here's my ...	İşte benim ...	eesh·te be·neem ...
(email) address	(e-posta) adresim	(e·pos·ta) ad·re·seem
fax number	faks numaram	faks noo·ma·ram
phone number	telefon numaram	te·le·fon noo·ma·ram

What's your ...?	Sizin ... nedir?	see·zeen ... ne·deer
(email) address	(e-posta) adresiniz	(e·pos·ta) ad·re·see·neez
fax number	faks numaranız	faks noo·ma·ra·nuhz
phone number	telefon numaranız	te·le·fon noo·ma·ra·nuhz

occupations

What's your occupation?	Mesleğiniz nedir? pol	mes·le·ee·neez ne·deer
	Mesleğin nedir? inf	mes·le·een ne·deer
I'm a/an ...	Ben ...	ben ...
artist	sanatçıyım m&f	sa·nat·chuh·yuhm
business person	iş adamıyım m	ish a·da·muh·yuhm
	kadınıyım f	ka·duh·nuh·yuhm
farmer	çiftçiyim m&f	cheeft·chee·yeem
manual worker	işçiyim m&f	eesh·chee·yeem
office worker	memurum m&f	me·moo·room
scientist	bilim adamıyım m&f	bee·leem a·da·muh·yuhm

background

Where are you from?	Nerelisiniz? pol	ne·re·lee·see·neez
	Nerelisin? inf	ne·re·lee·seen
I'm from ...	Ben ...	ben ...
Australia	Avustralya'lıyım	a·voos·tral·ya·luh·yuhm
Canada	Kanada'lıyım	ka·na·da·luh·yuhm
England	İngiltere'liyim	een·geel·te·re·lee·yeem
the USA	Amerika'lıyım	a·me·ree·ka·luh·yuhm
Are you married?	Evli misiniz?	ev·lee mee·see·neez
I'm married/single.	Ben evliyim/bekarım.	ben ev·lee·yeem/be·ka·ruhm

age

How old ...?	Kaç ...?	kach ...
are you	yaşındasın inf	ya·shuhn·da·suhn
is your son	yaşında oğlunuz	ya·shuhn·da o·loo·nooz
is your daughter	yaşında kızınız	ya·shuhn·da kuh·zuh·nuhz
I'm ... years old.	Ben ... yaşındayım.	ben ... ya·shuhn·da·yuhm
He/She is ... years old.	O ... yaşında.	o ... ya·shuhn·da

feelings

I'm/I'm not ...

cold	Üşüdüm./	ew-shew-*dewm*/
	Üşümedim.	ew-*shew*-me-deem
happy	Mutluyum./	moot-*loo*-yoom/
	Mutlu değilim.	moot-*loo* de-ee-leem
hot	Sıcakladım./	suh-jak-la-*duhm*/
	Sıcaklamadım.	suh-jak-*la*-ma-duhm
hungry	Açım./Aç değilim.	a-chuhm/ach de-ee-leem
sad	Üzgünüm./	ewz-gew-*newm*/
	Üzgün değilim.	ewz-*gewn* de-ee-leem
thirsty	Susadım./Susamadım.	soo-sa-*duhm*/soo-*sa*-ma-duhm
tired	Yorgunum./	yor-*goo*-noom/
	Yorgun değilim.	yor-*goon* de-ee-leem

Are you ...?

cold	Üşüdün mü?	ew-shew-*dewn* mew
happy	Mutlu musun?	moot-*loo* moo-*soon*
hot	Sıcakladın mı?	suh-jak-la-*duhn* muh
hungry	Aç mısın?	ach muh-*suhn*
sad	Üzgün müsün?	ewz-*gewn* moo-*soon*
thirsty	Susadın mı?	soo-sa-*duhn* muh
tired	Yorgun musun?	yor-*goon* moo-*soon*

entertainment

going out

Where can I find ...?	Buranın ... nerede?	boo-ra-*nuhn* ... *ne*-re-de
clubs	kulüpleri	koo-lewp-le-*ree*
gay venues	gey kulüpleri	gay koo-lewp-le-*ree*
pubs	birahaneleri	bee-ra-ha-ne-le-*ree*
I feel like going to a/the ...	... gitmek istiyor.	... geet-*mek* ees-*tee*-yor
concert	Konsere	kon-se-*re*
movies	Sinemaya	see-ne-ma-*ya*
party	Partiye	par-tee-*ye*
restaurant	Restorana	res-to-ra-*na*
theatre	Oyuna	o-yoo-*na*

interests

Do you like ...?	... sever misin?	... se-*ver* mee-*seen*
I like ...	... seviyorum.	... se-vee-yo-room
I don't like ...	... sevmiyorum.	... sev-mee-yo-room
art	Sanat	sa-*nat*
movies	Sinemaya gitmeyi	see-ne-ma-*ya* geet-me-yee
reading	Okumayı	o-koo-ma-*yuh*
sport	Sporu	spo-*roo*
travelling	Seyahat etmeyi	se-ya-*hat* et-me-yee
Do you ...?	... misin/misiniz? inf/pol	... mee-*seen*/mee-see-*neez*
dance	Dans eder	dans e-*der*
go to concerts	Konserlere gider	kon-ser-le-*re* gee-*der*
listen to music	Müzik dinler	mew-*zeek* deen-*ler*

food & drink

finding a place to eat

Can you recommend a ...?	İyi bir ... tavsiye edebilir misiniz?	ee-*yee* beer ... tav-see-*ye* e-de-*bee*-leer mee-see-*neez*
bar	bar	bar
café	kafe	ka-*fe*
restaurant	restoran	res-to-*ran*
I'd like ..., please.	... istiyorum.	... ees-*tee*-yo-room
a table for (five)	(Beş) kişilik bir masa	(besh) kee-shee-*leek* beer ma-*sa*
the nonsmoking section	Sigara içilmeyen bir yer	see-*ga*-ra ee-*cheel*-me-yen beer yer
the smoking section	Sigara içilen bir yer	see-*ga*-ra ee-chee-*len* beer yer

ordering food

breakfast	kahvaltı	kah-val-*tuh*
lunch	öğle yemeği	eu-le ye-me-ee
dinner	akşam yemeği	ak-sham ye-me-ee
snack	hafif yemek	ha-*feef* ye-mek

What would you recommend?
Ne tavsiye edersiniz?   ne tav·see·ye e·der·see·neez

I'd like (a/the)...	... istiyorum.	... ees·tee·yo·room
bill	Hesabı	he·sa·buh
drink list	İçecek listesini	ee·che·jek lees·te·see·nee
menu	Menüyü	me·new·yew
that dish	Şu yemeği	shoo ye·me·ee

drinks

(cup of) coffee ...	(fincan) kahve ...	(feen·jan) kah·ve ...
(cup of) tea ...	(fincan) çay ...	(feen·jan) chai ...
with milk	sütlü	sewt·lew
without sugar	şekersiz	she·ker·seez
(orange) juice	(portakal) suyu	(por·ta·kal) soo·yoo
soft drink	alkolsüz içecek	al·kol·sewz ee·che·jek
sparkling mineral water	maden sodası	ma·den so·da·suh
still mineral water	maden suyu	ma·den soo·yoo
(hot) water	(sıcak) su	(suh·jak) soo

in the bar

I'll have ...	... alayım.	... a·la·yuhm
I'll buy you a drink.	Sana içecek alayım.	sa·na ee·che·jek a·la·yuhm
What would you like?	Ne alırsınız?	ne a·luhr·suh·nuhz
Cheers!	Şerefe!	she·re·fe
brandy	brendi	bren·dee
cocktail	kokteyl	kok·tayl
cognac	konyak	kon·yak
a shot of (whisky)	bir tek (viski)	beer tek (vees·kee)
a bottle/glass of beer	bir şişe/bardak bira	beer shee·she/bar·dak bee·ra
a bottle/glass	bir şişe/bardak	beer shee·she/bar·dak
of ... wine	... şarap	... sha·rap
red	kırmızı	kuhr·muh·zuh
sparkling	köpüklü	keu·pewk·lew
white	beyaz	be·yaz

self-catering

What's the local speciality?
Bu yöreye has yiyecekler neler?   boo yeu·re·*ye* has yee·ye·jek·*ler* ne·ler

What's that?
Bu nedir?   boo ne·deer

How much (is a kilo of cheese)?
(Bir kilo peynir) Ne kadar?   (beer kee·*lo* pay·*neer*) ne ka·*dar*

I'd like ...	... istiyorum.	... ees·tee·yo·room
(200) grams	*(İkiyüz) gram*	(ee·*kee*·yewz) gram
(two) kilos	*(İki) kilo*	(ee·*kee*) kee·*lo*
(three) pieces	*(Üç) parça*	(ewch) par·*cha*
(six) slices	*(Altı) dilim*	(al·*tuh*) dee·*leem*

Less.	*Daha az.*	da·ha az
Enough.	*Yeterli.*	ye·ter·*lee*
More.	*Daha fazla.*	da·ha faz·*la*

special diets & allergies

Where's a vegetarian restaurant?
Buralarda vejeteryan restoran   boo·ra·lar·*da* ve·zhe·ter·*yan* res·to·*ran*
var mı?   var muh

Do you have vegetarian food?
Vejeteryan yiyecekleriniz   ve·zhe·ter·*yan* yee·ye·jek·le·ree·*neez*
var mı?   var muh

Is it cooked with ...?	*İçinde ... var mı?*	ee·cheen·*de* ... var muh
butter	*tereyağ*	te·re·ya
eggs	*yumurta*	yoo·moor·*ta*
meat stock	*et suyu*	et soo·*yoo*

I'm allergic to ...	... alerjim var.	... a·ler·*zheem* var
dairy produce	*Süt ürünlerine*	sewt ew·rewn·le·ree·*ne*
gluten	*Glutene*	gloo·te·*ne*
MSG	*Mono sodyum*	mo·*no* sod·*yoom*
	glutamata	gloo·ta·ma·*ta*
nuts	*Çerezlere*	che·rez·le·*re*
seafood	*Deniz ürünlerine*	de·*neez* ew·rewn·le·ree·*ne*

emergencies

basics

Help!	*İmdat!*	*eem*-dat
Stop!	*Dur!*	door
Go away!	*Git burdan!*	geet boor-*dan*
Thief!	*Hırsız var!*	huhr-*suhz* var
Fire!	*Yangın var!*	*yan*-guhn var
Watch out!	*Dikkat et!*	*deek*-kat et
Call ...!	*... çağırın!*	... cha-*uh*-ruhn
a doctor	*Doktor*	dok-*tor*
an ambulance	*Ambulans*	am-boo-*lans*
the police	*Polis*	po-*lees*

It's an emergency!
Bu acil bir durum.   boo a-*jeel* beer doo-room

Could you help me, please?
Yardım edebilir misiniz   yar-*duhm* e-de-bee-leer mee-see-*neez*
lütfen?   *lewt*-fen

Can I use your phone?
Telefonunuzu kullanabilir   te-le-fe-noo-noo-*zoo* kool-la-*na*-bee-leer
miyim?   mee-*yeem*

I'm lost.
Kayboldum.   kai-bol-*doom*

Where are the toilets?
Tuvaletler nerede?   too-va-let-*ler* ne-re-de

police

Where's the police station?
Polis karakolu nerede?   po-*lees* ka-ra-ko-*loo* ne-re-de

I want to report an offence.
Şikayette bulunmak   shee-ka-yet-*te* boo-loon-*mak*
istiyorum.   ees-*tee*-yo-room

I have insurance.
Sigortam var.   see-gor-*tam* var

I've been ...	Ben ...	ben ...
assaulted	saldırıya uğradım	sal·duh·ruh·ya oo·ra·duhm
raped	tecavüze uğradım	te·ja·vew·ze oo·ra·duhm
robbed	soyuldum	so·yool·doom

I've lost my ...	... kayıp.	... ka·yuhp
My ... was/were stolen.	... çalındı.	... cha·luhn·duh
backpack	Sırt çantası	suhrt chan·ta·suh
bags	Çantalar	chan·ta·lar
credit card	Kredi kartı	kre·dee kar·tuh
handbag	El çantası	el chan·ta·suh
jewellery	Mücevherler	mew·jev·her·ler
money	Para	pa·ra
passport	Pasaport	pa·sa·port
travellers cheques	Seyahat çekleri	se·ya·hat chek·le·ree
wallet	Cüzdan	jewz·dan

I want to contact my ...	... görüşmek istiyorum.	... geu·rewsh·mek ees·tee·yo·room
consulate	Konsoloslukla	kon·so·los·look·la
embassy	Elçilikle	el·chee·leek·le

health

medical needs

Where's the nearest ...?	En yakın ... nerede?	en ya·kuhn ... ne·re·de
dentist	dişçi	deesh·chee
doctor	doktor	dok·tor
hospital	hastane	has·ta·ne
(night) pharmacist	(nöbetçi) eczane	(neu·bet·chee) ej·za·ne

I need a doctor (who speaks English).
(İngilizce konuşan) (een·gee·leez·je ko·noo·shan)
Bir doktora ihtiyacım var. beer dok·to·ra eeh·tee·ya·juhm var

Could I see a female doctor?
Bayan doktora ba·yan dok·to·ra
görünebilir miyim? geu·rew·ne·bee·leer mee·yeem

I've run out of my medication.
İlacım bitti. ee·la·juhm beet·tee

symptoms, conditions & allergies

I'm sick.	Hastayım.	has·ta·yuhm
It hurts here.	Burası ağrıyor.	boo·ra·suh a·ruh·yor
I have a toothache.	Dişim ağrıyor.	dee·sheem a·ruh·yor
I have (a) ...	Bende ... var.	ben·de ... var
asthma	astım	as·tuhm
bronchitis	bronşit	bron·sheet
constipation	kabızlık	ka·buhz·luhk
cough	öksürük	euk·sew·rewk
diarrhoea	ishal	ees·hal
fever	ateş	a·tesh
headache	baş ağrısı	bash a·ruh·suh
heart condition	kalp rahatsızlığı	kalp ra·hat·suhz·luh·uh
nausea	bulantı	boo·lan·tuh
pain	ağrı	a·ruh
sore throat	boğaz ağrısı	bo·az a·ruh·suh
I'm allergic to ...	... alerjim var.	... a·ler·zheem var
antibiotics	Antibiyotiklere	an·tee·bee·yo·teek·le·re
anti-	Anti-	an·tee·
inflammatories	emflamatuarlara	em·fla·ma·too·ar·la·ra
aspirin	Aspirine	as·pee·ree·ne
bees	Arılara	a·ruh·la·ra
codeine	Kodeine	ko·de·ee·ne
penicillin	Penisiline	pe·nee·see·lee·ne
antiseptic	antiseptik	an·tee·sep·teek
bandage	bandaj	ban·dazh
condoms	prezervatifler	pre·zer·va·teef·ler
contraceptives	doğum kontrol hapı	do·oom kon·trol ha·puh
diarrhoea medicine	ishal ilacı	ees·hal ee·la·juh
insect repellent	sinek kovucu	see·nek ko·voo·joo
laxatives	müsil ilacı	mew·seel ee·la·juh
painkillers	ağrı kesici	a·ruh ke·see·jee
rehydration salts	rehidrasyon tuzları	re·heed·ras·yon tooz·la·ruh
sleeping tablets	uyku hapı	ooy·koo ha·puh

english–turkish dictionary

Words in this dictionary are marked as a (adjective), n (noun), v (verb), sg (singular), pl (plural), inf (informal) and pol (polite) where necessary.

A

accident *kaza* ka-*za*
accommodation *kalacak yer* ka-la-*jak* yer
adaptor *adaptör* a-dap-*teur*
address n *adres* ad-res
after *sonra* son-*ra*
air conditioning *klima* klee-ma
airplane *uçak* oo-*chak*
airport *havaalanı* ha-*va*-a-la-nuh
alcohol *alkol* al-*kol*
all *hepsi* hep-see
allergy *alerji* a-ler-*zhee*
ambulance *ambulans* am-boo-*lans*
and *ve* ve
ankle *ayak bileği* a-*yak* bee-le-*ee*
arm *kol* kol
ashtray *kül tablası* kewl tab-la-*suh*
ATM *bankamatik* ban-ka-ma-*teek*

B

baby *bebek* be-*bek*
back (body) *sırt* suhrt
backpack *sırt çantası* suhrt chan-ta-*suh*
bad *kötü* keu-*tew*
bag *çanta* chan-ta
baggage claim *bagaj konveyörü*
  ba-*gazh* kon-ve-yeu-*rew*
bank *banka* ban-ka
bar *bar* bar
bathroom *banyo* ban-yo
battery *pil* peel
beautiful *güzel* gew-*zel*
bed *yatak* ya-*tak*
beer *bira* bee-ra
before *önce* eun-je
behind *arkasında* ar-ka-suhn-*da*
bicycle *bisiklet* bee-seek-*let*
big *büyük* bew-*yewk*
bill *hesap* he-*sap*
black *siyah* see-*yah*
blanket *battaniye* bat-*ta*-nee-ye

blood group *kan gurubu* kan goo-roo-*boo*
blue *mavi* ma-vee
boat *vapur* va-*poor*
book (make a reservation) v *yer ayırtmak*
  yer a-*yuhrt*-mak
bottle *şişe* shee-she
bottle opener *şişe açacağı* shee-she a-cha-ja-*uh*
boy *oğlan* o-*lan*
brakes (car) *fren* fren
breakfast *kahvaltı* kah-val-*tuh*
broken (faulty) *bozuk* bo-*zook*
bus *otobüs* o-to-*bews*
business *iş* eesh
buy *satın almak* sa-tuhn al-*mak*

C

café *kafe* ka-*fe*
camera *kamera* ka-me-ra
camp site *kamp yeri* kamp ye-*ree*
cancel *iptal etmek* eep-*tal* et-mek
can opener *konserve açacağı* kon-ser-ve a-cha-ja-*uh*
car *araba* a-ra-ba
cash n *nakit* na-*keet*
cash (a cheque) v *(çek) bozdurmak*
  (chek) boz-door-*mak*
cell phone *cep telefonu* jep te-le-fo-*noo*
centre n *merkez* mer-*kez*
change (money) v *bozdurmak* boz-door-*mak*
cheap *ucuz* oo-*jooz*
check (bill) *fatura* fa-too-*ra*
check-in n *giriş* gee-*reesh*
chest *göğüs* geu-*ews*
child *çocuk* cho-*jook*
cigarette *sigara* see-*ga*-ra
city *şehir* she-*heer*
clean a *temiz* te-*meez*
closed *kapalı* ka-pa-*luh*
coffee *kahve* kah-*ve*
coins *madeni para* ma-de-*nee* pa-*ra*
cold a *soğuk* so-*uk*
collect call *ödemeli telefon* eu-de-me-*lee* te-le-*fon*
come *gelmek* gel-*mek*

computer *bilgisayar* beel-gee-sa-*yar*
condom *prezervatif* pre-zer-va-*teef*
contact lenses *kontak lens* kon-*tak* lens
cook v *pişirmek* pee-sheer-*mek*
cost n *fiyat* fee-*yat*
credit card *kredi kartı* kre-dee kar-*tuh*
cup *fincan* feen-*jan*
currency exchange *döviz kuru* deu-*veez* koo-*roo*
customs (immigration) *gümrük* gewm-*rewk*

D

dangerous *tehlikeli* teh-lee-ke-*lee*
date (time) *tarih* ta-*reeh*
day *gün* gewn
delay n *gecikme* ge-jeek-*me*
dentist *dişçi* deesh-*chee*
depart *ayrılmak* ai-ruhl-*mak*
diaper *bebek bezi* be-*bek* be-*zee*
dictionary *sözlük* seuz-*lewk*
dinner *akşam yemeği* ak-*sham* ye-me-ee
direct *direk* dee-*rek*
dirty *kirli* keer-*lee*
disabled *özürlü* eu-zewr-*lew*
discount n *indirim* een-dee-*reem*
doctor *doktor* dok-*tor*
double bed *iki kişilik yatak* ee-*kee* kee-shee-*leek* ya-*tak*
double room *iki kişilik oda* ee-*kee* kee-shee-*leek* o-*da*
drink n *içecek* ee-che-*jek*
drive v *sürmek* sewr-*mek*
drivers licence *ehliyet* eh-lee-*yet*
drugs (illicit) *uyuşturucu* oo-yoosh-too-roo-*joo*
dummy (pacifier) *emzik* em-*zeek*

E

ear *kulak* koo-*lak*
east *doğu* do-*oo*
eat *yemek* ye-*mek*
economy class *ekonomi sınıfı* e-ko-no-*mee* suh-nuh-*fuh*
electricity *elektrik* e-lek-*treek*
elevator *asansör* a-san-*seur*
email *e-posta* e-*pos*-ta
embassy *elçilik* el-chee-*leek*
emergency *acil durum* a-*jeel* doo-*room*
English (language) *İngilizce* een-gee-*leez*-je
entrance *giriş* gee-*reesh*
evening *akşam* ak-*sham*
exchange rate *döviz kuru* deu-*veez* koo-*roo*
exit n *çıkış* chuh-*kuhsh*

expensive *pahalı* pa-ha-*luh*
express mail *ekspres posta* eks-*pres* pos-*ta*
eye *göz* geuz

F

far *uzak* oo-*zak*
fast *hızlı* huhz-*luh*
father *baba* ba-*ba*
film (camera) *film* feelm
finger *parmak* par-*mak*
first-aid kit *ilk yardım çantası* eelk yar-*duhm* chan-ta-*suh*
first class *birinci sınıf* bee-reen-*jee* suh-*nuhf*
fish n *balık* ba-*luhk*
food *yiyecek* yee-ye-*jek*
foot *ayak* a-*yak*
fork *çatal* cha-*tal*
free (of charge) *ücretsiz* ewj-ret-*seez*
friend *arkadaş* ar-ka-*dash*
fruit *meyve* may-*ve*
full *dolu* do-*loo*
funny *komik* ko-*meek*

G

gift *hediye* he-dee-*ye*
girl *kız* kuhz
glass (drinking) *bardak* bar-*dak*
glasses *gözlük* geuz-*lewk*
go *gitmek* geet-*mek*
good *iyi* ee-*yee*
green *yeşil* ye-*sheel*
guide n *rehber* reh-*ber*

H

half n *yarım* ya-*ruhm*
hand *el* el
handbag *el çantası* el chan-ta-*suh*
happy *mutlu* moot-*loo*
have *sahip olmak* sa-*heep* ol-*mak*
he *o* o
head *baş* bash
heart *kalp* kalp
heat n *ısı* uh-*suh*
heavy *ağır* a-*uhr*
help v *yardım etmek* yar-*duhm* et-*mek*
here *burada* boo-*ra*-da
high *yüksek* yewk-*sek*

highway *otoyol* o-to-yol
hike v *uzun yürüyüşe çıkmak*
  oo-zoon yew-rew-yew-she chuhk-mak
holiday *tatil* ta-teel
homosexual *homoseksüel* ho-mo-sek-sew-el
hospital *hastane* has-ta-ne
hot *sıcak* suh-jak
hotel *otel* o-tel
hungry *aç* ach
husband *koca* ko-ja

I

I *ben* ben
identification (card) *kimlik kartı* keem-leek kar-tuh
ill *hasta* has-ta
important *önemli* eu-nem-lee
included *dahil* da-heel
injury *yara* ya-ra
insurance *sigorta* see-gor-ta
Internet *internet* een-ter-net
interpreter *tercüman* ter-jew-man

J

jewellery *mücevherler* mew-jev-her-ler
job *meslek* mes-lek

K

key *anahtar* a-nah-tar
kilogram *kilogram* kee-log-ram
kitchen *mutfak* moot-fak
knife *bıçak* buh-chak

L

laundry (place) *çamaşırlık* cha-ma-shuhr-luhk
lawyer *avukat* a-voo-kat
left (direction) *sol* sol
left-luggage office *emanet bürosu* e-ma-net bew-ro-soo
leg *bacak* ba-jak
lesbian *lezbiyen* lez-bee-yen
less *daha az* da-ha az
letter (mail) *mektup* mek-toop
lift (elevator) *asansör* a-san-seur
light n *ışık* uh-shuhk
like v *sevmek* sev-mek
lock n *kilit* kee-leet
long *uzun* oo-zoon

lost *kayıp* ka-yuhp
lost-property office *kayıp eşya bürosu*
  ka-yuhp esh-ya bew-ro-soo
love v *aşık olmak* a-shuhk ol-mak
luggage *bagaj* ba-gazh
lunch *öğle yemeği* eu-le ye-me-ee

M

mail n *mektup* mek-toop
man *adam* a-dam
map *harita* ha-ree-ta
market *pazar* pa-zar
matches *kibrit* keeb-reet
meat *et* et
medicine *ilaç* ee-lach
menu *yemek listesi* ye-mek lees-te-see
message *mesaj* me-sazh
milk *süt* sewt
minute *dakika* da-kee-ka
mobile phone *cep telefonu* jep te-le-fo-noo
money *para* pa-ra
month *ay* ai
morning *sabah* sa-bah
mother *anne* an-ne
motorcycle *motosiklet* mo-to-seek-let
motorway *paralı yol* pa-ra-luh yol
mouth *ağız* a-uhz
music *müzik* mew-zeek

N

name *ad* ad
napkin *peçete* pe-che-te
nappy *bebek bezi* be-bek be-zee
near *yakında* ya-kuhn-da
neck *boyun* bo-yoon
new *yeni* ye-nee
news *haberler* ha-ber-ler
newspaper *gazete* ga-ze-te
night *gece* ge-je
no *hayır* ha-yuhr
noisy *gürültülü* gew-rewl-tew-lew
nonsmoking *sigara içilmeyen* see-ga-ra ee-cheel-me-yen
north *kuzey* koo-zay
nose *burun* boo-roon
now *şimdi* sheem-dee
number *sayı* sa-yuh

O

oil (engine) *jağ* ya

old (object/person) *eski/yaşlı* es-kee/yash-luh

one-way ticket *gidiş bilet* gee-deesh bee-let

open a *açık* a-chuhk

outside *dışarıda* duh-sha-ruh-da

P

package *ambalaj* am-ba-lazh

paper *kağıt* ka-uht

park (car) v *park etmek* park et-mek

passport *pasaport* pa-sa-port

pay *ödemek* eu-de-mek

pen *tükenmez kalem* tew-ken-mez ka-lem

petrol *benzin* ben-zeen

pharmacy *eczane* ej-za-ne

phonecard *telefon kartı* te-le-fon kar-tuh

photo *fotoğraf* fo-to-raf

plate *tabak* ta-bak

police *polis* po-lees

postcard *kartpostal* kart-pos-tal

post office *postane* pos-ta-ne

pregnant *hamile* ha-mee-le

price *fiyat* fee-yat

Q

quiet *sakin* sa-keen

R

rain n *yağmur* ya-moor

razor *traş makinesi* trash ma-kee-ne-see

receipt n *makbuz* mak-booz

red *kırmızı* kuhr-muh-zuh

refund n *para iadesi* pa-ra ee-a-de-see

registered mail *taahhütlü posta* ta-ah-hewt-lew pos-ta

rent v *kiralamak* kee-ra-la-mak

repair v *tamir etmek* ta-meer et-mek

reservation *rezervasyon* re-zer-vas-yon

restaurant *restoran* res-to-ran

return v *geri dönmek* ge-ree deun-mek

return ticket *gidiş-dönüş bilet* gee-deesh-deu-newsh bee-let

right (direction) *doğru yön* do-roo yeun

road *yol* yol

room *oda* o-da

S

safe a *emniyetli* em-nee-yet-lee

sanitary napkin *hijyenik kadın bağı* heezh-ye-neek ka-duhn ba-uh

seat *yer* yer

send *göndermek* geun-der-mek

service station *benzin istasyonu* ben-zeen ees-tas-yo-noo

sex *seks* seks

shampoo *şampuan* sham-poo-an

share (a dorm) *paylaşmak* pai-lash-mak

shaving cream *traş kremi* tuh-rash kre-mee

she o o

sheet (bed) *çarşaf* char-shaf

shirt *gömlek* geum-lek

shoes *ayakkabılar* a-yak-ka-buh-lar

shop n *dükkan* dewk-kan

short *kısa* kuh-sa

shower n *duş* doosh

single room *tek kişilik oda* tek kee-shee-leek o-da

skin *cilt* jeelt

skirt *etek* e-tek

sleep v *uyumak* oo-yoo-mak

slowly *yavaşça* ya-vash-cha

small *küçük* kew-chewk

smoke (cigarettes) v *sigara içmek* see-ga-ra eech-mek

soap *sabun* sa-boon

some *biraz* bee-raz

soon *yakında* ya-kuhn-da

south *güney* gew-nay

souvenir shop *hediyelik eşya dükkanı* he-dee-ye-leek esh-ya dewk-ka-nuh

speak *konuşmak* ko-noosh-mak

spoon *kaşık* ka-shuhk

stamp *pul* pool

stand-by ticket *açık bilet* a-chuhk bee-let

station (train) *istasyon* ees-tas-yon

stomach *mide* mee-de

stop v *durmak* door-mak

stop (bus) n *durağı* doo-ra-uh

street *sokak* so-kak

student *öğrenci* eu-ren-jee

sun *güneş* gew-nesh

sunscreen *güneşten koruma kremi*
  gew-nesh-ten ko-roo-ma kre-mee
swim v *yüzmek* yewz-mek

T

tampons *tamponlar* tam-pon-lar
taxi *taksi* tak-see
teaspoon *çay kaşığı* chai ka-shuh-uh
teeth *dişler* deesh-ler
telephone n *telefon* te-le-fon
television *televizyon* te-le-veez-yon
temperature (weather) *derece* de-re-je
tent *çadır* cha-duhr
that (one) *şunu/onu* shoo-noo/o-noo
they *onlar* on-lar
thirsty *susamış* soo-sa-muhsh
this (one) *bunu* boo-noo
throat *boğaz* bo-az
ticket *bilet* bee-let
time *zaman* za-man
tired *yorgun* yor-goon
tissues *kağıt mendil* ka-uht men-deel
today *bugün* boo-gewn
toilet *tuvalet* too-va-let
tomorrow *yarın* ya-ruhn
tonight *bu gece* boo ge-je
toothbrush *diş fırçası* deesh fuhr-cha-suh
toothpaste *diş macunu* deesh ma-joo-noo
torch (flashlight) *el feneri* el fe-ne-ree
tour n *tur* toor
tourist office *turizm bürosu* too-reezm bew-ro-soo
towel *havlu* hav-loo
train *tren* tren
translate *çevirmek* che-veer-mek
travel agency *seyahat acentesi* seya-hat a-jen-te-see
travellers cheque *seyahat çeki* se-ya-hat che-kee
trousers *pantolon* pan-to-lon
Turkey *Türkiye* tewr-kee-ye
Turkish (language) *Türkçe* tewrk-che
Turkish Republic of Northern Cyprus (TRNC)
  Kuzey Kıbrıs Türk Cumhuriyeti (KKTC) koo-zay
  kuhb-ruhs tewrk joom-hoo-ree-ye-tee (ka-ka-te-je)
twin beds *çift yatak* cheeft ya-tak
tyre *lastik* las-teek

U

underwear *iç çamaşırı* eech cha-ma-shuh-ruh
urgent *acil* a-jeel

V

vacant *boş* bosh
vacation *tatil* ta-teel
vegetable n *sebze* seb-ze
vegetarian a *vejeteryan* ve-zhe-ter-yan
visa *vize* vee-ze

W

waiter *garson* gar-son
walk v *yürümek* yew-rew-mek
wallet *cüzdan* jewz-dan
warm a *ılık* uh-luhk
wash (something) *yıkamak* yuh-ka-mak
watch n *saat* sa-at
water *su* soo
we *biz* beez
weekend *hafta sonu* haf-ta so-noo
west *batı* ba-tuh
wheelchair *tekerlekli sandalye*
  te-ker-lek-lee san-dal-ye
when *ne zaman* ne za-man
where *nerede* ne-re-de
white *beyaz* be-yaz
who *kim* keem
why *neden* ne-den
wife *karı* ka-ruh
window *pencere* pen-je-re
wine *şarap* sha-rap
with *ile* ee-le
without *-sız/-siz/-suz/-süz* -suhz/-seez/-sooz/-sewz
woman *kadın* ka-duhn
write *yazı yazmak* ya-zuh yaz-mak

Y

yellow *sarı* sa-ruh
yes *evet* e-vet
yesterday *dün* dewn
you sg inf *sen* sen
you sg pol & pl *siz* seez

don't just stand there, say something!

To see the full range of our language products, go to:

lonelyplanet.com

What kind of traveller are you?

A. You're eating chicken for dinner *again* because it's the only word you know.

B. When no one understands what you say, you step closer and shout louder.

C. When the barman doesn't understand your order, you point frantically at the beer.

D. You're surrounded by locals, swapping jokes, email addresses and experiences – other travellers want to borrow your phrasebook or audio guide.

If you answered A, B, or C, you NEED Lonely Planet's language products ...

- **Lonely Planet Phrasebooks** – for every phrase you need in every language you want
- **Lonely Planet Language & Culture** – get behind the scenes of English as it's spoken around the world – learn and laugh
- **Lonely Planet Fast Talk & Fast Talk Audio** – essential phrases for short trips and weekends away – read, listen and talk like a local
- **Lonely Planet Small Talk** – 10 essential languages for city breaks
- **Lonely Planet Real Talk** – downloadable language audio guides from lonelyplanet.com to your MP3 player

... and this is why

- **Talk to everyone everywhere**
  Over 120 languages, more than any other publisher
- **The right words at the right time**
  Quick-reference colour sections, two-way dictionary, easy pronunciation, every possible subject – and audio to support it

Lonely Planet Offices

Australia
90 Maribyrnong St, Footscray,
Victoria 3011
☎ 03 8379 8000
fax 03 8379 8111
✉ talk2us@lonelyplanet.com.au

USA
150 Linden St, Oakland,
CA 94607
☎ 510 250 6400
fax 510 893 8572
✉ info@lonelyplanet.com

UK
2nd floor, 186 City Rd
London EC1V 2NT
☎ 020 7106 2100
fax 020 7106 2101
✉ go@lonelyplanet.co.uk

lonelyplanet.com